University of Kentucky Basketball Encyclopedia

University of Kentucky Basketball Encyclopedia
Revised and Updated

Tom Wallace
Foreword by Cotton Nash

SPORTS
PUBLISHING

University of Kentucky Basketball Encyclopedia

Sports Publishing books may be purchased in bulk at special discounts for sales promotion, corporate gifts, fund-raising, or educational purposes. Special editions can also be created to specifications. For details, contact the Special Sales Department, Sports Publishing, 307 West 36th Street, 11th Floor, New York, NY 10018 or sportspubbooks@skyhorsepublishing.com.

Sports Publishing® is a registered trademark of Skyhorse Publishing, Inc.®, a Delaware corporation.

Visit our website at www.sportspubbooks.com.

10 9 8 7 6 5 4 3 2 1

Library of Congress Cataloging-in-Publication Data is available on file.

Interior design by Jamie Barker

Cover design by Tom Lau

Cover photos: AP Images

All interior photos courtesy of UK Sports Information Department

ISBN: 978-1-61321-892-1

Ebook ISBN: 978-1-61321-893-8

Printed in China

This book is dedicated to Reggie Hanson, Deron Feldhaus,

John Pelphrey, Sean Woods, Richie Farmer and

Jamal Mashburn—six players who helped bring

UK back from the dead.

—T. W.—

Table of Contents

Acknowledgments viii

Foreword x

Introduction xii

Kentucky Coaches Since 1930 1

The Best of the Best 8

    Retired Jerseys 10

    All-Americans 12

Wildcat Profiles 14

UK Teams of Tradition 64

Year by Year with the Cats 68

UK Championship Victories 358

UK's Greatest Games 368

Famous Head-to-Head Showdowns 404

Wildcat VIPs 408

UK in the NCAA 414

UK in the SEC 418

UK's All-Time Leading Scorers 424

Records 432

All-Time Results 447

Acknowledgments

Once again, the list of those deserving mention for assisting or inspiring this book changes little from the first time around. As I stated then, writing may be a solitary endeavor, but getting a book published, especially one demanding hours and hours of research and writing, requires many helping hands.

Simply put, this book could not have happened were it not for those who were quick to lend a helping hand.

At the very top of this list are the UK Media Relations folks. From the initial edition in 2001 thru to this edition, they helped me without hesitation or reservation. From Brooks Downing (who got me involved in this project many years ago), to Scott Stricklin to Tony Neely to DeWayne Peevy, they have all been positive advocates for this project. Thanks, guys.

For this edition, I owe a big thanks to Eric Lindsey and Jake Most for coming through in the clutch by providing additional photos. Especially critical to the book were photos of Wildcats who played during the past five seasons. Virtually all photos of those players were provided by the UK Media Relations folks. If I were a rich dude, I'd buy lunch for Eric and Jake. They were true heroes.

I was especially thrilled when the great Cotton Nash agreed to write the Foreword for this edition. Cotton was not only one of UK's all-time greatest players, he was also one of my boyhood heroes. The first time I saw him play in person was during his sophomore season when the Cats took on Notre Dame in Freedom Hall. All he did that night was score 31 points and grab 17 rebounds.

But it was more than just his points or rebounds that hooked me; it was the way he carried himself, the smoothness in his moves, and those odd things he did, like always being the last player to come out of the dressing room, or how he would wipe his hands on the padding beneath the goal prior to shooting a free throw. I was totally mesmerized by the guy.

Wayne Chapman once told me that "when you saw Cotton walking across campus, you knew you were seeing an All-American." That's certainly how I felt when I watched him play that December night in 1961.

I had the chance to meet Cotton when I was working for Cawood, and it pleases me to say that he's everything you'd want your heroes to be. He's one of the good guys. I'm honored to have his name associated with this book.

Another name high on the list is the late Russell Rice, UK's former sports information director and the author of many books about the Wildcats, including the classic *Big Blue Machine*. I still maintain that a line in that book—"On the afternoon of Dec. 7, 1941, Kenny Rollins and Mulford "Muff" Davis walked out of a picture show and into a war"—is the single best line in my book. It's beyond perfect.

This book, like all books about UK sports, owes its lifeblood to the pioneering work Russell did in the past. He is the starting point from which we all travel.

Without question, the great Cawood Ledford's spirit can be found on every page of this book. Through my association with him, I had access to the UK program not granted to everyone. That was a blessing, one that played a big role in my being able to do this book.

Working for Cawood was one of the real joys of my life; getting to know him and become his friend was an even greater joy. Like Wildcat fans everywhere, I miss him deeply.

The late Bill Keightley, the venerable "Mr. Wildcat," was always a friend, believer, inspiration and a well-spring of information. He also remains one of the finest people I had the privileged to know. Long live the memory and spirit of "Mr. Wildcat."

Many of the photos in this book are the work of David Coyle, an old friend who can't seem to take a picture that isn't excellent. They say a picture is worth 1,000 words. If that's true, and it probably is, then David is responsible for far more words than I am. Thanks to David and all the folks at Team Coyle.

As with the previous editions, Jamie Barker worked his considerable magic to give the book its clean, easy-to-read look. Jamie's skills with graphics, design and layout are simply unbeatable. In truth, this book is as much Jamie's as it is mine.

Again, I must mention my thanks to good friends Gene Abell and Dan Metzger, the two guys responsible for getting me to Lexington—and inside Cawood's door—in the first place.

But in the end, the biggest thanks of all go to Marilyn Underwood. Not only does she continue to stand by me, she also gives advice (sought or otherwise), support, encouragement and love, all while quietly putting up with my constant kvetching. I couldn't have made it through this project without her faith and support.

Wildcat practices under Adolph Rupp were all business and famous for the silence.

Foreword

Only a select few sports teams, professional or amateur, have achieved the kind of success as the University of Kentucky basketball program, and then managed to keep that success at a consistently high level for such a long period of time. The Wildcats made their mark nationally back in the 1930s, and to this day they rank among the elite basketball programs in college hoops. In fact, UK has won more games than any other Division I program.

What makes UK's record even more impressive is that most of those wins didn't come against easy opponents. Almost from the beginning, going back to Coach Rupp's early years, the Wildcats consistently faced the strongest teams and the best individuals. That was certainly true when I played. During my three years as a Wildcat, I did

battle against Jeff Mullins of Duke, Billy Cunningham of North Carolina, Donnie Kessinger of Ole Miss, Jerry Lucas and John Havlicek of Ohio State, Rod Thorn of West Virginia and Les Hunter of Loyola of Chicago, just to name a few. Facing players of that caliber wasn't easy, but if you want to be the best you have to take on the best. UK players did that before I showed up, and they continue to do it these days. No one can ever accuse UK of shying away from a tough fight.

Having been a Wildcat myself, I know firsthand how much their basketball team means to the fans. Players come and go, coaches retire or move on, but the fans' loyalty to the program is unwavering. And no team has better or more faithful fans than UK. They are always behind the team and the players, no matter the situation. Home

Over the years Tom has written several articles about me, and in each one he always had an accurate assessment of my accomplishments. I know from those articles, and from previous editions of this book, that Tom gets his facts straight and that he writes in a style that is easy to read.

So when Tom asked me to write the Foreword for this fourth edition of the *Kentucky Basketball Encyclopedia*, I gladly said yes. I agreed because I know that this is easily the most-detailed, most-comprehensive book relating to UK basketball that you're going to find. If you're a Wildcat fan, either an old one or a new one, this is a book for you. It's all in here—stories on each season dating back to 1903, player profiles, game recaps, plenty of statistics and hundreds of terrific photos.

It was my great good fortune to be a Wildcat player and to be part of UK's long and glorious basketball tradition. Those four years are among the happiest and most-memorable of my life. Now I'm just another Wildcat fan, and as a fan I can tell you that this is a book you are going to enjoy and appreciate.

Tom has done a terrific job of detailing UK's rich basketball history for all Wildcat fans. It's all in these pages. Read and enjoy.

Cotton Nash

games in Rupp Arena are always sold out, and when the Cats hit the road, it's not unusual to see more UK fans in the stands than followers of the home team. There's a reason why UK fans are known as Big Blue Nation.

It seems to me that Wildcat fans love to read about or talk about the past almost as much as they look to the future. Fans are always asking me what it was like to play for Coach Rupp, or what was Harry Lancaster like, or what was my best game? They still send me copies of the issue of *Sports Illustrated* that had my picture on the cover and ask me to autograph it for them. That was many years ago, but Wildcat fans never forget. Once a member of the UK family, always a member.

I first got to know Tom back when he worked for Cawood Ledford, a man I had great respect and admiration for. For Tom, being able to work with Cawood and listen to his stories had to be the best education possible for undertaking a book such as the University of *Kentucky Basketball Encyclopedia*. I would imagine that going to work for Cawood every day was like taking a class in Wildcat basketball history. Tom couldn't help but absorb the information he heard on a daily basis.

Introduction

Throughout the University of Kentucky's long and magnificent basketball history, there have been three eras that can truly be called golden, and one that is most accurately described as a precursor. Any sports program that maintains such a high level of consistency decade after decade has had more than its share of successful eras. However, all other UK eras are overshadowed by these four, beginning with the precursor:

■ From 1930 through 1935, Adolph Rupp's first five teams had a won-loss record of 86-11, a winning percentage of 88.7. Two of those teams, 1932-33 and 1934-35, were named Helms Foundation National Champions. Six Wildcats were named All-Americans during this time frame, including Carey Spicer, Aggie Sale, Ellis Johnson, French DeMoisey, Leroy "Cowboy" Edwards and Dave Lawrence. Sale and Edwards were also named Helms Foundation National Player of the Year in 1933 and 1935,

respectively. This was the era that set the stage for what was to follow while also putting UK hoops on the national stage.

■ From 1945-46 through 1953-54, the Wildcats had a record of 241-20, which computes to an incredible winning percentage of 92.3. There were three NCAA championships ('48, '49, '51), one NIT title ('46), one undefeated team (1953-54), one Olympic gold medal (London, 1948) and SEC championships every season. Four of those teams won at least 30 games, and the most losses sustained in a season were five. All-Americans during those years included Ralph Beard, Alex Groza, Wah Wah Jones, Bill Spivey, Cliff Hagan and Frank Ramsey. A strong argument can be made that this is UK's greatest Golden Era.

■ From 1990-91 through 1997-98, the Wildcats' record was 240-40, a winning percentage of 85.7. There were a pair of national titles ('96, '98), one runner-up finish ('97)

Fabulous Five teammates Cliff Barker, Kenny Rollins, Wah Wah Jones and Ralph Beard are recognized by the Rupp Arena crowd during the golden anniversary of UK's 1948 NCAA title and Olympic gold medal. Missing is center Alex Groza, who passed away in 1995.

President Clinton was all smiles after receiving a Wildcat jersey from senior center Mark Pope. The president, an avid Arkansas fan, honored the 1996 championship Cats during the team's official visit to the White House.

and six SEC tourney championships. More important, this Golden Era restored glory to a program that had been hard hit by NCAA sanctions. Rick Pitino (with late help from Tubby Smith), was the architect of this rejuvenation. Jamal Mashburn, Tony Delk and Ron Mercer were Wildcats who earned All-America recognition during these years.

■ From 2009-10 through 2015-16, with John Calipari running the show, the Wildcats have a record of 217-47 for a winning percentage of .822 The 2011-12 team captured the national crown, four of his teams advanced to the Final Four—(2011, 2012, 2014 and 2015), and two teams had unblemished records in SEC action (2011-12 and 2014-15). Calipari-coached All-Americans include John Wall, DeMarcus Cousins, Terrence Jones, Anthony Davis, Michael Kidd-Gilchrist, Julius Randle, Willie Cauley-Stein, Karl-Anthony Towns, Tyler Ulis and Jamal Murray.

Sustained Excellence

In the original Introduction to the book, I argued that the two most successful sports teams of the 20th Century were the New York Yankees and the Kentucky Wildcats. That's a statement I stand behind 100 percent, and an argument I firmly believe I can win. After all, it's easy to win when the facts (wins) back you up.

The Yankees and the Wildcats were models of sustained excellence. Other teams soared across the sports firmament, only to flame out or disintegrate completely. Today's superpower became tomorrow's faded memory. But not UK or the Yankees. Those two teams reached the highest heights and remained there for almost the entire century.

However, the 21st Century has dawned much differently for both of those proud and mighty teams. The Yankees have claimed only a single World Series title since 2000, and making matters worse for pinstripe fans, they have at times performed in a most-ordinary manner. No doubt, those old pinstripe Hall of Fame Yankees who won a World Series ring virtually every October are wondering what went wrong.

For Big Blue fans, an almost-impossible bunch to satisfy, things went from "What's happened?" to "Hey, look folks, we're back on top." They were taken on an unsteady roller-coaster ride that went from the poorhouse back to the penthouse. From the depths of despair to the mountaintop.

Smooth Waters Once Again

There can be no denying the fact that the Big Blue

The giant shadow of legendary coach Adolph Rupp will forever loom over the UK program.

Nation faithful had to suffer through two years of agony and disappointment prior to John Calipari's arrival on the scene. Of course, those were the two years between Tubby Smith and Calipari. The infamous—and unsuccessful—Billy Gillispie Experiment.

Incredibly, Tubby, a man of dignity, class and honor, had worn out his welcome at UK, having alienated a vast segment of Big Blue fanatics, many of whom spent endless time and energy raking the coach over the coals for everything from recruiting failures to a boring style of play to, well, just about anything short of homicide. In the end, the coach labeled "10-Loss Tubby" by disgruntled fans could seemingly do nothing right. So, he bolted for Minnesota, taking over a basketball program that had hit rock bottom.

Mitch Barnhart, UK's athletics director, wasted little time choosing Smith's successor, plucking the little-known Gillispie

Joe B. Hall is one of the most-important figures in UK basketball history. His willingness to recruit black athletes helped UK shake its white only image and remain competitive at the highest levels.

made early commitments to join UK in upcoming years.

But Gillispie's instant popularity and fast start didn't last too long. Less than two months into the season, the combination of a slow start by the Wildcats, who often looked lost and disorganized on both ends of the court, and Legion's defection was enough to cause Big Blue fans to wonder if perhaps the jury was still out on the new coach.

Compounding the situation was Gillispie's personality. Or, his lack of a personality. There is simply no denying that he was something of an odd duck from the very beginning. He never really appeared to be comfortable in his role as UK coach. His lack of social skills, combined with an apparent unwillingness to accept the fact that the UK coach is more than a guy who pushes X's and O's around on a chalkboard, provided an undercurrent that ran through his two years at the helm. Gillispie failed to grasp a simple fact: the UK coach is a movie star and a rock star and a high-profile celebrity all rolled into one. In short, he is easily the most recognizable individual in the commonwealth. Gillispie never understood that.

But in the end, none of those things meant as much as a 40-27 record, no SEC success and a failure to make it into the NCAA tourney.

So long, Billy G; hello, Coach Cal.

A savior, at just the right moment.

And almost instantly, the UK ship was once again sailing on smooth waters.

Changing Times

Calipari was the perfect choice to rebuild the UK program. Successful coaching gigs at UMass and Memphis, along with a brief stint in the NBA, prepared him for the rigors—on-court and off—that go hand-in-hand with guiding the UK program. He didn't shy away from the challenge; he embraced it. He didn't run away from the spotlight; he sought it out. He didn't refuse to speak in front of UK alumni groups; he gladly made those appearances.

Of course, doing all the right things is only part of the deal. Racking up victories is what really matters. Moses come down from the mountain would be run out of town if he didn't win enough games. Winning is what it's ultimately all about.

And in that regard, Calipari is nothing but aces. The man had five straight 30-win seasons (the first coach to ever accomplish that) and seven overall. He has more than 600 wins as a college coach, a 78-percent winning rate, and he

from relative obscurity and throughsting him into the heated glare of UK's never-ending spotlight. Few coaches anywhere have gone farther faster than Gillispie did. From high school coach to head man at UK in just over a decade certainly qualifies as a meteoric rise within your chosen profession.

Gillispie, known as a workaholic and a master recruiter, had performed admirably during previous stints at UTEP (two years) and Texas A&M (three years). No doubt, his recruiting prowess played a key role in his landing the job. Remember, recruiting failures topped the list of grievances UK fans had against Tubby.

Gillispie, supremely confident, quickly proved that his reputation as a recruiter wasn't overblown. He landed Patrick Patterson and Alex Legion, two highly sought-after prep stars, and another half-dozen underclassmen who

has racked up enough coaching honors to fill a medium-size museum. He has sent a host of players to the NBA, including five first-round picks from his first UK team.

(You can bet that Coach Rupp is now looking down, nodding his head in approval, happy with what he is seeing.)

While he was nodding his approval, Coach Rupp would likely be shaking his head at how much the times have changed since he was running the show. No doubt, the Baron would be dazzled by the size, talent, strength and athleticism of today's players, while at the same time being dismayed that current players rarely hang around for more than a year or two. That's a far cry from "back in the day" when players stayed the full four years.

Even now, the debate rages concerning the merits (or lack thereof) of the so-called "one-and-done" situation. More than likely the divide is generational, with older fans still favoring the old way, while the younger fans, many who don't even remember the old way, are perfectly content with the current situation. In truth, most of Big Blue Nation cares about only one thing—winning.

Although many coaches are now beginning to accept the one-and-done model as a reality that can't be ignored, it was Calipari who first recognized and embraced it. He understood that it's better to have a John Wall or an Anthony Davis for only a single season than to not sign them, then have to deal with them in the NCAA Tournament. He wanted the best, even if he only had them for one season.

John Calipari led the Wildcats to their eighth national championship in 2012.

To many old-timers this isn't an ideal model. In their eyes, it violates the very principles of college athletics. College is about education (even for athletes) and should not simply be a stepping-stone to the NBA. Hence, their dislike for the one-and-done model.

But blaming Calipari (or any college coach) for opting to go that route is to point the finger in the wrong direction. If you're looking for a villain, then cast your eyes toward the NBA. There's your culprit.

And don't blame the players, either. If you had the choice between going to UK for one year, then signing an NBA guaranteed contract for $3 million per year, or staying in school, earning your degree, then finding a job (if you're fortunate) making $50,000 per year, what would you do? And besides, there is nothing that says a pro basketball player can't return to school and get his degree. Many have done just that.

In the final analysis, though, the ultimate success of the program rests where it always has—on the shoulders of the players who wear the blue and white, whether for one year

or four. They're the ones who put the ball in the basket, grab rebounds, hand out assists and play defense. They are the true pillars upon which the UK basketball empire was built. They have been the life blood, the warriors who set an unbelievably high standard of excellence and then have sustained it for more than 100 years.

Few programs have had more truly great players than the University of Kentucky. The roll call of Big Blue giants sounds like a Who's Who of college hoops. Their talent, dedication, sacrifice and athletic ability helped build a basketball program that gave all Kentuckians something to be proud of.

Thanks to them all, the four-year guys and the one-and-done players, we have all been able to journey down the "Glory Road."

Tom Wallace

5-27-2016

The UK basketball program has been a model of sustained excellence for a century. The Wildcats have won more games than any other Division I school.

Kentucky Coaches Since 1930

Adolph Rupp

UK Record: 876-190 (82.2%), 42 years
Alma Mater: Kansas (1923)
Hometown: Halstead, Kan.
Born: Sept. 2, 1901
Died: Dec. 11, 1977 (age 76)

Few coaches have had a more profound impact on a sport than Adolph Rupp had on college basketball. Without Rupp's driving insistence on excellence — and the fact that his teams consistently destroyed opponents — it's doubtful that college basketball would have risen to such heights, both in on-court performance and off-court popularity. That's especially true in the South, where, prior to Rupp's arrival at UK, basketball was little more than a club sport used

by football players to stay in shape. Rupp changed that forever by upping the ante. He took basketball seriously, thus forcing other Southern schools to improve their basketball program or risk continuing embarrassment at the hands of his fast-breaking Wildcat teams.

Rupp's basketball lineage can be traced back to the very beginning of the sport. He was tutored by the great Phog Allen at Kansas, and was a student of the game under Dr. James Naismith, the man who invented the game of basketball. After a high school coaching stint in Freeport, Ill., Rupp accepted the UK job in 1930, where, during the next 42 seasons, he took the Wildcat basketball program to the heights of glory, along the way becoming the winningest coach in all of college basketball.

Rupp went on to surpass his mentor, Coach Allen, on March 12, 1966, with his 747th victory against Dayton in the Mideast Regional. He achieved the top ranking when he passed Western Kentucky's Ed Diddle with victory No. 760 on Feb. 18, 1967, at Mississippi State.

The Baron at the drawing board. Adolph Rupp put UK basketball on the map, winning 876 games and four NCAA championships during his 42 years at the helm.

His teams dominated in league play, posting a 397-75 (84.1 percent) record against SEC competition. In the league's postseason tournament, Rupp's Wildcats were 57-6, winning 13 titles in 19 appearances.

By the end of his 42-year career, the man known as "The Baron of the Bluegrass" and "The Man in the Brown Suit" had been named National Coach of the Year four times and SEC Coach of the Year seven times. Rupp was inducted into the Naismith Hall of Fame in 1969.

Joe B. Hall

UK Record: 297-100 (74.8%), 13 years
Overall Record: 373-156 (70.5%), 19 years
Alma Mater: Kentucky (1955)
Hometown: Cynthiana, Ky.
Born: Nov. 30, 1928

Kentucky native Joe B. Hall had been a Big Blue fan, a Wildcat player and an assistant coach at UK, so he knew what he was in for when he stepped into the coaching vacancy created by Rupp's forced retirement. The pressure and the expectations were enormous. After all, Rupp was more than a legend. He was a towering figure, the winningest coach of all-time, and the only coach most Wildcat fans had ever known. Replacing a man of such stature is a daunting task, one few coaches have had to face.

But Hall, who grew up just 20 minutes north of the UK campus in Cynthiana, more than met the challenge, leading three teams to the Final Four (1975,'78 and '84) and winning the championship in 1978. It was the school's fifth NCAA title and first in 12 years. In addition, his 1976 club captured the NIT crown.

Hall began his association with UK as a student-athlete during the Fabulous Five era. As Hall would later say of that great team, "we had 12 guys on that squad, the 'Fabulous Five' and the 'Sorry Seven.' Naturally, I was one of the 'Sorry Seven'." He played one year on the junior varsity and one with the varsity before transferring to the University of the South in Sewanee, Tenn., where he finished his eligibility. Following his college career, Hall toured Europe with the Harlem Globetrotters in 1951. He then returned to UK and completed his degree requirements.

Rupp had 876 wins when he retired in 1972, a mark that stood until North Carolina's Dean Smith moved ahead during the 1997 season.

Among the many UK victories achieved by Rupp's teams were four NCAA titles (1948,'49,'51 and '58), one Olympic gold medal (1948), one NIT championship (1946) and 27 Southeastern Conference titles. In addition, his Wildcats were voted No. 1 in the final polls on six occasions.

Rupp coached some of college basketball's all-time greatest players, including Aggie Sale, Ralph Beard, Alex Groza, Cliff Hagan, Frank Ramsey, Johnny Cox, Vernon Hatton, Cotton Nash, Pat Riley, Louie Dampier and Dan Issel. Twenty-three of his players were voted All-Americans 35 times, and 52 players were honored 91 times as All-SEC performers.

He began his coaching career at Shepherdsville (Ky.) High School in 1956. From there, he went to Regis College in Denver, where he spent five years and fashioned a 57-50 record. After one season at Central Missouri State, he returned to UK on July 1, 1965 as an assistant to Rupp.

As UK's head coach, Hall won National Coach of the Year honors in 1978 and four SEC Coach of the Year awards. He had seven players earn All-America honors 11 times, while nine of his Wildcats were voted All-SEC on 18 occasions. Hall also saw 23 of his players drafted into the NBA, five in the first round.

Hall's teams registered a 172-62 (73.5 percent) record against SEC competition during the regular season, winning eight SEC titles in 13 seasons and one league tournament title in six tries.

After leaving UK, Hall spent several successful years in the banking business. He is now retired and lives in Lexington.

Eddie Sutton

UK Record: 88-39 (69.3%), 4 years
Alma Mater: Oklahoma A&M (1958)
Hometown: Bucklin, Kan.
Born: March 12, 1936

Known as a master defensive coach with a gift for building teams from scratch, Eddie Sutton came to UK in 1985 following a highly successful stint at Arkansas. At UK, Sutton found the cupboard anything but bare. With returning All-American Kenny Walker as the anchor, Sutton's first Wildcat team was his best, rolling to a 32-4 record and a berth in the Elite Eight. That Wildcat team was third in the final polls, finished with a 17-1 SEC record and captured the school's 36th league championship. All this after most prognosticators picked the Cats to finish no higher than third place in the SEC.

Sutton was honored for his efforts by being voted National Coach of the Year and SEC Coach of the Year.

The 1986-87 season, Sutton's second at UK, was far less successful. Riddled by injuries — at one point UK had only seven scholarship players — the best the Cats could do was an 18-11 record. But in Sutton's third year, UK bolted

to a 10-0 start that included impressive wins over Indiana and Louisville to earn a No. 1 ranking in the polls. The Cats were crowned SEC champs in both the regular season and the postseason but fell to Villanova in the Southeast Regional final 80-74.

Following the 1988 season, Sutton's reign came under siege by the NCAA when rules violations were discovered in the UK basketball program. The embattled coach's final Wildcat team finished with a 13-19 record in 1989, the school's first losing season since 1927. He resigned his post following the season.

Rick Pitino

UK Record: 219-50 (81.4%), 8 years
Alma Mater: Massachusetts (1974)
Hometown: New York, N.Y.
Born: Sept. 18, 1952

It's easy to forget just how low the UK basketball program was when Rick Pitino took over as coach. Equally, it's difficult to imagine any other coach who could have engineered such a miraculous turnaround in such a short period of time. From NCAA exile to NCAA champs, from "Kentucky Shame" to "Return to Glory" was accomplished in a mere seven years.

The brash and cocky 36-year-old Manhattan native came to UK from the New York Knicks, promising to win right away. And he did By the time Pitino left, UK's once-proud basketball dynasty had been resurrected from the dead, having achieved a sustained level of excellence that rivaled the glory period between 1946-1954.

Pitino came to UK with impressive credentials, especially as a rebuilder. His three previous teams, Boston College, Providence and the Knicks, had all experienced quick turnarounds under his guiding hand. His winning formula: the three-point shot and and a full-court press he dubbed "the mother-in-law press" because of its "constant harassment and pressure."

Pitino's first UK team, affectionately known as "Pitino's Bombinos," shocked the college basketball world by upsetting Shaquille O'Neal, Chris Jackson and the No.9-ranked LSU Tigers 100-95 en route to a 14-14 record.

But that season, surprising as it was, only provided a

Rick Pitino guided a stricken Wildcat program its highest level of sustained excellence since the "Glory Decade" from 1946 to 1954. Pitino's 1996 team won the NCAA Tournament. Here, Pitino discusses strategy with ex-UK All-American Ron Mercer.

99-95. After an Elite Eight finish in 1995, Pitino's next team captured the school's sixth NCAA title.

Although Pitino's last Wildcat team was hard hit by graduation (four Cats were taken in the 1996 NBA draft), and a devastating late-season injury to Derek Anderson, he somehow managed to guide them to a second straight national championship game before losing to Arizona 84-79 in overtime.

Along the way, Pitino's UK teams won five of six SEC Tournament titles, two ECAC Holiday Classics, the Maui Invitational and the Great Alaska Shootout. He had a 104-28 record against SEC teams, winning two league crowns, and an amazing 17-1 record in the SEC tourney.

He coached three All-Americans and eight All-SEC performers. The NBA drafted eight of his Wildcats, six in the first round, including three lottery picks.

Pitino left UK after the 1997 season to take over the Boston Celtics. He is now the coach of the University of Louisville.

Tubby Smith

UK Record: 263-83 (76%), 10 years
Alma Mater: High Point (N.C.) College, 1973
Hometown: Scotland, Md.
Born: June 30, 1951

Talk about starting fast out of the gate. All Tubby Smith did in his first year at UK was win the NCAA championship, the SEC championship and the SEC tourney championship. In addition, the team's 35 victories that season set a new NCAA record for the most wins by a coach in his initial season at a school.

The Wildcats, playing what came to be known as "Tubby Ball," came from 10 points down at halftime to beat Utah 78-69 in the championship game. It was UK's second NCAA title in three years, and its seventh overall. It came as no surprise, then, when Smith was named 1998 National Coach of the Year by Basketball Weekly and SEC Coach of the Year by The Associated Press.

Smith's second UK team went 28-9, won the SEC Tournament and reached the Elite Eight before losing to Michigan State.

glimpse into the future. The following year, although still banned from NCAA Tournament action, UK finished with the best record (14-4) in the SEC. Then in 1992, with NCAA sanctions finally lifted, the "Unforgettables" took eventual national champion Duke into overtime of the East Regional final before falling 104-103 in what many have called the greatest college basketball game ever played.

In 1993, with Jamal Mashburn leading the charge, UK advanced to the Final Four for the first time in nine years, losing to Michigan in overtime. The next year, the Cats recorded the biggest road comeback victory in NCAA history — 31 points with 15:34 remaining — to beat LSU

His 2003-04 club went 32-4, kicking off a three-year stretch in which the Wildcats were 87-15. Only Adolph Rupp racked up 100 victories at UK quicker than Smith. During his 10-years at the helm, Smith won 76 percent of his games.

The affable Smith was no stranger to the demands and pressures placed on the UK basketball coach, having served two years on Pitino's staff. Smith left UK after the 1990-91 season to take over the head coaching job at Tulsa. During his four seasons there, Smith's teams had a 79-43 record and twice advanced to the NCAA Tournament's Sweet 16.

In 1995, Smith moved to Georgia and began a highly successful two-year stint as the Bulldogs' top man. After directing Georgia to records of 21-10 and 24-9, Smith was UK Athletics Director C.M. Newton's first and only choice to replace the popular and successful Pitino.

Smith, a native of Scotland, Md. and one of 17 children, was a standout athlete at Great Mills High School, then later at High Point (N.C.) College. He began his coaching career at Great Mills High in 1973, eventually spending six years in the prep ranks before moving on to become an assistant at Virginia Commonwealth University from 1979-86 and South Carolina from 1986-89. Then in 1989 Smith answered Pitino's call to come to UK and help revive the NCAA-stricken program.

Smith is one of the most respected coaches in the business. When U.S. Olympic coach Larry Brown was putting together his staff for the 2000 games, Smith was one of his choices as an assistant. Smith also started a foundation to assist underprivileged children. To date, the foundation has raised in excess of $1 million.

Billy Gillispie

UK Record: 40-27 (59.7%), Two years
Alma Mater: Texas State, 1983
Hometown: Graford, Texas
Born: Nov. 7, 1959

His two-year stint as UK coach was rocky and unsuccessful, and featured some of the most ignominious losses in the school's long and illustrious history. Gillispie came to UK from Texas A&M, where he was named Big 12 Coach of the Year three times. Prior to his time at Texas A&M, he had been successful at UTEP.

His first UK club, after getting off to 6-7 start in pre-SEC action, finished league play with a 12-4 record, earning Gillispie co-Coach of the Year honors. That team, which had an 18-13 record overall, lost to Marquette in the first round of the NCAA Tournament.

Gillispie's second UK team ended the season with a 22-14 record, and failed to make it into the NCAA tourney for the first time since 1991.

Gillispie was fired as UK coach following the conclusion of the 2008-09 season.

Tubby Smith continued the winning tradition at UK, bringing the school its seventh national championship in 1998.

John Calipari

UK Record: 217-47 (82.2%), Seven years
Alma Mater: Clarion State (1982)
Hometown: Moon Township (Pa.)
Born: Feb. 10, 1959

During his seven years at the helm, John Calipari has restored UK to its rightful place among college basketball's elite teams, a run highlighted by the 2012 club capturing the school's eighth national title and the first since 1998. Calipari's record at UK is 217-47 for an astounding winning percentage of 82.2.

Twice, he has guided the Wildcats to 38-win seasons, going 38-2 in 2011-12 and 38-1 in 2014-15. During his coaching career, nine of his teams have had 30-win seasons.

Calipari has taken six teams to the Final Four, including four Wildcat clubs. He has been named National Coach of the Year six times by various organizations.

In only his second year at the helm, he took the Wildcats to their first Final Four in more than a decade. His first UK team, which finished with a 35-3 record, marked the fifth consecutive year that a Calipari-coached club won 30 or more games. He had done it in each of the previous four years at Memphis.

Calipari came to UK after serving nine years as head coach at Memphis. During his time at Memphis, Calipari's teams had a remarkable 252-69 record (78.5%). His 2007-08 team had a 38-2 record and finished as runner-up in the NCAA tourney. For his efforts, Calipari was named Naismith National Coach of the Year, making him only the second coach to receive the honor on more than one occasion. Duke's Mike Krzyzewski and Kansas' Bill Self are the other coaches to have won the award on multiple occasions.

Calipari made his coaching bones as the head man at UMass from 1988 through 1996. His UMass teams compiled a mark of 193-71 (73%). The 1995-96 team finished the season with a 35-2 record.

As a college coach, Calipari's overall record is 662-187 (78%).

He has also coached more than 30 players who have gone on to play in the National Basketball Association.

Kentucky Coaches Through the Years

Coach	Years at UK	Won	Lost	Pct.
W.W.H. Mustaine/Others	1903-09	21	35	.375
E.R. Sweetland/R.E. Spahr	1910	4	8	.333
H.J. Iddings	1911	5	6	.454
E.R. Sweetland	1912	9	0	1.000
J.J. Tigert	1913	5	3	.625
Alpha Brumage	1914-15	19	7	.731
J.J. Tigert/James Fark	1916	8	6	.571
J.J. Tigert/W.P. Tuttle	1917	4	6	.400
S.A. Boles	1918	9	*2-1	.792
Andrew Gill	1919	6	8	.428
George Buchheit	1920-24	44	27	.619
C.O. Applegran	1925	13	8	.619
Ray Eklund	1926	15	3	.833
Basil Hayden	1927	3	13	.187
John Mauer	1928-30	40	14	.740
Adolph Rupp	#1931-72	876	190	.822
Joe B. Hall	1973-85	297	100	.748
Eddie Sutton	1986-89	+88	39	.693
Rick Pitino	1990-97	219	50	.814
Tubby Smith	1998-2007	263	83	.760
Billy Gillispie	2008-09	40	27	.597
John Calapari	2010 – present	217	47	.822
Totals		**2205**	**682-1**	**.764**

* Unique tie resulted from scorer's error discovered after game.

No schedule played in 1953.

+ Three 1988 NCAA Tournament games vacated by decree of NCAA.

John Calipari offers words of wisdom to standout point guard Brandon Knight.

The Best of the Best

Without question, the ultimate honor for a Wildcat player or coach is to have his jersey retired. Through the years, 43 former players, coaches and contributors have been accorded this special recognition.

Tony Delk, star of the 1996 NCAA championship club, is the latest ex-Cat to see his jersey hanging from the Rupp Arena rafters.

According to Russell Rice, the former UK sports information director, Layton "Mickey" Rouse, an All-SEC guard and captain of the 1940 team, was the first Wildcat to have his first jersey retired. Coach Adolph Rupp surprised

Rouse by presenting him with his entire uniform at the annual banquet following the season.

The next to be honored were the five players who helped lead the Wildcats to back-to-back NCAA titles in 1948 and 1949. That group included Ralph Beard, Wah Wah Jones, Alex Groza, Cliff Barker and Kenny Rollins. It was during this ceremony that they were first called "the Fabulous Five" after Rupp commented that there would never be another team that "fabulous."

At the time, Rupp stated that

Ex-UK All-American Rick Robey had his jersey retired in 1999.

UK great Kevin Grevey had his uniform jersey retired in 1995. Grevey is UK's seventh all-time leading scorer.

Tony Delk is the latest Wildcat to have his jersey retired.

numbers remain active.

A trio of former UK coaches have also been honored—Rupp, Joe B. Hall and Rick Pitino.

Two long-time contributors to the UK basketball program have received this high honor. Those two are Cawood Ledford, the radio "Voice of the Wildcats" for 39 years, and Bill Keightley, the man known as "Mr. Wildcat" who spent five decades serving as UK equipment manager and father confessor to virtually every player who put on the blue and white.

those players' numbers would never be worn again. However, once the NCAA streamlined jersey numbers, it necessitated a change. Now, the jerseys are retired but the

Each recipient of this honor is presented with a framed jersey and the banner that is permanently on display in Rupp Arena.

In recognition of outstanding contributions to the University of Kentucky basketball program, the UK Athletics Department has retired jerseys honoring the following:

Basil Hayden
1920-21-22

Carey Spicer
1929-30-31

Adolph Rupp
Head Coach
1931-72

Forest "Aggie" Sale
1931-32-33

7 - John "Frenchy"
DeMoisey
1932-33-34

4-Layton "Mickey"
Rouse
1938-39-40

★26 - Kenny Rollins
1943-47-48

★15 - Alex Groza
1945-47-48-49

★12 - Ralph Beard
1946-47-48-49

★27 - Wallace Jones
1946-47-48-49

★22 - Cliff Barker
1947-48-49

*30 - Frank Ramsey
1951-52-54

★Member of "The Fabulous Five,"
1948 National Champions & Olympic Gold Medalists
*Member of 1954 Undefeated National Champions

*6 - Cliff Hagan
1951-52-54

*16 - Lou Tsioropoulos
1951-52-54

*42 - Billy Evans
1952-54-55

*20 - Gayle Rose
1952-54-55

Cawood Ledford
"Voice of the Wildcats"
1953-92

*22 - Jerry Bird
1954-55-56

*44 - Phil Grawemeyer
1954-55-56

50 - Bob Burrow
1955-56

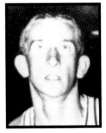

52 - Vernon Hatton
1956-57-58

24 - Johnny Cox
1957-58-59

Bill Keightley "Mr. Wildcat"
Equipment Manager
1962-2008

44 - Cotton Nash
1962-63-64

10 - Louie Dampier
1965-66-67

44 - Dan Issel
1968-69-70 UK's
All -Time Leading Scorer

Coach Joe B. Hall
Head Coach
1973-85

35 - Kevin Grevey
1973-74-75

21 - Jack Givens
1975-76-77-78

53 - Rick Robey
1975-76-77-78

4 - Kyle Macy
1978-79-80

32 - Richie Farmer
1989-90-91-92

12 - Deron Feldhaus
1989-90-91-92

34 - John Pelphrey
1989-90-91-92

11 - Sean Woods
1990-91-92

Rick Pitino
Head Coach
1990-1997

77 - Bill Spivey
1949-50

42 - Pat Riley
1965-66-67

24 - Jamal Mashburn
1991-92-93

Burgess Carey
1925-26

34 - Kenny Walker
1983-84-85-86

31 - Sam Bowie
1980-81-84

All-Americans

Basil Hayden
Forward-1921
Paris High School
Paris, Ky.

Burgess Carey
Guard-1925
Lexington Senior High School
Lexington, Ky.

Carey Spicer
Forward-1929,31
Lexington Senior High School
Lexington, Ky.

Paul McBrayer
Guard-1930
Kavanaugh High School
Lawrenceburg, Ky.

Forest Sale
Center-Forward-1932,33
Kavanaugh High School
Lawrenceburg, Ky.

Ellis Johnson
Guard-1933
Ashland High School
Ashland, Ky.

John DeMoisey
Center-1934
Walton High School
Walton, Ky.

LeRoy Edwards
Center-1935
Tech High School
Indianapolis, Ind.

Dave Lawrence
Forward-1935
Corinth High School
Corinth, Ky.

Bernard Opper
Guard-1939
Morris High School
New York, N.Y.

Lee Huber
Guard-1941
St. Xavier High School
Louisville, Ky.

Bob Brannum
Center-1944
Winfield High School
Winfield, Kan.

Jack Parkinson
Guard-1946
Yorktown High School
Yorktown, Ind.

Jack Tingle
Forward-1947
Trimble High School
Bedford, Ky.

Ralph Beard
Guard-1947,48,49**
Male High School
Louisville, Ky.

Alex Groza
*Center-1947,48**,49**
Martins Ferry High School
Martins Ferry, Ohio

Wallace Jones
*Forward-1949***
Harlan High School
Harlan, Ky.

Bill Spivey
*Center-1951***
Warner Robins High School
Warner Robins, Ga.

Cliff Hagan
Center-1952,54**
Owensboro High School
Owensboro, Ky.

Frank Ramsey
*Guard-1952,54***
Madisonville High School
Madisonville, Ky.

Bob Burrow
*Center-1956***
Wells High School
Wells, Texas

Vernon Hatton
Guard-1958
Lafayette High School
Lexington, Ky.

Johnny Cox
*Forward-1959***
Hazard High School
Hazard, Ky.

Cotton Nash
*Forward-Center-1962**,63**,64**
Lake Charles High School
Lake Charles, La.

12

Pat Riley
Forward-1966
Linton High School
Schenectady, N.Y.

Louie Dampier
Guard-1966,67***
Southport High School
Indianapolis, Ind.

Dan Issel
Center-1969,70*
Batavia High School
Batavia, Ill.

Kevin Grevey
Forward-1974,75
Taft High School
Hamilton, Ohio

Jack Givens
Forward-1977,78
Bryan Station High School
Lexington, Ky.

Rick Robey
Forward-Center-1977,78
Brother Martin High School
New Orleans, La.

Kyle Macy
Guard-1979,80*
Peru High School
Peru, Ind.

Sam Bowie
Center-1981
Lebanon High School
Lebanon, Pa.

Melvin Turpin
Center-1984**
Bryan Station High School
Lexington, Ky.

Kenny Walker
Forward-1985,86*
Crawford Co. High School
Roberta, Ga.

Jamal Mashburn
Forward-1993*
Cardinal Hayes High School
New York, N.Y.

Tony Delk
Guard-1996*
Haywood High School
Brownsville, Tenn.

Ron Mercer
Guard-Forward-1997*
Oak Hill Academy, Va.
Nashville, Tenn.

Tayshaun Prince
Forward-2001, 02**
Dominguez High School
Compton, Calif.

Jodie Meeks
Guard-2009
Pine Crest High School
Ft. Lauderdale, Fla.

John Wall
Guard-2010
Word of God High School
Raleigh, N.C.

DeMarcus Cousins
Center-2010
LeFlore High School
Mobile, Ala.

Anthony Davis
Center-2012
Perspectives Charter School
Chicago, Ill.

Michael Kidd-Gilchrist
Forward-2012
St. Patrick High School
Elizabeth, N.J.

Julius Randle
Forward-2014
Prestonwood Christian Academy
Dallas, Texas

Willie Cauley-Stein
Center-2015
Northwest High School
Olathe, Kan.

Karl-Anthony Towns
Center-2015
St. Joseph High School
Piscataway, N.J.

Tyler Ulis
Guard-2016
Marion Catholic
Chicago, Ill.

Jamal Murray
Guard-2016
Orangeville Prep
Kitchener, Ont., Canada

Wildcat Profiles

DEREK ANDERSON
(1996-97, 6'5", guard, Louisville, Ky.)

Transferred to UK after playing two seasons at Ohio State, where he scored 554 points. Made an immediate impact once he became eligible at UK, helping lead the Cats to a 34-2 record and the 1996 NCAA championship in his first season. Had a season-high 18 in the Cats' 101-70 NCAA tourney win over Utah. Scored 11 points, including a crucial three-pointer, in UK's 76-67 win over Syracuse in the title game. Was superb in the 1996 Mideast Regional, earning all-tourney recognition after scoring 30 points in wins over Utah and Wake Forest. Averaged 9.4 points and had 61 steals as a junior. Came back strong the following year, and was on his way to a possible MVP season when he went down with a torn ACL on Jan. 18 against Auburn. At the time of his injury, he was averaging 17.7 points. Scored a career-best 30 points twice, against Alaska-Anchorage and Indiana. Opened the season by scoring 77 points in UK's first three games. Finished second on the team in scoring, free throw shoot-

ing (81.1 percent), assists (3.5) and steals (1.9). His absence likely cost the Cats a second straight national title. With him watching from the sidelines, UK lost an 84-79 overtime thriller to Arizona in the final game. His blend of quickness, athleticism, offensive ability and defensive daring made him the quintessential Pitino-type player. Finished his college career with 1,228 points. Drafted by the Cleveland Cavaliers as the 13th pick overall in the 1997 NBA draft.

JIM ANDREWS
(1971-73, 6'11", center, Lima, Ohio)

An underrated player who has the rare distinction of being the starting center and leading scorer for Adolph Rupp's last team and Joe B. Hall's first team. Saw action in 24 games as a sophomore during the 1970-71 season, serving primarily as backup to Tom Payne. Came off the bench to score 19 points in only his seventh varsity game. Hit two late free throws and had a crucial blocked shot in the Cats' 82-79 win over LSU. Had 14 points and 12 rebounds in

a 102-83 SEC title-clinching win over Auburn. Became a full-time starter the next season, and immediately proved to be an offensive war horse. Averaged 21.5 points and 11.3 rebounds while making good on nearly 58 percent of his field goal attempts. Scored 37 in the season opener against Northwestern. Turned in a 34-point, 19-rebound effort against Mississippi State. Also had 34 against Vanderbilt and 32 against Georgia. His strong All-SEC performance helped Rupp's last team finish with a 21-7 record. As a senior, he was the anchor on a team that featured sophomore sensations Kevin Grevey, Jimmy Dan Conner, Mike Flynn and Bob Guyette. Had 33 points, 19 rebounds and five assists in a 95-68 win over Oregon. Racked up 57 points in back-to-back SEC wins over Florida and Georgia. Hit for 30 to help the Cats beat Austin Peay in the NCAA Tournament. Earned All-SEC honors after averaging 20.1 points and 12.4 rebounds for the 20-8 Wildcats. Ended his UK career with 1,320 points. His career field goal percentage of 56.3 is sixth best on UK's all-time list. Also ranks among UK's top dozen career rebounders with 783. Following a brief pro career in the NBA and overseas, he returned to Lexington, where he is now a vice president and director of marketing.

PHIL ARGENTO
(1967-69, 6'2", guard, Cleveland, Ohio)

Tough-minded, competitive backcourt player capable of blistering the nets on any given night. A solid defender and a superb marksman from the charity stripe. Flashed his great offensive potential in the final two games of the 1966-67 season, hitting for 21 against Vandy and 20 against Alabama. In that game against the Crimson Tide, he nailed 10 of 13 field goal attempts. Made good on 28 of 31 free throws as a sophomore. Averaged 5.2 points that year. Was having a solid junior campaign when he went down with an ankle injury that forced him to miss the last half of the season. Had 23 points and seven rebounds against Xavier, then came through with 18 points to lead the Cats to a come-from-behind victory over Notre Dame. In back-to-back efforts prior to his injury, he burned Vandy with a 25-point performance and Alabama with 24 points, including 23 in the second half. Averaged 13.2 points as a junior. Shot 48.7 percent from the field and 79.6 percent from the free throw line. In his final season, he canned 11 of 16 field goal attempts in a 27-point performance against Notre Dame. Had 21 points and five assists in a 103-89 win over Pete Maravich-led LSU. Cracked double figures 13 times during the 1968-69 season. Finished

his final year with a scoring average of 10 points per game. Shot 81.4 percent from the charity stripe and 49.3 percent from the field during his career. Drafted by the Los Angeles Lakers in the 10th round of the 1969 NBA draft.

KELENNA AZUBUIKE
(2003-05, 6'5", guard-forward, Tulsa, Okla.)

Another in a long line of quick, strong, athletic types who could do equal damage to opposing defenses from beyond the three-point arc or deep in the paint. Left UK after his junior season, finishing with 970 career points. Earned All-SEC tourney recognition in his final two seasons, and was voted second-team All-SEC as a junior. Came into his own as a sophomore, then really blossomed into a steady scorer during his final campaign. Averaged 14.7 points as a junior. Blistered Auburn with a career-high 30-point effort. Scored 24 against North Carolina and 21 against Tennessee Tech, Morehead State and South Carolina. Averaged 11.1 points per game during his sophomore season. Had a season-high 23 points against Georgia. Cracked double figures on 11 occasions. Played sparingly as a freshman, but did turn in one outstanding effort, ringing up 16 points in a 106-44 romp over Vanderbilt while hitting all six field goal tries, including two treys, and both free throw attempts. Shot 82 percent (23 of 28) from the charity stripe as a rookie. Left UK to pursue a career in the NBA. Had a brilliant prep career, leading Oklahoma in scoring in each of his final three seasons. Led his team to the state 4A title as a senior.

CLIFF BARKER
(1947-49, 6'2", guard-forward, Yorktown, Ind.)

The oldest member of the fabled "Fabulous Five," he was a magician with the basketball and a brilliant passer. Originally came to UK in the late '30s, played part of his freshman year, then dropped out of school, married and joined the Air Force. Landed in a German POW camp after being shot down while serving as an engineer and gunner on a B-17 bomber. Learned his magical ball-handling skills while playing around with a volleyball given to the prisoners by the Red Cross. Was a valuable sub on the 1946-47 club, then moved into the starting lineup one year later. It was the 1947-48 team, which featured Barker, Wah Wah Jones, Alex Groza, Kenny Rollins and Ralph Beard, that came to be immortalized as the "Fabulous Five." That magnificent team went 36-3, won the NCAA Tournament and the Olympic gold medal the fol-

Three-time All-American Ralph Beard is still regarded as the yardstick by which all UK guards are measured. The Wildcats went 130-10, won two NCAA championships and one NIT title during the four years Beard and Wah Wah Jones wore the Blue and White.

lowing summer in London. The next season, the 28-year-old Barker averaged 7.3 points as the Cats repeated as national champs. Although never a major scorer, his unselfish attitude (and that of Rollins) allowed more offense-minded players like Groza, Beard, Jones, Jim Line and Dale Barnstable the freedom to put up big numbers. Later joined with several of his fellow "Fabulous Five" teammates to form the Indianapolis Olympians in the NBA. Went on to become a high school coach in Charlestown, Ind., where he coached Cotton Nash for two years before the Nash family moved to Louisiana. The most unsung player on that "Fabulous Five" team. Also, one of the most essential.

DALE BARNSTABLE
(1947-50, 6'3" guard/forward, Antioch, Ill.)

An unheralded but important contributor on two UK teams that captured NCAA championships. Was especially critical to the Cats repeating as NCAA champs in 1948-49, stepping in to replace the graduated Kenny Rollins as the fifth starter, along with veterans Wah Wah Jones, Ralph Beard, Alex Groza and Cliff Barker. Averaged 6.1 points per game that season, hitting for a high of 15 against DePaul. Scored 13 against Georgia Tech, Ole Miss and Georgia. His efforts landed him a spot on the All-SEC third team. As a senior in 1949-50, he scored at a 5.9 clip. Hit for 18 against Western Ontario and Vandy. Tossed in 12 against Purdue and Mississippi State. Played little as a freshman in 1946-47, scoring just 71 points in 27 games. His season-best was an eight-point effort against Auburn. One year later, as a sophomore, he hit for a season-high 17 points in a win over DePaul. He also scored 10 against Georgia. Taken by Boston in the 1950 NBA draft. Came to UK from Antioch, Ill.

RALPH BEARD
(1946-49, 5'10", guard, Louisville, Ky.)

Still regarded to this day as the yardstick by which all UK guards are measured. Cheetah-quick and fiercely competitive, Beard was a guard for the ages and probably the most popular member of the "Fabulous Five." His list of accomplishments, both individual and team-wise, is truly astonishing. Three-time All-American, four-time All-SEC, four-time All-SEC tourney, 1,517 career points, Most Outstanding Player to play in Madison Square Garden in 1946, first player to grace the cover of *Sports Illustrated* magazine. More important, during his four seasons the Wildcats won

two NCAA championships, one NIT title, an Olympic gold medal, were 130-10 overall, 55-0 against SEC competition, had a winning margin of 28 points per game and won 27 games by margins in excess of 40 points. As a freshman, he scored a season-high 18 points to lead the Cats to a 55-44 win over Michigan State, Rupp's first triumph over the Spartans. Played brilliantly in the NIT, accounting for 37 points in three games. It was his free throw with 40 seconds left that beat Rhode Island 46-45 in the title game. Led the team in scoring as a sophomore with a 10.9 average. Scored 20 against Georgia Tech, 19 against Georgia and 18 against Wabash. He and Alex Groza combined for 35 points in UK's 60-30 rout of Notre Dame. Scored 31 points in UK's first two NIT games, then was held to a single point in the 49-45 championship game loss to Utah. Averaged 12.5 points during his junior year. Scored 13 against Holy Cross in the NCAA semifinal round and 12 as UK topped Baylor 58-42 to claim the first of its seven NCAA championships. Gave three memorable performances in the Olympic Trials, scoring 22 against Louisville, 13 in a rematch with Baylor and 23 against the Phillips Oilers. Averaged 10.9 as a senior, helping lead the Cats to a second straight NCAA title. Opened his final season with a 20-point performance against Indiana Central. Also hit for 20 in a 63-61 win over Bowling Green. Started three games at halfback for the UK football team before an injury led to his decision to concentrate solely on basketball. Came to UK after an outstanding prep career at Louisville Male High. Was an all-state selection his final two years, leading Male to the 1945 state championship. Made a smooth and successful transition to the NBA, where he was voted first-team All-NBA following the 1951 season, which turned out to be his last. Because of his involvement in the point-shaving scandal of the late '40s and early '50s, he was banned from playing in the NBA, thus bringing to an end a career that was just getting started. Had Beard not been derailed by the scandal, there is no doubt that he would be an NBA Hall of Fame legend. But nothing can tarnish Beard's legacy at UK, or diminish the enormity of his talent. He was a blur, a burner, one of the few old-time players with the speed and quickness to compete in today's game.

WINSTON BENNETT
(1984-86, 88, 6'7", forward, Louisville, Ky.)

A rugged combatant who combined great strength with agility. Scored 1,399 career points and grabbed 799

rebounds. Led the 1987-88 club in rebounding with an average of 7.8. Played three seasons, then had to sit out a year after suffering a severe knee injury. As a freshman, he came off the bench to score 11 points in a 74-67 UK win over the Hakeem Olajuwon-led Houston Cougars. Hit for a season-high 17 in wins over Alabama and Auburn. His critical three-pointer helped lift the Cats to a 72-67 win over Louisville in NCAA Tournament Mideast Regional final. Averaged 6.5 points as a freshman. Scored at a 7.2 clip as a sophomore with a season best of 14 against N.C. State and Florida. Had a superb junior season, averaging 12.7 points for Eddie Sutton's first UK team, which finished with a 32-4 record. Burned Louisville for 23 points in a 69-64 Wildcat victory. Scored 26 in a win over Tennessee and 20 in UK's SEC title-clinching 80-75 win over Georgia. Came back after missing the 1986-87 campaign to average a career-best 15.3 points per game while hitting 51.3 percent of his field goal attempts. Had 28 points and 10 rebounds against Miami (Ohio) and 24 points and 10 rebounds against Alaska. Pulled down a career-high 17 rebounds in a win over Vanderbilt. Scored 25 against Alabama and 24 against LSU. Had 56 points in UK's three SEC tourney wins. Earned All-SEC honors in 1986 and 1988. Shot 48.4 percent from the field and 71.3 percent from the free throw line during his UK career. Was a prep All-State performer at Male High in Louisville and Kentucky's 1983 Mr. Basketball. By signing with UK, he ended the school's more than decade long failure to land a top black player from Louisville. Played in the NBA with Cleveland and Miami, then joined Rick Pitino's coaching staff at UK and later at Boston.

JERRY BIRD
(1954-56, 6'6", forward, Corbin, Ky.)

The eldest brother in one of Kentucky's greatest athletic families. His brothers Calvin, Rodger and Billy all played football at UK, and his son Steve was a standout receiver at Eastern Kentucky University. He was a substitute on the unbeaten 1953-54 team, then moved into a starting role the following year. Averaged 10.7 points as a junior and 16.2 in his final season. Had a career-best 34-point performance against Dayton. Scored a team-high 22 points in UK's record-breaking 143-66 win over Georgia. Had 23 points in a losing cause against Iowa in the 1956 Eastern Regional final. Was drafted in the third round by the NBA's Minneapolis franchise. Currently lives in Corbin.

ERIC BLEDSOE
(2009-10, 6'1", guard, Birmingham, Ala.)

An excellent outside threat who shot 46 percent from the field and 38 percent from three-point range during his only season at UK. His great speed and jumping ability allowed him to compete successfully against taller opponents. Began his UK career with a 24-point effort against Morehead State. Hit for a career-high 29 points against East Tennessee State in NCAA tourney action. Burned Florida for 25 and Indiana for 23, helping the Cats secure tough road wins. Averaged 11.3 points per game at UK. Also had 52 steals. Earned a spot on the SEC All-Tournament team. Came close to averaging a triple-double during his senior season Parker High School. Scored at a 20.3 clip, handed out 11.5 assists and yanked down 9.4 rebounds per game. Led Parker High to a runner-up finish in the 5A championship. Named the No. 1 Super Senior by Birmingham *News*. Left UK for the NBA after his rookie season.

KEITH BOGANS
(1999-03, 6'5", guard, Alexandria, Va.)

Strong, tough competitor who possessed the outside shooting touch of a small guard and the physical strength to punish defenders on his way to the bucket. Ended his career as UK's fourth all-time top scorer with 1,923 points. His 743 three-point attempts are the most-ever by a Wildcat, and his 243 treys are second behind Tony Delk. Had one stretch of 29 straight games in which he accounted for at least one three-pointer. Wasted little time displaying his great potential, racking up 17 points against Maryland in only his third game. Hit double figures 23 times as a frosh, including season-best efforts of 25 points against Tennessee and Arkansas. Ended his rookie season with a 12.5 scoring average. Earned All-SEC Freshman team recognition for his efforts. Came back as a sophomore to average a team-leading 17 points per game, teaming with Tayshaun Prince to give the Cats a powerful 1-2 punch. Hit for a career-high 29 against Florida. Torched both Indiana and Georgia with 26. Named to the SEC all-tournament first team, and was a second-team All-SEC pick. Struggled through a disappointing junior campaign, yet still scored at an 11.6 clip. Hit for 20 points or better five times, including a 23-point performance against Notre Dame. Bounced back as a senior to score a team-best 15.7 points per game on a Wildcat club that went 32-4, won 25 straight games, finished 16-0 in SEC play, then capped things off by claim-

ing the SEC tourney title. Hit for double figures in 32 of 36 games. Scored a season-best 26 in a win over Tennessee State. Named SEC Player of the Year by league coaches. Started 122 games at UK, second only to Ralph Beard. Had 314 assists, placing him 13th on that list. Played his prep ball at legendary DeMatha Catholic High School.

SAM BOWIE
(1980-81, 84, 7'1", center-forward, Lebanon, Pa.)

One of the great "what-ifs" in UK basketball history. Among the most agile 7-footers to ever pick up a basketball. Capable of scoring inside or hitting a medium-range jumper. Also, an excellent rebounder and shot-blocker. Played his freshman and sophomore seasons, missed two years because of a leg injury, then returned for the 1983-84 campaign. Flashed his great promise by scoring 22 points and pulling down 17 rebounds against Duke in his UK debut. Played brilliantly in the SEC Tournament, scoring 66 points in three games, including a season-best 27 against Ole Miss in the semifinal game. Averaged 12.9 points, 8.1 rebounds and 2.1 blocked shots while hitting 53 percent of his field goal attempts during his freshman campaign. Came back the next season to average 17.4 points and 9.1 rebounds. Had 29 points and 16 rebounds in a win over Kansas, 29 points against Florida, and a 27-point, 12-rebound performance against Mississippi State. Earned All-SEC recognition in each of his first two years at UK. Returned after his two-year layoff to average 10.5 points and 9.2 rebounds as a senior. Scored 20 points three times that year. Also had 16 rebounds in a win over LSU. Finished his UK career with 1,285 points, 843 rebounds and a 52.2 percent field goal accuracy. Was the second overall pick in the 1984 NBA draft (Michael Jordan was third), going to Portland. Also played for the Nets and Lakers before injuries forced him into retirement. Currently lives in Lexington and is a former color analyst for the UK basketball broadcasts.

BOB BRANNUM
(1943-44, 47, 6'5", center, Winfield, Kan.)

Only played one full season at UK and it was a memorable one. A raw, brawny, tough character who loved nothing better than a physical battle. Averaged 12.1 points for the youthful 1943-44 "Wildkittens" club that surprised everyone by winning the SEC Tournament and finishing with a 19-2 record. Brannum's scoring clip was one of the highest in UK history at the time. Had 14 points, including a game-winning three-point play, in a 55-54 win over Notre Dame. Scored 18 in

wins over Cincinnati and Wright Field, and 17 in a tough 38-35 win over DePauw. At 17, he became the youngest player to earn All-America honors. Also made the All-SEC team. Left UK after his freshman season and entered the military. Upon returning to UK for the 1946-47 season, he found the talent pool so deep that he failed to make the 10-man traveling squad for the SEC tourney. Transferred to Michigan State, where he was an outstanding performer.

JEFF BRASSOW
(1990-91, 93-94, 6'5", forward/guard, Houston, Texas)

Had an outstanding career despite suffering a devastating knee injury that forced him to miss all but two games during his junior season. Known for his never-say-die spirit and for consistently dropping three-point bombs on opponents in crucial situations. A freshman on Pitino's first team, he was one the "seven men of iron" who led that undermanned club to a surprising 14-14 record. Averaged 6.8 points as a rookie. Scored 20 against Tennessee Tech in only his fourth game as a Wildcat. Later hit for a season-best 25 in a 94-81 loss to LSU. Averaged 8.1 points for the 1990-91 team that finished with a 22-6 record. Shot 81.5 percent from the charity stripe. Scored 18 points in a tough 93-85 win over Louisville. Had 15 points, 10 rebounds and four steals in the Cats' 81-65 win over Florida. Opened his junior campaign with a 23-point performance against West Virginia in the preseason NIT. Granted a medical redshirt after going down with a torn ACL. Came back the next season to average 3.9 points per game for the 1992-93 team that reached the Final Four. Scored a season-high 14 in an early 96-87 win over 13th-ranked Georgia Tech. Averaged seven points per game as a fifth-year senior. His miraculous last-second tip-in lifted the Cats past Arizona 93-92 in the championship game of the Maui Classic. Buried six of 12 three-point attempts and scored 25 points to lead UK to a 79-67 win over South Carolina. Scored 14 points and hit four crucial treys to help the Cats erase a 31-point second-half deficit and beat LSU 99-95 on the road. Had 44 points in three SEC tourney games, including 19 in a 95-76 first-round win over Mississippi State. Ended his career with 807 points and a 73.4 percent accuracy from the free throw stripe.

BOB BURROW
(1955-56, 6'7", center, Wells, Texas)

An excellent pivot man who came to UK after a scoring more than 2,000 points for Lon Morris Junior College.

Scored 1,023 points and pulled down 823 rebounds in his two seasons at UK. Averaged 19 points and 17.7 rebounds as a junior, 21.1 points and 14.6 rebounds during his final year. During those two seasons the Cats were 43-9. Exploded for 50 points in a win over LSU, making him one of only three Wildcats to hit the half-century mark in a game. (Dan Issel and Cliff Hagan are the other two.) His 34-rebound performance against Temple is still the UK single-game best. Reached the 1,000-point club in his 51st (and final) game. (Only Cotton Nash and Issel did it faster.) Earned All-America recognition in 1956, and was voted to the All-SEC team in 1955 and 1956. Played briefly in the NBA. Is now the assistant superintendent for the Fort Knox, Ky., schools. His son, Brett, played at Vanderbilt.

GERRY CALVERT
(1955-57, 5'11", guard, Maysville, Ky.)

The "fiery little redheaded pepperpot from Maysville" was a superb backcourt player and a double-figure scorer in each of his final two seasons. A heady playmaker with excellent skills on both ends of the court. Spent his sophomore season backing up Billy Evans, Gayle Rose and Linville Puckett before Puckett left the team. Finished the season strong, scoring 19 points in an 84-59 NCAA tourney win

Fiery guard Gerry Calvert was the second-leading scorer on the 1956-57 Wildcat club.

over Penn State. Moved into the starting lineup as a junior in 1955-56 and finished with an 11.2 scoring average. Opend the season with a 17-point performance in a 62-52 win over LSU. Hit for a season-high 19 in the Cats' 62-61 come-from-behind win over Maryland. Also scored 18 in a loss to Vanderbilt. Improved his scoring average to 15.2 as a senior, second only to Johnny Cox. Scored 40 points in two UKIT wins, including 22 against SMU. Scored 23 against Vandy, 21 against Auburn and 20 in each of the Cats' two easy wins over Tennessee. Served as co-captain of the 1956-57 club. Originally signed with the University of Louisville after finishing his prep career at Maysville High School, but soon changed his mind when assistant coach Harry Lancaster offered a scholarship to UK. Went on to become a successful lawyer in Lexington.

BURGESS CAREY
(1925-26, 6'0", guard, Lexington, Ky.)

Maybe the lowest-scoring All-American in college basketball history. Scored only 29 points in 18 games during the 1925-26 campaign, with a single-game high of five. Earned his All-America status because of his great prowess as a defensive player. Tall for the time, strong and rugged, Carey was a "back guard," a player stationed near the opponent's basket whose expressed purpose was to keep the enemy from scoring. Carey was captain of the 1925-26 club, which finished with a 15-3 record. Came to UK after leading Lexington Senior High School to state and national championships in 1922.

RALPH CARLISLE
(1935-37, 6'2", forward, Kavanaugh, Ky.)

A two-time All-SEC performer who was the Cats' leading scorer during his junior and senior seasons. Average 11.5 as a junior and 9.9 as a senior. In his junior year, he scored 20 in a come-from-behind 49-40 win over Xavier. Racked up 36 points in three games to help the Cats win the 1937 SEC tourney title. A solid rebounder and defender, and an excellent free throw shooter. Went on to become one of the most celebrated coaches in Kentucky high school history. His teams were known to be disciplined and exceptionally sound fundamentally. Coached at Kavanaugh, Highlands and Lexington Lafayette. Led Lafayette to state championships in 1950, 1953 and 1957. Among the players he coached at Lafayette were Wildcat standouts Vernon Hatton and Billy Ray Lickert.

MIKE CASEY
(1967-69, 71, 6'4", guard, Shelbyville, Ky.)

One of the great clutch performers in UK history. Rupp called him "the best money player I ever had." Came to UK after leading Shelby County High to the 1966 state tourney championship. Was part of a terrific class that included Dan Issel and Mike Pratt. Led the team in scoring as a sophomore with a 20.1 average. Scored 28 points in his first varsity game, the most-ever by a Wildcat rookie. His 26-point, six-steal performance in a comeback win over Notre Dame was indicative of his you-can't-beat-me attitude. Scored 60 points in two wins over LSU, including a season-high 31 in the first meeting. Had 30 against Mississippi State and 29 against Georgia. Led the team in field goal and free throw accuracy as a sophomore, and was named team MVP. Averaged 19.1 points and 4.6 assists during his junior campaign. Opened the 1968-69 season with a 29-point performance against Xavier. Scored 26 against North Carolina and 25 against Mississippi State. Led the team with 21 points in the NCAA tourney loss to Marquette. Joined the 1,000-point club in his 51st game. Suffered a broken leg in an automobile accident and had to miss the 1969-70 season, possibly costing UK another NCAA title. Came back a year later, and although a step slower, he still managed to average 17 points per game while hitting 50.4 percent of his shots. Scored 25 in his second game back, a 104-93 win over Michigan. Poured in 146 points during a six-game stretch, including 27 against Purdue and 26 against DePaul and Mississippi State. Finished his career with 1,535 points and an average of 18.7. Also handed out 260 assists. Was a three-time All-SEC selection. Kentucky's prep Mr. Basketball in 1966.

REX CHAPMAN
(1987-88, 6'4", guard, Owensboro, Ky.)

Possibly the most-heralded recruit in UK history, and certainly one of the most sought-after. Had a storybook career at Apollo High School in Owensboro, earning All-America and All-State recognition. Christened "King Rex" and "The Boy King" by legions of adoring UK fans. One sportswriter, after viewing Chapman-mania, suggested that Lexington be renamed "Rexington." Played the game with great flair, confidence and reckless abandon. An exceptional leaper who could dunk over taller opponents or step outside and

bury the trey. Had 18 points in his Wildcat debut. In a nationally televised game, he scorched Louisville for 26 points, hitting five of eight three-point attempts. Also had 26 in games against Indiana, Boston University and Tennessee. Hit five straight treys and scored 24 points in a win over Auburn. Knocked down a last-second bucket to beat Ole Miss 64-63. Ended his rookie season with a 16-point average. His 464 points are the most scored by a Wildcat freshman. Topped the club again in scoring as a sophomore, averaging 19 points per game. Hit for 29 against Ole Miss and 26 against Georgia. Scored 62 points and was voted MVP after leading UK to the SEC tourney title. Racked up 76 points in the Cats' three 1988 NCAA Tournament games, including a career-best 30 against Villanova. A two-time All-SEC performer. Finished his career with 1,073 points. Left UK after his sophomore season and was taken in the first round of the NBA draft by Charlotte. After a successful 12-year career, he retired from pro ball. His father, Wayne, played as a freshman at UK with Pat Riley and Louie Dampier, then transferred to Western Kentucky University.

TRUMAN CLAYTOR
(1976-79, 6'1", guard, Toledo, Ohio)

This Toledo, Ohio, native was a superb warrior on both ends of the court. A deadly outside shooter, he's another Wildcat guard who would have benefited tremendously had the three-point shot been around when he played. Scored 14 points in his debut effort against Northwestern as a frosh in 1975-76. He later hit two crucial free throws that helped the Cats clip Kansas 54-48. Scored 18 in a comeback win over Notre Dame. His late layup enabled the Cats to put away Niagara 67-61 in the NIT. Had several huge games as a sophomore in 1976-77, including a 29-point effort in the Cats' 93-78 win over VMI. In that game, he knocked down 13 of 15 field goal attempts. Scored 22 against Florida and 16 against Vandy. Came off the bench to score 12 points in a 72-58 NCAA tourney win over Princeton. Averaged 6.6 points as a sophomore. Was a solid, consistent performer for the powerful 1977-78 NCAA championship club, averaging 6.9 points per game. Had 17 points in a 101-77 win over Auburn and 16 in a win over St. John's. Handed out a career-best eight assists against Florida. Led the Cats with 16 points in that dramatic come-from-behind 85-76 NCAA tourney win

over Florida State. Scored eight points in the 94-88 title game win over Duke. Had an excellent senior season in 1978-79, finishing with an 8.7 scoring average while serving as co-captain. Scored 18 points to help the Cats battle back to beat Notre Dame. Was absolutely brilliant in the SEC tourney, scoring 84 points in four games. Hit 11 of 14 shots en route to a 25-point effort in UK's big 101-100 upset of Alabama, then followed that by scoring 20 against LSU. Scored 27 in the 75-69 OT loss to Tennessee in the championship game. His efforts earned him a spot on the All-SEC tourney team. Shot 77 percent from the free throw line and handed out 213 assists during his career. Taken by the Detroit Pistons in the sixth round of the 1979 NBA draft. Another underrated Wildcat.

LARRY CONLEY
(1964-66, 6'3", forward, Ashland, Ky.)

The heart and soul of the beloved "Rupp's Runts" team that came out of nowhere to finish with a 27-2 record and the runner-up spot in the NCAA Tournament. An exceptionally cerebral player and the most pin-point passer in Wildcat history. If there was an opening, no matter how small, he could get the ball to a teammate. Rupp called him "a coach on the floor." After that magical 1965-66 season, one sportswriter said Conley had been "the spirit of the team." Although wiry and frail-looking, he was a tough, durable player. Came in with Tommy Kron and Mickey Gibson, a talented trio dubbed the "Katzenjammer Kids" by Rupp. Started as a sophomore, averaging 12.2 points and 4.2 assists per game while leading the team with 49.3 percent field goal accuracy. Scored 17 points in his second game, then later came back with a season-high 20 against Florida. Shared team MVP honors with Cotton Nash. Averaged 11.6 points and 3.2 assists as a junior. Hit for a career-high 31 in a tough 91-90 loss to Vanderbilt. Scored 23 against Vandy in the second meeting. Prior to the start of the 1965-66 season, he and Kron unselfishly decided to sacrifice their own scoring, thus allowing Louie Dampier, Pat Riley and Thad Jaracz to become the principal offensive threats. (And get the lion's share of ink.) Still, Conley managed to average 11.5 points in that memorable season. His best scoring night was a 17-point effort against Florida. Had 14 points in UK's 84-77 win over Michigan in the Mideast Regional final. Scored 10 points in an 83-79 semifinal win over Duke despite suffering from the flu. Ended his career with 293 assists, a number that would be much higher were today's liberal assist standards used back then. Was a two-time

All-State performer at Ashland High School, leading his club to a state title in 1961 and a runner-up finish in 1962. The 1961 team is still considered by many to be the best in Kentucky history. Conley was a highly regarded college basketball analyst for several networks.

JIMMY DAN CONNER
(1973-75, 6'4", guard-forward, Lawrenceburg, Ky.)

A key member of the talented recruiting class that included Kevin Grevey, Mike Flynn, Bob Guyette, Steve Lochmueller, G.J. Smith and Jerry Hale. The steady Conner was always cool and calm, never buckling under pressure. Averaged 11.2 points and a team-leading three assists per game as a sophomore on Joe B. Hall's first team. Hit for a season-high 27 against Auburn. Scored 23 in an 86-81 victory over Tennessee. Also proved himself to be an excellent defensive player and rebounder. Averaged 12 points on the disappointing 1973-74 team. His high game that season was 24 in a 94-79 loss to Notre Dame. Scored at a 12.4 clip as a senior and was one of the leaders on that 1974-75 NCAA runner-up club. Blistered the nets for 35 in a big win over North Carolina, making good on 15 of 21 field goal attempts. Scored 27 against Auburn. Nailed three straight jumpers to help the Cats hold off Ole Miss for an 85-82 win. His two late free throws sealed UK's 91-90 win over Vanderbilt. Came up huge in UK's 92-90 upset of Indiana in the Mideast Regional final, scoring 17 points. Scored 1,009 points and shot 50 percent from the field during his career. Also had 264 career assists. Had a standout prep career at Anderson County, leading his team to a runner-up finish in the 1971 Sweet 16. Was named Kentucky's Mr. Basketball after his senior season. Drafted by Phoenix in the NBA, later played for the Kentucky Colonels in the ABA. Currently lives in Louisville.

DeMARCUS COUSINS
(2009-10, 6'11", center, Mobile, Ala.)

Powerful, unpredictable post player with a mercurial personality and prime-time NBA talent. Only played one year at UK, yet established himself as one of the school's best-ever centers. Also, one of the most colorful. Averaged 15.1 points and 9.8 rebounds despite playing only playing 23.5 minutes per game due to consistent foul trouble. Shot 56 percent from the field. Recorded 19 double-doubles, including one stretch of seven games in a row. Had career-best scoring nights of 27 against Sam Houston State and South Carolina. Scored 24 against UNC-Asheville and

21 against Vanderbilt. Pulled down 18 rebounds against Sam Houston State and Louisville. Had 19 points and 15 rebounds in a win over Tennessee. Named SEC Freshman of the Week four times and Player of the Week once. Voted to the All-SEC first team, and was named to the SEC All-Tournament team. Came to UK after a sterling prep career at LeFlore High, where he twice led his team to the Alabama Class 6A Final Four. Averaged 24.1 points and 13.2 rebounds per game as a senior. Earned McDonald's and Parade All-America recognition. Was a member of the 2009 USA Junior National Select Team. Went to the NBA as a first-round draft pick.

FRED COWAN
(1978-81, 6'9", forward/center, Sturgis, Ky.)

A slender inside player who more than held his own against bigger, stronger competitors. The third Wildcat in a 10-year span to hail from Union County. (Dwane Casey and Larry Johnson preceded him.) Finished his career with 975 points and 489 rebounds. Played sparingly as a freshman in 1977-78, scoring just 36 points. As a sophomore, he averaged 9.4 points and 5.5 rebounds per contest. Had a season-best 20 points and 10 rebounds against Georgia. Also had double-doubles against Ole Miss (17/12), LSU (16/13) and LSU again (10/10). Scored at a 12.5 clip as a junior in 1979-80, with a season-high 27-point, nine-rebound outing against LSU. Had 20 points against Vandy and gave a 19-point, 11-rebound effort against Alaska-Anchorage. Earned a spot on the All-Regional team after scoring 26 points in UK's NCAA tourney loss to Duke. Pulled down 5.7 rebounds per game. Came back to average 8.2 points as a senior. His best outings that year were 22 against Georgia and 19 against Kansas. Drafted in the sixth round of the 1981 NBA draft by Houston.

JOHNNY COX
(1957-59, 6'4", forward, Hazard, Ky.)

An All-American and one of the top guns on the "Fiddlin' Five" team that captured the 1958 NCAA championship. The best Eastern Kentucky "Mountain" Wildcat since Wah Wah Jones. Lean, leathery and tough as hickory, Cox possessed a wide variety of offensive weapons, most notably a deadly hook shot. Came to UK after leading Hazard to the 1955 state championship and was an instant force, averaging a team-high 19.4 points and 11.1 rebounds per game as a sophomore. Scored 34 points in a win over Mary-land, and had a 32-point, 23-rebound effort against Tennessee. Scored 25 against Houston in the UKIT final. Had 32 against Loyola of Chicago, 28 against Mississippi State and 26 against Florida. Also led the Cats with 26 in their 98-92 NCAA tourney win over Pittsburgh. Averaged 14.9 points and 12.6 rebounds for the "Fiddlin' Five." Twice hit for 23 during the regular season. Had 22 points and 13 rebounds in UK's 61-60 semifinal win over Temple, then followed that up with a 24-point effort in the 84-72 title-clinching victory over Seattle. In that game, Cox scored 16 of his points in the final 15 minutes. His performance earned him a spot on the all-tourney team. As a senior, Cox averaged 17.9 points and 12.2 rebounds for an unheralded UK team that ended up with a sparkling 24-3 record and a No. 2 ranking in the final polls. Kicked off his final season by ripping Florida State for 27 points in a 91-68 UK win. His 38-point, 17-rebound effort in a 69-56 win over Tennessee helped secure the Cats a spot in the NCAA tourney. Joined Jerry West, Oscar Robertson, Bob Boozer and Bailey Howell on the AP's All-America first team. Ended his career with 1,461 points and 1,004 rebounds, making him one of only four Wildcats to reach the 1,000 mark in those two areas. (Dan Issel, Frank Ramsey and Cliff Hagan are the others.) Was an All-SEC pick all three seasons. Played several years in the pros, then moved back to Hazard, where he currently resides.

JOE CRAWFORD
(2004-08, 6'5", guard/forward, Detroit, Mich.)

Another UK player who had the shooting ability to burn opponents from long-range and the strength to take them to the bucket. Had his shaky moments at UK, but steadily improved his numbers during his four years as a Wildcat. Accounted for 1,438 points wearing a Big Blue uniform, placing him 20th on the all-time scoring list. Played for Tubby Smith and Billy Gillespie. Had his best season as a senior, averaging 17.9 points per game. Saved his best for last, tossing in 35 points in UK's NCAA tourney loss to Marquette. Also had 35 against South Carolina and 32 against Texas Southern. Had 28 against Houston. Scored at a 14 points per game clip as a junior. Scored a season-best 29 against Georgia. Knocked in 24 against Tennessee and 23 against Ole Miss and South Carolina. Averaged 10.2 points as a sophomore. His season-best scoring efforts were 23-point outings against Ohio and Auburn. Cracked double figures 17 times as a sophomore. Averaged 3.2 points

as a freshman. Hit double digits three times, with a season-best 14 against LSU. Earned McDonald's All-America recognition as a senior after leading Renaissance High to a 27-0 record and the state championship. Originally committed to the University of Michigan before changing his mind and deciding to attend UK.

JOHN CRIGLER
(1956-58, 6'3", forward, Hebron, Ky.)

The starting forward opposite Cox on the 1958 championship club. A steady player who assistant coach Harry Lancaster called "the unknown and unsung player on the team." Started as a junior on the 1956-57 team that went 23-5, averaging 10.3 points per game. Hit for a season-high 24 to lead UK past Georgia Tech 95-72. Had 17 points in UK's memorable 85-83 triple-overtime win over Temple. Scored 64 points in a three-game stretch that featured wins over Alabama, Auburn and Tennessee. Averaged 13.6 points for the "Fiddlin' Five." Scored 26 in an easy UK win over Ole Miss. Had 21 points, including 17 in the first half, in a 65-61 win over Vanderbilt. His bucket with five ticks remaining lifted the Cats past Alabama 45-43 in overtime. It was his clever drives to the hoop that got Seattle All-American Elgin Baylor in early foul trouble in the championship tilt, a key factor in the Cats' 84-72 win. Crigler also contributed 14 points in that victory. Had a superb prep career at Hebron High School. Went on to become a successful coach and athletics director at Scott County High School.

LOUIE DAMPIER
(1965-67, 6'0", guard, Indianapolis, Ind.)

A member of "Rupp's Runts" and one of the all-time favorite Wildcats among Big Blue fans. A lethal outside shooter whose scoring numbers would have soared had the three-point shot been part of the college game when he played. (As he later proved during his pro career.) Scored 18 points in his first Wildcat game, then went on to lead the 1964-65 team in scoring with an average of 17 points per game. Also, shot 51.2 percent from the field and 84 percent from the free throw stripe that season. Made good on 17 of 24 field goal attempts en route to a season-high 37 points against Iowa State. Averaged 21.1 points during the unforgettable 1965-66 campaign while connecting on 51.6 percent of his shots. Had 23 points in UK's 83-79 semifinal win over Duke, then scored 19 in the championship game loss to Texas Western. His performance that season

garnered him first-team All-America recognition. Had a career-high 42 points against Vanderbilt. Averaged 20.6 in his final season, with a single-game high of 40 against Illinois. Topped the 30-point mark five times as a senior. Earned All-SEC honors during each of his three seasons as a Wildcat. Finished with 1,575 points and a career average of 19.7. Shot 50.8 percent from the field and 84.4 percent from the charity stripe, fifth best in UK history. Went on to have a brilliant pro career, helping lead the Kentucky Colonels to an ABA championship. The all-time leading scorer in ABA history with 13,725 points.

ERIK DANIELS
(2000-04, 6'8", forward, Cincinnati, Ohio)

A quiet, steady, unspectacular battler who succeeded while often playing under the radar and away from the spotlight. Scored 1,053 points, yanked down 522 rebounds and handed out 223 assists. Made good on 55 percent of his field goal attempts during his career. Had a superb senior season, finishing with a 14.5 scoring average while shooting 58 percent from the field, second-best in the SEC. Scored a career-best 24 points in a victory over Ole Miss. Tagged Arkansas for 23 points. Grabbed 14 rebounds in a 20-point win over Florida. Cracked double figures 26 times as a senior. Named first-team All-SEC by the league's coaches. Averaged 9.5 points while shooting 57 percent from the field as a junior. Scored 20 in wins over Ole Miss and Vanderbilt. Saw limited playing time during his first two years as a Wildcat, averaging 5.2 points as a freshman and 3.7 as a sophomore. Made an early impression on Big Blue fans by scoring 19 points in only his second game, a win over Jacksonville State. Scored in double figures seven times as a rookie. His best efforts as a sophomore were 10-point outings against Marshall and Kentucky State.

ED DAVENDER
(1985-88, 6'2", guard, New York, N.Y.)

Arguably the most underrated, underappreciated guard in UK history. The only Wildcat backcourt player to register more than 1,500 points and 400 assists. Another good clutch player who loved having the ball in his hands when the game was on the line. Came to UK after a sterling prep career at Boys and Girls High in Brooklyn. Averaged 8.5 points as a freshman. Scored 27 points against East Tennessee State in his first start. Also had 22 against LSU and 20 in a 92-89 win over 11th-ranked Kansas. Scored at an 11.5 clip for Eddie

Sutton's first UK club. Led that team in free throw percentage (79.4 percent) and steals (1.6). Hit for a season-high 22 points to lead UK past Indiana 63-58. Improved his scoring average to 15.2 as a junior, earning All-SEC honors for his efforts. Teamed with freshman Rex Chapman to give UK a deadly backcourt duo. Scored 36 points in the UKIT and was named MVP. His season-best scoring effort was 29 points, which he hit against Tennessee and Alabama. Led the Cats with 23 in their NCAA tourney loss to Ohio State. Shot 73.8 percent from the free throw stripe. Averaged 15.7 points and four assists as a senior, again garnering All-SEC recognition. Scored 27 against Tennessee and 24 against UNCC and Vanderbilt. Saved his best for last, hitting for a career-high 30 against Southern in the NCAA tourney. Also scored 23 in a 90-81 tourney win over Maryland. Finished his career with 1,637 points, 436 assists, 191 steals and a 79.2 percent accuracy from the free throw line.

TED DEEKEN
(1962-64, 6'3", forward, Louisville, Ky.)

Excellent inside player who provided solid support for Cotton Nash during the Cats' successful 1963-64 season. A late-bloomer who played little as a sophomore and didn't crack the starting lineup until midway through his junior year. Once he did, he proved to be a valuable asset as a scorer and rebounder. Averaged 18.5 points as a senior in 1963-64. Opened the season by scoring 99 points in UK's first four games, including 29 against Northwestern and 28 against Virginia. Later scored a career-best 34 in an easy romp past Auburn. Also tagged Georgia for 29 in Adolph Rupp's 700th win at UK. Burned Notre Dame for 27 in Freedom Hall. In all, he cracked the 20-point mark 10 times that season. Earned his first start as a junior during the disappointing 1962-63 campaign after coming off the bench to give three impressive performances. He began this stretch by registering a double-double (13 points, 14 rebounds) against Georgia Tech, which he followed by scoring 13 in a comeback win over LSU and 18 in a win over Tulane. His 18-point effort in his first start helped propel the Cats to a 78-69 overtime victory over Tennessee. Scored a season-high 25 in a tough 56-52 loss to Mississippi State in Starkville. Finished the year with a 9.8 scoring average, third-best on the team. Came to UK after helping guide Louisville Flaget to the 1960 state championship. Scored 14 in the title-game win over Monticello. Earned All-State recognition for his play that season.

TONY DELK
(1993-96, 6'1", guard, Brownsville, Tenn.)

UK's No.4 all-time scorer with 1,890 points and the leader in three-point buckets with a career total of 283. Also owns the record for most treys in a game, making nine against Texas Christian during the 1995-96 season. Had seven three-pointers in UK's 76-67 win over Syracuse in the 1996 NCAA championship game. Struggled early in his career, averaging just 4.6 points as a freshman. His best game as a rookie was an 18-point effort in an 87-66 win over South Carolina. Also hit for 15 against Tennessee. Moved back to his natural shooting guard position as a sophomore and responded with a 16.6 average. Opened the season by turning in a 19-point, 10-rebound, five-assist effort in a 78-70 win over Louisville. Scored a season-high 29 in the Cats' 95-76 SEC tourney win over Mississippi State. Led the Cats with 27 in a losing effort against Syracuse. Also had 27 against Georgia. Made 95 treys that season and shot 37.4 percent from beyond the three-point line. Improved his average to 16.7 as a junior in 1994-95. Burned Arkansas for 31 in a 94-92 UK loss. Scored 27 in an easy 127-80 romp past LSU. Topped the Cats during NCAA tourney action, scoring 76 points in four games. His 26 sparked the Cats past Arizona State 97-73 in the Southeast Regional. Averaged at a 17.8 pace during his final season for the title-winning Wildcats. Had a string of big-time scoring games, including 30 against Louisville, 29 against Iona and Georgia, and 28 against South Carolina. Buried a school-record nine three-pointers and scored 27 points in a 124-80 win over Texas Christian. Was absolutely brilliant during the Cats' run to the NCAA tourney championship. Scored 22 against San Jose State and 25 in an 83-63 win over Wake Forest that earned the Cats a trip to the Final Four. Led the Cats in those final two victories, scoring 20 in an 81-74 revenge win over UMass and 24 in the 76-67 championship game win over Syracuse. Those two performances were good enough to earn him MVP honors. Hit 39.8 percent of his three-point attempts as a Wildcat. A sticky defender who twice led the club in steals. Earned All-SEC recognition his final two years and was the SEC tourney MVP in 1996. Once cracked the 70-point mark in a high school game. Went to Charlotte in the first round of the 1996 NBA draft. Played several seasons with the Golden State Warriors. Currently works for the SEC Network.

JOHN "FRENCHY" DeMOISEY
(1932-34, 6'5", center, Walton, Ky.)

Rupp's third All-American, a prolific scorer and one of the first players to shoot a hook shot. After watching DeMoisey in action, one sportswriter said it was like seeing a "whirling dervish." Capable of posting big numbers offensively. Had 29 in a win over Vandy, 24 against Chicago, and during one stretch, he scored 70 points in four games. As a sophomore, DeMoisey averaged 10 points per game despite missing several games due to academic problems. Once scored 39 points in 39 minutes during a two-game span. In his junior season, he teamed with Aggie Sale to lead the Cats to a 21-3 record and the school's first SEC Tournament championship. Averaged 12 points that season. Scored 59 points in the SEC tourney. Averaged 12.5 points per game as a senior, leading the Cats to a 16-1 record. Was named All-American in 1934, and All-SEC in 1933 and 1934. His younger brother Truitt played for the Cats in the mid '40s.

LEROY EDWARDS
(1934-35, 6'5", center, Indianapolis, Ind.)

Only played one season at UK, but his performance that year was memorable enough to rank him among the all-time great Wildcats. In fact, many years later, Rupp was asked to name the greatest center he ever saw. His pick: Edwards. Known at times as "Cowboy," "Big Ed" or "Big Boy," Edwards was exceptionally strong physically. His great strength made him a difficult player to contain defensively, and, indeed, many opposing teams resorted to thuggery and mugging in an effort to shut him down. Averaged 16.3 points per game, the best by a Wildcat until Alex Groza showed up a decade later. His scoring and rebounding helped lead the 1934-35 club to a splendid 19-2 record. Single-handedly outscored the opposition in each of UK's first five games that season. His career-high 34 points against Creighton shattered the previous UK best held by DeMoisey. Also had 24 against Alabama and 23 against Xavier. Scored 343 points that season to set new UK and SEC records at the time. Earned All-America recognition and was chosen Helms National Player of the Year. Left UK after the season, returned to Indianapolis and began a successful pro career. Arguably Rupp's best inside player until Groza arrived on the scene.

ANTHONY EPPS
(1994-97, 6'2", guard, Lebanon, Ky.)

Hard-nosed point guard whose heady, consistent play silenced those critics who doubted his ability. A big-game player with a knack for making the right play at the right moment. Played in 141 games as a Wildcat, drawing 68 starts. Played very little as a freshman, but stepped up and became a valuable contributor during the 1994-95 campaign. Scored 15 points and handed out 13 assists in a 127-80 win over LSU on Seniors' Night. Also had 15 against Ohio University. Led the team in free throw shooting (85 percent) and assists (4.2). His steady leadership and willingness to distribute the basketball were big reasons why that super-talented 1995-96 club was able to claim the NCAA title. Scored a season-high 17 in UK's 88-73 win over Arkansas. Handed out 12 assists against Marshall, 11 against LSU and 10 against Tennessee. Had seven assists while playing all 40 minutes in UK's 1996 NCAA title-game win over Syracuse. Averaged 8.9 points as a senior on the 1996-97 NCAA runner-up squad. Hit for a career-best 22 points against Georgia in the 1997 SEC Tournament. Averaged 17.3 points per game in that tourney and was named to the all-tournament team. Had 15 points and six assists in the Cats' 72-59 NCAA tourney win over Utah. Hit a critical three-pointer to send the game into overtime in UK's 1997 championship loss to Arizona. Ended his UK career with 544 assists and 184 steals. Had 93 assists in NCAA tourney action. Was an 82 percent career free throw shooter at UK. Selected to the 1996 All-Midwest Regional team. Scored 881 points as a Wildcat. Earned All-State honors after leading Marion County High School to the 1993 Kentucky state championship. Also an All-State selection in football.

BILLY EVANS
(1952, 54-55, 6'1", forward, Berea, Ky.)

A much-underrated player and a key contributing member of the unbeaten 1953-54 Wildcat team, averaging 8.4 points per game. Hit for a season-high 17 against Georgia. Led the team in free throw shooting, hitting 77.8 percent of his freebies. Came back as a senior in 1954-55 campaign to average 13.9 points. Again led the team with 74.3 percent free throw shooting. Had his career-high scoring night when he hit for 26 against Tennessee. Matched the great Tom Gola with 20 points in UK's win over defending NCAA champ La Salle.

Also scored 20 in a thrilling 75-71 win over Vanderbilt. Ruled ineligible to participate in the NCAA Tournament because he was a fifth-year senior. Earned All-SEC recognition for his play during the 1954-55 season. A member of the 1956 U.S. Olympic team that captured the gold medal. Also excelled at tennis. Later became a highly successful executive with the Kentucky Fried Chicken Corporation.

RICHIE FARMER
(1989-92, 6'0", guard, Manchester, Ky.)

Much-beloved Wildcat, a solid competitor and one of the true Kentucky prep legends. Came to UK after leading Clay County to five straight Sweet 16 appearances, including the 1987 championship. Scored 317 points in state tourney action to break the old mark of 223 held by Wah Wah Jones. Hit for a championship-game high of 51 in a 1988 loss to Ballard. Kentucky's Mr. Basketball in 1988. Saw limited action as a freshman at UK, hitting for a season-high 15 against Western Carolina. Knocked down a three-pointer with two seconds left to give the Cats a 70-69 win over Ole Miss. One of the top gunners on the "Pitino's Bombinos" team that finished with a 14-14 record. Scored a season-best 21 in a loss to North Carolina. His six pressure-packed free throws in the final 1:05 sealed the Cats' stunning 100-95 upset of LSU. Led the club with 84.7 percent shooting from the free throw line. Averaged 10.1 as a junior for a UK team that had a 22-6 record. Scored 22 against Western Kentucky, 21 against Ole Miss and 20 against Auburn. Again led the team with 84.2 percent shooting from the charity stripe. Averaged 9.6 points for the probation-free 1991-92 team that finished with a 29-7 record and advanced to the Elite Eight. Buried five treys and scored a career-high 28 points in a 91-70 win over Notre Dame. Also hit for 22 in a win over UMass. Made 55 three-pointers as a senior to finish with 147 for his career. Left as UK's fourth-best from the free throw line, making good on 83.8 percent of his attempts.

DERON FELDHAUS
(1989-92, 6'7", forward, Maysville, Ky.)

This rugged second generation Wildcat blended a hard-nosed inside game with a soft shooting touch that also made him a threat from the outside. Another one of those warrior types who wasn't afraid to sacrifice his body for the good

of the team. Saw action as a starter and as a valuable sixth man during his outstanding career. Scored 1,231 points, shot 74.2 percent from the free throw line and connected on 37.5 percent of his three-point attempts. Played in 32 games as a freshman in 1988-89, averaging 3.7 points. Made his first start late in the season, scoring 11 points in a loss to Mississippi State. Had a double-double — 10 points, 10 rebounds — in a 70-69 win over Ole Miss. His two free throws with 12 seconds remaining sealed the Cats' 66-65 win over 18th-ranked Tennessee. Averaged 14.4 points as a sophomore on Pitino's first UK team. Scored 27 against North Carolina and 23 against Indiana. Had 19 points and 11 rebounds in a win over Tennessee. Also snared 13 rebounds against LSU and Shaquille O'Neal. Averaged 10.8 points as a junior. Scored a season-high 27 in a 93-80 win over LSU. Ended his career with a superb senior season, averaging 11.4 points while hitting 79.4 percent of his free throws and 37.5 percent from beyond the three-point arc. Had 22 against Arkansas and 19 against

Deron Feldhaus was a second-generation Wildcat, the son of Allen "the Horse" Feldhaus. Both were known for their rugged play and fearless attitude.

South Carolina. The youngest of three basketball-playing brothers, he was a standout performer for his father, ex-Cat Allen "the Horse" Feldhaus, at Mason County High School. Twice earned All-State honors. Enjoyed a long and successful pro career in Japan. One of the "Unforgettables" whose determined play and winning attitude helped bring the light back to UK basketball.

GERALD FITCH
(2001-04, 6'3", guard, Macon, Ga.)

A rock-solid performer whose consistency on both ends of the court has been matched by only a handful of past Wildcats. Fearless, tenacious and willing to take the big shot when necessary. Accounted for 1,391 points, 526 rebounds, 232 assists and 156 steals during his four-year career. Scored in double figures 73 times as a Wildcat. Twice named to the All-SEC team. Voted MVP of the SEC Tournament after leading the Cats to their 25th tourney title. Had 57 points in those three tourney wins. Averaged 16.2 points as a senior while leading the team in scoring 15 times. Had a career-best 36-point performance on 14-of-20 shooting in an easy win over Tennessee Tech. Scored 26 against Eastern Kentucky and Florida A&M, 25 against Michigan State and 24 against Marshall and South Carolina. Averaged 12.3 points during his junior season. Burned North Carolina and IUPUI for 25 points. Shot 48 percent from the field and 42 percent from behind the three-point line. Tossed in 8.9 points per game as a sophomore. Had season-high 17-point efforts against South Carolina and Georgia. Registered a pair of double-doubles — 16/10 against Tulane, 13/11 against Ole Miss. Scored 230 points and averaged 6.8 points per game during his initial season. His top rookie outing was a 17-point night against Arkansas. Cracked double figures 12 times that season. Recorded his first double-double when he had 11 points and 11 rebounds against Vandy. Ranks seventh all-time in three-point shooting (39.6 percent) and fourth in three-pointers made (199). Made good on 43 percent of his three-point attempts against SEC competion.

TRAVIS FORD
(1992-94, 5'9", guard, Madisonville, Ky.)

A rare backcourt ace who combined a point guard mentality with a shooting guard touch. The school's No. 2 all-time free throw shooter with a career mark of 88.2 percent. Hit a school-record 101 three-pointers in 1992-93. Shot an

SEC-record 52.9 percent from behind the three-point line that season. Made good on 44.5 percent of his three-point attempts during his Wildcat career. Also set a UK mark by handing out 15 assists against Eastern Kentucky. Finished his career with 428 assists. Transferred to UK after a successful freshman campaign at the University of Missouri. Played in 33 games in his injury-plagued initial season at UK, primarily serving as a backup to Sean Woods. Made three key treys to help the Cats ease past LSU 80-74. Averaged 3.5 points while handing out 65 assists that year. Assumed the point guard role the following season for a Wildcat club that went 30-4 and made it to the Final Four. Averaged 13.6 points and 4.9 assists while hitting 88.1 percent of his freebies. Canned seven treys and scored 29 points in an 81-78 win over Indiana. Scored 26 against Arkansas and 18 against LSU to capture the first of his two SEC tourney MVP awards. Connected on 14 of 22 three-point attempts in three SEC tourney games. Hit 10 of 11 shots in UK's 103-69 NCAA tourney win over Wake Forest. Earned All-SEC recognition that season. Averaged 11.3 as a senior in 1993-94 while matching Kyle Macy's single-season free throw mark of 91.2 percent. Dished out 5.8 assists per game to again lead the club in that category. Captured MVP honors in the Maui Classic by scoring 27 in a 100-88 win over Ohio State and 25 in the 93-92 championship game win over Arizona. Followed those performances with 27-point efforts against San Francisco and Georgia. Scored 39 points in three SEC tourney wins, again picking up the MVP trophy. Ended his UK career with 951 points. Averaged seven points and hit a school-record 96 percent of his free throws in his one season at Missouri. Scored 2,676 points during a brilliant prep career at Madisonville North Hopkins High School. A three-time All-State pick. Currently coaching at St. Louis University.

MIKE FLYNN
(1973-75, 6'3", guard, Jeffersonville, Ind.)

This member of the "Super Sophs" was an excellent backcourt player with a knack for playing some of his best basketball in the most crucial situations. Best remembered for his magnificent 22-point performance in UK's 92-90 win over unbeaten Indiana in the 1975 NCAA Tournament Mideast Regional final. Accounted for 14 of those points in the nerve-tingling second half to help the Cats earn their ticket to the Final Four. Averaged nine points as a senior while handing out just under four assists per game. Scored 22 in an 85-82 win over Ole Miss. Had 10 points in the championship-game loss to UCLA. Cracked the starting lineup midway through his sophomore season, finishing with an average of 9.1. His best scoring games included 22 against Georgia, 21 against Vanderbilt and 18 in a 95-93 win over Alabama. Led the 1972-73 team in free throw shooting with 73.3 percent accuracy. Scored at an 11.3 pace during his junior season. Twice hit for 20, once against Georgia and again against LSU. Also regarded as one of UK's premier backcourt defenders. Left UK and played three seasons in the NBA. Indiana's prep Mr. Basketball in 1971.

JACK GIVENS
(1975-78, 6'4", forward, Lexington, Ky.)

Silky-smooth lefty with one of the sweetest jump shots in Wildcat history, which he unleashed with a vengeance in his towering 41-point performance against Duke in the 1978 NCAA championship game. UK's third all-time leading scorer with 2,038 points. Surprisingly, he also ranks among the school's top rebounders with 793. A two-time All-American, a three-time All-SEC pick, the 1978 Final Four MVP and one of the most-consistent Wildcats of all-time. A homegrown Lexington product who played prep ball at Bryan Station High School, the "Goose" averaged 9.4 points for the 1974-75 UK club that was runner-up to UCLA in the NCAA tourney. Scored 19 against Florida in his first career start. Later scored 26 against Ole Miss and 24 against Syracuse in the semifinal game. Averaged 20.1 points as a sophomore for the NIT championship Wildcats. Made good on 82.9 percent of his free throws. Cracked the 30-point barrier three times, with a high of 33 in a win over LSU. Led all scorers with 26 in the final game played in Memorial Coliseum, a 94-93 overtime win over Mississippi State. Had 28 in UK's 79-78 NIT semifinal victory over Providence. Scored at an 18.9 clip and hit 83.2 percent of his freebies during his junior campaign. Hit 15 of 19 shots in a 30-point effort against Notre Dame in Freedom Hall. Had 26 in the Cats' 79-72 NCAA tourney loss to North Carolina. Averaged 18.1 points for the 1977-78 NCAA championship team that many consider to be UK's best-ever. Opened the season with a 30-point performance against SMU, then closed it with his majestic effort against Duke in the title game. Also led the Cats with 23 points in their 64-59 semifinal win over Arkansas. Hit 51.5 percent of his field goals and 79.8 percent of his free throws while at UK. Kentucky's Mr. Basketball in 1974. Drafted by the

Atlanta Hawks in the first round of the 1978 NBA draft. Played two seasons with the Hawks, then turned his attention to broadcasting.

PHIL GRAWEMEYER
(1954-56, 6'7", forward, Louisville, Ky.)

The guy known as "Cookie" was an outstanding performer whose career was hampered by injuries. A slim 6-7 lefty, he could score, rebound and defend. Came to UK after a standout prep career at Louisville Manuel High School. Was a valuable member of that powerful, unbeaten 1953-54 Wildcat club. Played in all 25 games and averaged 5.9 points per game. Hit for 17 in a win over Xavier and 13 in wins over La Salle and Tennessee. Cracked double figures five times as a sophomore. Was on pace for an all-star year in 1954-55 when he went down with a broken leg during UK's 20th game. Had scored in double digits 15 times in those 20 games, and was averaging 13 points per game. Scored 28 in the season opener against LSU, then followed that with a 27-point effort against Utah. Also had 21 against St. Louis, 20 against Florida and 19 against Georgia Tech. His scoring dipped to 8.4 during his final season in 1955-56, yet he still hit for double figures 11 times. Had a season-best 16-point performance against Tennessee. Finished his career with 703 rebounds in just 71 games. Drafted by Minneapolis.

KEVIN GREVEY
(1973-75, 6'5", forward, Hamilton, Ohio)

A two-time All-American, this lethal lefty is UK's sixth all-time leading scorer with 1,801 points. His 21.4 career scoring average trails only Dan Issel and Cotton Nash. Shot 51.7 percent from the field and 77.8 percent from the foul line for his career. His versatility and quickness made him a difficult target for defenders. When he got on a roll, he was virtually unstoppable. Averaged 18.7 as a sophomore after getting off to a slow start. Cranked it up later on, hitting for 33 and 29 in two wins over Alabama, 34 against Auburn and a career-high 40 against Georgia. Shot 53.5 percent from the field during his rookie campaign. Averaged 21.9 as a junior. Was the most-consistent player on that disappointing 13-13 team. Hit for 25 or more 11 times with a high of 35 against Florida. Also had 34 in a second meeting with Florida and 32 against Auburn. Topped the club in foul shooting, making good on 83 percent of his free throws. Led the 1974-75 Final Four team in scoring with

an average of 23.6. Cracked the 30-point barrier five times that season, including a 34-point effort in the championship game loss to UCLA. Had a season-high 37 against Auburn. Was named to the NCAA All-Final Four team. A three-time All-SEC selection and two-time UK team MVP. Came to UK after being named Ohio's Mr. Basketball in 1971. Had an outstanding NBA career with Washington and Milwaukee. Taken in the first round of the 1975 draft. After retiring, he opened "Grevey's," a popular restaurant in Washington, D.C. He also works as a radio broadcaster. His nephew, Ryan Hogan, lettered at UK in 1997-98 and 1998-99.

ALEX GROZA
(1945, 47-49, 6'7", center, Martins Ferry, Ohio)

A three-time All-American and the leading scorer for the "Fabulous Five." Left UK as the school's all-time leading scorer with 1,744 points. Still ranks No. 9 on that list. A very quick pivotman who had great hands and slick offensive moves. Averaged 16.5 points in 10 games as a freshman before entering the Army. Scored 91 points in his last four games prior to leaving the team. Came back to average 10.6 for the 1946-47 team that went 34-3. His high game that season was 21 against DePaul. Scored at a 12.5 clip to share scoring honors with Beard on the 1947-48 NCAA championship "Fabulous Five" club. Had 23 against Notre Dame and 22 against Georgia. Scored 54 points in the three tourney games, including 23 in the Cats' 60-52 semifinal win over Bob Cousy-led Holy Cross. Was named the NCAA tourney's MVP. Tossed in 33 points in a 77-59 win over Baylor in the Olympic Trials. Helped lead the 1948 U.S. Olympic team to a gold medal. His 78 points led the U.S. squad in scoring. Exploded as a scorer his senior year, averaging 20.5 points per game. Scored 30 or more on six occasions, including a career-high 38 against Georgia. Had 37 against Tulane in the 1949 SEC tourney title game. Racked up 82 points in three games to lead the Cats to a second straight NCAA title. Scored 25 in the championship-game win over Oklahoma A&M. Also repeated as the tourney MVP. Went on to make first-team All-NBA with the Indianapolis Olympians, but was later banned from the league for life because of his involvement in the point-shaving scandal. Another player who surely would have made it into the NBA Hall of Fame. Long-time Wildcat observ-

ers still rank Groza as one of the genuinely great players in Big Blue history.

CLIFF HAGAN
(1951-52, 54, 6"4", center, Owensboro, Ky.)

A two-time All-American and one of the five best players to ever put on a UK uniform. Strong, quick, athletic and graceful. Could score in many ways, but the hook shot was his chief weapon. His range and accuracy with the hook shot was amazing. Teamed with Frank Ramsey to give the Cats one of the greatest 1-2 combos in college basketball history. One of the few athletes to win championships at the high school, college and professional levels. Came to UK after leading Owensboro High to the 1949 state tourney championship. Scored 41 points in the title game. Joined the UK varsity midway through the 1950-51 season, playing in 20 games and helping lead that club to the NCAA championship. Hit for a season-high 25 points against Auburn. Came off the bench to score 10 points and help the Cats come from behind to beat Kansas State in the final game despite suffering from an infected throat. Took over at center when Bill Spivey was ruled ineligible and averaged 21.6 points and 16.5 rebounds for the 29-3 Cats during his junior season. Hit for a season-high 42 against Tennessee in the SEC tourney. Had 37 against Ole Miss, 34 against UCLA and 30 against Mississippi State. Led all scorers with 110 points in four SEC tourney games. Also led the Cats with 42 points in their two NCAA tourney games. Was named All-American and All-SEC for his performance that year. After UK's one year in exile, he opened the 1953-54 season with a 51-point effort against Temple. Outscored Tom Gola 28-16 in UK's 73-60 win over La Salle, the eventual NCAA champs. Scored 38 in an 88-62 win over Ole Miss and 32 in a 105-53 romp past Georgia Tech. Had a nine-game stretch in which he scored 243 points. Finished the season with a 24-point scoring average. Also averaged 13.5 rebounds for the unbeaten Cats. Made good on 45.5 percent of his field goal attempts. Was again named All-American. Ended his UK career with 1,475 points and 1,035 rebounds despite playing only 77 games. His 13.4 career rebounding average is second only to Bob Burrow's 16.1. Went on to have a distinguished pro career with the St. Louis Hawks in the NBA, earning All-NBA recognition. Helped lead the Hawks to the 1958 NBA championship. After a brief coaching stint in the pro ranks, he returned to UK and served as Athletics Director from 1975-88. Inducted into the Basketball Hall of Fame in 1977.

JOE "RED" HAGAN
(1936-38, 6'1", forward, Louisville, Ky.)

One of the most combative, irascible Wildcats of all-time. Feisty and fearless, he never met a confrontation he didn't like. He was also a superb basketball player, a three-year starter and the team's leading scorer as a senior. Scored 12 points in his second game, a 58-19 win over Berea. Later scored 15 against Tennessee, 12 against Notre Dame and a season-best 19 in the season finale against Vanderbilt. Averaged eight points as a sophomore, second only to Ralph Carlisle. Scored at a 7.3 pace as a junior, hitting for a season-high 17 in a 59-36 win over Creighton. Finished his career in a big way, averaging 10.1 points as a senior. Opened the season with a 16-point effort in a 69-35 romp past Berea. Scored nine points and led the Cats to a 40-29 come-from-behind win over Pittsburgh in the Sugar Bowl. Followed that by scoring 14 against Michigan State and 16 against Detroit. Scored 11 points and sank a 48-foot shot with 12 seconds left to give the Cats a 35-33 win over Marquette. Closed out the regular season by scoring 14 in a 29-26 win over Tennessee, then had a team-high 13 in a shocking 38-36 first-round loss to Tulane in the SEC Tournament. Voted the tourney's MVP despite UK's early exit. Came to UK after an outstanding prep career at St. Xavier High School.

REGGIE HANSON
(1988-91, 6'8", forward/center, Somerset, Ky.)

Versatile, tough inside player and one of the primary architects of UK's return to glory in the early 1990s. A solid performer on both ends of the court and one of the most personable UK players ever. Sat out as a freshman because of Prop 48, then moved into a starting role on Eddie Sutton's final Wildcat team during his sophomore season. Averaged 9.8 points that year while hitting a team-best 75 percent of his free throws. Had a season-high 20 points in a 76-65 win over Georgia. Flourished as a player in Rick Pitino's system, averaging 16.4 points, grabbing 7.2 rebounds and shooting 49.7 from the field as a junior. Voted that team's MVP. Had 24 points and 14 rebounds to help the Cats beat Ohio University 76-73 in Pitino's debut at UK. Scored 25 against Ole Miss and 24 against Louisville and Auburn. Snared 15 rebounds against Mississippi State. Averaged 14.4 points and 7.2 rebounds for the 1990-91 club that surprised everyone by finishing with a 22-6 record overall and a league-best 14-4 mark against SEC foes. Scored 28 against Tennessee, 27 against Eastern Kentucky and 24 against LSU. Canned a pair of clutch free throws to help the Cats escape Georgia 81-80. Finished his career with 1,171 points. Shot 50.5 percent from the field and 73.7 percent from the foul line. Named to the All-SEC team in each of his final two seasons. Came to UK after leading Pulaski County to the 1986 state championship. Reunited with Pitino for a brief stint with the Celtics.

VERNON HATTON
(1956-58, 6'3", guard, Lexington, Ky.)

A steel-nerved guard who made some of the most important and memorable shots in UK history. A three-year starter and the leading scorer for the "Fiddlin' Five" team that came out of nowhere to win the 1958 NCAA championship. Hit a 47-foot shot at the end of the first overtime to keep the Cats alive in their three-overtime 85-83 win over Temple, then came through with six points in the final OT to seal it. Later that same season, he burned Temple again when he dropped in a layup with 16 seconds left to give the Cats a 61-60 win in the national semifinal game. Scored 30 points in the title-game win over Seattle one night later. Cracked the starting five early in his sophomore year and finished with a 13.3 scoring average while leading the team in field goal percentage (49.4) and free throw percentage (66.7). Had a high game of 32 against DePaul that season. Scored the last five points in the Cats' 62-61 win over Maryland. Also had 25 against Auburn and 24 against Alabama. Averaged 14.8 as a junior with a season-best 26 in the opener against Washington & Lee. Missed seven games that season after undergoing an emergency appendectomy. Scored 25 in a 91-70 win over unbeaten Illinois. Topped the 1957-58 team in scoring (17.1), field goal shooting (41.9) and free throw accuracy (77.7). Twice hit for 26 during the regular season, then had his 30-point outburst in the NCAA final game. Named to the All-Final Four team after his standout performance. An All-American in 1958, and a three-time All-SEC selection. Finished his career with 1,153 points. Came to UK from Lexington Lafayette, where he led ex-Cat Ralph Carlisle's Generals to the 1953 state championship. After playing professionally for several years, he returned to Lexington and became a successful realtor and auctioneer.

BASIL HAYDEN
(1920-22, 6'0", forward, Paris, Ky.)

Holds the distinction of being UK's first All-American, earning that honor in 1921. He was also a key performer on the 1920-21 team that finished with a 13-1 record and won UK's first-ever tournament championship. Hit a crucial game-tying basket in the Cats' 20-19 championship-game win over Georgia in the 1921 Southern Intercollegiate Athletic Association Tournament. Averaged 9.6 points for that club. Suffered a knee injury prior to the 1921-22 season, but still managed to average five points per game. Led Wildcat teams to a 28-14 record during his three seasons. Was the team's top scorer with a 10.8 average as a sophomore in 1919-20. Coached at Stanford High School and Kentucky Wesleyan College before returing to UK as coach of the 1926-27 team.

CHUCK HAYES
(2001-05, 6'6", forward, Modesto, Calif.)

The archetypal blue-collar warrior who was always willing to do the grunt work necessary to help the Cats succeed. A team-first player and one of the classiest Wildcats ever. Scored 1,211 points and yanked down 910 rebounds during his career. Started 110 consecutive games at UK, tying Alex Groza for the school record. UK posted a 93-18 mark in games he started. Registered 23 double-doubles, including 10 during his senior season. Scored at a 10.9 clip in his final campaign, shooting 51 percent from the field. Had a season-best 18-point performance against William & Mary. Was a consensus first-team All-SEC pick as a senior. Voted the SEC's top defensive player by the league's coaches. Also earned honorable mention All-America recognition. Averaged 10.7 points as a junior. Made good on 10 of 14 field goal attempts and scored a career-high 23 points against Florida in the SEC Tournament. Scored 22 against Indiana and 21 against Notre Dame. Ended his junior campaign with seven double-doubles. Had a 17-point, 16-rebound performance against Notre Dame as a sophomore. Scored 16 in a 98-81 victory over North Carolina. Recorded double-doubles in both games against Georgia — 11/10 and 15/12. Cracked double digits twice as a freshman, with a 15-point effort against Tennessee being his best. Recorded his first double-double (10/13) against South Carolina. Ended his career with 128 blocked shots, 170 steals and 292 assists. Named a Parade All-American and California Division I Player of the Year as a senior as Modesto Chris-

tian High School. Averaged 25 points and 19 rebounds as a senior.

JOE HOLLAND
(1946-48, 6'4" forward, Benton, Ky.)

A steady, dependable forward who helped UK win a pair of championships — the 1946 NIT and the 1948 NCAA Tournament. Had his best season as a junior in 1946-47, averaging 6.2 points for the 34-3 Wildcats. Was outstanding in the SEC tourney that season, hitting for 15 in the championship win over Tulane and 14 against Georgia Tech in the semifinal game. Was one of five Cats named to the All-SEC tourney team that year. Had 14 points in UK's 70-50 win over St. John's in Madison Square Garden. His best game as a senior on the "Fabulous Five" team was a 12-point performance against Cincinnati. Earned his scholarship after impressing Rupp while playing for the Berea naval trainees team against UK in 1943. Later went on to play for the Indianapolis Olympians in the NBA. His son Joey lettered for the Cats in 1976. Owned successful automobile dealerships in Lexington and Charleston, W.Va.

DERRICK HORD
(1980-83, 6'6", forward/guard, Bristol, Tenn.)

Came to UK after a celebrated prep All-America career, and although he had his moments, he never quite lived up to his great promise. A very smooth player who, when he was playing well, was a joy to watch. Scored 1,220 points at UK while averaging 9.8 points per game. Had his best year in 1981-82 when his 16.3 average led the team in scoring and earned him All-SEC recognition. Saw action in 35 games as a freshman, finishing with a 5.9 scoring clip. Hit for a season-high 18 points on three occasions, against South Carolina, Vanderbilt and Florida. Moved into a starting position as a sophomore and upped his scoring average to 8.9. Had a season-best 24 points against Maine, connecting on 10 of 16 field goal attempts. Opened his outstanding junior season with a 28-point effort against Akron. His five points in overtime helped the Cats slip past Kansas 77-74. Was named MVP of the UKIT after scoring 38 points in those two wins. Had 26 against Vandy and 24 against LSU. After a fast start during his senior season, he went into a lengthy and mystifying slump. Scored 18 against Notre Dame, then came back with 26 in a win over third-ranked Villanova. Claimed the UKIT MVP award for a second straight year after scoring 31 points in wins over Duquesne and Tulane. Scored 23 against Kansas, then

went into his tailspin. Hit a buzzer-beater to give UK a 71-69 win over Auburn. Finished the season with an 8.9 scoring average and a team-high 82.3 percent from the charity stripe.

LEE HUBER
(1939-41, 6'0", guard, Louisville, Ky.)

Set-shot artist who made the All-American team in 1941. Tied for team scoring honors in 1940-41 season with 151 points. An All-SEC pick in 1941. As a sophomore, he scored six quick points to help the Cats come back and beat Ole Miss in the SEC tourney opener. Scored at a 5.4 clip as a junior. Won praise for his excellent guard play after scoring 17 points in a win over Clemson. Had 11 against Notre Dame and 12 against Tennessee before an illness slowed him for the remainder of season. Scored 25 points in the final two games of the 1941 SEC Tournament, earning a spot on the all-tourney team. Scored 12 points three times that season. Finished with a 5.9 scoring average. Came to UK on a tennis scholarship after twice winning the state singles title for St. Xavier High School. Also made the 1937 all-tournament team after leading the basketball Tigers to the semifinal round of the Sweet 16.

DAN ISSEL
(1968-70, 6'9", center, Batavia, Ill.)

UK's all-time leading scorer with 2,138 points, a two-time All-American and the holder of no fewer than 28 individual school records. Twice scored more than 50 points in a game, and went over the 40-point mark on six occasions. As a senior, he averaged 33.9 points and 13.2 rebounds while shooting 55.3 percent from the field and 76.4 percent from the free throw stripe. Hit for a school-record 53 points against Ole Miss and 51 against LSU. Started along with fellow sophomores Mike Casey and Mike Pratt on the 1967-68 club, averaging 16.4 points and 12.1 rebounds. His best game as a sophomore was a 36-point, 13-rebound effort against Marquette in the NCAA Tournament. Really blossomed into a scoring machine as a junior, averaging 26.6 points per game. Hit for 41 against Vanderbilt, and had an incredible 36-point, 29-rebound performance against LSU. Averaged 13.6 rebounds that season. Scored 47 against Alabama and 44 in a thrilling 109-99 win over Notre Dame in the NCAA tourney. Made the All-SEC team three times. Left UK as the all-time leader in points, average (25.7) and rebounds (1,078). UK was 71-12 during his three years, and likely would have won another NCAA title had it not been for the automobile accident that sidelined Casey for the entire 1969-70 campaign. Went on to have an all-pro career, first with the Kentucky Colonels, then with the Denver Nuggets. The second all-time leading scorer in the old ABA with 12,823 points. Teamed with Dampier and Artis Gilmore to lead the Colonels to the 1975 ABA championship. Finished his pro career with more than 25,000 points. Retired as coach and GM of the Nuggets. Inducted into the Basketball Hall of Fame in 1993.

THAD JARACZ
(1966-68, 6'5", center/forward, Lexington, Ky.)

The youngest member of "Rupp's Runts" and a double-figure scorer in each of his three years at UK. Averaged 13.2 points for the 1965-66 team that finished second to Texas Western in the NCAA tourney. Scored 22 points against Virginia in only his second game, then followed that with a 32-point performance in an 86-68 win over Illinois. Had 26 points and 13 rebounds against Florida. Later burned LSU for 25 in an easy 111-85 UK victory. Scored 17 points in the Cats' 86-79 NCAA tourney win over Dayton. Averaged 11.3 points and a team-leading 8.3 rebounds for the 1966-67 club that ended with a 13-13 record. Hit for a season-high 22 in a 98-97 overtime loss to Illinois. Had 20 in a 96-66 UKIT win over Oregon State. Closed out his career by averaging 11.3 points for the talent-rich 1967-68 club that featured sophomores Mike Casey, Dan Issel and Mike Pratt. Scored 23 in a win over Florida. Canned 12 of 16 shots and finished with 25 points against Georgia. Also snared 18 rebounds in that win over the Bulldogs. His 24 points helped the Cats overcome a 52-point performance by "Pistol" Pete Maravich and get the best of LSU 121-95. Played his prep ball at Lafayette High in Lexington. Retired from the Air Force as a Lieutenant Colonel.

ELLIS JOHNSON
(1931-33, 6'0", guard, Ashland, Ky.)

One of UK's truly great all-around athletes, lettering three years in basketball and football while also participating in baseball and track. A starting guard on Rupp's first team, which finished with a 15-3 record. More of a playmaker and defender than a scorer, he consistently earned high praise for his intelligent, heady play. Scored a career-high 14 against

Chattanooga during his junior season. In his final season, he averaged 3.8 points for the 21-3 Cats, helping them win the first SEC Tournament. Very popular with the fans, who chided Rupp anytime he removed Johnson from the game. Played exceptionally well in the SEC Tournament, earning a spot on the all-tourney team. Despite low scoring numbers, his defense and playmaking skills were good enough to land him on the 1933 All-America team. Led Ashland High School to the 1928 national championship. Went on to have a long and successful coaching career at Morehead State University.

LARRY JOHNSON
(1974-77, 6'2", guard, Morganfield, Ky.)

Very clever, very quick and one of the best backcourt defenders in UK history. Three times was voted the team's top defensive player. The first of three players to land at UK via the Union County pipeline. (Dwane Casey and Freddie Cowan followed.) Saw little action as a rookie, but gave several strong performances as a sophomore. Came off the bench to score 16 points and ignite a 113-96 victory over Notre Dame in Freedom Hall. Became a starter the following season, averaging 11.2 points for that NIT championship club. Scored a season-high 22 in a win over Florida. Had 18 against North Carolina and 16 against Indiana. Had UK's final five points, including the game-winning bucket with 13 seconds left, against Vanderbilt. His last-second jumper sent the Cats past Providence 79-78 and into the NIT championship game. Came through with 16 points in the 71-67 title game win over UNCC. Led the team in assists with an average of 3.3. Averaged 10.7 points and 4.8 assists as a senior. Had season highs of 21 against Florida, 20 against Indiana and 19 against Vanderbilt. Earned All-State honors at Union County High School.

WALLACE "WAH WAH" JONES
(1946-49, 6'4", forward/center, Harlan, Ky.)

Maybe *the* greatest all-around athlete to ever play at UK. An All-American in basketball and All-SEC in football, he also played baseball and was on the track team. He was rugged and fearless, a player who never backed away from a scrap. Arrived at UK with Beard in 1945, and during the four years they played, UK won 130 of 140 games, captured two NCAA titles, an NIT title, four SEC championships and an Olympic gold medal. He was an All-American in 1949, and a four-time All-SEC and All-SEC tourney selection. Left UK with 1,151 points and

a career scoring average of 9.1. Had a great rookie season, averaging 9.7 points per game. Scored 16 in a win over Notre Dame and 26 in two wins over Tennessee, a team he always killed. Had 16 in the NIT opener against Arizona, then came back with 10 in the championship win over Rhode Island. Injuries slowed him as a sophomore, yet he still scored six points per game. His best game that season was a 20-point effort against LIU in the NIT. Joined the fabled 1947-48 team after helping lead the gridiron Cats to a victory in the Great Lakes Bowl. Hit for 22 against Georgia and 18 against Tennessee in the SEC tourney semifinal game. Scored 42 points in UK's three NCAA tourney games, including 21 against Columbia. Averaged 9.3 points for the "Fabulous Five." Scored 42 points in the U.S. Olympic team's gold medal run. As a senior in 1948-49, he averaged 8.6 points to help the Cats defend their NCAA crown. Had a season-high 18 against Tulane in the Sugar Bowl. Also had 15 against St. John's in Madison Square Garden and 13 against Holy Cross in the Boston Garden. Took Harlan High School to the Sweet 16 all four years. Scored 23 points in the final game to help his team win the 1944 title. His 223 points in state tourney action are second only to ex-Cat Richie Farmer's 317. Went on to become a standout player for the Indianapolis Olympians in the NBA. After retiring, he did some broadcasting and served as sheriff of Fayette County. Owned several successful businesses in Lexington prior to his death in 2014. One of the most-famous and successful Wildcat players ever. A genuine Kentucky legend.

BRANDON KNIGHT
(2010-11, 6'3", guard, Ft. Lauderdale, Fla.)

UK hardly missed a beat when he stepped in to take over the point guard chores from the departed John Wall. Proved to be one of the smartest, most tough-minded Wildcats of all-time. Another guy who wanted the ball in his hands when the game was on the line. Hit game-winning buckets against Princeton and Ohio State during the Cats' run to the Final Four. Named Most Outstanding Player in East Region. Averaged 17.3 points per game. Handed out 159 assists. Reached double figures in 35 of 38 games, and recorded the most 20-point games (14) by a UK freshman. Hit for a career-best 30 points in UK's NCAA tourney win over West Virginia. Had 26 at Arkansas and 25 at Louisville. Twice hit for five treys in a game, against LSU and North Carolina. Had nine assists against

South Carolina. Earned All-SEC first-team honors. Had a standout prep career at Pine Crest High in Ft. Lauderdale, leading his school to four consecutive state title games, claiming the crown in 2008 and 2009. Averaged 32.5 points his senior campaign. Four-time class 3A-1A Player of the Year. Racked up 3,515 points during his prep career. The 2009-10 Gatorade High School Athlete of the Year. Averaged 31.2 points as a junior. Also, a standout in the classroom, posting a 4.3 GPA in high school.

TOMMY KRON
(1965-67, 6'5", guard, Tell City, Ind.)

Although a guard, he was the tallest of "Rupp's Runts." He was a superb defender, especially when playing the point on UK's 1-3-1 zone defense. A capable scorer, he averaged 12.3 as a junior and 10.2 on the 1965-66 NCAA runner-up club. Broke into the starting lineup midway through his sophomore season, scoring 13 points in a crucial SEC win over Tennessee. That game marked the first time Rupp used a zone defense at UK, and Kron's play at the point made it a success. Later scored a team-high 17 to lead the Cats past Tennessee a second time. Scored a career-high 30 against Syracuse during his junior season. Also had 24 against West Virginia and 21 against St. Louis. Scored 23 against Alabama and 22 against Tulane during the "Runts" season. Played excellent basketball in the NCAA tourney, scoring 14 and 12 in tough wins over Michigan and Duke. Led the "Runts" in free throw accuracy, connecting on 85.1 percent. Played several years in the pros, then retired and went into business in Louisville.

DAVE LAWRENCE
(1933-35, 6'1", forward, Corinth, Ky.)

An unsung hero who played in the shadow of Frenchy DeMoisey and Leroy Edwards, yet still managed to gain All-America honors for his play during the 1934-35 season. Also named to the All-SEC team that same year. A steady performer and a superb shooter. Played little as a sophomore, then moved into the starting lineup his final two seasons at UK. Averaged 7.9 points as a junior and 9.1 his senior year. UK teams were 56-6 during his three years. Topped his junior campaign with a season-best 19 points in a win over Tennessee. His career-high was 23 in the 1934-35 season-opening win over Chattanooga. Had 16 against Tulane, 15 against Tulane in a second meeting, 17 against Creighton and 10 in the season finale against Xavier. Served as dean of men at the University of Louisville for many years.

JAMES LEE
(1975-78, 6'5", forward, Lexington, Ky.)

UK's greatest sixth man and arguably the school's most-exciting slam dunk artist of all-time. Signed, sealed and delivered UK's 94-88 NCAA championship win over Duke by throwing down one of his patented monster dunks just ahead of the final horn. A Lexington native who earned All-State honors at Henry Clay High School. An excellent rebounder and defensive player. Offered a glimpse into the future by coming off the bench to score 11 points in his Wildcat debut. Scored in double figures four times as a freshman, with a high of 13 against Mississippi State. Moved into the starting lineup midway through his sophomore season after Rick Robey went down with an injury, averaging 9.3 points for that NIT championship team. Scored a season-high 21 against Alabama, then came back with successive 20-point efforts against Niagara and Kansas State in the NIT. Averaged 9.8 points as a junior. Had 13 points and 13 rebounds against Utah in the UKIT final. Scored 14 points and threw down several of his signature dunks in a big SEC win over Alabama. Scored 11.3 points per game for the 1977-78 NCAA championship team. Hit for a career-best 25 against Auburn. Had eight, including that rim-rattling dunk, in the win over Duke. Taken by Seattle in the second round of the 1978 NBA draft.

BILLY RAY LICKERT
(1959-61, 6'3", guard/forward, Lexington, Ky.)

A complete player who had the ability to score, pass, rebound and defend. Gave some of the greatest individual performances ever turned in by a Wildcat. A three-time All-SEC selection and the league's top sophomore in 1959. Flashed his great offensive potential with a 23-point effort in only his fourth varsity game. In a monster performance against Notre Dame, he scored 24 points and grabbed 17 rebounds while holding Irish All-American Tom Hawkins to 13 points, 11 below his average. Came back to score 18 as the Cats snapped Auburn's 30-game winning streak. Ended his rookie season with a 13.5 scoring average. His play helped that Wildcat team carve out a 24-3 record. Averaged 14.4 as a junior despite missing five games because of a leg injury. Opened the season strong, scoring 23 against UCLA, 20 against St. Louis and 27 against Temple. Had a huge 29-point effort in the Cats' 96-93 win over an Ohio State team that featured Jerry Lucas, John Havlicek and Larry Siegfried. Had an outstanding senior

season, averaging a team-best 16 points per game while also leading in field goal percentage (42 percent). His best outing was a 29-point, 12-rebound performance against St. Louis. Scored 83 points during one three-game stretch. Hit for 24 points as the Cats handed Florida its first SEC loss. Led the Cats with 28 points in their first-round NCAA tourney win over Morehead State. Accumulated 1,076 career points as a Wildcat, finishing with an average of 14.7. Made good on 74.7 percent of his free throws. Honed his skills at Lafayette High School under the watchful eye of ex-Cat Ralph Carlisle. Named Kentucky's Mr. Basketball after leading the Generals to the 1957 state championship.

JIM LINE
(1947-50, 6'2", forward, Akron, Ohio)

A dead-eye lefty who amassed 1,041 points during his four years at UK. Although not considered one of the "Fabulous Five," he was the fourth-leading scorer on that NCAA championship team with a 6.9 average. Despite being used only sparingly as a freshman in 1946-47, he had several big games, including 16 points against Texas A&M and 20 in the Cats' 98-29 victory over Vanderbilt in the SEC tourney. Also had 12 points in the NIT final game loss to Utah. His best game as a sophomore was a 22-point performance against Florida in the SEC tourney. Played some of his best ball in the 1949 NCAA Tournament after moving into the starting lineup, scoring 21 against Villanova and 15 against Illinois. Averaged 13.1 as a senior, second only to Bill Spivey. Opened the 1949-50 campaign with a 37-point showing in an easy win over Indiana Central. Scored 19 points to help the Cats upset top-ranked Bradley 71-66. Again made his presence felt in the SEC tourney, hitting for 19 against both Mississippi State and Tennessee. Named to the all-tourney team and the All-SEC team. Shot an excellent 42 percent from the field as a senior. Hit 74.5 percent of his free throws.

RONNIE LYONS
(1972-74, 5'10", guard, Maysville, Ky.)

A deadeye marksman from downtown whose long-range bombing could light up the scoreboard and the Big Blue faithful who packed Memorial Coliseum. Would have considered today's three-point line as little more than an extended free throw. Burst onto the scene with a vengeance as a sophomore in 1971-72, hitting for 12 against Kansas,

19 against Indiana and 16 against Michigan State. Scored 21 in the UKIT title game win over Princeton. Was superb during SEC play, hitting for 24 against Ole Miss, 23 against Vandy and 22 against Auburn. Led the Cats with 19 points in their 85-69 NCAA tourney win over Marquette. Shot 45 percent from the field and led the club with 87.5 percent accuracy from the charity stripe. Averaged 13.2 points, earning second-team All-SEC recognition. Scored at a 9.2 clip as a junior, while hitting 78 percent of his free throws. Burned Mississippi State for 54 points in two outings. Also had 17 against Florida and 15 against North Carolina. Came back to average 7.8 as a senior on that disappointing 1973-74 team, making good on 47 percent of his field goals and 82 percent of his free throws. Scored 16 in an 88-80 victory over Iowa, then hit for 21 in the 78-77 UKIT title game win over Stanford. Caught fire in February, hitting for 17 against Mississippi State, 21 against LSU, 14 against Georgia, 10 against Auburn and 12 against Ole Miss. Helped the Cats avoid their first losing season since 1926-27 by scoring 16 in a 108-69 win over Mississippi State in the finale. Finished his career as an 84-percent marksman from the free throw line. Came to UK after a superb career at Mason County High School.

KYLE MACY
(1978-80, 6'3", guard, Peru, Ind.)

An extremely popular Wildcat and one who had the cold blood of a reptile coursing through his veins. No UK player has ever come through more often in clutch situations than the guy known as "Cool Kyle." Also one of the most-imitated UK players ever. A generation of Kentucky prep players wouldn't dare shoot a free throw without first following Macy's ritual of bending over and drying his hands on his socks. Transferred to UK from Purdue, sat out the 1976-77 season, then became an instant floor general for the 1978 NCAA championship club. Scored 1,411 career points, earned All-America honors in 1979 and 1980, and set UK and SEC records by making good on 89 percent of his free throws. Handed out 470 assists during his days as a Wildcat. Averaged 12.5 points and 5.6 assists while hitting 89.2 percent from the charity stripe as a sophomore. Had a season high 30 against Florida, hitting 11 of 13 field goal attempts. Scored eight straight points to erase a three-point deficit and lift the Cats past Notre Dame 73-68. His 10 pressure-packed freebies helped

the Cats put away Michigan State 52-49 in the NCAA tourney. Came back the next season to average 15.2 points and 4.2 assists. Hit a last-second jumper and a free throw to cap UK's amazing 67-66 overtime win over Kansas. Was voted the SEC tourney MVP after scoring 32 against Ole Miss and 29 against LSU. Led the Cats with 20 points in their NCAA tourney loss to Clemson. As a senior, he averaged 15.4 points and hit 91.2 percent from the free throw line. Beat Auburn and LSU with last-second jumpers. Canned four straight free throws, then came up with a steal to give the Cats a 61-60 win over Purdue in the UKIT title game. Scored 57 points in two wins over Ole Miss and 28 against Georgia. Played several years in the NBA, then became a member of the UK broadcast team.

JAMAAL MAGLOIRE
(1997-00, 6'10", center, Toronto, Ontario, Canada)

Tough, aggressive post player and UK's all-time leader in blocked shots with 268. Struggled for much of his career with his offense — and his volatile temper — but once he cooled the volcano within, he became a solid scorer and team leader. Tested the NBA waters after his junior season, then opted to return to UK. Finished his career with 1,064 points and 789 rebounds. His final-season averages of 13.2 points and 9.1 rebounds were good enough to earn him a spot on the All-SEC first-team. Scored in double digits in 28 of UK's 33 games. Had 15 double-doubles as a senior, including 23 points and 15 rebounds in a win over Vanderbilt and 12 points and 16 rebounds against Maryland. Also had double-doubles against such powers as Louisville, Michigan State, Florida, Tennessee and LSU. Led the club in shooting with 50 percent accuracy. Also improved dramatically at the charity stripe, hitting on 68.5 percent of his attempts. Became the first Wildcat to be named SEC Player of the Week three times in the same season. Ranks among the top four all-time NCAA tourney shot-blockers with 37. Started 22 games as a freshman in 1996-97, averaging 4.9 points and 4.4 rebounds per game. His 79 blocked shots led the SEC and are the most-ever by a UK rookie. Was chosen to the SEC All-Freshman team. Came off the bench to score 16 points in only his second varsity game, an 87-53 win over Syracuse. Also hit for 13 points in wins over Tennessee and Alabama. Registered his first career double-double when he had 10 points and 10 rebounds against

Alaska-Anchorage. Came back to average 5.2 points and 4.2 rebounds as a sophomore on the 1998 NCAA championship club. Had 18 points and 17 rebounds to lead the Cats past Missouri in the Maui Classic. Scored 15 against Ohio University and 12 against Georgia Tech. Shot 71.4 percent from the field and 80 percent from the foul line during six NCAA tourney games. Had seven points, two rebounds and three blocked shots in the championship-game win over Utah. Was awarded UK's "Best Defender" award for a second straight year. Only made six starts as a junior, finishing with averages of seven points and 4.4 rebounds. Topped the team in blocked shots with 66, becoming only the fourth Wildcat to surpass the 200 mark in that category. Scored a season-high 15 points on two occasions, against Georgia Tech and Tennessee State. Registered three double-doubles, including a superb 14-point,11-rebound performance against Arkansas. Played well in the SEC tourney, averaging 10 points and 5.7 rebounds while shooting 61 percent from the field. Came to UK after leading Eastern High School to a 39-3 record and the provincial championship. Averaged 23.8 points, 14.7 rebounds and 7.2 blocked shots as a prep senior.

JAMAL MASHBURN
(1991-93, 6'8", forward, New York, N.Y.)

The single most important Wildcat in the post-probation era. Displayed plenty of courage by choosing to buck the odds and sign on with the scandal-scarred Wildcats. Had he not done so, the resurrection of UK's basketball program would have taken much longer. He was the athlete, the complete basketball player that Pitino needed to help kick-start the program and the recruiting process. Could score, pass, rebound and defend. Scored 1,843 points — fifth-best in UK history — although he only played in 98 games as a Wildcat. Was a consensus All-America pick in 1993. Averaged 12.9 as a freshman on Pitino's second UK team, which finished with a 22-6 record. Hit for a season-high 31 against Georgia, breaking UK's record for most points by a freshman. Also had 24 against Mississippi State and in the season finale against Auburn. Averaged a team-best 21.3 points and 7.8 rebounds as a sophomore. Gave a 28-point, 10-rebound performance in an early season 90-69 win over UMass. Had 33 points and 11 rebounds in a win over South Carolina. Scored 34 against Vanderbilt and 30 against Tennessee. Accounted for 64 points in three games to lead UK to the SEC tourney championship. Was voted the tourney's MVP. Played brilliantly in the NCAA Tournament. Had 27 against Iowa State, 30 in a second victory over UMass and 28 in UK's heartbreaking 104-103 overtime loss to Duke. Shot 56.7 percent from the field as a sophomore. In what turned out to be his final season at UK, he averaged 21 points and 8.3 rebounds. Had 38 points and 19 rebounds against Eastern Kentucky. Also hit for 30 against Georgia. Scored 29 in a big 81-78 win over Indiana. Was a model of consistency that season, hitting for 20 or more in 21 of UK's 34 games. Scored 23 in UK's 92-81 SEC tourney semifinal win over Arkansas, then came back with 17 in an 82-65 win over LSU in the title game. Had 19 and 23 in NCAA tourney wins over Utah and Wake Forest. Racked up 26 points before fouling out with 3:23 left in overtime in UK's 81-78 loss to Michigan in the Final Four. Earned All-SEC honors in each of his three seasons as a Wildcat. Finished with an 18.8 scoring average. Hit on 37.6 percent of his three-point attempts. Drafted by the Dallas Mavericks in the first round of the 1993 draft. Currently owns several successful businesses.

JIM MASTER
(1981-84, 6'5", guard, Fort Wayne, Ind.)

Lethal outside gunner and one of UK's all-time best free throw shooters. Another UK guard who would have loved the three-point shot. Scored 1,283 points during his career while hitting 84.9 percent of his free throws. His 89.6 free throw accuracy during the 1981-82 season is the third best in UK history and the best by a Wildcat sophomore. Averaged 6.5 points as a freshman, with a high of 16 on two occasions. Came off the bench to score 10 points in an early 68-66 win over Indiana. Scored 16 in his first start, a 71-68 double-overtime win over Georgia. Averaged 13.4 points as a sophomore. Had 54 points in two games against Auburn. Came back to average 12.5 as a junior. Blistered Vanderbilt for 26 points on 12 of 16 shooting from the field. Was outstanding in UK's 80-68 overtime loss to Louisville in the "Dream Game," scoring 18 points and sinking the 12-foot baseline jumper that sent the game into the extra period. Shot 53 percent from the field during his junior year. Averaged 9.6 points for the 1983-84 Final Four team. Opened his final season with a 19-point performance in UK's 65-44 win over Louisville. Scored 23 against Kansas and 22

against Mississippi State. Tallied 10 points and made a key assist to Kenny Walker in UK's 51-49 victory over Auburn in the SEC tourney championship game. Had 15 in UK's 72-67 NCAA tourney win over Louisville. Again led the team at the charity stripe, hitting 81.1 percent. Voted Indiana's Mr. Basketball in 1980 after a sterling prep career at Harding High School in Fort Wayne.

PAUL McBRAYER
(1928-30, 6'4", guard, Lawrenceburg, Ky.)

Started all three years at UK and was the school's last All-American prior to the arrival of Adolph Rupp. Was one of five sophomore starters on John Mauer's 1927-28 team that put together a 12-6 record after the previous year's club had finished with a dismal 3-13 mark. Averaged 5.5 points in his rookie season. Helped lead the Cats to records of 12-5 and 16-3 in his final two seasons. Was voted onto the All-America squad in 1930. Served as Rupp's assistant from 1934-43, and is credited with having a big influence on the Baron during those early years. McBrayer was an excellent tactician, recruiter and teacher of fundamentals. After a stint in the military, he returned to UK but wasn't rehired by Rupp. Went on to have a legendary career as coach and athletics director at Eastern Kentucky University.

WALTER McCARTY
(1994-96, 6'9", forward, Evansville, Ind.)

One of the most active and mobile big men in UK history. Ran the floor like a gazelle and had superb leaping ability. Owns one of UK's most-electrifying dunks ever, an in-your-face slam over Vanderbilt's J.J. Lucas that would have made James Lee proud. Known as "Ice" to his teammates. Sat out his freshman year due to Proposition 48. Had two huge games as a sophomore, scoring 24 against Ole Miss and 23 in the Cats' record-breaking 99-95 come-from-behind win at LSU. It was his trey with 19 seconds left that put the Cats in front for good at 96-95. Averaged 5.7 points per game. Came back the next season to score at a 10.5 clip. Scored 12 of UK's first 16 points and finished with 20 in a 97-58 victory over Notre Dame. Had 22 points and 10 rebounds in a 93-81 SEC tourney win over Auburn. His 17-point, 11-rebound effort helped key the Cats to an easy 113-67 romp past Mount St. Mary's in the NCAA Tournament. Closed out his career by averaging 11.3 points for the 1995-96 NCAA championship club. Shot a blistering 54.3 percent from the field that season. Hit for 20 against South Carolina. Had a total of 47 points in three SEC tourney games. Scored 24 against San Jose State in UK's NCAA tourney opener. Followed that by giving a 19-point performance in an 84-60 win over Virginia Tech. Taken by the New York Knicks in the first round of 1996 draft.

JODIE MEEKS
(2006-09, 6'4", guard, Norcross, Ga.)

A record-breaking standout who scored 1,246 points despite playing only 81 games during his three-year UK career. Had a monster junior campaign, racking up 854 points for a 23.7 scoring average. Scored 54 points against Tennessee, breaking Dan Issel's 39-year-old single-game mark of 53. Hit 15 of 22 shots from the field, including 10 of 15 from behind the three-point line, and all 14 of his free throws in that game. Scored 46 against Appalachian State and 45 against Arkansas. Topped the 30-point plateau on three other occasions. Shot 46 percent from the field and 41 percent from three-point range during his final season as a Wildcat. His 105 treys broke Travis Ford's single-season mark of 101. Named SEC Player of the Week a record four times. Earned All-America and All-SEC recognition. Injuries limited him to just 11 games as a junior. Averaged 8.8 points per game. Had 21-point efforts against Houston and Florida International. Averaged 8.7 points and earned Freshman All-America honors during his rookie season. Reached double figures 16 times. Had season-best 18-point performances against Louisville and LSU. Led Norcross High to the Class 5A state championship as a senior. Scored 32 points in the title game. Named 2006 Player of the Year by AJC, Gwinnett Daily Post and the Atlanta Tipoff Club. Took his talents to the NBA following his junior year at UK.

RON MERCER
(1996-97, 6'7", forward/guard, Nashville, Tenn.)

Easily ranks among the most supremely gifted and multi-dimensional Wildcats of all-time. Accounted for 1,013 points despite playing just 76 games. His 725 points during the 1996-97 campaign rank as the fifth-most by a UK player in a single season. Although known more for his slashing drives and arena-rattling dunks, he was also capable of burning defenses with his perimeter jumper. Drew 12 starts as a freshman on the talent-rich 1995-96 NCAA championship team, averaging eight points per game. Hit for 15 points in regular-season wins over LSU and Vanderbilt. Scored 17 in UK's 100-76 win over Florida in the SEC tourney. Saved his best for last, making good on eight of 12 shots and scoring 20 points in the Cats' 76-67 win over Syracuse in the NCAA championship game. Connected on three of four three-point attempts against the Orangemen. Named to the All-Final Four team. Averaged an SEC-best 18.1 points as a sophomore. Hit 13 of 16 shots and scored a career-high 30 points in a 101-87 win over Purdue. Scored 26 against Indiana and 25 against South Carolina. Scored 60 points in three games to lead UK to another SEC tourney title. Was voted the tourney MVP. Had 19 against St. Joseph's, 21 against Utah and 19 against Minnesota during NCAA tourney action. Held to 13 in the Cats' 84-79 overtime loss to Arizona in the championship game. Once again named to the All-Final Four team. Was a consensus first-team All-American, SEC Player of the Year and MVP of the West Regional and the Great Alaska Shootout. The prep 1996 Player of the Year as a senior at Oak Hill (Va.) Academy. Entered the NBA draft after his sophomore season and was taken in the first round by the Boston Celtics. Made the All-Rookie team in 1998.

DERRICK MILLER
(1987-90, 6'5", guard, Savannah, Ga.)

Rail-thin, long-range bomber connected on 191 three-pointers during his career and was the first Wildcat player to score 40 points in Rupp Arena. His 99 treys in the 1989-90 season are the most-ever by a UK senior. Struggled early in his career, and considered leaving UK after a sophomore season in which he averaged just six minutes of playing time. Averaged 5.2 points as a freshman and 1.3 as a sophomore. Had a season-high 15 in a loss to Georgia during his rookie campaign. Topped the club in three-point accuracy with 43.2 percent. Scored only 21 points and failed to crack double figures as a sophomore. Chose to stay at UK and was the third-leading scorer on Eddie Sutton's final team. Averaged 13.9 points that season while hitting 54 treys in 139 attempts. Hit his first 10 shots, including seven three-pointers, in a 36-point effort against California. Also had 34 against Louisville and 30 against Florida. Thrived as a senior in Pitino's up-tempo, launch-from-anywhere offense, averaging a team-leading 19.2

points per game. Nailed six treys in his record-breaking 40-point performance against Vanderbilt. Had 36 against Tennessee Tech and 32 against Kansas in back-to-back outings. Led the Cats with 29 points in their monumental 100-95 upset of powerful LSU. Accounted for 984 points in his final two seasons to finish with 1,156. An All-SEC pick in 1990.

CAMERON MILLS
(1995-98, 6'3", guard, Lexington, Ky.)

A former walk-on who left UK four years later as the school's most-accurate three-point shooter with a 47.4 percent accuracy. Hit an amazing 53.2 percent of his treys during his junior year in 1996-97. Had eight three-pointers in a career-high 31-point performance against Florida as a senior. He scorched the nets in 1996-97 postseason play, connecting on 63 percent of his three-point attempts, including five of six against St. Joseph's and five of seven against Montana. Also a superb free throw shooter, he shot 82.4 percent from the charity stripe during his career. Saw action in only 15 games during his first two seasons, scoring just 16 points. Hit double figures for the first time when scored 12 points in an 83-73 win over Arkansas midway through the 1996-97 season. Scored 30 points in UK's final two SEC tourney games, wins over Ole Miss and Georgia. Canned 10 of 16 three-point attempts during SEC tourney action. Tossed in 19 points to tie Wayne Turner for scoring honors in the Cats' 92-54 win over Montana in the NCAA Tournament opener. Also hit for 19 points against St. Joseph's. Hit a pair of treys and finished with 10 points in UK's 78-69 semifinal win over Minnesota. Came back with a 12-point effort in the Cats' 84-79 overtime loss to Arizona in the championship game. Finished the season with a 5.9 scoring clip. Averaged 4.4 points for Tubby Smith's 1998 NCAA championship club. Shot 43.7 percent from three-point range and 95.7 percent from the free throw line (22 of 23). Made good on 10 of 19 shots, including eight of 14 three-pointers, in his 31-point performance against Florida. Scored 12 points to help the Cats beat Arkansas 99-74 in the SEC tourney semifinal round. Hit a crucial trey, his first bucket in NCAA tourney action, to put UK in front of Duke 80-79 with 2:15 remaining. Came through with eight points in the Cats' 78-69 comeback win over Utah in the championship game. A two-time

All-State performer at Dunbar High School in Lexington. His father, Terry, was a three-year letterman at UK (1969-71).

DON MILLS
(1957-59, 6'6", center/forward, Berea, Ky.)

A solid inside player whose superb performance off the bench was a key reason why the Wildcats were able to beat Seattle 84-72 in the 1958 NCAA championship game. It was his hook shot that gave the Cats their first lead with just over six minutes remaining. Finished that game with nine points and five rebounds. Became a starter the following season, scoring at a 10.5 clip for a surprising Wildcat team that went 24-3. Shot 82.7 from the free throw line to lead the team in that category. Scored 20 points in the season-opening 91-68 win over Florida State. Had 24 points in a win over Marquette in the NCAA tourney. Averaged 12.7 points as a senior while pulling down a team-high 12.9 rebounds. Had 13 points and 11 rebounds in UK's great 96-93 win over an Ohio State team led by Jerry Lucas and John Havlicek. Registered back-to-back double-doubles in wins over Notre Dame (19/14) and Vanderbilt (16/17). Was named All-SEC in 1960. Had an outstanding prep career at Berea High School, earning All-State honors in 1955 and 1956.

DIRK MINNIEFIELD
(1980-83, 6'3", guard, Lexington, Ky.)

Big, tough, hard-nosed guard and UK's all-time assist leader with 646. Also scored 1,069 points and had 156 steals. Handed out 14 assists against Villanova during the 1982-83 season. Led the 1980-81 team in field goal shooting (55.4 percent) and free throw shooting (87.3 percent). Averaged five points per game as a freshman. Scored a season-high 14 in a win over Mississippi State. Nailed a 22-foot jump shot with two seconds left to give the Cats a 64-62 win over Auburn. Averaged 10.4 points and 5.4 assists as a sophomore in 1980-81. Had 20 against Mississippi State and 18 against Vandy. Scored at an 11.3 clip as a junior while handing out 6.3 assists per game. Hit for a season-high 25 against Alabama. Led the Cats with 22 points in a convincing 85-69 win over Indiana. Scored 20 in crucial SEC wins over Georgia and Ole Miss. His 49 points in three games earned him a spot on the SEC all-tournament team. Averaged 8.6 points and 5.8 assists as a senior. His 14 assists sparked

the Cats to their 93-79 win over third-ranked Villanova. Had 16 points against Ohio University in the NCAA tourney, then scored 12 in the 80-68 "Dream Game" loss to Louisville. Came to UK after leading Lexington Lafayette to the 1979 state championship. Named Kentucky's Mr. Basketball that same year. Was drafted by Dallas in the second round of the 1983 NBA draft. Also spent time with Cleveland, Houston, Golden State and Boston before retiring in 1988.

RANDOLPH MORRIS
(2005-07, 6'10", center, Atlanta, Ga.)

An unquestionably talented post player who is destined to go down as one of the great magnificent maybes in UK hoops history. Big Blue fans can only dream of what he could have accomplished had his career not been thwarted by his on-again/off-again flirtation with the NBA. Despite displaying a sometimes less than 100 percent interest in the collegiate game, he still finished his career with 1,123 points and 531 rebounds while making good on 57.8 percent of his field goal attempts. Left UK for the NBA after his junior campaign. Demonstrated his great potential as a junior, averaging a team-best 16.1 points per game. Had a dozen double-doubles, highlighted by a brilliant 29-point, 15-rebound effort against Mississippi State in the SEC tourney. Posted many of his double-doubles against top-flight competition — 23/13 against Santa Clara, 20/10 against Houston and 19/11 against Villanova. Also had a 25-point, 10-rebound outing against Eastern Kentucky. Shot 59.1 percent from the field during his junior season. Earned All-SEC recognition for his efforts. Sat out UK's first 14 games as a sophomore due to being suspended by the NCAA for dealing with professional agents. Returned to lead the team in scoring with a 13.3 average. Ripped Tennessee for 42 points in a pair of UK victories. Scored 19 against both Alabama and Arkansas. Accounted for 13 points and 11 rebounds against South Carolina. Shot 61 percent from the field. Started every game but one as a true freshman, averaging 8.8 points per game. Hit double figures 13 times, with a high of 25 in a win over Campbell. In that game, he connected on 11 of 14 shots. Scored 20 in the Cats' NCAA loss to Michigan State. Named to McDonald's All-America team after his senior season at Landmark Christian High School. Averaged 23 points, 16 rebounds and eight blocked shots as a prep senior.

COTTON NASH
(1962-64, 6'5", center/forward, Lake Charles, La.)

One of the most charismatic and popular Wildcats of all-time. Also one of the true greats. There seemed to be no limit to what he could do on a basketball court. He was smooth and graceful, sheer poetry in motion. Had a deadly outside jumper and enough slithery one-on-one moves to get to the rack against the finest defenders. Literally carried

Charismatic Cotton Nash (with wife Julie) acknowledges the crowd during a 1991 ceremony. The great Nash carried the UK program on his back from 1962-64 and left as the school's all-time leading scorer.

the program on his back during his three years at UK. He earned All-America and All-SEC honors in each of his three seasons. Left as the school's all-time leading scorer with 1,770 points in only 78 games. Has the distinction of reaching the 1,000-point milestone faster than any other Wildcat, surpassing that mark in his 45th game. Had a career scoring average of 22.7, and remains the only UK player to average 20 points three times. He also pulled down 962 rebounds, twice getting 30 in a single game. His 23.4 scoring average is the best-ever by a UK sophomore. Averaged 13.2 rebounds that season. Had 25 points and 17 rebounds in his Wildcat debut. Topped the 30-point mark nine times as a sophomore, including one string of four games in a row. Hit for a season-high 38 against Vanderbilt. An early season foot injury slowed him during his junior campaign, yet he still averaged 20.6 points and 12 rebounds. Also led the team in assists with 66. Scored 34 against Virginia Tech, 30 against West Virginia and 31 against Alabama. Averaged 24 points and 11.7 rebounds during his final season. Hit for 30 or more nine times, with a high of 34 on two occasions. Scored 30 in UK's 81-79 win over Duke in the final game of the Sugar Bowl tourney. Had 58 points in those two games to earn MVP honors. His 12.3 career rebounding average ranks fourth behind Burrow, Hagan and Issel on UK's all-time list. Left UK and became one of the few athletes to play both pro baseball and pro basketball.

BERNIE OPPER
(1937-39, 5'10", guard, New York, N.Y.)

This low-scoring backcourt player was chosen All-American in 1939. Helped direct the Cats to a pair of SEC Tournament titles in his three year-career. Recruited himself to UK by writing a letter to Rupp after seeing the Cats play in Madison Square Garden. Scored eight points in his Wildcat debut, but was noted more for his defense and ball-handling. Averaged 3.5 as a sophomore. Had several big games during his second season, including 14 against Michigan State and 10 against Alabama. Played two of his finest games in wins over Tennessee duing his senior year. Racked up a game-high 11 points in a 36-34 double-overtime win in the regular season encounter, then came back to score 13 in UK's 46-38 victory over the Vols in the SEC Tournament championship game. Was named to the All-SEC tourney team in 1938 and 1939.

SCOTT PADGETT
(1995, 97-99, 6'9", forward, Louisville, Ky.)

The classic comeback kid. Through hard work, determination and an iron will, he transformed himself from college dropout to college standout — in the classroom and on the hardwood. Scored 1,252 points, twice made the All-Final Four team, earned SEC all-tourney honors two times, was the tourney MVP in 1999, knocked down as many clutch buckets as any Wildcat ever has and was a two-time Academic All-SEC selection. All that after flunking out of college and spending 18 months working at several jobs back in Louisville. Played in 14 games as a freshman in 1994-95, scoring a total of 28 points. Sat out the entire 1995-96 championship season and the first eight games of the '96-'97 campaign. Ended his 18-month exile by scor-

Scott Padgett was drafted in the first round by the Utah Jazz.

ing 12 points and spearing seven rebounds against Georgia Tech. Went on to average 9.6 points per game that season. Had a season-best 24 in a 74-64 win over Tennessee. Made nine of 10 field goals and finished with 23 points against Western Carolina. Led the Cats with 17 points in their 84-79 overtime loss to Arizona in the NCAA tourney championship game. Averaged 11.5 points and shot 85.3 percent from the free throw line in 1997-98. Scored 24 against Alabama, 23 against Mississippi State and 20 against Tennessee. Was outstanding in tournament play. Had 12 points and 13 rebounds against Alabama, then combined with Jeff Sheppard for 25 first-half points in a 99-74 win over Arkansas. Scored 19 in the Cats' 94-68 win over UCLA and 12, including the go-ahead bucket, in an 86-84 come-from-behind win over Duke. Topped the Cats with 17 in their 78-69 comeback win over Utah in the NCAA tourney's final game. As a senior, he led the team in scoring (12.6) and rebounding (5.9). Hit 38.1 percent of his three-point attempts despite opening the season with a 0-for-18 slump. Scored 25 points and pulled down 13 rebounds in a 103-91 win over second-ranked Maryland. Had 29 points and 10 rebounds in the Cats' 92-88 overtime win against Kansas in the NCAA tourney. Hit the trey that tied the game against Kansas, then scored seven points in the OT to pull the Cats through. Came back to lead the club with 17 points in a 58-43 win over Miami of Ohio. An All-State performer at St. Xavier High School in Louisville. Currently coaching at Samford University.

TOM PARKER
(1970-72, 6'7", forward, Collinsville, Ill.)

Ranks up there with Grevey and Givens as one of UK's deadliest left-handed shooters. Finished with 1,238 points for a career average of 15.5. An All-SEC pick as a junior and senior. His strong play as a sophomore in 1969-70 helped the Cats offset the devastating loss of Casey. Broke into the starting quintet midway through the season and finished with a 10.4 scoring average and a 50.4 percent field goal accuracy. Had his first big game in only his fourth outing, coming off the bench to score 15 points in a 109-92 pasting of Indiana. Scored 18 in only his second start, then followed that by scoring 17 against Florida and 21 against Georgia. Had 14 points and 15 rebounds in a win over Alabama. Gave a solid 21-point performance in UK's season-ending 106-100 NCAA tourney loss to Jacksonville. Averaged a team-high 17.6 points as a junior in 1970-71.

Had several huge scoring efforts that season, topped by 32 against Mississippi State and 30 against Vanderbilt. Scored 23 in UK's loss to Western Kentucky University in the NCAA Tournament. Upped his scoring average to 18 in his final season as a Wildcat. Had a season-high 30 in the Cats' 83-67 victory over Notre Dame in Freedom Hall. Later had 29 against Auburn and 25 against Florida. Shot 49.3 percent from the field and 79.3 percent from the charity stripe during his career.

JACK PARKINSON
(1944, 46-48, 6'0", guard, Yorktown, Ind.)

The leading scorer on the 1945-46 team that went 28-2 and won the NIT. Earned All-America honors for his play that season. However, after serving in the military, he returned to UK and was relegated to the role of substitute during the "Fabulous Five" season. Cracked the starting line-up midway through his freshman campaign, averaging seven points for the youthful "Wildkittens" team of 1943-44 that finished with a sparkling 19-2 record. Played exceptionally well late in the season, scoring 27 against Tulane in the SEC tourney final and 20 in a win over Utah in the NIT. Scored at a 10.4 pace for the 1944-45 team that was 22-4. Accounted for 40 points in two games against Michigan State. Tallied a team-high 15 to lead the Cats past Tennessee 39-35 in the SEC tourney championship game. Averaged 11.3 for that NIT-winning 1945-46 team. Had 23 in a win over Vanderbilt and 20 in a bashing of Fort Benning. Topped the club with 56 points in four SEC tourney games. Made the SEC all-tournament team, the third time he achieved that honor. Scored 10 points and hit a critical basket in the Cats' 59-51 NIT semifinal win over West Virginia. Played very little after returning from the service. His high game during the 1947-48 season was a 12-point showing against Fort Knox.

PATRICK PATTERSON
(2007-10, 6'9", forward, Huntington, W.Va.)

Will undoubtedly forever be remembered as one of the classiest, hardest-working and most-unselfish Wildcats of all-time. Few UK players have represented the school with greater distinction. Handled himself well during the dark Billy Gillispie period. Came back for his junior year and was the anchor of that talented club that went 35-3 and restored UK to glory. Never complained when rookies Wall and Cousins grabbed the spotlight. Accounted for 1,564 points and 791 rebounds as a Wildcat. Shot 59 percent from the field during his career. Averaged 14.3 points as a junior. Posted nine double-doubles. Hit for a season-high 23 points against South Carolina. Had 19 points and 18 rebounds in a win over Rider, and 19 points and 11 boards against Indiana. Scored 22 in NCAA tourney action against East Tennessee State. Had a huge junior season, averaging 17.9 points and 9.3 rebounds while shooting 60 percent from the field. Had 15 double-doubles as a junior. Scored 33 against Tennessee State and 31 against Lamar. Had 28 points four times, against Longwood, LSU and twice against South Carolina. Pulled down 18 rebounds against Auburn. Named First-Team All-SEC. Had a superb rookie season, averaging 16.4 points and 7.7 rebounds. Missed six games due to injuries. Recorded six double-doubles. Tagged Tennessee Tech for 24 points and 15 rebounds. Finished with 23 points and 12 rebounds in a loss to Vandy. Also scored 23 points against Liberty. Named Second-Team All-SEC and Co-Freshman of the Year. Was a three-time all-state player at Huntington High School. Averaged 17 points and 12 rebounds as a senior. A McDonald's All-American in 2007.

JOHN PELPHREY
(1989-92, 6'7", forward, Paintsville, Ky.)

A remarkably intelligent and shrewd basketball player, one who possessed a fanatical work ethic and a near-limitless desire to excel. This overachieving "Unforgettable" is the perfect embodiment of the Wildcat tradition and spirit. Scored 1,257 points during his great career. A terrific passer and one of the best clutch players in UK history. Also a sneaky defender. Had 327 assists and 173 steals. Played sparingly as a freshman, averaging just 1.7 points per game. Moved into the starting lineup as a sophomore and finished with a 13-point scoring average. Hit for a season-high 24 in an overtime loss to Southwestern Louisiana. Shot 75.2 percent from the free throw stripe. Upped his scoring average to 14.4 as a junior while shooting 78.4 from the foul line and connecting on 62 three-pointers. Led the team in scoring on eight occasions, with a high of 29 in a 95-85 win over Ole Miss. Had 28 against Alabama and 24 against North Carolina and Florida. Canned two late free throws then made a steal and pass that led to a Jeff Brassow trey in UK's 89-81 win over Auburn. Averaged 12.5 points in his final season as a Wildcat. Opened his senior campaign with a 26-point performance in a 106-80 pre-season NIT victory over West Virginia. Also had 26 in the Cats' 103-89 win over arch-rival Louisville. Was outstanding

in the NCAA tourney, scoring 76 points in four games. Had 22 in an 88-69 win over Old Dominion and 20 in a 106-98 win over Iowa State. Scored 16 in that classic 104-103 overtime loss to Duke. His 160 three-point buckets rank him fourth on UK's all-time list. Chosen All-SEC in 1991 and was named to the SEC all-tournament team in 1992 and 1993. Had a magnificent prep career at Paintsville High School, earning All-State honors three times. Led the Tigers to the semifinals of the 1987 Sweet 16. Took his great basketball mind into the coaching ranks, joining ex-UK assistant Billy Donovan at Marshall University and Florida. Formerly coached at South Alabama and Arkansas.

MIKE PHILLIPS
(1975-78, 6'10, center, Manchester, Ohio)

One half of UK's vaunted "Twin Towers" duo that helped lead the Cats to a 102-21 won-loss record, an NCAA title, an NIT title and a second-place NCAA finish during the years between 1974 and 1978. Accounted for 1,367 points as a Wildcat while connecting on 55 percent of his field goal attempts. Averaged 7.8 points as a freshman. His high game that season was 26 against Mississippi State. Also scored 18 in wins over Washington State and LSU. Had a big game in UK's 92-90 win over Indiana, finishing with 10 points. Really stepped up as a sophomore, carrying much of the inside load after "Tower" mate Rick Robey went down with an injury. Averaged 15.6 points and 9.8 rebounds that season. Also shot 54.2 percent from the field. Scored 35 points and hauled down 28 rebounds against Tennessee. Had 30 points and 15 rebounds in a win over Vandy. Played superbly in the NIT, scoring 52 points in the Cats' final three wins. His crucial three-point play sealed the Cats' win over UNCC in the championship game. Came back as a junior to average 12.2 points per game. His best game that season was a 24-point, 19-rebound effort against LSU. In the 1977-78 championship campaign, he averaged 10.2 points while hitting nearly 60 percent from the field. Scored 22 in the season opener against SMU, then later hit for 23 against LSU. Led the Cats with 24 points in their NCAA tourney second-round win over Miami of Ohio. Had 10 points in UK's tough 52-49 semifinal win over Magic Johnson-led Michigan State. His 54.9 career field goal percentage ranks seventh on UK's all-time list. Was drafted into the NBA, but ended up having a highly successful pro career overseas.

MIKE PRATT
(1968-70, 6'4", forward, Dayton, Ohio)

Played in the towering shadow of Issel, yet still posted such good numbers that he has to be ranked among UK's all-time best forwards. Tough, fierce and exceptionally strong, he could score inside or outside. And no Wildcat ever set a better screen. Scored 1,359 career points and averaged 8.9 rebounds per game. His 42-point performance against Notre Dame in 1969 is among the greatest ever given by a Wildcat. It was during this game that Cawood Ledford said, "Pratt has picked up the banner and gone to war." The "gone to war" phrase became part of the UK lexicon, describing heroic performances by Wildcat players. Pratt cracked the starting lineup early in his sophomore season, and finished the year with a 14.1 scoring average. Scored 23 against Vandy, his best effort that season. Had 15 rebounds in a win over Dayton. Led the team in assists with 82. Averaged 16.9 as a junior. Hit for 23 against Vandy and 22 in consecutive wins over Auburn and Ole Miss. Led the club with 53.9 percent field goal shooting. Scored 28 in the 1969-70 season opener against West Virginia, the first in a long line of magnificent performances that year. Had 27 against North Carolina, a figure he later matched against LSU. Averaged 19.3 points while once again leading the team in assists with 99. Hit 48.4 percent of his field goal attempts at UK. A two-time All-SEC pick. Went on to play professionally in the old ABA. Now a member of the UK broadcast team.

JARED PRICKETT
(1993-95, 97, 6'9", forward, Fairmont, W.Va.)

This rugged rebounder/defender played in 143 games during his Wildcat career, a number topped only by Wayne Turner's 151. Missed making it into the 1,000-point club by a single bucket. Grabbed 777 rebounds while shooting 51.3 percent from the field. Recorded nine double-doubles in his career. Came to UK as part of a strong recruiting class that included Tony Delk, Rodrick Rhodes and Walter McCarty. Started 12 games as a freshman, hitting for a regular-season high of 16 against Arkansas. Also had 13 rebounds in that game. Gave a 22-point, 11-rebound performance in the Cats' 106-81 Southeast Regional final win over Florida State. Averaged 8.2 points and seven rebounds as a sophomore. Scored 16 points in UK's 93-92 Maui Classic win over Arizona. Had 10 points and 17 rebounds in a 79-67 win over South Carolina. Scored 17 points and snared 15 rebounds to help the Cats get past UMass 67-64. Pulled

down a career-high 20 rebounds against Arkansas. Served primarily as a backup during the 1994-95 season, averaging 6.7 points and 4.8 rebounds. Hit for a season-best 16 in wins over Vanderbilt and Mount St. Mary's. Played five games in 1995-96, then received a medical redshirt. Came back as a fifth-year senior to average 7.9 points and 5.9 rebounds. Shot 55 percent from the field that season. His best outing was a 16-point performance in a 101-87 win over Purdue. Spent several years playing professionally overseas.

TAYSHAUN PRINCE
(1999-2002, 6'9", forward, Compton, Calif.)

This long-arm California lefty proved himself to be one of the toughest, classiest, most-courageous Wildcats of all-time. An amazingly consistent player even though he was often the sole focus of opposing defenses. Made a string of clutch buckets during his outstanding career. Benefited greatly by electing to return to UK for his senior season. Finished with 1,775 points, eighth best among UK's all-time scoring leaders, and became the latest Wildcat to earn All-America honors (2001 and 2002). Also finished with 759 rebounds, 142 blocked shots and 255 assists. Started 11 games as a rookie, scoring 10 points against Eastern Kentucky in his first UK game. Hit for 15 versus Colorado and 12 against Michigan State in the NCAA tourney. Averaged 5.8 points per game as a frosh. Really blossomed as a sophomore, averaging 13.3 points and earning second-team All-SEC recognition. Scored in double figures 20 times. Had 21 against Maryland and Georgia Tech, and 20 against Louisville. Came through in the clutch in wins over Miami (Fla.) and Georgia. Finished the season strong, accounting for 88 points in UK's final five games. Scored a season-high 28 points in the NCAA tourney double overtime win over St. Bonaventure, including a pressure-packed trey with seven seconds left to tie the game at the end of regulation. His junior season ranks among the finest ever turned in by a Wildcat. He averaged 16.9 points, 6.5 rebounds, hit 84 percent of his free throws, 49.5 percent of his field goals, had six double-doubles and scored in double figures 31 times. Capped the season by being named second-team All-American, SEC Player of the Year and SEC Tournament MVP. Scored 27 against Holy Cross in the NCAA tourney, then followed that by tossing in a season-high 31 against Iowa. During regular-season action, he had 30 against Tennessee and 27 against Vandy in back-to-back

outings. Hit 12 of 15 field goal attempts and finished with 29 points against South Carolina. Racked up double-doubles in UK's final two SEC tourney games — 19/10 against Arkansas and 26/12 against Ole Miss. His two freebies lifted UK past Louisville, and his floater in the lane helped the Cats squeeze past South Carolina. Came back to average 17.5 points and 6.4 rebounds in his final season. Gave a majestic 31-point, 11-rebound performance against North Carolina, knocking down five early treys in a two-minute span. Scored 24 against Vandy, 23 against Morehead, and 22 against Tulane and Tennessee. Had 19 points and 10 rebounds in a win over Florida, one of his five double-doubles during the season. Blocked six shots against LSU. Hit 14 of 21 shots en route to a career-best 41-point effort against Tulsa in the NCAA tourney. Repeated as an All-SEC and All-American performer. Came to UK after a sterling prep career at Dominguez High School in Compton, Calif. Drafted in the first round by the Detroit Pistons.

LARRY PURSIFUL
(1960-62, 6'1", guard, Four Mile, Ky.)

One of UK's all-time great outside shooters, and one who would have loved the current three-point shot. Was Mr. Outside to Cotton Nash's Mr. Inside on the 1961-62 team that went 23-3 and tied for the SEC title. Averaged 19.1 that season, good enough to win a spot on the All-SEC team. Made 17 field goals in a 34-point effort against Tennessee in the UKIT. In that game, he scored 20 of UK's first 23 points. Burned Tennessee again later that year when he tossed in 30. Had 26 in regular-season wins over Kansas State and Florida. Again hit for 26 in UK's NCAA tourney win over Butler. Led the Cats with 21 in a 74-64 loss to Ohio State. Hit 51 percent of his field goal attempts that season and 81.6 percent of his free throws. Averaged 13.4 as a junior. Scored 21 points four times during the regular season, then matched that total again in the Cats' 88-67 playoff win over Vandy that secured a berth in the NCAA Tournament. Shot 83.8 percent from the charity stripe. Didn't play early during his sophomore season, but scored 15 points after drawing his first start in a late-season 75-55 win over Alabama. Another Wildcat who seldom gets the recognition he deserves.

FRANK RAMSEY
(1951-52, 54, 6'3", guard, Madisonville, Ky.)

Another of the truly bright stars in Big Blue history,

and probably the most successful on-court Wildcat of all-time. Won an NCAA title and enough NBA championship rings to open a jewelry store. Was a college All-American and an All-NBA pick. He and Hagan remain the most-electrifying 1-2 punch in UK history. A slashing, driving player who had a knack for coming through in the most crucial situations. Rupp said it best: "If we win by 30, Frank gets three points. If we win by three, he gets 30." Scored 1,344 points during his UK career, and despite playing a backcourt position he snared 1,038 rebounds, second only to Issel on the all-time list. Averaged 10.1 as a sophomore on the 1951 NCAA championship team. Had 20 twice that year, against Ole Miss and Loyola. Scored 19 in UK's easy 68-39 win over Kansas. Pulled down 434 rebounds that season, the most-ever by a UK sophomore. As a junior in 1951-52, his scoring, along with that of Hagan and Bobby Watson, helped the Cats go 29-3 despite the absence of Bill Spivey. Averaged 15.9 points and 12 rebounds that season. Smoked Xavier for 31 and Mississippi State for 29. Led the Cats with 24 in a 71-66 victory over Notre Dame. Came back after UK's one-year exile to average 19.6 points and nine rebounds for the unbeaten 1953-54 team. Had 37 against Tennessee, 29 against Georgia, 28 against Auburn and 27 against Xavier. But his finest performance came in the Cats' 63-56 league-clinching win over LSU. In that big win, he scored 30 points, including 10 in the final quarter, to pull the Cats through. A two-time All-American and a three-time All-SEC selection. Went on to become a standout player on those great Boston Celtics teams of the '50s and '60s. Helped the Celtics win seven NBA championships. Virtually invented the role of sixth man. Did some coaching after his retirement, then went into business in his hometown of Madisonville. Elected to the Basketball Hall of Fame in 1981.

RODRICK RHODES
(1993-95, 1993-95, 6'6", forward, Jersey City, N.J.)

Scored 1,209 points and averaged 12.2 points per game during a three-year career that was often troubled and turbulent. Came to UK after a glorious prep career, and was considered the jewel of a recruiting class that included Delk, McCarty and Prickett. Had all the tools to be a great one, yet never managed to fit comfortably into Pitino's system. Began his career in All-American fashion, scoring 27 points in his second game, a 96-87 win over 13th-ranked

Georgia Tech. Had 20 in an 88-68 win over Louisville, then earned MVP honors in the ECAC Holiday Festival after scoring 38 points in UK's two wins. His bucket with three seconds left was the difference in the Cats' 80-78 win over Auburn. Finished his freshman season with a 9.1 scoring average. Came back to average 14.6 points and 2.3 steals during the 1993-94 campaign. Shot 77.7 percent from the free throw line that year. Had 22 points and 10 rebounds against Florida. Also had 22 in a loss to Arkansas and 23 in an 82-67 win over Alabama. Hit for a season-best 24 against South Carolina. Tied for game-high honors with 22 in the Cats' 83-70 win over Tennessee State in the NCAA tourney opener. Averaged 12.9 points during the 1994-95 season, his last at UK. Had some outstanding moments early in the campaign, but virtually disappeared once tournament time rolled around. Scored a career-high 29 to lead UK to a 69-50 win over Tennessee. Had 23 during regular-season games against Texas Tech, Auburn, Ole Miss and Florida. Scored 16 in the Cats' 97-73 NCAA tourney win over Arizona State. Shot 76 percent from the free throw line during his career. Currently coaching high school basketball in Kentucky.

PAT RILEY
(1965-67, 6'4", forward, Schenectady, N.Y.)

The leading scorer and rebounder for the "Rupp's Runts" team that finished second to Texas Western in the NCAA Tournament. A marvelous all-around athlete with exceptional speed, quickness, agility and leaping ability. Although only 6'4", he jumped center and rarely failed to control the tip. Scored 1,464 points and averaged 18.3 during his three seasons at UK. Shot 47 percent from the field and 71.4 percent from the charity stripe. Averaged 15 points as a sophomore with a single-game high of 25 against Alabama. Also had 23 against St. Louis. Was absolutely brilliant during his junior year, averaging 22 points and 8.9 rebounds for the "Runts." Scored 36 against Notre Dame in Freedom Hall. Hit for 29 points on four occasions, including back-to-back NCAA tourney wins over Dayton and Michigan. Had 19 in each of UK's Final Four games, the win over Duke and the loss to Texas Western. Earned All-America recognition that year. An off-season back injury hampered his play during his senior year, yet he managed to average 17.4 points. Had a season-best 33-point performance against Northwestern. Scored 24 points and pulled down 13 rebounds in a 102-

72 win over LSU. Chosen to the All-SEC team in 1965 and 1966. Played several years in the NBA, then became a broadcaster for the Lakers. Moved from the broadcasting booth to the bench, guiding the Lakers to four NBA championships in the 1980s. Was named NBA Coach of the Decade. After leaving the Lakers, he coached the New York Knicks for several seasons. Currently the president of the Miami Heat.

RICK ROBEY
(1975-78, 6'10", forward/center, New Orleans, La.)

The other half of UK's great "Twin Towers" tandem, a two-time All-America and All-SEC selection. Scored 1,395 points. Left as UK's third deadliest shooter with a career field goal percentage of 58.1. His 63.5 percent accuracy, which he hit during his senior year, remains the second best for a single season. Led the team in rebounding three times, and was the team's best free throw shooter with an 81 percent mark during the 1974-75 campaign. Scored 25 against Oklahoma State in one of his first starts. Later had 28 against Vandy and 24 against Ole Miss. Scored 10 in that 92-90 NCAA tourney win over Indiana. Ended the season with a 10.4 scoring average. Hit 54.4 percent of his shots, still the best-ever by a UK freshman. Only played 12 games as a sophomore before being sidelined with an injury. Was scoring at a 15.6 clip when he went down. Had 24 in the opener against Northwestern, then ripped Miami of Ohio for 30. Scored 21 points, including two late buckets, to help the Cats survive Kansas 54-48. Averaged 14.2 points and 9.1 rebounds as a junior. Turned in a 22-point, 16-rebound effort in a win over Mississippi State. Scored 17 points and had 12 rebounds against Alabama. Played well in the NCAA tourney, scoring 20 in a win over Princeton and 15 in a losing effort against North Carolina. Averaged 14.4 points and 8.2 rebounds for the championship Cats. Had highs of 28 against Alabama and 26 against UNLV. Came up big in the championship game win over Duke, scoring 20 points and snaring 11 rebounds. Named to the All-Final Four team. Drafted by Indiana in the 1978 NBA draft. Played for the Pacers, Celtics and Suns before retiring.

KENNY ROLLINS
(1943, 47-48, 6'0", guard, Wickliffe, Ky.)

Unselfish captain of the "Fabulous Five" team that won the 1948 NCAA title and a gold medal in the summer

Olympics in London. A superb defender and passer who was always content to let his teammates put up the bigger scoring numbers. Averaged 5.3 points as a sophomore on the 1942-43 team, then spent nearly three years in the service. Scored 10 points on three occasions during his sophomore year. Teamed with Beard to give UK a great backcourt duo on that powerful 1946-47 team that went 34-3. Although not primarily a scorer, he had several big games that season, including 14 in a win over St. John's in Madison Square Garden, 17 against Tennessee and 16 in a 55-38 win over Tulane in the SEC tourney championship game. Averaged 8.4 points while hitting 80.3 percent of his free tosses. In that magical 1947-48 season, he averaged 6.6 points per game and led that high-powered offensive team in scoring five times. His best scoring effort that season was 16 in a win over St. John's. But it was his defensive effort against Bob Cousy in the NCAA tourney semifinals that was the high-point of his career. The great Holy Cross guard managed just three points against Rollins (he scored three more when Rollins went out), and the Cats won 60-52. Rollins was rewarded for his outstanding play, making the All-SEC team in 1947 and 1948.

RAJON RONDO
(2004-06, 6'1", guard, Louisville, Ky.)

Jet-quick guard with huge hands and enormous physical ability. His lack of an outside shot and his poor free throw shooting negatively impacted his career output. Despite those shortcomings, he still managed to post impressive numbers. Came to UK as part of a recruiting class that included Joe Crawford and Randolph Morris. Scored 654 points during his two seasons at UK for a 9.6 average. Also handed out 285 assists. Scored at an 11.2 clip as a sophomore. Burned Louisville for 25, had 22 against Florida, 21 against Indiana and 20 against North Carolina. Pulled down 19 rebounds against Iowa, a UK record for guards. Had 12 assists against Ole Miss. Posted a double-double — 17 points, 12 rebounds — in the season opener against South Dakota Sate. Had 69 steals as a sophomore. Averaged 8.1 points during his rookie campaign. Came through with clutch buckets against Louisville, South Carolina and Central Florida. Scored a season-best 18 versus Vanderbilt. Named to the SEC All-Freshman team. Played three years of prep ball at Louisville Eastern, then transferred to Oak Hill Academy for his final season. Averaged 21 points and 12 assists as a senior. Averaged 27.9 points as a junior at Eastern, earning All-State and 7th Region Player of the Year

honors. A McDonald's All-America pick in 2004.

LAYTON "MICKEY" ROUSE
(1938-40, 6'1", guard, Ludlow, Ky.)

A three-year backcourt starter and the first Wildcat player to have his uniform jersey retired. Moved into a starting position early in his sophomore season and helped lead the 1937-38 club to a 13-5 record. Averaged 4.4 points that season, with a single-game best of 11 in a huge win over Tennessee. Improved his average to 5.4 points as a junior. Scored 23 points in two easy wins over Vanderbilt. Also led the club with 10 points in a 37-31 win over Marquette. Came back as a senior to lead the team in scoring with an 8.3 average. That team finished with a 15-6 record and won the SEC tourney. Hit for a career-high 14 points in wins over Ohio State and Mississippi State. Scored 13 in a loss to Notre Dame. Had 12 points in the Cats' 51-43 SEC tourney championship win over Georgia. Earned All-SEC honors for his play during the 1939-40 campaign. Also named to the SEC all-tourney squad.

AGGIE SALE
(1931-33, 6'5", forward/center, Lawrenceburg, Ky.)

Rupp always considered Sale to be among the finest players he ever coached. Scored the first two points for Rupp at UK, and was the team's leading scorer with 19 points in the first of Rupp's 876 career victories. A two-time All-American and the 1933 Helms Foundation National Player of the Year. A very quick and agile inside player. Averaged 5.6 points as a sophomore despite being hampered by an injury. Developed into an outstanding player in his final two seasons, teaming with Frenchy DeMoisey to give the Cats a potent inside scoring tandem. Averaged a team-high 13.6 points during his junior season. Scored 21 against Tulane and 20 against Washington & Lee. Shook off a swarm of defenders to score 20 points in the Cats' 43-42 loss to North Carolina. Improved his scoring average to 13.8 in his final season. Saved his best for last, scoring 73 points in four games to help the Cats win the inaugural SEC Tournament. Had back-to-back 20-point showings against Florida and LSU in that tourney. Was also a prep All-American at Kavanaugh High School.

JEFF SHEPPARD
(1994-96, 98, 6'3", guard, Peachtree City, Ga.)

High-flying, exciting backcourt player and one of the most-unselfish Wildcats of all-time. No UK player of

comparable talent and skill ever spent as much time on the bench as he did. Or complained less. Still managed to finish his career with 1,091 points. Played three seasons, redshirted his senior year, then came back as a fifth-year senior to lead the team in scoring and earn Final Four MVP honors after leading the Cats to another NCAA title. Saw action in 29 games as a freshman in 1993-94, averaging 3.7 points per outing. Hit for 13 against San Francisco and Georgia. Started 27 of 33 games as a sophomore, finishing with an 8.3 average. Knocked down five first-half treys and scored a season-best 21 points against Marshall. Also hit five treys in an easy win over South Carolina. Made only one start as a junior, primarily serving as a backup to Delk and Epps. Averaged just 5.5 points and 12.8 minutes that season. Cracked double digits seven times, hitting for a high of 13 against Iona. Had a dunk and three crucial free throws in the Cats' 81-74 NCAA tourney semifinal win over UMass. Followed Pitino's advice and redshirted in 1996-97. Had a solid final season, helping lead UK to its second NCAA championship in three years and its seventh overall. Led the club in scoring with a 13.7 average while making good on 71 treys, sixth-best at UK for a single season. Scored 25 and 24 in back-to-back SEC wins over Auburn and South Carolina. Continued his superb play in the SEC tourney, turning in consecutive 17-point efforts in wins over Alabama and Arkansas. Sprained his ankle early in the second half against Arkansas and sat out the championship game against South Carolina. Came back in the NCAA tourney to score 18 against St. Louis, 19 against UCLA and 18 in that thrilling 86-84 comeback win over third-ranked Duke. Scored a career-high 27 in UK's 86-85 semifinal win over Stanford, then followed that by scoring 17 in the 78-69 title-game win over Utah. His baseline jumper put the Cats on top for good at 65-64 with 4:54 remaining. A third-team All-SEC pick as a senior. Finished his UK career with 288 assists. Earned prep All-State honors at McIntosh High School in Peachtree City, Ga. Also captured the state high jump championship. Spent a season playing for the Atlanta Hawks in the NBA. Currently runs several successful basketball camps.

ADRIAN SMITH
(1957-58, 6'0", guard, Farmington, Ky.)

Key member of the "Fiddlin' Five" title winners, and a player who was only beginning to develop into an outstand-ing player when he left UK. Went on to win an Olympic gold medal on that powerful 1960 U.S. team, then later had a successful NBA career as Oscar Robertson's backcourt mate on the Cincinnati Royals. Voted the MVP of the 1966 NBA all-star game. Spent his first two years at Northeast Missouri Junior College after being rejected by Rupp for being too small and too frail to play at UK. Transferred to UK for the 1956-57 campaign, and after getting off to a slow start, he flashed his great promise during the last half of the season. Had 24 and 20 in back-to-back wins over Georgia Tech and Georgia. Steady and dependable during that championship 1957-58 season, averaging 12.4 points per game. Scored 17 in that memorable three-overtime win over Temple and a team-high 21 in a win over St. Louis. Played a pivotal role in the Cats' 61-60 victory against Temple in the NCAA tourney semifinal game, hitting four clutch free throws to help erase a 59-55 deficit. Finished with 12 points in that win. Remained in Cincinnati after retiring from the pro ranks and became a successful banker.

SAUL SMITH
(1998-01, 6'2", guard, Lexington, Ky.)

Clever, heady point guard who faced the daunting task of running the club while playing for his father in UK's high-profile atmosphere. Few Wildcats have elicited more fan reaction — positive and negative — during their playing days, and none handled it with more character, grace and poise. A tough competitor who always left everything he had out on the court. Played in 143 games during his career, finishing with 363 assists, ranking him ninth among UK's all-time leaders. Also came up with 152 career steals. The Cats carved out a 110-33 record during his four years, capturing one NCAA crown and three SEC regular-season titles. Ended his career with a superb effort in the NCAA tourney loss to Southern Cal, nailing five treys en route to a 17-point, four-assist performance. Averaged 6.8 points during his senior season. Scored a career-high 18 against Vanderbilt. Hit for 17 against Eastern Kentucky University. Handed out a season-best 10 assists in the Cats' tough 46-45 loss to Michigan State. Had six assists and five steals in UK's easy win over Jacksonville State. Averaged 6.6 points while handing out 115 assists during his junior campaign. Also made good on 75 percent of his free throws. Came through with a steal and crucial jumper to help the Cats clip Utah in the Preseason NIT. Scored 15 points, all in the second half, in a loss at LSU. Had five three-pointers, 15 points and six assists against Maryland. Dished out eight assists against St. Bonaventure. Named the team's

Mr. Hustle for his hard-nosed efforts that season. Played in 37 games as a sophomore, drawing three starts at the shooting guard position. Averaged five points that season while handing out 61 assists and connecting on 35.6 percent of his three-point attempts. Came off the bench to score a team-high 17 points in a win over Ole Miss. Connected on 41.2 percent of his three-point attempts during seven postseason games. Saw action in every game as a freshman in 1997-98, drawing one start against Florida. Averaged 2.5 points. Scored a season-best eight points against Villanova and South Carolina. During one four-game stretch, he hit 10 of 11 field goal attempts, including six in succession. Also made six of seven three-pointers during that run. Came to UK after a superb prep career at Clarke Central High School. Averaged 20.3 points, 6.7 rebounds and 5.2 assists as a senior, leading his club to a 24-5 record and a quarterfinal finish in the Georgia Class 4A state tourney. Named Northeast Georgia Player of the Year by the Athens Daily News.

PATRICK SPARKS
(2004-06, 6'0", guard, Central City, Ky.)

Heady, super-intelligent guard known for his fierce take-no-prisoners competitive attitude and his uncanny knack for making big-time shots during crucial situations. Accounted for two of the most memorable plays in UK history — hitting three free throws with less than a second remaining to beat Louisville in Freedom Hall and knocking down a rim-rattling three-pointer at the buzzer against Michigan State that sent the game into overtime. Transferred to UK after two superb seasons at Western Kentucky. Scored 1,497 points during his collegiate career. Started 116 consecutive games. Averaged 11 points as a junior, earning him second-team All-SEC honors. Had a season-high 26 in a win at Alabama, including 20 in the second half. Canned seven of 10 treys in that victory. Scored 25 in that memorable win over Louisville and 20 against Coppin State. Cracked double figures 21 times. Named SEC and National Player of the Week after the Louisville game. Came back to average 9.7 points in his final campaign. Burned South Carolina for 26 points on eight of 11 shooting. Had 25-point efforts against West Virginia and Mississippi State. Finished on a high note, scoring a career-best 28 points in an NCAA tourney loss to UConn. Made good on 10 of 16 field goal attempts in that game. Named MVP of the Sun Belt Conference tourney as a sophomore at WKU.

Also, named first-team All-Sun Belt. Earned a gold medal as a member of the U.S. team in the World University Games. Led Kentucky in scoring as senior at Muhlenberg North High School, averaging 31.4 points per game. Finished his prep career with 2,653 points. Twice named first-team All-State.

CAREY SPICER
(1929-31, 6'1", forward, Lexington, Ky.)

The first All-American under Rupp and one of the two players most responsible for helping UK make a successful transition from the slow-down style employed by John Mauer to the more up-tempo style implemented by Rupp. (Louis "Little" McGinnis also made a smooth from the old style to the new.) Spicer actually made All-American under both coaches — Mauer in 1929, Rupp in 1931. His great adaptability is best reflected in the numbers he posted under the two coaches He averaged 5.7 and 6.5 in his two seasons with Mauer, then scored 10.6 points per game in Rupp's more open, fast-breaking system. Had his best night when he scored 27 in a 42-37 win over Vanderbilt. Also had a then-record 22 against Florida in the Southern Conference Tournament and 20 in a 38-34 regular-season win over Georgia Tech. Was named to the all-tournament team. An outstanding all-around athlete, he was also a superb halfback/quarterback who scored 75 points for UK during the 1930 football season. One sportswriter wrote that Spicer was "one of those quiet fellows back in the haze who can do things when things must be done."

BILL SPIVEY
(1950-51, 7'0", center, Warner Robins, Ga.)

Without question, the most tragic figure in UK history and one of the most unjustly treated athletes in all of sports. Ruled ineligible at UK as a senior, then later banned for life from the NBA even though he was never found guilty of being involved in the point-shaving scandal that rocked the college basketball world. He later sued the NBA and won a big judgment, but by then it was too late. The damage had already been done. Instead of proceeding on for what would surely have been a Hall of Fame career (and possibly the status as one of the premier pivotmen in basketball history), he was relegated to playing in second-class leagues and in exhibition games against the Globetrotters. In his two years at UK, he scored 1,213 points while leading the Cats to the 1951

NCAA championship and a 57-7 record overall. He pulled down 17.2 rebounds per game as a junior and hit a team-leading 72.7 percent of his free throws during his sophomore season. Started off with a bang, hitting for 16 points in his Wildcat debut. Outscored Bradley All-American Gene Melchiorre 22-20 in the Cats' 71-66 win. Scored 37 against Tennessee in the SEC tourney final. Finished his sophomore campaign with a 19.3 scoring average. Proved his superiority as a junior by completely outclassing Kansas center Clyde Lovellette in their head-to-head showdown, winning their scoring duel 22-10. Scored a career-high 40 points against Xavier. Was outstanding in the NCAA Final Four, scoring 28 in the semifinal win over Illinois and 22 in the 68-58 championship game victory over Kansas State. Averaged 19.2 points per game as a junior. A consensus All-America pick in 1951, and a two-time All-SEC selection. Volunteered to sit out his senior season until the matter concerning his involvement in the scandal was cleared up. Even as late as the SEC Tournament, he still had hopes of rejoining the team. That dream ended on the eve of UK's participation in the NCAA Tournament when the UK Athletics Board ruled him permanently ineligible. That UK team, led by Hagan, Ramsey and Watson, likely would have won another NCAA title had Spivey been allowed to play.

LARRY STEELE
(1969-71, 6'5", forward, Bainbridge, Ind.)

One of those players who used courage, effort, determination and spirit to overcome a lack of great natural ability. A non-stop baseline-to-baseline hustler. Also an excellent rebounder and defender. His tenacity and tremendous work ethic later paid huge dividends for him in the NBA, where he excelled for more than a decade with the Trail Blazers, first as a player, then later as their coach. Started as a sophomore at UK in 1968-69 and averaged 8.6 points. Scored 16 in his debut against Xavier. Hit for 18 in back-to-back wins over Florida and Tennessee. Averaged 8.8 points as a junior despite suffering an ankle injury that severely hampered his play during the last half of the season. Scored 21 in the opener against West Virginia. Later had 19 in a win over Ole Miss and 17 against LSU. Averaged 13.1 points as a senior while also handing out a team-high 3.9 assists per game. Tossed in 44 points as the Cats kicked off the 1970-71 campaign with wins over Northwestern and Michigan. After getting off to a

fast start, an injury (fractured hand) once again hampered his play. Finished his career in a big way, scoring 22 against Auburn, 24 against Tennessee and 20 against Marquette in the NCAA Tournament. His performance as a senior was good enough to earn him a spot on the All-SEC team.

JACK TINGLE
(1944-47, 6'3", forward, Bedford, Ky.)

Seldom gets much recognition but he had an outstanding career, starting all four years for Wildcat teams that had an overall record of 103-11. An All-American in 1947, and one of only three Wildcats to make All-SEC four times. (Beard and Jones are the other two.) Started as a freshman and averaged 8.4 points for the 1943-44 "Wildkittens" team that went 19-2. Scored 22 against Fort Knox and 18 against Oklahoma A&M in the NCAA tourney. Averaged 11.5 during his sophomore season. Accounted for 15 in a big win over Ohio State, then came back later in the campaign with back-to-back 21-point performances against Georgia Tech and Notre Dame. Had a 9.2 average for the 1945-46 NIT championship club. Led the team in scoring eight times. Hit for 19 against Georgia Tech, 17 against Fort Knox and 16 against Vanderbilt. Tagged Arizona for 13 and West Virginia for 16 in the first two NIT games. Scored five in UK's 46-45 title game win over Rhode Island. Continued his solid play as a senior although his scoring output dropped from previous years. His high-point total that year was 13, which he had in wins over Cincinnati and Tennessee. Also hit for 12 points on three occasions.

LOU TSIOROPOULOS
(1951-52, 54, 6'5", forward, Lynn, Mass.)

The super strong "Golden Greek" was a powerfully built inside player and, along with Hagan and Ramsey, one of "The Big Three" that carried the 1953-54 UK team to a perfect 25-0 record. Although known as a great rebounder and defender, he was also a surprisingly capable offensive player. Originally came to UK on a football scholarship, but once he got a taste of basketball he said farewell to the gridiron. Played very little as a sophomore on the 1951 NCAA championship team. His best outing that season was 14 points against Georgia Tech. Opened the 1951-52 season with a 22-point performance against Washington & Lee. Finished the year with a 7.9 scoring average. Chalked

up several big scoring nights during that unbeaten 1953-54 season, including a career-best 30 in a 105-53 win over Georgia Tech. In that game, he scored all of his points on field goals. Also scored 22 against Tulane. Had 20-point outings four times, including twice against Tennessee and once each against Florida and Vanderbilt. Scored 18 points in UK's 73-60 win over eventual NCAA champ La Salle. His superb defense held Bob Pettit to 17 points, 13 below his average, in the Cats' 63-56 win over LSU. Finished his final season with a scoring average of 14.5. Went on to become a successful high school and college coach.

WAYNE TURNER
(1996-1999, 6'2", guard, Boston, Mass.)

One of the most mentally tough Wildcats of all-time and the winningest UK guard since Ralph Beard. Played in a then-UK record 151 games, missing only one game in four years. The Wildcats were 132-20 during his career, winning two NCAA titles and finishing as runner-up once. The Cats also captured the SEC Tournament championship three times under his point-guard leadership. The school's all-time leading thief with 238 steals. Also had 1,170 points, 494 assists and 381 rebounds. Led the team in steals three times and assists twice. His almost-uncanny knack for scoring on drives to the bucket more than made up for a strange-looking outside jumper. Started eight games for the 1995-96 NCAA championship club. Averaged 4.5 points. Scored a season-high 13 in a 124-80 win over TCU. Averaged 6.6 points and had 79 steals as a sophomore. Moved into the starting lineup in postseason play and led UK to another SEC tourney title and the NCAA championship game. Had 19 points and five assists in a 92-50 win over Auburn in the SEC Tournament. Scored 61 points in UK's first four NCAA tourney games, including 19 against Montana in the opener. Upped his scoring average to 9.3 points as a junior. Had 16 points and eight steals in a win over George Washington University. Turned in a 17-point, 11-assist effort against Tennessee. Scored 20 to lead the Cats past Georgia 90-79. Was voted MVP of the SEC tourney after scoring 33 points and handing out 19 assists in UK's three wins. Had 11 points and nine assists against St. Louis in the NCAA Tournament. Scored 16 points, including nine inside the final 8:14, and handed out eight assists to help the Cats ease past Duke 86-84 and earn a trip to the Final Four. Voted the South Region

MVP. Averaged 10.5 points in his final campaign. Scored 17 as the Cats bumped off second-ranked Maryland 103-91 in an early season showdown. Came through with 21 of his game-high 24 points in the second half in a hard-earned 83-73 SEC tourney win over Ole Miss. Had 48 points in UK's three tourney victories. Scored 14 in the NCAA tourney opener, an 82-60 win over New Mexico State. Followed that with an outstanding 19-point performance in the Cats' 92-88 overtime win over Kansas. Reunited briefly with Pitino in Boston, but was later let go by the Celtics. Played one year with the Harlem Globetrotters.

MELVIN TURPIN
(1981-84, 6'11", center, Lexington, Ky.)

An All-American in 1984 and the second deadliest UK shooter of all-time with a career field goal percentage of 59.1. His 1,509 career points rank him No. 13 on UK's all-time scoring list. Twice led the team in rebounding and blocked shots. His 226 blocked shots is second best by a Wildcat. Averaged just 4.7 points as a freshman with a high of 17 against Florida. Stepped up as a sophomore by averaging 13.1 points and 7.1 rebounds while hitting 58.2 percent from the field. Had 28 against Tennessee and 24 against Ole Miss in the SEC tourney. Improved his numbers to 15.1 points and a scorching 61.7 percent shooting from the field as a junior. Hit for a career-high 42 points in a loss to Tennessee. Scored 25 against Auburn and 24 against Alabama. Played well in the NCAA tourney, scoring 16 in a win over Indiana and 18 in the "Dream Game" loss to Louisville. Teamed with Bowie to give the 1983-84 Final Four club an imposing frontline. Averaged a team-best 15.2 points that season while hitting on 59.3 percent of his shots. Had 35 points and 13 rebounds in a win over LSU. Hit clutch buckets to help the Cats escape with wins over Vandy and Georgia. Equaled his career high when he scored 42 points against Georgia in the SEC Tournament. Scored 67 points in three SEC tourney games and was named to the all-tournament team. Taken by Washington in the first round of the 1984 NBA draft, then traded to Cleveland. Also played for Utah and Washington before retiring after the 1990 season.

ANTOINE WALKER
(1995-96, 6'8", forward, Chicago, Ill.)

Another one of those athletic, multi-dimensional athletes that Pitino loved so much. Big, strong and quick.

Excellent at driving to the bucket or shooting from the outside. Also a sharp passer. Played the game with great confidence, swagger and showmanship. Scored 15 points in his UK debut, a 120-50 win over UT-Martin. Was named the 1995 SEC tourney MVP after coming through with 21 points against Florida and 23 in a 95-93 overtime win against Arkansas in the championship game. Had five points in the OT to help UK erase a nine-point deficit in that win over the Hogs. Pulled down 10 rebounds in the Cats' 97-73 NCAA tourney win over Arizona State. Moved into the starting lineup as a sophomore and averaged 15.2 points and 8.4 rebounds for the 1995-96 NCAA championship team. Scored 24 in an early season 89-82 victory over Indiana. Had 27 against Rider and 20 against Louisville. Canned 14 of 16 first-half shots and finished with a career-high 32 points in the Cats' 129-97 win over LSU. Scored 20 points and snared 11 rebounds in a win over Florida. Had 21 points in UK's 101-63 win over Vandy in the SEC Tournament opener, then came back the next night to give a spectacular 21-point, 14- rebound performance in a 95-75 win over Arkansas. Was again named to the SEC all-tourney team. Registered another double-double — 21 points, 11 rebounds — to lead the Cats past Virginia Tech 84-60 in the NCAA tourney. Followed that with a 19-point performance in a 101-70 smashing of Utah. Scored 14 in the team's 81-74 semifinal win over UMass, then had 11 in the 76-67 championship-game win over Syracuse. Undoubtedly would have ranked among UK's all-time top scorers had he not elected to leave UK and enter the NBA draft after his sophomore season. Picked sixth in the 1996 draft by the Boston Celtics. An NBA All-Star in 1998.

KENNY WALKER
(1983-86, 6'8", forward/center, Roberta, Ga.)

A two-time All-American and UK's second all-time leading scorer with 2,080 career points. One of UK's toughest, most-dependable and exciting players. Nicknamed "Sky" for his great leaping ability, he yanked down 942 rebounds and blocked 122 shots. Literally carried the 1984-85 team on his back, averaging 22.9 points and 10.2 rebounds per game. Turned it on late in his freshman year after getting off to a slow start. Scored 23 against Mississippi State, then had a 16-point, 18-rebound performance against Vanderbilt. Scored 19 points and speared 10 rebounds in UK's SEC-clinching 69-61 win over Tennessee. Had 17 points

in his first start, a 61-58 win over Ole Miss. Averaged 12.4 as a sophomore, with a high game of 21 against Tennessee. Teamed with Bowie and Turpin to give UK an NBA-caliber frontline. Topped the Cats with 20 points in their 74-67 win over Hakeem Olajuwon-led Houston. Exploded as a scorer during his sensational junior season, cracking the 30-point mark five times. Had 32 points and 15 rebounds against Louisville, and 36 points and 19 rebounds against Kansas. Shot 55.9 percent from the field and 76.8 percent from the free throw line. Racked up 75 points in UK's three NCAA tourney games. Averaged 20 points for Eddie Sutton's first UK team, which went 32-4 overall and 17-1 in SEC play. Had 33 against Hawaii, 31 against Ole Miss and 32 against Tennessee. Shot 55.3 percent from the field and 76.4 percent from the charity stripe. Made good on all 11 of his shots in a 32-point performance against Western Kentucky in the NCAA tourney. Twice named the SEC Player of the Year. Chosen by the Knicks in the first round of the 1986 NBA draft. Also played for Washington. Won the NBA Slam Dunk competition in 1989.

JOHN WALL
(2009-10, 6'4", guard, Raleigh, N.C.)

Quite possibly, the most naturally gifted Wildcat of all-time. Blessed with off-the-chart abilities and skills. From baseline to baseline, with ball in hand, no UK player has ever been faster. There simply seemed to be nothing he couldn't do on a basketball court. Came up with the "John Wall Dance," which became something of a sensation. Scored 616 points, the second most ever by a UK freshman, for a 16.6 average during his one season as a Wildcat. Also handed out 241 assists. Scored 19 points and hit the game-winning bucket in his debut performance against Miami (Ohio). Had a season-best 25 points against UConn. Scored 24 against Georgia, 23 against Stanford and Alabama. Dished out 16 assists against Hartford to break Travis Ford's record of 15. Cracked double figures in 34 of the 36 games he played in. Earned enough post-season honors to fill up a museum, including First-Team All-American, Yahoo Sports Player of the Year, MVP of the SEC tourney and SEC Player of the Year. Scored 22.1 points per game as a prep senior, leading Word of God High to a runner-up finished in the North Carolina Class 1A state tourney. Was named MVP of the Tournament of Champions at Missouri State University. Scored at an 18-point clip as a

title game win over Kansas State. Teamed with Hagan and Ramsey to make the 1951-52 season a huge success despite the absence of Spivey. Hit for a career-high 26 points in a win over Alabama. Ended his career with 1,001 points and a 10.4 average. A two-time All-SEC selection. Went on to become one of the most-successful high school coaches in Kentucky history, leading Owensboro High to state titles in 1972 and 1980.

SEAN WOODS
(1990-92, 6'2", guard, Indianapolis, Ind.)

A fierce competitor best remembered for making that daring, in-your-face layup over Christian Laettner to put UK ahead of Duke in that epic NCAA struggle. An outstanding assist man, and a defender Pitino loved for his ability to "lock up" opposing guards. Sat out his frosh season because of Prop 48, then stepped in as a sophomore to average 9.1 points and an SEC-best 5.9 assists per game. In just his third varsity game, he hit all seven field goal attempts en route to an 18-point performance against Mississippi State. Followed that effort by handing out 12 assists against Tennessee Tech. Had 32 points and 17 assists in two UKIT games. Scored 20 points against Florida and Georgia. His 164 assists are the most-ever by a first-year Wildcat. Averaged 9.7 points and 5.6 assists as a junior in 1990-91. Also had a team-high 50 steals. Hit for a career-best 25 points and handed out eight assists against Kansas. Burned Louisville for 20 points, hitting seven of 13 field goal attempts. Had 17 points and 11 assists against Ole Miss, and 12 points and 10 assists against Mississippi State. Destroyed Florida with 18 points, three rebounds, six assists and four steals. As a senior in 1991-92, he averaged 7.7 points and 4.6 assists. Also had 46 steals. Scored 16 in a 107-83 romp past Alabama. Was sensational in the NCAA tourney, scoring 16 against Old Dominion, 18 against Iowa State and 12 against UMass. Gave a 21-point, nine-assist performance in that Duke classic. Named to the NCAA All-Regional team and the SEC all-tournament team. Finished with 482 assists, placing him fifth on UK's all-time list. Came to UK after a brilliant prep career at Cathedral High School in Indianapolis, where he earned All-America and All-State recognition.

John Wall was the first player chosen in the 2010 NBA draft.

junior. Was a prep All-American. The first UK player to be drafted first overall in the NBA draft.

BOBBY WATSON
(1950-52, 5'10", guard, Owensboro, Ky.)

Superb team leader, sharp ball-handler and excellent outside scoring threat on some of UK's greatest teams. Averaged 10.4 points on the 1950-51 NCAA championship team and 13.1 on the 1951-52 team that went 29-3. UK was 86-10 during his three seasons. Although considered too small to be a success at UK, he quickly silenced the skeptics (including Rupp) with his outstanding performances. Scored 12 points in only his third game as a Wildcat. Twice hit for 15 points during his sophomore season. Finished with a 7.5 scoring average. As a junior, he scored a season-best 20 against Alabama and Ole Miss. Had 12 against St. John's in the NCAA tourney quarterfinal round and eight in the

Wildcat Profiles
2012-2016

DEVIN BOOKER
(2014-15, 6'6", forward, Grand Rapids, Mich.)

A deadly outside shooter who averaged 10 points per game despite limited playing time due to UK's platoon system. Scored a career-best 19 points against UCLA and UT-Arlington. Hit for 18 points on four occasions. Reached double figures in 20 games. Made good on 41 percent of his three-point attempts while connecting on 82 percent of his free throws. Earned SEC Sixth Man of the Year honors and was named to the All-SEC second team and the All-SEC Freshman Team. Also made the SEC Academic Honor Roll. Was named SEC Freshman of the Week four times. Scored 2,518 points during his prep career at Moss Point High School. Was named Mississippi Gatorade Player of the Year as a junior after averaging 29.7 points per game. Led Moss Point to the Region 8-4A championship. Averaged 30.9 points per game as a senior. Had a 54-point performance as a sophomore. Scored 31 points in the Alabama-Mississippi All-Star Classic. Selected as a McDonald's All-American.

Devin Booker guns from long range.

ISAIAH BRISCOE
(2015-16, 6'3", guard, Newark, N.J.)

A tough on-ball defender and a backcourt player with an exceptional knack for taking the ball to the bucket. Averaged 9.6 points and 5.3 rebounds per contest. Scored a career-best 20 points against UCLA. Hit for 18 points in a win over Illinois State, and had 15 points in wins over Wright State and Missouri. Notched a double-double against New Jersey Tech, finishing with 11 points and 12 rebounds. Pulled down 11 rebounds against Stony Brook and 10 against Tennessee. Twice handed out seven assists, once against Ohio State and again against South Florida. Played prep ball for Roselle Catholic, where he helped lead that school to consecutive Non-Public B championships. Averaged 22.1 points as a junior and 20.8 as a senior. Selected to play on the 2015 USA Basketball Under-19 team. Honored as an All-American by McDonald's, USA Today and Parade Magazine.

WILLIE CAULEY-STEIN
(2013-2015, 7'0", center, Olathe, Kan.)

An eclectic and sometimes flamboyant individual who always played the game with tremendous passion. A consensus first-team All-American in 2015. Also named National Defensive Player of the Year. Voted the SEC tourney MVP. Known for his hustle, rebounding and defense. Played three seasons and recorded 233 blocked shots, second best all-time in UK history. Also had 11 double-doubles. The first UK player to register more than 200 blocked shots and more than 100 steals. Averaged 8.9 points and 6.4 rebounds in his final season. Had 21 points and 12 rebounds in a win over Texas. Scored 18 against Auburn. Averaged 6.8 points and 6.1 rebounds as a sophomore. Hit for a season-best 18 points against Ole Miss. Had nine blocked shots against Providence and Boise State. Named to the SEC All-Defensive squad. Scored at an 8.3 clip as a freshman while averaging 6.2 rebounds per game. Burned Vanderbilt for 20 points. Had 60 blocked shots during his rookie campaign. Was named to the All-SEC Freshman team. A two-sport standout at Northwest High School. Averaged 15.8 points as a junior. Played wide receiver on

the football team, catching 57 passes for 1,140 yards and 14 touchdowns in nine games during the 2011 season.

ANTHONY DAVIS
(2011-12, 6'10", center, Chicago, Ill.)

By any standard of measurement, he ranks among the greatest Wildcats of all-time. Also, one of the most charismatic, personable and selfless. It is simply scary to think what he would have accomplished had he played three or four seasons. With his famous unibrow and a 1,000-watt smile, he may have looked like an angel but he played like a demon. Led the Cats to their eighth national title and, in so doing, captured virtually all post-season honors, including Final Four Most Outstanding Player, national Player of the Year, Defensive Player of the Year, USBWA National Freshman of the Year and SEC Player of the Year. All that despite putting up just the fourth most shots on the team. Averaged 14.2 points and 10.4 rebounds. Shot 62 percent from the field. Recorded 20 double-doubles. Scored 28 points against Vanderbilt and 27 against Arkansas. Yanked down 18 rebounds in a win over Chattanooga. Blocked 186 shots, with a season-best eight against both South Carolina and St. John's. Had seven blocked shots on six occasions. Only scored six points in the championship game win over Kansas, but he pulled down 16 rebounds and blocked six

Anthony Davis ranks as one of the greatest Wildcats of all-time.

shots. Played prep ball at Perspectives Charter School. Was 6'0" as a freshman, 6'10" as a senior. Handled the guard position until the growth spurt hit. Averaged 32 points, 22 rebounds and seven blocked shots as a senior. Named a McDonald's All-American.

MICHAEL KIDD-GILCHRIST
(2011-12, 6'7", forward, Elizabeth, N.J.)

Only wore the UK uniform for one season but established himself as one of those gritty players who wasn't shy about doing whatever it took to get a victory. Helped guide that 2012 club to the NCAA title. A tough defender and rebounder as well as a capable scorer. Always seemed to play his best against tougher competition. Had a monster performance against Louisville, scoring 24 points and grabbing 19 rebounds. Averaged 11.9 points and 7.4 rebounds while shooting 49 percent from the field. A second-team All-America selection and a first-team All-SEC pick. Came up big in the NCAA tourney East Regional, scoring 24 against Indiana and 19 against Baylor. Had 11 points and six rebounds in the title game win over Kansas. Scored 19 against LSU and 18 against Mississippi State and Lamar. Finished the season with 476 points and 297 rebounds. Had a standout prep career at St. Patrick High School in Elizabeth, N.J., earning All-America honors. Named USA Mr. Basketball in 2011. Was co-MVP of the McDonald's All-American game. Help lead the USA to a gold medal in the FIBA Under-17 World Championships in Hamburg, Germany.

ARCHIE GOODWIN
(2012-13, 6'4", guard, Little Rock, Ark.)

Another one of those gifted players who could score from outside or on the drive to the bucket. Scored 466 points and averaged 14.1 points per game in his one year as a Wildcat. His best scoring effort came against Morehead, when hit accounted for 28 points on 8 of 13 shooting from the field and 12 of 17 from the free throw stripe. Barely missed becoming only the second Wildcat to post a triple-double by finishing with 22 points, nine rebounds and nine assists against LIU-Brooklyn. He also had 22 points against Louisville and 20 against Georgia. Came to UK following a brilliant prep career at Sylvan Hills High School in Sherwood, Ark. Led his team to back-to-back state finals and the 2012 Class 5A championship. Named tourney MVP after scoring 27 points in the title game. Twice named

Gatorade Player of the Year in Arkansas, Also named to McDonald's and Parade All-American teams. The youngest American college player taken in the 2013 NBA draft.

AARON HARRISON
(2013-2015, 6'6", guard, Richmond, Texas)

Yet another Wildcat who earned a spot on the all-time Mr. Clutch list by knocking down last-second game-winning buckets against Michigan and Wisconsin in the 2014 NCAA Tournament. Averaged 13.7 points in his rookie season, while earning all-tourney recognition in the NCAA Mideast Regional and the SEC Tournament. Also named to the All-SEC squad. Torched Robert Morris for 28 points. Had 23 points against Belmont and 22 against both Eastern Michigan and Georgia. Scored at an 11.0 clip as a sophomore, again earning All-SEC tourney honors. Hit for double figures a team-best 24 times. Racked up 23 points in a come-from-behind win at Florida. Had a season-best 26-point performance against Ole Miss in the SEC opener. Averaged 23.1 points in helping Travis High School capture the Texas state championship during his senior season. Also led Travis to the 5A state title game as a junior, scoring 18.1 points per game. Named a McDonald's All-American.

ANDREW HARRISON
(2013-2015, 6'6", guard, Richmond, Texas)

The younger of the Harrison twins (by a minute), he had a solid two-year career as the Cats' point guard. Averaged 9.3 points, 3.6 assists and 2.2 rebounds as a sophomore, numbers good enough to earn him a spot on the 2015 Mideast Regional tourney and the All-SEC tourney teams. Scored 23 points and handed out seven assists in a win over Georgia. Had 18 points to help the Cats top 18th-ranked Arkansas. Opened the campaign by scoring 16 points against Grand Canyon. As a frosh, he averaged 10.9 points and four assists per outing. Handed out 159 assists as a freshman. Scored a career-high 26 points in a win over Tennessee. Posted a pair of 20-point performances in wins over Wichita State and Florida. Accounted for 18 points to lead the Cats past Louisville. Had 17 points and seven assists at North Carolina. Scored 15.8 points per game as a senior, leading Travis High School to the Texas championship in 2013. As a junior, he averaged 12.5 points to help Travis post a 36-4 record. A McDonald's All-American pick.

TERRENCE JONES
(2010-2012), 6'9", forward, Portland, Ore.)

A big-time point producer who posted some huge games during his two years as a Wildcat, including a 35-point outburst against Auburn as a freshman. Tallied 1,064 points, snared 608 rebounds and posted 17 double-doubles for the Cats. Averaged 12.3 points and 7.2 rebounds as a sophomore in 2011-12. Scored 27 points against LSU and 26 against St. John's. Had 22 points in a win over Western Kentucky and 20 against South Carolina. During his rookie season, along with his 35-point performance, he also posted big numbers against Oklahoma (29 points) and Notre Dame (27). Posted 25-point efforts against Vanderbilt and ETSU, and had 24 against both Georgia and UConn. Had 16 points, 17 rebounds and four blocked shots against Washington. Earned all-tourney recognition in the Maui Invitational after averaging 23 points and 11.3 rebounds. Averaged 30 points and 14 rebounds as a senior at Jefferson High School, leading that school to its third consecutive state championship. Played in the McDonald's All-American and Jordan Brand Classic All-Star games. Was a member of the 2010 USA Junior National Select team.

SKAL LABISSIERE
(2015-2016), 6'11", center, Port-au-Prince, Haiti)

A player talented enough to be ranked as one of the top incoming freshmen despite having virtually no high school experience. Got off to a good start as a Wildcat, struggled during the middle part of the season, then came on strong during the final three weeks. Averaged 6.6 points while shooting 51.6 percent from the field. Led the team in blocked shots on 12 occasions. A two-time SEC Freshman of the Week selection. Had a 26-point performance against NJIT in only his second outing as a Wildcat. Scored 17 points against South Florida and 16 against Boston University. Broke out of his slump by giving a strong effort against Florida—11 points, eight rebounds. Followed that by turning in his finest performance as a Wildcat, scoring 18 points on 8 of 10 shooting while yanking down nine rebounds against LSU. Participated in the Nike Hoop Summit and Jordan Brand Classic All-Star games. Registered 11 points, 12 rebounds and two blocked shots in Jordan Brand Classic game. Survived the 2010 earthquake in Haiti before moving to the United States.

DORON LAMB
(2010-2012, 6'4", guard, Queens, N.Y.)

A quiet assassin who was deadly from long range and from the charity stripe, this talented backcourt player tallied 1,018 points during his two years as a Wildcat. He connected on 47.5 percent of his three-point attempts and 81 percent of his free throws. Averaged 13.7 points as a sophomore in 2011-12. Was named to the Final Four All-Tournament team. Also named to the East Regional all-tourney squad. Scored season-high efforts of 26 points in wins over Samford and Penn State. Finished with 24 points and six rebounds against Chattanooga. Had 22 points against Kansas and 21 in a win over Indiana. Averaged 12.3 points per game as a freshman in 2010-11. Knocked down 11 of 12 field goal attempts, including seven of eight from three-point range, en route to a career-high 32 points against Winthrop. Scored 24 points on the road against North Carolina. Hit for 20 points three times, against Mississippi State, Ole Miss and ETSU in his college debut. Averaged 23 points as a senior at Oak Hill Academy, earning McDonald's and Jordan Brand Classic All-America honors.

Doron Lamb celebrates after knocking down a trey.

TREY LYLES
(2014-2015), 6'10", forward, Indianapolis, Ind.)

A supremely gifted player, one whose numbers would have been much more impressive had he not been part of a team so talent-rich it required a platoon system that considerably limited his playing time. Averaged 8.7 points and 5.2 rebounds. Scored in double figures 13 times, including eight of the season's final 14 games. Posted back-to-back 18-point efforts against Mississippi State and Arkansas. Put in 11 points and snared 11 rebounds in an NCAA tourney game against Cincinnati, and followed that up with 14 points and seven rebounds in an easy win over West Virginia in the next round. Had 10 points and 10 rebounds in a win over Eastern Kentucky. Opened his UK career by scoring 14 points against Grand Canyon. Named Indiana's Mr. Basketball and the state's Gatorade High School Player of the Year after averaging 23.7 points and 12.9 rebounds as a senior at Arsenal Tech. Led Tech to the 2014 state title. A McDonald's All-American. Scored 17 points in the Jordan Brand Classic game.

DARIUS MILLER
(2009-2012), 6'7", forward, Maysville, Ky.)

A true rarity on two fronts in today's world—a Kentucky kid who played four seasons at UK. Never a great player, but certainly a solid contributor who played in more games (152) than any previous Wildcat. Scored 1,248 points and was voted MVP of the SEC Tournament as a junior in 2010-11. Averaged 9.9 points and nailed 56 treys during his final season. Registered 19-point efforts on four occasions, against Indiana, Georgia, Iowa State and Portland. Also hit for 17 against Georgia on Senior Night. Represented the U.S. at the World University Games in China during the summer of 2011. Averaged 10.9 points as a junior, hitting for a career-best 24 points against Florida. Claimed the SEC Tournament MVP honor after averaging 13.3 points and 5.6 rebounds. Grabbed 11 rebounds in the season opener against ETSU. Averaged 6.5 points as a sophomore. Scored 20 points against Wake Forest and 18 against Arkansas. In the summer of 2009, he helped lead Team USA to a gold medal at the U-19 World Championship in New Zealand. Had several strong performances as a freshman, scoring 17 points against Tennessee and had 13 against Delaware State. Named Kentucky's Mr. Basketball after guiding Mason County High to the 2008 state title. Averaged 19.9 points, 7.9 rebounds and 3.6 assists as a senior.

Jamal Murray releases the Big Blue Arrow.

JAMAL MURRAY
(2015-2016), 6'4", guard, Kitchener, Ontario, Canada)

A tremendous long-range shooter who posted record-shattering numbers during his one season as a Wildcat. Set the high mark for most points scored (720) and scoring average (20.0) by a freshman. Became famous for launching an imaginary Big Blue Arrow after making a three-point bucket. Earned third-team All-America honors, along with first-team All-SEC and first-team All-SEC Tournament recognition. Also named to the SEC All-Freshman squad. Hit for 20-plus points 18 times, including one stretch of 12 straight. His 35-point effort against Florida tied Terrence Jones for most points scored by a rookie. Also scored 33 against both Ohio State and Vanderbilt. Other big scoring nights included 28 against Tennessee and 26 against South Carolina and Georgia. Made good on 113 treys while connecting on 41 percent of his three-point attempts. Had eight treys against Florida, seven against Ohio State and six against Georgia and Vanderbilt. Hit all 10 free throw attempts in a win over Wright State. Handed out eight

assists in the season-opening win over Albany. Was an experienced international player before landing at UK. He played for the Canadian team in the 2015 Pan American Games, averaging 16 points. He scored 30 points and was named MVP for his performance in the 2015 Nike Hoop Summit game, and was voted MVP of the 2015 BioSteel All-Canadian game.

NERLENS NOEL
(2012-2013, 6'11", center, Everett, Mass.)

Although he was limited in terms of offense, this slender inside player was an outstanding defender who possessed an uncanny knack for blocking shots. He swatted away 106 shots in his only season at UK, including a school-record 12 in a win at Ole Miss. Also pulled down 227 rebounds. He posted those numbers despite missing much of the season due to a serious knee injury. Named SEC Freshman of the Year and SEC Defensive Player of the Year. Earned first-team All-SEC recognition. Earned a spot on USBWA's Freshman All-America squad. Posted five double-doubles for the Wildcats. Scored a career-best 19 points to go along with 14 rebounds against Texas A&M. Had 16 rebounds and six steals against Baylor. Hit for 18 points, eight rebounds, five assists and five blocked shots in a win over LIU Brooklyn. Scored 16 points against Duke. Ripped down 13 rebounds and blocked eight shots against Alabama. Averaged 12.6 points and 7.2 rebounds as a senior at Tilton High School. Named USA Today National Player of the Year. Also earned Parade All-America honors. Played in the Jordan Brand Classic All-Star game. Was a member of the USA Junior National Select team for Nike Hoops Summit.

ALEX POYTHRESS
(2012-2016), 6'8", forward, Clarksville, Tenn.)

A shining example of a true student-athlete who excelled both on the basketball court and in the classroom. As a student, he graduated in three years and was on the SEC Academic Honor Roll for four straight years. He was named the 2016 Arthur Ashe Jr. Athlete of the Year. Had to battle through a devastating knee injury suffered during his junior season, which caused him to miss 29 games. Also missed five games as a senior. Averaged 11.2 points as a rookie, earning him a spot on the SEC All-Freshman squad. Became the first Wildcat to post four straight 20-point games since Jodie Meeks in 2008-09. Had a high of 22

points against both Lafayette and LIU-Brooklyn. Registered a double-double against LSU with 20 points and 12 rebounds. Also had a dozen rebounds against Florida. Averaged 5.9 points as a sophomore. Hit for 16 points against Texas A&M. Yanked down 12 rebounds against Michigan State. Had 10 points and 13 rebounds against UNC-Asheville. Came back as a senior to score at a 10.2 clip. Scored 25 points against Alabama and 21 against Eastern Kentucky. Recorded double-doubles against Wright State (10/10), Boston University (14/10), EKU (21/13) and Florida (12/10). Named Tennessee's Mr. Basketball and the state's Gatorade Player of the Year. Tabbed an All-American by McDonald's and Parade Magazine.

JULIUS RANDLE
(2013-2014), 6'9", forward, Dallas, Texas)

One of the most-impressive rookies to play at UK, this burly lefty led the team in scoring (15.0) and rebounding (10.4), earning him a host of awards, including first-team recognition on the All-SEC and the All-SEC Tournament squads. Named SEC Freshman of the Year. Set single-season freshman records for rebounds (417), double-doubles (24) and made free throws (204). Scored 29 points against Belmont and 27 against Michigan State. Poured in 25 points against Ole Miss. His bucket with 3.9 seconds remaining lifted the Cats past LSU 77-76 in overtime. Registered 23 points and 16 rebounds against UNC-Asheville. Had 22-point performances in wins over UT-Arlington and Northern Kentucky. Finished with 20 points and 14 rebounds in a loss at Arkansas. Scored 16 points to help the Cats get past Wisconsin in the Final Four. Had 10 points, six rebounds and four assists in the title game against UConn. Averaged 32.5 points and 22.5 rebounds as a senior for Prestonwood Christian Academy. Led that school to state championships during his freshman, junior and senior seasons. A McDonald's All-American. Voted co-MVP of the Jordan Brand Classic game after scoring 19 points and grabbing seven rebounds.

MARQUIS TEAGUE
(2011-2012), 6'2", guard, Indianapolis, Ind.)

Another in a long line of superb point guards coached by John Calipari, he started all 40 games in his one season as a Wildcat, averaging 10 points and 4.8 assists per outing. Scored a career-best 24 points to go along with seven assists in a win over Iowa State. Had 17 points against South Carolina. Twice hit for 16 points, once against Marist

and again against Vanderbilt. Recorded a double-double against Florida, scoring 12 points while dishing out 10 assists. Scored 15 points in a loss at Indiana, then matched that total in a win over Florida. Had seven rebounds and seven assists in a win at Georgia. Averaged 22.7 points, 5.9 assists and 4.2 rebounds as a senior at Pike High School. A McDonald's All-America selection. Scored 14 points and had seven assists in the Jordan Brand Classic game. Scored 18 points and had five assists in the Kentucky-Indiana All-Star game. Hit the game-winning bucket with 0.9 seconds remaining to give Indiana the victory.

KARL-ANTHONY TOWNS
(2014-2015), 6'11", center, Piscataway, N.J.)

A talented post player who earned All-America recognition in his only season as a Wildcat. Named Mideast Regional Most Valuable Player after leading the Wildcats to the Final Four. Voted SEC Freshman of the Year after averaging 10.3 points and 6.7 rebounds per game. Also blocked 88 enemy shots. Recorded eight double-doubles. Led the team in rebounding 18 times. Shot 81.3 percent from the

Karl-Anthony Towns powers his way to the bucket.

free throw line. Had his best scoring night against No. 8-ranked Notre Dame, finishing with 25 points on 10 of 13 shooting. Scored 21 points and yanked down 11 rebounds in an NCAA tourney win over Hampton. Hit for 19 points on four occasions, against Auburn, Florida, Georgia and Eastern Kentucky. Claimed the 2014 Gatorade National Player of the Year honor after leading St. Joseph to a 30-2 record and a title at the NJSIAA Tournament of Champions. Averaged 20.9 points, 13.4 rebounds and 6.2 blocked shots as a senior. Shot 66.1 percent from the field and 82.2 percent from the free throw line that season. A three-time first-team All-State selection. Performed as a member of the Dominican National Team.

TYLER ULIS
(2014-2016), 5'9", guard, Chicago, Ill.)

When the final history of UK hoops is written he will undoubtedly rank near the top as one of the Wildcats' all-time greatest guards. Earned first-team All-America honors, and was named SEC Player of the Year and SEC Defensive Player of the Year following his spectacular sophomore season. Captured the Bob Cousy Point Guard of the Year Award presented by the Naismith Memorial Basketball Hall of Fame. Scored 606 points, averaged 17.3 points and dished out 246 assists while playing 37 minutes per game. Those 246 assists broke John Wall's school record of 243. Accounted for 815 points and 381 assists during his UK career. As a sophomore, he went over the 20-point mark 15 times while recording eight double-doubles. Hit for 30 points against Texas A&M, 27 against South Carolina and Indiana, 26 against Kansas and 25 against Georgia. Handed out 14 assists against LSU and 12 against South Carolina. Despite seeing limited action on the 2014-15 team, he played well enough to land on the All-SEC Freshman team. Averaged 5.6 points per game. Scored 14 points against Arkansas and Louisville. Played prep ball for Marian Catholic, ending as the school's all-time leading scorer with 2,335 points. A two-time All-State selection and the Southtown Star Player of the Year. Was a McDonald's All-American. Also participated in the Jordan Brand Classic All-Star game.

Tyler Ulis directs traffic during a Wildcat victory.

KYLE WILTJER
(2011-2013, 6'10", forward, Portland, Ore.)

Only stayed at UK for two seasons, but proved himself to be a deadly outside gunner who could also score in close with a soft hook shot. Named SEC Sixth Man of the Year following his sophomore campaign. Averaged 10.2 points per game that season. Hit for 26 points against Ole Miss after coming off the bench. Scored 23 points and had 12 rebounds in a win over Lipscomb. Also had 23 points against Lafayette. Racked up 19 points against Maryland and 18 versus Tennessee. Tallied 17 points on three occasions, against Auburn, Tennessee and Eastern Michigan. Canned 35 three-pointers during his rookie season. Scored 26 points against Morehouse and 24 versus Loyola. Hit for 19 points against Penn State. Transferred to Gonzaga, where he earned All-America recognition. Averaged 19.6 points as a senior at Jesuit High School. Named a McDonald's All-American. Was voted Oregon's Class 6A Player of the Year, and was named 2011 Oregon Gatorade Player of the Year. A three-time Oregon Class 6A state champion.

JAMES YOUNG
(2013-2014), 6'6", forward, Flint, Mich.)

An underrated player and one who had a knack for putting the ball in the bucket on a regular basis. Averaged 14.3 points while knocking down 82 treys. Was a standout in the Final Four, scoring 17 points against Wisconsin, then following up with 20 against UConn. Was named to the Final Four All-Tournament team. Named second-team All-SEC. Hit for 26 points on two occasions, once against UT-Arlington and once against Mississippi State in the SEC opener. Was a thorn in LSU's side, finishing with 23 points and 21 points, respectively. Also had 23 points against Arkansas. Earned MVP honors of the UK-Louisville game after giving an 18-point, 10-rebound, four assists performance. Scored 21 points against Boise State and 20 against Missouri. Averaged 27.2 points and 16 rebounds as a senior at Rochester High School. As a junior at Troy High School, he scored at a 25.1 clip while pulling down 10.5 rebounds per game. Participated in the McDonald's All-America game and the Jordan Brand Classic game.

Kyle Wiltjer was SEC Sixth Man of the Year as a sophomore.

James Young was a standout during Final Four action.

A Big Blue trifecta. Rex Chapman, Jamal Mashburn and Kenny Walker — three of the most gifted and exciting Wildcats of all-time.

UK Teams of Tradition

The Wildkittens

This 1943-44 team featured such a youthful roster that Rupp said coaching them was like running a kindergarten. Rupp often referred to this gang of juveniles as "Beardless Wonders." Because so many veteran players had gone off to war, Rupp was left with 15 freshmen and two sophomores. Two of the freshmen, Don Whitehead and Walter Johnson, left the team after the 12th game to serve in the war effort. Despite the youth and inexperience, this team finished with a 19-2 record, won the SEC Tournament and came in third in the NIT. The key to the Wildkittens' success was the play of 17-year-old Bob Brannum, whose 12.1 scoring average was one of UK's best up to that point. Brannum was a rugged, fearless competitor who became the youngest player to earn All-America recognition. Sophomores Wilbur Schu and Tom Moseley, the club's two "old men," provided steady play, while a pair of freshmen, Jack Tingle and Jack Parkinson, consistently flashed the form that would later earn them All-America honors. Other Wildkit-

tens who made solid contributions were Truitt DeMoisey, Rudy Yessin and Buddy Parker.

The Wildkittens scored several big upsets during the season, including a 40-28 win over Ohio State and a 44-38 win over St. John's in front of 18,179 Madison Square Garden fans. They also gave Rupp a rare win over Notre Dame, beating the Irish 55-54 in Louisville.

Of the Wildkittens, only Tingle and Schu had four uninterrupted years at UK. Tingle went on to become one of only three Wildcat players to make All-SEC four times. Brannum and Parkinson eventually served time in the military, then returned to UK. Moseley later incurred Rupp's wrath and was dismissed from the team early in the 1944-45 season.

The Fabulous Five

One of the most frequently asked questions tossed at basketball historians and sports authorities is: "Who were the Fabulous Five at Kentucky?" Most Wildcat fans know the answer to that question long before they know the

Adolph Rupp with Fabulous Five greats Ralph Beard (12), Kenny Rollins (26), Wah Wah Jones (27), Alex Groza (15) and Cliff Barker (23) in their 1948 U.S. Olympic team uniforms. The five UK players helped the United States capture the gold medal. Rupp would later say that his proudest moment as a coach was watching these Wildcats receive their gold medals.

names of U.S. presidents. Alex Groza was the center, Ralph Beard and Kenny Rollins were the guards, and Wah Wah Jones and Cliff Barker were the forwards. What most fans don't know is that this unit didn't come together as starters until the 12th game of the season, a 67-53 win over Miami of Ohio on the night of Jan. 5, 1948. Prior to that game, Rupp had been juggling his starting lineup, looking for a winning combination. As Beard later said, "When he put that five together, he had found what he was looking for."

And a legend was born.

But not without a helping hand from Lady Fate and world events, namely World War II. Rollins, Barker and Groza were military veterans who migrated back to UK after leaving the service. By 1947, they were in their early to late 20s and hardened by the war they'd just experienced. Barker, in fact, spent 16 months in a German prisoner of war camp, where he mastered his ball-handling skills by playing around with a volleyball provided by the Red Cross. He'd also lost two front teeth to the butt of a German rifle. Rollins and Groza earned letters at UK before marching off to serve their country. Rollins was a starting guard on the 1942-43 team, Groza handled the pivot duties for the first 11 games during the 1944-45 season (UK was 11-0 at the time) before leaving for the Army. That trio was joined by the "kids" of the group, Kentucky schoolboy legends Jones and Beard, who were both barely out of their teens when the 1947-48 campaign rolled around.

This famous team, captained by Rollins, finished with a 36-3 record and won the school's first NCAA championship. The Fabulous Five then went on to participate as a unit in the 1948 Olympic Games in London, helping the USA team capture the gold medal.

Rollins graduated after the 1948 season, but the four returning starters led UK to a 32-2 record and a second consecutive NCAA title in 1949.

The Fiddlin' Five

Prior to the start of the 1957-58 season, Coach Adolph Rupp made this comment about his team: "They might be pretty good barnyard fiddlers, but we have a Carnegie Hall schedule, and it will take violinists to play that competition."

When the Wildcats became notorious for, as Rupp put it, "fiddlin' around and fiddlin' around, then finally pulling

it out at the end," the team was tagged with the nickname the Fiddlin' Five.

Perfect examples of this team's tenacity can be found in the two classic wins over Temple — 85-83 in three overtimes and 61-60 in the NCAA semifinal game. In each instance, the Cats appeared to be down for the count, only to rise up from the canvas and score last-second, heroic victories.

Who were the Fiddlin' Five? Johnny Cox and John Crigler were the forwards, Adrian Smith and Vernon Hatton were the guards, and Ed Beck was the center.

The Fiddlin' Five gave Rupp his fourth national championship when they defeated Elgin Baylor and Seattle 84-72 in the title game at Louisville's Freedom Hall. After the game, Rupp said, "Those boys are certainly not concert violinists, but they sure can fiddle."

Rupp's Runts

This 1965-66 UK team earned its moniker because the tallest starter was 6'5" guard Tommy Kron. Center Thad Jaracz, who worked his way into the starting lineup, was also 6'5", while forwards Larry Conley and Pat Riley were 6'4" and guard Louie Dampier was 6'0".

The team became one of Rupp's favorites during his long tenure at UK. Before the season started, Rupp said, "I honestly believe that man for man, we just might have

Adolph Rupp shares the NCAA hardware with Runts Larry Conley, Tommy Kron, Thad Jaracz, Pat Riley and Louie Dampier.

in the making a better team than we had in 1958 when we won the national championship."

However, not all UK fans shared Rupp's optimistic outlook.

Rick Pitino looks on as Unforgettables Sean Woods, John Pelphrey, Deron Feldhaus and Richie Farmer are honored following the 1992 season. This group of seniors was the heart and soul of UK's resurgence after the program had fallen on hard times in the late 1980s.

After all, the team was coming off a 15-10 record the season before, and with no starter taller than 6'5", Rupp's talk of another championship-caliber team seemed foolhardy.

But the Runts did indeed turn out to be one of the outstanding teams in UK's glorious history, compiling a sparkling 27-2 record. Their dead-eye shooting, superb passing, never-ending hustle and unselfish attitude also made them a favorite of Wildcat fans. Not even a disappointing 72-65 loss to Texas Western in the NCAA championship game could diminish the fans' love for the Runts, who remain to this day one of the most-cherished and beloved of all UK teams.

During the 1990-91 season, UK honored Rupp's Runts on the silver anniversary of their NCAA runner-up season.

The Unforgettables

During the Rick Pitino Era, several of his teams were christened with nicknames, among them "Pitino's Bombinos" and "The Untouchables." But no team captured the hearts of Wildcat fans more than The Unforgettables of 1991-92.

After two years of probation, the '92 team was eager to make its presence felt in postseason play. Led by seniors Richie Farmer, Deron Feldhaus, John Pelphrey and Sean

Woods and sophomore Jamal Mashburn, the Wildcats advanced to the East Regional final, where they faced Duke, the defending NCAA tourney champion. In that magnificent game, which many think is the best in college basketball history, Christian Laettner hit a last-second shot to give the Blue Devils a 104-103 overtime victory.

Athletics Director C.M. Newton summed up their accomplishments during a postseason ceremony in which the seniors' jerseys were retired. Newton said, "Today, our program is back on top, due largely to four young men who persevered, who weathered the hard times, and who brought the good times back to Kentucky basketball. Their contributions to UK basketball cannot be measured in statistics or record books."

Year by Year with the Cats

1903-20

The University of Kentucky basketball program, the winningest in history, began with a loss to Georgetown (Ky.) College on the afternoon of Feb. 6, 1903. The game was of such insufficient interest that the two Lexington newspapers couldn't agree on the final score. The *Herald* had it 17-6, the *Leader* said it was 15-6. The UK archives credit the *Leader's* 15-6 score as being official.

Back then, only 12 years after basketball had been invented, the school was known as Kentucky State College, and the team's nickname was Cadets. (It officially became Wildcats in 1909.) The first basketball team was put together by Walter W.H. Mustaine, the school's physical education director, with most of the players borrowed from the football team. That first team consisted of H.J. Wurtele, J. White Guyn, Joe Coons, R.H. Arnett, Leander Andrus, William Goodwin, Harold Amoss, J. Cronley Elliott, Ed Pierce and G.C. Montgomery. The players took up a col-

lection, raising $3 to purchase a basketball. They were also responsible for furnishing their own uniforms and shoes.

The first of UK's more than 1,800 victories came on Feb.18, when the Cadets beat the Lexington YMCA 11-10. They closed out that initial season with a 42-2 loss to Kentucky University (now Transylvania College).

Despite the relative indifference on the part of educators, the sport of basketball was an instant hit. Within a year's time, both the Lexington YMCA and its counterpart in Louisville had formed teams that would compete against each other and against various college teams. Basketball, whether the academic types liked it or not, was here to stay.

From 1903 until 1911, the Wildcats had only one winning season and a 30-49 record overall. Those early teams were run by student managers, while the task of actually coaching the team fell to the elected captain. The school's first true coach was E.R. Sweetland, a native of Dryden, N. Y., and a former standout athlete at Cornell University. Since Sweetland already coached the UK football team, he

Members of UK's unbeaten 1911-12 team included, from left to right, Brinkley Barnett, D.W. Hart, W.C. Harrison, R.C. Preston and Jake Gaiser. Kneeling is team manager Giles Meadors.

was the logical choice to take over the fledgling basketball program as well.

Sweetland coached part of the 1909-10 season, then left Kentucky because of poor health. He returned two years later, and his strong presence was felt immediately. The 1911-12 team finished with a 9-0 record, becoming the first of only two Wildcat teams to go through an entire season undefeated. This was a high-scoring team that averaged 32.2 points per game, including a high of 52 against Central University. The leading scorer was junior forward Binkley Barnett with a 7.1 average. Other members of that perfect Wildcat team were D.W. Hart, W.C. Harrison, Jake Gaiser, R.C. Preston, H.L. Farmer and William Tuttle.

After the season, the gypsy-like Sweetland again left UK, this time for good. J.J. Tigert, a philosophy professor, coached the 1912-13 team to a 5-3 record and served as athletics director from 1915 until 1917. The 1913-14 club, coached by Alpha Brumage, was one of UK's strongest early teams, ending the season with a 12-2 record. Preston led that team with a 6.1 average. The remainder of the scoring

was rounded out by Tom Zerfoss (6.0), Karl Zerfoss (4.7), William Tuttle (3.9) and Herschel Scott (3.2).

The Wildcats finished 7-5 one year later, then, thanks to Derrill Hart, the school's first double-figure point producer, they were 8-6 in 1915-16. Hart, a senior forward, averaged 13.3 points per game. Other scorers on that team included Jim Server (5.7), Robert Ireland (5.6), Karl Zerfoss (3.3) and George Gumbert (2.4).

The decade ended with UK posting only one winning record between 1916 and 1920. The 1917-18 squad, led by H.C. Thomas, had a record of 9-2-1. The only tie in UK history came against Kentucky Wesleyan, 21-21, when a scorer's error was discovered after the game had ended. The two teams scheduled a rematch to settle the issue, but the game was never played. Thomas was that team's best scorer with a 10.8 average. He was followed by J.C. Everett (6.6), Bob Lavin (5.0), Tony Dishman (3.3) and Ed Parker (3.3).

UK's first 18 teams produced a record of 95-88-1. Above average, but nothing special. Certainly no indicator of the enormous success that would eventually be achieved. The

program, like most in those early days, was unstable and in need of a strong, consistent guiding hand. The decade to come, the 1920s, would, to a certain extent at least, provide some measure of stability. It would also sow the seeds of greatness that lay ahead.

1921-30

The most positive aspect of the UK program at the end of the previous decade was the arrival of George C. Buchheit as basketball coach. Buchheit stayed from 1919 through 1924, making his five-year tenure the longest until Adolph Rupp took over in 1930. With Buchheit as coach and S.A. Boles as athletics director, the UK basketball program was, at last, in good hands.

In 1920-21, Buchheit's second Wildcat team, led by Basil Hayden and Bill King, had a 13-1 record and captured the school's first championship, winning the Southern Intercollegiate Athletic Association Tournament in Atlanta.

The Cats won their first six games, then suffered their lone setback of the season against Centre College, 29-27 in Danville. They bounced back to beat Georgetown 56-11, Centre 20-13 and Vanderbilt 37-18 to take a 9-1 mark into the SIAA tourney.

The high level of play continued into the tournament. The Cats easily moved through the draw, beating Tulane 50-28, Mercer 49-25 and Mississippi A&M 28-13 to set up a championship game showdown against Georgia.

The title game was tense and close from beginning to end, with the two clubs never separated by more than three points. UK was up 8-7 at the intermission, but after a see-saw second half, the Bulldogs pulled in front 19-17 with a minute remaining. With 45 seconds left, Hayden broke free and scored for UK to tie the game at 19-19.

On the ensuing center jump, UK's Bobby Lavin came up with ball, then rifled a pass to an open Paul Adkins beneath the bucket. As Adkins went in to shoot, he was fouled hard by a Georgia player.

In those days, one player was usually designated to shoot all of his team's free throws. King was UK's man. Also, in those days the clock continued to tick while free throws were being shot. However, a game could not end until the player had finished shooting. As King eyed the bucket, the timer signaled that the clock had run out. In a hushed gymnasium, King calmly launched his free toss. The ball hit the rim, eased slightly to the right, then fell through, giving UK a 20-19 victory and the tournament title. Hun-

dreds were on hand to meet the triumphant Wildcats when they arrived back in Lexington. This was the first time that UK fans celebrated a championship with their conquering heroes. It would not be the last.

King led that team in scoring with an 11.4 average. Hayden, who was named UK's first All-American, averaged 9.6. Along with Adkins and Lavin, other team members included Sam Ridgeway, Gilbert Smith, Jim Wilhelm and Bill Poynz.

Basketball was now beginning to take shape. UK, along with West Virginia, Washington & Lee, Virginia Military Institute, North Carolina, North Carolina State, Clemson, Georgia Tech, Georgia, Alabama, Tulane, Alabama Polytech, Mississippi A&M and Tennessee, joined together to form the Southern Athletic Conference. In addition, UK's championship win and the growing popularity of basketball soon had fans clamoring for a new and larger gym. The result of this outcry was a drive to solicit the funds needed to build a new home for the Wildcats.

With a veteran team returning, UK had high hopes for a second straight championship season. But that dream ended when Ridgeway was sidelined for the year because of an illness and Hayden suffered a knee injury prior to the first game. Hayden played, but was never as effective as he had been before the injury. The weakened Cats still managed a respectable 10-6 record despite the run of bad luck. Adkins was the team's top scorer with an 8.8 average. He was followed closely by King's 8.3 scoring clip. Lavin averaged 5.2, Hayden 5.0 and Poynz 2.9.

Buchheit's final two UK teams were a study in contrast. The 1922-23 club had a dismal 3-10 record, while the 1923-24 team finished with an outstanding 13-3 mark. Carl Riefkin averaged 10.2 to lead the 1922-23 team, which lost nine straight during one stretch, the longest losing skid in UK history.

An outstanding group of sophomores, led by Jim McFarland and Lovell "Cowboy" Underwood, was chiefly responsible for UK's turnaround 13-3 mark a year later. McFarland was the team's leading scorer with a 9.9 average. Will Milward was second with a 5.3 average, followed by Underwood's 4.9.

The most-heralded member of that class, and UK's second All-American, was guard Burgess Carey. Carey played as a freshman, then enrolled at Washington & Lee. After a brief stay at Washington & Lee, he transferred back to UK, but had to sit out a year. By the time he was eligible for the

1924-25 season, Buchheit had been replaced by C.O. Applegran and the Wildcats had their new home, 2,800-seat Alumni Gym.

Applegran led his only UK team to a 13-8 record, then was replaced by Ray Eklund, who guided the Cats to a 15-3 record and the third round of the Southern Conference Tournament. That Wildcat team lost its first two games — 38-29 to DePauw and 34-23 to Indiana — then reeled off 15 straight wins before falling to Mississippi A&M 31-26 in the tourney's semifinal game.

Carey, a low-scoring defensive wizard, was named All-American after the 1925 season. McFarland led the 1925 team with a 7.1 average, while Gayle Mohney's 11.1 average topped the 1926 club.

Eklund's sudden resignation a week before the 1926-27 season began forced UK officials to put in an emergency call to Hayden, asking the old Wildcat All-American to take over the reins. Hayden was out of coaching when he received his summons, having gone into the insurance business, and his basketball rust was apparent. Making matters worse was a roster filled mainly with football players. Despite his best efforts, Hayden could do no better than lead his team to a 3-13 record.

John Mauer, a former standout player at the University of Illinois, came in as UK's coach in 1927, bringing with him a deliberate, controlled "submarine" attack that consisted primaily of bounce passes and steady movement. Mauer was strict, organized and focused, and his style of play was new and somewhat mystifying to his players. At the time, most offenses designated certain players for specific roles. Mauer's plan was radically different. He incorporated all five players into the attack, thus giving equal importance to guards, forwards and centers.

Paul McBrayer was a standout from 1928-30. He was the last UK All-American prior to the arrival of Adolph Rupp. Later, he became Rupp's assistant.

Mauer's arrival at UK coincided with an influx of gifted, intelligent basketball players who were quick to master his complex new system. With such players as Paul McBrayer, Cecil Combs, Irvine Jeffries, Lawrence "Big" McGinnis, Paul Jenkins, Louis "Little" McGinnis and Carey Spicer leading the way, Mauer's three UK teams went 40-14. Two of his players, Spicer and McBrayer, earned All-America honors.

But Mauer brought an element to UK basketball that was more important than wins and losses — he brought a demand for excellence. Mauer was a tough, demanding coach, and he expected his players to take a serious approach to the game. Basketball, under Mauer, developed into something more than a disorganzied game played by a rag-tag group of players. It was no longer something akin to indoor football; rather, there was logic, precision and structure. Mauer became, according to the school newspaper, the "Moses" who led the sport out of the wilderness and into the dawn of a new era.

Mauer's first team, the 1927-28 group, finished with a 12-6 record, losing to Ole Miss 41-28 in the semifinal round of the Southern Conference Tournament. That was the first UK team to have more than one player to average in double figures. Jeffries led the club with an 11.5 average, while Combs was next at 10.3.

The 1928-29 team, led by Stan Milward and "Little" McGinnis, had a 12-5 record. Those Wildcats also beat Notre Dame 19-16 in the first meeting between the two schools. The Cats disposed of Tulane 29-15 in the first round of the Southern Conference Tournament, then lost a tough 26-24 decision to Georgia when a last-second shot by McGinnis rattled around the rim and fell off.

Mauer's final team was his best. That club, featuring

veterans Combs, Spicer, Milward, "Little" McGinnis and McBrayer, went 16-3 before losing to Duke 37-32 in the third round of the postseason tournament in Atlanta. Combs led a balanced scoring attack with a 6.6 average. Spicer was next at 6.5, followed by Milward (5.9), McGinnis (5.4) and McBrayer (4.8).

Less than two months after the season ended, Mauer resigned as UK coach and accepted the head coaching position at Miami University in Ohio. Once again, UK officials had a coaching vacancy to fill. This time, however, there was no lack of interest in the job. Because of UK's rising status within the college basketball community, and because of the vast wealth of talent in the Commonwealth, particularly in Lexington, the applications soon began pouring in. In all, 70 men applied for the job. That list was eventually narrowed down to two. On March 23, 1930, the job was officially offered to — and accepted by — a brash young man whose basketball lineage could be traced back to the very roots of the sport.

Adolph Frederick Rupp.

1930-31

While being interviewed for the vacant coaching position at Kentucky, Adolph Rupp was ask why he, rather than one of the other 70 applicants, should be hired. With classic bravado, Rupp said, "Because I'm the best damned basketball coach in the nation."

The never-too-modest Rupp got the job. And thus began one of the longest, most-successful coaching reigns in sports history.

Rupp came to UK from Halstead, Kan., by way of Freeport (Ill.), High School, where he spent three years coaching basketball and football. His Freeport teams had a 66-17 record, won two district titles and one sectional title.

Rupp learned the game while playing three seasons for legendary Kansas coach Dr. Forrest "Phog" Allen. Another strong influence on Rupp was none other than James Naismith, the man who invented basketball in 1891. Naismith was a professor at the University of Kansas during Rupp's years there, and the young Rupp got to know the game's inventor very well.

Hard times were mainly responsible for Rupp's decision to scrap his initial goal of becoming a banker in favor of getting into the teaching and coaching professions. He spent a year coaching wrestling at Burr Oak High School in Kansas, then took the job at Freeport High the following

year. After his three seasons there, he was chosen to replace Mauer at UK.

Rupp inherited a program that was on solid footing. Under Mauer, the Wildcats posted a 40-14 record while becoming a hot item at the ticket window. Even more important, Mauer brought consistency, style and precision to what had evolved into a slam-bang game. It was during Mauer's tenure that the cobblestones for the "Glory Road" were first laid.

But Mauer's submarine style of play, though successful, wasn't always exciting to watch. It was slow and deliberate. It was also the exact opposite of the style Rupp intended to install.

After watching a preseason scrimmage, Lexington *Herald* sports editor Neville Dunn wrote, "UK fans will get their first opportunity to pass judgment on Coach Adolph Rupp's system of playing basketball... Spectators at the game tonight will see the Wildcats using a system of offense that has been out of order at the University of Kentucky for the past three years. The slow-breaking, guard offense of Coach Johnnie Mauer, a system that won many big games for Kentucky, has given way to the old, but much improved and ever fascinating and thrilling fast-break."

Despite the enthusiasm generated by a new system, there were many who doubted that Rupp would succeed, citing the loss of such key players as McBrayer, Combs, "Big" McGinnis and Milward as being too much of an obstacle to overcome.

The *Kernal*, UK's school paper, went so far as to proclaim that "If Coach Rupp does come through with a winning team, he will be hailed as a miracle man."

But one important fact was being overlooked: the UK talent pool was far from empty. Spicer, an All-American, was back. So were "Little" McGinnis, George Yates and Jake Bronston. This group of versatile players was responsible for the smooth and successful transition from Mauer's slow style to Rupp's more frenetic pace. And joining them were Aggie Sale and Ellis Johnson, a pair of sophomores who would both earn All-America recognition before their playing days were finished.

Rupp unveiled his new system on the night of Dec. 19, 1930. With Sale scoring 19 points and McGinnis adding 17, the Wildcats stormed past Georgetown College 67-19.

Harry Lancaster, later to become Rupp's assistant, led the Tigers in scoring with 10 points.

The Rupp Era was off to a blazing start.

Adolph Rupp with his first UK team. Front row: Ercel Little, George Yates, Carey Spicer, Aggie Sale and Bud Cavana.
Middle row: George Skinner, Alan Lavin, Bill Trott, Jake Bronston, Louis McGinnis and Cecil Bell. Back row: Rupp,
Bill Congleton, Bill Kleiser, Ellis Johnson, Charles Worthington, Darrell Darby and manager Morris Levin.

The Cats continued to give impressive performances, easily beating Marshall 42-26, Berea 41-25 (despite hitting just 19 of 90 field goal attempts for 21 percent), and Clemson 33-21. Thanks to Rupp's new system, which gave his players great freedom on offense, UK featured a balanced scoring attack that was difficult to defend against. In UK's first four games, McGinnis scored in double figures four times, Sale three times (he missed one game due to an injury) and Yates twice.

The Cats' first real test came against unbeaten Tennessee. With 4,000 fans looking on, the Cats had to overcome an early 13-7 deficit before eventually pulling away to post a 31-23 victory. McGinnis led UK with 10 points.

Despite several close shaves, the Cats managed to remain unbeaten through their first 10 games. With Sale sidelined,

Spicer stepped up as UK's most-consistent scorer, posting some modern-day numbers. He had 27 points in a tough 42-37 win over Vanderbilt, 14 in a 36-32 overtime win at Tennessee and 20 in a 38-34 win over Georgia Tech.

Rupp's first loss as UK coach came when Georgia topped the Cats 25-16 in Athens. Georgia's defense completely dominated the game, limiting UK to five buckets and Spicer to a single point.

The Cats' shooting woes continued the next night in a 29-26 loss at Clemson. UK led 19-13 at the half, but managed just three field goals after the intermission.

McGinnis and Yates each scored 12 points as the Cats snapped their losing skid by blasting Georgia Tech 35-16. In the regular-season finale against Vanderbilt, Spicer had 14 points and Yates 12 in an easy 43-23 Wildcat win.

UK took an impressive 12-2 record into the Southern Conference Tournament in Atlanta. However, UK's hopes of capturing the crown were hurt by the absence of Sale and Johnson, both of whom were out with injuries.

Spicer, McGinnis and Yates each scored 10 points as the Cats opened postseason action with a solid 33-28 win over N.C. State. One night later, McGinnis erupted for 18 points to lead UK to a 35-30 victory over Duke.

UK stormed into the championship game on the strength of a record-setting 56-35 semifinal win over Florida. The Cats' point total was the highest in Southern Conference Tournament history, while Spicer's 22 points were the most ever by a single player. Spicer received strong support from Yates and McGinnis, who chipped in with 16 and 13, respectively.

The championship matchup against Maryland turned out to be a classic down-to-the-wire thriller. Baffled by Maryland's zone defense, the Cats fell behind early and trailed 18-7 at the half. But with McGinnis, Yates and Bronston leading the charge, UK fought back into contention, eventually taking a 27-25 lead on a McGinnis bucket with just under a minute remaining.

But UK was denied the title, thanks to Maryland's Bozzy Berger. After hitting a layup to knot the score at 27-27, Berger nailed a long shot with 10 seconds remaining to give the Terrapins a 29-27 win and the tourney championship.

Bronston paced UK with 14 points. Berger, Maryland's hero, led his team with 12 points.

McGinnis was the tourney's top scorer with 48 points. He made the All-Southern team along with Yates and Spicer, who was held scoreless in the championship game.

Rupp's first season at UK was a resounding success. His team finished with a 15-3 record despite the lengthy absence of Sale and Johnson. But even more important, Rupp's high-powered offense brought a new dimension to what had primarily been a slow and cautious game.

Rupp had the Wildcats on the move. And he was only beginning. In a few short years, the rest of the college basketball world would be racing to catch up.

1931-32

Rupp's second season could have turned out to be a disaster had it not been for the emergence of John "Frenchy" DeMoisey as a super player. Originally, DeMoisey, a sophomore from Walton, Ky., hadn't figured prominently in Rupp's plans for the upcoming campaign. But when

Yates was lost for the season because of a shoulder injury sustained during a UK football game and Bronston was declared ineligible, the 6'6" DeMoisey got his chance, which he quickly made the most of.

Joining DeMoisey in the starting lineup for the opener against Georgetown were Sale, Johnson, junior forward Darrell Darby and senior guard Charlie Worthington.

The powerful Cats jumped to a 23-1 lead against the Carey Spicer-coached Tigers en route to a 66-24 win. Sale led UK with 12 points, while DeMoisey, whose specialty was a unique hook shot, had 11 in his debut effort.

In its next outing UK faced Carnegie Tech, one of the top teams in the East at the time. With DeMoisey scoring 15 points and Sale adding 13, the Cats battled to a 36-34 win. After the game, Carnegie Tech coach Horgan declared UK to be "as good a team as there is in the East."

Following easy wins over Berea (52-27) and Marshall (46-16), DeMoisey and Bill Davis were declared academically ineligible. With DeMoisey out, Sale shifted from forward to the pivot spot and Howard Kreuter moved into Sale's old forward position.

Darby and Sale led the Cats to a pair of wins over Clemson and a 30-20 victory over Sewanee. With a 7-0 record, the Cats traveled to Knoxville for a game against the Volunteers. After blowing a 22-13 halftime advantage, the Cats won it 29-28 on a pair of Worthington free throws inside the final minute. Sale's 10 points led UK in that win.

DeMoisey rejoined the team against Washington & Lee, scoring 10 points off the bench in a 48-28 win. Sale's 20 points topped UK in scoring.

In UK's next game, a 61-37 win at Vanderbilt, DeMoisey scored 29, giving him 39 points in 39 minutes of action since returning from academic exile. After the game, one Nashville sportswriter described the DeMoisey hook shot as a "whirling dervish."

By now UK basketball under Rupp had become an immensely popular must-see event. Crowds were big, loud and raucous. Tempers were sometimes short, often leading to fist fights among irate Big Blue spectators.

UK's popularity hit an all-time peak when a then-record 5,000 fans crammed into the UK gym to watch Sale, DeMoisey and Darby lead the Cats to a 50-22 destruction of Alabama. Sale had 17 points, DeMoisey 12 and Darby 11 to pace UK.

The Cats needed wins in their final two games to close out the regular season with an unblemished record. They

Adolph Rupp's powerful second UK team. First row: Cecil Bell, Ercel Little, Gordon George, Harvey Mattingly, Evan Settle and Bill Kleiser. Middle row: Bill Davis, C.D. Blair, Darrell Darby, Ellis Johnson, Howard Kreuter and Charles Worthington. Back row: Assistant coach Len Miller, James Hughes, Frenchy DeMoisey, Aggie Sale, George Skinner and Rupp.

moved one step closer to their goal by beating Tennessee 41-27 behind Sale's 15 points. Johnson, who contributed eight points, was praised for his excellent defensive effort.

But the dream of a perfect season ended when Vanderbilt handed the flu-stricken Cats a disappointing 32-31 home-court loss. DeMoisey and Worthington led UK with nine points each, while Sale, who did not start because of the flu, had just four.

Although several players were still feeling the effects of flu-like symptoms, the Cats had no trouble beating Tulane 50-30 in the Southern Conference Tournament opener. UK led 13-0, only to watch as Tulane closed the difference to 18-16. But two buckets by DeMoisey and one by Sale enabled the Cats to build a 24-16 lead by intermission. UK then outscored Tulane 13-1 at the start of the final half to turn the game into a rout.

Sale led UK with 21 points, while Darby added 17.

In the quarterfinal round, the heavily favored Cats suffered a stunning 43-42 loss to North Carolina. It was a back-and-forth struggle that saw the Tar Heels rally from a 36-27 deficit midway through the final half to take a 39-38 lead. After DeMoisey and North Carolina's Virgil Weathers swapped buckets, Worthington hit a pair of free throws to give UK a 42-41 lead. Then with the final seconds ticking away, Weathers scored again to lift the Tar Heels to victory.

Sale was brilliant in defeat, scoring a game-high 20 points despite being swarmed by North Carolina defenders.

The loss left UK with a final mark of 15-2, giving Rupp a 30-5 record during his first two seasons at the helm. Sale was the team's top scorer with a 13.6 average, the best in school history at the time. For his efforts, Sale was named to the All-America team. DeMoisey was second in scoring with an average of 10 points per game.

Aggie Sale was a two-time All-American and the 1933 Helms Foundation National Player of the Year.

1932-33

When Rupp gathered his troops for preseason practice prior to the 1932-33 campaign, he found himself surrounded by a host of familiar faces. Sale, DeMoisey, Johnson, Darby and Davis were back, giving Rupp the nucleus of a potentially powerful team. Joining that group of veterans was a pair of talented sophomores — Dave Lawrence and Jack Tucker.

Also on hand was Yates, who had missed the previous season because of a shoulder injury. Although Yates had been the third-leading scorer two years earlier, he would see limited action this season. Yates became the first in a long line of standout Wildcat players who rejoined the team only to find themselves lost in Rupp's increasingly rich and deep talent pool. It was a fate shared by future Wildcats Bob Brannum, Jack Parkinson and Jim Jordan.

The 1932-33 season offered something new — the Southeastern Conference. During the off-season, UK joined with 12 other schools to form the SEC. Other charter members included Alabama, Alabama Polytech (Auburn), Ole Miss, Mississippi State, Georgia, Georgia Tech, LSU, Tennessee, Tulane, Florida, Sewanee and Vanderbilt.

On the eve of the season opener against the UK Alumni,

Rupp sounded like anything but the coach of a talented and experienced team. In particular, Rupp voiced his concerns about the backcourt, wondering who would step in and fill Worthington's shoes. He needn't have worried. Davis teamed with the wily Johnson to give the Cats a superior backcourt duo. Rounding out the starting quintet were Sale and Darby at the forward positions and DeMoisey in the middle.

This UK team was unlike any that had come before it, scoring points in such a rapid-fire manner that dazed opponents were left to wonder what had hit them. In their first four games, the Cats won by scores of 52-17, 62-21, 57-27 and 53-17. And the points came from everywhere. DeMoisey was the hottest Wildcat, registering 70 points in those four wins. Sale, Darby and Johnson all had double-figure efforts during that stretch.

No previous Wildcat team had averaged more than 37 points per game; this one was on course to shatter that mark in a big way. After four games, these Cats were scoring at a 56 points per game clip, prompting Lexington sportswriter Brownie Leach to write that, "Point a minute basketball is a thing of the past; this team is the 'half a hundred' boys."

After a 42-11 win over Tulane, Rupp took his team North for a matchup against Chicago. As many of Rupp's friends from Freeport looked on, the Cats, paced by DeMoisey's 24 points, rolled to an easy 58-26 victory. The Chicago fans were dazzled by what they witnessed. So were the Chicago sportswriters. In the game story the next day, one writer wrote that "the Southern hurricane blasted the Maroon defenses to pieces, whipping the ball down the court in whirlwind fashion."

The flamboyant DeMoisey was a particular favorite of fans and writers, who constantly referred to him as "the free-wheeling wizard."

The streaking Cats returned home to face Big Ten strongboy Ohio State. It turned out to be a night in which the best action took place in the stands and outside the gym. More than 5,000 fans were inside, with another 2,000 outside clamoring to get in. So unruly was the mob that ticket holders had difficulty gaining entrance into the gym. It was after this wild spectacle that the cry began for UK authorities to install a system that would prevent similar occurrences in the future. As sportswriter Brownie Leach wrote, "It's time that the seating situation should no longer be handled with gloves."

Inside, the Cats fared no better than the ticket holders did on the outside, dropping a 46-30 decision to the Buck-

UK's 1933 Helms Foundation National Champions. Front row: Biggerstaff, Evan Settle, Gates, Nugent, Jack Tucker, Jackson, Dave Lawrence. Middle row: Adolph Rupp, S.A. Boles, Ralph Kercheval, Bill Davis, Ellis Johnson, Darrell Darby, trainer Frank Mann, Assistant coach Len Miller. Back row: Crittenden Blair, Berkley Davis, Morris, Aggie Sale, Frenchy DeMoisey, George Yates, Howard Kreuter, manager Charles Maxson.

eyes. The game was close early, but Ohio State assumed command in the second half, building a 21-point lead (38-17) before settling for the final 16-point win. It was the worst loss ever by a Rupp team, either at the high school or college level.

Sale led UK with 11 points. The Buckeyes' leading scorer was Wilmer Hoskett with 15 points. This would not be the last time a Buckeye named Hoskett dealt a cruel blow to the Cats. In the 1968 NCAA tourney, Wilmer's son, Bill, scored 21 points in an 82-81 Buckeye win that knocked UK out of a trip to the Final Four.

The first loss of the season sent the Cats into a funk. They split a pair of games against Creighton, winning 32-26 behind the combined 21 points by DeMoisey and Sale, then losing 34-22 in a game that saw DeMoisey held scoreless. Sale carried the Cats in their next two games, scoring 15 in a 44-36 win over South Carolina and 20 in a 42-21 win over Tennessee.

The Cats regained their old scoring form in a 67-18 pasting of Clemson. Sale continued to shine, leading the Cats with 22 points. Johnson chipped in with 10.

After wins over Tennessee (44-23), Vanderbilt (40-29) and Clemson (42-32), the Cats were handed their third setback of the season, losing 44-38 at South Carolina. Each team had 16 field goals, but the Gamecocks used a 12-6 free throw advantage to notch the upset. Sale and Davis shared scoring honors for UK with 15 points apiece.

UK shattered all previous scoring records in an 81-22 laugher against Mexico University. It was the most points scored by a Wildcat team to date, and their 37 field goals set another school record. DeMoisey had 23 points for UK, while Sale added 20. Lawrence also hit double figures with 10.

Behind the solid 1-2 scoring punch of Sale and DeMoisey, the Cats won their final three regular season games to clinch the SEC title with a perfect 8-0 league mark.

Sale had 19 points to lead UK past Georgia Tech 45-22, then DeMoisey came through with 12 in a 35-31 win over Alabama. In the final regular season game, UK gunned down Vandy 45-28 as Sale matched the Commodores' scoring output.

UK opened SEC tourney action in Atlanta with an

easy 49-31 win over Ole Miss. The Cats broke out to a quick 7-0 lead and were never threatened. Sale led the Cats with 17 points, while DeMoisey added 16. Despite the margin of victory, Rupp said his team's performance was "disappointing."

Next up for the Cats was Florida, a team many were calling the tourney's dark horse. Given the outcome, dead horse would have been the more appropriate description. UK barely broke a sweat, dispatching the overmatched Gators 48-24. Sale and DeMoisey again paced the Cats, scoring 20 and 11 points, respectively, while the backcourt pair of Johnson and Davis earned high praise from Rupp for their outstanding defense.

UK captured the SEC tourney title by beating LSU 51-38 in semifinal action and Mississippi State 46-27 in the championship tilt. In those two games, Sale scored 34 points and DeMoisey had 32.

Not surprisingly, Sale was acclaimed as the greatest player ever seen in Atlanta. He was also named the Helms National Player of the Year for the 1932-33 season. And UK, which averaged 46.9 points per game while scoring a record 1,125 points during the season, was hailed as the best team to ever participate in the 11 tournaments played in Atlanta. The Cats were also accorded the honor of being chosen the Helms National Champions.

Sale led the team in scoring for the second straight year, averaging a new UK-best 13.8 points per game. DeMoisey followed with an average of 12 points.

Ashland native Ellis Johnson was a terrific all-around athlete who played four sports while at UK. He was a starter on Rupp's first UK team, and earned All-America recognition in 1933.

UK finished with a final record of 21-3, marking the first 20-win season in Wildcat basketball history.

1933-34

With All-Americans Sale and Johnson having graduated, along with Darby and Yates, Rupp now faced his first real rebuilding challenge at UK. Fortunately for Rupp, the UK coffers, despite such heavy losses, were far from depleted. For starters, DeMoisey, the "whirling dervish," was back, and it would be upon his shoulders that Rupp would rebuild.

DeMoisey was joined in the starting lineup by Jack Tucker, Bill Davis, Dave Lawrence and sophomore guard Andy Anderson. First off the bench for the Cats was another sophomore guard, Garland Lewis.

As the season approached, Rupp said his club had potential but needed plenty of hard work. Whatever Rupp did to tap that potential paid off in a big way. The Wildcats, virtually unheralded before the season began, sailed through their regular season without sustaining a single loss. Although the season would end on a bitter note, it was a remarkable effort by the Wildcat players. In many ways, it may also have been Rupp's finest coaching performance to date.

With DeMoisey leading the way, the Cats opened by ringing up impressive wins over the UK Alumni (53-20), Georgetown (41-12) and Marshall (48-26). In those three games, DeMoisey accounted for 42 points.

The Cats' first real test came against dangerous Cincin-

nati, a team Rupp called "the best passing team I've ever seen." Led by 6'4" standout Carl Austing, the Bearcats managed to hang with UK until the late stages of the game. But as the final minutes ticked down, UK, sparked by DeMoisey and Davis, pulled away for a 31-25 victory. DeMoisey had 12 points to lead UK, while Davis added 11. Austing led all scorers with 13.

Davis got the hot hand in UK's next two games, scoring 27 points in back-to-back road wins over Tulane. Then, following a three-week layoff, the Cats, behind Tucker's 14 points, swamped Sewanee 55-16 for their 15th straight win, a UK record at the time.

The Cats crushed Tennessee 44-23 in Knoxville behind DeMoisey's 20-point effort, then returned home to smack Chattanooga 47-20 as Lawrence and Davis combined for 21 points.

UK's winning ways had become such standard fare at this juncture that the team was beginning to be taken for granted by Big Blue fans, a fact sportswriter Brownie Leach was quick to point out in a post-game column: "The fact that it is no longer news for the Wildcats to win was reflected in the slim attendance (1,500) that turned out Saturday night."

The Cats sailed past Tennessee 53-26 to set up a crtical battle against unbeaten Alabama in Birmingham. With the SEC lead at stake, the Cats rode 11 for 13 marksmanship at the charity stripe to a hard-earned 33-28 win. Tucker led UK with nine points, while DeMoisey chipped in with eight.

UK cruised past Vanderbilt 48-26, then cemented its hold on the SEC lead by beating Alabama 26-21 in front of 4,000 fans. The Cats closed out their perfect regular season with wins over Georgia Tech (49-25), Sewanee (60-15) and Vanderbilt (47-27). The win over Vandy was notable for two reasons: DeMoisey had 25 points in just 27 minutes of action, and it was UK's 24th straight win, which equaled the modern record set by Duquesne.

With a 16-0 record and the SEC regular season title to their credit, the Cats were heavily favored to win the postseason tournament in Atlanta. Sportswriter Leach called UK "the biggest favorite since Reigh Count went to the post in the 1928 Kentucky Derby."

Certainly no one expected the Cats to have any trouble in their opener against Florida, which was invited to the tourney only after illness-plagued Ole Miss declined to participate.

From the opening tip-off it was obvious that the Wildcat players believed what the prognosticators were saying. UK fell behind early, and was on the short end of a 22-21 halftime score. Midway through the second stanza, buckets by Davis and DeMoisey put UK on top 27-24. Finally, it looked as though the tide had turned in UK's favor. But the Gators refused to buckle. After two DeMoisey free throws put UK in front 31-30, the Gators went on an 8-1 run to pull off an upset of major proportions.

The final: Florida 38, UK 32.

DeMoisey, who led all scorers with 16 points, admitted that he and his teammates were looking ahead rather than focusing on lowly Florida. When asked to explain what happened, DeMoisey said, "We just came down here to play in the finals. That was our main goal. We were wondering all along whether it would be Alabama or LSU that we would meet Tuesday night."

The loss also added to Rupp's distaste for the postseason SEC Tournament. As one of three league coaches opposed to the event, Rupp incurred the wrath of coaches, fans and sportswriters. Rupp was unmoved, arguing that the real reason why most SEC schools sought a quick end to basketball season was so they could get spring football practice under way. He wanted more regular-season games, which meant pushing the SEC tourney back to a later date.

The tournament was disbanded the next season, prompting a firestorm of verbal bombs to be hurled in Rupp's direction. The main brunt of the attack focused on what one sportswriter termed "Rupp's attitude of victory first and championships above all."

It was a charge Rupp would have leveled at him on many occasions in the future.

Though the acid-tongue Rupp could trade barbs with the best of them, he preferred to answer his critics in the only way that mattered — by winning basketball games. In four seasons at UK, Rupp's teams had carved out a 67-9 record, won the SEC regular season title in each of that league's first two years in existence, captured the SEC tourney once and set new standards for points scored in a season and in a game.

And there was no end in sight to UK's reign of terror. Even though the All-American DeMoisey and the reliable Davis were graduating, a steady stream of talented players continued to drift toward UK. Waiting in the wings was a player with such rare offensive skills that, despite

playing just one season, he is still regarded by many as being among the greatest Wildcats of all-time.

The player's name: Leroy Edwards.

1934-35

Prior to 1934, all seven Wildcat All-Americans had been native Kentuckians. Indeed, the vast majority of UK players in those early years were home-grown products who honed their skills in small towns like Paris, Walton, Lawrenceburg, Ashland and Lexington. Given the wealth of basketball talent virtually at his back door, Rupp felt little need to recruit out of state.

Then Rupp heard about Leroy Edwards, a 6'5" schoolboy standout at Indianapolis Tech High School who was being overlooked by Indiana, Notre Dame and Purdue. Intrigued, Rupp made one visit, watched Edwards play, and realized immediately that he'd found a special player.

Leroy Edwards was an All-American and the National Player of the Year in his only season as a Wildcat.

Edwards agreed to become a Wildcat, and although he only played one season, his talent was such that he left an indelible impression on those who saw him in action.

Many years later, Rupp said Edwards was the greatest pivot man he'd ever seen and the strongest player he ever coached. Because of his tremendous strength and his advanced offensive skills, Edwards proved to be a forerunner to the centers and power forwards that were to come.

Edwards came to the varsity along with two other outstanding sophomores — Warfield Donohue and Ralph Carlisle. That trio, which had been at the heart of an undefeated freshman team the previous season, joined with returning veterans Lawrence, Tucker, Lewis and Anderson to give Rupp yet another formidable club.

Edwards flashed his brilliance from the beginning, single-handedly outscoring the opposition in each of UK's first

five victories. That early season stretch included wins over the UK Alumni (55-8), Ogelthorpe (81-12), Tulane (38-9 and 52-12), and Chicago (42-16). In those games, Edwards chalked up point totals of 18, 22, 10, 16 and 26.

Thanks in no small part to the growing interest in Edwards, the Cats, now 5-0, were invited to the Mecca of college basketball — Madison Square Garden — to take on powerful NYU as part of a double-header put on by promotor Ned Irish. It marked the first time a UK team played in New York City, where Rupp knew his growing program could receive greater national exposure.

The game was brutal from the tip-off, especially for Edwards, who bore the brunt of a NYU defense that often resembled a Times Square mugging. Constantly shadowed by a pair of burly defenders, Edwards was forever being held, poked, tripped and ridden. Although he never got untracked, scoring just six points, Edwards was loudly cheered by a Garden crowd that was unhappy with NYU's strong-arm tactics.

To make matters worse (and Rupp angrier), the officials, while ignoring the lawlessness taking place under the basket, consistently whistled fouls against the UK players for setting illegal screens. Rupp argued that what his players were doing was legal in the South and Midwest, but his pleas were ignored by the officials.

Despite everything, the Cats led 22-18 with less than two minutes remaining and appeared to be on the verge of picking up their sixth straight win. Then the bottom fell out. After NYU scored four unanswered points to tie it at 22-22, Edwards was whistled for an illegal screen. With just eight seconds left, Sidney Gross connected on a free toss to give NYU a 23-22 win.

UK may have lost on the basketball court, but not in the court of public opinion. The tough Madison Square Garden fans loved the Cats' gritty effort, while the New York sportswriters were quick to say that UK had been robbed. Immediately after the game, Ned Irish apologized to Rupp for the poor officiating.

When asked his opinion of what happened, Rupp offered one of his most memorable lines: "We were strangers and they took us in."

Unaffected by the loss in New York, the Cats won their next nine games by an average margin of 28 points. Although Edwards continued to rack up big numbers (24 against Chattanooga, 21 against Alabama, 23 against Xavier), he received plenty of help from his teammates, especially Lawrence. The senior forward from Corinth, Ky., scored a season-high 23 in the 66-19 win over Chattanooga, then followed that performance by scoring 16, 14 and 15 in two wins against Tulane and one against Tennessee.

In early February, after a 57-30 win over Georgia Tech, Rupp announced that UK would not participate in the SEC Tournament because of a scheduling conflict. As it turned out, it didn't matter. There was no SEC Tournament that year.

Michigan State ended the Cats' nine-game run, winning 32-26 in East Lansing despite 16 points from Edwards. The Cats escaped disaster in their next outing, edging home-standing Tennessee 38-36 on a late bucket by Lewis. Lawrence led UK with 11 points.

Edwards set a new single-game high in UK's next game, scoring 34 points in an impressive 63-42 win over a very good Creighton team. Edwards' output topped the previous high of 29 held by DeMoisey.

After beating Creighton 24-13 in

Dave Lawrence was a silent assassin who helped lead the Wildcats to a 35-3 record during his final two years.

a rematch, the Cats closed out their season with wins over Vanderbilt (53-19) and Xavier (46-29) to finish with a 19-2 record. Against Vandy, Donohue was the leading scorer with 14 points, followed by Edwards with nine. In the season finale against Xavier, a flu-stricken Edwards scored 16 points despite playing only half the game.

The Xavier game turned out to be Edwards' last at UK. After the season, Edwards returned home, married his childhood sweetheart, got a job in a plant and signed to play pro basketball.

Although Edwards' time as a Wildcat lasted but one year, he remains one of the brightest stars in the UK galaxy. In his single season at UK, the player affectionately known as "Cowboy," "Big Ed," and "Big Boy," averaged 16.3 points per game, while setting UK and SEC records for most points in a season with 343.

For his efforts, Edwards was named All-American and was chosen Helms National Player of the Year.

The Kentucky-only All-American lineage had finally been broken.

1935-36

The loss of Edwards after the 1934-35 campaign was of such magnitude that it took Rupp eight years to find a suitable replacement. It wasn't until 1943, with the arrival of 17-year-old Bob Brannum, that the Cats once again had a genuine big-time scorer.

During those eight years, from 1935-36 through 1942-43, Wildcat teams were good but not spectacular. The players, though talented, hard-working and tough-minded, lacked the exceptional skills of those who had preceeded them. There were no high-scoring All-Americans like Sale, Spicer, DeMoisey, Edwards or the much-underrated Lawrence. In fact, over the

The 1934-35 Wildcats featured Helms National Player of the Year Leroy Edwards (25) and All-American Dave Lawrence (26). Another standout performer was All-SEC forward Ralph Carlisle (14).

next eight years only three Wildcats averaged in double figures. That absence of a superstar to build around was reflected in UK's winning percentage. In Rupp's first five years, the Cats won 89 percent of their games (86-11); over the next eight seasons, that figure dipped to a still-respectable 74 percent (129-46).

The 1935-36 club was typical of those Wildcat teams in the years between Edwards' departure and Brannum's arrival. Led by the fearless Carlisle, these Rupp-driven Cats often succeeded far beyond their talent level, as they would do time and time again over the years. They were capable of beating the best; however, lacking consistency, they were susceptible to baffling upsets.

For the season opener against Georgetown College, Rupp fielded a lineup consisting of seniors Lewis and Anderson, juniors Carlisle and Donohue, and feisty sophomore Joe "Red" Hagan, a former prep standout at St. Xavier High in Louisville.

The Cats opened strong, beating Georgetown 42-17 behind Carlisle's game-high 13 points. In their next game, Lewis scored 19 and Hagan 12 as the Cats ripped Berea 58-30.

Despite those two impressive wins, Rupp, always the alarmist, sounded the trumpet of despair when assessing his team's chances against Pittsburgh, a team famed for its complicated and elaborate "figure eight" offense.

"Pitt can beat us as much as it wants to," Rupp lamented. "We just haven't got it this year."

The final: UK 35, Pitt 17. And it could have been worse. With his team leading 22-2 at the break, Rupp called off the dogs, clearing his bench early in the second half. Carlisle again led the Cats with 12 points.

After three home wins the Cats were off to New York for a rematch against NYU in Madison Square Garden. The outcome differed little from the previous year — NYU won 41-28 despite a marvelous 17-point performance by Carlisle.

In Rupp's view the referees hadn't improved much either. Still upset that screening plays were not being recognized, Rupp said, "UK probably would not play again in New York until the officiating becomes standard."

UK's next game, a 36-32 win at Xavier, was such a foul-plagued affair that the two coaches agreed to change the disqualification number from four to five. The Cats won, thanks to the late clutch play by Carlisle, who finished with 17 points.

Carlisle remained hot, accounting for 41 points in two wins over Tulane and one over Michigan State. Against the Spartans, Carlisle tallied 16 points as the Cats overcame a 13-12 deficit at the half to revenge last season's loss to the

Big Ten powerhouse.

In UK's wild 40-31 win over Tennessee, it was the officals and not the Vol defense that finally managed to stop Carlisle. Early in the second half of what was a fiercely fought battle between bitter rivals, Carlisle was tossed for hitting a Tennessee player. In Carlisle's absence Hagan and Lewis stepped up, scoring 15 and 10 points, respectively, for the winning Wildcats.

Vanderbilt, unbeaten in SEC play, whipped the Cats 33-24 in Nashville. UK rebounded with back-to-back wins over Alabama — 32-30 in Tuscaloosa and 40-34 in Lexington. In the second of those two wins, sophomore J. Rice Walker came off the bench to spark the Cats' late comeback surge.

No one could rescue the Cats in their next game, an embarrassing 41-20 drubbing at Notre Dame. The Irish smoked UK early, running out to a 29-7 lead by halftime. It was UK's worst loss in nine years. The game was a personal nightmare for Carlisle, who was held scoreless. Hagan was the only bright spot for UK, scoring 12 points after coming off the bench.

After an easy 39-28 win over Butler, the Cats dropped a 39-28 decision to Tennessee in Knoxville. UK was done in by Ashland native Alvin Rice, whose three long bombs late in the game enabled the Vols to pull away for the win.

Carlisle snapped out of his scoring slump by ringing up 20 points in a 49-40 win over Xavier. With Xavier leading 18-17, Carlisle scored seven unanswered points to give the Cats a 24-18 advantage at the half. Once in command, the Cats were never again seriously challenged. Hagan and Lewis also gave superb performances, contributing 11 points apiece to the Cats' cause.

In what was perhaps their finest effort of the season, the Cats demolished Creighton 68-38 in the first game of a two-game homestand. Lewis led UK with 22 points, while Carlisle added 18.

If the first game against Creighton was the high mark for UK's season, the rematch proved to be the absolute nadir. Creighton switched gears in the second game, slowing the pace to a crawl. The antsy Cats, thrown completely off their game, fell behind early and never caught up. Creighton won it 31-29, halting UK's home-court winning streak at 39.

Hagan scored 19, Carlisle 18 and Lewis 11 as the Cats ended their regular season with a 61-41 revenge win over

Vanderbilt. It was a rugged game that saw 38 fouls called and featured a heated exchange between Vandy coach Josh Cody and referee Frank Lane. The win over Vandy gave the Cats some much-needed momentum to take into the SEC Tournament, which, after a one-year hiatus, had been revived. It had also been shifted from Atlanta to Knoxville.

UK began tourney action with a 41-39 come-from-behind win over Mississippi State. Although heavily favored to win, the Cats, in Rupp's words, "played very poorly." Hagan and Carlisle rescued the struggling Cats, scoring 13 and 12 points, respectively.

Tennessee ended the Cats' up-and-down season by rolling to a 39-28 win in the quarterfinal round. Playing in front of a vocal home crowd, Tennessee won with ease by holding the lethargic Cats to just seven field goals for the game. Carlisle was the lone Wildcat standout, scoring 17 points. His performances earned him a spot on the All-SEC tourney team. He was also the team's leading scorer for the season with an 11.5 average.

UK's 15-6 record was Rupp's worst since taking over six years earlier. Already Rupp had raised the bar of expectation so high that a 15-6 record was viewed as mediocre. There were more "mediocre" years on the horizon, but it was during this period that Rupp was laying the groundwork for an explosion that would rock the world of college hoops.

1936-37

Few Wildcat teams in history have been more inconsistent and unpredictable than this one. These Cats, led by Carlisle, Donohue and Hagan, managed to put together a fine 17-5 record, yet lost three games to teams they had already defeated. In mid-February, following back-to-back losses to Alabama and Tennessee, the Cats were already being written off as a team with no shot at winning the SEC Tournament. And yet, when the final bucket had been made, it was Rupp's Cats who walked away with championship trophy.

Rupp's starters for the opener against Georgetown were Carlisle and Hagan at the forward positions, Walker in the middle, with Donohue and sophomore Bernie Opper in the backcourt.

Carlisle had 16 points and Opper added eight in his varsity debut as the Cats won 46-21. The Cats struggled early, and were only leading 19-15 at the half, before finally pulling away in the second frame. When

it was over, an unhappy Rupp said his club had been given a "great scare."

After blasting Berea 70-26, the Cats got their first test of the season against Xavier in Cincinnati. The Cats, behind some late-game heroics by Carlisle, squeaked past Xavier 34-28 in overtime. With his team trailing 26-20, Carlisle scored a field goal and a free throw to key a 7-1 spurt that sent the game into the extra period. The Cats continued their run in the OT, outscoring Xavier 7-1 to notch the victory. Carlisle's 18 points led the Cats.

Although the Cats easily defeated Centenary 37-19 in their next game, Rupp was so displeased with his team's effort that he ordered an immediate post-game practice. While Rupp may indeed have been punishing his players for their performance against Centenary, it's more likely that his true motive for calling the midnight workout was to begin early preparations for UK's next two opponents — Michigan State and Notre Dame.

The Cats earned a split in those two outings, beating Michigan State 28-21, then being smeared by the Irish 41-28 in front of more than 6,000 fans in the Jefferson County Armory. It was the largest crowd to see a basketball game in Kentucky at the time, and the first time Rupp took a team to Louisville. Notre Dame, led by Paul Novak's 18 points, completely dominated the outclassed Cats in all areas of the game.

Facing Creighton at home, the Cats broke away from a 22-22 tie and went on to post a 59-36 victory. Hagan had 17 points to lead UK, while Carlisle finished with 11.

More late-game heroics decided the outcome of UK's rematch with Michigan State; only this time, it was the Spartans' Howard Kraft who wore the hero's robes. Michigan State won 24-23 on a late free throw by Kraft. The Cats had a chance to pull it out, but shots by Carlisle and Opper inside the final 15 seconds failed to find their mark.

The Cats bounced back, winning their next four games in convincing fashion. Included in that streak were easy wins over SEC foes Tennessee (43-26), Vanderbilt (41-26) and Alabama (37-27). Sophomore Homer "Tub" Thompson played well for the Cats, coming off the bench to score nine points against Vandy and 13 against the Crimson Tide.

But the Cats' good fortunes were fleeting, and over the next five games they lost to Tulane, Alabama and Tennessee. The 34-31 loss to Alabama was particularly disturbing because it came on UK's home court. Also, it was the first time a Rupp-coached team lost to Alabama.

In the 26-24 loss to Tennessee in Knoxville, the Cats held a 24-18 lead, only to watch as Ashland native Alvin Rice once again sparked a Volunteer comeback. Rice had six points, all coming on outside buckets late in the game. Carlisle, now mired in a horrible scoring slump, and Walter Hodge had five points each to lead UK in scoring.

The Cats closed out their regular season by beating Vanderbilt 51-19 and Xavier 23-15. Hagan was UK's top scorer in those two wins with 18 points. Carlisle sat out the Xavier game because of the flu.

Even though this team was given little chance of capturing the SEC tourney title in Knoxville, it would, like many future Wildcat clubs, shine the brightest when it counted the most. These Cats did what successful teams do — saved their best for last.

So did Carlisle, who broke out of his scoring drought to end his UK career by giving three of his finest performances.

It was Carlisle's scorching second-half shooting that enabled the Cats to break open a close game and easily handle LSU 57-27 in the opener. Carlisle, still weakened by the flu, didn't play in the first half, which ended with UK leading 19-15. But in the final 20 minutes, Carlisle made good on five of seven field goal attempts to turn the game into a yawner. Thompson paced UK with 11 points, while Walker and Carlisle each had 10.

The Cats' semifinal game against Georgia Tech followed a similar pattern. After five first-half ties, the last at 18-18, four points by Carlisle and two by sophomore Fred Curtis put the Cats on the road to a 40-30 victory. Carlisle's 16 points were tops for UK. Hodge and Curtis had nine each.

The championship game against Tennessee was never in doubt. Although the Vols were favored to win, UK won its second SEC tourney title in four tries by rolling to a surprisingly easy 39-25 win. Carlisle had 10 points in his final game for UK.

Thanks to the All-SEC efforts by Carlisle, Donohue, Walker and Hodge, it was a satisfying finish for a team that had read its own obituary only a month earlier.

1937-38

Prior to the start of the season Rupp surveyed his talent, then predicted this to be the "weakest scoring outfit he has ever worked with at Kentucky."

Rupp had good reason to be concerned. Gone were Carlisle and Donohue, a pair of tough-minded players who

had been through the wars and who knew how to win. Adding to Rupp's bleak outlook was the sudden loss of Hodge, who was forced to miss the entire season after going down with a serious knee injury only weeks before the opener against Berea.

Still, though, Rupp wasn't left empty-handed. Returning were battle-tested veterans Hagan, Opper, Thompson, Walker and Curtis. They were joined by Marion Cluggish, a 6'8" sophomore center from Corbin, and Layton "Mickey" Rouse, a 6'1" sophomore guard from Ludlow.

What this team may have lacked in natural ability, it more than made up for in intensity and the willingess to go toe-to-toe with the opposition. With the quick-tempered and irascible Hagan in the dual roles of team leader and lightning rod for danger, it was perhaps inevitable that this would turn out to be one of the roughest, most-physical UK teams in history. One thing is for certain: This was not a Wildcat team that won with finesse.

The season began on a successful if somewhat odd note. The Cats routed Berea 69-35, but Rupp wasn't on hand for the game. He was home in bed with the flu. Assistant coach Paul McBrayer handled the coaching chores in Rupp's absence. Thompson led UK with 12 points, while Cluggish made a successful debut by scoring 11.

The short-fused Cats were involved in their first altercation during a 38-21 win over Cincinnati. At the center of this melee was UK sub Bob Davis, who was ejected for throwing a punch at one of the visiting Bearcats. Sportswriter Neville Dunn described Davis' punch as "a roundhouse right... a haymaker." Players from both benches ran onto the court. Unfortunately, so did some overly enthusi-

New York City native Bernie Opper recruited himself to UK after watching the Wildcats play in Madison Square Garden.

astic Wildcat fans.

The Cats beat Centenary 35-25, then hit the road to New Orleans for a Sugar Bowl matchup against Pittsburgh. With Thompson scoring 11 points and Curtis adding 10, the Cats won 40-29 for their fourth victory in as many outings.

And their last for nearly a month.

Facing a brutal three-week stretch against top-flight opponents, the road-weary Cats lost at Michigan State, Detroit and Notre Dame. It marked the first time a Rupp-coached team dropped three games in succession.

The twin evils of cold shooting and hot tempers were at the core of UK's sudden collapse. The Cats made just four of 13 free throws in the 43-38 loss at Michigan State, then, displaying what one sportswriter later called "rotten marksmanship," they fell 34-26 at Detroit. The only Wildcat to rise above the muck was Hagan, who had 30 points in those two setbacks.

In yet another game marred by several on-court altercations Notre Dame continued its mastery over UK, beating the Cats 47-37 behind a 20-point performance by Johnny Moir. The loss left Rupp with an 0-3 record against the Irish.

The action almost didn't end after 40 minutes. Tempers got so hot near the end of the game that players from both teams threatened to take the warfare outside. Finally, cooler heads prevailed and the two combatants went their separate ways.

The Cats returned home and took out their frustrations on Tennessee, winning easily 52-27. The rapidly improving Curtis led UK's attack with 15 points, while Rouse had 11. But rough play and constant fouling continued to plague

the Cats. At one point, though his team was in no danger of losing to the Vols, Rupp became so angry with the officiating that he was hit with a technical.

The victory against Tennessee ignited a run that saw the Cats win nine of their final 10 regular-season games. Xavier put the only blemish on the Cats during that period, winning 39-32 in Cincinnati.

It was a streak that had it all — impressive wins over Michigan State (44-27) and Xavier (45-29), last-second heroics (a 35-33 win over Marquette on a Hagan bucket from near mid-court), a Wildcat player from Nashville (Curtis) scoring a career-best 21 points in a 48-24 win over Vanderbilt and the naming of a new athletics director (Bernie Shively).

And, of course, more rough-and-tumble play. After watching the Cats dispensed with Alabama 28-21, sportswriter Dunn wrote that "UK is playing a rougher brand of basketball than is wholly admirable."

Admirable or not, after edging past Tennessee 29-26 in Knoxville, the Cats owned a record of 13-4 overall and 6-0 in league play heading into the SEC Tournament in Baton Rouge.

UK was a solid choice to beat Tulane in the opening round, but after a 27-hour train ride the Wildcat players had little left to give. Taking advantage of the sluggish, foul-prone Cats (three of whom were tagged with three fouls in the first half), Tulane pulled off the 38-36 upset.

Ironically, out of what was a rather ordinary season rose one of UK's most-extraordinary and influential figures — Bernie Shively. On Feb. 21, 1938, Shively, or "Shive," was unanimously approved as UK's new AD, a position he held until his death in 1967. Without question, Rupp and Shively are the two central figures in UK's rise to prominence in college basketball.

1938-39

By the end of the 1930s, Kentucky had established itself as the premier basketball program in the South and one of the best in the nation. The driving force behind UK's rise to national prominence was, of course, Rupp. More than anything else, it was his dynamic personality, his will to win and his unwillingness to accept anything less than total dedication from his players that were the building blocks upon which the UK basketball empire was constructed.

And make no mistake, Rupp ruled his kingdom with an iron fist. He was absolute boss. As both judge and jury, his

verdict was the only one that counted. In the words of Lexington sportswriter Larry Shropshire, Rupp was "der fuehrer of basketball doings at the University of Kentucky."

Rupp was also deserving of his growing reputation as a great coach. He had proved his ability to win with star-studded teams and with teams of average talent. His ninth UK team, which fell into the average group, was a prime example of Rupp's knack for getting the maximum out of his players. Though little was expected of the 1938-39 club, this bunch of Wildcats would, by the end of the season, become one of the great overachieving teams in UK hoops history.

So equal were the UK players that Rupp had a difficult time deciding on a starting lineup for the opener against Georgetown. In the end, Rupp finally went with veterans Thompson, Rouse and Opper, junior James Goodman and promising sophomore Keith Farnsley, a 6-foot forward from New Albany, Ind. But that lineup didn't last long. After Curtis came off the bench to lead UK to a 39-19 win over the Tigers, he replaced Goodman as a starter.

Curtis justified Rupp's lineup change by leading the Cats to convincing wins over Kentucky Wesleyan (57-18) and Cincinnati (44-27). In those two outings, Curtis, a 6'2" senior from Nashville, registered 24 points.

UK upped its record to 4-0 with a solid 67-47 win over Washington & Lee. Thompson was the top scorer with 17 points, while Curtis added 10. The Cats also got 10 points from Lee Huber, a talented 6-foot guard from Louisville St. Xavier High.

For UK's next game, Rupp took his team back to the scene of the crime (Madison Square Garden) for a matchup against Long Island University. Although Rupp voiced few complaints about the officiating, his team fared no better on this visit to the big city than it had in previous years. Haunted by miserable shooting, the Cats, who failed to make a single field goal during the first 10 minutes, were soundly thrashed 52-34.

After beating St. Joseph's 41-30 behind Curtis' 17 points, the Cats faced Notre Dame in Louisville. The game was close, with seven lead changes in the second half, but the Irish parlayed a big advantage at the free throw stripe into a 42-37 victory. The Cats had four more field goals (14-10), but Notre Dame prevailed by connecting on 22 freebies to UK's nine. Curtis led UK with 11 points.

UK next faced Tennessee, which was now coached by

John Mauer. In the first meeting between Rupp and his predecessor at UK, it was Mauer's more deliberate style that won the day.

Tennessee won a shocker 30-29, handing Rupp and his team an embarrassing loss in front of the home crowd. When the final horn sounded, a jubilant Mauer rushed onto the court to congratulate his victorious players.

UK's slide continued when George Prather, the SEC's leading scorer, powered Alabama to a 41-38 win in Birmingham. The Cats led 37-35, but were outscored 6-1 in the final two minutes.

Having lost four of their last five games, and with the regular season barely at the halfway point, the slumping Cats now found themselves just two losses shy of matching the most ever suffered by a Rupp-coached team. To avoid that odious distinction, the Cats needed to rediscover their early season form. That's exactly what they did. In one of the most-amazing turnarounds in UK history, the Cats marched through the remainder of their schedule without suffering a single loss. The team that once stood on the brink of failure somehow managed to transform itself into a team of splendid accomplishment.

Included among UK's victims were Alabama and Tennessee, two teams that conquered the Cats in earlier meetings. Against Alabama, Thompson had 13 points and Curtis 11 as the Cats won convincingly 45-27. Equally vital in that win was UK's defense, which held the high-scoring Prather to one bucket and seven total points.

In the rematch against Tennessee in Knoxville, the Cats revenged their home-court embarrassment by nipping the Vols 36-34 in double overtime on a late basket by Farnsley. The score was knotted 32-32 at the end of regulation and 34-34 after the first extra period. Opper and Farnsley led UK with 11 and 10 points, respectively.

Unselfishness and teamwork were at the heart of this club's success. So was a balanced scoring attack, which seemed to produce a different hero in each game. Five different Wildcats led the team in scoring in those final eight regular-season wins.

The Cats carried a 13-4 record into their SEC Tournament opener against Ole Miss. Trailing 28-27, the Cats broke loose for 16 points during a three-minute span to send them on their way to a 49-30 win. Huber keyed that game-deciding spurt by sinking three field goals.

Thompson scored 10 and Farnsley nine as the Cats crushed LSU 53-34 to set up a championship battle — and the rubber match — against arch-rival Tennessee. With the Vols holding an 18-11 lead, Opper scored three quick baskets to help the Cats fight back and take a 24-19 lead at the half. The second half was all UK. Making good on 14 of 20 free throws, the Cats claimed their second SEC tourney title in three years by beating Tennessee 46-38. Opper, UK's top scorer with 13 points, was voted to the all-tournament team along with Farnsley. Opper also earned All-America recognition that season.

When it was over, Rupp, never one to shy away from a little embellishment, claimed to have lost 30 pounds during the three-day tourney. Later, speaking to a group of reporters, Rupp said, "Boys, it's great to get this one. We certainly had a struggle, and I'm glad it's over."

This was perhaps Rupp's finest coaching job since taking over at UK. His Cats finished 16-4, won the SEC regular-season title and the SEC Tournament.

Those were facts that required no embellishing.

1939-40

Rupp's 10th Wildcat team figured to be a good one. And it was. Built around the nucleus of Rouse, Farnsley, Cluggish and Huber, the Cats put together another superb season, finishing with a 17-5 record (which could have been better; a mid-season flu attack likely cost the team two wins) and a second straight SEC Tournament championship.

Several Wildcats filled in the fifth starting spot, with Waller White, Jim King, Carl "Hoot" Combs and Ermal Allen all getting considerable playing time.

The Cats got an early wake-up call in only their second game of the season, losing 39-30 at home to Cincinnati. The Bearcats were led by Eddie Jucker's 12 points. Jucker later became the coach at his alma mater, directing the Bearcats to NCAA titles in 1961 and 1962.

Some onlookers attributed the loss to Rupp for his failure to open up the offense in the second half. They felt that Rupp played it close to the vest rather than reveal anything to the scouts from Ohio State who were in the stands. The Buckeyes were UK's opponent in the upcoming Sugar Bowl. Rupp, however, laid the blame squarely on his players, saying he was "totally befuddled" by their performance.

The Cats bounced back to win their next five games, including three on the road. Huber's 17 points helped the Cats destroy Clemson 55-31, then Rouse came through with 14 in a 36-30 Sugar Bowl win over the spying Buckeyes. The Cats' biggest scare came against Xavier. With the score tied 39-39 in overtime, White's bucket and free throw were enough to give the visiting Cats a 42-41 win. Farnsley led UK with 12 points.

UK's winning ways were halted by Notre Dame, the one team that continued to mystify Rupp and dominate the Wildcats. The Irish, paced by Eddie Riska's 17 points, beat UK 52-47.

It was after beating Tennessee 35-26 that the flu bug found a home inside the Wildcat compound. Huber and King were the hardest hit, and without them, the Cats lost to Alabama (36-32) and Vanderbilt (40-32). The Cats somehow managed to beat a good Marquette team 51-45 even though King, White and Carl Staker didn't see action at all and Huber played only five minutes. Farnsley and Rouse came up big for the Cats with 18 and 12 points, respectively. But the big hero was Don Orme, a little-used sub who never earned a letter at UK. Orme had nine points, including back-to-back baskets that broke a 39-39 deadlock.

Proof of how important Huber and King were to the team became clearly evident in a rematch with Alabama. Without Huber and King, UK lost 36-32. With them in the lineup, the Cats won 46-18. Rouse and Combs scored nine points each for the Cats, while strong interior defense by Cluggish held Prather to just three points.

Cluggish turned offensive minded in UK's next outing, ringing up 11 points in a 37-29 win over Xavier. One night later, Farnsley and Rouse each scored 14 as the Cats topped Mississippi State 45-37.

The Cats ended the regular season on a down note, losing two of their final three games, at Tennessee and Georgia Tech. That streak almost extended to a third straight defeat, and likely would have had it not been for Cluggish. His 22-point effort brought the Cats back from a 24-17 halftime deficit and carried them to a 43-38 win over visiting Vanderbilt.

The scenario was similar in the first game of the SEC tourney in Knoxville. UK again faced Vandy, and Cluggish again (with solid support from Allen) proved to be the difference. Cluggish had 13 and Allen 12 as the Cats beat the Commodores 44-34.

Farnsley provided the fireworks in UK's 30-29 overtime thriller over Tennessee in the semifinals. Farnsley scored 11 points, including seven inside the final three

minutes, to help the Cats survive. It was the second time in six meetings between Rupp and Mauer that it took an overtime to decide the outcome. The win gave Rupp a 4-2 record against Mauer. However, the Baron was 2-0 in tournament play.

After surviving against Tennessee, there was no way the Cats were about to lose to Georgia in the championship game. With the title on the line, UK opened a 31-19 halftime lead, then rolled on to post a 51-43 victory. Four Cats cracked double figures, including all-tourney picks Farnsley and Rouse with 12 each, White with 11 and Cluggish with 10.

Rouse was also a first-team selection on the All-SEC squad.

In Rupp's first decade at UK, his teams had a record of 162-37 for an 81.4 winning percentage. Four times his teams won the SEC Tournament, and his 1933 team was declared national champs. Six of his players achieved All-American status, while two — Sale and Edwards — were named National Player of the Year.

But as momentous as that decade had been, it didn't begin to compare to the turbulent decade that lay ahead. Coming up was a World War that threatened the free world and a basketball team that would forever define greatness.

1940-41

If the previous team was one of Rupp's great success stories, then this one, the last in peace time until the 1945-46 season, was one of his biggest disappointments. Despite having a solid core of veteran players back, the Wildcats could do no better than a 17-8 record. No Rupp-coached team had ever lost as many as eight games in a season, and no Wildcat team would again lose that many for another 20 years.

At one point, even the possibility of a winning season was up for grabs. Through their first 14 games the Cats' record was a break-even 7-7. A season that began with a great deal of promise was rapidly deteriorating into Rupp's worst nightmare.

But the cagey Rupp rose to the challenge, demonstrating once again why he was already being ranked among the coaching elite. Only on a handful of occasions during his 42-year career at UK did Rupp do a better job of coaching than in the second half of this season. Under Rupp's whip, the Wildcats, once no better than a .500 team, won 10 of their last 11 games, becoming at the end the team everyone

expected from the beginning.

A key reason why Rupp was able to salvage the sinking Wildcat ship was the emergence of sophomores Mel Brewer and Milt Ticco. Both played splendidly, and were, especially during the latter stages of the campaign, among the most consistent of all Wildcats.

The Cats won their first three games, beating up on the UK Alumni (62-25), West Virginia (46-34) and Maryville College (53-14). White, Ticco and Staker claimed scoring honors in each of those three wins.

Then the Cats hit the road, heading West for encounters with Nebraska and Creighton. It was not a successful journey. The Cats dropped both games, falling to Nebraska 40-39 and Creighton 54-45.

After wins over Kansas State (28-25) and Centenary (70-18), the Cats lost five of their next seven games, including one that was decided by the official scorer after the final gun sounded.

Facing Notre Dame in Louisville, the Cats overcame a 36-19 second-half deficit to tie the score at 47-47 and send the game into overtime. Or so the Wildcats thought. As players from both teams waited to begin the extra period, the official scorer summoned the referees and coaches to the scoring table, informed them that the gentleman in charge of the scoreboard had failed to count a late Notre Dame free throw and that the final score should read 48-47 in favor of the Irish.

The Cats limped through the remainder of January, suffering subsequent losses to West Virginia, Tennessee and Xavier. There were a few shining individual performances (Ticco's 26 points against Xavier, White's 15 against Notre Dame), but the overall consistency necessary for victory against quality opponents was lacking.

Lee Huber's superb backcourt play earned him All-America honors in 1941.

All that changed when the calendar page flipped to February. With Rupp ill at home and McBrayer calling the shots, the Cats began their 10-game winning streak by edging Vanderbilt 51-50 in Nashville. Down by six late in the game, the Cats came back to tie it at 46-46 on a bucket by Huber, then took the lead for good on back-to-back baskets by Allen and Farnsley. Brewer led the Cats with 13 points. Allen finished with 10.

Behind some big scoring by Brewer and Allen, the Cats took a pair from Alabama, winning 38-36 and 46-38. Brewer had 14 in the first game, Allen 15 in the rematch.

Tennessee was the only team to throw a scare into the Cats during their final four regular-season games. After falling behind by nine, the Cats battled back to secure a 23-22 lead on a Farnsley free throw. With Marvin Akers tossing in 12 points and King adding eight, the Cats pulled away for a 37-28 win.

As the SEC Tournament got underway, the Cats had two reasons to feel good about their chances of winning a third consecutive title. They were playing their best basketball of the season, and the tourney had been moved from Knoxville to Wildcat-friendly Louisville.

With a highly partisan crowd cheering them on, the Cats waltz through their first two games, beating Ole Miss 62-52 and Tulane 59-30. In the win over Ole Miss, King led the way with 12 points, while Huber and Akers each had 10. King came up big again against Tulane, scoring 15 points to go along with 17 by Farnsley.

The Cats' 39-37 semifinal win over Alabama offered proof (again) that in the world of sports good luck and bad luck eventually balance out. Lady Fate can work against a team, as she did in UK's loss to Notre Dame (the scorekeeper's error), or she can help a team, as she did in the

Alabama game.

With the score tied at 37-37 Huber launched a last-second shot that appeared to be on target, only to be batted out of the basket by an Alabama player. The officials got together, discussed what had happened, then ruled that Huber's bucket would count. That decision gave the Cats a 39-37 win. Huber was the Cats' top scorer with 13 points.

It came as no surprise to anyone that UK and Tennessee were the two teams left to fight it out for the championship. What did come as a surprise, however, was the outcome. This time it was the Vols who silenced a hostile crowd, clipping the Cats 36-33 to claim the tourney hardware.

Huber again led the Cats with 12 points in a losing cause. Both he and Farnsley were all-tournament selections. Huber was also chosen to the All-America team.

Few may have realized it at the time, but in nine short months the world would be at war. Many of the same Wildcat players who fought so hard on the basketball court would be sent to foreign shores to fight a different kind of war, one to preserve this country's freedom.

Sadly, some would never return.

Scrappy Ermal Allen helped the Cats score important SEC wins over Vanderbilt and Alabama.

1941-42

In his great book *Big Blue Machine*, former UK sports information director Russell Rice described in one perfect sentence what happened next.

"On the afternoon of Dec. 7, 1941, Kenny Rollins and Mulford "Muff" Davis walked out of a picture show and into a war."

Only a few hours earlier, the two freshmen were on hand to watch their varsity brethren open the season with a 35-21 win over Miami of Ohio. Led by White's 10 points and seven from Brewer, the Cats hardly broke a sweat against the visitors from Oxford.

It was an uneventful game, an uneventful Saturday night. Then Rollins and Davis exited the movie theater that Sunday afternoon to learn that all hell had broken loose. Japan had bombed Pearl Harbor, the United States was at war, and everyone's future was clouded in uncertainty.

There was almost immediate speculation about the future of sports, both amateur and professional. Many argued in favor of suspending all sports until the war ended. It was their contention that all energy should go toward the daunting task of defeating the Axis powers. Others deemed that to be an unwise option, pointing out that it would only serve to further deflate the spirit of an already reeling nation. President Roosevelt came down strong in favor of allowing sports to continue. It was his belief that sports like Major League Baseball and college basketball would help Americans stay sane during this traumatic period. In the end, Roosevelt's view prevailed.

Over the next four years, the UK roster was often at the mercy of the draft board. Some Wildcat players left for the military prior to the start of a season. Others were called up after the season was underway. A final-game lineup card might look drastically different than the one Rupp turned in for the opener three months earlier.

For UK's next game, a 43-41 loss at Ohio State, Rupp started White and Ticco at forward, Brewer at center, Staker and junior Ken England in the backcourt. That lineup was never set in stone, and Rupp, blessed with a deep bench, never hesitated to make changes. After much early shuffling

of personnel, Rupp inserted veterans Akers and Allen into the starting quintet, replacing England and Ticco. Other Cats who made big contributions during the season included King, Ed Lander, Vince Splane and Lloyd Ramsey.

Following the loss to Ohio State, the Cats won nine of their next 10 games. The lone setback was a 46-40 loss at Tennessee despite an excellent 17-point effort from Allen. The Cats' two biggest wins during that stretch came against Xavier and Georgia Tech, both on the road. It was a pair of Allen freebies that lifted the Cats past Xavier 40-39, and a 20-point performance from Brewer that sparked the 63-53 win over Georgia Tech. In those nine wins, five different Wildcats led the team in scoring, including Brewer, Ticco, Akers, Allen and Lander.

Alabama halted the Cats' winning ways, posting a 41-35 win in Tuscaloosa. That was followed by a 46-43 loss at Notre Dame, thus improving the Irish's record to 7-0 against Rupp. UK led 22-15 at the half, but with the score tied 38-38, Buster Hiller hit a basket to put the Irish in front for good. Notre Dame's Bob Rensberger led all scorers with 17 points. Brewer and Staker had seven each for the Cats.

The Cats avenged a pair of earlier losses in their next two games, beating Alabama 50-34 and Tennessee 36-33. Brewer provided the big numbers for UK, scoring 13 points in each game.

The Cats closed out their regular season with solid home-court wins over Georgia Tech (57-51) and Xavier (44-36). Akers was the top gunner in those two wins, scoring 18 against Tech and 12 against Xavier.

In the SEC Tournament, again played in Louisville, the Cats opened with a 42-36 win over Florida. The Cats led 20-11 at intermission, and were never seriously threatened despite giving what Rupp termed "a listless effort." Staker was the top scorer for UK with 10 points. Akers had nine and Allen eight.

The Cats played much better in their next game, a 59-32 rout of Ole Miss. Ten different Cats hit the scoring column, topped by Brewer's 11 points.

King came off the bench to score 11 points and power the Cats to a come-from-behind 40-31 win over Auburn in semifinal action. After a dismal first half that ended with Auburn leading 18-11, the Cats rallied to even the score at 28-28. Then King took charge, hitting three baskets in a 10-0 run that tamed the Tigers and sent UK into a championship matchup against Alabama. King led the Cats with 11 points, while the steady, aggressive

Allen added nine.

The final was a heart-stopper that featured another gutsy, clutch performance by a Wildcat sub. The hero on this night was England, who came off the bench to lead UK with 13 points. With the score tied at 31-31, a bucket by White and two free throws by England helped the Cats scratch out a 36-34 victory.

Allen was named first-team All-SEC, while teammates King and Akers made the second team.

With almost a month's wait before appearing in the NCAA Tournament for the first time, Rupp agreed to play the Great Lakes Navy squad in a benefit game. Great Lakes raced to a 21-4 lead, then went on to easily handle the Cats 58-47. Brewer, Ticco and England each scored 10 points for UK. Ex-Wildcat All-American Lee Huber had five points for the winners.

On a day that was a Lexington sports fan's dream, the Wildcats tangled with Illinois' celebrated Whiz Kids in the NCAA Eastern Regional in New Orleans. In fact, so much was going on that Lexington radio station WLAP rated the UK-Illini game as no better than third on the priority list. The station planned to carry the Lafayette-Berry state high school quarterfinal game, switch to coverage of Sugar Ray Robinson's fight against Norman Rubio, then cut in on UK's game once the fight ended.

The magnificent Sugar Ray won on a seventh-round TKO. Desite giving his usual sweet performance, Sugar Ray didn't outshine the Cats, who were equally brilliant that night.

With Ticco ringing up 13 points and Staker adding nine, the Cats turned the Whiz Kids into Fizz Kids, nipping the youthful Illini 46-44. Illinois, which started five sophomores and had an 18-4 record, had been favored to win.

Incredibly, after giving one of their best efforts of the season, the Cats stunk up the place one night later, losing to Dartmouth 47-28. Akers had 11 points for the Cats, who ended their season with a 19-6 record.

That night, back in Louisville, Lafayette beat Harlan 44-32 to win the state championship. The leading scorer in the game was a gifted Harlan freshman. He had 16 points.

His name: Wallace "Wah Wah" Jones.

1942-43

With the war now entering its second year, and with the call to military duty taking so many players out of school early, the powers that be made the decision to

Kenny Rollins didn't let the misspelling of Kentucky on his jersey keep him from taking the ball to the bucket against Georgia Tech.

allow incoming freshman to participate on the varsity level. That change was a savior for UK, which lost Allen, White, Staker and King to graduation, and England and Ramsey to the service.

Rupp's starting lineup featured a mixture of youth and experience. Seniors Brewer, Ticco and Akers were joined by sophomores Rollins and Davis. Lander, another proven player, offered support off the bench, along with Paul Noel, Clyde Parker and Bill Barlow.

The Cats were impressive in their first two outings, blasting Cincinnati 61-39 behind Ticco's 15 points, then beating Washington University 45-38 as Brewer led the way with 13.

Then came successive losses to Indiana (58-52) and Ohio State (45-40). The Cats were on top at intermission in both of those games, and were still holding the upper hand during the late going, only to come unglued in the final few minutes. Ticco had 10 against Indiana, Akers 12 in the loss to the Buckeyes.

The slumping Cats needed a breather, which they got in a 64-30 romp past Fort Knox. It was the beginning of an

impressive seven-game winning streak that included successive road wins against Xavier, Tennessee, Georgia and Georgia Tech, followed by UK's first triumph over Notre Dame during the Rupp era.

In Knoxville, the Cats, once again frustrated and confused by Mauer's patient style of play, managed just eight points in the opening half. With only two minutes remaining, the Vols were still in control, holding a 26-20 lead. Then the Cats caught fire. After buckets by Parker and Ticco keyed a charge that cut the Vols' lead to 28-27, Parker accounted for three unanswered points to give the Cats a 30-28 victory. Ticco paced the Cats with 12 points, while Parker finished with nine.

The win gave Rupp a 7-5 edge over Mauer, the man he replaced at Kentucky. In eight of those 12 bitterly fought battles, the outcome was decided by six points or less.

In what turned out to be another escape-from-the-grave performance, the Cats finally broke the Notre Dame jinx, winning 60-55 in Louisville. The Cats trailed by six at the break, then watched as the Irish, led by Rensberger, upped their advantage to 37-27 at the start of the second half.

Refusing to buckle, the Cats battled back to take a 50-49 lead on a three-point play by Akers with nine minutes remaining. The score was tied nine times in the second half, but the Cats, despite losing Akers, Ticco and Rollins to fouls, hung on for the win. Akers was UK's top point-getter with 17. Ticco finished with 16 and Davis 12. Rensberger tied Akers for top honors with 17.

After the game, Akers, known to his teammates as "Big Train," said, "It was a great night for Adolph Rupp. He is now thoroughly convinced that all things come to those who wait."

The Cats dodged another bullet against Vanderbilt, winning 39-38 in their first home appearance in three weeks. Rollins and Akers each had 10 points for the cold-shooting Cats, who connected on just 13 of 67 field goal attempts for 19.4 percent.

Alabama slowed the Wildcat momentum, but only briefly. After losing 41-32 in Tuscaloosa, the Cats came back to win five straight, including a 53-29 trouncing of hated foe Tennessee. Ticco had 17 to head the UK attack. Davis and Rollins each contributed 10.

The Cats also ripped Alabama 67-41, making 28 field goals to only nine by the Tide. Davis had 19 points for the Cats, while Ticco added 14.

For their final regular-season game, the Cats traveled

to Chicago for a marquee matchup against DePaul and All-American center George Mikan. The Cats were in terrible shape heading into the game, especially at the pivot position. Brewer had an injured arm, Lander was out with a broken leg, and third-stringer Carl Althaus had recently been called into the Army Air Corps.

Brewer did play (and scored eight points), but neither he nor the Wildcats could handle Mikan. With 16,000 fans looking on in Chicago Stadium, the Cats went six minutes before making their first field goal, fell behind 19-3 and were never in the game. Mikan scored 18 points to lead DePaul to an easy 53-44 win. Ticco had 13 for the Cats, who, Rupp complained, were victimized by Mikan's constant goal-tending tactics.

The Cats had little trouble in their first two SEC Tournament games, beating Tulane 48-31 and Georgia 59-30. Akers had 17 against the Green Wave, Noel 16 off the bench in the win over Georgia.

In a hard-fought — and costly — semifinal against Mississippi State, Ticco scored 18 and Brewer 11 to push the Cats to a 52-43 win. The Bulldogs pulled to within 37-33 in the second half, but baskets by Noel, Ticco, Davis and Akers turned the momentum back in favor of the Cats. The win was costly because Rollins sustained an injury that prevented him from playing against Tennessee in the championship game.

Mauer's club edged the Cats 33-30 to claim the title and disappoint the Big Blue faithful in Louisville. It was a typical UK-Tennessee struggle. After a pair of Noel free throws gave the Cats a 27-25 advantage, Tennessee answered with eight straight points to earn the win.

The Cats again suffered through a horrendous shooting night, especially in the first half. In those 20 minutes, the Cats made good on just four of 33 attempts.

Brewer led UK with 10 points. Tennessee's Bernie Mehen had a game-high 13 for the Vols. Brewer, Akers and Ticco were named to the all-tournament squad.

The Cats closed out their season with another benefit game against Great Lakes, losing 53-39 in Louisville. The loss gave them a final record of 17-6.

Given the circumstances, it had been a successful year for the Wildcats. But the continuing war effort was exacting such a heavy toll on young manpower that many colleges, including UK, considered shutting down all sports programs until the conflict was over. UK did, in fact, put its football program on hold during the 1943 season.

There was also talk about suspending the basketball program, but Rupp argued against such a move. If there was ever a basketball program that could have used a break, it was Kentucky's. With Ticco, Akers and Brewer having graduated, and Rollins scheduled to go into the service, Rupp was, for the first time, facing a virtually blank roster. But Rupp wanted to march on, saying that he could find enough youngsters to field a competitive team.

And he did. When the next season opened, UK's roster consisted of two sophomores and 15 freshmen. By the time that season ended, those youthful Cats had given Rupp and Big Blue fans one of the most unexpected, successful and inspiring campaigns in UK history.

1943-44

Whenever Rupp was asked to describe this team, the word that popped up most often was "kindergarten." With 15 incoming rookies and two sophomores, this ranks as the youngest team in Wildcat history. Because the players were so young — most were no older than 18 — this was the first of many UK teams to be given a nickname — the "Wildkittens." One of Rupp's favorite terms for describing his

Seventeen-year-old Bob Brannum's rugged, fearless and high-scoring play was a key reason why the unheralded 1943-44 "Wildkittens" finished with a surprising 19-2 record.

UK's Bob Brannum and Adolph Rupp at an All-American dinner with Oklahoma A&M's Henry Iba and Bob Kurland at Toots Shor's restaurant in New York City. Brannum and Kurland were both first-team All-Americans in 1944. At 17, Brannum is the youngest player ever chosen to the All-America first-team.

gang of juveniles was "Beardless Wonders."

The two "old men" were Wilbur Schu, a 6'3" forward from Versailles, and Tom Moseley, a 6'3" guard from Lexington. Those two sophomores were in the starting lineup throughout the season, and were two of the steadiest Wildcats.

Among the rookies were Don Whitehead and Walter Johnson, who, after getting off to terrific starts, were called into the military after playing in only 12 games. What remained was a rag-tag collection of misfits and military rejects that included Jack Tingle, Jack Parkinson and Truitt DeMoisey, younger brother of ex-UK All-American Frenchy DeMoisey. Fortunately for Rupp, those three were outstanding — and durable — basketball players.

However, this team couldn't have achieved what it did (19-2 record, SEC tourney title, third place in the NIT) were it not for the presence of 17-year-old Bob Brannum, a talented 6'5" Kansas cyclone whose game totally lacked either finesse or fear. Brannum was a brawny bruiser, a banger, one of those physical players who seem to thrive best when the action gets down and dirty. The rougher things got, the better he played. But Brannum also knew how to put the ball in the basket, and would, by season's end, distinguish himself as a most-prolific scorer. His 12.1

scoring average was the best since that of the great Leroy Edwards in 1934-35.

Brannum had 11 and Moseley eight as Rupp's young Cats opened with a 51-18 trouncing of Fort Knox. Brannum had 15 in a 54-40 win over Berea, then Johnson came through with 13 as the Cats ripped Indiana 66-41.

The Cats notched a second straight win over a Big Ten foe, pulling off a 40-28 upset at Ohio State. Whitehead had 14 and Brannum 13 for the Cats, whose solid defense limited Buckeye All-American (and future NBA great) Arnie Risen to two points.

After demolishing Cincinnati 58-30, the Cats lost a 43-41 thriller to Illinois when Howard Judson hit the game-winner with 40 seconds left. Judson and Brannum tied for scoring honors with 15 points each.

To virtually everyone's surprise, the Cats wouldn't lose again until the semifinal round of the NIT more than two months later. Along the way, there were stunning upsets of St. John's and Notre Dame, and a revenge win over the Illini. A season that many had projected to be a dud turned out to be a shining diamond.

Taking on St. John's in front of 18,179 hostile Madison Square Garden fans, the Cats grabbed control early, led 22-17 at intermission and went on to win 44-38. Brannum had 12 to lead the Cats, while Tingle added 10. St. John's

was paced by Dick McGuire's 16 points. (McGuire's brother Al would later become well-known to Big Blue fans.)

It was a three-point play by Brannum with 37 ticks left that lifted the Cats to their 55-54 win over Notre Dame. The Cats led 29-26 at the half, then watched as the Irish fought back to take the lead in the second stanza. With his team trailing 54-52, Brannum made a basket in close and drew a foul from Notre Dame's George Todorovich. Brannum sank the free toss to give Rupp his second consecutive win over the Irish. Johnson paced UK with 15 points, Brannum had 14 and Tingle 12. Todorovich led Notre Dame with 15.

In their rematch against Illinois, the Cats, behind Brannum's 16 points, broke open a close game late in the second half and edged away for a 51-40 win. The game was tied three times, the last at 34-34, before the Cats assumed command. Tingle continued his excellent play, scoring 12 points.

There were a few scares during the season, most notably a 38-35 comeback win against lowly DePauw at home, but most of the Cats' wins came without much trouble. UK beat Carnegie Tech 61-14, Wright Field 61-28, Ohio University 51-35 and Fort Knox (again) 76-48. Against Fort Knox, the Cats hit just 30 of 108 field goal attempts for 28 percent. Afterward, Rupp said, "The boys were definitely off the beam."

Superb play wasn't the only factor contributing to UK's success this season. The schedule was a big help. Due to the war and the uncertainty surrounding college athletics at the time, the Cats didn't face an SEC opponent until the postseason tournament. Not having to invade such traditional enemy territories as Knoxville, Tuscaloosa and Nashville provided the Cats with something of a "breather" schedule compared to what they typically would have faced.

The Cats' first meeting with a conference rival came against Georgia in the SEC tourney opener at Louisville. Brannum and Tingle each scored 12 points and Parkinson added 10 as the Cats advanced with a 57-29 win.

Tingle scored 13 and sub Rudy Yessin had seven to lead the Cats to a 55-28 semifinal win over LSU. Facing Tulane in the title game, the Cats, with Parkinson exploding for 27 points, captured their fourth tourney crown in six years with a 62-46 victory. Brannum chipped in with 15 for the winners. Parkinson, Brannum and Tingle were named to the All-SEC team.

Immediately after winning the SEC Tournament UK accepted an offer to play in the NIT. The Cats' first-round foe was Utah, a club that didn't strike fear into Rupp's heart.

"I think we'll be all right," Rupp said. "I understand that Utah hasn't got one of those out-sized centers that Phog Allen calls mezzanine-peeping goons. Such being the case, we'll be in the ball game."

But after a 16-day layoff the rust was apparent in the Cats' hard-earned 46-38 victory over the Utes. The game was close throughout, and had it not been for another big effort by Parkinson, the Cats likely would have fallen. Parkinson ended up with 20 to lead all scorers, while Brannum had 11. Utah was led by Herb Wilkinson with 15 and future NBA great Arnie Ferrin with 13.

St. John's halted the Cats' magnificent winning streak at 13 with a 48-45 semifinal win. St. John's battled back to overcome an eight-point Wildcat lead and tie the score at 41-41. The score was later tied at 43-43 and 45-45 before Don Wehr scored to put St. John's in front for good. Schu and Tingle led UK with 15 and 11 points, respectively. The St. John's defense limited Brannum and Parkinson to a combined total of 11 points.

In the consolation game against Oklahoma A&M, the Cats managed to win 45-29 even though Brannum went scoreless. Tingle had 18 for UK, while 7-foot Bob Kurland had 14 for the Aggies.

Brannum joined Kurland and McGuire on the first-team All-America squad, thus becoming the youngest player to earn that honor. Rupp was also honored at the end of the season. He was elected to the Athletic Foundation Collegiate Basketball Hall of Fame.

This season turned out to be Brannum's shining moment in a Wildcat uniform. Once the NIT had concluded he and his wife returned home to Kansas. After spending time in the military, Brannum would rejoin the Wildcats, only to discover that someone had moved in to take his place.

Alex Groza.

1944-45

No one was going to mistake Alex Groza for Leroy Edwards or Bob Brannum. For one thing, Groza, at 6'7", was taller than either of those two other great Wildcat centers. And unlike his muscular, rugged predecessors, Groza was rail thin, smooth and extremely agile for a big man. His game was more about grace and finesse; theirs was about power and destruction.

Not that Groza wasn't tough. He was. He had to be, growing up in the industrial town of Martins Ferry, Ohio, and being the youngest of four athletic-minded brothers,

Alex Groza led the 1944-45 team to 11 straight wins before being called into the Army. He returned to UK after the war and was at the center of some of UK's all-time greatest teams.

one of whom, Lou, was the Hall of Fame place-kicker for the Cleveland Browns. In that setting, he had to be tough just to make his presence known.

But unlike Edwards and Brannum, Groza was a very polished player. He had a variety of slick moves around the bucket, and was very adept at tipping the ball into the basket. Groza, like his future teammate Ralph Beard, was a modern-day player who just happened to play in the 1940s.

He was also a prolific scorer who, by the time he left UK in 1949, was the school's all-time leading scorer with 1,744 points, a three-time All-American and twice the NCAA Tournament's MVP.

All that despite a freshman season in which he played in just 10 games before being called into the Army. However, in that brief period, Groza offered Wildcat fans a sneak peek into the future by giving a series of high-level performances.

Groza couldn't have come to UK at a better time. Bran-

num was gone, taking with him his 12.1 points-per-game scoring clip. So was Moseley, who was booted off the team for missing practice. That left Tingle, Parkinson and Schu as the only remaining starters from the previous year's club. Fortunately for Rupp, Groza, along with fellow freshmen Johnny Stough and Kenton "Dutch" Campbell, were more than able to step in and fill the missing holes. Groza took over Brannum's spot in the pivot and Stough replaced Moseley in the backcourt.

From the very beginning, Groza's season was clouded by the possibility of military duty. On the day the Cats opened the season with a 56-23 win over Fort Knox, Groza was in Columbus, Ohio, taking his physical. He managed to get back to Lexington in time to score nine points in his Wildcat debut. Tingle had 14 in that win, while Parkinson added 12.

Behind the hot shooting of Schu, the Cats racked up easy wins over Berea (56-32), Cincinnati (66-24) and Indiana (61-43). Schu, a southpaw, had 13 in the win over Berea and 16 against the Hoosiers. Two days after UK defeated Indiana, Groza received his notice to report for military induction on Jan. 4, 1945.

The Cats' first test came against an Ohio State club that had Risen and Don Grate, two outstanding players. But with Groza scoring 16 points and Tingle and Parkinson 15 each, the Cats fought their way to a 53-48 overtime win. Grate and Risen combined for 30 points for the Buckeyes.

More tough games followed for the Cats, including a 50-46 win over Wyoming, a 45-44 win over Temple on Groza's last-second basket and a 62-52 overtime win over Long Island University in which the Cats rallied from a 44-29 deficit to earn the victory and remain unbeaten. Groza, by now virtually unstoppable, had 27 against Temple and 25 against LIU, including six of the Cats' 11 points in the overtime.

Groza had 25 in a 59-46 win over Ohio University, then did not play in his team's 75-6 win over Arkansas State. However, because his induction date had been pushed back to Jan. 15, he was able to help the Cats beat Michigan State 66-35, scoring 14 points in his final game of the season.

Parkinson's 23 points were tops for the Cats.

Campbell took over the center position, and although he was a solid performer, he was no Groza. The impact of Groza's absence was felt immediately. Without their leading scorer (Groza was averaging 16.5 when he went into the Army), the Cats fell to Tennessee 35-34 in Knoxville.

Tingle picked up some of the slack, scoring 21 points in each of the Cats' next two games, a 64-58 win over Georgia

Tech and a 59-58 overtime loss to Notre Dame. The Irish prevailed in that game when future coach Johnny Dee sank the game-winner.

Groza's absence was felt most keenly in a rematch with Michigan State, a team the Cats crushed by 31 points earlier in the season. Without Groza the Cats proved to be easy prey, dropping a 66-50 decision to the home-standing Spartans. Parkinson had 17 to lead the Cats.

The Cats regrouped to win their final three regular-season games, beating Tennessee 40-34, Ohio University 61-38 and Cincinnati 65-35 to finish with a 17-3 record.

In their SEC tourney opener, the Cats, led by Parkinson's 15 points, pounded Florida 57-35. Buddy Parker came off the bench to score 12 for the Cats, while Campbell contributed 11.

Tingle knocked in 14 points and Schu had 11 as the Cats easily handled LSU 68-37 to advance to a semifinal matchup against dangerous Alabama. In the only meeting between the two teams that season, the Cats, after an early struggle, walked away with a 52-41 victory. Parkinson's 14 points led a balanced UK scoring attack that also saw Campbell and Tingle hit double figures with 13 and 10 points, respectively.

Pitted against Tennessee in the championship game, the Cats battled their way to a 39-35 win to claim another SEC tourney title. Parkinson again topped the Cats with 15 points. Tingle finished with nine. Parkinson, Tingle and Campbell were named to the all-tournament team.

For their NCAA Tournament opener, the Cats faced a familiar, tough opponent — Ohio State. In the first meeting between the two clubs, won by the Cats 53-48 in overtime, Groza had 16 points. This time around, though, it was a different story. The Cats, forced into battle without their top gun, fell behind early and were never able to catch up. The Buckeyes, with Grate scoring 15 points, got their revenge with a 45-37 win.

The disappointed Cats beat Tufts 66-56 in the consolation game to end their season with a 22-4 mark. Schu led the Cats with 21 points.

The season had been a good one, and likely would have been even better had Groza been on board all the way. It would be two years before he again slipped on a UK jersey and did battle as a Wildcat.

The war would end before the 1945-46 season rolled around. For the first time in four long years Americans were able to breathe a sigh of relief, and Big Blue fans could once again turn their full attention to their beloved Wildcats.

What they were about to see would be dazzling and spectacular. For in the next eight years, University of Kentucky basketball would rise to its greatest heights.

Sadly, five former Wildcats would not return from the war. Jim King, Mel Brewer, Walter Johnson, Jim Goforth, and Ken England were among those U.S. soldiers killed in combat. It was their hard work and sweat that helped give rise to a basketball empire. It was their lives that helped a nation preserve its freedoms.

1945-46

In September 1945, two exceptional athletes arrived at the University of Kentucky. One was 6'4", rugged as a mountain man and multi-talented; the other was 5'10", quicker than a lightning bolt and fiercely competitive.

"Wah Wah" Jones and Ralph Beard.

Although the seeds of greatness had already been planted by the players who had preceded them, it would be upon the shoulders of these two native Kentuckians that the Wildcat program would rise to a different level. Jones and Beard, perhaps more than any other Wildcats, were responsible for putting the basketball program on what Rupp would later call the "Glory Road."

During the four years Jones and Beard played, UK had a 130-10 record, won two NCAA championships, one NIT title, an Olympic gold medal, had a 55-0 record against Southeastern Conference opponents and 27 wins with margins in excess of 40 points.

It should be noted that the UK program wasn't exactly languishing when Jones and Beard arrived. Quite the contrary. During Rupp's first 15 years at UK, his teams had won 80 percent of their games and he had produced seven All-America players.

Despite that success, none of those teams were as powerful or dominant as the ones led by Jones and Beard. Earlier Wildcat teams won; the Jones-Beard teams destroyed.

World events played a hand in UK's fortunes. The end of World War II saw the return of several players who, when combined with the players already on the scene, would provide Rupp with his deepest and most-talented teams. Two of those players — Bob Brannum and Jim Jordan — would find the well of talent to be so deep that they transferred to other schools. And Jack Parkinson, an All-American in 1946, was relegated to a substitute's role when he returned to UK.

The opening-night lineup against Fort Knox featured

Members of the 1945-46 NIT championship team included, kneeling, Manager Humzey Yessin, Muff Davis, Buddy Parker, Ralph Beard, Jack Parkinson and Bill Sturgill. Standing, trainer Frank Mann, Elmer Gilb, Jack Tingle, Dutch Campbell, Adolph Rupp, Wah Wah Jones, Wilbur Schu and Joe Holland.

forwards Tingle and Joe Holland, center Malcolm McMullen, and guards Parkinson and Beard. Schu missed the Cats' first four games because of scholastic difficulties, while Jones, an All-SEC football performer and quite possibly the finest all-around athlete to ever wear a UK uniform, didn't crack the lineup until the third game. This became a standard routine throughout Jones' career. After ending the football season against Tennessee on a Saturday, Jones would then join the basketball squad at practice the following Monday. (Beard also played football, starting at halfback in UK's first three games. But after injuring his shoulder, Beard gave up his gridiron career, choosing instead to concentrate on basketball.)

The Cats cruised through their first seven games, winning by an average margin of 23 points. Tingle was superb during that stretch, leading the club in scoring on four occasions. Only two teams, Western Ontario and Oklahoma, managed to make things interesting. But the Cats simply had too

much weaponry and too much ammunition for their upset-minded opponents. Parkinson came up big in both wins, scoring 17 in a 51-42 win over Western Ontario and 12 in a 43-33 win over Oklahoma. Beard also had a dozen points against the Sooners, while Jones added 10.

The Cats' most-impressive early showing came in a 73-59 win over St. John's in Madison Square Garden. Thanks to a 27-point effort from Harry Boykoff, St. John's stayed close until the final minutes. But the Cats refused to cave in, taking charge for good when Tingle and Schu wrapped a free throw apiece around a Parkinson layup. Schu came off the bench to lead his team in scoring with 18 points. Other Cats in double figures included Parkinson (14), Tingle (12) and Campbell (11), who also came up big in a sub's role.

A late cold spell proved fatal in the Cats' next game, a 53-45 loss to Temple in Philadelphia. Leading 27-26, the Cats went the next five minutes without a field goal. By the time the dry spell ended, Temple was holding a comfortable

40-27 lead. Parkinson paced UK with 14 points.

After routine wins over Ohio University (57-48) and Ft. Benning (81-25), the Cats secured their first-ever win at Michigan State, coming out on top 55-44. Beard's 18 points led the Cats in that victory.

On Jan. 15, 1946, the big news in Kentucky was the naming of Paul "Bear" Bryant as the new Wildcat football coach. Before the ink had dried on Bryant's contract, Rupp found himself fighting off charges that he dominated athletics at UK. Rupp blamed Southern sportswriters for "seeking to cause a breach" between him and Bryant even before the two men met.

The Cats were derailed only once more during the remainder of the season, that coming in a 56-47 loss to Notre Dame in Louisville. The Irish led 28-24 at the half, then pulled away for the win. Jones had 16 for the Cats and Parkinson added 11. Beard was held scoreless. All-American Vince Boryla led Notre Dame with a game-high 18.

The SEC Tournament, once again held in Louisville, was a laugher, with UK winning four games by a total margin of 134 points. The fallen included Auburn (69-24), Florida (69-32), Alabama (59-30) and LSU (59-36). Those wins, along with six during the regular season, were the start of UK's total domination of Southeastern Conference action. The Cats would not lose again in league play until 1950.

Parkinson was the Cats' top scorer in the tourney with 56 points. He was named to the all-tournament team along with Tingle, Jones and Beard.

In a rematch against Temple prior to the NCAA Tournament, Jones scored 17, Schu 13 and Beard nine as the Cats came from behind to beat the Owls 54-43 in Louisville.

Freshman Ralph Beard's late free throw gave the Cats a spine-tingling 46-45 victory over Rhode Island in the championship game of the 1946 NIT in Madison Square Garden.

The Cats trailed 18-9, and were on the short end of a 28-25 score at the half, before taking charge in the final 20 minutes.

In the NIT, UK opened with a 77-53 victory over Arizona. The Cats broke to a 43-22 lead at the half and were never challenged. Jones headed a balanced attack with 16 points. Parkinson had 14, Tingle 13, and Beard and Schu nine each.

Three late buckets by Tingle and one by Parkinson enabled the Cats to break away from a 51-51 deadlock and beat West Virginia 59-51 in semifinal action. The game was tied on 14 occasions before Tingle took over. Tingle led the Cats with 16 points, while Beard had 15 and Parkinson 10.

That win set up a championship game against Rhode Island, a pairing that most experts felt would result in a UK blowout. At tip-off the Cats were 11-point favorites.

UK raced to a 23-16 lead, and appeared to have things under control. However, a late Rhode Island surge gave the Rams a 27-26 lead at intermission. The lead changed hands several times in the second half, with neither team able to manage more than a three-point advantage. With Rhode Island leading 45-44, Campbell sank a free throw to draw the Cats even. Moments later, with a Madison Square Garden crowd of 18,475 looking on, it was the gum-chewing, precocious freshman Beard who stepped to the charity stripe and sank the free throw that gave UK a 46-45 victory and the school its first NIT title. The win also gave the Cats a 28-2 record, the most wins ever by a UK team.

Beard and Jones accounted for half of UK's points, scoring 13 and 10, respectively. Schu added nine.

Parkinson, the team's leading scorer with an 11.3 average, earned All-America honors. He then went into the

military, and upon his return to UK found himself relegated to the bench.

UK's scoring balance showed in the final averages. Jones finished with a 9.7 clip, Beard 9.3 and Tingle 9.2.

The next season would see the return of several familiar faces, including Groza, Brannum, Rollins and Barker. The pieces for the Fabulous Five were beginning to come together.

1946-47

Alex Groza returned from World War II bigger, stronger and, like all veterans, more mature. At 6'7", and possessing tremendous skills around the basket, Groza would anchor the Wildcats for the next three seasons. By the time he left, he would be UK's all-time leading scorer.

Two other military veterans returned as well — smooth and steady guard Kenny Rollins and slick-passing forward Cliff Barker, who had sharpened his ball-handling skills during his time as a prisoner in a German POW camp.

Rollins and Beard gave UK a rock-solid backcourt while Groza patrolled the middle with absolute authority. The two forward spots, however, weren't quite so cut and dried. Several players filled those postions at different times during the season. Barker, Tingle, Joe Holland and freshman Jim Line, who is said to be the first Wildcat to shoot a one-handed shot, all got their share of playing time. (Of course, once Jones worked out the football kinks and got into basketball shape, one of the forward spots became his.)

This club, the first UK team to win 30 games, was labeled a "vaunted basketball machine" by one sportswriter. In truth, a strong argument could be made that this team was better than either of the two more-celebrated NCAA championship clubs that followed. (Had Rupp opted for this team to play in the NCAA rather than the more prestigious NIT, it's likely that UK would have one more championship trophy.) After all, it was this team that had All-Americans Brannum and Jordan sitting on the bench. It was this team that had such depth that it could win 34 games even though one of its best players (Jones) was slowed throughout the season by a series of injuries.

Tingle, Holland, Groza, Rollins and Beard comprised the starting lineup in an opening-night 78-36 win over Indiana Central. Beard and Holland had 15 each for the Cats.

Jones drew his first start in the Cats' fifth game, a 65-35 win over Idaho, but departed just two minutes into the action after spraining an ankle. Beard had 14 points and Groza 12, but it was Barker's ball-handling skills that caught the attention of sportswriter Babe Kimbrough, who

wrote that the Wildcat forward "could do everything with a basketball except make it talk."

DePaul and St. John's, two clubs expected to put up a tough struggle, were easy prey for the rampaging Cats. Facing DePaul in Louisville, the Cats, behind Beard's 15 points and 10 each from Groza and Holland, stormed to an easy 65-45 win. Against St. John's in Madison Square Garden, Holland and Rollins each had 14 points as the Cats broke away in the second half to win convincingly 70-50. Beard chipped in with 13, while Groza had 12.

Jones scored four points in his first game back, a 75-34 win over Baylor. Beard again led UK with 12 points. Rollins and Brannum each contributed 11.

The Cats shattered the school's old scoring record in their next outing, a 96-24 win over Wabash. All 14 Cats

Rugged forward Wah Wah Jones is arguably the greatest all-around athlete to ever play at the University of Kentucky.

Adolph Rupp was all smiles after five of his players dominated the 1947 SEC all-tournament first team. The honored Wildcats are Wah Wah Jones, Jack Tingle, Joe Holland, Ralph Beard and Kenny Rollins.

scored, led by Beard's 18 points.

With a record of 11-0, the Cats headed to New Orleans to take on Oklahoma A&M in the Sugar Bowl. In a classic matchup of contrasting styles, Henry Iba's patient Aggies shocked the run-oriented Cats 37-31. The Aggies took the lead late in the first half and never trailed again. Rollins was the Cats' leading scorer with eight points.

After beating Ohio University (46-36), Dayton (70-29) and Vanderbilt (82-30), the Cats traveled to Knoxville to tangle with Tennessee. Tingle and Beard each scored 13 to lead the Cats to a hard-earned 54-39 victory. Following the game, Tennessee coach John Mauer said this was "the finest UK team I've ever seen."

Rupp's 300th win as UK coach came in Athens, where the Cats beat Georgia 84-45. Beard had 19, Holland 14

and Groza 10. Rupp's record now stood at 300-65.

Two of the Cats' finest efforts came in back-to-back wins over a pair of teams that traditionally proved troublesome — Michigan State and Notre Dame. In an 86-36 thrashing of the Spartans, it was Brannum who led the way with 14 points. Ironically, when the two teams met again in less than a year, Brannum would be wearing a Spartan uniform.

The expected down-to-the-wire tussle with Notre Dame never materialized. Groza hit a free throw, Beard followed with a bucket and the Cats were on their way to a 60-30 win. Groza finished with 18 points and Beard had 17.

Although still hampered by a knee injury, Jones came off the bench to score nine points and spark the Cats to a 48-37 win at Alabama. After a tense first half that featured three ties, Jones scored on a close-in bucket to put the Cats

on top for good. Rollins paced the Cats with 14 points.

DePaul obtained a measure of revenge, beating the Cats 53-47 in Chicago. It was DePaul's defense that made the difference. Neither Beard nor Tingle managed to score a single basket against the inspired Demons. Groza was the game's top scorer with 21 points. DePaul was led by Whitey Kachan with 18 and Ed Mikan (George's younger brother) with 15.

The Cats closed out the regular season with six straight wins, giving them a 27-2 mark heading into the SEC Tournament in Louisville. No one expected the Cats to be seriously challenged in the tourney, and they weren't. The average margin of victory in the four games was 43.5 points.

Line had his best game of the season in the opener, coming off the bench to score 20 points in a 98-29 win over Vanderbilt. The 98 points represented a new high for UK and the SEC tourney. Beard had 19 for the Cats, while Jones and Buddy Parker each had 12.

A healthy Jones continued to play well, hitting for 18 points in the Cats' 84-18 win over Auburn. Holland and Parker scored 14 apiece and Jones had 12 as the Cats moved into the championship game by trouncing Georgia Tech 75-53. With Rollins scoring 16 and Holland 15, the Cats captured the crown with a 55-38 win over Tulane.

Tingle, Holland, Jones, Rollins and Beard were named to the All-SEC first team, while Groza was chosen to the second five.

In a tune-up prior to the NIT, the Cats, behind 15 points from Groza and 13 from Jones, demolished Temple 68-29 in Louisville.

A few days later Rupp named the players who would make up the traveling squad for the NIT trip to New York. When Brannum learned that his name wasn't on the list, he immediately announced that he would leave UK at the end of the quarter. Brannum left, eventually transferring to Michigan State, where he would soon cross swords with his old teammates.

In the NIT opener against Long Island University, the Cats, after blowing an 11-point halftime lead, rode the clutch play of Jones to a 66-62 victory. With the score knotted at 62-62, Jones put in the go-ahead bucket, then stole the ball and hit Tingle for an easy layup that sealed the win. Jones had 20 points to lead the Cats. Beard finished with 16 and Groza 10.

It was while the team was in New York that rumors began to swirl that Jordan, Line and Holland were planning

to transfer after the season ended. When asked about it, all three players offered staunch denials.

The Cats' 60-42 semifinal win over N.C. State was a much closer game than the final score indicates. The score was tied 20-20 at intermission, and the underdog Wolfpack actually went in front 24-23 during the early moments of the second half. But that would be N.C. State's last gasp. A short jumper by Rollins put the Cats back on top and sparked a second-half explosion that doomed the Wolfpack. Beard again topped the Cats with 15 points.

But this season, glorious as it was, was destined to end on a sour note — a 49-45 loss to Utah in the championship game. Much like the previous year's title game, this one wasn't expected to be close. Utah was fortunate to even be in the final game, having gotten there by the slimmest of margins — a one-point win over Duquesne and a two-point win over West Virginia. UK went into the game heavily favored to win.

But Utah bucked the odds by controlling the tempo and never allowing the run-oriented Wildcats to shift into overdrive. The Utes led all the way, and thanks to excellent free throw shooting and big buckets at crucial times by Arnie Ferrin and Vern Gardner, they were able to shock the record Garden crowd of 18,493 with the big upset.

Groza and Line led UK with 12 points each. But Beard, UK's leading scorer for the season, would suffer through a nightmare game in which he managed only a single free throw.

This team finished with a 34-3 record. Beard and Groza were chosen first-team All-Americans, and Tingle was named to the second team. Also, the New York sportswriters voted Beard as the most outstanding visiting player to perform in Madison Square Garden that season.

Record-wise, this had been the best Wildcat team to date. However, good as it was, there was an even better team on the horizon.

Coming up: The Fabulous Five.

1947-48

Beard, Jones, Groza, Barker, Rollins... Wildcat fans learn those names before they learn the presidents.

The Fabulous Five.

This is UK's most-legendary team, the one that set a standard of excellence that all future Wildcat teams would be measured against. Thirty-six wins (still a school record) and just three losses, an NCAA championship and later that sum-

The 1947-48 national championship club is still considered by many to be UK's greatest team.
Members inlcuded, sitting, Adolph Rupp, Johnny Stough, Ralph Beard, Kenny Rollins, Cliff Barker, Dale Barnstable and
assistant coach Harry Lancaster. Standing, manager Humzey Yessin, Garland Townes, Jim Jordan, Joe Holland,
Alex Groza, Wah Wah Jones, Jim Line, Roger Day and trainer Bud Berger.

mer a gold medal in the 1948 Olympic Games in London.

Despite its legendary status, it wasn't until UK's 12th game of the season, against Miami of Ohio on the night of Jan. 5, 1948, that Beard, Jones, Groza, Rollins and Barker — The Fabulous Five — finally came together as a unit.

Prior to that night, Rupp had been groping for a starting combination, shuffling a variety of players around the core trio of Beard, Groza and Rollins. Jones, as was always the case, earned his usual forward spot after working out the football kinks. However, it wasn't until Rupp inserted the clever Barker into the forward position opposite Jones that Rupp had what he was looking for — a basketball machine that cut down foes with alarming ease.

It was a unique team, if for no other reason than the vast age differences among the players. Barker and Rollins were both nearing 30, while Jones and Beard were barely out of their teens. Some players were married and had families; others were single. Despite those differences, they had one thing in common — they could play.

Joining Rollins, Groza and Beard in the opening-night starting lineup against Indiana Central were forwards Line and Barnstable. The Cats romped 80-41. Beard was the leading scorer with 17 points. In all, 16 of the 19 Cats who saw action hit the scoring column.

When Jones concluded his gridiron duties, which were extended due to the Cats' appearance in the Great Lakes Bowl, he joined the basketball team, debuting with three

points in a 74-50 win over DePaul.

Beard injured his hip in a 67-31 win over Cincinnati, causing him to miss his only game in four years at UK, a 79-37 smashing of Xavier. Holland had 12 against Cincinnati, Groza 18 against Xavier.

With Beard still hobbled by his injury, and Jones sidelined with an injured foot, the unbeaten Cats (7-0) hit the road for a game against Temple in Philadelphia. The Owls took advantage of a less-than-healthy Beard and an absent Jones, upsetting UK 60-59 in a thriller that went down to the final seconds. Nelson Bobb was the Cat-killer, hitting a bucket and a free throw to erase a 58-57 deficit and put Temple ahead 60-58. Rollins drew a foul with only seconds left, sending him to the charity stripe with a pair of free throws that could send the game into overtime. The senior guard hit the first free toss, but when the second one rimmed out, the Owls had their win. Groza had 16 points for the Cats. Temple's Eddie Lerner claimed game-high honors with 22.

Rollins redeemed himself in the Cats' next game, scoring 16 in a 52-40 win over St. John's in Madison Square Garden. Jones had 15 in a 65-23 thumping of Creighton, and Beard, healthy again, came off the bench to score 18 in a 98-41 pasting of Western Ontario.

The quintet that became immortalized as the "Fabulous Five" finally came together against Miami (Ohio) in the first of six straight road games. It wasn't a particularly striking effort. The Cats won 67-53, with Barker and Beard each scoring 13 points.

Next up for the Cats was Michigan State and ex-teammate Bob Brannum. The Spartans, fueled by a brilliant 23-point performance from an inspired Brannum, nearly pulled off the upset. But with Rollins hitting for three points inside the final 45 seconds and Barnstable coming through with seven clutch points, the Cats managed to edge Brannum and Company 47-45. Rollins finished with 12 points, while Groza, clearly outplayed by Brannum, had 10.

The Cats stumbled only once the rest of the way, falling 64-55 at Notre Dame. The Irish led 34-32 at the half, then steadily pulled away in the final 20 minutes to hand the Cats their second loss of the season. Groza and Beard paced the Cats with 23 and 17, respectively.

The Cats blitzed through their remaining nine regular-season games. Included among the fallen was Temple, an earlier conquerer of the Cats. In the revenge match, Jones and Beard each scored 12 points and Groza added 11 as the Cats posted an easy 58-38 victory.

The SEC tourney featured more of the same, four UK wins by a total of 111 points. Line had 22 in the opener, an 87-31 win over Florida, then Groza came through with 15 to lead his club past LSU 63-47 in quarterfinal action. Jones scored 18 in a 70-47 win over Tennessee, the school he almost attended (and his brother Hugh did attend).

In the championship game, Rollins had 14, Groza 13 and Beard 11 as the Cats, after leading 26-25 at intermission, broke away in the second half to beat Georgia Tech 54-43.

All five Wildcat starters earned All-SEC recognition. Jones, Beard and Rollins were named to the first team, Groza and Barker to the second five.

Prior to the NCAA Tournament, True magazine named Beard Player of the Year for the second time. Beard also was named first-team All-American, while Groza was voted on the second-team.

After Jones scored 19 points in an easy 76-53 win over Columbia in the NCAA tourney opener, the Cats found themselves up against Holy Cross, a red-hot team that had won 19 straight and was unbeaten that season in Madison Square Garden. The Crusaders had several formidable weapons, most notably sophomore guard Bob Cousy, who came in averaging just under 20 points per game. But Cousy would never be a factor, thanks to the brilliant defensive effort by Rollins. The Cats' senior captain, with occasional relief from Barnstable, limited Cousy to a lone field goal and just six points overall.

After an early struggle, Beard led a scoring burst that put the Cats in front for good. The UK lead swelled to 14 before Holy Cross managed to trim the difference to four. Then, following a timeout, UK reeled off seven unanswered points — five by Jones and two by Groza — to put the game away. The final score was 60-52.

Groza had been brilliant, scoring 23 points, while the duo of Beard and Jones added 13 and 12, respectively. Rollins, the defensive wizard, also contributed eight points.

The championship game against Baylor was almost anticlimactic. UK jumped to a 24-7 lead, then went on to win 58-42 and take home the school's first NCAA championship trophy. Groza, the tourney's MVP, had 14 points to lead UK. Beard had 12, while Jones and Rollins each had nine.

Following the regular season, UK participated in the Olympic Trials, which were also held in Madison Square Garden. With Beard scoring 22 points and Jones adding 19, UK scorched Louisville 91-57, then followed that win

by once again easily handling Baylor 77-59 behind Groza's 33-point outburst.

In the final game against the AAU champion Phillips 66ers, a game some called "the greatest of all-time," UK blew a late lead and lost 53-49. Seven-foot center Bob Kurland hit three crucial buckets inside the final minutes to help seal UK's doom. UK was also hampered by the absence of Barker (broken nose) and Jones (fouls). Beard carried the Cats, giving an electrifying 23-point performance to lead all scorers.

After the game, Phillips coach Bud Browning said, "that little Beard. He is absolutely the best I ever saw." Browning also offered his assessment of the Wildcats, calling them "the greatest team we faced all year."

As a result of this tournament, the five Wildcat starters were members of the 14-player U.S. Olympic team. In London, the U.S. team won eight straight to capture the gold medal. Groza was the team's leading scorer with 76 points.

1948-49

With four starters returning (only Rollins was gone), there was no doubt that Kentucky was the odds-on favorite to repeat as national champs. Barnstable, a 6-3 junior, easily moved into Rollins' guard spot opposite Beard, while Line and junior Walt Hirsch were usually the first ones off the bench.

Rupp's Wildcats didn't disappoint the experts. Only a handful of teams were capable of staying close. In all, only three teams played UK to within 10 points. And only one team, St. Louis, was able to knock off the Cats. The Billikens upset UK 42-40 in the final game of the Sugar Bowl tournament in New Orleans.

Beard scored 20 as the Cats kicked off the season by smashing Indiana Central 74-38. Their second game, against DePaul, was billed as a "real test" by Rupp. It wasn't. Beard and Barnstable each scored 15 and Groza added 12 as the Cats won easily 67-36.

It wasn't until game five that Rupp's real test warning came true. Squaring off against Holy Cross in front of 14,000 Boston Garden fans (one of whom tried to start a fight with Rupp), the Cats built a big early lead then hung on down the stretch to claim a 51-48 win. Groza paced the Cats with 17, Jones had 13 and Beard 11. Cousy led Holy Cross with 11.

Two nights later in Madison Square Garden, the Cats held St. John's to only nine field goals en route to a 57-30 victory. Groza topped the Cats with 21 points. Jones added 15.

In their 42-40 loss to St. Louis, the Cats blew a nine-point halftime lead, then were beaten on a late basket by

the Billikens' Louis Lehman. The highly anticipated battle between big men Groza and Ed Macauley ended in a virtual standoff. Groza finished with 13 points, one better than Macauley.

Upset-minded Bowling Green came within a bucket of handing the Cats their second straight setback. Only the late free throw accuracy of Beard and Hirsch enabled the Cats to come away with a 63-61 win. Beard had 20 for the Cats.

It was at this stage of the season that Groza began to put up huge numbers. He led the club in scoring in 13 of UK's final 15 regular-season games. Groza became virtually unstoppable, scoring 31 against Vanderbilt, 30 against Bradley, 34 against Tennessee and a UK/SEC record 38 against Georgia. This stretch of high-scoring performances, unmatched in UK history, propelled Groza past predecessors Edwards and Brannum and earned him his standing as one of the greatest Wildcat pivotmen of all-time.

Groza's hot streak also propelled the Cats to a string of easy victories, beginning with a 66-51 win at Tennessee. Georgia Tech and DePaul did manage to make things interesting for awhile, but both eventually fell by identical 56-45 scores. Beard had 16 in each game, while Groza's 18 led the scoring against DePaul.

Although Groza had clearly established himself as the dominant scorer, he was by no means the lone Wildcat inflicting damage on opponents. One of the strong points of this team was its balanced scoring. In nine of UK's final 15 games, at least three Wildcat players hit double figures. Four players hit for double digits against Georgia Tech, and five did it in the first of two wins against Xavier.

The Cats received only two minor scares during the remainder of the regular campaign. Bradley battled the Cats hard, but fell 62-52. The Braves never found a cure for Groza, who punished them with 30 points.

Xavier was the one team that did put up a serious fight. The Cats eventually won 51-40, but not before Xavier accomplished two rare feats — shut down Groza and lead the Cats (34-30) in the second half. Barker and Jones picked up the scoring slack, racking up 15 and 11 points, respectively.

Barker's 65-foot bucket highlighted a 70-37 win over Vanderbilt in the final home appearance for the seniors. Barker launched his historic shot despite the protests of Rupp, who was screaming from the sidelines for Barker to just tuck it away and let the clock run out. Groza had 23,

The 1948-49 team made it two NCAA titles in a row. Team members included, sitting, Adolph Rupp, Jim Line, Cliff Barker, Johnny Stough, Ralph Beard, Joe B. Hall, Garland Townes and assistant coach Harry Lancaster. Standing, Dale Barnstable, Walt Hirsch, Wah Wah Jones, Alex Groza, Bob Henne, Roger Day and manager Humzey Yessin.

Jones 18 and Barker 13 in that UK win.

As the season wound down, Rupp decided to go for a "Grand Slam" by competing in the NIT and the NCAA tournaments. By choosing to do so, Rupp put his team in a position to accomplish something that had never been done — win both events in the same year.

The Cats' first priority, however, was the SEC tourney, which they won by beating Florida (73-36), Auburn (70-39), Tennessee (83-44) and Tulane (68-52). Groza scored 94 points in those four games, including 37 in the championship win over Tulane. Again, Groza had plenty of support, especially from Beard and Jones. Jones was the top scorer against Tennessee with 17, while Beard had 11, 15 and 13 in the Cats' final three tourney games. Not surprisingly, that trio, along with Barker, were named to the all-tourney team.

The Cats, fresh from winning four SEC tourney games by a combined total of 123 points, figured to have little trouble with Loyola of Chicago in the NIT opener. But Loyola humbled UK — and shocked the basketball world — by scoring a 67-56 upset. Loyola's big win was sparked by Jack Kerris' 23-point performance. UK was led by Beard's 15 points. Groza and Barker each contributed 12.

Seven days later, UK was back in New York, site of the NCAA tourney's Eastern Regional. The embarrassed Cats were also back to their old ways, beating Villanova 85-72 and Illinois 76-47 to earn a trip to Seattle for a matchup against Oklahoma A&M in the title game.

Groza had 30 points in the win over Villanova. Line came through with a 21-point effort and Barker had 18. Villanova's Paul Arizin tied Groza for high-point honors with 30.

Groza and Line were the top guns in the win over Illinois. Groza had 27, Line 15. Beard and Jones finished with nine each.

The title game, which UK won 46-36, belonged to Groza. In his final performance as a Wildcat, Groza once again came up big, scoring 25 points despite fouling out with just over five minutes left to play. In addition, foul problems forced Groza to the bench for nearly eight minutes earlier in the second half.

He was, to no one's surprise, the unanimous pick as the tourney's MVP.

Groza, Beard and Jones all were named All-Americans for their performance in 1948-49. Also, they left UK as the school's three all-time leading scorers, having accounted

It was once said that Cliff Barker could do everything with a basketball except make it talk.

for 4,412 points. Groza, the first UK player to average 20 points in a season, finished as the school's top scorer with 1,744 career points. It's a mark that stood until 1964, when it was surpassed by Cotton Nash.

Beard ended his career with 1,517 points, while Jones had 1,151.

With so many great players soon to graduate, some onlookers took great delight in predicting an end to UK's reign of terror. But their predictions of doom proved to be premature. Rupp had plenty of cards left to play, including seven-foot Bill Spivey.

1949-50

The secret of Bill Spivey's success? Food. And, even more specifically, milk shakes.

When Spivey arrived at UK from Warner Robins, Ga., he was seven-feet tall and skinny as a reed. Additional weight, muscle and strength were needed if Spivey hoped to become a successful collegiate player. So the task of beefing up Spivey was given to assistant coach Harry Lancaster, who immediately instructed Spivey to eat numerous meals each day. In addition, Spivey was ordered to drink several milk shakes.

During the summer, Lancaster sent several telegrams to Rupp, informing the Baron that all was going well, and that Spivey was indeed gaining weight. With each correspondence, Lancaster would proudly boast about the vast quantities of food Spivey had consumed. Finally, after hearing enough of this, Rupp sent a telegram back to Lancaster, saying, "I know he can eat, but can he play basketball?"

Rupp needn't have worried — Spivey could play. From the very outset, Spivey proved himself to be the finest big man in the college ranks, one who, had it not been for a tragic miscarriage of justice, likely would have gone on to become one of the great players of all-time.

Spivey's towering presence helped offset the loss of the four great stars who had graduated the previous year. He was joined by returning veterans Barnstable, Line and Hirsch, and a whole host of newcomers, including Bobby Watson, Lucian "Skippy" Whitaker, Len Pearson and Guy Strong. Another rookie, Shelby Linville, became eligible during the second semester and was a valuable addition to the team. In all, 10 of the 14 players were sophomores, making this the youngest UK team since the 1943-44 "Wildkittens."

Rupp's lineup for the opener against Indiana Central was comprised of Line, Hirsch, Spivey, Barnstable and Pearson. While all eyes were closely scrutinizing Spivey's every move, it was the veteran Line who stole the show. The 6'2" southpaw forward was on fire, hitting 13 of 16 field goal attempts and 11 of 12 free throws for a career-best 37 points. With Spivey adding 16 in his debut, the Cats romped to an 84-61 victory.

After beating Western Ontario 90-18, the Cats went to New York to tackle a strong St. John's team. The Redmen roared to a 23-point first-half lead, then went on to spank UK 69-58. The Cats closed the gap to 50-41 in the second half, but three straight points by Al McGuire crushed the comeback effort. Spivey was the game's leading scorer with 17 points. Strong had 14 and Watson 12 for the Cats. All-American Dick McGuire led St. John's with 13 points.

Extra meals and plenty of milk shakes beefed up rail-thin Georgia native Bill Spivey and transformed him into one of the game's dominant big men.

In their next game against DePaul in Louisville, the Cats overcame a 32-23 halftime deficit to nip Ray Meyers' club 49-47. Trailing 47-45 with 45 seconds left, the Cats tied it on a pair of free throws by Whitaker. After a DePaul miss, Whitaker was again fouled. He hit one of two free tosses to give UK a 48-47 advantage. Again, DePaul failed to score and was forced to foul. This time it was little-used Garland Townes who stepped to the line, hitting one of two free throws to account for the final score. Spivey's 15 points were tops for UK.

Rupp's youthful Cats, faced with a difficult early slate, were quickly coming of age. They won at Purdue 60-54, then followed that with a 57-56 overtime win over Villanova in the Sugar Bowl opener. It was 51-51 at the end of regulation, but a quick Whitaker bucket put the Cats in

front 53-51. After Arizin and Whitaker swapped baskets, a freebie by Benny Stewart pulled Villanova to within 55-54. Following a two-pointer by Arizin, Line broke free to score the clinching basket on a layup. Arizin, another consensus All-American, won the duel of centers, outscoring Spivey 24 to 14. Barnstable had 11 for the Cats.

It didn't get any easier in the championship game against a heavily favored Bradley team that was led by the outstanding Gene Melchiorre. But with Spivey scoring 22 and Line 19, the Cats took the Sugar Bowl title with a hard-earned 71-66 win. Melchiorre had 20 for the Braves.

Tennessee snapped the Cats' 65-game SEC winning streak with a 66-53 victory in Knoxville. The Vols' Art Burris scored 28 points, while the defense limited Spivey to 12. Line led UK with 15.

The Cats split their next four games, beating Georgia Tech 61-47 and DePaul 86-53, and losing to Georgia 71-60 and Notre Dame 64-51. Six-eight Bob Schloss keyed Georgia's win, scoring 28 points. Watson had 15 for the Cats. The loss marked the first time since the 1941-42 season that UK lost two SEC games.

Spivey's 27 points weren't enough to fight off the home-standing Irish, who beat the Cats 64-51. It would be the Cats' last loss until the NIT.

Line scored 20 and Spivey had 16 as the Cats bounced back to beat Xavier 58-47 in Cincinnati. The young Cats now owned a 12-4 record despite having played 13 of 16 games away from home.

Returning home for the first time in nearly six weeks, the revenge-minded Cats held Schloss to just six points and beat Georgia 88-56. Four Cats hit double figures, led by Hirsch's 21. Spivey had 18, Whitaker 13 and Line 11.

Thanks to three late points by Watson, the Cats beat Alabama 66-64 to give Rupp victory No. 400 at UK. It was Watson's field goal and free throw that broke a 60-60 deadlock and assured the win for Rupp. Spivey was also instrumental in the win, ringing up 27 points.

In a 79-52 win over Tennessee, the rapidly maturing Spivey gained a measure of personal revenge by outscoring Burris 34-12. Later, in a 97-62 win over Georgia Tech, Spivey scored 40 points, breaking Groza's UK/SEC record for most points in a game.

In the season finale against Vanderbilt, and the last game to be played in Alumni Gym, the Cats had to fight back from a 12-point halftime deficit to beat the Commodores 70-66. It was the Cats' 84th consecutive home win, giving

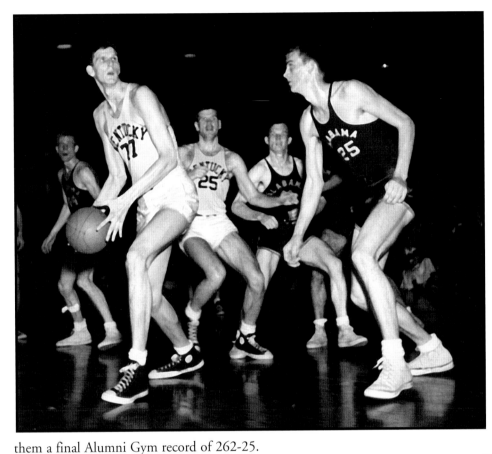

Bill Spivey prepares to launch a shot as an Alabama defender closes in. Spivey averaged 19.2 points for the 1951 NCAA championship team.

slaughter with 26 points. Spivey's 15 topped UK's scoring.

Although the Cats hobbled home after their NIT loss, the season had been a success. A young team that played 20 of 30 games on the road had finished with a 25-5 record. Spivey, who had averaged 19.3 in his rookie season, would be back. So would Linville, Watson, Hirsch and Whitaker. And joining them would be a trio of talented sophomores — Frank Ramsey, Cliff Hagan and Lou Tsioropoulos. Another golden season lay ahead.

them a final Alumni Gym record of 262-25.

UK took an 11-game winning streak into the SEC tourney opener against Mississippi State. With Spivey experiencing a miserable night (one bucket, four points), it turned out to be a much tougher struggle than anticipated. But Line again came through, scoring 19 points to lift the Cats to a 56-46 win. Hirsch and Barnstable also aided in the win, hitting for 12 points each.

After vanquishing Georgia 79-63 in the semifinals, the Cats, behind Spivey's 37-point performance, routed Tennessee 95-58 to win the title. Line had 19 for UK, while Hirsch and Watson connected for 15 apiece.

With his team sitting on an impressive 24-4 record, Rupp was confident that the NCAA would select UK to respresent District 3 in the tournament. But the Selection Committee wanted UK to play N.C. State, with the winner getting the bid. When Rupp refused, the committee chose N.C. State. With UK out of the NCAA Tournament, Rupp promptly accepted a bid to play in the NIT.

The end came swiftly and without mercy, and it certainly wasn't what Rupp or Big Blue fans expected. City College of New York blasted the Cats 89-50, handing Rupp his worst defeat as a coach. Ed Warner led the

1950-51

After racking up 84 consecutive victories in Alumni Gym, the Wildcats moved into Memorial Coliseum, an 11,500 seat structure that cost just under 4 million dollars. The building, which serves to honor the Kentuckians who died in World War II and the Korean conflict, was called a "white elephant" by those skeptics who doubted that the sport of college basketball was popular enough to consistently fill a building with such a large capacity. It was the same criticism hurled at the 2,800 seat Alumni Gym when it opened in 1924.

With 10,000 fans on hand, the Cats christened their new home with a 73-43 rout of West Texas State. Rupp's lineup for the opener was made up of Spivey, Linville, Hirsch, Watson and Ramsey.

While this wasn't the deepest team Rupp ever had, it was one with great balance. In all, four Wildcats averaged in double figures for the season, the first time that had ever happened. Along with the five starters, Whitaker, Tsioropoulos, C.M. Newton and Hagan, who joined the team at midseason, all saw considerable playing time.

An early season 68-39 home win over Kansas proved just

how good Spivey had become. In what was billed as a "battle of the giants," a crowd of 13,000 looked on as Spivey completely dominated 6'9" Clyde Lovellette, winning the scoring battle 22-10. Spivey's superiority could have been even greater had Rupp not removed his star center from the game when Lovellette fouled out with just over 12 minutes remaining. Ramsey also played well, scoring 19 points. Hirsch added 10.

St. John's tried the deep-freeze approach, but a marvelous 12-point, 13-rebound performance by Ramsey lifted the Cats to a 43-37 win. Spivey had 15 and Linville 12 for UK.

In Sugar Bowl action, the slow-down tactics employed by St. Louis proved to be more successful. The Billikens won a 43-42 overtime thriller to halt the Cats' winning streak at six. UK had a chance to pull out the victory, but failed to do so when Hirsch misfired on a pair of late free throws.

The Cats caught fire after that loss, and two reasons why were Watson's continuing improvement and the addition of the great Hagan to the team. The 5'10" Watson went from being a steady, assist-oriented playmaker to a serious — and steady — offensive threat capable of racking up big numbers. He scored 17 to help the Cats dispose of DePaul 63-55 and 20 in a 65-48 win against Alabama.

Hagan made his UK debut in game 15, scoring 13 points in the Cats' 74-49 win over Vanderbilt in Nashville. Hirsch led four Wildcats in double figures with 17. Watson finished with 16, while Spivey matched Hagan with 13.

The three Western Kentucky natives — Ramsey, Watson and Hagan — put on a big show for the locals in the Cats' 86-39 win over Ole Miss in Owensboro. Playing in front of their home-town fans, Watson and Hagan had 20 and 13, respectively, while Ramsey, from nearby Madisonville, tied

UK's 1950-51 NCAA championship team. Front row: Lindle Castle, Skippy Whitaker, Bobby Watson, Guy Strong and Ches Riddle. Middle row: Adolph Rupp, Cliff Hagan, C.M. Newton, Walt Hirsch, Paul Lansaw, Dwight Price and assistant coach Harry Lancaster. Back row: Frank Ramsey, Shelby Linville, Bill Spivey, Roger Layne, Lou Tsioropoulos and Read Morgan.

for game-high honors with 20.

Spivey scored 40 in a 78-51 victory over Xavier, then followed that with a 23-point performance that helped the Cats survive a tough 60-57 struggle against DePaul.

While Rupp was beset by a series of illnesses during the final weeks of the season, his team continued to play spectacular basketball, winning its final 18 games. The Cats closed the regular season with an 89-57 win over Vanderbilt to finish with a 24-1 record and a No. 1 ranking in the national polls. Spivey led the Cats with 21 against Vandy. Linville had 19, Watson 17 and Hagan 12.

A sore throat forced Spivey to miss the SEC tourney opener against Mississippi State. But even without their All-American center, the Cats didn't miss a beat, winning easily 92-70. Four UK players scored in double figures, including Hirsch with 21, Hagan 20, Watson 19 and Ramsey 14.

Hagan had 25 and Spivey 23 in the Cats' 84-54 win over Auburn, then Spivey came back with 19 and Tsioropoulos added 14 as the Cats moved into the championship game by beating Georgia Tech 82-56.

In the tourney final, the Cats faced Vanderbilt, a team they had defeated by 25 and 32 points in the two previous meetings. But this night belonged to the Commodores, who fought back from nine down in the second half to register a stunning 61-57 upset. It marked the first time in eight years that the Cats failed to win the SEC tourney crown. With the score tied 55-55, Vandy took the lead for good on a basket by Gene Southwood. Spivey had 21 for the Cats. Bob Dudley Smith led Vandy with 15.

UK prepared for its NCAA tourney appearance with 97-61 win over Loyola of Chicago. Spivey, Hagan and Ramsey combined for 61 points in that win.

As the NCAA Tournament rolled around UK's depth was cut by one when Hirsch, the team's captain, was ruled ineligible because this was his fourth year on the varsity. Rupp filled that vacancy by moving Hagan into the starting lineup, a change that probably served to strengthed an already-strong team as it headed into the expanded NCAA Tournament. (It now took four wins to capture the title.)

UK opened with a hard-earned come-from-behind 79-68 win over Louisville in Raleigh, N.C. After leading 44-40 at the half, the Cats fell behind 64-60 with 9:35 left to play. To make matters even more desperate, Spivey had been hit with his fifth personal foul. But with Linville leading the charge, UK rattled off 10 unanswered points to regain the momentum and survive the scare.

Linville led UK with 22 points. Whitaker finished with 16, Ramsey 14 and Spivey 10. Bob Brown and Bob Naber led the Cardinals with 15 points each.

With that win, the Cats moved on to Madison Square Garden for a second matchup against St. John's. The Redmen led 24-23 at the half, and the two teams were dead even with just under six minutes left. But a Linville one-hander, followed by a perfect Ramsey to Spivey pass that led to a bucket, keyed a late surge that enabled UK to put away the Redmen 59-43.

The Cats again featured a balanced scoring attack, led by Ramsey's 13 points. Watson and Spivey each had 12. Bob Zawoluk had 15 for St. John's.

Next up for the Cats was Big 10 champ Illinois. The Illini came out on fire, and by the half were sitting on a 39-32 lead. But with Spivey snapping out of his scoring slump, UK slowly chipped away at the deficit, finally taking a 74-72 lead on a bucket by Linville. Then with only 12 seconds remaining, and the score knotted at 74-74, Linville again came through, sinking the game-winning basket for the Cats. Illinois had one final shot at sending the game into overtime, but a last-second attempt missed its mark.

Spivey, who had scored just 22 points in the two previous games, finished with 28 points and 16 rebounds. Linville had 14, while the backcourt duo of Watson and Whitaker each had 10. Rod Fletcher led Illinois with 21 points.

It was on to Minneapolis for a date with Kansas State in the championship game. Despite a 31-2 record, UK went into its third title game in four years as the underdog. And puny underdogs at that. Hagan was fighting the flu and Spivey had a cold, leaving the Cats with only six healthy players.

Early on, Kansas State looked as if it was going to take advantage of UK's medical woes, bolting to a quick 9-4 lead. Rupp countered by inserting the ailing Hagan into the lineup, a move that quickly turned things in UK's favor. The Cats battled back, finally taking a 24-22 lead on a Spivey layup. But Kansas State quickly regained the momentum, eventually taking a 29-27 lead at the half.

The second half, though, was all UK. With Spivey and Hagan dominating the rebounding, UK took the lead for good at 31-30 on a Linville free throw. That lead would reach 15 points (54-39) with 10 minutes remaining. Spivey and the UK defense made the difference. During one eight-minute stretch, while Kansas State was going without

a field goal, Spivey scored six buckets for the Cats.

Kansas State mounted one final charge, closing to within 58-48 with 4:40 left to play. But Hagan answered with two buckets, Spivey had a free throw and Whitaker scored on a layup to put the game out of reach.

UK claimed its third NCAA championship in four years with a 68-58 victory. In what turned out to be his final game in a UK uniform, Spivey led the Wildcats with 22 points and 21 rebounds. Hagan finished with 10 points, while Ramsey and Whitaker each had nine.

Spivey led UK's balanced attack that season, scoring 19.2 points per game. Others in double figures include Linville (10.4), Watson (10.4) and Ramsey (10.1). Hirsch finished with an average of 9.1.

Spivey, who was named first-team All-American, also pulled down 567 rebounds, still a UK and SEC record.

Cliff Hagan puts up his patented hook shot as a helpless Georgia defender looks on.

his death. And, indeed, Spivey was never convicted. Despite his plea of innocence, Spivey was eventually ruled ineligible for his senior season. He was also banned for life from playing in the NBA, thus denying him the opportunity to do battle against early NBA giants like George Mikan, Bill Russell and Wilt Chamberlain. Spivey would later sue the NBA and win. But it was too late; the damage had already been done. Spivey's tragic fate still remains one of the great injustices in the history of sports.

When the Cats opened their season against Washington & Lee, Spivey, who three weeks earlier had undergone knee surgery, was still on crutches. Although his name was being linked to the scandal, Spivey still had hopes of playing once his injury healed. But even without Spivey, UK had no trouble in the opener, beating W&L 96-46. Tsioropoulos scored 22 and Ramsey added 17 for the Cats.

1951-52

If the past four seasons had been filled with unlimited glory and success, the next three would be filled with an equal amount of frustration and what-ifs. The point-shaving scandal of the late 1940s rocked college basketball, and no program was more affected than Kentucky's. Because of sanctions and rulings handed down by the NCAA, Kentucky missed the chance to win three more national championships.

In 1951-52, Rupp had a powerful team coming back. Spivey, the game's best big man, was set to return for his final season, and he would be joined by Hagan, Ramsey, Watson, Tsioropoulos, Whitaker, Linville and newcomer Billy Evans. It was a formidable club in every respect.

But while UK looked unbeatable on the court, it was handed a severe setback in the court — Spivey was charged with taking money from gamblers. It was a charge he denied until

After Hagan and Ramsey combined for 54 points in a 97-72 win over Xavier, the Cats suffered their first setback of the season, dropping a 61-57 decision at Minnesota. The Cats were on top 36-31 in the third quarter and seemed to be on their way to a win when Ramsey was whistled for his fifth foul. After that, it was all Minnesota. Ed Kalafat, a 6'6" sophomore, killed UK with 30 points. Watson topped the Cats' scoring with 16.

Led by 25 points apiece from Hagan and Watson, the Cats gave one of their finest performances ever in an 81-40 win over St. John's. It was UK's 100th consecutive home-court victory. UK totally dominated every aspect of the game, hitting 44.4 percent from the field to 16.6 by the Redmen. For the night, St. John's made just 10 field goals, while Zawoluk was held to one bucket and seven points.

Prior to playing UCLA, (UK won 84-53 behind Hagan's 34 points), Spivey asked that his name be removed from

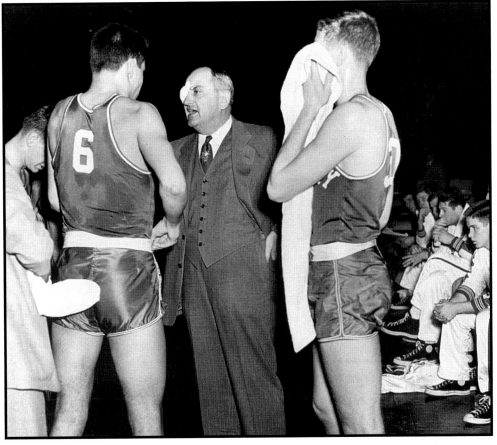

Even an eye infection couldn't keep Adolph Rupp off the sidelines. Here, the Baron barks orders to his All-American duo of Cliff Hagan (6) and Frank Ramsey (30).

Shaking off the controversy caused by the point shaving scandal, and by Spivey's uncertain future, the Cats continued to play impressively. Especially Ramsey, who had 31 against Xavier, 24 against Notre Dame and 29 against Mississippi State. In a surprisingly difficult 71-67 win at Alabama, Ramsey bailed out the Cats by scoring 12 of his 13 points in the second half. Watson had 26 against the Tide, while Hagan finished with 30 against Mississippi

the eligibility list until the matter concerning the scandal was cleared up. In the upcoming weeks and months, Spivey would testify on several occasions, and even take a lie detector test in an effort to prove his innocence.

For the second time in two years St. Louis got the best of UK in the Sugar Bowl. The Billikens won 61-60 on a tip-in by Tom Lillis with 10 seconds left. Watson put up a final shot for the Cats, but it was off the mark. The Sugar Bowl had become something of a graveyard for the Cats, who, in nine appearances, had a 7-6 record.

The Cats returned to Owensboro to face Ole Miss, and with local heroes Hagan and Watson once again putting on a big show, they shattered the SEC scoring record with a 116-58 win. Hagan had 37 for UK and Watson added 18.

LSU wasn't such an easy conquest for the Cats. In the first of three terrific battles contested over the span of three years, the Cats, sparked by Evans, parlayed a big third quarter into a 57-47 victory. Trailing 29-18 at the half, the Cats outscored LSU 27-9 in the decisive third quarter to take control of the game. Watson had 13 for the winners, Tsioropoulos added 11 and Evans had seven. LSU was led by the great Bob Pettit, who topped all scorers with 22.

State.

But the role of hero wasn't limited to superstars Hagan, Ramsey and Watson. Sometimes an unlikely source stepped up and captured the spotlight. Like Willie Rouse, who broke free to score the deciding bucket (his only one that night) and give the Cats a 63-61 win at DePaul in the final game of the regular season.

Even as the SEC tourney approached, Spivey felt confident that he would soon rejoin the team. He had just returned from New York, where a grand jury heard his testimony. It was his belief that the UK Athletics Board would reinstate him. But it was not to be. On March 1, the final day of the SEC Tournament, Spivey learned his fate — he had been declared permanently ineligible.

The determined Cats blocked out the off-court distractions and easily won their first three SEC tourney games. Hagan was marvelous, scoring 91 points in those three games, including a tourney-record 42 in an 81-66 win over Tennessee in the semifinal game.

Despite the presence of high-powered scorers Hagan, Ramsey and Pettit, the title game against LSU turned out to be a classic defensive struggle. UK led 31-17, and despite

Lou Tsioropoulos fights for the ball despite being surrounded by a host of St. John's players. That's future coach Al McGuire (18) on the right.

1952-53

This was the season in which the UK basketball program felt the full wrath of the NCAA's fury — a one-year suspension. This dictate stemmed from the point-shaving scandal, in which several Wildcat players had been implicated. Hardest hit were All-NBA standouts Beard and Groza, members of the successful Indianapolis Olympians, who saw their careers come to an end, and Spivey, the potentially great pivotman, whose career ended before it began.

In addition, there was a scathing indictment of the program from the New York judge who handled the case. In a no-holds-barred 63-page statement, he detailed numerous wrongdoings and excesses within the basketball program, charging athletes and UK officials with a wide variety of infractions. Eighteen pages of the report were devoted to Rupp, who the judge said, "failed in his duty to observe the amateur rules, to build character and protect the morals and health of his charges."

The University of Kentucky launched its own internal investigation, and while acknowledging that certain players did take bribes to "shave" points (win by less than the gamblers' point spread), no evidence was found that Rupp was aware of — or encouraged — such practices.

Although no member of the 1952-53 team was around when the scandal broke, they would be the ones who paid the price by having to sit idle for a full season.

While the NCAA's ruling prohibited the Wildcats from competing in intercollegiate play, it did not keep them from practicing. Along with the daily practices (which the players said were among the toughest), the team held four public scrimmages. In all, more than 35,000 fans turned out to see those games.

Rupp, furious at the NCAA and at some of his coaching brethren, used the season in exile to sharpen his team's skills to a razor-like finish. He wanted nothing less than to unleash his full vengeance on the college basketball world.

making just three field goals in the second half, somehow managed to hold on for a 44-43 victory. After Pettit, who had 25 points, put the Tigers in front 43-42, Tsioropoulos came through with the winning basket for UK. Hagan finished with 19 for the Cats.

With Hagan scoring 25 points, UK blasted Penn State 82-54 in the NCAA tourney first round to set up a rematch against St. John's. In one of the great turnarounds in college basketball history, St. John's, a 41-point loser to UK earlier in the season, bounced the Cats out of the championship hunt with a 64-57 win. Zawoluk, held to only seven points in the first meeting, had 32 this time around. Hagan led UK with 22, while Ramsey added 14.

Hagan finished with a 21.6 scoring average, the highest-ever by a Wildcat. He also pulled down 16.5 rebounds a game. Ramsey, the slashing 6'3" guard, scored at a 15.9 clip, while the feisty 5'10" Watson averaged 13.1 points per game.

It was a disappointing finish to what had been a marvelous season. The Cats had carved out a 29-3 mark despite the absence of Spivey, the game's most dominant player. They had another unbeaten record in SEC play, and finished with a No. 1 ranking in the AP and UPI polls. UK fans could only wonder what might have been had Spivey been allowed to play. But the disappointments and the what might have beens were only beginning.

Cliff Hagan proudly accepts the game ball from Adolph Rupp after scoring 51 points against Temple in the 1953-54 season opener.

An enraged Rupp said: "I'll not retire until the man who said Kentucky can't play in the NCAA hands me the national championship trophy."

Rupp made good on his promise. He would get his trophy.

1953-54

In the vast firmament of UK stars, few have shone brighter than Cliff Hagan and Frank Ramsey. They were UK's version of Butch Cassidy and The Sundance Kid, two players with such exceptional skills that by the time they fired their last shot more than a decade later they were considered among the greatest to ever play the game at any level. And never have two Wildcat players been more closely linked. Hagan and Ramsey — seldom is one name mentioned without the other.

Hagan was 6'4", strong, smooth and exceptionally talented. It's impossible to pick an all-time UK starting five that doesn't include Hagan. He was that good. Although he could score in a variety of ways, the main weapon in his arsenal was the hook shot. Few players in basketball history can match Hagan's accuracy with that particular shot.

The 6'3" Ramsey was a slashing, driving blur of perpetual motion. He never seemed to stop moving. Ramsey was a great all-around player. Though less dominant than Hagan, Ramsey was equally effective, especially when the

stakes were high. Ramsey was the ultimate big-game player. Rupp once remarked that "if we win by 30, Ramsey gets three. But if we win by three, Ramsey gets 30."

Rupp relied heavily on the combined talents of Hagan and Ramsey to punish his enemies and destroy opposing teams. Hagan and Ramsey, together with the tough Tsioropoulos, came to be forever immortalized as "The Big Three," and with that trio leading the way, Rupp's Wildcats painted a masterpiece season of perfection — 25 wins without a loss.

Few teams in UK history were as powerful and dominant as this one. The average margin of victory was 27.2 points, and, incredibly, only two teams played the Cats to within 10 points. Yet, despite going unbeaten, it would be a bittersweet season, thanks once again to the NCAA.

Hagan, Ramsey, Tsioropoulos and Evans usually held down starting spots. Two players — junior Gayle Rose and sophomore Linville Puckett — split time at the guard position opposite Ramsey. Phil "Cookie" Grawemeyer, a 6'7" sophomore, drew several starts at forward ahead of Evans, while 6'6" Jerry Bird, another sophomore, saw plenty of action once he recovered from an early season injury. Other reserves included Rouse, Dan Chandler, Jess Curry, Pete Grigsby, Bill Bibb, Harold Hurst, Hugh Coy and Clay Evans.

Kentucky's return to action after 20 months in the wilderness was highlighted by Hagan's record-breaking 51-point performance against Temple. Hagan scored at will against the Owls, leading UK to an easy 86-59 win. With that win, Rupp's Cats announced to the college basketball world that they were back in full force. With his magnificent individual effort, Hagan reminded everyone that he was one of the game's finest players.

Ramsey inflicted the major damage in the next game, scoring 27 points in an 81-66 win at Xavier. After beating Wake Forest 101-69 at home, the Cats went to St. Louis for a game against Coach Ed Hickey's Billikens. Ramsey had 21, Hagan 18 and Tsioropoulos 15 in a

wild 71-59 UK win. Tsioro-poulos was nearly involved in a brawl, a St. Louis fan took a swing at UK athletics director Bernie Shively, and UK assistant coach Lancaster did slug Pat Hickey, the coach's son, for firing the timer's pistol too close to his leg.

Although no one knew it at the time, the UKIT turned out to be this team's NCAA Tournament. The Cats beat Duke 85-69 in the first game, then took on La Salle and high-scoring Tom Gola in the championship tilt one night later. With Hagan outscoring Gola 28-16, the Cats rolled to a 73-60 victory. Three months later, as La Salle was winning the NCAA tourney championship, the unbeaten Wildcats were watching from the sidelines. Big Blue historians and fans always point to the win over La Salle as evidence that this UK team would have captured another NCAA title.

Tough-in-the-clutch Frank Ramsey came through with 30 points in UK's SEC title-clinching 63-56 win over LSU.

Unbeaten Minnesota was the next to fall, dropping a 74-59 decision to the Cats. Ramsey led UK with 23. Hagan had 20, Evans 12 and Grawemeyer 11.

Xavier did throw a scare into the Cats before eventually falling 77-71. UK led by 22 points, then had to fight off a spirited Xavier comeback in the final minutes. Hagan had 20, Tsioropoulos 18 and Grawemeyer 17.

The Big Three combined for 83 points in the Cats' 105-53 win over Georgia Tech. Hagan led the way with 32 points, while Tsioropoulos hit a career-high 30 (all on field goals) and Ramsey added 21.

The Cats unleashed their full fury in a 94-43 destruction of Tulane. It was a game Rupp would have won by 100 points if possible. The Green Wave were coached by Cliff Wells, one of the coaches who voted to suspend UK and a man Rupp bitterly despised. The Big Three, perhaps feeling their own

resentment toward Wells, combined for 71 points in that win. Ramsey had 25, Hagan 24 and Tsioropoulos 22.

Ramsey reached his career high with a 37-point performance in UK's 97-71 win over Tennessee, then followed that with 24 points in an 85-63 win at Vanderbilt and 29 in a 106-55 romp past Georgia.

Hagan then took over, leading the team in scoring in the next seven games. As Hagan chalked up huge numbers, the Cats continued to win in ridiculously easy fashion. In those seven games, only a 76-61 win over DePaul was even remotely competitive. Hagan had 29 in that win, while Evans chipped in with 15. Hagan's best outing in that stretch came against Ole Miss. He had 38 points to lead UK to an 88-62 win.

Ramsey interrupted Hagan's lock on scoring honors, hitting for 28 against Auburn. Hagan finished with 25 in that 109-79 win, while Tsioropoulos had 19, Evans 14 and Rose 13.

UK ended its regular season with a 68-43 win over Alabama, which was coached by Johnny Dee, another of Rupp's arch-enemies. Hagan led a balanced UK scoring attack with 24 points. Tsioropoulos, Ramsey and Puckett each contributed 11.

UK and LSU both finished with 14-0 records in SEC play; however, because of a scheduling disagreement they had not met during the regular season. On March 9, the two clubs squared off in Nashville for a one-game playoff, with the winner earning the SEC championship ring and a trip to the NCAA Tournament.

Ramsey was sensational, scoring 30 points to help UK come back from a second-half deficit to post a 63-56 win. After the Tigers erased an 11-point deficit and took a 49-48 lead, Ramsey hit back-to-back buckets to put the Cats on

top for good. Ramsey scored 10 of his 30 points in the deciding fourth quarter. In the battle between first-team All-Americans (and future St. Louis Hawks teammates) Hagan and Pettit finished with 17 points each.

But UK's joy didn't last. Moments after the victory, it was announced that UK would not participate in the NCAA Tournament. Hagan, Ramsey and Tsioropoulos were ruled ineligible because they were no longer undergraduates (they had already earned their college degree), and at that time postgraduates were not allowed to play in the NCAA Tournament. In a terrible bit of irony, The Big Three were being penalized because they had been successful in the classroom.

The players voted 9-3 in favor of participating in the postseason event, but Rupp quickly vetoed that vote. Rupp said there was no way UK was going to participate in the NCAA Tournament without the three players most responsible for the team being there in the first place.

The 1953-54 UK team is the only one in the history of college hoops to finish with an unbeaten record and not win a national title.

Hagan ended his career with 1,475 points and 1,035 rebounds despite playing only 77 games. Ramsey accounted for 1,344 points and 1,038 rebounds, the second-most in UK history and the most-ever by a guard. The two players had long and successful all-star NBA careers — Hagan with the Hawks, Ramsey with the Celtics.

Both players are enshrined in the College Basketball Hall of Fame in Springfield, Mass.

1954-55

Throughout his career, Rupp had opted not to recruit players from the junior college ranks. However, that would change with the addition of 6'7" Bob Burrow to the UK lineup.

In an effort to offset the loss of The Big Three (in particular, the magnificent Hagan), Rupp went to Lon Morris Junior College in Jacksonville, Texas, and found Burrow, the 1954 JUCO Player of the Year. Burrow had plenty of offensive scoring tricks, was a savage rebounder and a solid defender. With Burrow in the middle, Rupp hoped that UK's run of high-powered, dominating pivot-men would continue. And Burrow wouldn't disappoint. In his two years, he more than held his own with predecessors Groza, Spivey and Hagan by accounting for 1,023 points and 823 rebounds, including a school-record 34 against Temple.

Burrow was surrounded by a strong veteran group that included Evans and Puckett, starters from the previous unbeaten season, along with Rose, Grawemeyer and Bird. Rupp had every reason to feel confident that this would be a strong team. The pollsters agreed, ranking the Cats in the top five during much of the season.

But the season turned out to be one of discontent and disappoint-

Steady Billy Evans goes up for an easy two against LSU.

The 1954-55 team included, sitting, Adolph Rupp, Sonny Corum, Gayle Rose, Billy Evans, Gerry Calvert, Dan Chandler and Harry Lancaster. Standing, trainer Rusty Payne, Earl Adkins, Ray Mills, Jerry Bird, Bob Burrow, Phil Grawemeyer, Harold Hurst, John Brewer and manager Bill Surface.

ment, highlighted by a stunning home-court loss to Georgia Tech and an open rebellion that led Rupp to dismiss the talented, hard-headed Puckett from the team. And when the end came, it came swiftly. Despite a 22-2 record and a 10-game winning streak, the Cats fell to Marquette 79-71 in the opening round of the NCAA Tournament.

Grawemeyer, Bird, Burrow, Evans and Puckett were the starters in the Cats' 74-58 win over LSU in the opener. Grawemeyer came through with 28, while Evans added 17. Burrow scored just two points in his Wildcat debut.

Burrow finally made his presence felt with a 25-point showing in the Cats' 101-69 win over Temple. Burrow received strong support from Ray Mills, who came off the bench to score 24.

The Cats won six straight to improve their record to 7-0. Included among the list of victims was defending NCAA champ La Salle. For the second straight year, UK topped La Salle and Tom Gola in the championship game of the UKIT. The Cats won 63-54. Evans paced UK with 20 points. Burrow had 18 and Grawemeyer 14. Gola scored 20 to tie Evans for high-point honors.

Then on Jan. 8, 1955, the unthinkable happened — after 129 straight home wins, UK lost to lowly Georgia Tech. It was the first time many Wildcat fans had ever seen their team lose a game. When the final buzzer sounded, and as the Yellow Jacket players celebrated on the court, Memorial Coliseum was a tomb. Disbelieving fans, shocked into silence, remained in their seats for several minutes, unable to comprehend what they had just witnessed. After 12 seasons, an NCAA record home-court winning streak had ended.

It was a stunner of major proportions. Rupp and his coaching staff were so confident of victory that they didn't bother to scout the lightly regarded Yellow Jackets. UK led most of the game, but with just seconds remaining, Tech's Joe Helms knocked down a short jumper to give his team a 59-58 lead. UK had two chances to escape the upset, but a shot by Puckett and a tip-in attempt by Grawemeyer both missed their mark.

Helms led Georgia Tech with 23 points. Grawemeyer was UK's top scorer with 19.

Rupp would later tell legendary UK announcer Cawood Ledford that the two worst disasters in his lifetime were

Pearl Harbor and the Georgia Tech loss in Memorial Coliseum.

The Cats easily beat DePaul and Tulane, then had to fight hard to come away with a 64-62 win at LSU. Grawemeyer had 18 for the Cats. Others in double figures included Burrow (16), Evans (12) and Puckett (10).

Evans and Bird were the heroes in UK's exciting 75-71 win over Vanderbilt in Nashville. With the score tied at 60-60, Bird and Evans scored a basket each to put the Cats on the road to victory. The two players had 20 points each for UK. High-point honors went to Vandy's Babe Taylor. The Frankfort native had 25 in a losing cause.

Almost incredibly, Georgia Tech stung the Cats a second time, winning 65-59 in Atlanta. The Yellow Jackets built a 32-24 halftime lead, then used a huge advantage at the charity stripe to hold off the Cats. UK had seven more field goals (27-20), but Georgia Tech cashed in on 25 free throws to just five by the Cats to secure the win. Helms and Bobby Kimmel led Georgia Tech with 24 and 20, respectively. Burrow's 20 topped UK.

Prior to taking on Florida, Rupp announced that Puckett had been dismissed from the team for missing practice. When asked about it, Puckett responded by saying that basketball at UK was "a matter of life and death," equating the experience with that of going to war. Puckett withdrew from UK and migrated to Owensboro, where he played several seasons for Kentucky Wesleyan.

Puckett's open rebellion (the first during Rupp's tenure) and subsequent dismissal from the squad seemed to have little, if any, affect on the Cats. The same can't be said about the loss of Grawemeyer, who was sidelined for the season when he suffered a broken leg in the Cats' 76-72 win over DePaul. When he went down, Grawemeyer was averaging 13 points per game and was one of the team's best clutch players. Without him, the Cats were never the same.

Bob Burrow broke new ground by becoming the first junior college transfer to play for Adolph Rupp.

One of the most bizarre events in UK basketball history occurred prior to the game against Alabama in Memorial Coliseum. As the two clubs were warming up, a fight broke out at midcourt between UK's Dan Chandler and Bama's Jim Bogan. Although the 5'10" Chandler was at a distinct size disadvantage against the 6'7" Bogan, he was declared the fight's winner by the many sportwriters who witnessed the brawl.

Chandler's teammates also came away victorious in the main event, beating Alabama 66-52 behind Burrow's 26 points and 14 from John Brewer.

The Cats finished the regular season on a high note, routing Tennessee 101-64. Evans, in his final game as a Wildcat, led UK with 26 points. Burrow had 24 and Rose added 20.

By tournament time, UK, already without Puckett and Grawemeyer, lost yet another player — Evans. The team captain — and one of the most-underrated players in UK history — fell victim to the same rule that caused Hagan, Ramsey and Tsioropoulos to miss the 1954 NCAA tourney. Like them, Evans was a fifth-year senior, and thus ineligible to participate in the tournament.

The absence of three opening-night starters was too much for the Cats to overcome. Despite a glowing record and high national ranking, the Cats, although a solid favorite to win, lost to Marquette 79-71 in the Eastern Regional at Evanston, Ill. UK led 38-36 at the half, but the final 20 minutes belonged to the Warriors.

Rose played well, scoring 20 points in his final game as a Wildcat. Burrow had 19, while Brewer finished with 16.

The Cats came back one night later to beat Penn State 84-59 in the consolation game. Burrow led a balanced scoring attack with 22 points. Gerry Calvert and Bird finished with 19 and 17, respectively.

It had been a mixed-bag of a season for the Cats, who finished with a No. 2 ranking in both the AP and UPI polls. Burrow proved himself by averaging 19 points and 17.7 rebounds per game. Evans was his typical solid self, averaging just under 14 points before being ruled ineligible, while Bird scored at a 10.7 clip. Burrow and Evans were both named to the All-SEC team.

1955-56

Burrow, now a legitimate All-America candidate, was back for his final season. So were Grawemeyer, Bird, Calvert and Brewer. Joining that group of veterans were sophomores Vernon Hatton, a talented 6'3" guard from Lexington Lafayette, and John Crigler, a 6'3" forward from Hebron.

But this team, despite a core of solid players, never lived up to its expectations. A major reason for this failure was lack of depth. Once Rupp got past his first seven players, the quality of talent dropped considerably.

By this time, Rupp was no longer recruiting as aggressively as he once had. Many of the top in-state players, once a lock to attend UK, were choosing to go elsewhere. During the next few years, several who did sign (Corky Withrow, Roger Newman, Jackie Moreland, Bobby Slusher, Howard Dardeen) either didn't attend at all or showed up but didn't stay.

To fill the holes, Rupp looked to a source he once had scorned — the JUCO ranks. Hoping to find more jewels like Burrow, Rupp, over the next five years, raided the JUCO coffers and found such players as Adrian Smith, Sid Cohen, Bennie Coffman, Vince Del Negro and Doug Pendygraft. Some met with success, others failed to provide Rupp with the help he needed.

It became apparent early that the 1955-56 team wasn't up to recent standards. After opening the season with a hard-earned 62-52 win at LSU, the Cats came home and were soundly beaten by Temple 73-61. Temple's backcourt duo of Guy Rodgers and Hal Lear did most of the damage, combining for 43 points. Ray Mills came off the bench to lead UK with 14 points.

The Cats turned escape artists in their next two games, beating DePaul 71-69 at home and Maryland 62-61 on the road. In the DePaul game, the score was tied 10 times and there were an equal number of lead changes before Bird won it with a last-second layup. Hatton saved the Cats against Maryland. With his team trailing 60-57, Hatton

Forward Jerry Bird was the second-leading scorer on the 1956 SEC runner-up club.

scored the final five points to lift the Cats to victory.

Hatton's heroic performance earned him his first start against Minnesota in the UKIT opener. The Cats won 72-65 behind Burrow's 27 points. However, near the end of the game, UK's big center went down with a sprained ankle, causing him to sit out the championship encounter against Dayton. Bird had a terrific 34-point performance, but the weakened Cats were no match for Dayton. With seven-foot Bill Uhl scoring 20 points, the Flyers won 89-74. It marked the first time the Cats failed to win their own tournament.

Burrow came back from his injury by turning in a pair of strong performances. He scored 40 points in a 101-80 victory over St. Louis, then teamed with Hatton to lead the

Cats to a 104-51 waltz past Georgia Tech. Burrow had 24, while Hatton hit for 21.

But Burrow's finest hour as a Wildcat came in a 107-65 victory over LSU. In that game, Burrow hit 19 field goals and 12 free throws to finish with 50 points, thus becoming only the second UK player to hit the half-century mark. (Hagan was the first.)

A pair of native Kentuckians were the villains in Vanderbilt's 81-73 upset win over UK in Nashville. Frankfort's Babe Taylor led Vandy with 25 points, while Guthrie's Al Rochelle added 24. Calvert's 18 topped UK's scoring.

Hatton scored 25 and Burrow had 19, including the game-winning jumper with nine seconds left, as the Cats edged past Auburn 82-81. Hatton stayed hot, scoring 32 in a disappointing 81-79 loss to DePaul. The Cats owned a 72-66 lead with less than five minutes left, then fizzled down the stretch.

After Burrow scored 34 points in a 76-55 revenge win over Vanderbilt, league-leading Alabama handed the Cats a humiliating 101-77 loss. It was the first time an opponent cracked the century mark against a Rupp-coached team. UK trailed 51-50, but had no answers when the Crimson Tide went on a 27-2 run that turned the game into a laugher. Once again it was a Kentucky native who inflicted the heaviest damage. Jerry Harper, a Louisville Flaget graduate, had 37 for Alabama. Burrow scored 26 for UK and Hatton had 24.

Following the loss to Alabama, UK rebounded with back-to-back devastating performances to close out the regular season. Playing Georgia in the Louisville Armory, the Cats rolled to a record-breaking 143-66 victory. Bird led UK with 22 points, while Burrow added 21. In all, 13 different Wildcats scored.

In the season finale, UK again topped the 100-point mark, beating Tennessee 101-77. Hatton had 20 for the Cats and Bird added 17.

UK finished with a 12-2 record in SEC action, two games off the pace set by Alabama. Although the Tide cruised through SEC action with a perfect 14-0 record, they declined the chance to participate in the NCAA Tournament. UK, by virtue of its second-place finish, was then given the bid.

Coming off those final two explosive wins, UK took a 19-5 record and a high degree of confidence into the Eastern Regional at Iowa City, Iowa.

Matched up against Wayne State in the opening round,

UK, after struggling early, trailed 38-36 at the break. But with Burrow asserting his superiority inside, UK quickly took charge and eventually rolled to an easy 84-64 win.

Burrow was dominant, scoring 33 points to lead all scorers. Calvert had 14, while Hatton and Bird each had 10.

The Cats' season ended one night later when Iowa, led by All-American Carl "Sugar" Cain's 34 points, rolled to an 89-77 win. Burrow also turned in an All-America effort, scoring 31 points for the Cats. Bird chipped in with 23.

Burrow, who averaged 21.1 points and 14.6 rebounds, was again named to the All-SEC team. In addition, he was chosen second-team All-America. Bird averaged 16.2 points, while Hatton, who finished with a 13.3 scoring average and a team-best 49.4 percent field goal accuracy, was voted SEC Sophomore of the Year.

1956-57

For UK to have a successful season, someone needed to step in and fill Burrow's shoes. And someone did — a tall, skinny, tough kid named Johnny Cox.

Cox, a 6'4" native of Hazard, came to UK after leading his high school to the 1955 state championship. Initially, Rupp and Harry Lancaster had doubts that Cox could make the grade in the classroom and tried to persuade him to choose a different college. But Cox would not be deterred, and as UK fans soon learned, when Johnny Cox put his mind to something, he usually succeeded. As Lancaster later recounted, "Johnny said, 'I'll do 'er' and when John said, 'I'll do 'er', he did it."

Cox had an excellent jump shot, and along with ex-Cat Cliff Hagan, one of the best hook shots in the history of college hoops. Even more important, perhaps, the long-armed Cox was a superb rebounder. With Burrow and Bird now departed, strong board work by Cox was essential if the Cats hoped to be successful.

Hatton, now a junior, and Cox were being counted on to provide the nucleus of UK's attack. Joining them in the starting lineup were Calvert, Crigler and Ed Beck. Top reserves were Adrian Smith, Billy Ray Cassady and Earl Adkins.

The Cats struggled early, losing two one-point decisions in their first five games. Hatton got the team off on the right foot with a 26-point performance in an opening-night 94-66 win over Washington & Lee. After ripping Miami 114-75, UK, fueled by Cox's 23 points, topped Temple 73-58 despite 27 points from Guy Rodgers.

Jack Mimlitz tagged the Cats for 25 points to lead St. Louis to a 71-70 victory. Hatton had 21 for UK, while Cox

scored 20. Duke handed the Cats their second loss, coming from 15 points down to post an 85-84 win. The Cats led 84-79 with 50 seconds left, and appeared to have a victory tucked away. But when Duke cranked up the defensive pressure, the Cats quickly crumbled, coughing up the ball on three straight possessions. The Blue Devils took advantage of UK's carelessness, scoring the game's final six points to earn the comeback win. Cox and Hatton had 22 points apiece for UK.

The Cats captured the UKIT title with impressive wins over a pair of excellent teams — SMU and Illinois. Calvert's 22 points sparked a 73-67 win over SMU, then Hatton tossed in 25 and Calvert added 18 as the Cats knocked off the unbeaten Illini 91-70.

In the Sugar Bowl opener against Virginia Tech, baskets by Adkins and Brewer inside the final 14 seconds enabled the Cats to survive a 56-55 thriller. With his club down 55-52, Adkins canned a jumper with 14 seconds remaining to make it 55-54. Then with time running out, Brewer intercepted a pass and put in the game-winner. Beck led UK with 16 points.

One night later, Cox scored 25 and Crigler added 18 as the Cats blasted Houston 111-76 to win their second tournament in eight days. Beck, who had 10 points in the final game, was voted tourney MVP.

An emergency appendectomy sidelined Hatton, but even without their ace guard the Cats opened SEC play with a solid 95-72 win against Georgia Tech. Crigler paced the Cats with 24 points. Brewer, filling in for Hatton, added 12.

UK ran its win streak to seven before dropping a 68-60 decision at Tulane. The Cats shaved a 17-point Tulane lead

Lanky Johnny Cox averaged 19.4 points for the surprising 1956-57 team. His effort earned him Sophomore of the Year honors in the SEC.

down to four but could get no closer. Cox's 16 points topped UK's scoring.

With Hatton watching from the sidelines, the pressure fell on Cox to step up and become UK's main go-to guy. And the talented sophomore from the mountains of Eastern Kentucky more than rose to the challenge. In UK's next four games, all wins, Cox scored 95 points.

Smith was another Wildcat who began to make some noise. The sharp-shooting guard known as "Odie" tallied 44 points in wins over Georgia Tech and Georgia. Hatton saw his first action in three weeks against Georgia, scoring two points in six minutes of playing time.

Even with Hatton healthy once again and Cox continuing to sizzle, the Cats were no match for Mississippi State and Bailey Howell. The 6'7" Howell scored 37 points and pulled down 20 rebounds to lead the Maroons to an 89-81 victory in Starkville. Cox had 28 for UK.

Hatton made his first start since undergoing surgery, scoring 20 points in a 115-65 win over Loyola of Chicago. Cox led the Cats with 32 points.

After escaping with an 80-78 home-court win over Vanderbilt, the Cats defeated Alabama 79-60 and Auburn 103-85 to clinch the SEC title. In the win over Auburn, four Wildcat players scored 20 or more points, the first time in UK history that had happened. Hatton had 24, Calvert and Crigler 21 each, and Cox 20. Beck also played well, pulling down 17 rebounds.

With the league championship already secured, the Cats took care of business by blasting Tennessee 93-75 in the final regular-season game. Calvert and Cox paced the Cats with 20 points each, while Hatton added 17.

UK went into postseason play with a 22-4 record and a

Memorable game-winning buckets in two wins over Temple cemented Vernon Hatton's reputation as one of UK's greatest clutch performers.

No. 3 ranking in the AP and UPI polls. Cox, who had a monster rookie season, was voted SEC Sophomore of the Year. He led the team in scoring (19.4) and free throw percentage (76.6), and was second to Beck in rebounding with an average of 11.1 per game.

Calvert was second in scoring behind Cox with an average of 15.2, while Hatton (14.8) and Crigler (10.3) also hit double figures.

With the Mideast Regional being played in Lexington, UK was a solid choice to advance to the Final Four. The Cats opened tourney play by posting a tough 98-92 win

over Pittsburgh. Cox scored 26 for the Cats and Hatton had 24, but it was Brewer's clutch free throw shooting that made the difference. Brewer connected on all eight of his charity tosses to help UK hold off the Panthers.

In the regional final against Michigan State, the Cats appeared to be on their way to an easy win. They dominated the first half, and were sitting on a 47-35 lead at the intermission. But Michigan State proved to be too quick and too strong for the Cats to contain for the full 40 minutes. With Jack Quiggle scoring 22 points and Jumpin' Johnny Green controlling the boards, the Spartans stormed back to rip UK 80-68. Calvert's 18 points led UK. Cox and Hatton finished with 17 and 15, respectively.

Although the past three seasons had been good ones by most standards (a 66-14 record), clearly the Wildcats' achievements failed to rise to the level of excellence attained by UK teams during the "Glory Decade" of 1945-46 through 1953-54. Some were even beginning to question Rupp's coaching ability. The first murmurs were being heard that perhaps it was time for the Baron to step down. Rupp, though, would have none of it. All he needed was one more miracle to silence the doubters.

He would get it, thanks to an unlikely gang that came to be forever immortalized as "The Fiddlin' Five."

1957-58

Rupp couldn't have felt much confidence heading into the season. Certainly, he had no way of knowing that this team would give him his fourth and final NCAA championship.

Rupp was surrounded by a solid group of veterans. Hatton, Crigler, Smith and Beck, all seniors now, were joined in the starting lineup by Cox. For backup, Rupp had Cassady, Adkins, Don Mills and Lincoln Collinsworth. It was a good team, but not one that brought on visions of a national title.

Even Rupp said as much: "We're fiddlers, that's all. They're pretty good fiddlers — be right entertaining at a barn dance. But I'll tell you, you need violinists to play at Carnegie Hall. We don't have any violinists."

Perhaps not. But Rupp did have two factors working in his favor. First, this was a gritty group of players who knew how to win big games, some in spectacular fashion. Second, in Hatton, UK had one of the greatest clutch players in the school's history.

The Cats displayed that toughness by beating Duke 78-74 and Ohio State 61-54 in their first two outings. Hatton had 46 points for UK in those two victories.

Then came one of the most unforgettable and exciting games in UK history — an 85-83 triple-overtime win over Temple. It was in this thrilling victory that Hatton cemented his reputation as Mr. Clutch. With one second left in the first overtime, and with his team trailing 71-69, Hatton took an inbounds pass from Crigler and launched a 47-foot shot that found its mark. Then, after the two teams were deadlocked at 75-75 at the end of the second extra frame, Hatton took over. In the final overtime, following two free throws each by Crigler and Smith, Hatton scored the next six points to help the Cats finally put away the Owls. Cox led UK with 22 points, while Hatton, Crigler and Smith each finished with 17. Rodgers and Mel Brodsky each scored 24 for Temple.

As fate would have it, this was the first of two meetings between the two clubs that season. The second encounter, which had far more at stake, turned out to be even more pressure packed than the first.

Following the win over Temple, UK went into a slide, losing three of its next four games. Included among those setbacks was a 77-70 loss to West Virginia in the UKIT opener. Lloyd Sharrer had 21 for the Mountaineers and Jerry West chipped in with 15. Cox led UK with a game-best 23. The loss was Rupp's 100th since taking over at UK in 1930. His record now stood at 565-100.

With his team sitting on a 4-3 record, and with an outlook that was anything but bright, Rupp's description of his players as barnyard fiddlers was proving accurate. He was also accurate when he said his team lacked consistency.

But the courageous Cats weren't ready to be written off as losers. With every player stepping up his performance level, the Cats managed to turn things around and win 15 of their final 18 games to finish with a 19-6 record. Their 12-2 mark in SEC play was good enough to capture the league crown.

Members of the 1958 NCAA championship team included, sitting, Rupp, Adrian Smith, Johnny Crigler, Ed Beck, Don Mills, Johnny Cox, Vernon Hatton and Harry Lancaster. Standing, manager Jay Atkerson, Earl Adkins, Bill Smith, Phil Johnson, Billy Ray Cassady, Lincoln Collinsworth and Harold Ross.

Standing between the Cats and another league championship was Bailey Howell and his Mississippi State teammates. UK built a 34-24 halftime lead, then played the Maroons on even terms in the final 20 minutes to come away with a crucial 72-62 win. Howell's 28-point effort was offset by the combined 57 points scored by the UK trio of Cox (22), Hatton (18) and Crigler (17).

The Cats did stumble once during the final month of the regular season, and it was a shocking fall. Loyola of Chicago, which UK defeated 75-42 earlier in the season, scored a major 57-56 stunner when Art McZier sank 15-foot hook shot at the buzzer. Hatton paced UK with 22 points. It was his jumper with four seconds left that put the Cats on top 56-55 and set the stage for McZier's heroics.

The Cats bounced back to win three of their final four games, losing only to Auburn 64-63 on the road. They beat Vanderbilt 65-61, Alabama 45-43 in overtime on a last-second basket by Crigler, and Tennessee 77-66.

Despite their strong finish, the Cats weren't given much of a chance to win the national championship. But they did have one huge plus in their favor — all of their games would be played in Kentucky. The Mideast Regional was to be held in Memorial Coliseum, and the Final Four in Louisville's Freedom Hall.

The Cats gave two of their finest performances of the season in the Mideast Regional. With Cox scoring 23 points and Smith adding 18, the Cats opened with a 94-70 romp past Miami of Ohio. That was followed by a surprisingly easy 89-56 victory over a good Notre Dame team. In fact, the Irish, led by Tom Hawkins, were favored to win. But the game was never in doubt. UK took the lead early and won going away.

Balance was the key to UK's win. All five starters scored in double figures, with Hatton's 26 points earning game-high honors. Smith finished with 16, Cox 14, Crigler and Beck 11 each.

Next up: a rematch with Temple, and more late-game magic from Hatton.

With nearly 19,000 fans looking on, UK and Temple picked up where they left off in December. The two clubs dueled, fought and scraped like a pair of great boxers. Each had the other on the ropes, but couldn't deliver the knockout punch. The score was 31-31 at intermission, and 42-42 with just under 11 minutes remaining.

Then Rodgers took over, hitting four quick baskets to give Temple a 59-55 advantage. But UK wouldn't go

away. Over the next two minutes, Smith wrapped four free throws around a single freebie by Temple's Dan Fleming to make it 60-59 with 29 seconds left.

UK's Collinsworth then fouled Rodgers, but the Temple All-American missed. Following a UK timeout, Hatton drove the baseline and scored on a layup to give his team a 61-60 lead. The Owls had the ball and 12 seconds to work with, but their hopes were dashed when Bill "Pickles" Kennedy lost the ball out of bounds.

Cox led UK in that win with 22 points. Hatton and Smith, both of whom were superb down the stretch, had 13 and 12, respectively. Rodgers had 22 for the Owls.

All that now stood between Rupp and his fourth national title was Seattle. The Chieftains, like the Wildcats, were an unlikely finalist. But with Elgin Baylor providing the scoring and rebounding punch, Seattle fought its way into the title game by registering an impressive 73-51 semifinal win over heavily favored Kansas State.

Seattle dominated early, taking a 29-18 lead with 7:44 left in the first half. But UK battled back, and by intermission, trailed by three (39-36) thanks to strong efforts by Hatton and Crigler. Then less than four minutes into the second half, Baylor was whistled for his fourth personal and the momentum suddenly shifted in UK's favor. With Cox on fire from the outside, the Cats built a 67-60 lead. Seattle did manage to make one final charge, closing to within 68-65. But two free throws by Cox sparked a late UK run that put Seattle away for good.

Hatton had 30 points to lead UK. Cox finished with 24, 16 of which came in the final 15 minutes. Crigler, whose early driving to the basket resulted in Baylor's foul problems, had 14. Mills also gave a terrific effort, scoring nine points. It was his hook shot that put UK in front for good at 61-60.

Baylor led Seattle with 25 points.

Rupp had delivered on his promise. The NCAA, which had severely punished UK and harshly reprimanded Rupp in the early 1950s, once again put the championship trophy in his hands. Rupp's fiddlers had played a winning tune.

1958-59

With Cox as the only returning starter, and with a host of new and unproven players on hand, expectations for the Wildcats were lower than they had been in years. In fact, most experts gave the Cats no chance of making any noise on a national scale.

Adolph Rupp with Sid Cohen, Al Robinson, Don Mills, Ned Jennings, Billy Ray Lickert, Bennie Coffman and Dick Parsons prior to the 1958-59 season. This group helped lead the Wildcats to a 24-3 record.

But the experts couldn't have been more wrong. What many predicted to be a disastrous season quickly turned out to be one of the most surprising — and pleasant — seasons in UK history.

Rupp knew going in that he had the rugged Cox to build around. Now a senior and an bona fide All-America candidate, Cox would be the Cats' leader. Rupp also had the 6'7" Mills to handle the center position. Mills had finished the previous season on a high note, and was now being counted on to add offensive punch and solid board work.

However, once Rupp got beyond Cox and Mills, he was navigating in uncharted waters. The remainder of the UK roster consisted of nothing but question marks. There was a mixture of JUCOs (Sid Cohen, Bennie Coffman) and sophomores (Billy Ray Lickert, Bobby Slusher, Dickie Parsons, Ned Jennings), none of whom had proven themselves at this level. Little wonder, then, that no one considered these Cats to be much of a threat.

But from the opening tipoff it was apparent that the experts were way off base in their quick dismissal of this

club. The Cats startled everyone by winning their first 11 games, including a 97-91 upset of Jerry West and West Virginia in the UKIT, and a miraculous 58-56 comeback victory against Maryland in overtime.

Cox, Mills, Lickert, Slusher and Cohen were the starters in UK's 91-68 opening win against Florida State. The two veterans, Cox and Mills, led UK with 27 and 20 points, respectively. Louisville native and future coach Hugh Durham scored 30 for the Seminoles.

Cox had 22 and Mills 17 to lead the Cats past Temple 76-71, then Cohen had 19 and Parsons 14 in a 78-64 win over Duke. Lickert, the former Mr. Basketball from Lexington Lafayette, had his first big scoring outburst, knocking down 23 points as the Cats defeated SMU 72-60. Cox then came through with 27 in a 76-57 win over St. Louis.

Perhaps no win more clearly exemplified the grit and determination of this team than the one against Maryland. Down 54-51 with 10 seconds left, Rupp called a timeout and ordered one of his guards, either Parsons or Coffman, to drive straight for the basket, score and, hopefully, draw a foul in the process. Coffman did just that, going for a layup, and in the process, drawing a foul from Maryland's Al Bunge. Coffman made the freebie to send the game into the extra period. Given new life, the Cats quickly took over. Cox sank a field goal and Parsons hit one of two free throws to give UK a lead it wouldn't relinquish. Final: UK 58, Maryland 57.

The unbeaten Cats went into their UKIT first-round matchup against Ohio State at less than full strength. But even with Mills and Lickert out because of a stomach virus, the Cats, behind 23 points each from Cox and Slusher, had little trouble beating Ohio State 95-76.

Lickert also missed the championship game, but Mills played and scored 17 points in the Cats' 97-91 win over West Virginia. Cohen had 23, Slusher 19 and Cox 16 for the winners. West gave one of the great performances ever

seen in Memorial Coliseum, finishing with 36 points.

The Cats, unheralded and unranked when the season began, had climbed to No. 1 in both polls by the time they squared off against Vanderbilt in Nashville. It was here that UK's 11-game winning streak came to an end. Vandy took advantage of a miserable shooting night by the visitors (23 of 77 for 29.9 percent) to bump off the unbeaten Cats 75-66. Jim Henry had 29 for the victorious Commodores. Lickert's 14 was tops for UK.

After losing at Vandy, the Cats came back to win seven straight and 12 of their final 13. One of those wins, a 108-55 victory over Georgia, was No. 600 for Rupp against just 104 losses. Five Cats hit for double figures in that game, led by Slusher with 17 and Lickert and Mills with 15 each.

Billy Ray Lickert earned SEC Sophomore of the Year recognition for his performance during the 1958-59 campaign.

The lone setback came when the All-American Howell led Mississippi State to a conference-clinching 66-58 win over the Cats in Starkville. Howell had 27 points and 17 rebounds, but it was the Maroons' tight zone defense that was the big difference. The baffled Cats, who managed only 16 first-half points, made good on just 21 of 60 attempts for 35 percent.

However, because of its refusal to play against black players, Mississippi State once again declined its automatic berth in the NCAA tourney, thus allowing UK to participate.

One of UK's strongest showings, and perhaps Lickert's finest-ever in a Wildcat uniform, came in a 71-52 thumping of Notre Dame. Lickert was simply magnificent, scoring 24 points and grabbing 17 rebounds while holding Notre Dame All-American Tom Hawkins to 13 points, 11 below his average.

Auburn came to Lexington riding a 30-game winning streak that spanned two years, but with Cox and Lickert each scoring 18 and Coffman adding 16, the Cats won with ease 75-56. Cox hit his career high of 38 in UK's 69-56 win over Tennessee, then learned that he had been named to the

AP's first-team All-America quintet along with West, Howell, Cincinnati's Oscar Robertson and Kansas State's Bob Boozer.

UK ended the regular season with a 23-2 record, a second-place finish in the SEC and a No. 2 ranking in the AP and UPI polls. Not bad for a team that no one had taken seriously when the season began. For his role in molding another championship-caliber team, Rupp was voted national Coach of the Year.

Cox had been brilliant throughout, scoring 17.9 points per game and averaging 12.2 rebounds. By the time he finished his career, Cox had accumulated 1,461 points and 1,004 rebounds, making him one of only four players in UK history to score more than 1,000 points and grab more than 1,000 rebounds. Dan Issel, Frank Ramsey and Cliff Hagan are the other three.

But Cox wasn't the only Wildcat to shine during this amazing season. Coffman and Mills both averaged in double figures, while Cohen, Slusher and Parsons turned in consistent and solid efforts.

And in Lickert, UK had yet another in a long line of talented sophomores who stepped in and played far beyond anyone's expectations. Lickert averaged 13.5 points per game, second only to Cox. For his outstanding play, Lickert was named SEC Sophomore of the Year.

However, as sweet as UK's season had been, it ended in the worst way imaginable for Big Blue fans — a stunning 76-61 loss to in-state rival Louisville in the opening round of the Mideast Regional.

The Cats seized control early, and when Lickert hit a short jumper, they were sitting on a 27-12 lead. UK was still on top 36-28 at intermission, but the Cardinals, thanks to a successful full-court press and strong ownership of the boards, dominated the second half. Louisville won the battle of the boards 46-37, while holding the Cats to just 33 percent shooting from the field (22 of 67). The Cardinals, meanwhile, hit 25 of 55 for 46 percent.

Lickert led UK with 16 points. Coffman had 13 and Cox, who connected on just three of his 15 shots, added 10. Louisville's Don Goldstein topped all scorers with 19 points.

This would be the last time the two teams faced each other until the "Dream Game" in 1983.

One night later, UK rode the hot shooting by Coffman to a 98-69 win over Marquette in the consolation game. The victory gave the Cats a final 24-3 record. Coffman made good on 13 of 18 field goal attempts and finished with 28 points. Mills also had a big night offensively, scoring 24 points.

A season begun under a dark cloud of doubt had turned into one of the brightest in UK history. It would be three years before those rays of sunshine broke through again.

1959-60

With a cast of familiar characters returning from the previous season, the Cats were projected to have another successful campaign. But that wouldn't be the case. Facing a brutal pre-SEC schedule that included road games against UCLA, USC, St. Louis and Kansas, and home games against West Virginia (yet another meeting with Jerry West), North Carolina and Ohio State, the Cats struggled early and never really got untracked. By season's end the Cats could manage only a mediocre and disappointing 18-7 record. Their 10-4 SEC record was far off the championship pace set by Auburn, thus eliminating the Cats from postseason play.

Individually, many of the UK players acquitted themselves well. Lickert, despite missing five games, led the scoring with a 14.4 average. Mills scored at a 12.7 clip and had a team-best 12.9 rebounding average, while the backcourt duo of Cohen and Coffman averaged 10.7 and 10.2, respectively. Off the bench, UK had good performances from Jim McDonald, Carroll Burchett, Larry Pursiful and Allen Feldhaus.

Coffman came off the bench to score 18 points as the Cats opened with a strong 106-73 victory over Colorado State. Parsons and McDonald each contributed 14 points. Rupp's starters for the opener included Lickert, Feldhaus, Jennings, Cohen and Parsons.

Members of the 1959-60 team included, sitting Adolph Rupp, Dick Parsons, Eddie Mason, Larry Pursiful, Bennie Coffman, Al Robinson, Sid Cohen, Billy Ray Lickert and Harry Lancaster. Standing trainer Sam Pressman, Herky Rupp, Roy Roberts, Harry Hurd, Ned Jennings, Don Mills, Allen Feldhaus, Jim McDonald and manager Tommy Thompson.

After 14 ties and the same number of lead changes, it took five late points by Cohen to lift the Cats past UCLA 68-66 in Los Angeles. Lickert paced UK with 23 points.

The second leg of UK's West Coast journey didn't turn out so successfully. Southern Cal raced to an easy 87-73 win over the foul-plagued Cats. Jennings had 21 for UK before being hit with his fifth foul. Lickert and Coffman also fouled out.

Red-hot St. Louis broke open a tight game in the second half and went on to beat the road-weary Cats 73-61. Pete McCaffrey had 21 points for the Billikens, who shot 52 percent from the field for the game. Lickert's 20 was tops for UK.

After the game, a "terribly disappointed" Rupp said, "If these boys get whipped a few more times, maybe they'll realize the folks at home don't appreciate them loafing around."

Playing on the road for a fourth straight game, the Cats snapped their two-game losing streak with a 77-72 overtime win over Kansas. Jennings led UK with 27 points, Coffman had 18 and Mills 13. Kansas star Wayne Hightower turned in a supreme effort, scoring 33 points and snatching 14 rebounds for the Jayhawks.

The Cats returned home to face North Carolina in the UKIT. With Coffman hitting for 23 and Lickert adding 15, the Cats squeezed past the Tar Heels 76-70 to set up a championship game matchup with West Virginia.

Lickert's early defense on West enabled the Cats to stay close throughout much of the first half. But when Lickert was tagged with his fourth personal foul prior to intermission, West took over. Despite playing with a broken nose, West, who Rupp always considered to be among the two or three best players he ever coached against, finished with 33 points to lead his Mountaineers to a title-clinching 79-70 win. Coffman had 20 to lead UK in scoring.

Many years later, when recalling the difficult task of guarding West, Lickert said, "I think the guy scored six points during the National Anthem."

The Cats followed the West Virginia loss by giving two of their finest performances of the season, beating Temple 97-92 and Ohio State 96-93. Lickert was outstanding, scoring 56 points in those two wins.

The win over Ohio State will forever rank as one of the most memorable games ever played in Memorial Coliseum. This was the Buckeye team that had Jerry Lucas, John Havlicek, Larry Siegfried, Mel Nowell and Joe Roberts. It was a young, powerful and imposing team, which it proved three

months later by winning the national title with a 75-55 win over California.

To upset the Buckeyes, UK had to overcome a brilliant 34-point performance by Lucas and an eight-point Ohio State lead inside the game's final 10 minutes.

After falling behind by 15 in the first half, the Cats, who trailed 59-49 at intermission, suddenly caught fire. With Lickert and Coffman igniting the assault, the Cats pulled to within 67-66 with 13:58 left. But Ohio State answered, outscoring the Cats 13-6 over the next four minutes to take an 80-72 lead.

The Cats responded with a flurry of points, and when Coffman knocked in a short jumper with 5:13 remaining, they had taken an 85-84 advantage. After the Buckeyes nudged ahead 86-85, Mills hit a free throw and a spinning jump shot in the lane to give UK an 88-86 lead with 3:06 left to play. That marked the 10th and final lead change of the game.

Trailing 90-86 and desperate to get the ball, Ohio State began to foul. At first, it looked like the ploy might work. Twice the Cats missed the front end of the bonus, allowing Ohio State to close to within 90-89 with just 45 ticks left on the clock.

But with the game on the line, UK connected on six free throws — four by Cohen, two by Burchett — inside the final 35 seconds to hang on for the victory.

Lickert and Coffman were sensational, combining for 54 points. Lickert had 29, while Coffman had 26. Mills and Burchett each contributed 13 points and 11 rebounds.

Ironically, Coffman also had a broken nose at the time. He suffered his injury against West Virginia, the same game in which West had his nose broken.

UK opened SEC action with a 62-54 home-court loss to Georgia Tech and a 76-59 win at Vanderbilt. Then the Cats were hit with a double dose of bad luck. First, Lickert went down with an injury that sidelined him for five games. (This club was slowed by injuries all season. Parsons, Jennings and McDonald also missed considerable playing time due to being injured.)

The second bit of bad news involved Roger Newman, a talented 6'4" Greenville native who Rupp was counting on to strengthen the Cats. Newman averaged 16.1 points as a freshman, then was ruled ineligible because of academic problems. Newman redeemed himself in the classroom and was initially given the OK to play by SEC Commissioner Bernie Moore. However, upon learning that Newman

had played for the Lexington YMCA team, Moore quickly reversed his decision and ruled Newman ineligible.

Despite the injuries and the inconsistent play, the Cats went to Auburn with a 9-2 league record and an outside shot at getting into postseason action. But those hopes were dashed when Jimmy Fibbe dropped in two free throws with four seconds left to give the Tigers a 61-60 win. Lickert, Mills and Cohen each had 14 for UK. Ray Groover led Auburn with 22, while Fibbe, a Frankfort native, finished with 17.

In his first start, Pursiful pitched in 15 points to help UK beat Alabama 75-55. Lickert was UK's top scorer with 18. Tennessee came to Lexington and handed the Cats their third

In his only season as a Wildcat, Roger Newman led the 1960-61 team in rebounding and was the second-leading scorer.

home-court loss of the season, winning 65-63 on a 20-foot jump shot by Dalen Showalter with six seconds remaining. Lickert had 20 for UK and Mills added 15.

Lickert hit for 21 and Cohen had 13 as the Cats closed out their season with a 73-66 victory over Pittsburgh. The win left UK with a final record of 18-7.

Rupp had suffered through one of his most disappointing seasons at UK. With little help on the way from the recruiting ranks, the immediate future didn't look particularly bright.

1960-61

This season marked the lowest point during Rupp's first 30 years as UK's head coach. The team would finish with a 19-9 record, the most losses a Rupp team had ever suffered.

Despite the high number of marks in the loss column, this team was, in some ways, an overachiever. There wasn't much size or depth, yet these Cats scored impressive wins over North Carolina, Notre Dame, Georgia Tech and eventual SEC champ Mississippi State. They ended the season ranked in the Top 20 (No.18) and earned a spot in the NCAA Tournament by beating Vanderbilt in a one-game

playoff to decide the SEC's representative. (Mississippi State again rejected its chance to participate because of a steadfast refusal to play against black players.)

Lickert was back for his final season, and it was around him that Rupp built this team. Pursiful, a slim 6'1" junior guard with a deadly outside jumper, was also being counted on to provide scoring punch. Veterans Burchett, Jennings, Parsons and Feldhaus were all slated for their share of playing time. So was 6'5" JUCO transfer Vinny Del Negro. Missing from the team was the talented Slusher, who had been dismissed for disciplinary reasons.

Joining this mix was Newman, who, after four years in basketball exile, was finally eligible to play. Newman was part of a 1956 recruiting haul by Rupp that quickly turned sour. Newman, Corky Withrow, Jackie Moreland and Don Mills were among the top players in the nation as high school seniors, and all four opted to sign with UK. But of those four, only Mills played four years at Kentucky. Withrow signed a pro baseball contract, Moreland chose instead to play at Louisiana Tech and Newman, after a successful freshman year, began his well-publicized odyssey. (Another player in that '56 class was the legendary "King" Kelly Coleman, the Wayland Wonder, who, despite being heavily courted by Rupp, spurned UK and signed with West Virginia.)

After nearly four years out of action, Newman finally migrated back to UK. His presence was a big reason why this UK team achieved what it did. Newman was versatile enough to play guard or forward, and he had the ability to score from long range or in close. In addition, his great leaping ability helped the smallish Cats hold their own against most opponents on the boards. Despite being just 6'4", Newman led the team in rebounding with a 9.5 average.

Newman had 20 points and 17 rebounds in UK's 72-56

win over VMI in the opener. Lickert, Feldhaus, Del Negro and Pursiful rounded out UK's starting quintet. Despite the Cats' win, the big talk that night centered on freshman Cotton Nash, who scored 40 points in the preliminary game.

UK's woes began with a 63-58 home-court loss to Florida State. That was followed by wins over Notre Dame (68-62) and North Carolina (70-65). Lickert had 21 against the Irish, while Jennings had 19 points and 14 rebounds in the win over North Carolina. Doug Moe led the Tar Heels with 25 points.

The Cats entered SEC play by winning three of their last five pre-conference games. Temple, led by guard Bruce Drysdale's 25 points, beat the Cats 66-58. St. Louis also got the best of UK, claiming the UKIT title with a 74-72 overtime win. The UK wins came against Illinois (83-78), Missouri (81-69) and Miami of Ohio (70-58). Lickert, Newman and Pursiful were all playing well, but beyond those three, the play was inconsistent. Lickert had 29-point efforts against St. Louis and Missouri, Pursiful had 21 against Illinois and Missouri, while Newman accounted for 24 points and 12 rebounds against Illinois and 17 points against Missouri.

The shoddy, erratic play continued once SEC action began. After Lickert scored 25 in an 89-79 win over Georgia Tech, the Cats lost four of their next five games, all of which were on the road. Vanderbilt edged the Cats 64-62 in Nashville, then LSU, which had never beaten UK in 19 tries, pulled off a 73-59 shocker. A pair of two-point losses — 72-70 to Tulane and 62-60 to Georgia Tech — plunged the slumping Cats toward the bottom of the SEC standings. The lone victory in that sting of dismal efforts came against Tennessee. Pursiful's 20 points led the Cats to an 83-54 win over the Vols.

At this stage, the Cats were 2-4 in SEC play and all but out of the title chase. With an 8-7 record overall, even a winning season wasn't a foregone conclusion. But just when the Cats reached their lowest ebb, they suddenly caught fire. Playing flawlessly and with great heart, they won their final nine regular-season games. Miraculously, the pendulum had swung in a different direction. It's one of the great turnarounds in UK hoops history.

The streak began when Lickert and Jennings combined for 46 points in a sound 89-68 thumping of previously unbeaten Florida. Lickert had 24, Jennings 22 in that win. Then Newman snapped out of a scoring slump with a 24-point effort in the Cats' 74-67 win over Georgia. Newman and Pursiful each scored 18 and Parsons added 12 as

the resurgent Cats upped their winning streak to three with a 74-60 win over Ole Miss.

Any remaining doubts about this UK team's astonishing turnaround, or its grit and courage, were laid to rest in Starkville, Miss. In a near-perfect performance, the Cats upset heavily favored Mississippi State 68-62. Newman led the way with 24 points. Pursiful finished with 16, while Lickert and Jennings each had 13. Jerry Graves had 26 points and 12 rebounds for the Maroons.

Newman continued his brilliant play with a 26-point, 18-rebound performance in the Cats' 77-76 non-conference win over UCLA. That gave Newman 92 points in UK's last four games. Pursiful also made life miserable for the Bruins, hitting for 21 points.

Two crucial buckets by Feldhaus and a short jumper by Jennings lifted the Cats to a 60-59 win over Vanderbilt. Pursiful had 19 for UK, Lickert 10 and Feldhaus six.

The Cats routed Alabama 80-53 and Auburn 77-51 at home, then ended the season with a 68-61 win at Tennessee. With the two teams dead even at 58-58, Burchett decided the matter in UK's favor by scoring eight points in the final three minutes. Five Cats scored in double figures, headed by Jennings with 18.

The nine straight wins left UK with a 10-4 SEC record, good enough to tie Vanderbilt for second place. With league champ Mississippi State out of the postseason picture, UK and Vandy were scheduled for a one-game showdown in Knoxville to decide which team would be the SEC's representative in NCAA Tournament action.

The two clubs split their regular-season games, with Vandy winning 64-62 in Nashville and UK scratching out a 60-59 win in Lexington. The playoff game was expected to be another close and fierce war.

But the great battle never materialized. Playing perhaps its finest game of the season, UK utterly demolished the Commodores, winning 88-67 to earn a spot in the NCAA Tournament. Once again, five UK players cracked double figures, led by Pursiful with 21 and Newman with 18. Lickert and Jennings each had 14, while Parsons had 13.

UK's 10-game winning streak was stopped by Marquette in a final pre-tournament tune-up in Chicago. The Warriors dominated all the way, easily winning 88-72.

The Cats were paired against Ohio Valley Conference winner Morehead State in the NCAA tourney's Mideast Regional. Despite being a big underdog, Morehead State

gave the Cats all they wanted, before eventually coming up on the short end of a 71-64 score.

Lickert was the driving force behind UK's win, scoring 28 points. Newman and Burchett also hit double digits with 14 and 12, respectively. Granny Williams had 20 for the Eagles.

On deck for the Cats was Ohio State, the defending NCAA champs. This time, Lucas, Havlicek and Co. were too much for the Cats to handle. With Lucas scoring 33 points and grabbing 30 rebounds (one more than the entire UK team) and Siegfried adding 20 points, the Buckeyes had little trouble posting an 87-74 win.

Newman paced the Cats with 31 points, including 17 of 22 from the charity stripe. Lickert closed out his UK career with a 17-point performance.

Lickert was UK's leading scorer for the season, averaging 16 points per game. For his efforts, Lickert was again named to the All-SEC team. Other double-figure scorers included Newman (14.1), Pursiful (13.4) and Jennings (11.5).

After consecutive disappointing seasons, UK fans were desperate for something positive to happen. They wanted a return to the glory days. There was no arguing that the UK program, reeling from several years of recruiting failures, no longer held its place of prominence among the hierarchy of college basketball's elite teams.

What the once-mighty UK program needed was a savior. Fortunately for UK and its fans, one was on the way.

Cotton Nash.

1961-62

Few players in UK basketball history have captured the fans' imagination quite the way Cotton Nash did. Blonde, handsome, charismatic and exceptionally talented, the 6'5" Nash burst upon the UK scene like a meteor. Smoother than the finest silk, Nash was that rare basketball player who seemed capable of doing virtually anything he wanted to do. He could score from far beyond what is now the three-point line, or he could slither past defenders and score an easy layup.

Nash was also independent-minded, a fact that oftentimes got him in hot water with Rupp. The two men, both possessed of strong personalities, clashed often during the next three years. Theirs would always be an uneasy alliance.

But to UK fans, starved for the glory that once was, none of that mattered. To them, Nash was the player who could lift UK back to the pinnacle of college hoops. He was, from the very beginning, an instant hero. And yet, because of his great talent and the huge expectations he generated, Nash caught more than his share of heat from the fans. No matter what he did, it never seemed to be enough.

Perhaps Cawood Ledford said it best in his autobiography: "I've never understood why Cotton Nash took so

Adolph Rupp and three-time All-American Cotton Nash show off UK's four NCAA championship trophies. An uneasy alliance is the best way to describe the relationship between these two strong-willed, independent-minded personalities.

many knocks from the fans. Even though he was a three-time All-American, he was never able to satisfy everyone. As far as I'm concerned, they ought to build a monument to the guy. After UK had gone 19-9 in 1960-61, he absolutely carried the program on his back for the next three years."

Despite the presence of Nash, few expected the Cats to have the kind of season they had — a 23-3 record, co-SEC champs and a No. 3 national ranking in both polls.

One of the main concerns for this UK team was the lack of a true pivotman. Nash, a natural forward, spent most of the season (indeed, most of his career) playing out of position. On those occasions when Nash went outside to do his damage, Feldhaus or Burchett usually handled the post play. This was, all in all, one of the smallest UK teams in history.

But it was also a team with great chemistry. Burchett, Feldhaus, Scotty Baesler and Roy Roberts were marvelous role players. Feldhaus was as mean a player as UK has ever had, Roberts was an in-your-face defender, Baesler was a smart team leader and Burchett was a scoring threat and a terrific rebounder.

But what made this team so exceptional was its great inside-outside scoring duo of Nash and Pursiful. Because Pursiful developed into one of UK's best-ever outside shooters, opposing defenses never had the luxury of concentrating solely on stopping Nash. If the defenses collapsed, Pursiful made them pay dearly. When they sought to stop Pursiful, Nash was free to work his magic in close.

Nash made his mark early, scoring 25 points in the season-opening 93-61 win over Miami of Ohio. Then, just two nights later, Nash and Rupp collided for the first time. After making several turnovers, Nash was benched for the final 11 minutes against Southern Cal. The result was a 79-77 home-court loss.

Nash got back on track in his next game, scoring 30 points and snaring 17 rebounds in an 86-77 win over St. Louis. Baesler also had a big game, hitting for 20 points. The Cats beat Baylor 94-60, then came back to blast Temple 78-55. In that game, Nash had 20 points and a whopping 30 rebounds.

The UKIT, which UK won with wins over Tennessee and Kansas State, was a showcase for Pursiful. He scored 34 against the Vols, including 20 of UK's first 23 points, and 26 in the championship game against Kansas State. In UK's final pre-SEC game, Nash dazzled the Freedom Hall fans with a 31-point, 17-rebound performance in a 100-53 pasting of Notre Dame.

The surprising Cats, now ranked in the Top 10, went into SEC play with a 9-1 record. Nash continued to post big numbers, hitting for 35 against Georgia Tech, 31 against Vanderbilt and 26 against LSU. The Cats rose to No. 2 in the polls behind Ohio State after Pursiful and Nash each scored 30 in a fight-marred 95-82 win at Tennessee. Nash and Tennessee's Sid Elliott were involved in the altercation, after which Feldhaus chased Elliott down the court before cooler heads prevailed.

UK's first real SEC struggle was a come-from-behind 81-69 win at Florida. Feldhaus provided the spark that brought the Cats back from a 10-point deficit, scoring 16 points. Pursiful paced the winners with 26. Pursiful also led the Cats to an 83-60 win over Ole Miss, scoring 23 points. Nash had 22 points and 22 rebounds, while future Chicago Cubs shortstop Donnie Kessinger scored 21 for the Rebels.

Then came a home game against a veteran Mississippi State team that was led by Leland Mitchell, W.D. "Red" Stroud and Kentucky native Joe Dan Gold. Bulldog coach (and Rupp nemesis) Babe McCarthy, certain that a high-octane game would favor UK, devised a plan to slow down the rampaging Cats by spreading the court, driving to the bucket and taking only high-percentage shots.

McCarthy's plan, flawlessly executed by his veteran players, worked to perfection. The Bulldogs made good on 18 of 28 shots, including seven of eight in the second half, and came away with a 49-44 win. After the game, a Mississippi State team manager placed a wreath on UK's goal. Nash had 23 for the Cats. Stroud led Mississippi State with 17.

The Cats rebounded by winning their final five games to finish with a 22-2 record overall and 13-1 in SEC play. Nash sizzled in those five wins, scoring 157 points and locking up the SEC scoring title. He scored 38 in an 87-80 win over Vandy, then followed that with consecutive 30-point efforts in wins over Alabama (73-65) and Auburn (63-60). Nash had 31 points and 17 rebounds in the Cats' 97-72 win over Tulane and 28 points in a 90-59 drumming of Tennessee.

Despite their record, the Cats weren't alone at the top of the SEC standings. Mississippi State also had a 13-1 record, but for the third time in four years declined to participate in the NCAA Tournament.

In the Mideast Regional at Iowa City, Pursiful scored 26 points and Nash added 23 as UK opened by crushing Butler 81-60. That win set up another meeting against

Ohio State, the top-ranked team in the country. The Buckeyes won 74-64, thanks in no small measure to the terrific defensive job Havlicek did on Nash, who managed just 14 points on five of 19 shooting.

Lucas again proved to be too much for the Cats to handle. He scored 33 points, including 25 in the first half, and hauled down 15 rebounds. During a one-minute stretch in the opening half, Lucas scored three straight three-point plays. Pursiful was UK's top scorer with 21.

UK's season was over, and it had by all standards been a good one. Nash led the team with a 23.4 scoring average, the best by a UK player since Cliff Hagan. Nash was also the leading rebounder with an average of 13.2. He was named to the All-SEC first team, and to several All-America teams.

Pursiful, another All-SEC pick, finished with a 19.1 scoring average, while leading the team in field goal accuracy with 51 percent and free throw accuracy with 81.6 percent. Baesler was the top assist man, dishing out 4.3 per game.

With Nash returning, expectations were high for the 1962-63 season. For the first time in nearly four years, UK fans could once again dream the ultimate dream — seeing their Wildcats capture another national title. However, it wouldn't take long for that dream to vanish.

1962-63

It has often been remarked that the only two sure things in life are death and taxes. For UK fans, a third could be added — a Wildcat victory in the season opener. Indeed, no Rupp-coached team had ever suffered a season-opening loss. In fact, only once did the Cats win their season opener by fewer than 10 points. (UK beat Duke 78-74 to kick off the 1957-58 campaign.)

So when the Cats took the

floor against Virginia Tech on Dec. 1, 1962, no one expected anything other than a win. Opening game wins were, after all, automatic.

But Virginia Tech did something that 31 other UK opponents failed to do — pin an opening-night loss on Rupp's Cats. Virginia Tech upset UK 80-77 despite 34 points from Nash. In Memorial Coliseum, no less.

It was the beginning of a long and disappointing season for the Wildcats, one in which they fell from a lofty preseason perch to a 16-9 record overall and a middle-of-the-pack fifth-place finish in the SEC standings.

The reason for the Cats' tumble into mediocrity was simple: lack of talent. There was Nash, the All-American, but little else. No UK team before or since has ever depended so much on a single player. For UK to win, Nash had to post huge numbers.

But with no consistent outside shooter like Pursiful to keep defenses honest, Nash was a marked man. Teams could double- and triple-team him without fearing that another Wildcat would pick up the slack. As a result, Nash was forced to carry the load by himself. Although he acquitted himself well under difficult circumstances (averages of 20.6 points and 12 rebounds per game), he was unable to save this team or the season.

Nash did get some offensive support from Charles "Chili" Ishmael during the early part of the season. Ishmael averaged 11.1 points per game before being declared ineligible for the second semester.

Another Achilles' heel for this team was its inability to come through in close games.

Cotton Nash averaged 20.6 points and 12 rebounds during the disappointing 1962-63 season.

Of the nine losses, six were decided by four points or less. Two came in overtime. And five were in Memorial Coliseum, the mighty fortress where the Cats were once thought to be unbeatable.

The opening-night lineup consisted of Nash, Roberts, Baesler, Don Rolfes and Sam Harper. But that lineup changed regularly throughout the season. At various times, Rupp pencilled in Ishmael, Randy Embry, Ted Deeken and Terry Mobley as starters.

Embry's bucket broke a 52-52 tie and lifted the Cats to their first victory of the season, a 56-52 win over Temple. That was the beginning of a run in which the Cats won seven of their next eight games. The only loss came against North Carolina 68-66. It was Billy Cunningham's steal and layup that enabled the Tar Heels to come out on top. Larry Brown had 19 points for North Carolina. Rolfes paced UK with 18.

Despite suffering from a deep stone bruise in his foot, Nash gave two sterling performances in the UKIT. He had 27 points in a 94-69 win over Iowa, then came back one night later with a 30-point, 15-rebound effort in UK's 79-75 win over West Virginia. Roberts and Baesler had 19 and 14 points, respectively, for UK, while West Virginia guard Rod Thorn matched Nash with 30 points.

UK's good times ended with an 87-63 loss at St. Louis. It was the worst whipping a UK team had received since the 89-50 loss to CCNY in 1950. Georgia Tech then came into Memorial Coliseum and slipped out with an 86-85 double-overtime win. Ishmael had 22 for the Cats. Jim Caldwell led the Yellow Jackets with 19.

With Nash racking up 78 points, UK won three straight, beating Vanderbilt 106-82, LSU 63-56 and Tulane 81-72. Deeken saved the Cats against LSU, scoring 13 points after coming off the bench with his team down by seven. Deeken followed that with back-to-back 18-point performances against Tulane and Tennessee. His play in the win over Tulane earned him a spot in the starting lineup for the rest of the season.

Other Cats did have some shining moments. Rolfes scored all 20 of his points in the second half to lead UK past Notre Dame 78-70. Baesler had 22 against Vanderbilt, Embry had 14 against Ole Miss and Mobley had 13 against Dartmouth. But the team's fortunes clearly rested on Nash's shoulders. When he played well, the Cats had a shot at winning; when he was held in check, they lost.

Ishmael had his best game against Florida, scoring 30 points to lead UK to a 94-71 win. But that would be his last hurrah. After the Cats struggled to a hard-earned 75-69 win over Ole Miss, Ishmael, the team's second-leading scorer at the time, was declared academically ineligible. To make matters worse for the Cats, the 6'6" Rolfes missed several games due to tonsilitis.

Nash scored 14 points in the win over Florida, pushing him past the 1,000-point mark for his career. It was only his 45th game in a UK uniform, giving him the distinction of joining the 1,000-point club quicker than any Wildcat. It's a record Nash still owns.

Deeken's play was one of the few bright spots in the final month of the season. He had 25 against Mississippi State, 16 against Vandy and 17 against Auburn. Nash's best moments came when he scored 31 against Alabama and 28 against Auburn.

UK's final game was a fitting end to a dreadful season. With Rupp sick at home because of the flu, the Cats played poorly in a 63-55 loss at Tennessee. A.W. Davis led the Vols with 23. Nash's 16 topped UK.

Nash was once again named to several All-America teams, and was the lone Wildcat to make All-SEC.

Although the season had been a major disappointment, it wasn't hard to feel positive about the way the 1963-64 campaign was shaping up. Nash, the All-American, would be back for his final season. So would Ishmael, Embry, Mobley and the rapidly improving Deeken. And ready to join them was a talented trio of sophomores that Rupp tagged as the "Katzenjammer Kids."

1963-64

The arrival of "Katzenjammer Kids" Larry Conley, Tommy Kron and Mickey Gibson, along with veterans Deeken, Mobley, Ishmael and Embry, meant that Nash was at last surrounded by a deeper and more talented supporting cast. And it showed. Nash went on to have another All-America season, and the Cats, despite a dismal tournament showing, rose to No. 1 in the nation for the first time since 1959.

Of the three rookies, Conley, a native of Ashland, made the strongest impact. The son of a former coach, Conley was then — and remains so today — one of the smartest players to ever put on a UK uniform. There was nothing about the game that Conley didn't know and understand. He was an excellent shooter, a good defender, and despite his frail-looking appearance, a better-than-average rebounder. But above all else, Conley excelled at passing

the basketball. He is still considered by many to be the finest passer in UK history.

Nash was the chief beneficiary of Conley's deft passing ability and unselfish attitude. Another Cat who thrived was Deeken, who, until his senior year, had been little more than a role player. But with Conley distributing the ball, and with Nash still drawing the brunt of opponents' defensive efforts, the 6'4" Deeken emerged as a legitimate scoring threat. As a shooter capable of having big scoring nights, Deeken, like Pursiful two years earlier, was able to draw some of the heat away from Nash.

Nash and Deeken each scored 28 points as the Cats opened with a 95-64 win over Virginia. Also in the starting lineup that night were Mobley, Embry and 6'7" junior John Adams.

The Cats, behind Nash's 33 points, blistered Texas Tech 107-91 in their second outing of the young season. Other Cats in double figures included Deeken (20), Conley (17), Embry (16) and Mobley (10).

Conley made his first start against Northwestern, scoring 12 points in a 95-63 romp. Deeken led UK with 29, while Nash had 27.

In their first real test of the season, the charged-up Cats rolled to a 100-80 win over a good North Carolina team. UK's balanced scoring attack, which featured five players in double figures, was enough to offset a brilliant 32-point, 20-rebound performance by Billy Cunningham. Nash led the way with 23, Mobley and Deeken each had 22, Ishmael 17 and Conley 15 for the victorious Wildcats.

Gibson made his first appearance after gaining his academic eligibility, scoring nine points in UK's 108-85 win over Wisconsin in the UKIT opener. Nash topped UK with 33 points, while Deeken and Mobley added 23 and 20,

Terry Mobley's last-second jumper beat Duke 81-79 in the championship game of the 1963 Sugar Bowl tournament. The win also sent UK to No. 1 in the polls for the first time since 1959.

respectively. One night later, the Cats won the title with a 98-75 win over Wake Forest. Once again, all five starters cracked double figures, led by Nash with 28.

After Nash scored 33 and Deeken 27 in a 101-81 win over Notre Dame, the Cats beat Loyola of Louisiana 86-64 in the first round of the Sugar Bowl tournament in New Orleans. That win set up a meeting with tall and talented Duke.

The Blue Devils had a giant front line that featured a pair of 6'10" players — Jay Buckley and Hack Tison. They also had an All-American, former Kentucky native Jeff Mullins. The 6'4" Mullins, a Lexington Lafayette graduate, had been Kentucky's Mr. Basketball in 1960.

Duke led early, and took a 47-37 lead into the locker room at intermission. But with Nash scoring 20 of his 30 points in the second half, the Cats managed to take a 72-70 lead when Deeken hit a hook shot. Duke again reclaimed a two-point advantage at 79-77, but UK was able to draw even at 79-79 on a Mobley jumper. Duke's attempt to hold for a last-second shot was foiled when Deeken knocked the ball away from Tison. The alert Kron scooped it up and immediately called for a timeout.

The obvious choice to take UK's last shot was Nash. But with only seven seconds left, and with Nash unable to get free, it was left to Mobley to fill the role of hero. He moved down the left side of the foul lane, pulled up and hit a jump shot with four seconds left to give UK the two-point win.

Nash, who scored 58 points in the two games, was named the tournament's MVP.

When the AP and UPI polls were released the following Monday, the Cats, now 10-0, held down the top spot.

Larry Conley goes in for an uncontested layup. Conley is still regarded by many as the best passer in UK history.

But the glory didn't last long. Within the next three days, after losing 76-67 at Georgia Tech and 85-83 at Vanderbilt when John Ed Miller sank a 25-footer with one second left, the Cats tumbled from No. 1 in the nation to last in the SEC. Gibson had his best game in the loss to Vandy, scoring a team-high 19 points.

A 103-84 win over LSU triggered a second 10-game winning streak that helped lift the Cats back into first place in the SEC. During that stretch, the red-hot Cats went over the century mark five times. But in a must-win game against Tennessee, it was UK's defense rather than its offense that made the difference. With Kron making his first start, and with UK using a zone defense for the first time under Rupp, the Cats beat Tennessee 66-57.

Conley hit for 20 in a 77-72 win over Florida, then Nash and Deeken combined for 62 points to lead the

Cats past Georgia 103-83 and give Rupp his 700th win. Now in his 34th season at UK, Rupp had guided his teams to a 700-136 record.

Mississippi State came to Lexington and gave the Cats a scare before falling 65-59. Deeken had 19 to lead UK. Nash scored 32, Ishmael 20 and Conley 17 as the Cats got revenge against Vanderbilt with a 104-73 win. In the Cats' next game, a 99-79 win over Auburn, Deeken scored 34 points and Nash had 33.

Then came one of the most-perplexing and disappointing finishes ever experienced by a UK team. Just when it looked like the Cats were rolling toward great postseason success, the thunder suddenly vanished from the offense. During their final three regular-season games, a team that had scored 100 or more points on 10 occasions averaged an anemic 53.7 points. The player most missing in action was Nash, who scored just 30 points in those three games.

UK's lone win, 42-38 at Tennessee, was sandwiched between a 65-59 loss at Alabama and a 67-60 loss to St. Louis in Memorial Coliseum. Despite a 21-4 record, the SEC championship and a No. 4 ranking in the polls, the shaken Cats staggered into the NCAA Tournament.

They also went in without Gibson, who, one day before the team departed for Minneapolis, was kicked off the squad for disciplinary reasons. Although he was only 6'2", Gibson possessed exceptional leaping ability. His loss was a big blow to a team that needed all the rebounding help it could get.

Earlier in the season, after losing two straight, the Cats had been able to turn things around and get back into high gear. That wasn't the case this time. Cold shooting continued to plague the Cats, who were upset 85-69 by Ohio University in the Mideast Regional in Minneapolis.

UK, which hit just 31 of 80 shots for 39 percent, trailed 40-24 at the half and was never in the game. Conley and Mobley each had 17 points to lead the Cats. Nash was lim-

ited to just 10.

In the consolation game against Loyola of Chicago, it was the defense that failed the Cats. UK found its shooting touch, but the Ramblers, led by Les Hunter's 27 points and 18 rebounds, raced to a 100-91 victory. The loss left UK with a final record of 21-6.

Nash paced the Cats with 23 points. Mobley finished with 21, while Conley and Deeken had 15 and 12, respectively.

For his career, Nash scored 1,770 points to surpass Alex Groza as UK's all-time leading scorer. Nash averaged 24 points and 11.7 rebounds in his final season. He remains the only UK player to average 20 points for three seasons. His 22.7 career scoring average is second only to Dan Issel's 25.8.

Deeken also had a strong senior season, averaging 18.5 points per game. Conley scored at a 12.2 clip while handing out 4.2 assists per game.

The great Nash was gone, taking with him 1,770 points and 962 rebounds. Rupp knew that replacing those numbers wasn't going to be easy. But the Baron had two players waiting in the wings who just might be able to do it — a tough, talented New Yorker and a quiet long-range gunner from Indiana.

1964-65

Pat Riley and Louie Dampier were two-thirds of a recruiting class that Rupp was counting on to do big things at UK. The third member of that trio was Wayne Chapman, a 6'6" Owensboro native whose son Rex would later become a star Wildcat.

Pat Riley averaged 15 points as a sophomore, then came back the next season to lead the 1965-66 NCAA runner-up team in scoring with a 22-point average.

As freshmen, Riley, Dampier and Chapman had been sensational. All three averaged better than 20 points per game. But what made them so special was their versatility. Riley and Chapman could play inside or out on the floor with equal efficiency, while Dampier seemed to have unlimited shooting range. All three were smart, hard-nosed players who were unafraid to mix it up.

By blending them in with Conley, Kron, Mobley, Embry and Adams, Rupp knew he had the perfect ingredients for a small, highly intelligent and versatile Wildcat team, one capable of beating opponents in a variety of ways.

However, before Rupp had a chance to see what he had on his hands, one of those ingredients decided to take his skills elsewhere. The trio of sophomores was reduced by one when Chapman chose to transfer to Western Kentucky University.

Chapman's absence had an enormous impact on this UK team. The depth, which was shaky to begin with, was even thinner now, and the versatility factor wasn't as strong. It also meant that without the 6'6" Chapman, UK was even more susceptible on the boards.

Rupp's lineup for much of the season consisted of Conley and Riley at forward, Adams in the middle, and Kron and Dampier in the backcourt. Mobley and Embry, both seniors, were UK's only true veterans off the bench.

But what hurt this team more than lack of size and depth was the lack of any real on-court chemistry. Rupp went public several times during the season, chiding his players

for their selfish play. Without size, depth and chemistry, this Wildcat team was doomed from the start. And it didn't take long to realize that this season was going to be a struggle. After the first 10 games, the Cats owned a 5-5 record.

There were some bright moments and some excellent individual performances. Dampier scored 37 points, hitting hit 17 of 24 field goal attempts, in a 100-74 win over Iowa State. He hit for 31 and Kron had 30 as the Cats pounded Syracuse 110-77. Conley had 31 aganst Vanderbilt, Riley had 25 against Alabama and Adams had 24 against West Virginia. But the consistency so necessary for success wasn't there.

After winning four of their first five games, the Cats' season quickly began to unravel with successive losses to Illinois, St. Louis and Notre Dame. The Illini won the UKIT with a 91-86 win, thanks to a 27-point, 22-rebound effort by Skip Thoren. Dampier paced the Cats with 16.

Riley scored 23 and Kron pitched in 21, but it wasn't enough to beat St. Louis. The Billikens roared back from a 39-33 halftime deficit to beat UK 80-75. Notre Dame, fueled by Ron Reed's 32 points, smashed the Cats 111-97 in Freedom Hall. Dampier had 32 to match Reed for high-point honors.

The Cats beat Dartmouth 107-67, then watched as All-American Clyde Lee scored 41 points and grabbed 17 rebounds to lead Vanderbilt to a 97-79 win in the SEC opener. After losing two of their next five SEC games, giving them a 3-3 league mark, the Cats strung together a five-game winning streak that breathed life into their once-dormant title chances.

The streak began with a 102-82 win at Georgia. Riley and Dampier each scored 21 for the Cats and Adams added 20. Dampier and Adams combined for 41 points in UK's next outing, a 78-61 win over Florida. After beating Georgia again 96-64, the Cats smashed Ole Miss 102-65 as six players hit in double digits. Dampier led UK's attack with 17, while Conley and Mobley each contributed 14. The Cats captured their fifth straight win by beating Mississippi State 74-56. Riley's 20 points led UK. Conley had 19 and Mobley 13.

The Cats' streak was snapped at five game, but not before they turned in one of their best performances of the season. Playing league-leading Vanderbilt in Nashville, the Cats fought hard before eventually dropping a 91-90 decision. Conley and Dampier paced UK with 31 and 24, respectively. Vandy was led by Lee with 33 and

Miller with 30.

After back-to-back losses to Auburn (88-69) and Alabama (75-71), the Cats closed out their season with home wins over Tennessee and Alabama. A Conley field goal and two Dampier free throws inside the final 1:26 enabled UK to edge past Tennessee 61-60. Riley scored 17, Dampier 15 and Conley 14 in the season-ending 78-72 victory over Alabama.

In conference action, UK could only manage a 10-6 record, which was far off Vanderbilt's league-best 15-1 mark. Overall, the Wildcats ended with a 15-10 record. It was the first time a Rupp team had suffered that many setbacks in a single season.

Dampier and Riley averaged 17 and 15 points, respectively, to lead a balanced scoring attack that saw all five starters score in double figures. Following the two sophomores were Kron (12.3), Adams (11.8) and Conley (11.6).

Adams was the team's top rebounder, Conley again handed out the most assists, and Dampier, the deadeye from Southport, Ind., made good on 51.2 percent of his field goal attempts and 84 percent of his free throws.

By this time, UK fans were seriously beginning to question whether or not Rupp still had it. There were more disappointing seasons than good ones, and the recruiting coffers were practically empty. Also, by refusing to actively recruit black players, UK may have missed out on such tremendous in-state talents as Tom Thacker, Wes Unseld, Clem Haskins and Butch Beard. The times were, indeed, changing, and Rupp seemed reluctant to change with them.

But Rupp wasn't ready to let the critics write his epitaph. He had a few surprises left, beginning with the next season, which turned out to be one of his finest accomplishments.

Thanks to a bunch of Runts.

1965-66

The situation at UK had seldom looked much bleaker. With little in the way of big-time talent coming in to join the four returning starters, preseason hopes for this team were at an all-time low. UK wasn't ranked in anyone's Top 20, and no one gave them any chance of winning another SEC crown.

However, by the time the season was over, UK had captured the imagination of the entire basketball world, Rupp was once again voted Coach of the Year, and two Wildcats — Dampier and Riley — earned All-America honors.

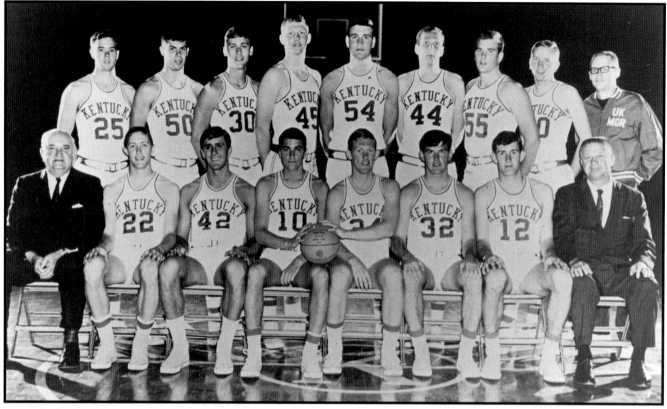

The beloved 1965-66 team included, sitting, Adolph Rupp, Gene Stewart, Pat Riley, Louie Dampier, Bobby Tallent, Steve Clevenger, Jim LeMaster and Harry Lancaster. Standing, Tommy Porter, Gary Gamble, Tommy Kron, Cliff Berger, Larry Lentz, Brad Bounds, Thad Jaracz, Larry Conley and manager Mike Harreld.

This team, which came to be known as "Rupp's Runts", became not only Rupp's all-time favorite team, but the favorite among Wildcat fans as well. Few UK teams have endeared themselves to the Big Blue faithful quite the way the Runts did.

It's easy to see why there were such low expectations prior to the season. The problems that plagued the 1964-65 team, lack of size and depth, were still present. In fact, with 6'5" sophomore Thad Jaracz taking over for Adams in the pivot, UK's starting five was even smaller than the previous season. As for depth, there were more players on hand, but few who had proven themselves in the heat of battle. There was simply no reason for optimism in the Wildcat camp.

And yet, this Wildcat team won its first 23 games, captured the SEC title, earned a No. 1 ranking with a final 27-2 record, and finished as runner-up in the NCAA Tournament. It was, in every way, a truly magical season.

How was such a turnaround accomplished? Why was this team, thought to be average at best, able to become a

great team? There were many reasons why, among them:

1: It was a superbly conditioned team. Joe B. Hall had been hired as an assistant, and one of his first moves was to put in an off-season conditioning program. The UK players groaned and griped at Hall's strict regimen, but the end result was a Wildcat team that was still going strong at the end of 40 minutes. It was a team that never seemed to run out of gas.

2: The reserves were better than expected. At various times during the season, the Wildcats got strong play from a host of back-up players, including Cliff Berger, Bobby Tallent, Jim LeMaster, Gary Gamble, Tommy Porter and Steve Clevenger. The bench, which was thought to be a liability, turned out to be a big plus for the Cats.

3: Shooting, passing and defense. This was a Wildcat team capable of blistering the nets on any given night. In an era when 50 percent field goal shooting was a rarity, this team did it on a consistent basis.

4: Dampier and Riley. The two juniors turned in All-America performances this season. Riley led the team in scoring with a 22 points per game average, while Dampier

was close behind with a 21.1 clip.

5: Team chemistry. Unlike the previous season, this Wildcat team thrived because of its unselfish attitude. The glory of one was never as important as was the glory of all.

6: Conley and Kron. In assessing the success of the Runts, the role played by these two Wildcats cannot be overstated. In later years, many who were present, including Riley and assistant coach Harry Lancaster, have gone on record as saying that Conley and Kron were the real MVP's of this team. It was from their willingness to sacrifice individual achievements for the good of the team that the unselfish attitude was born. As a result, Riley, Dampier and, in particular, Jaracz were able to thrive.

The Cats opened fast, winning their first five games by an average margin of 25 points. The victims were Hardin-Simmons 83-55, Virginia 99-73, Illinois 86-68, Air Force 78-58 and Indiana 91-56. Dampier gunned in 112 points in those five wins, while Riley hit for 29 against Virginia and Jaracz had 32 against the Illini.

Then it was Riley's turn to get the hot hand. In UK's next three games, Riley scored 89 points, including 36 in a

103-69 win over Notre Dame.

Jaracz came up with a 26-point, 13-rebound performance to help the Cats successfully open conference play with a 78-64 win at Florida. Conley had 17 points for the winners.

Thanks to four crucial free throws by Berger, the Cats survived their first real scare of the season by clipping Georgia 69-65 in two overtimes. Berger canned the four freebies inside the final two minutes. Dampier's 23 points were tops for UK.

The Cats shot a scorching 55 percent from the field in a 96-83 win over dangerous Vanderbilt. Dampier had 28 and Riley 24 for UK. Vandy's Lee led all scorers with 30.

LSU ran into an even hotter-shooting UK team. The Cats shot 72.7 percent in the first half, then went on to crush LSU 111-85. Auburn had no answers, either. UK shot 60 percent against the Tigers, winning easily 115-78. Dampier dazzled Auburn with 32 points, while Riley added 25.

UK played one of its finest games in Nashville, beating Vandy 105-90 behind Dampier's 42-point performance. Riley also had a big night for the Cats, finishing with 28 points.

Rupp's Runts Larry Conley, Louie Dampier, Thad Jaracz, Tommy Kron and Pat Riley reunited for a 1991 ceremony marking the 25th anniversary of that glorious 1965-66 season.

A rare cold-shooting night at Mississippi State almost cost the Cats their perfect record. Despite hitting just 41.7 percent, the Cats were able to hang on for a 73-69 win. Balanced scoring saved UK. All five starters hit double figures, led by Riley with 21. Dampier had 13, Kron 11, Conley and Jaracz 10 each.

Tennessee ended UK's run at 23 straight with a 69-62 win in Knoxville. The two clubs sparred on even terms until late in the game, then the Vols assumed command when Howard Bayne, Red Robbins and Ron Widby scored three straight key baskets. Widby and UK's Riley shared scoring honors with 22.

After ending the regular season with a 103-74 win over Tulane, the Cats moved on to Iowa City for a Mideast Regional matchup against Dayton. The Flyers, led by 7-foot center Henry Finkel, led 40-38 at the half. But with Dampier on fire from the outside, the Cats came back to post an 86-79 win. Dampier ended the game with 34 points. Riley and Jaracz had 18 and 17, respectively. Finkel led all scorers with 36 points.

UK played one of its finest games of the season against Michigan, winning 84-77 to earn a trip to the Final Four. Once again, it was the Cats' ability to hit the basket that pulled them through. Although outrebounded 42-35, UK was able to overcome the Wolverines by hitting 37 of 72 field goal attempts for 51 percent. Riley was the hottest Cat, scoring 29 points. Dampier had 15, while Kron and Conley each contributed 14. Cazzie Russell matched Riley's 29 to tie for game-high honors.

With UK and Duke ranked 1-2 in the polls, it was assumed by many that their semifinal matchup in College Park, Md., would be for the national championship. The other two Final Four participants, Texas Western and Utah, were given little chance of winning it all.

UK and Duke played splendid basketball, with both teams giving championship-level performances. The game was close from start to finish, and wasn't decided until the final minute. But in the end, UK, behind Dampier's 23 points, won 83-79. Riley had 19 for the Cats, Kron had 12, and Conley, who was weakened by the flu, added 10. Lefty Jack Marin led Duke with 29 points.

The championship game against Texas Western was supposed to be a cinch for the Cats. But Texas Western fooled the experts. Their quickness stunned the Cats. Lightning-fast Bobby Joe Hill proved to be the biggest thorn in UK's side. His two early steals resulted in layups that gave the

Miners a lead they would never relinquish. In the second half, after UK had closed to within a single point, Hill and Orsten Artis combined for six straight points as the Miners pushed their lead to nine. UK charged repeatedly, but the Miners, tough, steady and brave down the stretch, hung on for a 72-65 win and the national championship.

Riley and Dampier paced UK with 19 points each, while Conley, in his final game as a Wildcat, had 10. The larcenous Hill led all scorers with 20.

Not even a loss in the final game could dim the luster of what had been a terrific season and a total team effort. Riley and Dampier became the first two Wildcats to average 20 points in the same season, while Jaracz (13.2), Conley (11.5) and Kron (10.2) all averaged in double digits.

Later that summer, the Runts traveled to Tel Aviv, Israel, where they easily won the International Universities Tournament.

If UK fans had low expectations prior to the 1965-66 season, the opposite was true as the 1966-67 campaign drew near. The excitement was sky-high. With Riley, Dampier and Jaracz returning, how could it not be? But little did anyone know then just how much Conley and Kron would be missed.

1966-67

When the UK players returned to school in the fall, Rupp was shocked to learn that Riley had injured his back while water skiing. Riley, Dampier and Jaracz were expected to be the top guns for the Cats, and now Riley, the Runts' leading scorer, was hobbled by an injury. Fortunately, the injury wasn't serious. But it would nag Riley throughout the season, a season that turned out to be the worst in Rupp's distinguished career.

Rupp initially toyed with the idea of letting Riley sit out the season. That way, Riley's back would have time to heal properly. But Rupp discarded that notion, based perhaps on his feeling (and those of the rest of the college basketball world) that this was a Wildcat team with the potential to win the national championship.

There was good reason to expect big things from the Cats. Joining Riley, Dampier and Jaracz was a cast of veteran players, including Berger, Tallent, Gamble, Porter, LeMaster, Clevenger and talented sophomore guard Phil Argento.

Despite the positives — and the high hopes — it didn't take long for the season to become a disaster. The Cats lost three of their first five games, and, incredibly, all three were in Memorial Coliseum. It was a downward slide

from which the Wildcats never recovered. In all, the Cats suffered seven home setbacks, including four in overtime.

Not surprisingly, the Cats' fortunes went hand in hand with Riley's play. When he felt good, the Cats were a high-scoring, competitive club. Seven times during the season, UK scored more than 100 points. But Riley's painful back never allowed him to develop any real consistency. That left Dampier to carry much of the load by himself, and although he had another outstanding season, without the steady play from Riley, and without other players stepping up their game, UK was a beatable team on virtually any given night.

Riley, Gamble, Jaracz, Dampier and Tallent were the starters in the opener against Virginia. Dampier scored 31 and Riley added 23 as the Cats won easily 104-84.

Illinois came into Memorial Coliseum and nipped the Cats 98-97 in overtime. Dampier's 40 points led the Cats, who battled back from a 12-point second-half deficit to send the game into the extra period.

UK won its next game, a wild 118-116 thriller at Northwestern. A pair of Riley free throws with two seconds remaining decided the outcome. Riley had 33 to lead UK, while Dampier finished with 32, including 24 in the second half. Jaracz scored 23 and Tallent added 20.

Larry Miller scored 24 to lead visiting North Carolina to a 64-55 win, then Gary Keller had 25 in Florida's 78-75 win over the Cats.

UK won its own Christmas tournament, beating Oregon State 96-66 and Kansas State 83-79. Dampier scored

Louie Dampier doing what he did best — launching from long range. He went on to become the all-time leading scorer in the old ABA.

30 in the opener, Tallent had 25 in the championship game. Then came one of the most inglorious moments in UK history, a 92-77 loss to Cornell. Six-foot junior guard Greg Morris burned UK for 37 points to lead the Ivy League school to its big upset.

UK, already 0-1 in SEC play after the earlier loss to Florida, quickly dropped to 0-4 with successive losses to Vanderbilt, Florida and Georgia. Only the Vandy game was close. The Commodores won 91-89 in overtime when Bo Wyenandt hit a layup with seven seconds left to play. Florida beat the Cats a second time, winning 89-72 in Gainesville, then Georgia applied the brakes in its 49-40 win over UK. The Bulldogs trailed 8-6 at intermission, then pulled away in the second half for the win.

Tallent soon emerged as the only Wildcat other than Dampier to play well on a consistent basis. He scored 25 against Kansas State, 28 against Notre Dame and 26 in the second loss to Florida. It was his 15-foot jumper with seven seconds left that beat Auburn 60-58 and snapped the Cats' three-game skid.

Perhaps inevitably, the strain of such a miserable and disappointing season was bound to manifest itself in other ways. In this instance, it was a clash between Rupp and Tallent, an incident that led to Tallent's dismissal from the team and a public rebuke of Rupp by UK President John Oswald.

Tallent, an excellent shooter, had drawn Rupp's criticism — much of it through the media — for being a poor ballhandler and for lacking good leadership skills. Hard feelings between Rupp and Tallent had been growing, and their feud finally reached the boiling point during UK's 76-57 loss in

Knoxville. After being yanked from the game following a mistake, Tallent and Rupp exchanged harsh words. When the Cats got back to Lexington, Tallent was told that he had been dismissed from the team. Most UK fans felt that Rupp was coming down too hard on his junior guard. So did Oswald, who reprimanded Rupp for the way he treated Tallent.

By this time, with UK's season all but a washout, much of the excitement was being generated by the freshman team. Hall, who was now chiefly responsible for the recruiting, had brought in a strong freshman class, headed by Mike Casey, Dan Issel and Mike Pratt. It was this trio that gave UK fans a glimmer of sunshine in what was otherwise a rainy season.

After losing three straight, the Cats, now 12-13, went into the finale against Alabama needing a win to avoid the first losing season in Rupp's career. With Riley scoring 28 points and Argento adding 20, the Cats saved face with a 110-78 win.

The 13 losses and the .500 won-loss mark were by far the worst-ever for Rupp.

Dampier led UK in scoring with an average of 20.6. Riley, despite his back injury, still managed a 17.4 scoring average. Jaracz and Berger finished with identical 11.3 averages. Jaracz pulled down 8.3 rebounds per game to lead the team in that category.

Dampier and Riley went on to have outstanding pro careers. Dampier, who scored 1,575 points in a Wildcat uniform, became the all-time leading scorer in the American Basketball Association, while Riley, who had 1,464 points at UK, guided the Los Angeles Lakers to four NBA titles in the 1980s. He currently coaches the Miami Heat.

1967-68

Seldom in UK's illustrious history has the arrival of three rookies been the cause for such high expectations and so much excitement. It was on the shoulders of Mike Casey, Dan Issel and Mike Pratt, dubbed the

"Super Sophs" after posting a brilliant 18-2 record as freshmen, that UK's hopes for a return to the college basketball limelight rested.

They didn't fail. By the time that threesome ended their careers, they had accounted for 5,032 points and taken UK back to No. 1 in the national polls. And had it not been for an unfortunate automobile accident, they may well have brought UK another NCAA championship.

From their first game, a 96-79 win over Michigan that saw Casey score 28 points and Issel 18, it was clear that this trio was special. Casey was a tough competitor who loved having the ball in his hands when the game was on the line; Issel, still a work in progress, had the potential to be UK's best true pivot man since Spivey; Pratt was a warrior who could score, rebound and defend.

The 6'4" Pratt didn't crack the starting lineup until several games into the season. Neither did Argento, who eventually claimed one of the guard spots. Rupp's lineup in the Michi-

Rupp poses with juniors Mike Casey (34), Dan Issel (44) and Mike Pratt (22) prior to the start of the 1968-69 season. This celebrated trio accounted for 5,032 points for the Wildcats.

gan opener featured Casey and Jaracz at forward, Issel in the middle, and Clevenger and LeMaster in the backcourt.

The Cats easily won their next three games, beating Florida 99-76, Xavier 111-76 and Pennsylvania 64-49. Three different Wildcat players led the scoring in those victories — Jacacz had 23 against Florida, Argento 23 against Xavier and Clevenger 13 after coming off the bench to spark the win over Penn.

North Carolina, with its huge front line, dealt the Cats an 84-77 setback in Greensboro. After the Cats took a 64-63 lead on a short jumper by Berger, the Tar Heels rattled off eight straight points to take control of the game. Jaracz paced UK with 19 points, while Pratt and Issel each had 13. North Carolina was led by 6'11" center Rusty Clark with 23 points and Larry Miller with 19.

Phil Argento claimed a starting backcourt spot early in his sophomore year. He averaged in double figures in each of his final two seasons at UK.

Casey pumped in 27 and Argento added 17 as the Cats got back on the winning track with a tough 88-85 win over Dayton in the first round of the UKIT. UK led 45-31 at the break, then had to hold off the fast-charging Flyers down the stretch. Pratt had a double-double for UK, scoring 15 and picking off 15 rebounds.

Former Georgia Tech coach Bobby Cremins scored 17 points for South Carolina, but it wasn't enough to derail the Cats, who won 76-66 to claim the championship. Casey and Pratt led UK with 19 and 17, respectively.

Casey gave a giant performance against Notre Dame, scoring 27 points and coming up with six steals to lead the Cats to a come-from-behind 81-73 win in Freedom Hall. UK trailed throughout the game, then outscored the

Irish 18-3 in the final four minutes to come away with the victory. With that win, number 772 for his career, Rupp surpassed his old mentor Phog Allen as the all-time winningest coach in college basketball.

The Cats hit 13 of their first 16 shots, built a 49-19 first-half lead, then cruised to a surprisingly easy 94-74 win over Vanderbilt in Nashville. Argento and Casey each scored 25 for the red-hot Wildcats, while Pratt added 20.

Argento had 24 points, including 23 in the second half, to help lift the Cats past upset-minded Alabama 84-76. Pratt scored 20 for the Cats, who overcame a 76-72 Alabama lead in the final five minutes.

After beating Alabama, the league-leading Cats suddenly fell into a funk, losing three of their next four games. Florida beat UK 96-78 behind Neal Walk's 28 points and 23 rebounds; Auburn won 74-73 on two Tom Perry free throws; and Tennessee handed the Cats their worst SEC loss 87-59. UK's only victory was a 104-73 win over Georgia. Casey scored 29 in that game, while Jaracz, who connected on 12 of 16 shots, added 25.

The embarrassing loss to Tennessee would be UK's last during the regular season. Beginning with a wild 121-95 win over Pete Maravich-led LSU, the Cats won their final 11 regular-season games to capture another SEC championship.

In the first of his six battles against UK over the next three seasons, the talented, flamboyant "Pistol" Pete scored 52 points, hitting 19 of 51 field goal tries and 14 free throws. Maravich would score 312 points against the Cats, yet come up empty in the win department.

Casey's 31 points led UK in that first meeting. Other Cats in double figures included Jaracz (24), Pratt (18) and Issel (17).

Issel had his best game of the season in the second matchup against LSU, scoring 21 points and grabbing 20 rebounds in a 109-96 victory. Casey led the Cats with 29 points. Maravich finished with 44.

Even with Argento sidelined by an injury, the Cats kept on winning. Much of the credit for UK's strong finish goes to Issel, who was only now beginning to flash the offensive potential that carried him to the top of UK's all-time scoring list. Issel led UK in scoring in five of the last eight games, hitting for 31 in a 106-87 win over Georgia and 28 in a 96-83 win over Alabama.

Casey also continued to shine, leading the scoring parade three times in the final eight games. His high was 30 in the Cats' 107-81 win over Mississippi State.

The two most crucial wins in the final month came against Tennessee and Vandy. UK claimed the SEC lead by beating the Vols 60-59 in Memorial Coliseum. Trailing 57-56, the Cats scratched out the victory when Casey and Issel hit consecutive buckets inside the last minute. UK beat Vandy 85-80, thanks to the strong work by subs Porter and Gamble. Porter scored 16 points and Gamble had seven, including five clutch free throws down the stretch. Gamble also hauled down 12 rebounds. Issel led UK with 23 points.

Rupp's young Cats finished with a 21-4 record and a league-best 15-3 mark. Going into NCAA tourney play, UK was ranked No. 5 in both the AP and UPI polls.

Even better, the Mideast Regional was slated to be played in Memorial Coliseum. Marquette, coached by the always combative Al McGuire, was UK's opening opponent.

Handling the Warriors on the court turned out to be easier for the Cats than handling McGuire off the court. Prior to the game, McGuire, in an obvious effort to anger Rupp, was only too happy to play the role of villain. He refused to join the other coaches on Rupp's TV show, demanded that his team be allowed to dress in the home team's locker room and sit on the home team's bench, and balked at playing the game with a basketball that had Rupp's name on it. Rupp's reply to McGuire: "Find a ball with your name on it and that's the one we'll use."

What McGuire's antics did, of course, was to fire up the Wildcats. With Issel scoring 36 points (on 14 of 18

shooting from the field) and pulling down 13 rebounds, the Cats rolled to a convincing 107-89 win. Casey and Pratt also put the hurt on McGuire's club, scoring 19 and 18 points, respectively.

By defeating Marquette, the Cats were now within one win of earning a trip to the Final Four. All that stood in their way was Big Ten champ Ohio State, a team the Cats had twice faced — and been defeated by — in NCAA tourney action during the 1960s. But unlike those encounters, this time the Cats, playing on their home turf, were favored to prevail.

Ohio State led 44-40 at intermission, but the Cats charged back to take an 81-80 lead on an Issel tip-in with 27 seconds left. The Buckeyes missed a go-ahead shot, then got a second chance when Casey fumbled the rebound out of bounds. Given a reprieve, the Buckeyes got the ball to Dave Sorenson, who banked in the game-winner with three seconds remaining.

Issel had 19 for UK and Casey added 16. Sorenson led all scorers with 22, while his teammate Bill Hosket was close behind with 21.

Despite the sudden and disappointing end, the three sophomores had more than lived up to their advanced billing. Casey's 20.1 scoring average was the best by a Wildcat sophomore since Nash. Issel's average of 16.4 offered only a glimpse of what was on the horizon, while Pratt finished with a solid 14.1 scoring clip. UK's other two starters also averaged in double figures — Argento 12.3 and Jaracz 11.3.

Issel was the top rebounder with a 12.1 average.

1968-69

It was during this season that Issel went from being an above average post player to an all-out scoring machine. By the time the season was over, Issel had shattered all single season scoring records. "Big Dan", as he came to be known, averaged 26.6 points during his junior year, more than two points per game better than the previous best held by Hagan and Nash.

With Issel having blossomed into a bona fide All-America candidate, and with Casey, Pratt and Argento returning, the Cats were formidable. Larry Steele, a 6'5" sophomore who always seemed to be in perpetual motion, rounded out the Cats' usual starting lineup. Terry Mills, who drew several early starts, Bob McCowan and Randy Poole also turned in consistently excellent efforts in supporting roles.

Even with an injured Pratt sitting out the first two

games, UK had little trouble getting off to a fast start. Casey and Issel each scored 29 and Steele added 16 in his debut as the Cats blasted Xavier 115-77 in the opener. In UK's second game, an 86-77 win over Miami of Ohio, Issel scored 22, Casey 20 and Argento 18.

Pratt's return wasn't enough to keep the Cats from falling to North Carolina for the third straight year. Charlie Scott scored 19 and Eddie Fogler canned several clutch free throws to help propel the Tar Heels to an 87-77 win. Casey led UK with 26.

The Cats easily handled Pennsylvania 102-78, then beat Michigan 112-104 in a thrilling UKIT opener. Issel scored 34, Pratt 20 and Argento 17 for the winning Wildcats. Michigan was paced by Rudy Tomjanovich and Dennis Stewart with 26 each. One night later, Issel and Pratt combined for 42 points as UK won the title with an 80-65 win over Army. Jim Oxley led Army with 18, while current Duke coach Mike Krzyzewski had six.

The Cats split their last two pre-conference games, beating Notre Dame 110-90 and losing to Wisconsin 69-65 in Chicago. Issel tossed in 31 points and Argento added 27 in the win over Notre Dame. Against the Badgers, cold-shooting UK rallied from a 63-46 deficit to make it interesting, but never could take the lead. An uncharacteristic 38-percent shooting night led to UK's downfall. Issel was UK's top gun with 22 points.

In the SEC opener at Ole Miss, it was Poole's turn to play the role of hero. Poole scored six unanswered points to break a 52-52 deadlock and send the Cats on to a 69-59 win.

The Cats continued to roll, easily beating Mississippi State 91-72, Florida 88-67 and Georgia 88-68. The win

Mike Pratt makes his move on an Alabama defender. Pratt's monumental 42-point "gone to war" performance against Notre Dame is one of the greatest ever by a Wildcat.

over Georgia was a milestone for the UK program. It was the school's 1,000th win, making UK the first Division I program to win 1,000 games.

A five-year Knoxville drought came to an end when the visiting Cats edged Tennessee 69-66. Issel had 21 to lead UK. Steele scored 18 and Pratt added 17. Bill Justus paced the Vols with 25.

It was the same old story when the Cats tangled with LSU in Baton Rouge — "Pistol" Pete put on a spectacular fireworks display, hitting for 52 points, but UK won the game 108-96. Issel had 25 to lead UK. Casey finished with 23, Pratt 21 and Poole, in another strong performance off the bench, chipped in 13.

Issel scored 33 and UK outscored Alabama 19-6 in the overtime period to give Rupp his 800th career victory, an 83-70 win in Tuscaloosa.

Issel, Casey and Pratt were rapidly becoming the most prolific scoring trio in UK history. In UK's next four games, wins over Vanderbilt 103-89, Auburn 105-93 (despite 42 points from John Mengelt), Ole Miss 104-68 and Mississippi State 91-69, the junior threesome accounted for 263 points.

UK's 11-game winning streak, and its perfect SEC mark, ended when Boyd Welch sank a pair of free throws with nine seconds remaining to lift Florida to an 82-81 win. The Cats again had trouble handling burly Neal Walk, who finished with 19 points and 18 rebounds. Casey and Issel each scored 20 for UK.

McCowan came off the bench to score 16 points and spark the Cats to an 85-77 win over Georgia. The Bulldogs led 40-39 at the half, but the Cats, behind McCowan's hot hand, took the lead early in the final 20 minutes and never

looked back. Pratt and Casey shared high-point honors with 21 points apiece.

In a brilliant duel between All-Americans Maravich and Issel, the Wildcats, after trailing 47-46 at intermission, roared back to beat LSU 103-89. Maravich scored 45, hitting 21 of 53 field goal attempts. But it was Issel who had the better all-around game, scoring 36 points and pulling down 29 rebounds. Issel also had a better supporting cast. Argento had 21, Casey 20 and Pratt 19 for UK.

The Cats finished the regular season by winning three of their final four games. They beat Alabama 108-79, Auburn 90-86 and Tennessee 84-69. Only the Alabama win was easy. Auburn took the Cats to the wire, only to come up short in its upset bid. The Tigers never found a way to stop Issel, who ended the night with 34 points. Tennessee fought UK to a 34-34 first-half standstill, but once again the Cats had enough late-game firepower to avoid the upset. Four Cats hit double figures, led by Issel with 23. Casey had 18, Steele 16 and Pratt 15. The always-dependable Justus scored 18 for the Vols.

The Cats' loss came against Vanderbilt in Nashville. The Commodores overcame a 41-point performance by Issel to beat UK 101-99. Rudy Thacker paced Vandy with 23 points, while Tom Hagan and Perry Wallace each contributed 22. Casey and Pratt had 21 apiece for UK.

UK ended the regular season with a 22-4 record and another SEC title. The UPI poll had the Cats as the No. 5 team in the country, while the AP had them at No. 7.

Waiting for the Cats in the NCAA Tournament was Marquette and the cagey Al McGuire. But unlike the previous year, when the Mideast Regional was held in Lexington, this time the two teams would meet in Marquette's own backyard — Madison, Wis.

It was an ugly, physical and mean-spirited game, and a potentially dangerous situation. McGuire used race to fire up his all-black team against the all-white Wildcats, and it didn't take long for tempers to get out of control. On several occasions, players squared off and nearly came to blows.

McGuire's strategy, along with excellent defense against Issel, worked to perfection. Marquette led 36-33 at the half, then went on to post an 81-74 victory. The Cats, perhaps flustered by the stormy situation, never got untracked. It also didn't help that Casey, Steele, Pratt and Argento all fouled out.

George Thompson had 22 points for the winners and Dean "the Dream" Meminger added 20. Casey led UK with 24, Pratt had 17 and Argento 16. Issel was held to just 13 points but did come up with 16 rebounds.

In the consolation game, Issel bounced back with 36 points and Steele added 12 as the lethargic Cats slipped past Miami of Ohio 72-71.

The Cats ended the season with a 23-5 record. Issel was a consensus All-American, and he, Casey and Pratt were named to the All-SEC team. Casey averaged 19.1 points per game and Pratt averaged 16.9.

Later that summer, on June 9, Tom Payne inked a scholarship with UK, thus becoming the first black player to sign with the Wildcat basketball program. The 7'2" Payne had been an all-state center at Shawnee High School in Louisville.

Attention quickly turned to the 1969-70 season. Hopes were running high, and for good reason. Issel, Casey, Pratt, Steele, Mills and McCowan were all returning. They would be joined by Tom Parker, a sharpshooting forward, and Kent Hollenbeck, a quick guard. It figured to be UK's strongest team since the undefeated days of Hagan, Ramsey and Tsioropoulos.

But all those big dreams and high hopes would soon be dealt a crushing blow.

1969-70

When Rupp first learned that Mike Casey had suffered a severely broken leg in an automobile accident, he said, "Well, there goes the national championship." And Rupp wasn't wrong, either. Although the Cats put together a sparkling record (25-1 in the regular season and a No. 1 ranking in both polls), and even though Issel shattered virtually every scoring record in the books, this UK team was never as good as it would have been had the dependable and tough-minded Casey been aboard.

Once again, when the season was over, Wildcat fans were left to wonder "what if."

Issel, Pratt and Steele were locked in as starters, while a youthful gang of backcourt players vied for the two guard spots. During the season, all five — Mills, McCowan, Hollenbeck, Stan Key and Jim Dinwiddie — had moments of excellence, thus helping to fill the void created by Casey's absence.

The presence of Parker, a 6'6" lefty from Collinsville, Ill., was an enormous plus, thanks to his uncanny shooting touch. More than anyone else, it was Parker who replaced Casey as the Cats' main outside scoring threat. His ability to keep defenses honest also helped open up the low-post

Dan Issel puts up a short jumper as four Georgia defenders look on. Issel left as UK's all-time leading scorer and rebounder.

area for Issel.

The always-hustling Steele gave the Cats extra grit, while Pratt, in his final season as a Wildcat, was rock-solid. Although he was overshadowed by Issel's record-setting numbers, Pratt was instrumental to this club's success. His final season remains one of the best-ever by a Wildcat player.

But if Pratt was outstanding, then Issel was nothing short of brilliant. He led the team in scoring (33.9), rebounding (13.2), field goal percentage (55.3) and free throw percentage (76.4). Twice that season, he topped the 50-point mark in a game, including a school-record 53 against Ole Miss, and on six other occasions he scored more than 40 points. By the time he left UK, Issel was the all-time leader in points (2,138), rebounds (1,078) and career scoring average (25.7).

Issel picked up where he left off the previous season, hitting for 34 points in UK's 106-87 win over West Virginia in the opener. Pratt finished with 28 and Steele added 21. Rounding out the starting lineup that night were Mills and Dinwiddie.

UK's next three games proved that this club, even without Casey, was one that had to be reckoned with. Kansas, North Carolina and Indiana, three formidable and dangerous opponents, could find no way to stop Issel and the rampaging Wildcats. Issel scored 29 as the Cats began that impressive three-game sweep by destroying Kansas 115-85. Pratt had 18, Steele 17 and Mills 15 for UK.

The Tar Heels fared even worse in their attempt to stop Issel. His 41-point, 15-rebound performance keyed the Cats to a 94-87 victory. Pratt also hurt Dean Smith's club, scoring 27 points. Charlie Scott led North Carolina with 29.

The Cats shot 68.4 percent in the first half, raced to a 63-38 halftime lead, then went on to beat Indiana 109-92. Issel led a balanced UK attack with 32 points. Parker had his first big game, coming off the bench to score 15.

McCowan turned in two superb performances in the UKIT, racking up 41 points to walk off with the MVP award. The Cats beat Navy 73-59 in the first game. Issel led UK with 40 points and 18 rebounds, while McCowan

scored 16. In the championship matchup with unbeaten Duke, Pratt scored 26, McCowan 25 and Issel 20 in a 98-76 Wildcat victory. Duke's Randy Denton had 28 points and 21 rebounds in a losing effort.

Next up for the Cats was a ferocious struggle against Notre Dame in Freedom Hall. Thanks to Pratt's monumental 42-point performance, the Cats remained perfect by posting a 102-100 victory. Issel finished with 35 for UK and McCowan had 14. All-American Austin Carr led all scorers with 43. These two clubs were destined to run across each other again later in the season, and the second encounter, which had far more riding on the outcome, would be equally exciting and memorable.

The Cats ran through their first seven SEC games, facing only one serious challenge along the way. Georgia pushed the Cats to the limit before finally falling 72-71. Issel had 32, but it was Hollenbeck who saved the Cats. He came off the bench to score 12 points, hitting on six of his eight field goal attempts.

Maravich lit up the Memorial Coliseum scoreboard for one final time, scoring 55 points in LSU's 109-96 loss to the Cats. Issel and Mills led UK with 35 and 22, respectively. Other Cats in double figures included Pratt (19), Steele (17) and McCowan (12).

The Cats took their 15-0 record and No. 1 ranking to Nashville for a battle against Vanderbilt. The Commodores grabbed control early, then held on for an 89-81 win. Vandy's accurate free throw shooting, especially by Tom Arnholt, was the difference. Arnholt finished with 28 points, hitting 14 of 15 freebies. Issel's 26 led the Cats.

The loss to Vandy was UK's last during the regular season, although it took some late-game heroics by Mills to avoid a second straight slip-up. Mills knocked down a last-second

jump shot to lift the Cats past Auburn 84-83. Issel had 28 and Pratt 20 for the Cats, who rallied from 11 points down to get the win.

Issel broke Hagan's record for most points in a game when he scored 53 in the Cats' 120-85 smearing of Ole Miss. Hagan's old mark was 51, which he scored against Temple in the 1953-54 season opener.

Parker was inserted into the starting lineup when Steele went down with an injury, and the sophomore forward wasted no time making his presence felt. He scored 56 points in UK's next three games, wins over Mississippi State (86-57), Florida (110-66) and Georgia (116-86). Issel had 40 against the Bulldogs. Pratt finished with 23, Parker 21 and Mills 18.

Despite the wins and the lofty national ranking, all was not well within the Wildcat camp. McCowan and Poole, two valuable reserves, were booted off the team after being spotted in a Starkville tavern on the afternoon prior to playing Mississippi State. Their absence further weakened an already thin bench, a fact that would haunt the Cats in NCAA tourney action.

In the final head-to-head battle between Issel and Maravich, "Pistol" Pete again won the scoring honors 64 to 51

LSU's talented, flamboyant "Pistol" Pete Maravich scored a whopping 312 points in his six battles with UK yet never came away with a victory. His 64 points in a 1970 game are the most ever by a UK opponent.

and UK again won the game 121-105. Issel came back with 47 in a 98-89 win over Alabama and 31 in a hard-earned 90-86 revenge win over Vandy. Parker continued to justify his spot in the starting quintet, accounting for 53 points in those three wins. He also pulled down 15 rebounds against Alabama.

UK closed out its regular season by beating Auburn 102-81 at home and Tennessee 86-69 on the road. In their last game in front of Wildcat fans, Issel scored 42 points and Pratt had 20 in the win over Auburn. Parker and Issel shared high-point honors against the Vols with 20 each.

First up for the Cats in the Mideast Regional was a rematch against eighth-ranked Notre Dame. With Carr striking from everywhere en route to a 52-point performance, the Irish built an early lead and were on top 53-48 at the half. But the Cats, led by Issel, closed to within 87-86 with three minutes remaining. After a Notre Dame miss, the Cats took the lead when Parker hit a short jumper. Issel followed with a bucket and two free throws, and the Cats were on their way to a 109-99 win.

Issel's 44 points led a balanced UK attack that saw five players hit double figures. Pratt had 14 points, Mills 13, Parker 12 and Dinwiddie 11.

For the game, UK made good on 43 of 72 field goal attempts for 59.7 percent.

UK's next foe, Jacksonville, featured two seven-footers, one of whom was the great Artis Gilmore, and a superb guard named Rex Morgan. In the end, however, the Dolphins' most valuable player may have been guard Vaughn Wedeking. It was Wedeking who slipped in behind Issel, drawing the fifth and final foul on the Wildcats' star center.

An injury suffered in an automobile accident forced Mike Casey to miss the 1969-70 season. Adolph Rupp felt that Casey's absence cost UK another NCAA title.

Prior to being whistled for his fifth foul, Issel scored nine points in less than two minutes to single-handedly pull UK back from a 72-60 deficit. But with Issel out, and Pratt soon to follow with 8:07 left, the Cats lost 106-100.

Issel ended his career with a 28-point, 10-rebound performance. Parker contributed 21 points and Mills added 18. Morgan keyed the Dolphins with 28 points. Gilmore also made his presence felt, scoring 24 points and grabbing 20 rebounds.

Although UK's final record was an excellent 26-2, Wildcat fans were once again left with an empty feeling. UCLA went on to win yet another NCAA title, one that may well have gone to the Wildcats had Mike Casey been able to play.

1970-71

With the arrival of Tom Payne onto the scene, the University of Kentucky had at last broken the color barrier. The 7'2" Payne signed with UK, then ran into academic problems that forced him to play on an AAU team his freshman season. Although Payne was thought to be something of a project when he arrived in the UK camp, he turned out to be much farther along than anyone expected. It quickly became apparent that he had the potential to be a more than adequate replacement for the now-departed Issel. And, indeed, Payne did acquit himself well during his one and only season in a Wildcat uniform, averaging 16.9 points and 10.1 rebounds.

While the racial barrier had finally been crossed, there was no denying that by dragging its feet, UK missed out on many of the best black prep players who grew up within the Commonwealth borders. Superbly talented players such

Kent Hollenbeck makes a move on an Auburn defender as Jim Dinwiddie and Tom Parker set a double screen. A series of injuries kept the talented Hollenbeck from fulfilling his promise as a Wildcat.

as Wes Unseld, Clem Haskins, Butch Beard, Mike Redd, Jerome Perry, Jim McDaniels, Jim Rose and the Smith brothers, Dwight and Greg, having been passed over by UK, choose instead to cast their lot with other Kentucky schools. The failure to actively recruit those players was a mistake on UK's part, and by season's end, the magnitude of that mistake would ring loud and clear.

Payne's massive presence in the middle, along with the return of veterans Steele, Parker, Mills, Key, Hollenbeck and Mark Soderberg gave the Cats a solid nucleus to build around. Also on hand were promising sophomores Jim Andrews and Larry Stamper.

But the big news centered around the return of Casey.

His return brought with it a litany of obvious questions. Would he be the same player he was prior to the accident? Would his injured leg withstand the rigors of a college basketball season? Would he perhaps be a step slower than he was before he got hurt?

As the season progressed, it became clear that Casey was in many ways the same player as before. He was tough, fearless and brave in clutch situations. But the accident had taken its toll. Casey, for all his determination, had been robbed of his quickness.

The Cats opened the season in strong fashion, winning their first five games, three of which were on the road. In four of those five games, the offensive-minded Cats cracked the century mark.

Six Wildcats hit for double figures in the season-opening 115-100 road win over a good Northwestern team. The Cats had to come from behind 15 times in that game before finally taking control. Parker led UK with 23, while Steele added 20. Other Cats in double figures included Soderberg (15), Payne (14), Mills (13) and Hollenbeck (11). Casey, who started in the backcourt, had five.

Casey found his rhythm in the Cats' second game, hitting for 25 in a 104-93 win over Michigan. Steele finished with 24 and Payne added 17 for UK.

Key came off the bench to score nine crucial points, including the go-ahead bucket, and spark the Cats to a 106-100 victory over West Virginia in Morgantown. The two clubs traded leads until Key's jumper put UK in front for good at 78-77. Parker paced the UK scoring attack with 24 points. Hollenbeck had 23, Casey and Payne 19 each.

The Cats' most-impressive early performance came against Indiana in Bloomington. Despite the absence of Steele and Mills, both of whom were out with injuries, the Cats beat Indiana 95-93 in overtime. Parker and Hollenbeck again led UK with 24 and 19 points, respectively. Casey finished with 18, Payne and Soderberg 13 each. IU's George McGinnis had 38 points and 20 rebounds.

The win over Indiana catapulted UK to No. 3 in the national polls. But other news inside the Wildcat com-

pound wasn't so positive. Steele had a fractured bone in his hand and the talented Soderberg, disgruntled due to lack of playing time, quit the team.

The discord was felt almost immediately. After beating DePaul 106-85 in the UKIT opener, the Cats lost to Purdue 89-83 in the championship game. Casey scored 53 points in the two games to lead UK.

Thanks to Andrews, the Cats returned to their successful ways with an 84-78 win over Oregon State. Andrews, who hadn't scored all season, came through with 19 second-half points to help his team overcome a 42-37 halftime deficit and pick up its sixth win in seven games.

No one could save the Cats against Notre Dame. With Austin Carr exploding for 50 points, the Irish beat UK 99-92. The Cats tried to make it two losses in a row, blowing a 24-point lead before finally hanging on for a 103-95 win over Ole Miss. Three late baskets by Mills enabled the Cats to survive the Ole Miss charge. Casey led UK with 23, Parker had 21, Payne 18 and Mills 14. Ole Miss guard Johnny Neumann scored 47 to lead all scorers.

It was a 1-3-1 zone that saved UK in its 79-71 win

Members of the 1970-71 team included, sitting, left to right, Adolph Rupp, Stan Key, Terry Mills, Mike Casey, Larry Steele, Jim Dinwiddie, Kent Hollenbeck and assistant coach Joe B. Hall. Standing, left to right, manager John Ferguson, trainer Claude Vaughn, Steve Penhorwood, Tom Parker, Tom Payne, Jim Andrews, Clint Wheeler, Larry Stamper and assistant coach T.L. Plain.

over Mississippi State. With his team trailing by 13, Rupp ordered the switch from man-to-man to zone. The Bulldogs, unable to solve the 1-3-1 puzzle, quickly came unglued. Casey and Payne combined for 50 points, enabling UK to roar back for the win.

The Cats easily won their next two games, beating Florida 101-75 and Georgia 79-66. Then came a 75-71 loss to Tennessee in Knoxville. Volunteer guard Dickie Johnston, the game's smallest player at 5'8", hit eight straight free throws in the final three minutes to hold off the Cats. Casey had 18 for UK. Tennessee's Jimmy England was the game's top scorer with 25.

Andrews hit two critical free throws, then blocked a shot by Al Sanders in UK's 82-79 win over LSU. Parker had 19 for the Cats. Sanders finished with 24 for LSU.

The Cats followed the win over LSU by giving five straight outstanding performances. They beat Alabama 86-73, Vanderbilt 102-92, Auburn 114-76, Ole Miss 121-86 and Mississippi State 102-83. There were great individual efforts, as well. Parker had 32 against Mississippi State and 30 against Vandy. Payne scored 24 against Ole Miss and 23 against Auburn. Hollenbeck had 21 against Alabama and 20 against Ole Miss.

A hospitalized Rupp stayed in Lexington when his team departed for a two-game swing through Florida and Georgia. With Hall at the helm, the Gators derailed the rampaging UK express by scoring a 74-65 upset. The Cats, who had been scorching the nets, shot a cool 33 percent from the field. Parker was the only UK bright spot, finishing with 20 points. Florida was led by Tom Purvis and Earl Findley with 24 and 22, respectively.

That loss was UK's last until tournament time. Payne

Terry Mills came off the bench to score 13 points in his final home appearance, an 84-78 win over Tennessee. A quarter-century later, his son Cameron would become one of UK's all-time best outside shooters.

personally made sure of that. He scored 74 points and grabbed 34 rebounds in UK's next two games, a 107-95 win over Georgia and a 110-73 win over LSU. The Cats continued to register big numbers, beating Alabama 101-74, Vanderbilt 119-90 and Auburn 102-83. The win over Vandy was especially dominating, given that the game was played in Nashville. The visiting Cats went on an early 19-2 run to break away from a 15-15 deadlock and build a 55-37 lead by intermission. Parker paced UK with 26 points. Steele, Casey and Dinwiddie each finished with 17.

Payne had 30 points and Steele added 22 in the SEC-clinching win over Auburn. Andrews also turned in a solid effort, scoring 14 points and getting 12 rebounds.

Mills made his final home appearance a memorable one by coming off the bench to score 13 clutch points in the Cats' 84-78 win over Tennessee. The two teams played on even terms until Mills helped deliver the knockout blow for UK. Steele was UK's leading scorer with 24. Payne had 20 and Parker 16. England led the Vols with 21.

With all five starters averaging in double figures, this was the most offensive-minded team in UK history. Fifteen times during the season the Cats scored more than 100 points. That remains the school record. During one 10-game SEC stretch, they scored 100 or more points nine times.

The Cats were on a roll when they faced off against in-state rival Western Kentucky University in the Mideast Regional at Athens, Ga. But what many felt would be another easy UK win turned out to be a stunning and convincing loss. In a game that was never close, the Hilltoppers stormed to an easy 107-83 victory.

UK had lost crucial NCAA tourney games to predomi-

Adolph Rupp fought to keep his job despite reaching the mandatory retirement age of 70. When UK President Otis Singletary refused to make an exception, the coaching career of the man who won more games than anyone was finished.

nantly black teams before (Texas Western, Marquette, Jacksonville), but perhaps more than any of those, it was the WKU game that offered the clearest evidence of just how far behind UK had fallen.

The WKU starters — McDaniels, Rose, Clarence Glover, Jerome Perry and Jerry Dunn — were quicker, more athletic and hungrier than the UK players. They were also black kids who hailed from Kentucky. Led by McDaniels' 35 points and 11 rebounds, the Hilltoppers soundly thrashed UK in every department. Rose scored 25 points for WKU, while Glover had 18 points and 17 rebounds.

Parker topped the Cats with 23 points. Payne had 15 points and 10 rebounds, and Casey, in his last game, chipped in with 12.

UK closed out its season with a 91-74 loss to Marquette in the consolation game. Those back-to-back losses left UK with a final record of 22-6.

Although the loss to WKU draped a dark curtain over the season, the truth is, this is a somewhat underrated UK team. It faced a difficult schedule, won many games in treacherous places, overcame injuries and defections, and had enough character and mental toughness to come from behind and win on numerous occasions.

Parker was the Cats' leading point producer for the season, averaging 17.6 points per game. Casey's 17-point average was next, while Payne followed with a 16.9 average. Hollenbeck and Steele finished with averages of 14 and 13.1, respectively.

Almost as soon as the season concluded, a firestorm of controversy began to swirl. It was a firestorm that would last throughout the next season, and nearly cost UK its next coach.

1971-72

Adolph Rupp turned 70 during the 71-72 campaign, and 70 was, for UK employees, the mandatory retirement age. Rupp, however, refused to acknowledge that this would be his final season at the helm. Thus, for virtually the entire season, the team's accomplishments on the court were overshadowed by the debate concerning Rupp's future. Would he be forced to retire, or would an exception be made in his case?

Rupp remained fairly silent on the issue, but it was no secret that behind closed doors he was marshaling his forces for the battle against UK president Dr. Otis Singletary. Rupp worked through the media, hoping to win the public's support. In addition, there were petitions signed by former players and prominent Kentuckians arguing that Rupp should be allowed to remain as coach. For his part, Dr. Singletary made it clear that no special favor would be granted to Rupp. The battle lines had been drawn.

Caught in the middle was assistant coach Joe B. Hall, the man many saw as the logical successor to Rupp. Hall had, after all, played for Rupp back in the late 1940s before returning as an assistant during the 1965-66 season. It was Hall who had upgraded UK's recruiting, and was the force behind the shattering of the color barrier.

But the bitter Rupp, rather than seeing his young assistant

as an heir apparent, treated Hall like an arch-rival. Instead, Rupp openly praised Gale Catlett, another assistant coach. At one point, a frustrated Hall took the St. Louis coaching job, only to be persuaded by friends to remain at UK.

It was an uncomfortable, unpleasant situation, and there can be no doubting that it had an impact on the team's performance. Also impacting the team was the absence of Payne, who declared hardship and went into the NBA, and a pair of injuries that limited the talented Hollenbeck's playing time.

Despite the distractions, this team was solid if not spectacular, finishing with a 21-7 record, the SEC championship and a No. 14 ranking in the final polls. The 6'11" Andrews, now a junior, emerged as a tremendous low-post player, while little sophomore guard Ronnie Lyons gave the Cats an excellent outside scoring threat. The remainder of the starting quintet usually consisted of veterans Parker, Key and Stamper. Also returning was McCowan, who had once again earned Rupp's good graces after the disaster that occurred during the 1969-70 season.

Andrews helped the Cats get off on the right foot, scoring 37 points in a 94-85 win over Northwestern. Key also had a big game, finishing with 20. Andrews scored 26 in UK's second outing, but it took three straight long-range jumpers by Lyons to put away Kansas 79-69. Lyons had connected on just one of his first 12 attempts before hitting those three. He ended the night with 12 points.

The Cats beat Kansas State 71-64, then took on a Bobby Knight-coached Indiana team for the first time. With Steve Downing scoring 47 points and pulling down 25 rebounds, Knight's Hoosiers clipped UK 90-89 in double overtime. Andrews led the Cats with 22.

After losing to Michigan State 91-85, the Cats bounced back to win the UKIT, beating Missouri 83-79 and Princeton 96-82. McCowan, the 1969 UKIT MVP, single-

Lefty Tom Parker remains one of UK's deadliest shooters. Parker averaged 15.5 points during his three seasons in a Wildcat uniform.

handedly pulled the Cats through against Missouri. With his team on the short end of a 58-51 score, McCowan took charge, scoring 15 points on seven of nine shooting over the next 10 minutes to key the comeback win. In the championship game win over Princeton, Andrews had 28, Parker 23 and Lyons 21.

The Cats, behind Parker's 30 points, beat Notre Dame 83-67 to take a 6-2 mark into their SEC opener against Ole Miss. On the day the NCAA announced that freshmen would be allowed to play at the varsity level beginning next season, Lyons scored 24 to lead UK to a 93-82 victory over the Rebels. Two nights later, Andrews and Parker combined for 62 points and 36 rebounds in a 104-76 smearing of Mississippi State.

UK's first SEC road trip resulted in losses to Florida and Georgia. The Cats blew a 15-point lead against Florida, then lost 72-70 when Jerry Hoover scored on a layup with six seconds left. The story in Athens was exactly opposite. The Cats overcame a 16-point deficit, closing the difference to 72-71, before finally dropping an 85-73 decision.

After seeing their league record fall to 2-2, the Cats came home to edge Tennessee 72-70 on an Andrews bucket with three seconds remaining. The Cats followed that win by trouncing Vanderbilt 106-80 on the strength of 34 points from Andrews and 61 percent shooting from the field.

Andrews and Key had 27 and 24, respectively, in an 89-71 win over LSU, then Parker scored 22 and Stamper 18 to help the Cats fight off Alabama 77-74. The win over Alabama was costly, however. Hollenbeck, who missed UK's first nine game because of a broken foot, was lost for the season when he suffered another foot injury.

The Cats won their next six games to run their streak to 10 straight. Included in that string of victories were wins in three traditional Wildcat death chambers — Nashville, Auburn and Starkville. UK beat Vandy 85-80 in overtime,

Auburn 78-72, Ole Miss 90-82 and Mississippi State 63-55. The Cats then returned home to beat Florida 95-68 and Georgia 87-63. Parker scored 25 against the Gators, while Andrews led the way with 28 in the win over Georgia.

UK's road show success hit the skids with back-to-back losses at LSU and Alabama. LSU shot 60 percent from the field, and Bill Newton scored 31 points, in an 88-71 win over the Cats. Alabama came from four down at halftime to nip the Cats 73-70 in Tuscaloosa.

In what turned out to be Rupp's final game in Memorial Coliseum, Parker scored 29 and Key added 23 as the Cats blasted Auburn 102-67. On hand for the game that night were many of Rupp's greatest pivotmen, including Aggie Sale, Alex Groza, Bill Spivey, Cliff Hagan, Bob Burrow, Cotton Nash and Dan Issel.

Going into the final game of the season, the Cats needed a victory over Tennessee in Knoxville to secure a spot in the NCAA Tournament. They got it, sneaking past the Vols 67-66 when Mike Edwards missed the front end of a bonus with no time showing on the clock. Andrews led UK with 20 points. Tennessee's Len Kosmalski had 24.

After the game, a somber Rupp told reporters that, "they can leave me with the team or they may as well take me out to the Lexington Cemetery. I know there are thousands of petitions coming in to the president. I guess that puts pressure on him. I don't want them to stick me off in some office a mile from the coliseum and let me make speeches. This school and this team and basketball have been my life. I want to stay in basketball."

For the fourth time in five years, UK was paired against its old nemesis Marquette in postseason action. This time, however, the second-ranked Warriors went into the game as heavy favorites. In fact, many thought Al McGuire's team to be the chief threat to UCLA for the national title. But Marquette's chances were dealt a severe blow when star center Jim Chones signed a pro contract in February and left the team.

The Warriors led UK 34-33 at intermission, and were on top by six in the second half when George Frazier went down with an ankle injury. His absence, along with UK's red-hot shooting (55 percent), proved to be too much for Marquette to overcome. The Cats stormed back to take an 85-69 victory.

Lyons led UK with 19 points, while Stamper and Andrews each contributed 17. Key finished with 14 and Parker added 12.

Having dispatched Marquette, the Cats now faced Flor-ida State, a dangerous team coached by Louisville native Hugh Durham. The game was close for a half, but Florida State pulled away in the final 20 minutes for an easy 73-54 win. To UK fans, it must have seemed like *deja vu*. Florida State had too much quickness and athletic ability for the Cats to cope with. And just as it had been the previous year against Western Kentucky, it was a pair of Kentucky kids, ex-Louisville Central standouts Ron King and Otto Petty, who put the major hurt on the Cats. King led all scorers with 22 points, while Petty had 13 points and eight assists.

Andrews concluded his fine season with a 17-point, 11-rebound performance. Parker and Lyons each had 10 points.

A few weeks later, it was officially announced that Hall would be the new UK coach. At the press conference introducing Hall, Rupp was conspicuous by his absence.

Rupp's tenure at UK was done. But the magnitude of what the man achieved is astonishing. In 42 years, his teams had a combined record of 876-190 for a phenomenal winning percentage of 82.2 percent. His teams did even better in SEC play, posting a record of 397-75 for an 84.1 winning percentage. He led UK to four national championships, one NIT title, an Olympic gold medal and 27 SEC titles. Four times he was voted national Coach of the Year, and seven times he was the SEC Coach of the Year. On six occasions, his teams were voted No. 1 in the final polls. Twenty-three of his players were named All-Americans, and 52 were chosen to the All-SEC team.

Not surprisingly, in 1969 Rupp was inducted into the Naismith Hall of Fame.

Hall was now the man sitting on the hot seat. But he wasn't coming in empty-handed. Thanks to his own excellent recruiting efforts, Hall had filled the UK coffers with a group of freshmen that were the cause of great excitement and high anticipation.

1972-73

It could be argued — and it was — that attempting to fill Rupp's shoes was an impossible undertaking. After all, Rupp *was* Kentucky basketball. He ran the Wildcat ship for 42 memorable seasons. To the vast majority of Big Blue fans, Rupp was the only UK coach they had known.

So the pressure that fell on Hall's shoulders was enormous. But that pressure was eased somewhat by the talent he had surrounding him. Andrews, Lyons and Stamper were returning. Joining them would be one of

Joe B. Hall had the unenviable task of following the winningest coach of all-time and the only coach most UK fans had ever known.

the most-heralded sophomore classes in UK history, a group known as the "Super Kittens." As freshmen, this talented group put together a perfect 22-0 record. The "Super Kittens" consisted of Jimmy Dan Conner, Kevin Grevey, Mike Flynn, Bob Guyette, Steve Lochmueller, Jerry Hale and G.J. Smith. It was a closely knit band of brothers who possessed size, quickness, basketball savvy and plenty of confidence.

Hall's usual starting lineup, especially if he opted for a taller version, featured Andrews in the middle, Grevey and Guyette as the forwards, and Lyons and Conner in the backcourt. On those occasions when Hall went with a smaller, quicker lineup, Flynn moved into a backcourt spot, with Conner shifting to Guyette's forward position. Lochmueller also saw plenty of action, particularly on those occasions

when the Cats needed better rebounding and defense.

The "Super Kittens" were anything but super in the early going, losing three of their first four games. Only Guyette played with any consistency, while Grevey, the most heralded of the rookies, played so poorly that he briefly lost his starting spot. For the closely scrutinized Hall, UK's poor start only served to provide more ammunition for those critics who continued to lament Rupp's dismissal.

The Cats opened with a 75-66 win over Michigan State, then suffered consecutive losses to Iowa (79-66), Indiana (64-58) and North Carolina (78-70). The only area of consistency in those three losses was poor shooting. Against Iowa, the Cats made good on 29 of 70 attempts for 41 percent. UK went into the dressing room with a 32-28 halftime lead over Indiana, only to go sour in the final 20 minutes. North Carolina, led by George Karl's 22 points, took advantage of UK's cold shooting to build an early 20-point lead that proved to be insurmountable.

Grevey finally began to find the range in the Cats' two

UKIT wins. He scored 20 and Conner added 15 to lead the Cats past Nebraska 85-60 in the opener. Andrews had 33 and Grevey 14 as the Cats captured the title with a 95-68 win over Oregon.

The Cats closed out the pre-SEC schedule with a pair of gritty wins over Kansas and Notre Dame. Grevey and Guyette each scored 17 and Andrews added 16 as the Cats beat the Jayhawks 77-71. Then Andrews lit it up for 20 to lead UK to a 65-63 win over the Irish in Freedom Hall.

Ole Miss spoiled the Cats' SEC opener, using a huge 53-34 rebounding advantage to score a 61-58 upset. Fred Cox, the Rebels' 7-foot center, had 18 points and 15 rebounds.

Andrews went on a scoring rampage in the next three games, racking up 81 points to lead the Cats past Mississippi State 90-81, Florida 95-65 and Georgia 89-68.

A trio of native Kentuckians stepped up in crunch time to lead Tennessee and Vanderbilt to wins over UK. Kentuckian Rodney Woods scored the game's final four points to give the Vols a 65-64 win, then Mayfield's Joe Ford canned two free throws with three seconds remaining to lift Vandy past the Cats 76-75. Hart County native Terry Compton led Vandy with 17 points.

After Andrews scored 24, Grevey 22 and Guyette 19 in an 86-71 win over LSU, the Cats gave one of their best performances of the season against Alabama, winning 95-93 behind Grevey's 33-point outburst. UK had to overcome Alabama's 1-2 punch of Leon Douglas and Wendell Hudson, who combined for 65 points.

Vanderbilt waltzed into Lexington and beat the Cats 83-76, ending UK's 49-game home winning streak against SEC teams. Compton again did the most damage, scoring 23 points. Flynn led UK with 21.

The Cats now stood 5-4 halfway through the SEC slate,

Kevin Grevey (35), Ronnie Lyons (14) and Jim Andrews (55) were named to the all-tourney team after leading the Wildcats to the 1972 UKIT title.

and appeared to be out of the race. But Hall's Cats, showing plenty of moxie, weren't ready to raise the flag of surrender just yet. They needed to win out to have a shot at the SEC crown, and that's what they did. With their backs squarely against the wall, they surprised everyone by winning their final nine games to finish 14-4 in league play and win another SEC championship.

The main reason for UK's late-season surge was Grevey. After what had been a hit-and-miss rookie campaign, the southpaw from Hamilton, Ohio, suddenly began to scald the nets. In UK's final seven games, Grevey posted Issel-like numbers, scoring 203 points.

But Grevey wasn't the only Wildcat hero. Conner had a big game in UK's 88-57 win over Auburn, finishing with 27 points. Andrews tagged Ole Miss for 24 in an 88-70 win, and Lyons put in 28 to ease the Cats past Mississippi State 100-87 in overtime. Lochmueller's defense against Tim Bassett was instrumental in UK's 99-86 win at Georgia. Bassett scored 36 points, but managed just eight against Lochmueller in the final 14 minutes.

Still, it was Grevey's consistent scoring that elevated this team to a championship-caliber level. He hit for a season-high 40 against Georgia, then followed that with a 26-point effort in the Cats' 94-76 win over LSU. Conner also had 26 points against the Tigers.

The Cats gave another terrific performance against Alabama, hitting 56 percent from the field in a 111-95 win. Five Wildcats scored in double figures, led by Grevey with 29. Lochmueller finished with 18, Conner and Flynn 16 each, and Andrews 14. Hudson paced C.M. Newton's Crimson Tide with a game-high 31 points.

UK took the SEC lead by beating Auburn 91-79, then clinched the title with

an 86-81 win over Tennessee. With his team trailing 65-61, Grevey hit four straight jumpers to put the Cats on top for good at 69-67. Grevey had 62 points in those two wins, Andrews had 48 and Conner had 41.

UK's opening-round foe in the Mideast Regional was Ohio Valley Conference champ Austin Peay. The Governors were a high-scoring team led by James "Fly" Williams, a player with unlimited shooting range and a willingness to launch from anywhere inside the arena.

Although Williams had an off-night shooting (13 of 31 from the field), the Governors took UK into overtime before finally succumbing 106-100. Andrews led all scorers with 30 points, while Grevey added 21. Williams finished with 26 for Austin Peay.

That win set up a rematch against Indiana. The Hoosiers jumped to an early lead, and were in front 45-32 at the half. UK clawed its way back, eventually taking a 61-59 lead with less than eight minutes left. But the Hoosiers, led by Downing and Quinn Buckner, regained the upper hand and came away with a 72-65 win.

Downing finished with 23 points and 13 rebounds. Buckner had 16 points and 11 rebounds.

Andrews ended his UK career with a 23-point, 10-rebound effort. He averaged 20.1 points and 12.4 rebounds per game as a senior. As a Wildcat, Andrews scored 1,320 points, while making good on 56.3 percent of his field goal attempts.

Grevey and Conner also had excellent sophomore seasons, averaging 18.7 and 11.2 points, respectively.

Despite a fine 20-8 record, it had been a somewhat topsy-turvy season for the young Cats. If nothing else, though,

Kevin Grevey was the steadiest performer on the disappointing 1973-74 team that finished with a 13-13 record.

they had demonstrated great courage by winning 10 of their last 11 games. With that momentum to build on, and with virtually all key personnel returning, there was no reason to doubt that next season would be even better.

1973-74

Few UK seasons have begun with more high hopes than this one. And few have turned out to be more dismal. By season's end, what was thought to be a championship-caliber team could do no better than break even. The Cats' 13-13 record matched the one recorded by the 1966-67 club.

Despite a wealth of talent, experience and depth, the absence of a true big man in the middle proved to be a season-long problem the Cats could never overcome. With the 6'9" Guyette and the 6'7" Lochmueller handling the center position, the Cats were often overmatched physically in the low-post area.

Just as with the previous season, the Cats won their opener, then dropped three straight. But unlike the previous year, this team was never able to put together a winning streak of any length. Only twice during the season were the Cats able to win three in a row.

Individually, several Wildcats did have a decent season. Grevey averaged 21.9 points per game, hitting nearly 51 percent of his shots. Guyette, Conner and Flynn also scored at a double-digit clip, and Guyette, despite being small for a center, averaged eight rebounds per game. But the individual efforts, no matter how good, never translated into outstanding or consistent overall team play. From the very first game, an 81-68 win over Miami of Ohio, to the final game three months later, which the Cats had to win to avoid a losing season, this UK team never rose above mediocre. There wasn't a single win against a ranked opponent, and for the first time since the Rupp Era began in 1930, the Cats lost four in a row.

The opener against Miami should have been an indicator of what lay ahead. Although heavy favorites to win easily, the Cats had to struggle before finally putting away from the pesky Redskins. Grevey's 29 led UK.

What followed next was a repeat of the previous year's script — three straight losses. Roger Morningstar scored 20 points to lead Kansas to a 71-63 win over the Cats, then Indiana, behind John Laskowski's 23-point effort, claimed a 77-68 victory in Freedom Hall. Rebounding was the difference in UK's 101-84 loss to North Carolina. The Tar Heels, led by Bobby Jones' 21 points, owned a huge 42-26

advantage on the glass. Grevey scored 72 points in those three losses to lead UK.

Grevey pitched in 29 points and Lyons added 16 as the Cats snapped their losing streak with an 88-80 win over Iowa. A severe tongue lashing from Hall spurred the Cats to a 102-77 win over Dartmouth in the UKIT opener. Early in the second half, with his team not executing the 1-3-1 zone to his satisfaction, Hall scolded his players, saying, "two more minutes of this stuff and I'll empty the bench." Grevey again led UK in scoring with 25. Conner finished with 19 and Guyette 12.

UK won its own tournament with a 78-77 win over Stanford despite a 26-point, 27-rebound performance by 7-foot Cardinal center Rich Kelly. The Cats trailed 71-70 when Stanford was hit with a technical. Lyons made the free throw to tie the score, then seconds later Conner came up with a steal and layup that put UK in front for good. Grevey had 25 and Lyons 21 for the Cats.

Powerful Notre Dame had little trouble against the Cats, winning easily 94-79. John Shumate led the Irish with 25, while super-talented freshman Adrian Dantley had 22. Grevey and Conner led UK with 25 and 24, respectively.

UK's trip through the SEC, which began with a 95-84 loss to LSU, proved to be just as mystifying, frustrating and disappointing as the December portion of the schedule had been. There were no impressive victories, no truly spectacular performances. So lackluster was this team that the boo-birds, rarely heard in Memorial Coliseum, vented their feelings several times during the season.

After beating Georgia 80-74 and Auburn 79-58, the Cats lost to Tennessee 67-54. Or, more specifically, they lost to Ernie Grunfeld, who outscored the Cats 12-0 in the final 5:48. Grunfeld finished with 20 points to lead all scorers.

The Cats blasted Ole Miss 93-64, then gave a respectable performance in an 81-77 loss at Alabama. UK was up 44-39 at the half, but the Crimson Tide, led by Douglas, Cleveland and Odums, had enough firepower to avoid being upset. Douglas had 24 for the Tide. Guyette's 23 led UK.

Grevey hit for a season-high 35 points in a 91-82 win over Florida. It was the start of the team's most-successful stretch during the season, four wins in five games. Following an 82-65 loss to Vanderbilt, the Cats beat Mississippi State 82-70, LSU 73-70 and Georgia 86-72. The Cats split their next two games, losing to Auburn 99-97 in overtime and beating Tennessee 61-58. Auburn came out the gate on fire,

hitting 10 of its first 13 shots, yet the Cats had a chance to send the game into a second extra period and possibly win their fourth straight. But those hopes died when Jerry Hale missed the front end of a bonus after time had expired.

After beating Tennessee, the Cats began their disasterous four-game slide by dropping a 61-60 decision to Ole Miss. Rebel freshman Gary Yoder's steal and layup with 10 seconds left decided the issue. A 94-71 loss to Alabama, UK's worst at home since the 1926-27 season, was quickly followed by a 75-65 loss to Florida and a 71-69 loss to Vanderbilt.

The Cats now stood at 12-13 and in need of a win over Mississippi State in their final game to avoid the school's first losing record since 1926-27.

With Grevey scoring 25 points, the Cats escaped total humiliation by easily defeating Mississippi State 108-69 in Memorial Coliseum. Guyette had 17 for the Cats and Lyons added 16.

Later that summer, Hall took his team to Australia for an important 19-game exhibition tour. UK played well down under, winning all but two of those games. That tour proved to be pivotal, because it helped the shaken Wildcat players regain much of their shredded confidence.

With a new-found faith in their own abilities, along with the arrival of four gifted freshmen, the Cats were ready to regain their lost honor. And they would, coming within a single win of capturing another NCAA title.

1974-75

The problem that plagued UK the previous season — lack of size inside — was soon to be double-teamed and put to rest. The arrival of another exceptional freshman class included two 6'10" post players, Rick Robey and Mike

Jimmy Dan Conner hit 15 of 21 shots and scored 35 points in UK's pivotal 90-78 come-from-behind win over North Carolina.

Phillips, who later became known as the "Twin Towers." For the next four years, Robey and Phillips gave the Cats an inside presence second to none in the college ranks.

Robey and Phillips were joined in that rookie group by an outstanding pair of Lexington natives, Jack "Goose" Givens and James Lee. Givens, was "Silk," a smooth player and a deadly shooter, while Lee, nicknamed "Steel," was known for his rebounding, defense and thunderous dunks.

When that talented foursome joined ranks with the veteran senior class, UK had its deepest, most-talented team in years. The Cats were ranked high in the preseason polls, and they justified that ranking by opening with wins over Northwestern and Miami of Ohio. Grevey scored 32 and Lee came off the bench to chip in 11 as the Cats rolled past Northwestern 97-70. In UK's 80-73 win over the Redskins, Guyette had 17, Grevey 16 and Givens 10.

Then came one of the most lopsided and humiliating losses in UK history — 98-74 to powerful Indiana in Bloomington. It was a big-time spanking, and it could have been worse had IU coach Bobby Knight not substituted liberally in the late stages. Led by the 1-2 punch of All-Americans Kent Benson and Scott May, the Hoosiers raced to a 54-38 halftime lead and never looked back. Benson had 26 points and 12 rebounds, while May added 25 points. Grevey led the Cats with 22.

It was in the waning minutes of the game that an incident took place involving Hall and Knight. The two former fishing buddies finished arguing an official's call, and as Hall turned to walk away, Knight cuffed him on the back

of the head. Knight claimed it was a playful gesture, a claim the UK coaches and fans were quick to reject.

That loss, devastating as it was, seemed to harden the Cats' resolve. Facing a tough North Carolina team in Freedom Hall, the Cats fell behind 31-16 in the first half and appeared to be on their way to a second straight decisive loss. But with Conner picking up the banner, the Cats outscored North Carolina 26-3 over the next few minutes to take control of the game. UK went on to beat the Tar Heels 90-78. Conner was the driving force behind the victory, hitting 15 of 21 shots to finish with 35 points.

The win over North Carolina ignited a seven-game winning streak that included a 100-63 romp past Kansas and an impressive 113-96 win over highly ranked Notre Dame. The Cats also won their own Christmas tournament, beating Washington State 97-75 and Oklahoma State 90-65. Grevey had 51 points in those two wins, while Robey had 25 points and 10 rebounds against Oklahoma State.

Larry Johnson came off the bench to spark the Cats to their win over Notre Dame. The Irish were sitting on a 36-28 lead when Johnson entered the game. The Cats

immediately went on a 15-0 run to claim a 43-36 lead and the game's momentum. Grevey led a balanced UK attack with 28 points. Guyette had 18, Johnson 16, Conner 15, Robey and Phillips 14 apiece. Notre Dame's Dantley had 39 to lead all scorers.

Grevey scored 20 to lead the Cats to a 115-80 win over LSU, then came back to hit for 32 in a 96-77 win over Georgia. Phillips had 18 against the Tigers, Guyette had 19 against Georgia.

Auburn opened the second half by hitting 14 of its first 19 shots, then went on to upset the Cats 90-85. Mike Mitchell was Auburn's main gun with 31 points. Grevey had 29 for UK, while Conner added 27.

Excellent play by Grevey, Conner and the rapidly improving Givens helped carry the Cats to hard-earned wins over Tennessee, Ole Miss and Alabama. Grevey scored 24 and Givens had 18 in the Cats' 88-82 win over Tennessee. Grunfeld's 26 led all scorers.

Conner buried three straight jumpers to lift the Cats past upset-minded Ole Miss 85-82. Grevey led UK with 27. Flynn finished with 22, Conner and Robey with 13 each. In a crucial SEC showdown against Alabama, Grevey dropped in three pressure-packed free throws to stem the Tide and give UK a 74-69 victory. Grevey's 20 paced the Cats. Douglas had 27 points and 25 rebounds for Alabama.

In his first start, Givens hit eight of 11 shots and finished with 19 points as UK toppled Florida 87-65. Grevey led UK with 26. Conner stepped to the free throw line and hit a pair of late free throws to seal the Cats' 91-90 win over Vanderbilt in Nashville. Grevey again led UK with 27 points. Conner had 18 and Phillips added 12.

After Givens scored 18 in an easy 112-79 win over Mississippi State, the Cats sneaked past LSU 77-76 despite missing the front end of four straight bonus situations in the final three minutes. Conner and Grevey each had 17 for UK. LSU's Glenn Hansen had 29 to claim game-high honors.

The Cats beat Georgia 75-61 and Auburn 119-73 to improve their SEC record to 11-1 and put them in a tie for first place with Alabama. Grevey continued to shoot well, hitting for 20 against Georgia and 37 in the win over Auburn.

The Cats' stay at the top of the SEC standings was shortlived, thanks to Tennessee's Bernard King. After the Cats

Mike Flynn's brilliant 22-point performance sparked the Wildcats to a 92-90 win over Indiana in the Mideast Regional. Flynn was Indiana's Mr. Basketball in 1971

had battled back from a 56-44 halftime deficit to close to within 90-88, King connected on a bucket and two free throws to quell the uprising and send the Vols to a 103-98 win. Grunfeld led all scorers with 29. King and Mike Jackson each had 24 for the Vols. Grevey had 24, Givens 20 and Robey 18 for UK.

Freshmen Givens and Robey combined for 50 points as the Cats tuned up for a crucial showdown with Alabama by beating Ole Miss 109-89. Grevey, benched for 15 minutes because of poor play, scored 12 of his 16 points after climbing out of Hall's doghouse to lead the Cats to an 84-79 win over Alabama and a share of first place in the SEC standings. Givens and Guyette had 17 each for UK. Alabama's Douglas led everyone with 34.

Once again, UK's stay at the top proved to be brief. A 10-minute scoring drought by UK was all Florida needed to wipe out a 54-50 deficit and beat the Cats 66-58. Grevey and Florida's Gene Shy shared scoring honors with 20 each.

UK closed out its regular season with easy wins over Vanderbilt and Mississippi State to finish with a 15-3 league record and a tie for first place with Alabama. Robey and Grevey each scored 28 against the Commodores. Grevey had 30 and Phillips 26 in the win over Mississippi State.

Although UK and Alabama finished with identical 15-3 SEC records, the Cats, by virtue of their two regular-season wins, won the automatic tourney bid. However, because of the expanded NCAA Tournament field, C.M. Newton's club also received an invitation to the big party.

The Cats opened tourney play against (who else?) Marquette in Tuscaloosa, Ala. After trailing 28-25 at the half, UK came back to win easily 76-54, thanks to a strong defense that completely shut down the Warriors in the final 20 minutes. For the game, Marquette hit just 32 percent from the field.

Grevey paced the Cats with 19 points, while Guyette had 14 points and 15 rebounds.

With five players scoring in double figures, UK beat a good Central Michigan team 90-73 in the next round at Dayton, Ohio. Grevey led the balanced attack with 17 points. Phillips had 15, Givens 12, and Robey and Flynn 11 apiece. Future NBA standout Dan Roundfield had 20 points and 11 rebounds for Central Michigan.

The Cats were now one win away from making their first trip to the Final Four since 1966. But standing in their way was Indiana, which owned a flawless 31-0 record and that earlier 98-74 win over the Cats. To earn a ticket to San Diego, the Cats had to win the rematch with the unbeaten and top-ranked Hoosiers.

The game, which the Wildcats won 92-90, still ranks as one of the greatest and most-exciting in UK basketball history. It was tense, emotional, pressure-charged and close from start to finish. Both teams had leads of up to eight points, only to see them slip away. Each team had 37 field goals, and each shot just under 50 percent from the field.

Late in the game, Phillips accounted for six points to give UK an 89-81 lead, and although the Hoosiers fought back, the Cats were able to hang on for the victory.

Flynn, Indiana's 1971 high school Mr. Basketball, came up big for the Cats, scoring 22 points. Conner and Grevey each had 17, while Robey and Phillips each had 10.

Benson, IU's great center, had a brilliant game with 33 points and 23 rebounds. May, IU's leading scorer during the season, scored only two points in seven minutes of action. This game marked his return after breaking his wrist late in the season.

In the national semifinal game, the Cats won a surprisingly easy 95-79 victory over Syracuse. A huge 51-38 rebounding advantage was instrumental in that win. Givens, the freshman, turned in a sparkling performance, hitting 10 of 20 shots, scoring 24 points and pulling down 11 rebounds. Grevey and Conner had 14 and 12 points, respectively.

UK's opponent in the championship game was UCLA, which had scored a 75-74 overtime win over Louisville in the other semifinal game. Prior to the final game, Bruin coach John Wooden announced that he would retire at the end of the season. After 27 seasons as UCLA's coach, the Wizard of Westwood, whose Bruin teams had won nine of the past 11 NCAA titles, was calling it quits. The timing of Wooden's announcement was shrewd and calculated. No group of players ever had more motivation to win than these Bruins.

Wooden used only six players that night, but they had enough in them to claim a 92-85 win. Surprisingly, despite being outsized physically, the Bruins won the battle of the boards 55-49. They also shot well from the field (49 percent), while holding the Cats to just 38-percent shooting. Perhaps even more important, the Bruins held UK big men Robey, Phillips and Dan Hall to a combined total of eight points.

Grevey closed out his UK career by scoring 34 points against the Bruins. Guyette and Flynn, in their final game, had 16 and 10 points, respectively.

Richard Washington led UCLA with 28 points. Dave Meyers added 24.

Grevey earned All-America honors, averaging 23.6 points per game as a senior. He left UK with 1,801 points, which at the time was second only to Dan Issel, and is still the sixth-highest point total in UK history.

Conner also shot his way into UK's elite scoring fraternity, ending his outstanding career with 1,009 points.

Although UK came up one win shy of capturing another national championship, there was little reason for disappointment. With Givens, Robey, Phillips, Johnson and Lee set to return, the outlook for next season was bright.

1975-76

Throughout UK's glorious basketball history, few seasons have been more schizophrenic than this one. The Cats were projected to be a contender for the national title, yet after the first 20 games, the best they could do was break even. What began as a season of big dreams had quickly

Larry Johnson's defensive quickness was a key element in the 1975-76 team's late season turnaround. After a 10-10 start, the Cats won their final 10 games and the NIT championship.

turned into an all-out struggle for survival.

Then, just when it began to look like there would be a replay of the 1973-74 season, the Cats got hot, winning their final 10 games to finish with a 20-10 record.

And, amazingly, the NIT championship.

One big reason why the Cats faltered was the absence of Robey. A series of injuries limited UK's talented power forward to just 12 games that season, and without his size and experience, the Cats were severely crippled.

Even without Robey, the Cats had plenty of talent but not much proven depth. Givens, Phillips and Johnson were staters throughout the season. The always-exciting Lee moved up from his usual sixth-man role

to take over a forward spot when Robey went down. At various times during the season, Reggie Warford, Merion Haskins, Danny Hall and Truman Claytor got the nod for the fifth starting position. Other valuable reserves who made important contributions included high-jumping Bob Fowler and Dwane Casey.

The Cats stumbled right out of the gate, losing 89-77 at Northwestern. It was UK's first opening-night loss since 1962. Northwestern led 42-34 at the half, then increased that lead to 65-42 with 10 minutes left. Robey topped UK's scoring with 24 points. Givens finished with 15 and Claytor had 14 in his Wildcat debut. Northwestern guard Billy McKinney led all scorers with 31.

Mitch Kupchak scored 24 points and Walter Davis added 19 as North Carolina defeated the Cats 90-77 in Charlotte. The score was tied 42-42 at the half, but a quick 31-16 spurt by the Tar Heels at the start of the second half broke the game open. Givens had 24 points to match Kupchak for top honors. The 0-2 start marked the first time since the 1926-27 season that the Cats had opened with back-to-back losses.

With Givens and Robey combining for 61 points, UK put its first mark in the W column with an easy 91-69 win over Miami of Ohio. Givens had 31, Robey 30. The big news that night was a lineup change — Dan Hall replaced Phillips at the pivot position. Hall finished with two points.

Despite drawing that early start, Hall's stay at UK would be brief. By midseason, a disgruntled Hall, unhappy with his lack of playing time, left UK and transferred to Marshall University.

Two clutch buckets by Robey and a pair of late Claytor free throws helped lift the Cats to a 54-48 victory over Kansas. Robey led UK with 21 points.

The Cats gave one of their finest efforts of the season in a heart-breaking 77-68 overtime loss to Indiana in Freedom Hall.

The Hoosiers, who would go undefeated and win the NCAA championship, were lucky to escape the Cats. UK led by two late in the game and had the ball. But following a miss by Johnson, the Hoosiers rebounded and got the ball to Scott May. May put up a shot that was off the mark, but a fluke tip-in by IU center Kent Benson tied the score at 64-64 and sent the game into overtime. The extra frame belonged to the Hoosiers, who outscored UK 13-4 to notch the win. Benson and May each had 27 points for Indiana. Givens led UK with 20.

The Cats won their own Christmas tournament, beating Georgia Tech 66-64 and Oregon State 82-74. Robey had

18 in the opener, Phillips had 27 points and 15 rebounds in the championship game.

A second-half defensive switch from man-to-man to a 1-3-1 zone proved to be the savior in UK's 79-77 comeback win over Notre Dame in Freedom Hall. With his club on the short end of a 39-32 score at the break, Hall ordered the defensive change. It was a saving move by the UK coach. Notre Dame failed to adjust, and the momentum soon swung in UK's direction. Claytor and Phillips each had 18 for the Cats. Notre Dame All-American Adrian Dantley led all scorers with 28.

Those three wins gave the Cats a 5-3 record heading into SEC play. But any hopes of winning another league title were quickly laid to rest, thanks to successive losses to Mississippi State (77-73), Alabama (76-63) and Tennessee (90-88 in overtime). Each of those three losses, which sent the Cats crashing to the bottom of the league standings, was a dagger in the heart.

The Cats led Mississippi State 42-36 at the half, only to come apart in the final 20 minutes. They had two more field goals than Alabama, but shot just 13 free throws to the Tide's 37. And the Cats were on the verge of upsetting Tennessee when Bernard King hit an impossible shot while falling backward. It was in this game that Tennessee's Ernie Grunfeld, who finished with 43 points, shot four free throws that should have been shot by a teammate.

UK beat Georgia 92-76 but lost Robey to a season-ending injury. Givens keyed the Wildcat victory with 26 points. Haskins and Warford each came off the bench to score 12.

Johnson was the main man in UK's next two wins — 77-76 over Vanderbilt and 89-82 over Florida. Johnson scored UK's final five points, including the game-winning jump shot with 13 seconds remaining, in the win over Vandy. Phillips was the Cats' leading scorer with 30, while Johnson added 15. Johnson followed that performance with a 22-point effort against the Gators.

The Cats lost to Auburn 91-84 in overtime after leading by 14 in the first half. They bounced back to beat Ole Miss 89-81 and LSU 85-71. Givens scored 28 points against the Rebels, Phillips had a 35-point, 20-rebound performance against LSU.

In a nasty, physical game that saw seven technical fouls called and two players (Claytor and Johnny Darden) ejected for fighting, Tennessee again beat the Cats 92-85. Grunfeld led the Vols with 32, while King contributed 22. Phillips and Givens paced UK with 20 and 18, respectively.

Two more losses followed — 86-81 to Georgia and 69-65 to Vanderbilt. At Vandy, the Cats had only nine players suited up, including UK quarterback Derrick Ramsey. A pair of Cats, Fowler and Joey Holland, had been suspended for violating team rules.

With a 10-10 record overall, a 5-7 mark in SEC play and an outlook that offered little promise, this group of Wildcats couldn't sink much lower. There would be no SEC title, no NCAA Tournament appearance. A losing record was a distinct possibility. At that low point, certainly no one could have imagined what was about to unfold.

Like so many past Wildcat teams that found themselves facing the firing squad, this one somehow marshalled enough inner resources to dodge the killing bullet. With Givens and Phillips providing the most firepower, the Cats beat Florida 96-89 to kick off a six-game winning streak that included an impressive 90-85 upset of Alabama, the eventual SEC champs.

And it didn't stop there. Before the uniforms were put away for good, this unlikely team would win 10 straight, finish with a 20-10 record and claim the school's second NIT championship.

Givens was sensational during this late-season surge, scoring 110 points in UK's next four games. He had 20 against the Gators, then 27 in a 93-82 win over Auburn. Phillips and Lee also damaged the Tigers, scoring 24 and 17, respectively. Givens came back with 30 and Phillips added 24 as the Cats made it three in a row by beating Ole Miss 94-87. In a tough rematch against LSU, Givens racked up 33 points to lead UK to an 85-70 victory. Phillips had 18 points and 15 rebounds in that win.

Phillips scored 25, Lee 21 and Givens 18 in UK's big upset of Alabama. Reggie King led the Tide with 25 points.

UK's final regular-season game was against Mississippi State, and it would be the last one played in Memorial Coliseum. It would also be one of the most thrilling games ever played in the place UK had called home for 26 years.

With Rupp, Lancaster and a host of former UK All-Americans looking on, the Cats battled back from a seven-point deficit with just 1:23 left to play, sent the game into overtime, and then claimed a 94-93 victory. And they did it without Phillips, who was ejected from the game with 6:55 left in regulation play.

Trailing 84-77, and playing with an extremely small lineup, the Cats went on an 8-1 run to even the score at 85-85 and force the overtime. Two buckets by Johnson, one

by Warford, and 12-foot jumper by Givens with eight seconds remaining were enough to bring about the deadlock. After State took an 87-85 lead, baskets by Givens, Johnson and Fowler put the Cats in front for good.

Givens led all scorers with 26 points, while Phillips had 22 before getting tossed. The backcourt duo of Johnson and Warford also played well, scoring 16 and 12 points, respectively.

UK took its 16-10 record to Madison Square Garden for its first appearance in the NIT since 1950. If the UK players were disappointed by not being in the NCAA tourney, they didn't show it. With Lee scoring 20 points, the Cats edged past Niagara 67-61 in the opener. After watching a 10-point lead whittled to two, the Cats needed a critical three-point play by Fowler and a steal and layup by Claytor to finally put Niagara away.

The Cats overcame a nine-point second-half deficit to beat Kansas State 81-78 in the second round. Lee was once again UK's top point producer with 20. Phillips finished with 17, while Givens and Johnson each had 15.

Johnson's jump shot with a single tick left on the clock lifted the Cats past Providence 79-78 and into the championship game. Givens led UK with 29. Phillips had 19 and Johnson 12.

Awaiting the Cats in the title game was UNCC, which was coached by Lexington native Lee Rose and led by Cedric "Cornbread" Maxwell.

The game turned out to be a showcase for Warford. UK's lone senior, who had never lettered until this season, scored 10 of his 14 points inside the final minutes to help lift the Cats to a 71-67 victory. Twice, Warford hit buckets that gave UK the upper hand, including a 15-footer that put the Cats in front for good at 64-63.

Phillips and Johnson led UK in scoring with 16 each. Maxwell was the game's top scorer with 24.

It was a fitting end for Warford, the Drakesboro (Ky.) native whose positive attitude, intelligence and winning personality were instrumental in helping UK shed its all-white image. Warford followed Tom Payne as the second black to sign with UK, and it was with much help from him that UK was able to land Johnson, Haskins, Givens, Lee, Claytor and Casey.

Givens was UK's leading scorer for the season, averaging 20.1 points per game. Phillips scored at a 15.6 clip, while Johnson averaged 11.2. Robey averaged 15.6 points in his 12 games.

1976-77

The Cats moved into Rupp Arena, and with a veteran

group of players returning from the NIT championship team, there was every reason to expect big things this season. And the Cats lived up to the high expectations, finishing with a 26-4 record overall, a 16-2 SEC mark (co-champs with Tennessee), and a No. 6 ranking in the final AP poll.

Givens, Robey, Phillips and Johnson were joined in the starting lineup by freshman guard Jay Shidler, who, because of his blond hair and his ability to light up the scoreboard from long rang, was immediately dubbed "White Lightning" by adoring Wildcat fans. Lee, Claytor and Casey provided solid support off the bench.

The Cats opened in their new home with a 72-64 win over Wisconsin. It wasn't an impressive performance (UK was outscored by two in the second half), but with Rupp looking on, the Cats did enough to make their Rupp Arena debut a success. Robey led the Cats with 13. Givens and Johnson each had 12, while Lee came off the bench to score 11.

After that uninspired effort, the Cats turned in a succession of performances that were

James Lee goes up to ram home one of his patented dunks. Few Wildcats could ignite a crowd faster than "Jammin" James.

nothing short of overpowering. They beat Texas Christian 103-53, Indiana (in Bloomington) 66-51, Kansas 90-63, South Carolina 98-67 and Bowling Green State 77-59 in the UKIT opener.

Givens led the scoring in three of those games, hitting for 15 against Kansas and 28 against both South Carolina and Bowling Green. Robey was high man with 21 against TCU, while Johnson and Shidler each tallied 20 against the Hoosiers.

With a 6-0 record, and clearly on a roll, the Cats weren't

expected to have much trouble against a good Utah team in the UKIT championship game. But with Phillips, Shidler and Claytor suspended for a curfew violation, the Cats, now No. 3 in the national polls, suffered a stunning 70-68 setback when Utah's Earl Williams knocked down a jumper just ahead of the final buzzer.

Robey paced UK with 19 points. Lee had 13 points and 13 rebounds, and Casey finished with 12 points. Utah's Jeff Judkins led all scorers with 24.

Before heading into league play, the Cats, fueled by Givens' 30-point performance, blistered top-ranked Notre Dame 102-78 in Freedom Hall. Givens burned the Irish defense, making good on 15 of 19 field goal attempts. Robey followed Givens with 18 points.

Clutch play by Lee and Robey helped the Cats go 2-0 in SEC action by claiming a pair of thrilling wins over Georgia and Vanderbilt. Four late points by Lee lifted the Cats past Georgia 64-59 in overtime, then Robey hit a last-second shot to nip the Commodores 64-62. Givens had 17 against Georgia, Robey had 21 against Vandy.

In their next outing, another overtime thriller, the Cats failed to conjure up enough late-game magic to pull out the win. With Grunfeld scoring 22 points and King collecting 19 rebounds, Tennessee beat the Cats 71-67. Givens led UK with 23 points.

That would be the Cats' last loss until the two teams collided again almost two months later. In between, the Cats reeled off an impressive 14-game winning streak, including seven victories on the road. It was a marvelous stretch,

highlighted by a series of gritty, courageous performances by a club that seemed to improve with each game.

The streak began when Givens scored 20 points in a 75-68 win over Auburn. Shidler's two free throws with four seconds remaining sent the Cats past Florida 73-71. After those two close calls came a pair of blowouts. Phillips had 24 points and 19 rebounds to lead UK past LSU 87-72, then Givens scored 19, Johnson 18 and Lee 14 as the Cats smacked Ole Miss 100-73.

The Cats received a big scare at Alabama before finally coming away with a hard-earned 87-85 win. With the score tied at 83-83, Robey sank a pair of free throws to give UK the lead for good. Givens led the Cats with 23 points. Robey and Phillips each had 16, and Shidler contributed 12. Alabama's Rickey Brown topped C.M. Newton's club with 21 points.

After beating Mississippi State 92-85, the Cats turned in two of their most-devastating performances, ripping Vandy 113-73 and Florida State 97-57. The Cats shot 55 percent from the field against Vandy, and had five players in double figures. Phillips had 24, Givens 21, Johnson 19, Robey 18 and Claytor 16.

Complete control of the boards was the deciding factor in the win over Florida State. UK won the rebounding battle 56-28. Givens' 28 points paced the Cats. Phillips and Robey combined for 33 points and 27 rebounds.

Following wins over Auburn (89-82), Florida (104-78) and LSU (90-76), the Cats beat Ole Miss 81-69 to give Hall his 100th victory since taking over for Rupp five years earlier. Phillips scored 20 points in that memorable win.

Lee came off the bench to score 14 points, including several on his patented dunks, as the Cats beat dangerous Alabama 85-70. Six Cats scored in double figures against the Tide, led by Johnson with 16. Alabama's Reggie King was the game's leading scorer with 21.

It took 83.3 percent second-half shooting (15 of 18) to carry the surging Cats past Mississippi State 77-64. Robey had 19 for UK, while Lee turned in another terrific performance, finishing with 14.

UK's streak ended in Knoxville, where the Vols, led by King's 36 points, scored an 81-79 comeback win. It was the Vols' fifth straight victory over UK. The Cats led 47-42 at the break, then stretched that advantage to 55-44 early in the second half. But with King leading the charge, the home-standing Vols battled back to earn the win and a share of the SEC lead. Both UK and Tennessee ended the season with identical 16-2 SEC records.

The Cats closed out the season by beating Georgia 72-54, giving them a superb 24-3 record overall. Balanced scoring, excellent shooting and a big rebounding advantage over opponents were the keys to this club's successful campaign. Givens led the scoring with an 18.9 average, while Robey (14.2), Phillips (12.2) and Johnson (10.7) also scored in double figures. Lee came in at just under double digits with a 9.8 average.

The Cats shot 50.1 percent from the field, 70.5 percent from the free throw stripe, and had a seven-rebound advantage over their opposition.

Hot shooting enabled the Cats to easily defeat Princeton 72-58 in their NCAA Tournament opener. The Cats made good on 29 of 50 shots for 58 percent. Robey paced the Cats with 20 points, while Claytor came off the bench to chip in with 12.

The Cats faced VMI in the second round, and with Claytor hitting 13 of 15 shots en route to a 29-point performance, they came away with a 93-78 win. The game was close for a half (UK led 44-41 at intermission), but behind the blistering shooting by Claytor and Givens, the Cats were able to pull away and win easily.

Givens had 26 points for the Cats, who hit 39 of 65 field goals attempts for 60 percent.

Next up for the Cats was powerful North Carolina, led by Walter Davis, John Kuester and Phil Ford. The Tar Heels grabbed the upper hand early, taking a 53-41 lead into the dressing room at the break. After the Cats pulled to within 71-70 on a three-point play by Robey, Tar Heel coach Dean Smith ordered his team to go into its celebrated four-corner spread offense. With Ford handling the ball almost exclusively, and with UK forced to foul, the Tar Heels were able to hang on for a 79-72 win.

UK had five more buckets than North Carolina (28-23), but the Tar Heels countered that by hitting 33 of 36 from the charity stripe. Davis topped the Tar Heels with 21 points, while Kuester added 19, including 13 of 14 from the free throw line.

Givens had 26 to lead UK.

Losing to North Carolina in a slow-down game was a bitter way to end the season. However, that bitterness couldn't dim the excitement Wildcat fans felt about next year's club. Only Johnson would be departing, and standing in the wings, ready to replace him was Kyle Macy, a clever 6'3" guard who had transferred to UK from Purdue.

Macy was seen as the final piece of the puzzle, and long before the first tipoff, fans and media had already projected the Cats to be a heavy favorite to capture the national title.

Those expectations would place a heavy burden on Hall and his players.

1977-78

Because of the enormous pressure to win it all (anything less than a national championship would be seen as a failure), this became known as the season without any joy. In many regards, it was a long, strenuous season for the Wildcat players and coaches. But when the final shot had been taken, it would be this UK team, which some still maintain is the school's best-ever, that stood alone on the mountaintop holding the championship trophy.

In every way this was a team worthy of its high ranking and lofty expectations. There were no glaring weaknesses or deficiencies. It was a team with size, strength, depth and experience. It had the ability to pound teams inside or step out and score from long range. The players were veterans who had been war-tested and battle-hardened. They wanted to win, and they knew how to do it. If any team could succeed under such intense pressure, it was this one.

The starting lineup was expected to consist of Robey, Phillips and Givens along the frontline, with Macy and Shidler in the backcourt. However, during the first week of practice, Shidler broke a bone in his foot and was replaced in the starting quintet by Claytor. That turned out to be a blessing in disguise for the Cats. Claytor provided steady play and excellent outside shooting, while Shidler was

Rick Robey puts up a short jumper despite being challenged by a Northwestern defender. Robey's strong inside presence helped the 1977-78 team capture the NCAA championship.

instant offense off the bench.

During the season, Hall was a stern and unrelenting taskmaster. On several occasions, despite a glowing won-loss record, he publicly lambasted his players. Once, after losing in overtime to LSU, he said the team should be known as the "Folding Five." Criticism, frequent substitutions and a never-ending demand for excellence were Hall's way of guarding against over-confidence and complacency.

With Givens scoring 30, Hall's top-ranked club opened with an easy 110-86 romp past SMU. UK's Twin Towers, Robey and Phillips, had 23 and 22, respectively, while Macy gave a sterling debut performance, scoring 16 points and handing out 10 assists.

In a rough, foul-plagued game (55 fouls were called), the Cats topped Indiana 78-64 in Rupp Arena. Givens led UK with 22. Mike Woodson had 20 for the Hoosiers.

After those two wins, the Cats traveled to Kansas, where they posted a 73-66 win. Macy was UK's top scorer with 15.

After the game, the coaches and players were told that Adolph Rupp had died. The man who single-handedly built the University of Kentucky basketball empire was dead after a lengthy battle with cancer. Appropriately, "the Baron of the Bluegrass" passed away while the Cats were facing his alma mater.

The Cats easily won their next four games, including two in the UKIT. They beat South Carolina 84-65, Portland State 114-88, St. John's 102-72 and Iona 104-65. Virtually every Wildcat who played made solid contributions. There were several big efforts turned in by UK substitutes. Lee, of course, was his usual self, scoring 55 points in those

Joe B. Hall got a victory ride after the Wildcats won the 1975 UKIT. Two seasons later, Hall's club went on to claim a bigger prize — the 1978 NCAA championship.

four wins. Chuck Aleksinas had 17 against Portland State and 12 against Iona, while Tim Stephens had 12 in the win over Portland State.

Macy's late-game heroics enabled the Cats to fend off Notre Dame 73-68 in Freedom Hall. With his team down 66-63, Macy hit for eight straight points to steal the shamrock from the Irish and put the Cats on the road to their eighth victory without a loss. Macy and Givens each finished with 18 points.

The Cats improved their record to 14-0 by winning their first six SEC games. Lee had 17 in a 72-59 win over Vanderbilt, then Macy came through with 20 to lead the Cats past Florida 86-67. Givens rammed in 29 as the hot-shooting Cats beat Auburn 101-77. In that game, UK made good on 39 of 69 shots for 56 percent. Claytor finished with 17 and Robey added 16.

While LSU coach Dale Brown was complaining that UK "was brutalizing the game of basketball," the Cats raced to a 55-28 halftime lead then went on to beat the Tigers 96-76. Macy led UK with 23 points, Robey had 18, Givens 17 and Lee 12. Louisville native Rudy Macklin and Jordy Hultberg each had 16 for LSU.

After beating Ole Miss 76-56 and Mississippi State 75-65, the Cats were knocked from the ranks of the unbeaten by Alabama. The Tide went on an early 13-0 run to take a lead they never relinquished. Reggie King led Alabama with 26 points. Robey was the game's leading scorer with 28.

It was a poor performance, and Hall was quick to make his players aware of his dissatisfaction. In particular, Hall came down hard on Givens, who was accused of playing scared and with no heart.

Givens scored 19 as the Cats rebounded with a 90-73 win over Georgia. Macy and Lee each contributed 18 in that victory. Macy followed that effort by turning in one of the greatest performances ever by a Wildcat guard. In UK's 88-61 win over Florida, Macy scored 30 points by hitting 11 of 13 field goal attempts and all eight of his free throws. Then, with Boston Celtic legends Red Auerbach and K.C. Jones looking on, the Cats stormed to a 104-81 win over Auburn. Lee had 25 to lead the Cats. Givens finished with 22, Robey 21 and Macy 17.

UK's second — and final — loss of the season came at LSU. The Tigers, led by Macklin's 23 points, nipped UK 95-94 in overtime. Robey had 18 for the Cats, who fought back from a 12-point second-half deficit only to come up a point shy of victory.

It was after this loss that Hall dubbed his team the "Folding Five." Hall, who had been stern before, now became an absolute tyrant. He was not about to let this team underachieve.

The Cats played poorly but managed to beat Ole Miss 64-52, then beat Tennessee 90-77 to give Hall his 200th win at UK. Five Wildcats hit double figures against the

While Joe B. Hall clues James Lee to the plan of attack, Jack Givens offers words of advice to Kyle Macy.
The 1977-78 Wildcat team is still regarded by many as the school's all-time best.

Vols, headed by Robey with 18 points.

After surviving Mississippi State 58-56 in another less-than-shining effort, the Cats beat Alabama 98-84, Tennessee 68-57 and Georgia 78-67 to clinch another SEC title. Givens was UK's top scorer in those three wins, accounting for 55 points.

The Cats ended their regular season with a 92-70 non-conference win over UNLV and a 78-68 win over Vanderbilt. Robey scored 26 against the Runnin' Rebels and Macy had 22 against Vandy.

UK finished with a 25-2 record and a No. 1 ranking. The Cats ended the season exactly where they had begun — atop the polls. Despite the ranking and the regular-season accomplishments, the real test was only now beginning for the Cats, who, in the eyes of many, would be seen as failures if anyone else cut down the nets in St. Louis.

The Cats' march to the national title got off to a bumpy,

almost-disastrous start. Facing a quick and inspired Florida State team, the Cats found themselves trailing 39-32 at the half. Thoroughly disgusted by the lackluster performance, Hall benched Givens, Robey and Claytor at the start of the second half, replacing them with Casey, LaVon Williams and Freddie Cowan. It was a gutsy — and risky — move by Hall, one that could not only cost the Cats the game, but one that could possibly cost him his job.

With the three subs providing much-needed energy and inspiration, the Cats clawed their way back into contention, eventually taking a 54-53 lead when Macy swished a 15-foot jump shot with 8:33 left. When Hall finally reinserted his starters into the game, the Cats promptly went on a 14-0 run to break the game open. The Cats won it 85-76.

Claytor led UK with 16 points. Phillips and Macy each had 14, while Robey had 12.

The Cats played well in their next outing, demolish-

ing Miami of Ohio 91-69. UK, led by Phillips' 11 of 13 shooting, made good on 41 of 66 attempts for 62 percent. Phillips finished with a game-high 24 points.

On deck for the Cats was a young Michigan State team led by freshman sensation Earvin "Magic" Johnson. The upstart Spartans used a patient offense and a 3-2 zone defense to grab control of the game. At the half they were in front 27-22, and were still leading until a Lee dunk tied it at 35-35.

During the final stretch, as the game went down to the wire, Macy went to work at the free throw line. The ever-so-cool Macy cemented his reputation as one of UK's greatest clutch players by hitting 10 straight freebies. His calm under fire helped lift the Cats to a 52-49 victory.

Macy paced the Cats with 18 points, while Givens finished with 14. Johnson, who would lead his team to the national championship one year later, hit just two of 10 shots and finished with six points. Greg Kelser led the Spartans with 19.

In the semifinal game, UK faced Arkansas and its talented "triplets" — Sidney Moncrief, Marvin Delph and Ron Brewer. The Razorbacks were coached by Eddie Sutton, a man UK fans would soon get to know up close and personal.

The Wildcat players later said that Arkansas was the best team they faced all season. And they said this for good reason. The Razorbacks, hampered by early foul trouble, fell behind by nine points in the second half, only to go on a run and pull to within a single point with 3:23 remaining. But with Givens coming through with several key buckets, the Cats were able to hang on for a 64-59 win.

The outstanding 23-point performance by Givens was only a preview of what was to come. Two nights later, he would give one of the greatest individual performances ever turned in by a Wildcat.

After 31 games, all that now stood between the Cats and a national title was a young, talented Duke team. The Blue Devils, who didn't have a single senior in the starting lineup, defeated Notre Dame in the other semifinal game. They were also playing at the top of their form heading into the championship showdown with UK.

But any illusions the Blue Devils may have had about running out the table were quickly shattered by the white-hot Givens, who lit up the Checkerdome for 41 points. In the final game of his great career, Givens shot the Cats to a 94-88 victory and the school's fifth national championship.

As *Sports Illustrated* said on its cover, the Goose was golden.

Givens scored 16 of UK's final 18 first-half points to give his team a 45-38 lead at the break. The Cats later stretched their advantage to 16 (66-50) following a three-point play by Givens. With the victory seemingly secure, Hall removed his starters with a little more than a minute left to play. However, after the Blue Devils closed to within 92-88, Hall was forced to put his starters back in.

Fittingly, UK's final bucket of the season came on a thunderous dunk by Lee. It was the perfect exclamation point to what had been a tremendous season.

Givens' 41 points is the third-best in championship game history, trailing only Bill Walton's 44 in 1973 and Gail Goodrich's 42 in 1965. In that game, Givens connected on 18 of 27 shots.

Robey also played well, scoring 20 points and hauling down 11 rebounds.

During the season, five Wildcats scored in double figures, including sixth-man Lee, who averaged 11.3. Givens led the team with an 18.1 average, Robey was next with a 14.4 clip and Macy averaged 12.5. Phillips was the fifth Cat in double figures with an average of 10.2.

Macy set the school record for free throw accuracy, hitting 115 of 129 for 89.2 percent.

Givens departed UK with 2,038 career points, second only to Dan Issel on UK's all-time scoring list. Robey and Phillips also earned membership into the elite 1,000-point club. Robey finished with 1,395 points, while Phillips was close behind with 1,367.

During their four years at UK, the foursome of Givens, Robey, Phillips and Lee led the Cats to a 102-21 record, two NCAA championship games, one NCAA title and the NIT crown.

Thanks to them, UK was back on top of the college basketball world.

1978-79

All it took was a quick look at the roster to know that this wasn't going to be a big and physical Wildcat team. The UK frontline, which for four years had been dominated by the imposing presence of Robey, Phillips and Lee, now featured Aleksinas, Freddie Cowan and LaVon Williams. While Aleksinas did have some size and strength, and was the team's only true center, the 6'8" Cowan and the 6'7" Williams were a pair of slender sophomores who weren't likely to strike terror into opposing players.

The backcourt was solid and experienced, with Macy, Claytor and Shidler all returning. If the Cats had a strength, it was their perimeter game.

The bench was young and talented, but largely untested in battle. Leading that group was Stephens, now a junior, and Clarence Tillman and Chuck Verderber, two tough rookie forwards. However, Aleksinas and Stephens would quit the team during the season, thus leaving Hall with only 10 scholarship players.

There was one freshman who did stand out — Dwight Anderson. The 6'3" Anderson is one of the most naturally gifted athletes to ever play at UK, and although his career lasted less than two years, he remains one of the brightest comets to ever blaze across the Big Blue skies. Nickname "the Blur" by longtime UK announcer Cawood Ledford, Anderson played with flash, courage and panache. Few Wildcats have been more exciting to watch. But Anderson's UK career would be brief, and his great promise would go unfulfilled.

The Cats opened with easy wins over La Salle (109-77) and West Texas (121-67) before taking on fifth-ranked Kansas in Rupp Arena. That game, which the Cats won 67-66 in overtime, featured one of the most memorable comebacks in UK history.

Trailing 66-60 with 31 seconds left in overtime, UK scored seven straight points to walk away with the improbable win. Anderson and Macy were at the heart of the Cats' amazing

Dwight Anderson earned the nickname "the Blur" after dazzling a national television audience during UK's 81-76 win over second-ranked Notre Dame in Freedom Hall. Despite his great gifts, Anderson's career at UK came to a sudden end.

death-defying act. It was an Anderson layup that started UK's comeback drive. Then, at the 16-second mark, Anderson was fouled but missed the front end of a bonus. In the ensuing scramble for the ball, he drew a foul. This time, Anderson made both free throws to cut the Kansas lead to 66-64. They were the only four points Anderson scored during the game.

After the Jayhawks inbounded the ball, Anderson managed to knock the ball loose from Kansas' Mac Stallcup and straight into the hands of Macy, who calmly hit a 15-foot jump shot to tie the score.

When Macy's shot went in, Kansas' star guard Darnell Valentine immediately called for a timeout. It was an instinctive act by Valentine. And a disasterous one. Because the Jayhawks had already used all of their timeouts, they were whistled for a technical foul. Macy stepped to the free throw line and hit the game-deciding freebie.

Macy led UK with 15 points, while Williams added 10. Valentine, in a superb performance, led all scorers with 27 points.

After surviving against Kansas, the Cats dropped two of their next three games. In a see-saw battle against Indiana, the Cats came from nine points down to go ahead 58-55 with less than two minutes left. But a three-point play by Mike Woodson tied the score and sent the game into overtime. The Hoosiers, led by Woodson's 27 points, eventually edged UK 68-67. Macy had 11 to top UK's scoring.

Texas A&M came into Rupp Arena and upset the Cats 73-69 in the opening round of the UKIT. It was only the second time in the tournament's 26-year history that UK got bounced in the first round. In the consolation game, Aleksinas scored 20 and Anderson added 17 as the Cats beat Syracuse 94-87.

With a national television audience looking on, the ever-improving Anderson stole the show by scoring 17 second-half points to lift the Cats to an 81-76 come-from-behind victory over second-ranked Notre Dame in Freedom Hall.

The Cats were on the short end of a 61-49 score with 10:23 left. That's when Anderson began to dodge, dart and dazzle. He hit two free throws and an acrobatic layup to trim the Irish lead to 61-53. Despite more good work by Anderson, Claytor and Tillman, Notre Dame was still clinging to a 70-66 advantage with less than five minutes left. That lead quickly crumbled, thanks to a bucket by Anderson and a tip-in by Tillman that locked the score at 70-70. With 2:43 remaining, Anderson hit two free throws, then stole the ball, drove the length of the court and scored on a high-flying dunk that upped the Cats' lead to 74-70. The stunned Irish never caught up.

Claytor's 18 points topped UK's balanced scoring attack. Williams and Aleksinas each had 12, while Macy contributed 11. Notre Dame's Kelly Tripuka was the game's high scorer with 21 points.

Due to lack of size, and ultimately, lack of manpower, the Cats struggled through the SEC part of the schedule, finishing in sixth place with a 10-8 league record and a 16-10 mark overall. In past years, that record would have meant the end of the season.

However, after a 27-year hiatus, the league decided to renew the SEC Tournament, thus giving the Cats a second life. And they made the most of it.

The Cats needed that second life; five losses in their first six SEC games all but knocked them out of contention for another league regular-season championship. Florida started the Cats on their downward spiral, winning 76-65 in Gainesville. LSU inflicted an even more painful setback, beating the Cats 93-89 in Rupp Arena. It was LSU's first win in Lexington in 21 tries.

After Cowan scored 17 and Williams had 15 in a 90-64 win over Ole Miss, the Cats came up short in successive losses to Alabama, Mississippi State and Tennessee. The Crimson Tide missed 11 of their first 13 shots, hit just 24-percent from the field, yet still managed to beat the Cats 55-52. Williams had 16 to lead UK. Reggie King's 22 points and 11 rebounds paced Alabama.

Mississippi State held the ball for nearly six minutes, then won a 63-61 thriller on a last-second shot by Ray White. Tennessee had less trouble with the Cats, winning 66-55 in Rupp Arena. Reggie Johnson led the Vols with 20. Williams had 19 for UK, while Macy followed with 18.

By the time the Cats beat Georgia 73-64, Stephens and Aleksinas had both called it quits. With Aleksinas gone, Cowan shifted into the pivot spot and Anderson moved into the starting lineup. That gave the Cats a backcourt-heavy team, with Macy, Claytor and Anderson on the perimeter, Cowan and Williams on the inside. Shidler and Verderber were usually the first subs in, and in the last half of the season both came through with several excellent performances.

It was a steal and layup by Shidler, followed by two Williams free throws, that enabled

Freddie Cowan lays in a deuce for the Cats. Although only 6'8", Cowan spent much of his time handling the pivot duties for the 1978-79 team.

Truman Claytor accounted for 84 points during the 1979 SEC tourney, including 25 in a 101-100 quarterfinal win over Alabama.

the Cats to ease past Auburn 86-83 in overtime. Anderson led UK with 19 points, while Verderber came off the bench to score 10.

The Cats ran their winning streak to four by beating Florida 87-81 and Auburn 66-59. Anderson was UK's leading scorer in both games, hitting for 25 against the Gators and 13 against Auburn. Verderber also came up with a pair of solid efforts, scoring 32 points in the two wins.

The Cats broke even in their next six outings, beating Ole Miss 87-82, Alabama 80-71 and Mississippi State 80-65, while losing to LSU 70-61, Vandy 68-58 and Tennessee 101-84. There were some worthy individual efforts — Macy had 24 against Vandy, Anderson had 26 against Mississippi State, including a UK record 18 of 23 from the free throw line — but they were often offset by inconsistent team play. Against LSU, the anemic Cats managed just 17 first-half points. In

the loss to Tennessee, UK's defense was virtually non-existent.

Thanks to Anderson, the Cats were able to end on a strong note by winning their final three regular-season games. Anderson scored 23 in a 90-74 win over Georgia, then followed that by coming up with 19 to help the Cats slap Vandy 96-70. In the season finale, Shidler made good on eight of nine field goal attempts and finished with 20 points as UK beat South Carolina 79-74. Anderson scored 16 in that UK win.

The Cats continued to shine in the SEC Tournament, beating Ole Miss 82-77 in the opener behind Macy's 32 points. Trailing 53-52, the Cats outscored Ole Miss 25-8 to take control of the game. Other Cats in double figures included Williams (14), Anderson (13) and Claytor (12). Ole Miss' John Stroud led all scorers with 39.

Claytor was the man in the Cats' exciting 101-100 upset of Alabama in the quarterfinal round. UK's senior guard blistered the nets, hitting 11 of 14 field goal attempts in a 25-point performance. Macy and Anderson scored 22 and 19, respectively for the Cats, who hit 43 of 63 from the field for 68 percent. Reggie King led the Tide with 38.

Macy and Claytor combined for 49 points to lead the Cats past LSU 80-67 and into a championship showdown against Tennessee. Macy had 29 and Claytor had 20 in what proved to be a costly win for the Cats. Anderson fell and broke his wrist only 23 seconds into the game.

In the title tilt, Tennessee overcame a 44-37 halftime deficit then went on to beat the Cats 75-69 in overtime. Gary Carter led the Vols with 22. Claytor had a game-high 27 for UK, while backcourt mate Macy was voted the tourney's MVP.

The Cats' strong finish earned them a spot in the NIT and a first-round matchup against Clemson. Despite playing in front of a friendly Rupp Arena crowd, the Cats, with Anderson among the spectators, lost to Clemson 68-67 in overtime. Macy again led the Cats with 20 points.

After the game, an irate Hall blasted the officials, saying "there was no semblance of order out there."

The Cats ended with a 19-12 record, and given all they had gone through, the defections and injuries, this has to be considered a successful campaign. Macy averaged 15.2 points, while earning All-America and All-SEC honors. Anderson, the brilliant freshman, finished with a fine 13.3 scoring clip.

Away from the court, Hall's recruiting efforts were beyond successful. Hall and chief recruiter Leonard Hamilton had inked Sam Bowie, Derrick Hord, Dirk Minniefield

and Charles Hurt. With those new faces coming in to join the returning talent, the Cats' future looked bright. And it would be. But not without some dark moments.

1979-80

Seldom has a UK team had a more intriguing blend of veterans and rookies than this one. It was also a team that was deep at all positions. Macy and Shidler gave the Cats a deadly and experienced backcourt, while Anderson, Cowan, Williams, Verderber and Tillman provided depth and versatility in the frontcourt. And the freshman class, headed by McDonald's All-Americans Bowie and Hord, figured to make an immediate impact.

Bowie, especially, was being counted on for big things. At 7'1", Bowie was UK's tallest player since Tom Payne. However, unlike Payne — and UK's other 7-footer Bill Spivey — Bowie was an exceptionally mobile and graceful big man. He could run the court like a guard, and he could step outside and hit the medium-range jumper. One look at Bowie and you knew he was something special.

UK's depth chart was reduced by one in October when Tillman decided to leave school. It was the first of two defections this season. In December, the gifted Anderson left amid a swirl of controversy and questions.

The Cats' season began and ended with heartbreaking losses to Duke. But sandwiched in between those setbacks was some extraordinarily strong and consistent play. This was a team that displayed a great deal of maturity, especially in December when the Anderson situation arose. A team

Sam Bowie ranks as one of the most agile and mobile big men the college game has ever seen. There is no limit to what he may have accomplished had his career not been hampered by injuries.

lacking fortitude and maturity could easily have come unglued. But this team was fortunate to have Macy as its unquestioned leader, and it was largely due to his steady leadership that the Cats were able to shake off the controversy surrounding Anderson's departure. Even without Anderson, they went on to forge a 26-4 record in the regular season and a 15-3 mark in SEC play.

Despite Bowie's magnificent 22-point, 17-rebound debut performance, the Cats opened with an 82-76 overtime loss to Duke in the Hall of Fame Classic. The Cats led 65-56, but Duke fought back to tie the score at 72-72 and send the game into the extra period. With Mike Gminski scoring five straight points, the Blue Devils took control of the OT and eventually put UK away. Gminski led Duke with 21 points.

That loss was the only bump in the road for the Cats during the non-conference part of the schedule. They won their next 12 games, beginning with a championship run in the Great Alaska Shootout. The Cats beat Bradley 79-58, Alaska 97-68 and Iona 57-50 in the title game. Macy scored 15 in the final game, including several late jumpers that helped UK hold off upset-minded Iona.

Following an easy 80-46 victory over Baylor, the Cats set a new Rupp Arena standard in their 126-81 romp past South Carolina. Macy paced a balanced UK attack with 24 points. Bowie had 23, Anderson 19 and Hord 18.

The Cats' next two wins were hard-earned and impressive. They edged Kansas 57-56, then upset top-ranked Indiana 69-58, thanks to a supreme defensive effort that held Bobby Knight's club to 19 second-half points. Bowie had 17 points

and 14 rebounds in the win over Kansas, while Macy had 12 and Shidler and Williams 11 apiece against Indiana.

Macy scored 28 and Anderson added 20 as the Cats blasted Georgia 95-69 in Atlanta. Next, the Cats beat California 78-52 in the UKIT opener to set up a championship matchup with Purdue and its All-American center Joe Barry Carroll. UK won 61-60 when Macy, the ex-Boilermaker, hit four straight free throws to put his team in front then swiped the ball from Keith Edmonson to preserve the win. Macy and Cowan each had 18 to lead UK. Carroll had 25 for Purdue.

Two days before taking on Notre Dame in Freedom Hall, it was announced that Anderson was leaving the team, citing "personal reasons" as the cause for his departure. Anderson was averaging 10.7 points at the time. One day later, Bowie and Minniefield were hit with a one-game suspension for violating team rules.

Despite the absent players and the controversy, the Cats shocked the unbeaten and third-ranked Irish 86-80. Five Cats scored in double figures, headed by Macy with 21. Cowan finished with 16, Williams with 13, and freshmen Hord and Hurt with 10 each. The win over Notre Dame gave the Cats an 11-1 record heading into SEC action.

The Cats broke even in their first four SEC games, with the two wins coming courtesy of Macy. He nailed a 25-foot jumper with two seconds left to beat Auburn 67-65, then came through with a 29-point effort in a 79-73 UK win over Ole Miss. The two Wildcat losses in those four games

Charles Hurt gave the Wildcats solid rebounding and defense. His 59.3 percent field goal accuracy is third-best all-time at UK .

came against Tennessee 49-47 and Alabama 78-64.

After that four-game split, the Cats went on to win 12 of their next 13 against league foes, losing only to LSU 65-60 in Rupp Arena. Surprisingly, two of the Cats' three league losses occurred in front of the home crowd.

The Cats bounced back to score revenge wins against all three of their conquering opponents. They beat Tennessee 83-75, Alabama 73-63 and LSU 76-74 in overtime. Once again, Macy was at the heart of all three of those crucial SEC wins. He had 22 against the Volunteers, 20 against Alabama and the game-winning bucket at the buzzer in UK's SEC title-clinching win over LSU.

Other Cats also made their presence felt during the team's climb up the SEC standings. Minniefield hit a last-second jumper in a 64-62 win over Auburn; Shidler's 18 points helped the Cats slip past Alabama; Bowie had 20 points, nine rebounds and six blocked shots in a 91-73 victory over Vanderbilt; Cowan had 27 in that overtime win over LSU. Also included in that run was a 95-70 thrashing of Florida, UK's 500th SEC win.

With Bowie registering back-to-back double-doubles, the Cats beat Auburn 69-61 and Ole Miss 70-67 in their first two SEC tourney games. Bowie had 19 points and 10 rebounds in the opener, followed by a 27-point, 11-rebound effort against the Rebels.

In semifinal action, LSU claimed the rubber match by knocking off the error-prone Cats 80-78. DeWayne Scales was high man for the Tigers with 26 points, but it was the

clutch play of Ethan Martin that proved to be the difference. He finished with 14 points. All-tourney picks Bowie and Macy led UK with 20 each.

With a 28-5 record and a No. 3 ranking, the Cats were paired against Florida State in the opening round of the NCAA Tournament. UK dominated the rebounding 54-31 en route to an easy 97-78 win. Macy paced UK with 16 points, while Bowie had 13 points and 11 rebounds. Cowan and Williams also hit double figures with 14 points each. Shidler came off the bench to score 10.

Next up for UK was a rematch against Duke in Rupp Arena. The Cats were a slight favorite to get revenge for their season-opening loss, but the experienced Blue Devils came out hot, building a 37-23 lead by intermission. UK charged back, and actually had a chance to win, but Macy, who had come through in clutch situations so many times in the past, missed an 18-foot jumper with five seconds left. Duke escaped with a 55-54 win.

Cold shooting doomed the Cats. For the game, they hit just 19 of 47 for 40 percent. Conversely, Duke, which was outrebounded 31-20, made good on 22 of 40 for 55 percent.

Cowan led all scorers with 26 points. Duke was led by Gminski with 17 and Lexington native Vince Taylor with 15.

Macy closed out his great career with 1,411 points and 470 assists. In addition, he holds the UK/SEC record for career free throw accuracy, making good on 89 percent of his attempts. "Cool" Kyle remains one of the most-popular Wildcats of all-time.

1980-81

This was the first of two straight mystifying seasons that saw talented Wildcat teams post excellent regular-season records and earn Top 10 rankings only to suffer inglorious first-round losses to lesser opponents in NCAA tourney action.

With Macy gone, Bowie was now the Cats' main bread-and-butter guy. He was usually joined on the frontline by forwards Cowan and Verderber, and by Hord and Minniefield in the backcourt. Hord, a natural small forward, struggled at the guard position, but Minniefield, who inherited the playmaker role from Macy, quickly proved to be a player with legitimate NBA talent.

That group, along with junior Charles Hurt, was strengthened by the addition of another bumper crop of freshmen that included guards Jim Master and Dicky Beal, forward Bret Bearup and center Melvin Turpin.

During December, the Cats were as good as advertised, with only a 67-61 loss to Notre Dame keeping them from having an unblemished record heading into conference play. The early part of the campaign was highlighted by back-to-back wins over Indiana and Kansas. The Cats clipped Indiana 68-66 in Bloomington, then bombed the Jayhawks 87-73 behind Bowie's 29 points and 16 rebounds.

In UKIT action, the Cats beat Alaska 91-56 and UAB 61-53 to claim the championship. Hurt led UK in the opener with 16 points, Bowie had 25 in the final game. This wouldn't be the last time the Cats ran into UAB. The two clubs were destined to cross paths again three months later, and the results would be disastrous for UK.

After losing to Notre Dame, the Cats, behind 24

Dirk Minniefield possessed NBA-caliber backcourt skills. Minniefield holds the UK record for most assists with 646.

Charles Hurt, Dirk Minniefield and Derrick Hord prior to tip-off. This trio was part of a talented recruiting class that also included Sam Bowie.

Tough wins over Vanderbilt (78-64) and Mississippi State (71-64) were followed by an even tougher 71-68 double-overtime win at Georgia. In that close call, it was the gutsy play by Master and Verderber that enabled the Cats to survive. Verderber dropped in a pair of free throws to seal the win, while Master made good on his first starting assignment by scoring 16 points, including eight in the two overtimes. The great Dominique Wilkins led Georgia with 32 points.

UK's last loss of the regular season came in Knoxville, where Dale Ellis scored 22 and Gary Carter 18 in an 87-71 Tennessee victory. Bowie's 26 weren't enough for the Cats, who played poorly in the final 20 minutes after trailing by only four at intermission.

Bowie continued to rack up All-America-type numbers, hitting for 25 in a 62-55 win over Ole Miss and 21 in a 77-62 revenge win over Alabama. Bowie also had 14 rebounds against the Tide, while Minniefield added 16 points.

After Verderber scored 16 points to lead the Cats past Florida 69-56, it was the defense that dominated in an 80-48 win over Vanderbilt. UK outscored Vandy 54-25 in the second half, holding the visitors to just six field goals in the final 20 minutes. Bowie had 19 for the Cats, Minniefield 17 and Cowan 11.

The Cats ended the regular season by notching another pair of close wins, beating Mississippi State 78-74 and LSU 73-71. Minniefield had 20 and Bowie 18 against the Bulldogs. Bowie, Minniefield, Turpin and Verderber each scored 11 in the win over LSU.

The confident Cats went into the SEC tourney with a 22-4 record and a No. 8 ranking in both polls. Their quarterfinal foe was Vanderbilt, a team they had destroyed by a combined 46 points in their two previous meetings. The Cats beat Vandy 78-64 in Nashville and 80-48 in Lexington.

points from Hord and 15 from Master, savaged Maine 100-54 to kick off a five-game winning streak. Cowan picked up the Cats in their next three games, accounting for 39 points in wins over Georgia (76-62) and Auburn (79-66), then hitting the game-winner in a 48-47 victory over Tennessee. A difficult 64-55 home-court win over Ole Miss ended the run and gave the Cats a 4-0 SEC record.

Then came successive losses at Alabama and LSU. The Tide slipped past cold-shooting UK 59-55. LSU blitzed the Cats early, jumping to a 13-point halftime lead, then went on to post an 81-67 win.

UK responded with another five-game winning streak, beginning with a 102-48 laugher against Florida. Bowie's 29 points led UK, while Minniefield and Turpin each contributed 17.

Despite being an odds-on favorite to make it three straight over the Commodores, it was the stunned Cats who found themselves on the losing end of a 60-55 score when the final horn sounded. UK had the edge in field goals (23-19), but the Commodores overcame that difference by connecting on 22 free throws to nine by the Cats.

The game was a nightmare for the Cats, and yet, bad as it was, it didn't compare to what lay ahead.

Ten days after losing to Vandy, the Cats were paired against another team they had defeated during the regular season — UAB in the NCAA Tournament's Mideast Regional at Tuscaloosa.

Once again, a huge free throw advantage by the opponent proved to be UK's undoing. Although UAB made just 19 field goals (UK had 23), 31 of 40 shooting from the charity stripe was enough to secure a 69-62 win.

Verderber had a strong game for the Cats, scoring 16 points and grabbing nine rebounds. Minniefield and Hurt finished with 14 and 11 points, respectively.

For a team that had played so well, this was a sad and disappointing way to end the season. The sting became even more painful three weeks later when Indiana, another UK regular-season conquest, captured the NCAA championship.

Even though the final days had been dark and unsuccessful, UK's future had rarely looked brighter. Everyone but Cowan would be returning. And in Bowie, the Cats had a genuine franchise player. The ingredients for another NCAA championship run were in place.

However, those hopes were quickly dashed by a broken bone.

1981-82

When Joe Hall landed Sam Bowie, he brought to the school what is commonly known as a franchise player. He was also unique — at 7'1", Bowie was exceptionally quick and mobile. He could score, defend, rebound and pass. He was an "eraser," a post defender whose presence allowed his teammates to gamble on defense, then erase their mistakes when one was beaten by an opponent. Bowie, by his very presence, made the Cats a formidable team.

Bowie had more than lived up to the high expectations. In his first two years as a Wildcat, he scored 928 points, grabbed 530 rebounds and blocked 153 shots. After finishing his sophomore season with a 17.4 scoring average, it was apparent to everyone that "Big Sam" was poised on the brink of becoming perhaps UK's best big man ever. The future for Bowie appeared to be limitless.

But prior to the start of the 1981-82 campaign, Hall announced that Bowie had a broken bone in his leg and would have to sit out the entire season. In fact, it would be a full two years before Wildcat fans saw Bowie on a basketball court again.

Fortunately for the Cats, Turpin, a 6'11" sophomore

Melvin Turpin stepped up and filled the void created by Sam Bowie's injury. Turpin developed into one of UK's most-efficient inside scoring threats.

from Lexington Bryan Station, was able to step in and give the team a commanding presence in the middle. Although not nearly as quick or mobile as Bowie, Turpin was a superb shooter and a decent rebounder. During his career at UK, Turpin made 59.1 percent of his field goal attempts, second-best in school history.

Turpin's inexperience was offset by a supporting cast of veteran teammates. Minniefield and the lethal-shooting Master started in the backcourt, while Hord, now back at his more-

Junior Derrick Hord had his best year during the 1981-82 season. His 16.3 average topped the team in scoring.

comfortable forward spot, and either Verderber or Hurt joined with Turpin on the frontline. Even though Bearup opted to redshirt, UK's bench was deep. Dicky Beal, Troy McKinley, Tom Heitz, Mike Ballenger and Bo Lanter all made strong contributions during the season.

Despite Bowie's absence, the Cats started the season in an impressive fashion, winning their first six games. Hord scored 28 in an 83-64 season-opening victory over outclassed Akron, then Minniefield came through with 18 points, 14 in the second half, to lead the visiting Cats past Ohio State 78-62. Minniefield stayed hot in the Cats' next game, hitting for 22 points in an 85-69 win over Indiana. The Cats, behind 25 first-half points by Minniefield and Master, raced to a 47-25 halftime lead over Indiana and never looked back. Master finished with 17 for UK.

Hord's five points in overtime helped the Cats survive a 77-74 thriller at Kansas. Master led UK with 27, while Hord had 13.

The Cats barely broke a sweat in the UKIT, rolling past Jacksonville 107-91 and Seton Hall 98-74. Seven Wildcats hit for double figures against Jacksonville, led by Hord with 17. Hord had 21 to lead the Cats in their win over Seton Hall. Turpin also had a big night, scoring 19 points and pulling down 13 rebounds.

UK fell from the ranks of the unbeaten when top-ranked North Carolina thumped the Cats 82-69 in East Rutherford, N.J. The Cats trailed by only three (38-35) at the intermission, but the Tar Heels, sparked by James Worthy and Sam Perkins, slowly pulled away in the second half. Worthy had 26, Perkins 21 and Michael Jordan 19 for the winners. Hurt, now having replaced Verderber in the starting lineup, led UK with 18.

UK bounced back to edge Notre Dame 34-28 in an overtime thriller at Freedom Hall. After the two teams battled to a 23-23 standstill (literally, thanks to Notre Dame's stall tactics), Turpin opened the extra frame by sinking a short jumper to give UK a 25-23 lead. After that, the Cats hit seven free throws — four by Hord, two by Master and one by Minniefield — to avoid the upset. The Cats hit 13 of their 17 field goal attempts for 76.5 percent. Turpin was UK's leading scorer with 11. John Paxson had 12 for the Irish.

It was slow-down strategy like the one employed by Notre Dame's Digger Phelps, along with the four-corner offense used by North Carolina's Dean Smith, that eventually prompted the NCAA hierarchy to follow the NBA example and bring in the shot clock. UK fans, who detested the stall tactics, couldn't have been more delighted with the change.

As often happened with Hall's teams, the Cats struggled in the month of January, losing three times. During his 13-year tenure at UK, Hall's teams lost 37 times in January. Because of this tendency to shine in December, then slump the following month, it became known as the "January swoon."

Turpin's last-second basket got the Cats off on the right foot in SEC action, a 68-66 win over Georgia despite 28 points from Wilkins. Then Master, Hord and Heitz turned in terrific performances as the Cats held off Auburn and Charles Barkley 83-71. Master led UK with 26 points, Hord had 22 and Heitz had 12. "Sir Charles" paced Auburn with 25 points and 17 rebounds.

The Cats fell to 2-2 in league play when they dropped a pair of squeakers to Tennessee and Ole Miss. With Michael Brooks scoring 15 of his 19 points after the break, the Vols overcame a six-point halftime deficit — and 28 points by Turpin — to beat UK 70-66. Ole Miss built a 34-23 halftime cushion, then held on down the stretch to upset the

Cats 67-65 in Oxford. Carlos Clark led Ole Miss with 23. Master's 20 was UK's top effort.

With a different player leading the point parade in each game, the Cats won four straight to improve their SEC mark to 6-2 and get back in the title chase. Minniefield scored 25 in an 86-69 win over Alabama, Master's 22 led the Cats past Florida 91-76, Hord had 22 in a 67-58 win over Vanderbilt and Turpin rang up 20 in a 76-65 win over dangerous LSU.

Just when it looked as though the Cats had shaken free of the January blues, they suffered two losses in their next three games. An 82-73 victory over Georgia was sandwiched between a 56-51 loss at Ole Miss and an 83-81 overtime loss at Auburn. Suddenly, the Cats were 6-4 in league play and in the middle of the standings. They needed to put together a hot streak if they hoped to have a chance at another SEC crown, and that's exactly what they did. Beginning with a 77-67 win over Tennessee, the Cats won their next six games to once again thrust themselves into the title chase.

After beating Tennessee, the Cats scored the game's final nine points at the charity stripe to come from behind and beat Ole Miss 56-49. Then with Master scoring 18 and Hord adding 16, including 14 in the second half, the Cats came through with a crucial 72-62 win at Alabama. That was followed by an 84-78 win over Florida in which the Cats shot 58 percent from the field.

Homestanding Vanderbilt bolted to a 40-30 halftime advantage and threatened to snap UK's winning streak, but the gritty Cats, fueled by 24 second-half points from Hord and Minniefield, came back to escape with a 73-69 win. Hord had 26 for UK, while Cawood (Ky.) native Phil Cox led Vandy with 18.

UK ended the regular season by splitting its final two games, beating Mississippi State 71-54 and losing to LSU 94-78. On the strength of those six wins in their final seven games, the Cats claimed a share of the league title with Tennessee, finished with a 20-6 record overall and a 13-5 mark in SEC action.

For the first time since its rebirth, the SEC tourney was being held in Rupp Arena. First up for the Cats was another meeting with Auburn and Charles Barkley. This time, however, "Sir Charles" was no factor. The Cats won easily 89-66, while Barkley was held to four first-half points and just 18 overall. Minniefield led UK with 18 points, but it was the inspired play by Beal, who came off the bench to score 12 points, that ignited the easy win.

Ole Miss proved to be a more difficult challenge, taking the Cats to the wire before finally losing 62-58. Turpin and Minniefield saved the Cats, scoring 24 and 20 points, respectively. Clark had 20 for the Rebels.

The Cats were denied the tourney championship when Eddie Phillips nailed a last-second jumper that gave Alabama a stirring 48-46 victory. It was the only basket in the second half for Phillips, who led the Tide with 13 points. Minniefield had 11 for UK and was voted the tourney's MVP.

The big news as UK headed to Nashville for a first-round NCAA Tournament matchup against Middle Tennessee was the presence of Louisville in the same bracket. The two teams, now bitter rivals despite having not played each other since 1959, were only a single win away from a much-anticipated showdown.

Louisville, under Denny Crum, had risen to prominence in college hoops, claiming the NCAA crown in 1980 and becoming virtual Final Four regulars. Naturally, Louisville fans wanted a piece of the Big Blue. Most basketball observers sided with Louisville, arguing that the in-state matchup was a natural.

But Hall and UK athletics director Cliff Hagan stubbornly disagreed. Adhering to Adolph Rupp's belief that nothing good could come from playing other Kentucky schools, Hall and Hagan held their ground and refused to schedule Louisville. If the two teams were ever going to meet, it would have to be in postseason play.

With so much anticipation and media hype swirling around a possible UK-UL showdown, the Cats' opener against Middle Tennessee got lost in the storm. All eyes were looking forward to a battle between the blue and the red, where in-state bragging rights would finally be settled.

But the eagerly awaited showdown never materialized. The Cats, perhaps with their thoughts cast too far into the future, turned in a retched, humiliating performance against Middle Tennessee, losing 50-44. It was a game without a single UK highlight. The Cats shot just 38 percent from the field and were outrebounded 35-23 by the smaller Raiders. Not a single Wildcat player managed to score in double figures.

That loss left the Cats with a final mark of 22-8. Hord, in his finest season as a Wildcat, led the team in scoring with a 16.3 average. He was named All-SEC and honorable mention All-American. Master was next in scoring with a 13.4 scoring clip, while Turpin and Minniefield also finished in double figures with respective averages of 13.1 and 11.3.

Despite the dismal finish, the Cats had fashioned

another successful season. Turpin had done an admirable job filling in for the absent Bowie, and Hord had finally fulfilled his great promise. The future looked bright. All five starters would be returning, and, hopefully, a healthy "Big Sam" would be there to join them.

1982-83

The news coming out of the UK camp wasn't good — Bowie's stress fracture was slow to heal and would require bone-graft surgery. He would have to sit out another season.

It was the first hint of the frustrating, trying season that lay ahead.

But if any UK team had the manpower to overcome the loss of a super player like Bowie, it was this one. All five starters were back. So were Beal and Bearup. And the three freshmen, Kenny Walker, Todd May and Roger Harden, looked like exciting, promising players with the potential to step in and make immediate contributions.

Bowie would be missed — you can't escape the absence of a player of his magnitude — but

Indiana native Jim Master was a deadly marksman from the perimeter and from the charity stripe.

ranked Villanova 93-79. Once again, the Cats burned the nets, making good on 35 of 55 shots for 63.6 percent. Hurt and Turpin each scored 15 points, while Minniefield set a new UK record by dishing out 14 assists.

The Cats sailed through their next four games, beating Detroit 83-46, Illinois 76-57, Duquesne 55-42 and Tulane 80-61 in the UKIT title game. Hord, who scored 31 points in the tourney, was named MVP.

Prior to the UKIT, May, the former Mr. Basketball from Virgie High School, left the team, citing lack of playing time as his reason for leaving.

The Cats had been on fire through their first seven games, hitting 61.4 percent from the field. But that was before they ran into undefeated and fifth-ranked Indiana. Against the Hoosiers' sticky man-to-man defense, the Cats managed just 41.4 percent shooting. The result was a 62-59 loss. The Cats led 44-37 with 13:13 left, but Indiana, sparked by Randy Wittman and Ted Kitchel, came back for the win. Turpin paced UK with 17 points. Wittman

with so much talent, experience and depth on hand, his absence shouldn't prove fatal. Even without Bowie, UK had enough weaponry and firepower to make a serious run at the national title.

Early on, it looked as if the Cats might do just that. They bolted from the gate, winning 10 of their first 11 games. They opened with a 90-53 rout of Butler, then followed that by hitting 75 percent from the field in a 58-45 win over Notre Dame. Master had 21 to lead the Cats in the opener, while Hord's 18 was tops against the Irish.

In a prime-time early season showdown, Hord erupted for 26 points to lead the second-ranked Wildcats past No.3-

and Kitchel had 17 and 16, respectively, for IU.

With Hord scoring 23 and four of his teammates also hitting double figures, the Cats bounced back strong by ripping Kansas 83-62 in their last game before the SEC wars heated up. Turpin had 14, Hurt and Minniefield 13 each, and Beal 10.

January, always a difficult month for Hall's teams, turned out to be even more cruel than usual — the Cats won just five of nine games. And it could have been worse. After struggling to a 72-60 win over Ole Miss, the Cats survived two overtime games — 59-53 against Mississippi State, 82-77 against Vanderbilt — slipped

past LSU 52-50 thanks to a late blocked shot by Turpin and came from behind to beat Florida 70-63, once again courtesy of Turpin, who led the comeback charge with 17 second-half points.

The four January losses were to Alabama 74-67, Auburn 75-67, Georgia 70-63 and Tennessee 65-63, despite a heroic 42-point performance by Turpin. Two of those losses were especially painful. The Cats led Alabama by five late in the game, then committed three turnovers and missed three free throws inside the last two minutes. Against Georgia, the Cats were sitting on a comfortable lead, only to be outscored 19-2 during one stretch in the second half.

Turpin, Master and Walker were the most-consistent Wildcats during this slump. Along with his great individual effort against the Vols, Turpin had 24 against Alabama and 23 against Florida. Master hit 12 of 16 shots en route to 26 points against Vandy, while Walker came off the bench to contribute 14 points in the win over Vandy and 12 in the loss to Georgia.

If the UK team slumped in January, then Hord crashed completely. His game took a nose dive to such an extent that the senior forward eventually lost his starting spot. Hall, frustrated and perplexed, lashed out publicly, perhaps hoping to light a fire within Hord. But Hall's plan didn't work. The more he ripped into Hord, the worse Hord played.

The cold winds of February saw the return of the hot-shooting Wildcats. They won all seven of their games that month, climbing to the top of the SEC standings in the process. They began their march toward the top by beating Alabama 76-70 and Mississippi State 88-67. Master led the Cats against Alabama with 17 points. Walker's 23 points and 13 rebounds, along with some strong early play by Bearup, keyed the win over Mississippi State.

The much-maligned Hord came through against Auburn, hitting a buzzer-beater to give the Cats a 71-69 victory. Turpin had 25 for UK, while Master added 20. Chuck Person led Auburn with 17. The Tigers were forced to play without Barkley, who was tossed two minutes into the game for committing a flagrant foul against Hurt.

After Master scored 40 points in wins over Florida (73-61) and Vanderbilt (82-63), Beal, in his first game back after a three-week absence, came off the bench to spark the Cats past Georgia 81-72. Walker turned in a 19-point, 10-rebound performance to help the Cats beat Tennessee 69-61 and clinch the SEC championship. Turpin scored 18 points in that win, while Beal had seven points and six assists. Tennessee's Dale Ellis led all scorers with 31 points.

UK split its last two regular-season games, beating Ole Miss 61-58 and losing to LSU 74-60. Turpin had 23 points against the Rebels, but it was Walker who made the difference. Walker, now starting in Hord's spot, finished with 17 points, including 11 straight during the second half. LSU took advantage of 22 UK turnovers to post its win. Carter led the Tigers with 23 points. Master had 19 for UK.

With eight wins in their final nine games, the Cats had improved their record to 21-6. Even more important, they were playing tough, solid basketball heading into postseason action.

But the Cats were anything but tough and solid in their SEC tourney opener against Alabama. Suddenly, they were once again the January Cats, blowing a 14-point lead and eventually dropping a 69-64 decision to the Crimson Tide. Ennis Whatley hit 11 of 15 free throws and finished with 21 points for the winners. Master had 20 for UK.

The quick departure from the SEC Tournament wasn't the confidence builder Hall envisioned as his team headed into NCAA Tournament action against Ohio University in Tampa.

Ohio U. tried to control tempo against the heavily favored Wildcats, and managed to do so for a half. The Cats led 21-17 at the break, but quickly took control once the second half got underway. With Minniefield scoring 16 points and Turpin adding 14, the Cats, who shot 50 percent from the field and hit 21 of 25 free throws, went on to win easily 57-40.

Next up was a Mideast Regional rematch against Indiana in Knoxville. Once again, looming in the distance just one win away, was the long shadow of Louisville.

Thanks to a marvelous effort by Walker, the Cats avenged their early season loss to the Hoosiers, winning a 64-59 thriller. Walker was perfect off the bench, making all six of his field goal attempts and finishing with 13 points. Turpin's 16 points paced the hot-shooting Cats, who connected on 27 of 43 attempts for 63 percent. The UK backcourt of Master and Minniefield contributed 12 and 11 points, respectively.

When Louisville upheld its end of the bargain by defeating Arkansas 65-63, the long-awaited "Dream Game" had become a reality. And in one of those rare instances, the game more than lived up to the hype.

Fiercely contested and well-played from beginning to end, with both teams displaying comeback courage, and with heroes wearing blue and red, the game was every bit the war everyone predicted. Or hoped to see.

UK led 23-10 halfway through the first 20 minutes, only to watch as the Cardinals, led by Lancaster Gordon and Milt Wagner, roared back to take a five-point lead late in the game. Then it was UK's turn to dig deep into its heart and mount a comeback that knotted the score at 60-60. With the clock ticking down, Minniefield saw an opening to the basket and went for it, only to have his shot tapped away by Charles Jones. Gordon raced to the other end and banked in a jumper that put the Cards in front 62-60 with 11 seconds left. UK needed a miracle, which it got when Master swished a 12-foot baseline jumper just ahead of the buzzer to send the game into overtime.

It had been a brilliant, thrilling and pulsating 40 minutes of basketball, and still the outcome had yet to be decided. But it would be, and more quickly that anyone in the Stokely Athletic Center or watching on TV could have predicted.

In the overtime period, the Cards unleashed a full-court press that was relentless in its fury and successful in its outcome. On UK's first seven possessions in the OT, the Cards caused five turnovers.

The press was, Master later said, "like a calvary charge."

While UK was withering under the pressure, the Cards scored 14 straight points in the overtime to take a commanding lead. When it was all done, the "Dream Game" belonged to Louisville — 80-68.

Both teams acquitted themselves in an exemplary manner. UL hit 34 of 57 shots for 60 percent, while UK made good on 32 of 57 for 56 percent. Gordon and Wagner accounted for 42 points for the Cards — 24 and 18, respectively. Master and Turpin led UK with 18 points each, while Minniefield added 12.

With the first "Dream Game" having been such a success, the clamor began in earnest for the two schools to meet on a regular basis. UK officials, fans, and even the governor began lobbying hard for Hall and Hagan to change their policy against playing in-state schools, particularly Louisville. Under mounting pressure from the UK Board of Trustees, the Athletics Board, after a spirited debate, voted 12-6 in favor of exploring the possiblity of a UK-UL series. Two months later, Hagan and UL AD Bill Olsen agreed on a four-year series that would alternate games between Rupp Arena and Freedom Hall. The first game would be in Rupp Arena, and would be the season opener for both teams.

The Cats would open next season against the team that had ended this one.

Only this time, "Big Sam" would be back.

1983-84

A healthy Sam Bowie returned to action after a two-year absence and helped take the Wildcats to the 1984 Final Four.

For the first time in three years there was no bad news coming out of the Wildcat camp. Everything was positive. Bowie was back and healthy. So were veterans like Master, Turpin, Beal, Bearup, Walker, Harden, McKinley and Heitz. Joining them was a pair of gifted freshmen Winston Bennett and James Blackmon. The Cats were loaded, with or without Bowie. But having the big guy back, with his talent and his leadership skills, made this an exceptionally deep and talented club. The experts agreed. In virtually every preseason poll, the Cats were seen as one of the prime contenders for the national title.

Despite the high expectations and the even higher talent level, several questions lingered as the Cats headed into their season opener against Louisville. How would Bowie respond after two years on the sidelines? Could Bowie and Turpin blend together as well as the earlier "Twin Towers" tandem of Robey and Phillips? How much quickness did Beal have left after his knee surgery? Those were legitimate concerns for Hall. And with Louisville as the opening opponent, it wouldn't take long for him to get some answers.

"Dream Game II" quickly turned into Cream Game for the Wildcats and Nightmare City for Louisville. The Cats turned the tables on their archrivals, using quickness on defense to post a stunningly easy 65-44 victory. And the game wasn't as close as the final score indicates. Leading 22-16 with just over five minutes left in the first half, the Cats, fueled by rookies Bennett and Blackmon, went on a 13-4 run to take a 35-20 lead at intermission. UK's blitz continued in the second half, and after another 20-6 run, the Cats owned a commanding 55-26 advantage.

UK's aggressive man-to-man defense was the difference, holding the Cards to just 36 percent shooting while causing

20 turnovers, 12 of which were steals. So dominant was UK's defense that the UL backcourt of Gordon and Wagner was limited to a combined 12 points.

Master again proved to be the thorn in UL's side, scoring a game-high 19 points. Turpin finished with 16, while Walker added 13. Despite showing the obvious rust from two years' inactivity, Bowie turned in a strong effort. He scored only seven points, but he had 10 rebounds, five blocked shots, five assists and three steals.

Thanks to the clutch play of Blackmon, the heavily favored Cats managed to subdue Indiana 59-54 in their next game. Blackmon, a Marion, Ind., native, scored 14 points, including five in the final minutes to help the Cats survive. After that win, the No. 2-ranked Cats went on the road and handed Kansas a 72-50 defeat, the third worst home loss ever for the Jayhawks. Turpin had 25 in that game, while Master finished with 23.

The Cats routed Wyoming 66-40 and BYU 93-59 to capture the UKIT, then beat Cincinnati 24-11 in a game that left Hall and the Big Blue faithful pleading even louder for the introduction of the shot clock into college basketball.

With the clock winding down, Blackmon banked in a short jumper to give the Cats a 56-54 win at Illinois. The Cats used tough defense and a balanced scoring attack to overcome a 33-26 Illini halftime lead and remain unbeaten. Bowie and Master each had 11 for UK, while Walker added 10. Blackmon chipped in with six.

Turpin hit for 22 and Walker had 18 as the Cats closed out the non-conference part of their schedule by easily

Freshman James Blackmon got off to a fast start as a Wildcat, scoring 14 in a win over Indiana, then banking in the game-winner against Illinois.

beating Purdue 86-67. The Cats bolted to a 53-27 half-time lead and were never seriously threatened. Bennett came off the bench to score 10 for the victorious Wildcats.

The Cats improved their record to 12-0 overall and 4-0 in SEC action by beating Ole Miss 68-55, LSU 96-80, Alabama 76-66 and Mississippi State 51-42. None of those wins was easy. Blackmon, starting in place of the suspended Master, scored 15 points and Bennett added 13 as the Cats broke away from a 26-26 halftime deadlock to finally put away Ole Miss. It took a 35-point, 13-rebound effort by Turpin and 51 percent team shooting to get past LSU in Baton Rouge. Walker also had a big game against the Tigers with 22 points.

Beating Alabama was an even more difficult challenge. With the score tied 52-52, Hall inserted Beal, Bennett and Blackmon into the lineup, then switched from a man-to-man defense to a 2-2-1 full-court press. The result of Hall's strategic maneuvering was a 14-0 UK run that broke the game open. Walker and Bennett led UK with 17 points each.

After a listless 51-42 win over Mississippi State, the Cats went to Auburn and were soundly beaten 82-63. Chuck Person and Charles Barkley combined to score 46 points for the Tigers. Turpin's 22 paced UK.

Florida made it two losses in a row for the Cats, winning 69-57 in Gainesville. The Cats trailed 34-18 at intermission and were never able to mount a serious comeback effort. Eugene McDowell had 16 for the Gators. Master led all scorers with 18.

Dicky Beal came through with five points in the final 43 seconds to give the Cats a 54-51 win over Illinois and a spot in the Final Four.

Unlike recent UK teams, those were the only two January glitches. The Cats lost just twice more during the regular season — at Alabama (69-62) and at Tennessee (63-58) — but they never sputtered and stumbled like their recent predecessors.

The Cats took a break from SEC play in late January when they hosted powerful Houston and its All-American center Hakeem Olajuwon. After falling behind 11-1, the Cats, keyed by a strong performance off the bench by Harden, roared back to score a 74-67 victory. Walker had 20 points to lead the Cats, while Turpin added 19. Bowie's 18 rebounds helped UK win the battle of the boards 51-45. The gifted Olajuwon, blanketed by Bowie and Turpin, was held to just 14 points.

The Cats avenged their loss to Auburn, coming from behind to post an 84-64 win. Trailing 30-22, the Cats, sparked by eight points from Bennett, went on a 15-2 run to grab a 37-32 lead at the half. Bennett and Beal, neither of whom started, each scored 17 for the Cats. Barkley had 18 to lead Auburn.

Despite missing four free throws inside the final minute, the Cats, thanks to two layups by Blackmon, edged past Florida 67-65 to avenge another earlier setback. In UK's next two wins, both squeakers, it was Turpin and Beal who came through in the clutch. Turpin hit an 18-foot jumper and Beal dropped in two free throws to break a 54-54 tie and send the Cats to a 58-54 win over Vanderbilt. Against Georgia, with the score even at 62-62, Turpin hit a short jump shot and Beal hit a pair of freebies to give the Cats a 66-64 victory. Turpin led the Cats with 40 points in those two wins.

Bowie scored 20 and Bennett added 13 as the Cats clinched the SEC title by beating Ole Miss 76-57. Bowie came back to score 20 points and grab 16 rebounds in the Cats' 90-68 season-ending win over LSU.

The Cats had more than lived up to their advance notices, posting a 23-4 mark heading into the SEC tourney. Turpin's 42-point outburst was enough to lift the Cats past Georgia 92-79 in the tourney opener. Turpin's point total and his 18 field goals tied the SEC tourney records set by Hagan in 1952. In addition, Turpin pulled down 16 rebounds in that UK victory.

In a semifinal battle against Alabama, Beal hit two free throws with three seconds left to give the Cats a 48-46 win and a date with Barkley, Person and dangerous Auburn in the championship game.

The final was a classic heart-stopper, with 12 ties and 18 lead changes. Neither team led by more than four points. And befitting such a closely contested game, the outcome wasn't decided until the final seconds.

Master, under pressure from the Auburn defense, found Walker behind a double screen at the top of the key. Walker took the pass, went above a trio of Tiger defenders and hit the game-winning 15-foot jumper just a second before the final horn sounded. It was UK's first SEC tourney title in 31 years, and its first since the tournament was renewed in 1979.

Turpin led UK with 13 points. Walker had 12 and Master 10. Barkley and Person each had 14 for the Tigers.

If the Wildcat players felt a sense of *deja vu* during the NCAA Tournament, it was with good reason. Their first three opponents were teams they had met — and conquered — during the regular campaign. First up was Brigham Young, a 93-59 loser to the Cats in the championship game of the UKIT. The second meeting proved to be a virtual rerun of the first game. With five players scoring in double figures, the hot-shooting Cats, led by Walker's 19 points and Beal's 14 assists, stormed to an easy 93-68 win.

What that win got the Cats was a third meeting with Louisville in 12 months. Suddenly, two teams that had not seen each other in a quarter-century were fast becoming familiar opponents.

But this meeting, unlike the December blowout, was another white knuckler that could have gone either way. UL, behind major efforts from Gordon and Wagner — a combined 47 points, compared to the 12 they had in the opener — assumed early control and led 36-32 at the half.

But in the end, superior shooting and rebounding, along with a superb performance from Beal, were enough to lift the Cats to a 72-67 win.

Beal and Master each had 15 points to lead UK. Bowie's 12 rebounds helped give the Cats a decisive 35-23 rebounding edge.

Illinois was all that stood between UK and a trip to the Final Four. The first meeting between the two teams had been decided by a Blackmon jumper at the last second. This game, although contested in Rupp Arena, figured to be just as close. It was. But in the end, UK came away with a 54-51 win. Once again it was Beal, the smallest player on the court, who stood the tallest. He scored five points in the final 43 seconds, including two free throws with 14 seconds remaining, to secure the Cats their first trip to the Big Dance since 1978. For his heroic efforts, Beal was voted the Mideast Regional's MVP.

UK's experience in the Final Four was short, memorable and more painful than a bad visit to the dentist. Facing Georgetown and its star center Patrick Ewing, the Cats jumped to an early 27-15 lead and were on top 29-22 at the half. What followed next was so horrendous that it almost became comical. The Cats, after playing near-perfect basketball in the opening half, suddenly went icy cold. Shot after shot was off the mark. In all, the Cats made just three of 33 field goals attempts in the final 20 minutes. What had once looked like a possible UK win quickly turned into an easy 53-40 Georgetown victory.

Despite the bitter taste left by the Georgetown loss, the Cats had their best season since the 1978 championship team. They finished with a 29-5 record, won both the SEC regular-season and tourney titles, went to the Final Four and ended with a No. 3 ranking in the AP and UPI polls.

With such a big hit coming via graduation, the Cats would now look to Walker as their main bread-and-butter guy. Although he did everything that was asked of him, it turned out to be a difficult, disappointing season, one that ended with a surprise announcement.

1984-85

For the first time in his 13 years as UK's head coach, Joe B. Hall faced a major rebuilding challenge. The loss of Bowie, Turpin, Master and Beal left this UK team short on experience, quickness, shooting ability and size. With the 6'9" Bearup now the tallest starter, the intimidation factor provided by the Twin Towers was no longer present.

But Hall's war chest was far from empty. Walker was a genuine All-American candidate, and Bennett, although only 6'7", was a rugged and fearless warrior. Blackmon and Harden were also back, giving Hall a pair of solid backcourt players. And in a freshman class that included Richard Madison, Cedric Jenkins and Rob Lock, the clear standout was Ed Davender, a 6'2" prep All-America from Brooklyn.

Although most Wildcat fans expected the team to struggle, no one was prepared for the disaster that was soon to unfold. After opening with a lackluster 63-54 win over Toledo, the Cats lost to Purdue, Indiana and Louisville on the road and to SMU in Rupp Arena. It marked the first time in the modern era that a UK team had a 1-4 record after five games.

The team's play in that string of setbacks was ugly, inconsistent and lacking inspiration. The Cats had 22 turnovers and committed 34 fouls in the 66-56 loss to Purdue. They blew a late lead in their embarrassing 56-54 homecourt loss to SMU, eventually getting beat on a last-second jump shot by Butch Moore. They were totally dominated in their 81-68 loss at Indiana. And in their 71-64 loss to Louisville, the Cats, after leading at the half, came unglued down the stretch.

Davender, in his first start, scored 27 points and Bearup added 13 as the Cats beat East Tennessee State 69-54 in the opening round of the UKIT. One night later, Walker scored 18 and Blackmon and Madison each had 12 as the Cats beat Cincinnati 66-55 to claim the title. Walker was named the tourney's MVP.

That UKIT sweep would be the first of seven straight wins for the Cats. They followed those two wins by giving

Bret Bearup fires from the corner. Bearup averaged 6.3 points as a fifth-year senior in 1984-85.

one of their best performances of the season, beating 11th-ranked Kansas 92-89 in Freedom Hall. Walker was spectacular, scoring 36 points and pulling down 19 rebounds. Davender also turned in a big effort with 20 points. Danny Manning led Kansas with 30.

The Cats continued to roll, beating Auburn 68-61, North Carolina 78-62, Vanderbilt 75-58 and Ole Miss 57-45. Although the Cats were winning, Walker was the lone mark of consistency. He accounted for 102 points in those four wins. This was a trend that would carry through until the end of the season. Walker could be counted on to produce every night, but his teammates were shaky and unpredictable. Not since the days of Cotton Nash had a single player been asked to carry such a heavy load by himself.

A cold start doomed UK in its 60-58 loss at Alabama. The Cats, after missing on 11 of their first 13 shots, fell behind early and were never able to overtake the Crimson Tide. Walker's 25 led all scorers.

The Cats rallied from five points down at the break to clip Mississippi State 58-57 and take over first place in the SEC standings with a 4-1 league mark. Two free throws by Harden put UK in front for good at 50-49 with 4:38 left. UK's 1-2-2 zone defense was the difference. The Cats went to the zone in the second half after Mississippi State shot 71.4 percent in the opening 20 minutes.

Successive losses to Florida, Georgia and Tennessee quickly exposed the Cats as little more than imposters to the SEC throne. Florida beat UK 67-55 in Lexington, then Georgia, after trailing most of the way, scored on 16 of 20 possessions

to beat the Cats 81-73. Tennessee, led by Michael Brooks' 34 points, virtually closed the book on UK's title hopes by winning 81-65 in Knoxville.

The Cats won their next five games, beating LSU 53-43, Auburn 49-47 in overtime, Vandy 68-62, Ole Miss 67-52 and Alabama 51-48. Walker was a one-man Delta Force for UK, racking up 119 points in those five wins, including 31 against Vandy and 33 against Ole Miss.

Amazingly, the one-time imposters to the throne were now back in first place in the league standings. But once again, the Cats' stay at the top was short-lived. In their next game, the Cats were humbled by Mississippi State, losing 82-69. They bounced back to beat Florida 76-68, then suffered a disasterous 79-77 loss to Georgia in Rupp Arena. It was Georgia's first win in Lexington since 1923, and it was a huge blow to UK's remaining title hopes. Horace McMillan scored the final six points for the Bulldogs, who were led by Joe Ward with 18 points. Walker had 25 for the Cats, while Bearup finished with 12 and Harden 11.

The Cats ended the regular season by splitting their final two games. They beat Tennessee 92-67 behind a 33-point, 18-rebound performance by Walker, then shot just 38.5 percent in a 67-61 loss to LSU. That split left the Cats with a 16-11 record overall and an 11-7 mark in SEC play, which landed them in a tie for third place.

The Cats faced Florida in the SEC tourney opener, and for the third time in five years they were bounced in the first round. The Cats led all the way, and were on top 51-47 with just over three minutes remaining. That's when things began to come apart. With Andrew Moten and Vernon Maxwell taking charge, the Gators outscored UK 11-4 to come away with the win. Moten had 16 points, while Maxwell added 12. Bennett paced UK with 14 points. Davender and Walker each had 13.

In previous years, given their mediocre season-long performance and their early exit from the SEC tourney, the best the Cats could have hoped for postseason-wise was an invitation to play in the NIT. However, thanks to the NCAA's expanded 64-team format, the Cats, despite an 18-12 record, were invited to the NCAA Tournament.

Facing Washington in the opening round, UK rode 34 of 40 shooting from the charity stripe to a 66-58 win. Walker was outstanding for the Cats, scoring 29 points. Madison also turned in a superb effort, coming off the bench to spear 10 rebounds.

Hot shooting (26 of 47 for 55 percent) and a key defen-sive play by Walker in the final minute enabled the Cats to scratch out a 64-61 win over UNLV in the second round. Walker topped the Cats with 23 points, hitting 10 of 14 field goal attempts. Davender chipped in with 13 points. However, UK's win wasn't sealed until Walker blocked a potential go-ahead shot by Richie Adams, then picked up the ball and sprinted downcourt for a dunk.

The Cats moved on to Denver, where they squared off against a St. John's team that featured future NBA players Chris Mullin, Walter Berry, Bill Wennington and Mark Jackson. The Redmen led 39-38 after a see-saw first half in which the two teams hit 63 percent from the field. The score remained close until midway through the second half. After a Davender bucket pulled UK to within 66-62, Mullin and Jackson each scored four points to give the Redmen a 74-62 advantage and control of the game.

St. John's ended the Cats' season by posting an 86-70 victory.

The Cats had one more field goal than St. John's, but the Redmen more than made up for it by hitting 26 free throws to just eight by UK.

Walker had 23 points for the Cats despite getting poked in the eye early in the game. Harden and Davender finished with 13 and 11, respectively, while Troy McKinley connected on four jumpers for eight points.

Mullin led all scorers with 30 points.

Walker finished the season with a 22.9 scoring average, the best by a Wildcat since Kevin Grevey's 23.6 average in 1974-75. Walker also led the team in rebounding with an average of 10.2.

It had not been the happiest season in UK basketball history. On the court, the Cats had been an average team at best, finishing with an 18-13 record. To make matters worse, *The Courier-Journal* and the *Herald-Leader* were involved in lengthy investigations into possible improprie-ties on Hall's part.

Deciding that he'd had enough, and that the time was right, Hall announced after the St. John's game that he was stepping down as UK's head coach. The man who had the unevial task of succeeding the almost-mythic Adolph Rupp was calling it quits after 13 seasons at the helm. Fittingly, Hall's final game was played in Denver, the city where his college coaching career began with a five-year stint at Regis College.

Hall's UK teams had a record of 297-100. There was an NCAA championship, an NIT title, three Final Four

appearances and eight SEC championships. He was voted National Coach of the Year in 1978.

Less than two weeks later, after interviewing such men as Lute Olson, Gene Bartow and Lee Rose, UK announced that it was hiring Eddie Sutton as the new coach. Sutton had played for Rupp's old friend Henry Iba at Oklahoma State in the mid-'50s, then gone on to have outstanding coaching stints at Creighton and Arkansas. Known as a master defensive coach, Sutton would inherit a veteran UK team led by the All-American Walker.

He would also inherit a lot more than that, most of which had little to do with basketball.

1985-86

Eddie Sutton's turbulent four-year reign as coach began and ended

Kenny Walker's All-American effort enabled Eddie Sutton's first Wildcat team to finish with a glittering 32-4 record.

was introduced as the next Wildcat coach.

Sutton's tenure began with a bang, a truly magical season that saw an overachieving Wildcat team carve out an unexpected 32-4 record. Yet, while Sutton's coaching philosophy — heavy on defense, cautious on offense — was successful on the basketball court, it wasn't always as popular in the court of public opinion. To Wildcat fans born and raised on the up-tempo, fast-breaking Adolph Rupp style, Sutton's more deliberate Henry Iba-influenced approach took some getting used to. Not all Wildcat fans did.

Still, though, there can be no denying that Sutton's first Wildcat team remains one of the most successful and most appreciated in UK hoops history. What that team accomplished far

while UK was the prime target of an NCAA investigation. The first investigation was not of Sutton's making (it was Joe B. Hall who was under the NCAA's microscope), but the second one was. And by the time it was over, Sutton was gone and the UK basketball program was in shambles.

Without question, it was the lowest point in Wildcat basketball history.

Sutton came to UK with glowing credentials, having been a big winner at Creighton and Arkansas. Despite his past accomplishments, most college basketball observers and Big Blue fans were surprised when Sutton was hired. But Sutton actively campaigned for the job throughout the interview process, which took place during the 1985 Final Four weekend in Lexington. And he prevailed. Two days after the Final Four, Sutton

exceeded anyone's expectations. The sticky man-to-man defense and the patient offense that Sutton preached were a perfect fit for a UK club that usually started three guards, lacked a true center and was short on depth. The Cats won because Sutton was able to disguise and overcome whatever shortcomings the team faced.

Of course, it didn't hurt that Sutton inherited a group of highly intelligent veteran players, led seniors Walker and Harden, who were quick to embrace and adapt to his system. Walker, fresh from an all-everything junior season, provided the Cats with offensive punch, while Harden was a coach on the floor and a tremendous pressure player. They were joined in the starting lineup by Bennett, Davender and Blackmon, with Madison, Lock,

Paul Andrews, Leroy Byrd and Cedric Jenkins offering support off the bench.

Few Wildcat teams have been more consistent from start to finish than this one. And no UK team has been better defensively. Throughout the entire 1985-86 season, only one team managed to score 80 points against the Cats. On 18 occasions, UK held the opposition to under 60 points. For the year, opponents shot just 46 percent from the field and averaged 61.4 points per game.

The Cats won 10 of their first 11 games, beginning with an easy 77-58 victory over Northwestern (La.) State. Bennett led the UK attack with 18 points. Walker and Davender chipped in with 13 apiece.

With Walker totaling 82 points, the Cats spanked Chaminade 89-57, Hawaii 98-65 and Cincinnati 84-54 to improve their record to 4-0 heading into a showdown against Indiana in Rupp Arena. The two clubs battled on even terms until a Jenkins five-footer put UK on top for good at 44-42 with just under 12 minutes left. Davender paced UK with 22 points. Ricky Calloway had 22 for the Hoosiers, who were without their standout guard Steve Alford. Alford was serving a one-game suspension for violating an NCAA rule.

Hot-shooting Kansas handed Sutton his first loss as UK's coach, hitting 61.5 percent from the field en route to an 83-66 victory. Danny Manning had 22 points to lead Kansas. Walker, Bennett and Blackmon each had 12 for the Cats.

After beating East Carolina 86-52 and Pepperdine 88-56 to win the UKIT, the Cats rode a strong 23-point performance by Bennett to a 69-64 win over Louisville. The Cats also got a big lift from Madison, who came off the bench to toss in 10 points. Milt Wagner had 19 for the Cardinals.

Winston Bennett heads upcourt as Richard Madison and a pair of Cincinnati defenders give chase. Bennett brought toughness and grit to the Cats, especially on the boards.

The Cats destroyed VMI 93-55, then opened SEC play with an 80-71 win at Vanderbilt. Walker had 25 against the Commodores, while Davender and Bennett finished with 19 and 16, respectively.

Auburn momentarily derailed the UK express by scoring a 60-56 upset at home. The Tigers, behind 18 first-half points by Person, built a 34-20 lead by intermission and were still holding onto a 54-42 advantage when the Cats began to rally. A bucket by Blackmon and eight straight points by Walker closed the gap to 54-52. But the Tigers used four free throws by Gerald White and two by Jeff Moore to hold off the fast-charging Wildcats. Person finished with 24 points for the Tigers. Walker's 22 led UK.

That loss to Auburn turned out to be the only blemish on UK's SEC record. The Cats would win their next 16 conference games, including seven on the road, to finish with a league-best 17-1 mark and the school's 36th SEC championship. The only stumble by the Cats during the remainder of the regular season was a 54-51 non-conference loss to N.C. State.

Few UK teams have been more courageous, gritty or tougher in pressure situations than this one. These Cats

Roger Harden passes to a teammate as Alabama's Jim Farmer closes in. The fearless Harden had a knack for knocking down last-second game-winning buckets.

found ways to win. Each night seemed to produce another hero. Harden hit last-second buckets that beat LSU 54-52 and Alabama 73-71. Madison, who hadn't scored a field goal in four games, hit for 13 points to help the Cats survive Ole Miss 62-58. Bennett had 26 points in a 74-57 win over Tennessee, Blackmon came through with 22 to lead UK past Vandy 73-65, and Davender scored 17 in a win over Florida.

There were incredible shooting nights — 72.2 percent in an 88-62 win over Mississippi State, 58.2 percent in an 80-69 win over Florida. There were historic wins — 80-75 over Georgia for the school's 1,400th victory, and 62-60 at Tennessee, giving the Cats their first win in Knoxville in eight years.

And, of course, there was Walker, whose steady scoring, rebounding, defense and leadership were at the very heart

of this team's astounding success. Although still the center of attention for opposing defenses, Walker averaged 20 points and 7.4 rebounds per game while hitting 58.2 percent from the field. His best scoring efforts in SEC action were 31 against Ole Miss and 32 in that UK win at Knoxville.

UK's 17-1 league record was its best since the Issel-led 1970 team, and it marked the Cats as odds-on favorite to win the SEC tourney in Rupp Arena.

UK opened tourney play with a convincing 95-69 victory over Ole Miss. Walker had 28 for the Cats, who connected on 39 of 68 shots for 57 percent. Blackmon also gave a solid performance, finishing with 18 points.

Harden came through again against LSU, sinking a 22-foot jumper with eight seconds left to seal a 61-58 Wildcat victory. In the championship game against Alabama, Walker scored 20 points and Harden added 18 as the Cats captured the crown with an 83-72 win. Jenkins also hit double figures with 13 points, while Harden handed out seven assists.

The Cats had now defeated LSU and Alabama three times. However, it wouldn't be the last time they crossed paths with those two ancient adversaries.

The Cats took an 11-game winning streak into their NCAA Tournament opening round matchup against Davidson in Charlotte, N.C. With Walker posting a double-double (20 points, 10 rebounds), the Cats jumped to an early lead and were never threatened, winning 75-55. UK shot 55 percent from the field, and made good on 21 of 32 free throws. Bennett had 14 points and Davender added 11, while Blackmon finished with nine points and 11 rebounds.

That win set up UK's first meeting with Western Kentucky since 1971, when the Hilltoppers thrashed the Cats 107-83. In that game, UK had no answer for WKU center Jim McDaniels, who scored 35 points. This time around, however, the situation was reversed. UK had Walker, and he proved to be a force that couldn't be stopped.

Walker hit all 11 of his shots, scored 32 points and pulled down eight rebounds to lead UK to a 71-64 victory. His superb performance was helped by Bennett's 13 points, and by another solid defensive effort that limited WKU to a cool 42 percent shooting from the field.

UK advanced to Atlanta, where its biggest opponent was familiarity. For some inexplicable reason, the NCAA put three SEC teams in the same region. Looming next for the Cats was a fourth meeting with Alabama. And as fate would have it, a fourth showdown with LSU.

The Cats' balanced scoring attack and some timely buckets were enough to earn them a 68-63 win over the Crimson Tide. Walker topped the Cats with 22 points, while Bennett had 14 points and 12 rebounds. Davender and Blackmon had 13 and 11 points, respectively for UK, which shot 52 percent from the field compared to 43 percent by Alabama.

To beat a team four times in a single season is a difficult achievement, and UK's string of miracles ran out against LSU. The Tigers, led by John Williams and Don Redden, came back from a 34-33 halftime deficit to clip UK 59-57.

Walker had 20 points in his final game as a Wildcat, ending his career with 2,080 points, second only to Dan Issel on UK's all-time scoring list. Harden also went out on a positive note, scoring 12 points. Blackmon had 10 points, while Bennett, in what would be his last game for two years, grabbed a dozen rebounds.

UK's first season under Sutton had been an amazing success story. Defense, teamwork, intelligence and a willingness by certain players to accept their designated role were instrumental in this team's 32-4 record and No. 3 ranking in the AP and UPI polls.

The magnificent Walker earned first-team All-America recognition for a second straight year. In addition, he was named the SEC Player of the Year for the second time. Sutton also received his share of accolades, being named National Coach of the Year and SEC Coach of the Year.

To Wildcat fans, the disappointment of losing was more than tempered by the excitement of what lay ahead. The boy king was on his way.

Rex Chapman.

The enormity of Rex Chapman's popularity was such that one sportswriter suggested that Lexington should change its name to "Rexington." Chapman's blend of talent, savvy and moxie made him one of the most-exciting players to wear the blue and white.

Ed Davender is arguably the most underappreciated guard in UK history. He ended his career with 1,637 points, 436 assists and 191 steals.

1986-87

Rex Chapman was christened the "Boy King" and "King Rex" long before he ever played his first game in a UK uniform. He generated a level of excitement unmatched by any of the great Wildcat freshmen who preceded him. Fans eager for their first glimpse of Chapman waited in line for days outside of Memorial Coliseum to assure admittance to Midnight Madness, the annual practice session that marks the official start of the basketball season.

Such was the enormity of his popularity — and his legend — that one local sportswriter suggested that Lexington change its name to "Rexington."

Chapman, a slender 6'4" bundle of talent, savvy and moxie, came to UK after a storybook career at Apollo High School in Owensboro, Ky., where he earned All-America recognition. After a difficult recruiting battle, one in which Michael Jordan made a personal pitch for his alma mater North Carolina, UK managed to sign Chapman.

The son of Wayne Chapman, the ex-Cat who left UK for Western Kentucky University after his freshman season, Rex was blessed with exceptional leaping ability and the fearless-

ness to take the ball to the basket against bigger opponents. He played the game with great flair, was an odds-defying passer, and a shooter willing to take the last-second shot.

Chapman's arrival at UK coincided with the arrival of the three-point shot in college basketball. His presence also helped offset the loss of Bennett, who injured his knee in preseason practice and was forced to sit out the season. Without Bennett's toughness and inside strength, UK came to rely heavily on the outside shot. Sutton, who realized early on the value of the new rule, became one of the first coaches to embrace — and successfully utilize — the three-point shot.

The strength of this UK team was its backcourt duo of Davender and Chapman, who was the first freshman to ever start a season opener for a Sutton-coached team. In truth, Sutton mostly used a three-guard lineup, with the 6'3" Blackmon listed as a small forward. Joining them in the starting lineup were a pair of juniors — 6'8" Richard Madison and 6'11" Rob Lock. The UK bench, which was dangerously thin, was led by three-point shooting whiz Derrick Miller, 6'8" Irv Thomas, 6'3" Paul Andrews and 6'9" Cedric Jenkins.

Chapman justified his starting nod by scoring 18 points and handing out six assists in a 71-69 win over scrappy Austin Peay. The Cats blew a 12-point second-half lead, then won it on a 10-footer by Thomas and a free throw by Andrews. Davender led UK with 20 points.

After Davender scored 23 points in a 66-60 win over Texas Tech, the Cats took Indiana down to the wire before eventually coming out on the short end of a 71-66 score. The Cats trailed by eight and appeared to be down for the count when the wondrous young Chapman took over. Chapman wrapped a pair of treys and a three-point play around an IU bucket to bring UK to within 60-59. But the Hoosiers, led by Steve Alford's 26 points, managed to fight off the Cats and claim the win. Chapman, who scored 13 of UK's final 15 points, matched Alford for game-high honors with 26.

A smothering defense helped the Cats win their next three games. They beat Lamar 71-56, then topped Iona 75-59 and Boston University 81-69 to win the UKIT. After missing 11 of their first 21 free throws against BU, the Cats connected on 12 of their final 13 freebie attempts to put away BU. Lock had 19 against Iona, while Chapman's 26 was tops against BU. Davender, who totaled 39 points in the two games, was voted the tourney's MVP.

Although Chapman had more than lived up to his press clippings, it wasn't until the seventh game against arch-rival Louisville in Freedom Hall that the magnitude of his talents and flair for the game came into full bloom.

With a national television audience looking on, Chapman scored 26 points to lead the Cats to an 85-51 victory. He destroyed the Cardinals in every way imaginable — dunks, finger rolls, and, of course, from the outside, where he hit five of eight three-point attempts, two of which were well beyond the NBA distance of 23'9". It was a spectacular performance, one of the most-memorable in UK history.

It was also the best team effort turned in by the Cats that season. UK hit 11 of 17 three-pointers. Davender had 16 points and five assists, Madison pulled down 17 rebounds and Blackmon hit all three of his treys.

But as good as Chapman was, the Cats, without Bennett's steadying influence, were seldom more than an above-average team for the rest of the season. Never again were they able to put it all together like they did against Louisville. The Cats could do no better than 10-8 in SEC play. Along the way, they even suffered their own embarrassment, a 76-41 home-court drubbing at the hands of LSU.

Georgia handed the cold-shooting Cats a rare Freedom Hall loss, pulling off a stunning 69-65 shocker in the SEC opener. UK's trio of outside gunners — Davender, Chapman and Miller — were a combined 15 of

Rob Lock looks to move into Mr. (David) Robinson's neighborhood. In one of the greatest individual performances ever given against UK, Robinson had 45 points, 14 rebounds, 10 blocked shots and eight dunks. Despite his supreme effort, UK beat Navy 80-69.

44 from the field. Davender led UK with 16, while Miller had 15. Georgia's Toney Mack topped all scorers with 24.

Chapman rescued the Cats at Auburn, nailing five straight treys and scoring 21 of his 24 points after intermission in a 63-60 win. No one could rescue the team in its next two games — losses to Alabama and Tennessee. The Crimson Tide shot 57.7 percent from the field and out-rebounded the Cats 32-23 en route to a 69-55 win in Rupp Arena. Derrick McKey had 25 for Alabama. Madison's 15 paced UK.

Tony White scored 32 points as Tennessee dropped the Cats to 1-3 in league action by posting a 75-68 win. The loss nullified a superb 29-point effort by Davender.

The Cats beat Mississippi State 57-47 and Florida 67-62, then suffered their humiliating 76-41 home loss to LSU. It was UK's worst setback since 1950. LSU, which led by just four at the half, held the Cats to 12 field goals and 25 per-

cent shooting. Anthony Wilson led the LSU slaughter with 28 points.

The Cats came back to win their next two games, beating Vanderbilt 71-65 on the strength of Blackmon's two clutch three-pointers and Navy 80-69, despite an other-worldly performance by David Robinson. In what is without question the greatest one-man show ever witnessed in Rupp Arena, the "Admiral" had 45 points, 14 rebounds, 10 blocked shots and eight dunks in a losing cause.

After losing 76-65 to Ole Miss, the Cats won four straight, beating Mississippi State 50-36, Auburn 75-71 (thanks to Blackmon's 27 points), Alabama 70-69 and Tennessee 91-84 in overtime.

That streak featured some exceptional moments, most-notably thrilling comebacks in the wins over Alabama and Tennessee. Against the ninth-ranked Crimson Tide, who earlier had defeated UK by 14 in Rupp Arena, the Cats erased a six-point deficit in the final 1:23 and pulled off the upset when Davender hit a 12-foot jumper with six ticks remaining. Davender finished with 29 in that win.

In their game against Tennessee, the Cats performed an even greater miracle, coming back from 10 points down with just 1:13 left to tie the score and force an overtime. With Chapman, Davender and Jenkins coming up big in crunch time, the Cats went on to post a 91-84 win. Davender and Chapman combined for 51 points against the Vols, while Jenkins added 11.

Along with battling opponents on the court, the Cats were fighting rumors of dissension and conflict among the players off the court. Chapman, the sensational and highly publicized freshman, was at the heart of rumors, which had him fighting with veterans Davender and Blackmon. At the press conference following the Mississippi State game, Chapman addressed the situation, saying the rumors were unfounded and had no merit. Davender and Blackmon agreed that the rumors were just that — rumors.

Whether or not the off-court controversy played any role in the team's on-court performance is uncertain, but the Cats, after beating Tennessee, lost three of their next four games to all but kill any hopes for a late run at the SEC title. The losses were to Florida 74-56, LSU 65-52 and Georgia 79-71. The lone victory was a 65-54 win over Vandy.

The regular season ended on a positive, if precarious, note — one-point wins over Ole Miss (64-63) and Oklahoma (75-74), thanks to last-second buckets by Chapman and Madison.

UK's postseason life turned out to be brief and disap-

pointing. The Cats fell to Auburn 79-72 in the SEC tourney opener. Davender and Chapman each had 17 for the Cats. Auburn's Jeff Moore was the game's top scorer with 23.

In the NCAA Tournament, Ohio State, led by Dennis Hopson's 32 points, pulled away in the second half and beat the Cats 91-77. The Buckeyes were deadeyes from the field, hitting 33 of 50 shots for 66 percent. Davender had 23 points for UK, while Lock and Chapman finished with 14 and 13, respectively.

The back-to-back tourney losses left UK with a final record of 18-11.

Chapman's 16-point average made him the first freshman since Alex Groza to lead the team in scoring. In addition, Chapman led the team in assists, averaging 3.6.

The steady Davender also played well, averaging 15.2 points and two steals per game. Madison was the top rebounder with an average of 7.4.

This team was never able to overcome the absence of Bennett. Had he been able to play, the Cats would almost certainly have been a far superior team. On the positive side, Bennett's surgically repaired knee was on the mend. He would be back for the next season, joining a solid group of veterans, headed by Davender and Chapman, and an exciting bunch of rookies, featuring prep All-Americans Eric Manuel and LeRon Ellis.

It promised to be another exciting, championship-caliber team. Instead, it turned out to be an unhappy season, and by the time it came to an end a king would abdicate his throne and dark clouds were beginning to gather on the Big Blue horizon.

1987-88

The relationship between Sutton and Chapman was always delicate at best. Their styles and personalities virtually assured conflict. Sutton liked control, Chapman enjoyed freedom. Sutton was more on the conservative side, Chapman played with flair and reckless abandon. Adding fuel to an already delicate situation was the fans' god-like worship of Chapman. For a successful and celebrated coach like Sutton, a man with no lack of ego, having to stand in the huge shadow cast by one of his players was no easy pill to swallow.

So it was inevitable, then, that coach and player would clash. And they did. As the season progressed, their relationship became strained and more distant. The chief cause for their split was the issue of Chapman's shot selection and

the way it was handled. Sutton criticized Chapman publicly through the media; Chapman felt the matter should be handled internally.

The rift between Sutton and Chapman almost overshadowed the fact that this was an excellent Wildcat team with NCAA championship potential. Bennett's return gave the team added toughness and experience. Davender, in his final season, continued to carve his name on the list of great UK guards. Seniors Madison, Lock and Jenkins never gave anything less than 100 percent effort. Manuel, a multi-talented rookie from Georgia, played with the poise of a true veteran. The bench, led by Miller, Ellis and Reggie Hanson, provided excellent backup at all positions. And, of course, there was Chapman, whose All-America skills, talents and unpredictability elevated the team to the title-contender level.

Cedric Jenkins scored a buzzer-beating tip-in to give the Wildcats a 76-75 win over upset-minded Louisville in Rupp Arena.

Bennett's presence was vital to this club's success, and as the season wore on and he left behind the rust gathered from a year on the sidelines, his performance level soared. Bennett had 28 points and 10 rebounds against Miami. He had a 24-point, 10-rebound effort against Alaska. Even more important, his maturity served as a steadying influence on a team that at times appeared to be on the verge of internal combustion.

The unbeaten Cats had to rally from a nine-point second-half deficit to beat Vanderbilt 81-74 in their SEC opener. Trailing 65-56, the Cats scored 11 unanswered points, including seven in 21 seconds, to gain control of the game. Davender paced the Cats with 24 points. Chapman had 21 and Lock added 18, while Bennett yanked down 17 rebounds.

Davender, Chapman and Bennett combined for 67 points as the Cats came from behind to down Georgia 84-77 in Athens. Willie Anderson had 19 for the Bulldogs, who were in front 45-43 at the break.

The Cats opened strong, winning their first 10 games and rising to No. 1 in the weekly polls. Included in that streak was an 82-76 overtime win over Indiana in Indianapolis and a 76-75 home-court victory over revenge-minded Louisville. Last-second heroics saved the Cats in both games. Chapman and Madison accounted for UK's final seven points in overtime to put away Indiana. The win over Louisville was even more dramatic. With his team down by one, Jenkins scored on a tip-in just ahead of the buzzer to deny the Cardinals their sweet revenge. Davender had 42 points in those two wins, while Chapman had 41.

Other early Wildcat victims included Hawaii 86-59, Cincinnati 101-77, Miami (Ohio) 85-71, UNCC 84-81 and Alaska 100-58. Lock's play during December was superb. The California native scored 18 in each of UK's first two games and 17 against Miami.

After ripping Mississippi State 93-52 to improve to 10-0 overall and 3-0 in SEC action, the Cats faced off against Auburn in Rupp Arena. The game didn't figure to be close. But the underdog Tigers, taking advantage of a dreadful UK performance, pulled off a stunning 53-52 upset. Forward John Caylor's last-second jumper from the left side proved to be the difference.

By now, the rift between Sutton and Chapman had become obvious to everyone. Nowhere were their feelings better exemplified than in a now-classic photo showing coach and player sitting side by side at the post-game press conference following the Auburn loss. The expression on their faces spoke louder than words.

Despite the internal turmoil, the Cats rebounded from the Auburn loss by beating Alabama 63-55 and Tennessee

Few photos ever spoke louder than this one. By the halfway point of the season, the rift between Eddie Sutton and Rex Chapman had become obvious to everyone, and a stunning home-court loss to Auburn didn't help matters.

83-65. Davender's 17 led the Cats in their win at Alabama, while Chapman scored 23 against the Vols.

UK offered up another clunker performance in a 58-56 loss to Florida in Rupp Arena. The icy Cats made good on 16 of 57 shots from the field for 28.1 percent. Chapman was the coldest Cat, turning in a five-for-19 shooting performance. Bennett led UK with 20 points and 11 rebounds.

The Cats split their next two games, beating LSU 76-61 and losing to three-point minded Vanderbilt 83-66. Vandy connected on 13 of 20 trey attempts to bump off the Cats. Kentucky natives Scott Draud and Barry Goheen combined for 39 points to lead Vandy. Chapman topped UK with 18.

A 23-point performance by Davender and 14 points from Ellis in his first start lifted the Cats past Notre

Dame 78-68 and triggered a five-game winning streak. But once again, all was not well within the UK camp. In UK's 94-65 win over Ole Miss, Davender was benched for the final 24 minutes, further sparking rumors of great unrest among the players and coaches. In addition, Miller, miffed at his lack of playing time (six minutes per game), was sulking and unhappy.

Davender was back in the starting lineup against Mississippi State, scoring 21 points in an 83-59 victory. Chapman scored 25 to lead the Cats past Auburn 69-62, then Bennett had 25 in an 82-68 win over Alabama. The Cats dropped their next two games, falling to Tennessee 72-70 and Florida 83-76. Greg Bell and Vernon Maxwell were the primary villains in those two UK setbacks. Bell canned a 12-footer with two seconds left to save the Vols, while Maxwell raked UK's defense for 32 points to

propel the Gators to their win.

The Cats closed out the regular season by giving a string of solid performances, beating LSU 95-69, Syracuse 62-58 (despite the absence of Chapman), Georgia 80-72 and Ole Miss 78-71. The big news during this stretch was Chapman's back injury, which he sustained in the LSU game. Of lesser note was the insertion of Manuel into the starting lineup. Manuel made good on his opportunity, scoring 14 points against LSU and 11 against Syracuse, including six of the team's final seven points. Chapman bounced back from his injury to score 29 points in the season finale against Ole Miss.

Despite all the controversy and unrest, the Cats finished with a 22-5 record overall, a league-best 13-5 mark in SEC action and a No. 6 ranking in the final regular-season polls.

Bennett and Chapman each tallied 19 points as the Cats beat Ole Miss 82-64 in the SEC Tournament opener. Manuel's 17 second-half points enabled the Cats to fight back from a 40-35 halftime deficit and beat LSU 86-80 in semifinal action. Manuel led UK with 24 points, while Bennett and Chapman finished with 23 and 20, respectively.

Chapman put his name on the MVP trophy by scoring 23 points in UK's 62-57 championship game win over Georgia. The Bulldogs were in front 58-57, but a bucket by Bennett and four straight Chapman free throws sealed it for UK.

With the SEC regular-season and tourney titles under their belt, and riding the crest of a seven-game winning streak, the Cats headed into NCAA Tournament action on a high note. Boasting one of the premier backcourt duos (Davender and Chapman) in college basketball (and UK history), the Cats were poised to make a serious run for another NCAA title.

The run of strong performances continued into the NCAA tourney. Davender erupted for 30 points and Chapman added 23 as the Cats rolled to an easy 99-84 win over Southern. Manuel also gave a terrific effort, scoring 13 points and grabbing 10 rebounds.

In second-round action against Maryland, UK's balanced scoring attack again proved to be the difference in a tough 90-81 win. For the second straight game, UK shot well (32 of 56 for 57 percent) and all five starters scored in double figures, led by Chapman and Davender with 23 points each. Bennett turned in a giant effort with 17 points and 12 rebounds, while Manuel and Lock finished with 13

Eric Manuel turned in a series of strong performances late in his rookie campaign. Because of the NCAA investigation, the talented Georgia native only played one season at UK.

and 10 points, respectively.

Next up for UK was Villanova, a team the red-hot Cats were expected to easily handle. But Rollie Massimino's scrappy club played a flawless first half, building a 43-32 lead at intermission. UK, behind Chapman's 30-point performance, chopped into the lead in the final 20 minutes, yet was never able to claim the upper hand. When the smoke cleared, Villanova was an 80-74 winner.

UK ended with a 27-6 record. Chapman led the team in scoring with a 19 point average, while also becoming the first Wildcat sophomore to join the 1,000-point club. And despite criticism of his shot selection, Chapman hit

41.5 percent of his three-point attempts.

Davender finished with a 15.7 scoring average and 1,637 career points (ninth best in UK history), 436 assists and 191 steals. Bennett, who averaged 15.3 for the season, left UK with 1,399 points.

With the season over, one huge question hung in the air: Would Chapman stay at UK or would he turn pro? It's safe to conclude that the agony of his decision was lessened to a great degree by an incident that happened in early April — the discovery of the infamous Emery package containing $1,000 that was earmarked for the father of UK recruit Chris Mills in Los Angeles.

Once the NCAA got wind of such a major rules violation, it quickly launched an in-depth investigation into the UK basketball program. By the time that investigation was over, UK was the scourge of college basketball, having been hit with NCAA sanctions, forced to vacate three NCAA Tournament games and surrender the SEC regular-season title. Sutton, one of the game's most-respected coaches resigned in disgrace. Hagan, the school's AD and one of UK's greatest players ever, was also among the casualties. And two players with All-America potential — Manuel and Mills — would each play only one season in a UK uniform.

Chapman, perhaps sensing the dark scandal-dominated days ahead, made the decision to take his game to the NBA.

The boy king was gone.

1988-89

Chris Mills, one of the most-complete players in Wildcat history, was at the center of the controversy that eventually led to UK being severely penalized by the NCAA. Like Eric Manuel, Mills only played one season for the Cats.

The 11-month period between the discovery of the Emery package and the end of the 1988-89 season was without question the bleakest in UK's long and illustrious basketball history. Never had the program come under such intense scrutiny, and never had the stakes been higher.

The NCAA investigators weren't the only detectives on the scene. UK President Dr. David Roselle ordered an internal, no-holds-barred probe into the program, and both the Lexington and Louisville newspapers also launched their own investigations.

The UK basketball program suddenly became an isolated compound under siege from all directions.

Not surprisingly, it was a period filled with almost-daily doses of rumors, suspicions, innuendoes, denials and accusations. Virtually anyone who might possibly come under the investigation's microscope hired an attorney. There were enough busy lawyers involved to start a good-size law firm.

At the heart of the investigation was the $1,000 that the NCAA accused UK assistant coach Dwane Casey of sending to Claud Mills, the father of UK signee Chris Mills. It was a charge that Casey — and the rest of the UK coaching staff — adamantly denied.

However, as the various probes continued, other possible infractions began to pop up, most notably one alleging that Manuel, with help from the UK coaching staff, cheated on his college entrance exam. Although Manuel denied then (and still does) that anything illegal occurred,

he would never again be allowed to play for any NCAA member institution.

Despite everything, most Wildcat fans had high hopes for the upcoming season. Even without Chapman and Manuel, this was still a team with some talent. The 6'7" Mills was one of the most-complete players to ever put on a UK uniform. Ellis, at 6'10", was an exceptionally mobile big man, and Miller possessed enough proficiency from beyond the three-point arc to give him high-scoring potential anytime he suited up.

Joining them in the starting lineup were a pair of sophomores, 6'7" Reggie Hanson and 6'1" Sean Sutton, the coach's son. Backing them up were Mike Scott and a trio of young Kentucky natives who would later make an indelible mark on UK basketball — redshirt freshmen John Pelphrey and Deron Feldhaus, and true freshman Richie Farmer.

While this wasn't the least-talented team in UK history, it was the team that faced the most off-court distractions. The investigation hovered over everything like a death shroud, causing the focus of attention to be on the ramifications of the investigation and various possible scenarios rather than on basketball.

The result was predictable — an unmitigated disaster. UK finished with a 13-19 record, the school's first losing mark in 61 seasons. During one stretch, the Cats lost six straight games, the first time that had happened since the 1922-23 season. It was the longest, coldest and bleakest winter in UK hoops history.

In many ways, the drama of what UK was about to go through, both on and off the court, was summed up in the season opener against Duke. Prior to the game, TV analyst Dick Vitale called for Sutton to resign "for the good of the UK program." Vitale's blasphemy, which initially caused great outrage among the Big Blue faithful, would eventually become the prevailing sentiment as this long, dark season progressed.

The situation on the court was equally appalling. Duke pounded the overmatched Cats 80-55, handing UK its worst opening-season loss since the 1926-27 campaign. In what was to become a trend during the season, the Cats stayed with Duke through the first half — the two clubs

were deadlocked at 43-43 with 17 minutes remaining — only to fall apart in the late going.

The Cats finished with a 5-7 pre-SEC record. Along the way there were several outstanding individuals performances. Miller knocked down seven treys and finished with 36 points in an 89-71 win over California; Ellis had 37 points against Northwestern State and 33 against Marshall; Mills scored 17 points and pulled down 20 rebounds in that 91-78 win over Marshall. He later recorded the first "triple-double" in UK history, scoring 19 points, grabbing 10 rebounds and handing out 10 assists to lead the Cats past Austin Peay 85-77.

But the Cats, no matter how intense the effort, were little more than easy prey for quality opponents like Louisville, Indiana and Notre Dame. Those three ancient foes beat the barely competitive Cats by a combined total of 62 points.

Even as the world was closing in around him, Sutton, to his great credit, somehow managed to coax every ounce of energy and every drop of sweat from this beleaguered group. Although this team's record is UK's worst in nearly three-quarters of a century, no one can fault the players for

LeRon Ellis had some shining moments during the disastrous 1988-89 season. The Cats finished with a 13-19 mark, giving the school its first losing record in 61 seasons.

lack of effort. In fact, given the Perry Mason circumstances surrounding the on-going investigation and the myriad of daily distractions, it's a tribute to the players that they were able to achieve what they did. They handled themselves well and with great class despite being caught in the middle of a truly nightmarish situation.

If there was an upbeat moment during the season, it came early in SEC action. The Cats won their first three league games, beginning with a 76-65 victory over Georgia. Hanson led UK with 20 points, while Ellis and Mills each contributed 18. Mills also had a dozen rebounds.

Miller hit for 27 and Ellis added 17 as the Cats held on to beat Vanderbilt 70-61 despite six three-pointers by Kentucky native Barry Goheen, who finished with 20 points. With Miller exploding for 30 points, the Cats made it three wins in a row by upsetting Florida 69-56 in Gainesville. Dwayne Schintzius had 20 points and 13 rebounds for the Gators.

With less than five minutes remaining in their battle against LSU, the Cats stood on the verge of going 4-0 in SEC action. They owned a 55-48 lead, and appeared to be in control. But LSU's Chris Jackson had other ideas. The flashy All-American guard scored 16 straight points, including two game-deciding free throws with six seconds left, to give his Tigers a 64-62 win.

Total domination of the glass wars led to the Cats' 76-64 loss at Alabama. The Crimson Tide outrebounded UK 36-20. Michael Ansley led the winners with 19 points and 13 rebounds. Miller tied for game-high honors with 19.

Miller scored 23 points and Feldhaus cashed in a pair of free throws with 12 seconds left to seal the Cats' 66-65 upset over No.18-ranked Tennessee. Bell paced the Vols with 22.

The Cats turned in perhaps their finest overall performance of the season in an 86-76 win over Auburn. Miller scored 16 points to lead the Cats, who shot 53.4 percent from the field. Mills had 15 points and 11 rebounds, while Ellis and Sean Sutton finished with 14 and 13, respectively.

But even one of the rare good days couldn't escape the bad news coming from the investigation — Manuel's ACT score was thrown out. Officials ruled that Manuel had in all likelihood cheated, and that the UK coaching staff was behind the skulduggery. It was a charge Manuel, Sutton and the UK coaches strongly denied.

Despite the distractions, the Cats were sitting near the top of the SEC standings with a 5-2 record. But that was an illusion; the heaviness of what was surrounding them was about to take its toll. Seven losses in their next eight games sent the Cats plunging toward the bottom of the pack. Even worse, it left them with 16 losses, the most-ever by a UK team. And there was still almost a month left in the season.

Events began to accelerate during the final days of the season. What had seemed almost surreal suddenly now became very real. When the Cats beat Tennessee 76-71, the most-telling headline in the Lexington *Herald-Leader* wasn't about the game, it was about Sutton's status. "Sutton Out, Lee Rose in, Paper says." The article listed other coaches who were being considered as possible replacements, including Jeff Mullins, Rick Pitino, Jim Crews, Joe Dean Jr. and Lynn Nance.

Also, C.M. Newton agreed to leave Vanderbilt and become UK's new athletics director on April 1, 1989. Newton's predecessor, Cliff Hagan, was the first casualty of the mess surrounding the basketball program.

UK's long season officially ended with a 77-63 loss to Vanderbilt in the SEC tourney opener. Even this moment wasn't without irony and surrealism. The opposing coach was, of course, Newton, the man who, in a few shorts weeks, would face the daunting task of rebuilding the UK program from out of the ashes.

Nine days after the loss to Vanderbilt, Sutton went on national TV and announced that he was resigning as UK coach. He departed UK after four seasons, during which his teams compiled an overall 88-39 record.

On May 19, exactly two months after Sutton stepped down, the NCAA guillotine fell on UK. Three years probation, a two-year ban on postseason play, no television appearances and a reduction in scholarships. The NCAA had unleashed all its fury on the Cats.

Upon learning the sanctions, the NCAA-approved exodus of players began immediately. Mills transferred to Arizona, Ellis to Syracuse and Sean Sutton to Purdue. As for Manuel, he would eventually wind up at Oklahoma City College, an NAIA school.

Hanson, Pelphrey, Farmer and Sean Woods, who sat out the season as a Prop 48 case, also considered leaving, but decided to stay and tough it out. Their decision to remain as Wildcats would have far-ranging consequences that no one could have imagined at the time.

But for Newton, the first order of business was to hire a coach. He approached ex-Cat Pat Riley, then the L.A. Lakers coach. Riley quickly declined, choosing instead to remain in Los Angeles. Pitino, another NBA coach, was

also high on Newton's list. But Pitino, coach of the New York Knicks at the time, said he wouldn't discuss it until his team had finished its season.

Not to be deterred, Newton then spoke to Arizona's Lute Olson and Seton Hall's P.J. Carlesimo. But Olson and Carlesimo, perhaps influenced by the stiff NCAA penalties and UK's bleak prospects, opted to stay put.

By this time, the Knicks had been eliminated from the NBA playoffs, so Newton approached Pitino a second time. Although Pitino had resurrected the Knicks in just two seasons, his well-documented differences with general manager Al Bianchi had taken their toll. Unhappy coaching the Knicks, he decided to come to Lexington, listen to Newton's pitch and look the situation over.

On June 2, 1989, Pitino agreed to take the job.

The man who had rebuilt struggling programs at Boston College, Providence and with the Knicks was now accepting his most-difficult challenge yet — taking over a program that had been pinned to the mat by the NCAA, had a shortage of talented players and poor prospects on the recruiting trail.

Few believed that Pitino could possibly have the same quick turnaround at UK that he'd had elsewhere. Even the most optimistic UK fan figured it would take four to five years before the Cats would once again be competitive at the highest

levels.

Only one person believed otherwise.

Rick Pitino.

And he would be right.

1989-90

No one ever accused Rick Pitino of lacking brashness or confidence. So it came as no big surprise when he made the bold proclamation that UK would win, and win right away. Given the situation, and the total destruction left behind by the NCAA's juggernaut, Pitino's words were met with great skepticism by Big Blue fans and college basketball experts. It's one thing to turn around a team that has Patrick Ewing as its anchor; it's a totally different proposition when the anchor is Reggie Hanson.

Pitino's confidence level registered much higher than the talent level. In all, thanks to the mass exodus of players and the reluctance of high school recruits to sign on with a fallen program, Pitino had but eight scholarship players available. Of that eight, only two — Hanson and Miller — had proved themselves to be capable Division I players.

Everything was thumbs-up once Rick Pitino took over the fallen UK program. The cocky and brash New Yorker came in promising that the Cats would win immediately.

Walk-ons were elicited to help fill out the roster, and during the preseason, assistant coach Billy Donovan participated in the scrimmages.

Knowing that his thin troops were far from ready to play his up-tempo, all-out, pressing style of play, Pitino turned his preseason conditioning program into a Marine-type boot camp. There were 5 a.m. practices. The weight training program, under the guidance of Rock Oliver, was brutal, driving the players to the very edge of endurance. Pitino's goal wasn't limited to developing physical toughness — he wanted his players mentally tough as well.

Pitino's confidence was matched only by his love of the three-point shot. He had been among the first college coaches to see its potential, and in 1987, with Donovan as his principal long-range missile launcher, Pitino took a marginally talented Providence team to the Final Four.

He also believed in the full-court press, the "mother-in-law" press, as he termed it, one that would cause "constant pressure and harassment."

Derrick Miller became the first UK player to score 40 points in Rupp Arena as the Cats pounded Vanderbilt 100-73.

them. Their drive to succeed was propelled by the winning tradition they were now part of.

And it did turn out to be an excellent team in Rupp Arena, going 13-2 in front of the home crowd. But on the road, it was a different story — just a lone win, 78-74 at Florida. (Ironically, later Pitino teams were known for their amazing ability to win in front of hostile crowds.)

With the exception of one outright disaster, a 150-95 loss at Kansas, the Cats were competitive even in defeat. Of their losses, six were by seven points or less. What kept them in most games, even against vastly superior teams, was the three-point shot, which Pitino green-lighted the players to take at every opportunity. The Cats put up 810 three-point attempts during the season, enough to be immortalized as "Pitino's Bombinos" by sports columnist John McGill.

Pitino's debut was a success, a 76-73 win over Ohio in Rupp Arena. Hanson led the Cats with 24 points and 14 rebounds. Miller chipped in with 18.

Starters in Pitino's first game were Feldhaus and Pelphrey at the forward spots, Hanson in the middle, with Miller and Sean Woods in the backcourt. Farmer and freshman Jeff Brassow provided backup off the bench. Though thin and scrawny-looking, that group, later dubbed "the seven men of iron" by sportswriter Billy Reed, turned out to be one of the grittiest, most mentally tough teams in UK history.

Everyone believed that Pitino would win — just not with this team. Most UK fans felt that this club would be lucky to win 10 games. Cawood Ledford predicted the Cats to win eight games, and told Pitino that if the team won 10, he should be National Coach of the Year.

But what no one, including Pitino or Cawood, could have predicted was the depth of pride, courage and heart in this group of Wildcat players. These were young men with unlimited character. It also didn't hurt that four of the players — Hanson, Feldhaus, Farmer and Pelphrey — were Kentucky kids who had grown up following the Big Blue. Wearing a Wildcat uniform had been a life-long dream for

Their second game, a 71-69 loss to heavily favored Indiana in Indianapolis, offered a hint that this team might be better than expected. The pressing Cats forced Indiana into 25 turnovers, but couldn't overcome a chilly 36-percent shooting performance. Feldhaus had 23 for the Cats, who

shot an even colder 29.7 percent in the second half.

The Cats connected on 31 treys in their next two games — a 102-97 win over Mississippi State and a 111-75 pasting of Tennessee Tech. Miller was the deadliest Wildcat, scoring 57 points in those two wins. Hanson had 37, and Brassow came off the bench to toss in 20 against Tennessee Tech.

Any hopes that this exciting, surprising UK team was ready for prime-time were quickly put to rest by Kansas. The powerful Jayhawks shattered a host of NCAA records by blasting UK 150-95. The Cats stayed with Kansas for much of the first half, and were trailing 64-57 with less than five minutes remaining before intermission. But the Jayhawks went on a 16-4 run to take an 80-61 lead at the break. The second half was all Kansas, which had six players in double figures, led by Terry Brown with 31. Miller had 32 for the Cats, while Pelphrey and Farmer added 20 and 19, respectively.

The Cats shook off that destruction, bouncing back to beat Furman 104-73 and Portland 88-71 in the UKIT opener. Miller had 21 against Furman, Woods led with 20 against ex-Cat Larry Steele's Portland club. But in the championship game against Southwestern Louisiana, the Cats blew a six-point lead inside the final two minutes and dropped a 116-113 overtime thriller. Pelphrey paced UK with 24 points.

That disappointing setback was the start of a slide that saw the Cats lose five straight and six of their next seven. Three Wildcats hit for 20 points or more, but it wasn't enough to keep North Carolina from ringing up a 121-110 win. Feldhaus had 27, Miller 26 and Farmer 21 for UK. King Rice led the Tar Heels with 22.

It took 60-percent shooting for eighth-ranked Louisville to register a hard-earned 86-79 victory in Rupp Arena. LaBradford Smith had 22 for the Cards. Hanson's 24 earned him game-high honors.

Back-to-back road losses to Georgia (106-91) and Vanderbilt (92-85) were followed by an 89-81 win over Florida. Two Miller free throws and a Hanson three-pointer kicked off a late 17-8 run that put away the Gators and broke UK's five-game losing skid. Woods led the Cats with 20, followed by Hanson with 19 and Pelphrey with 16.

UK's 94-81 loss at LSU was spiced by a heated nose-to-nose confrontation between Pitino and Dale Brown. The two coaches, after venting some steam at the officials

following an on-court altercation, quickly turned the situation into a private and highly charged *tete-a-tete*. Chris Jackson led the powerful Tigers with 28 points. Shaquille O'Neal had 14 points and 15 rebounds. Brassow was UK's top gun with 25.

With Hanson hitting for 20 and Feldhaus chipping in 19, the Cats gave a terrific performance in an 82-65 win over Alabama. They followed that by ringing up 17 three-pointers in a 95-83 victory over Tennessee. Miller burned the Vols for 28 points, while Feldhaus had a 19-point, 11-rebound effort.

The Cats lost two of their next three, blowing a 17-point lead in a 74-70 loss at Auburn and dropping a tough 87-86 overtime decision at Mississippi State. Sandwiched between those two losses was a 98-79 win over Ole Miss.

What followed next was a remarkable four-game stretch — all wins — that included one of the greatest and bravest performances ever given by a UK team. The streak began with Woods scoring 20 and Hanson adding 18 in an 88-77 revenge win over Georgia. Then Miller hit for six second-half treys and became the first Wildcat to score 40 points in Rupp Arena as the Cats rolled past Vandy 100-73. Woods was the hero at Florida, coming through with a crucial three-point play that gave the Cats a 78-74 win and their first road victory in 16 games. Feldhaus had 17 in that win over Florida.

But this team will forever be remembered for — and defined by — a single game, against LSU on the night of Feb. 15, 1990. In those 40 minutes, all the elements embodied by this group of players crystallized into a towering performance that resulted in a memorable victory.

The Tigers had two seven-footers, O'Neal and Stanley Roberts, plus Jackson, the finest guard in the college ranks at the time. An easy LSU blowout wouldn't have surprised anyone.

But the scrappy Cats rocked LSU, jumping to a 41-18 lead with 6:24 left in the first half. Hot shooting by Miller and Feldhaus (they finished with 29 and 24 points, respectively), coupled with a pressing defense that caused the frustrated Tigers to commit numerous turnovers, enabled the Cats to take charge from the opening tipoff.

However, it was in the home stretch, after Jackson's brilliant 41-point performance put his team in a position to win, that the fire within the heart of these Wildcats burned the brightest.

Refusing to fold, the gallant Cats hung on for the electrifying 100-95 win. Every UK player stood tall, but none more so than Farmer, the legend from Clay County. It was his six pressure-packed free throws inside the final 1:05 that sealed the win for UK.

That win gave the Cats a 13-10 mark and the golden opportunity to finish with a winning record. It wasn't to be. Four losses (all on the road) in their last five games left the Cats with a 14-14 record. Hanson, so crucial to this team's fortunes, was superb during that final stage of the season, scoring 86 points in the last four games.

In years past, a break-even record would have been considered a failure. But this wasn't a normal year. Given what this team had achieved under such extraordinary circumstances, this rates as one of the most-successful teams in UK history.

Pitino had more than delivered on his promise. His team was exciting, played hard and won games. Even more important, their style of play put the fun back into it for Wildcat fans. The joy that had been missing for almost two years had returned with a bang.

What Pitino needed now was a super player who could take the program to a higher level. But getting such a player wasn't going to be easy — nowhere is the pain of NCAA sanctions felt more severely than in recruiting. The

Jamal Mashburn is without question the single most important player in the post-probation era. He had the courage to choose UK at a time when the future of the basketball program was shaky and uncertain.

top prep players, keenly aware of UK's situation, were quick to turn a deaf ear to Pitino's sales pitch.

One didn't. A chubby young man from New York with a reputation for being lazy and unmotivated decided to buck the trend by casting his lot with Pitino and UK.

Jamal Mashburn.

It would be on his broad shoulders that the UK program reclaimed its place among the giants of college basketball.

1990-91

If Pitino was the lightning that ignited the fire of UK's basketball rebirth, then Jamal Mashburn was the thunder. At 6'8", Mashburn had a blue-chip game, all-around NBA skills and a team-first attitude. He also had the courage to choose UK at a time when the future of the basketball program was on shaky grounds.

There is no way to overstate the importance of Mashburn's role in UK's dramatic turnaround from down-and-out basketball bad boy to top-of-the-world team of the 1990s. Had there been no Mashburn, it's hard to envision those two NCAA championship rings and four Final Four appearances in a six-year span. Had Mashburn decided not to attend UK, it's doubtful that later talents like Antoine Walker, Tony Delk, Ron Mercer and Derek Anderson would have worn the blue and white.

Mashburn brought all-around skills and physical pres-

ence to a team that had an abundance of heart, character, intelligence and mental toughness. He was the first true "Pitino-type" recruit, a super-athlete who could run the floor, shoot, pass and defend.

Mashburn was also quick to blend in with his veteran teammates. Sometimes too much so, in fact. If he had a shortcoming in his initial season, it was the deference he showed to the older players. More often than not, Pitino had to prod the reluctant Mashburn to assert himself rather than remain hidden out of the spotlight.

It was evident from the first game that this was not simply an extension of last year's rebuilding team. The club was formidable in every respect. Pitino's complex system was now fully in place, and the players finally had a firm grasp on what he was attempting to do. The press could be devastating, while the offense, with its constant motion, back-door cuts and that "extra pass" Pitino wanted, consistently puzzled opposing defenses. The strength and conditioning program also paid big dividends, transforming the players into believers that the game's final five minutes belonged to them.

It only took five games for this team to show just how good it was and how far Pitino had advanced the program in a single year. After Hanson scored 15 in an easy 85-62 over Penn, the Cats showed their great mental toughness by hanging on down the stretch for a 75-71 win at Cincinnati, the first of their nine wins away from Rupp Arena. Hanson again topped UK with 20 points. Mashburn finished with 18 and Brassow added 12.

Farmer scored 19, Hanson 17 and Pelphrey 15 as

the Cats overcame a five-point halftime deficit to beat Notre Dame 98-90 in Indianapolis.

But it was in Game 4 that all lingering doubts about the state of the program were forever laid to rest. The Cats, sparked by Woods' 25-point, eight-assist performance, rolled to an 88-71 win over Kansas. That's an incredible 72-point turnaround from the previous year's 150-95 loss to Roy Williams' club. Once again, the Cats' conditioning and mental toughness were the difference. With the Cats leading 63-62, Mashburn connected on two straight jumpers to ignite a 19-0 run that broke the game open. Mashburn and Hanson each had 15, while Pelphrey chipped in with 12.

Although Game 5 resulted in a disappointing 84-81 to North Carolina in Chapel Hill (the Cats blew an 81-77 lead), it once again proved how far the program had traveled. The Tar Heels, remember, had easily handled UK 121-110 in Freedom Hall during Pitino's first season; in this squeaker, they had to score the final seven points to get the victory. Pelphrey paced UK with 24 points. Pete Chilcutt, Rick Fox and King Rice each had 14 for North Carolina, which shot 32 free throws to UK's 11.

The North Carolina game showed something else as well — Pitino's teams were no longer fair game on the road. Throughout his final seven seasons at UK, Pitino's teams would enjoy amazing success in hostile environments.

The Cats finally got a breather, blasting Tennessee-Chattanooga 86-70. Pelphrey and Farmer led UK with 17 points apiece. Hanson had another strong game, scoring 13 points and pulling down 12 rebounds.

Indiana scored the game's final five points to slip past the Cats 87-84 in Bloomington.

Sean Woods split two defenders to score a bucket for the Wildcats. Woods was a tough-minded leader from his point-guard position.

Rick Pitino's off-beat sartorial attire poked fun at Alabama coach Wimp Sanderson's penchant for plaid coats. Celebrating the Cats' 79-73 victory are Jamal Mashburn, Richie Farmer, Sean Woods, Deron Feldhaus and John Pelphrey.

The Cats erased an 11-point second-half deficit, eventually drawing even at 82-82 on a Mashburn trey. But the Hoosiers, behind great efforts from Calbert Cheaney and Damon Bailey, dug in and held on for the win. Pelphrey topped UK with 21 points. Cheaney had 23 and Bailey 16 for Indiana.

After the loss at Indiana, the Cats ran off 10 straight wins to up their record to 16-2. That impressive streak began with wins over a pair of in-state schools — Western Kentucky and Eastern Kentucky. Farmer's 22 led the Cats past WKU 84-70, then Hanson had 27 in a 74-60 win over EKU.

Facing a third straight in-state club, the Cats knocked down 13 three-pointers in a 93-85 win over arch-rival Louisville in Freedom Hall. Four Cats hit double figures, topped by Woods with 20. Others included Brassow (18), Hanson (17) and Farmer (14). LaBradford Smith led all scorers with 26.

Two free throws each by Hanson and Mashburn inside the final five seconds lifted the Cats past Georgia 81-80 in their SEC opener. Pelphrey led UK with 21, while Mashburn had 17 points and 15 rebounds. Georgia's Litterial Green burned the Cats for 38.

Feldhaus and Hanson combined for 51 points, but it took a pair of three-pointers by walk-on Junior Braddy to help hold off fast-charging LSU and give the Cats a 93-80 win. The Cats owned a 49-32 advantage at the half, but LSU, keyed by Shaquille O'Neal's 28-point, 17-rebound performance, closed to within seven midway through the final 20 minutes. That's when Braddy nailed his back-to-back treys to put the momentum back in UK's corner. Braddy finished with eight points for the Cats.

Twenty-four points by Mashburn and a Rupp Arena record 23 steals enabled the Cats to waltz past Mississippi

State 89-70. Two late free throws by Woods and one by Hanson were enough to give UK a 78-74 win over Tennessee. Six Wildcats hit for double figures against the Vols, led by Hanson with 17. Tennessee's outstanding guard Allan Houston had 20 points in a losing effort.

On the night the Gulf War began, the Cats, behind Pelphrey's 29-point performance, beat Ole Miss 95-85 in Oxford. Three nights later, the Cats, after receiving a scathing halftime sermon from Pitino ("a typical chalk-throwing extravaganza," Pelphrey called it), came from behind to beat Vanderbilt 58-50. Mashburn's 17 led the Cats, whose 19-point first-half output prompted Pitino's reprimand.

A marvelous performance by Brassow (15 points, 10 rebounds, four steals) highlighted the Cats' 10th consecutive victory, an 81-65 win over Florida. But Brassow wasn't the only Wildcat to shine against the Gators. Woods had 18 points, Pelphrey had 14 and Hanson finished with 10 points and 14 rebounds.

Alabama ended the Cats' run by scoring an 88-83 win in Tuscaloosa. Melvin Cheatum and James Robinson inflicted most of the damage, finishing with 26 and 21 points, respectively. Pelphrey had a game-best 28 for UK.

The Cats escaped a second-straight loss, edging past Auburn 89-81. After trailing most of the way, the Cats took the lead for good at 80-78 on a pair of Pelphrey freebies with 1:53 remaining. Pelphrey then intercepted a pass and got the ball to Brassow, who drained a three-pointer that put away the Tigers. Feldhaus paced UK with 17 points. Wesley Person led Auburn with 22.

The combination of overwhelming defense and a record-shattering performance by Mashburn resulted in a 96-84 Wildcat win over talented and dangerous Georgia. Mashburn hit for 31 points, the most-ever by a UK freshman. (Rick Robey held the old record with 28.) But it was the Wildcats' defense that made the difference in this game. The Cats blocked 16 shots and held Georgia to just 39 percent shooting from the field.

The worm turned in the Cats' next outing, a 107-88 loss to LSU. In this game, the Cats were done in by Arctic-like 29.2 percent shooting (including eight of 40 from three-point range) and a porous defense that was unable to shut down the Tigers (67.2 percent shooting) or O'Neal (33 points).

After dropping an 83-82 decision at Mississippi State, the Cats bounced back to beat Tennessee 85-74 and Ole Miss 89-77. Hanson had 28 in the win over the Vols, Farmer's 21 led the way against the Rebels.

In a game Pitino would never forget, and one in which he was ejected, the Cats lost to Vanderbilt 98-87 in Nashville despite having 11 more field goals than their hosts. What angered Pitino (and led to his early exit) was Vandy's huge advantage at the free throw stripe. The Commodores hit 40 of 51 freebies to UK's four of seven. Pitino would later say, "That's the greatest discrepancy I've ever seen since I've been a coach." Farmer scored 19 to lead the Cats.

Back-to-back treys by Brassow and Feldhaus broke a 59-59 deadlock and sent the Cats on their way to a 90-74 win at Florida. Pelphrey had 24 against the Gators, while Feldhaus added 18. The Cats followed that win by beating Alabama 79-73 in Rupp Arena. It was the 1,500th win in UK basketball history and victory No. 200 in Rupp Arena. Farmer was UK's leading scorer with 16.

With a 13-4 SEC record going into the season finale against Auburn in Rupp Arena, the Cats needed a victory to insure the best record in league action. Although banned from postseason play, or from being listed as the "official" SEC champion, a victory over the Tigers would seal the deal as to who was the league's best team on the court.

As 24,310 fans looked on, the Cats turned in their most-powerful performance of the season, ripping Auburn 114-93 to lay claim to the SEC's best record. UK, which led 65-43 at intermission, bombed the Tigers from three-point range, making good on 16 of 34 attempts. Six Wildcats scored in double figures, led by Mashburn with 21 and Farmer with 20. Brassow had 13, Pelphrey 12, Hanson and Braddy 11 each.

That win gave UK a 22-6 record overall and a 14-4 mark against SEC foes.

Following the game, the UK players and coaches celebrated by cutting down the nets. After a huge banner proclaiming "SEC #1, 1991" was unfurled and paraded onto the court, athletics director C.M. Newton announced that the team would be honored with a downtown parade.

The good times were back, and with all the principal players set to return, and with NCAA sanctions now a fading memory, UK was once again a major player in the world of college hoops. But even the most optimistic Big Blue fan wouldn't have dared to imagine what lay ahead. On the horizon was yet another magnificent season, one that included what many consider to be the greatest college basketball game of all-time.

John Pelphrey listens as Rick Pitino lays down the law. The cerebral Pelphrey was a foxy player who used his great basketball IQ to consistently beat more talented opponents.

1991-92

Pitino's first two teams had not only brought the fun back for UK fans, they had also overachieved far beyond anyone's wildest expectations. Even Pitino, never one to lack for confidence, admitted surprise at how well those two teams had performed.

But the talent on those two clubs, particularly the second one, has always been underrated. True, with few exceptions, they weren't blessed with great speed, quickness or athleticism. What those players did have, however, and what allowed them to overachieve, were extremely high basketball IQs. Hanson, Pelphrey, Mashburn, Feldhaus, Woods, Farmer, Brassow and Braddy were the equivalent of basketball intellectuals. They understood the game, and it was that understanding, combined with determination, savvy and heart, that enabled them to consistently beat more talented teams.

UK's surprising on-court success didn't alleviate the one major problem area still facing Pitino — recruiting. The top prep players were still reluctant to sign on with the Cats. Despite the lingering effects of the NCAA sanctions, and the negative image of UK projected by opposing recruiters, Pitino still managed to bring in five new faces, freshmen Chris Harrison, Aminu Timberlake and Andre Riddick, JUCO Dale Brown and Travis Ford, a transfer from Missouri now eligible after sitting out the previous season.

The true miracle of Pitino's first two teams is that they were able to overachieve despite such a manpower shortage.

In two seasons, nine players had logged more than 90 percent of the playing time for the Cats. That situation, Pitino hoped, would be rectified to a certain degree by the incoming four players. Even with Hanson having graduated, the additional bodies meant the Cats would have a deeper bench.

But it didn't turn out that way. Brassow was lost for the season after playing only two games, and of the four eligible rookies, only Brown would make a noticeable contribution. Given the circumstances, the schedule and on-going personnel shortcomings, what this team achieved not only rivals but surpasses the accomplishments of Pitino's first two Wildcat squads.

The season began on a rocky note. After disposing of West Virginia 106-80 in the preseason NIT, the Cats turned in a clunker of a performance in their second-round 85-67 loss to Pittsburgh in Rupp Arena. In that nightmare outing, the Cats' defense was a virtual no-show. Pitt consistently shredded UK's press, scored at will on the inside and shot 52 percent from the field. Pitt center Darren Morningstar did the most damage with 27 points. Mashburn's 26 led UK.

The Cats, still shell-shocked by the dismal effort against Pittsburgh, were dealt an even more severe blow — the gutsy, dependable Brassow was out for the season. Brassow, who had 23 points in the opener, suffered a torn ACL that required major reconstructive surgery. His absence was certain to be felt on both ends of the court. Offensively, he was a zone-buster and a terrific clutch player. Defensively, he was a Tasmanian devil type whose constant motion made him particularly effective on the press.

With the situation suddenly very dicey, Mashburn stepped up and personally began to carry the team on his broad shoulders. He had 28 points and 10 rebounds in a 90-69 win over UMass, then followed that with a 21-point performance that helped UK ring up a 76-74 upset of ninth-ranked Indiana in Indianapolis. In the Cats' next two games, easy wins over SW Texas State (82-36) and More-head State (101-84), Mashburn scored 42 points, giving him 91 in this four-game stretch.

Although Mashburn was the hottest Cat, he wasn't the only one to take his game to a higher level. Farmer scored 22 against UMass, Feldhaus had 19 against Indiana and Pelphrey tallied 18 in the win over Morehead.

Newcomer Brown made his first significant contribution in the Cats' 94-68 win over Arizona State. The 6'2" Brown buried six three-pointers and finished with 24 points. Mashburn had 16 for the Cats, who hit 37 of 61 shots for 61 percent.

Georgia Tech built a 20-point second-half lead, then held off the Cats down the stretch for a thrilling 81-80 victory in the Kuppenheimer Classic. Brown again paced the Cats with 21 points. Jon Berry led the Yellow Jackets with 24. One person who missed the furious finish was Pitino. The fiery UK coach, upset with the officiating, was ejected in the second half.

Mashburn hit for 23 and Pelphrey added 14 as the Cats beat stubborn Ohio University 73-63 to begin an impressive eight-game winning streak. Eleven three-pointers, 54-percent shooting and a combined 51 points from Pelphrey and Mashburn were enough to put away Louisville 103-89. Pelphrey scored 26 and Mashburn had 25 for the Cats. Greg Minor led Louisville with 18.

It was the irrepressible Farmer who shot holes in Notre Dame's defense, hitting five treys and scoring 28 points in an easy 91-70 UK win. Mashburn gave another monster performance in the Cats' 80-63 win at South Carolina. Mashburn ended the night with 33 points and 11 rebounds.

Feldhaus and Braddy came off the bench to score 15 points each to help the Cats beat Georgia 78-66 for their fifth straight win. UK's blitzkrieg defense also played a big role in that important SEC victory. The Cats forced

16 turnovers and held Georgia to 33-percent shooting from the field.

Mashburn tossed in 18 points and Ford handed out eight assists in an 81-60 romp past Florida. The Cats, behind Mashburn's 21 points and 15 rebounds, topped Vanderbilt 84-71 to snap a four-game losing streak in Music City. With 11 different players scoring, led by Mashburn with 18, the Cats made it eight straight by winning an 85-55 laugher over outgunned Eastern Kentucky.

One mark of Pitino's UK teams was their ability to bounce back from a loss. The concept of a prolonged slump simply didn't exist. Amazingly, only four times in his final seven years did the Wildcats lose back-to-back games.

The first of those four occasions came in successive losses to Tennessee and Arkansas. The Vols rode 56-percent shooting and a 36-point performance by Allan Houston to a convincing 107-85 win in Knoxville. SEC newcomer Arkansas, with

Richie Farmer came to UK after a record-breaking prep career at Clay County High School. Farmer typified the on-court intelligence and never-say-die attitude of Pitino's early UK teams.

its "40 minutes of hell," marched into Rupp Arena and whipped the Cats 105-88 in the first of many legendary battles between the two teams. Lee Mayberry led the Hogs with 23 points. Pelphrey and Feldhaus each had 22 for the Cats, while Mashburn was held to a season-low four points.

The Cats split their next two games, beating Ole Miss 96-78 at home, then getting drubbed by LSU 74-53 in Baton Rouge. In that game, the unstoppable O'Neal had 20 points and 20 rebounds.

The Cats snapped back to win their next seven games and eight of their final nine in the regular season to finish with a 23-6 record overall and a 12-4 mark in SEC action. The lone blemish was a 69-62 loss at Florida. UK's victims included Auburn 85-67, Alabama 107-83, Western Kentucky 93-83, Mississippi State 89-84, Georgia 84-73, South Carolina 74-56, Vanderbilt 80-56 and Tennessee 99-88.

That stretch featured a host of outstanding team and individual performances. Gimel Martinez, in his two best games of the season, scored 17 against Auburn, then came back with 26 points and 10 rebounds

Gimel Martinez followed a 17-point performance against Auburn with a 26-point, 10-rebound effort in a win over Alabama.

against Alabama. Mashburn scored 34 against Vandy, 30 against Tennessee and 26 against WKU and Georgia. Brown hit all seven of his shots, including four treys, and had 18 points in the win over Georgia. Feldhaus accounted for 55 points in wins over WKU, Mississippi State and South Carolina. And the Cats burned up the outside with 12 three-pointers against both Alabama and Tennessee.

The Cats opened SEC tourney play by demolishing Vanderbilt 76-57. Mashburn led the destruction with 24

points and 10 rebounds. Farmer and Woods chipped in with 10 points each.

Pelphrey scored 17, Martinez added 14 and Ford drilled three big treys as the Cats put away Shaq-less LSU 80-74 in semifinal action. O'Neal was suspended for fighting in his club's opening-round game. Without his presence in the middle, LSU was unable to make it three straight wins over the Cats. Justin Anderson had 21 for LSU.

In the title game against Alabama, the Cats, after trailing 32-29 at the break, gave a text book exhibition of basketball during the final 20 minutes to claim the crown with an 80-54 win. Mashburn, the tourney MVP, had 28 points and 13 rebounds, while the rejuvenated Martinez scored 12.

The Cats continued their dazzling play in the NCAA East Regional at Worcester, Mass., beating Old Dominion 88-69 and Iowa State 106-98. Pelphrey was superb in those two wins, accounting for 42 points. Mashburn had 27 against Iowa State, which was led by the high-scoring backcourt duo of Justus Thigpen and Ron Bayless. They combined for 62 points to help keep Iowa State in the game.

Philadelphia was the site of the East Regional final and a rematch with UMass. Behind hot shooting by Mashburn and Pelphrey, the Cats built a 50-42 lead by intermission. UMass refused to cave in, and appeared to be on the verge of making a serious run at the Cats when coach John Calipari was hit with a questionable technical with 5:47 left to play. That call provided a big lift for the Cats, who pulled away for an 87-77 win. Mashburn paced UK with 30 points. Pelphrey finished with 18. Jim McCoy led UMass with 21.

Jamal Mashburn yanks down a rebound as Duke's Christian Laettner and John Pelphrey look on. Laettner's last-second bucket gave Duke a 104-103 overtime win in what many have called the greatest college basketball game ever played.

to eyeball with the top-ranked Blue Devils, trading punch for punch, matching bucket for bucket. It was an epic battle, a game for the ages.

Duke, pushed to the edge of defeat, prevailed 104-103 in overtime when Christian Laettner nailed a turnaround 17-foot jumper just as the final horn sounded. It was Laettner's 10th field goal in 10 tries. He also hit all 10 of his free throws to finish with 31 points. It took nothing less than perfection to finally put away the Wildcats.

The Cats had their share of heroes as well, with none standing taller than Woods, who finished with 21 points, including two on a bold in-your-face 13-footer over Laettner that put the Cats in front 103-102 with 2.1 seconds remaining. Mashburn led the Cats with 28 points, while Brown and Pelphrey added in 18 and 16, respectively.

The loss left UK with a final record of 29-7. Mashburn's 21.3 average was the best by a Wildcat since Kenny Walker scored at a 22.9 clip in the 1984-85 season. Mashburn also led the team in field goal percentage (56.7) and rebounds (7.8). His efforts earned him All-SEC honors for a second straight year.

Incredibly, UK, only one year removed from basketball purgatory, was now a single victory away from reaching the Final Four. But standing in the way was powerful Duke, the defending national champ and a heavy favorite to repeat. Most experts predicted a Duke blowout. The Blue Devils had too many weapons, too much tournament experience. But the gritty Wildcats would have no part of the experts' blowout scenario. For 45 minutes they stood eyeball

But at the heart of this club, which became known as "The Unforgettables," were the four seniors — Pelphrey, Woods, Feldhaus and Farmer. All had acquitted themselves well in their final season. Pelphrey ended his career with 1,257 points. Feldhaus had 1,231. Woods handed out 482 assists, fourth best in UK history. Farmer's 83.8 career free throw percentage ranks him fourth behind Kyle Macy, Travis Ford and Jim Master.

Statistics and career numbers can never accurately measure the contribution these four players made to the UK

program. They chose to stay at UK at a time when it would have been easy to jump ship. During those dark days, when UK basketball was at its lowest ebb, few would have blamed them if they had opted to go elsewhere. Their willingness to stay, to tough it out, to bear the sins of others was the foundation upon which Pitino was able to rebuild the shattered UK basketball program.

During a postseason ceremony in which the four players had their jerseys retired, C.M. Newton offered his own praise: "Today, our program is back on top, due largely to four young men who persevered, who weathered the hard times, and who brought the good times back to Kentucky basketball. Their contributions to UK basketball cannot be measured in statistics or record books."

1992-93

Winning, more than anything else, is the quickest cure for athletic ills. Put enough marks in the W column and everyone pays attention. Nowhere is that more evident — or more important — than in the area of recruiting. Players gravitate toward programs that are winners. That's why the University of Kentucky has had so little trouble attracting great players throughout its rich basketball history.

In his first three years at UK, Pitino's recruiting had met with mixed success. There were hits (Mashburn, Brassow, Martinez), misses (Toomer, Timberlake), strikeouts (the often-injured Henry Thomas) and question marks (Harrison, Riddick). In addition, there had been a pair of transfers (Ford, Brown) and a gritty walk-on (Braddy) whose timely arrival at UK couldn't have come at a more opportune time.

But Pitino's luck was about to change. Thanks to three

New Jersey native Rodrick Rhodes was considered the jewel in a talented freshman class that included Tony Delk, Walter McCarty and Jared Prickett. Rhodes got off to a fast start, scoring 43 points in his first two games.

overachieving teams that put the UK basketball program back into the prime-time spotlight, Pitino was able to get what he desperately needed — a super recruiting class that could step in and offset the loss of Pelphrey, Woods, Feldhaus and Farmer.

Rodrick Rhodes, Tony Delk, Jared Prickett and Walter McCarty, impressed by what Pitino had done and by the style his teams played, were quick to sign on with UK. So was Rodney Dent, a JUCO from Texas. Finally, Pitino had what he needed — a group of players with the athleticism and quickness so necessary to making his system successful.

It was a diverse group. Delk, a shooter with unlimited range, once cracked the 70-point mark in a high school game; Prickett was a rugged rebounder and defender; McCarty, who would sit out his first season because of Proposition 48, was a big man who had small-guard quickness; Dent was a 6'10" wide-body who could score and defend in the paint.

But without question, Rhodes was the jewel of this group. He was 6'6", wiry, strong, quick and athletic. He'd been a prep All-American while playing for Bob Hurley at St. Anthony's High School in Jersey City, N.J. Every college coach in America coveted Rhodes, who was seen as a can't-miss All-American and future NBA star. Pitino prevailed in the intense recruiting war for Rhodes, but it was a victory with mixed results. Although Rhodes had his shining moments as a Wildcat, his career at UK — and his relationship with Pitino — was often rocky and troubled. Indeed, Rhodes would be long gone by the time classmates Delk, McCarty and Prickett experienced the joy of winning a national championship.

Rhodes got off to an All-American start, scoring 43

points in his first two games. He and Ford each scored 16 in the Cats' 81-65 win over Wright State in the opener. Dent also made his presence felt, scoring 14 points and pulling down 12 rebounds in his debut effort.

Rhodes and Mashburn each had 27 points and Brassow added 14 as the fifth-ranked Cats handed 13th-ranked Georgia Tech a 96-87 defeat. In their next outing, the Cats, behind Mashburn's 38-point, 19-rebound performance, came from behind to beat upset-minded Eastern Kentucky 82-73. Trailing 73-72 with 2:21 remaining, the Cats closed in a rush, scoring the game's final 10 points, including six on a pair of Brassow treys, to hold off the Colonels.

Against ninth-ranked Louisville, the Cats, after falling behind 30-20, rallied to post an easy 88-68 victory in Freedom Hall. Fifty-five percent shooting enabled the Cats to wipe out the 10-point deficit and eventually build a 27-point advantage of their own in the second half. Mashburn led the Cats with 27. Rhodes had 20, while Martinez came off the bench to score 14.

Mashburn scored 50 points in the Cats next two games, a 108-65 win over Morehead State and a 65-49 win over Miami of Ohio. Mashburn also led the Cats with 22 points in their 89-67 win over Rutgers in the ECAC Holiday Festival at Madison Square Garden. The Cats, fueled by Rhodes' 23 points, beat St. John's 86-77 to capture the title. Rhodes was named the tourney's MVP. Martinez gave another strong performance off the bench, scoring 15 points against the Redmen.

Ford's sensational outside shooting was enough to help the Cats hold off Indiana 81-78 in Freedom Hall. Ford made good on 10 of 15 shots, including seven of 10 from three-point range, to finish with 29 points. It was a pair of Ford treys and one by Mashburn that put the Cats in front for good at 77-74. Mashburn, Calbert Cheaney and Matt Nover all scored 29 points apiece to tie Ford for game-high honors.

The Cats opened SEC action by beating Georgia 74-59 and Tennessee 84-70. Mashburn had 26 against the Bulldogs, who coughed up the ball 27 times against the relentless UK press. Brown scored 23 and Mashburn had 21 in the win over the Volunteers.

With an 11-0 record, the Cats were voted the No. 1 team in the country. It was the first times since 1988 that UK held the top spot in the national rankings.

Thanks to a blistering performance by Vanderbilt, UK's stay at the top proved to be brief. The Commodores shot 63.3 percent (31 of 49) and easily knocked off the top-

Rodney Dent goes above the shooter, teammate Travis Ford and the basket to challenge a shot. Dent, a JUCO transfer, gave the Wildcats an intimidating inside presence.

ranked Cats 101-86. Billy McCaffrey had 22 points and 14 assists for Vandy. Rhodes and Ford led UK with 19 and 18 points, respectively.

With Mashburn scoring 24, the Cats beat Alabama 73-59 to begin a six-game winning streak in which the average margin of victory was 23 points. Other UK victims included South Carolina 108-82, LSU 105-67, Florida 71-48, Mississippi State 87-63 and Vanderbilt 82-67. Mashburn led the Cats in three of those five victories, scoring 27 against LSU, 22 against Florida and 17 against Vandy. Rhodes and Dent each had 17 in the win over South Carolina, while Ford hit for 21 against Mississippi State.

Arkansas' stifling defense and the clutch play of Corliss Williamson and Robert Shepherd were enough to lift the

Travis Ford loosens up before a game. His superb play in the SEC Tournament earned him the first of his two MVP honors.

Razorbacks past UK 101-94 in Fayetteville. The Cats shot just 42.5 percent from the field and had 21 turnovers. Williamson had 22 to lead Arkansas. Shepherd finished with 20. Mashburn and Ford each had 20 for the Cats, who also benefited from a strong 16-point, 13-rebound performance by Prickett.

Mashburn scored 22 in an 81-62 win over Notre Dame, then Delk, in his best performance of the season, knocked down four treys and finished with a team-high 18 points to lead the Cats past South Carolina 87-66. Mashburn's 30 points and 14 rebounds enabled the Cats to win their third straight, an easy 86-70 win over Georgia.

A bizarre game-winning three-point play in the final seconds decided the outcome in the Cats' disappointing 78-77 loss to Tennessee in Knoxville. With his team trailing 77-74, Allan Houston hit the first of two free throws, then intentionally missed the second. The Vols claimed the rebound, shot and missed. But Corey Allen rebounded, layed in the bucket and drew a foul on the play. He then dropped in the free throw to give the Vols their miraculous comeback victory. Houston led all scorers with 27 points.

Mashburn had 26 for UK and Ford added 22.

Rhodes saved the Cats from a second straight setback by sinking a game-winning jump shot with three seconds left in an 80-78 win over Auburn. Mashburn paced the Cats with 22 points. Wesley Person had 24 for the Tigers. After the game, Mashburn announced his decision to enter the NBA draft at the end of the season.

The Cats closed out the regular season by beating Ole Miss 98-66 and Florida 85-77. Mashburn had 22 against the Rebels, while Ford's 23 led the way in the win over Florida.

Ford continued his brilliant play in the SEC tourney, earning MVP honors after connecting on 14 of 22 three-pointers in UK's three wins. The Cats were equally brilliant, opening tourney play with a dominant 101-40 blowout of Tennessee. The Cats raced to a 14-0 lead and were leading 41-17 at the half against a bewildered Tennessee club that committed 30 turnovers. Seven Wildcats scored in double figures, led by Delk with 15.

The Cats bolted to a 17-0 lead against Arkansas in semifinal action, then had to hold on down the stretch for a 92-81 victory. Ford hit six of seven three-point attempts and finished with 26 points for UK. Mashburn had 23 and Brown added 12.

In the title game, Ford scored 18 points (all on treys) and Mashburn had 17 as the Cats beat LSU 82-65 to capture their second consecutive SEC tourney crown. Riddick and Brown also hit double digits with 15 and 11, respectively.

The Cats had no trouble in their two NCAA Tournament Southeast Regional games in Nashville, beating Rider 96-52 and Utah 83-62. The Cats shot 60 percent against Rider and 54 percent against Utah, a team they would

face — and conquer — four times in NCAA Tournament action during the 1990s. Mashburn had 36 points in those two easy UK wins.

UK continued to sizzle from the outside, hitting 16 of 24 three-point attempts in a 103-69 win over Wake Forest. The Cats, behind Ford's 10 of 11 shooting, built a 60-26 halftime lead and were never threatened. Ford ended the night with 26 points to lead all scorers. Mashburn tossed in 23 and Brown added 16.

A strong performance by Prickett (22 points, 11 rebounds) and a 12-2 spurt early in the second half were enough to shoot the Cats past Florida State 106-81 and into their first Final Four appearance since 1984. Prickett received solid support from Ford, who finished with 19 points. Other Cats in double figures included Mashburn and Brown with 12 each and Martinez with 10. Bobby Sura had 17 for Florida State.

UK's foe in the Final Four semifinal game was Michigan and its fabled "Fab Five." The Wolverines, led by Chris Webber and Jalen Rose, were in front 40-35 at the intermission. But the Cats, despite poor shooting (41 percent) and the loss of Brown to an injury with more than six minutes remaining, battled back to tie the score at 71-71 and send the game into overtime.

Even though Mashburn fouled out with 3:23 left, the Cats were in a position to pull off the win. When Delk sank a pair of free throws, the Cats owned a 78-75 lead with less than a minute remaining.

Then the bottom fell out for UK. Ray Jackson hit a four-foot jumper to make it 78-77. Seconds later, Webber scored on a layup to give Michigan a one-point lead. When the Cats had no answer, Rose sealed the outcome by dropping in two free throws.

Mashburn scored 26 points in his final game as a Wildcat, giving him 1,843 for his career. Brown had 16 before going down with his injury and Ford had 12. Webber had 27 points and 13 rebounds for Michigan. Rose finished with 18.

UK ended the season with a final record of 30-4. It was UK's first 30-win season since 1985-86.

In just four years, and in only the second year off probation, Pitino had taken the Wildcats to the Final Four. They won their second straight SEC tourney title, reached No. 1 in the country and finished with a No. 2 ranking in the final polls.

Kentucky basketball was back.

Jeff Brassow was a fearless player in clutch situations. His acrobatic tip-in at the buzzer gave the Cats a 93-92 win over unbeaten Arizona in the Maui Classic championship game.

1993-94

Expectations were sky-high for this UK team, which entered the season ranked as the No. 1 team in the country. The pollsters weren't going too far out on a limb by tabbing the Cats as the team to beat. Even though Mashburn and Brown were gone, UK was deep, talented, experienced and athletic. It was a team with definite national championship potential.

Much was also expected of Rhodes, now a sophomore with a full season under his belt. The talented, versatile Rhodes was being counted on by Pitino to step up and fill Mashburn's shoes. But Rhodes and Pitino were never a comfortable match, and by season's end, the rift between them was deep and obvious.

Rhodes' inconsistent play, along with a career-threatening knee injury to Dent only 11 games into the season, hurt this club's chances of living up to its preseason hype. Although the Cats finished with a fine 27-7 record and won a third straight SEC Tournament championship, it was an unsatisfying season that left a bitter aftertaste.

Rhodes and Dent were joined in the opening-night lineup by Prickett, Delk and Ford. Reserves included veterans Brassow, Martinez, Riddick and Harrison. Newcomers included McCarty, now academically eligible, and a pair of freshmen — Jeff Sheppard and Anthony Epps — who would leave their names in the UK record books.

Delk scored 19 points, grabbed 10 rebounds and had five assists to lead the Cats past Louisville 78-70 in the opener. Riddick contributed 15 points and Ford added 14. Clifford Rozier had 29 points and 13 rebounds for the Cardinals.

After Rhodes scored 21 points in an easy 115-77 rout of Texas Tech, the top-ranked Cats were upended by Indiana 96-84. The Hoosier defense held the Cats to 35 percent shooting from the field, including just nine of 33 from three-point range. Damon Bailey led IU with 29 points. Ford topped the Cats with 20.

The Cats took out their anger on a pair of in-state rivals, beating Eastern Kentucky 107-78 and Morehead State 99-61. Six Cats scored in double figures against the Colonels, led by Dent with 16. Ford finished with 12 points, while setting the UK mark for most assists in a game with 15. Dent also led the Cats against Morehead, tossing in 24 points. In those two wins, the Cats outrebounded their opponents 103-60.

In the Maui Classic, Ford once again showed that tournament time was Travis time. He walked off with the MVP trophy, scoring 52 points in the final two games, and the Cats came away as tourney champs.

The Cats opened with an easy 86-61 win over Texas. Delk led a balanced UK attack with 15 points. Prickett

Rick Pitino welcomes Rodrick Rhodes to the bench during the final moments of a UK victory. The relationship between player and coach wasn't always so cordial.

had 14, Martinez 12 and Dent 11.

Ford and Delk nailed seven treys and combined for 50 points in the Cats' 100-88 semifinal win over Ohio State. Ford had 27 and Delk 23 for UK. Derek Anderson, soon to be a familiar face to Big Blue fans, paced the Buckeyes with 23.

Ford came back to score 25 in the title game, but the real hero was Brassow, whose acrobatic tip-in at the buzzer lifted the Cats to a 93-92 victory over unbeaten Arizona. Brassow reached back, grabbed Rhodes' errant three-point attempt and somehow managed to guide the ball into the bucket. Delk and Prickett had 18 and 16 points, respectively, while Brassow's game-winning basket gave him six for the night. Arizona was led by its great backcourt duo of Khalid Reeves and Damon Stoudamire, who combined for 59 points.

Two strong performances by Sheppard helped the Cats close out their pre-SEC schedule with wins over San Francisco (110-83) and Robert Morris (92-67). Sheppard scored 31 points in those wins, including a game-high 18 against Robert Morris. Ford had 27 and Rhodes 20 against the Dons.

Hot-shooting UK opened SEC play by smacking Vanderbilt 107-82 in Rupp Arena. The Cats shot 60 percent from the field and had double-digit scoring from five players, including Rhodes with 20 and Delk with 18. It was an impressive — but costly — win. Less than four minutes into the game, Dent went down with his season-ending knee injury.

With Dent on the sidelines, Riddick and Martinez would split the pivot duties for the rest of the season. Both performed admirably, but without Dent's wide-body presence in the middle, the Cats were never the same team.

The Cats kicked off the post-Dent era by ripping turn-

over-prone Notre Dame 84-59. In all, the Irish turned the ball over 34 times against UK's pressure defense. Delk led the Cats with 16 points, while Martinez added 14.

It was after UK's 94-90 overtime loss at Georgia that the rift between Pitino and Rhodes first became public. Pitino benched Rhodes for the final 15 minutes after Rhodes was hit with a technical for swearing at a Georgia player. Then, following the game, Pitino vented his anger and frustration, saying, "I'm fed up with him."

No doubt adding to Pitino's unhappy mood was UK's horrendous free throw shooting. The Cats hit just 12 of 30 freebies. Delk scored 27 points in a losing cause. Charles Claxton had 21 to lead Georgia.

McCarty made the most of his first start, scoring 24 points in a 98-64 win over Ole Miss. Rhodes, benched after the Georgia game, and Prickett each had 18.

Rhodes again came off the bench to give another strong performance, hitting for 22 points and pulling down 10 rebounds to lead the Cats past Tennessee 93-74. Delk paced UK with 23 points.

Dent's absence was keenly felt in the Cats' 59-57 loss at Florida. Without Dent's help on the boards, UK was outrebounded 51-39. Gator center Andrew DeClercq had 20 of the Gators' rebounds.

In what Pitino called "our most-important game outside of the (NCAA) Tournament in four-and-a-half years," the Cats overcame a four-point halftime deficit to beat Mississippi State 86-70 and snap a two-game losing streak on the road. The Cats trailed 38-34 at intermission, but took command early in the second half against a Bulldog team

that came out of the dressing room firing blanks. The Bulldogs missed their first eight shots in the second half. Ford scored 17 points to lead UK.

Brassow buried six treys and had 25 points as the Cats beat South Carolina 79-67. Prickett turned in a double-double performance with 10 points and 17 rebounds.

The Cats upped their winning streak to five by beating Auburn 91-74, Alabama 82-67 and UMass 67-64. Delk accounted for 62 points in those three wins, while Prickett had a second double-double (17 points, 15 rebounds) against UMass.

Arkansas, behind 20 second-half points from Scotty Thurman, roared from behind to knock off the Cats 90-82 in Rupp Arena. Thurman led all scorers with 26 points, including 10 in the final 6:35. Rhodes paced the Cats with 22. Prickett gave another marvelous effort, scoring 11 points and hauling down 20 rebounds.

UK dropped its second straight game, losing 93-85 at Syracuse. Adrian Autry had 30 for the Orangemen, who hit 36 of 60 from the field for 60 percent. Delk scored 27 to lead the Cats.

While Delk continued to shoot well, the usually reliable Ford was mired in a terrible shooting slump. In his last 11 games, the UK point guard had connected on just 24 of 83 shots for 28.9 percent.

A third-straight loss seemed inevitable when the Cats found themselves on the short end of a 68-37 score with 15:34 left to play at LSU. Tiger fans were ready for a Mardi Gras-type celebration, while back in the Bluegrass, the Big Blue faithful were turning off

Versatile Walter McCarty scores over a pair of defenders. McCarty's long-range bombing sparked the Cats' improbable 99-95 comeback win at LSU.

their TVs and radios. They shouldn't have. For what happened next will forever rank among the high points in UK basketball history.

Behind the three-point shooting of Brassow, Harrison and McCarty, the Cats staged a miraculous on-the-road comeback. Bucket by bucket, the Cats cut into LSU's rapidly vanishing lead, and when McCarty nailed a trey with 19 seconds left, they had taken a 96-95 lead. After LSU missed two chances to reclaim the lead, the Cats hit three free throws to ice the improbable comeback. In all, the Cats made 15 treys, including four by Brassow and two each by Harrison and McCarty. McCarty led UK with 23 points. Other Cats in double figures included Brassow (14), Martinez (13), Rhodes (11) and Ford (10). LSU got 36 points from Ronnie Henderson and 32 from Clarence Caesar.

Having slipped free of the hangman's noose, the rejuvenated Cats won their next four, beating Vanderbilt 77-69, Tennessee 77-73 (without the suspended trio of Ford, Prickett and Martinez), Georgia 80-59 and Florida 80-77.

None of those wins came easy. Ford snapped out of his shooting slump to score 22 points against Vanderbilt. At Tennessee, the Cats rallied from 14 down in the second half, then used clutch free throw shooting by Epps and Rhodes to hold on for the victory. It took an 18-0 run at the start of the second half to put away Georgia, and in the win over Florida, the Cats had to score on 11 of their final 13 possessions before the outcome was decided.

The Cats ended the regular season on a down tick, suffering a shocking 75-74 loss at South Carolina. Emmett Hall's layup with two seconds left was the difference. Hall had 20 points to lead South Carolina. Rhodes scored 24 for UK.

Rhodes wasn't in uniform for the Cats' SEC tourney

opening 95-76 victory over Mississippi State. Having once again run afoul of Pitino, Rhodes was hit with a one-game suspension. Brassow earned the starting nod and responded with a 19-point performance. Delk had 29 to lead all scorers.

Defense was the Cats' main weapon in their 90-78 semifinal win over Arkansas. The Cats held Arkansas to 32.1 percent shooting while limiting the All-American Williamson to just eight of 21 from the field. After the Razorbacks cut an early UK lead to 61-58, back-to-back buckets by Martinez keyed an 11-3 run that shifted the momentum back to the Wildcats. Delk paced UK with 16 points.

In the title game, the Cats faced a red-hot Florida club that was riding the sizzling outside shooting of guards Dan Cross and Craig Brown. They came into the championship game having connected on 13 of 19 three-pointers in two previous Gator victories.

But once again, UK's defense was dominant. The Cats claimed the championship with a 73-60 win, holding Cross and Brown to just two three-pointers in 11 attempts. Rhodes was the Cats' top scorer with 15 points. Delk and Brassow each had 13, while Ford, named the tourney MVP, added 10.

The Cats, fresh off their third consecutive SEC tourney title, were paired against Tennessee State in first-round NCAA Tournament action. The heavily favored Cats were expected to win easily, but the game turned out to be a tough struggle. After leading 25-24 at the half, the Cats eventually prevailed 83-70, thanks to a

Only a handful of Wildcats have had more pure talent than Antoine Walker. He may have been all cocky swagger on the outside, but inside beat the heart of an assassin.

Chris Harrison and Anthony Epps were all smiles after the Wildcats came from behind to beat Florida in Rupp Arena. Harrison's three-point shooting triggered the comeback.

standout 22-point performance by Riddick. Rhodes also tossed in 22 points for the victorious Wildcats.

Any hopes these Wildcats may have had about a second straight Final Four trip were quickly laid to rest by Marquette. The Warriors, taking advantage of a miserable effort by the Wildcats, built an early 42-24 lead then coasted to a 75-63 victory.

The Cats couldn't have played much worse, or been more uninspired. They shot just 31 percent from the field and were soundly whipped on the boards. Had it not been for Delk's 24-point performance, the outcome likely would have been worse.

It was a sudden and disappointing end to what had been a mixed-bag of a season. This was a team loaded with talent but lacking in chemistry. Delk was its leading scorer with a 16.6 average. Rhodes finished with a 14.6 scoring clip and Ford, in his final season, averaged 11.3.

1994-95

With the exception of Ford, Brassow and Martinez, all the principles were back from the previous season. With veterans Delk, Rhodes, Prickett, Riddick, McCarty, Epps, Sheppard and Harrison all returning, the Cats had talent and experience at every position. In addition, several new

faces ready were set to join the mix — freshmen Antoine Walker, Allen Edwards and Scott Padgett, transfer Mark Pope and walk-on Cameron Mills, the son of ex-Cat Terry Mills. And waiting in the wings was Derek Anderson, the talented Louisville native who was sitting out after transferring to UK from Ohio State.

Pitino was no longer grubbing for players; now he was stockpiling talent.

The incoming players were an intriguing group. Pope was cerebral, gritty and extremely hard working; Edwards had great versatility and an impeccable basketball pedigree (brothers Doug and Steve were standout college players); Padgett, the Louisville St. Xavier All-State performer, combined power forward ruggedness with a small forward's shooting touch.

But the rookie who was expected to make the most immediate impact was Walker, a 6'8" bundle of pure talent and athletic ability. Walker, a Chicago native, was Rodrick Rhodes with an outside shot. He could run, jump, score, pass, rebound and defend — and he did it all with a cocky swagger. The only thing Walker loved more than a camera was winning. Inside this hot dog beat the heart of an assassin.

Despite the depth and talent, this group of Wildcats again came up short in their quest for the national title. They strung together another excellent season — 28-5 record, No. 2 ranking in the final AP poll, SEC regular-season and tournament championships. They sailed through three NCAA Tournament games, giving high-caliber performances that left Mount St. Mary's, Tulane and Arizona State wondering what hit them. Then the magic vanished, and the Cats turned in an atrocious effort that eerily resembled the one they gave against Marquette a year earlier. The result was a loss to North Carolina. A second-straight season of high hopes ended in a disappointing and unsatisfying manner.

Rebounding and defense were at the heart of Jared Prickett's game. He played in 143 games as a Wildcat, missing the 1,000-point club by a single bucket.

With seven players scoring in double figures, the Cats began the season with a near-record 124-50 victory over UT-Martin. Prickett paced the Cats with 21 points. Delk finished with 17, Rhodes 16 and Walker 15 in his Wildcat debut. The 74-point margin was just three shy of UK's all-time record of 77 set in that 143-66 win over Georgia in 1956.

Some excellent clutch play by Rhodes inside the final minute enabled the Cats to slip past Ohio University 79-74 in their second outing. After the Cats saw a once-comfortable 14-point lead whittled down to one, Rhodes settled the issue by canning a free throw and a short jumper. McCarty

and Delk paced UK with 17 points each. Epps scored 15, while Pope fashioned his first double-double by giving an 11-point, 11-rebound performance.

Facing eventual NCAA champ UCLA in Anaheim, the Cats once again built a late lead, only to see it evaporate down the stretch. The Cats led 81-78 with 45 seconds left when UCLA center George Zidek scored on a hook shot. Following a UK turnover, McCarty was whistled for a controversial foul against J.R. Henderson with six-tenths of a second left on the clock. Henderson, a freshman, hit both free throws to give the Bruins an 82-81 win. All-American Ed O'Bannon was the game's top scorer with 26 points. Rhodes had 16 and Sheppard 14 for UK.

Against Indiana in Freedom Hall, it was the Cats' turn to rise from the coffin and emerge with a come-from-behind 73-70 win. Trailing 47-41, the Cats fought back to take a 70-69 lead on a three-point play by Delk. McCarty followed with a trey, then the UK defense did the rest, holding the Hoosiers to a single free throw in the final three minutes. McCarty had 16 to lead the Cats. Brian Evans and Neil Reed each scored 17 for Indiana.

After those two heart-stoppers, the Cats won their next three games with ease, beating Boston University 90-49, Texas Tech 83-68 and Marshall 116-75. Four different Cats led the team in scoring in those three victories. Delk and Walker scored 13 apiece against Boston University, Rhodes had 23 against Texas Tech and Sheppard ripped the Thundering Herd for 21.

Louisville turned the tables and used the Cats' chief weapon — the three-point shot — to post an 88-86 win in Freedom Hall. It was the Cards' first win over UK since 1989. DeJuan Wheat led the uprising, knocking down back-to-back treys to key a 14-2 run that wiped out a 54-49 UK lead and put the Cardinals in front for good. Wheat and UK's Delk shared scoring honors with 23 each.

Rhodes scored 23 and Delk added 18 as the Cats kicked off SEC action by blasting Auburn 98-64. They followed that by hitting 17 three-pointers in an easy 80-55 win at South Carolina. Delk and Sheppard led UK with 18 and 15 points, respectively, with all of their points coming from behind the three-point line. In all, only 10 UK buckets weren't three-pointers.

The Cats gave a terrific all-around performance in their 83-67 win over Florida. They hit 32 of 56 from the field for 57 percent, while holding the Gators to 18 of 52 for 34.6 percent. Rhodes and Delk each scored 17 for UK. Dan Cross had 21 to lead the Gators.

Pitino was less than pleased with his club's next effort, an 83-71 win over Georgia. Following the game, Pitino, upset at the lack of intensity, ordered his players back into the gym for a midnight practice. Delk's 17 paced UK.

The Cats ran their winning streak to seven by beating Ole Miss 82-65, Vanderbilt 81-68 and Tennessee 69-50. Free throws (33 of 42) were the difference in the win over Ole Miss. Rhodes led UK with 23 points, 16 from the charity stripe. A 20-0 second-half run, highlighted by McCarty's classic dunk over J.J. Lucas, sent the Cats past Vandy. Delk had 24 for UK in that win. Rhodes came through with a season-best 29 points against a Tennessee team that shot just 29.4 percent from the field and had 27 turnovers against the Wildcat defense.

In one of the most exciting games of the season, Arkansas won the battle of nerves and beat the Cats 94-92 in Fayetteville. A three-point bucket by Scotty Thurman with 11 seconds left put the Razorbacks in front 93-92. Following a UK miscue, Clint McDaniel hit one of two free throws to account for the final margin. Delk was splendid in defeat, scoring 31 points. Williamson had 28 to lead Arkansas, while Thurman added 22.

After Rhodes scored 19 points in a 90-72 win over South Carolina, the Cats stepped outside of league play to beat Syracuse 77-71 in Rupp Arena. The game was anything but an artistic masterpiece — neither team shot better than 42 percent while combining for 58 turnovers. It was close, however. With the two teams knotted at 60-60, Delk buried a trey and Sheppard hit a pair of free throws to ignite a 13-4 UK run that put the game away. Delk, who wasn't expected to play because of a shoulder injury, led the Cats with 16 points. McCarty followed with 15. Andrew Moten had a game-high 23 for the Orangemen.

Delk and Prickett combined for 34 points in a 68-48 win over Tennessee, then McCarty came through with 20 points, including 12 of his team's first 16, to lead the Cats

A glum Rick Pitino was dumbfounded by his team's performance during a 74-61 NCAA tourney loss to North Carolina. Pitino said his players were selfish and lacked a team-first attitude.

to a 97-58 drubbing of Notre Dame.

The Cats' inability to defend against the three-point shot resulted in their fourth setback of the season, a shocking 76-71 loss to Mississippi State in Rupp Arena. The Bulldogs, who shot a red-hot 57 percent from the field overall, connected on 11 of 21 three-pointers. Marcus Grant had 23 points to lead the Bulldogs. Delk's 16 paced the Cats.

With former heavyweight boxing champ Muhammad Ali sitting on the bench, the Cats prevailed 87-77 in a tough come-from-behind struggle against Florida. The Gators assumed control early, building an 11-point lead. But Harrison stroked a trey to trigger a 7-0 run that closed the difference to 40-33 by intermission. The second half saw 10 lead changes before a Prickett jumper put UK on top for good at 72-71. Rhodes had 23 to lead UK. Other Cats in double figures included Delk (19), Pope (14) and Harrison (11).

Rhodes scored 16 and McCarty and Delk each added

14 as the Cats sailed past Alabama 72-52 to improve their record to 19-4. Win No. 20 didn't come so easily. After falling behind Vandy 16-6, Pitino, angry at his team's porous defense, called a 20-second timeout and laced into his players with full vengeance. His message was duly noted — the Cats stormed back to beat Vandy 71-60. Delk led the UK comeback with 22 points.

Six Cats hit for double figures in a 97-74 win at Georgia. It was the worst home loss for Hugh Durham during his 17 years as the Bulldog coach. Delk again led the UK scoring parade with 16 points. Rhodes finished with 15, Riddick 14, Walker 11 and McCarty and Sheppard 10 each for the Cats.

In the season finale, the Cats used 20 of 35 three-point shooting to destroy LSU 127-80. Delk continued his hot shooting, scoring a game-high 27 points. Rhodes had 17, while Harrison, in his final home appearance, chipped in with 16. Epps also gave a standout performance, scoring 15 points and handing out 13 assists.

The Cats, 14-2 in league play, began defense of their SEC tourney title with a 93-81 win over Auburn. A 49-37 rebounding edge was the difference. McCarty and Pope each had a double-double for the Cats. McCarty had 22 points and 10 rebounds, while Pope finished with 19 points and 10 boards.

With Walker coming off the bench to score 21 points, the Cats rolled past Florida 86-72 in semifinal action. In all, the Cats got 55 points, 16 rebounds and 13 assists from the bench. Pope was second to Walker in scoring with 16 points. Cross had 24 for the Gators.

Walker scored 23 points and notched MVP honors after leading the Cats to a thrilling 95-93 overtime win over Arkansas in the title game. Twice, the Cats had to pull off their best Dracula act and come back from the dead. They trailed by 19 (35-16) in the first half and were down 91-82 with only 1:39 left in overtime. But just when it looked like the Cats had finally run out of miracles, a three-point play Walker and a Pope tip-in sliced the difference to 91-87. After McDaniel cashed in a pair of free throws, Delk knocked down a trey and Walker scored on the inside to make it 93-92. Epps then swiped the in-bounds pass, drew a foul, and dropped in two free throws to put UK in front 94-93. Following a Thurman miss, Delk hit one of two free throws to seal UK's fourth straight SEC tourney championship.

Delk ended the night with 15 points. Pope had 12 points and 10 rebounds. Williamson led Arkansas with

22 points.

UK, top-seeded in the Southeast Regional, opened NCAA Tournament play by bashing Mount St. Mary's 113-67. Delk led the onslaught with 20 points. McCarty had 17 points and 11 rebounds, while Prickett also hit double figures with 16 points.

An 18-0 Wildcat blitz turned an expected difficult challenge into a relatively easy 82-60 win over Tulane in second-round action. Six different Wildcats contributed during that crucial run. Rhodes snapped out of a scoring slump to lead the Cats with 14 points. Delk and Sheppard each contributed 11.

With Delk scoring 26 points on 11 of 18 shooting, the sizzling Cats rocked a good Arizona State team 97-73 in Birmingham. In giving one of their best performances of the season, the Cats shot 56 percent from the field and whipped the Sun Devils 40-32 on the boards. Rhodes, who connected on six of eight shots, had 16 points and eight assists. Riddick chipped in with 15 points and Walker picked off 10 rebounds. Ron Riley scored 20 for Arizona State.

Then disaster hit. In an Elite Eight match up between the two winningest programs in college basketball history, the Cats stunk up the joint, dropping a 74-61 decision to North Carolina. At no time during the game did the Cats even remotely resemble the team that came in riding the crest of an 11-game winning streak. Poor shot selection, failure to make the extra pass, not attacking the low post — these were the sins that lead to UK's downfall. The numbers told the story: UK hit 21 of 75 from the field (28 percent), seven of 36 from three-point range (19 percent) and were outrebounded 43-38.

Pitino's assessment? Selfishness on the part of his players.

"I'm dumbfounded by the way we played tonight," Pitino said. "We had a great team coming in here, and now we're going home as individuals."

Delk led the Cats with 19 points. Donald Williams and Jerry Stackhouse each scored 18 for the Tar Heels. Stackhouse also grabbed 12 rebounds.

With the season having come to a quick — and perplexing — end, the Cats could only watch as UCLA claimed another NCAA championship one week later. They could also begin thinking about the upcoming season, one that held tremendous promise. Once again, all the key players would be returning. Plus, Anderson, the talented Ohio State transfer, was ready to take the hardwood again after sitting out the season. That group would be joined by an incoming

The 1996 NCAA championship team included, sitting, left to right, assistant coach Delray Brooks, Rick Pitino, Allen Edwards, Derek Anderson, Jeff Sheppard, Tony Delk, Anthony Epps, Cameron Mills, associate coach Jim O'Brien and assistant coach Winston Bennett. Standing, left to right, equipment manager Bill Keightley, administrative assistant George Barber, Jason Lathrem, Oliver Simmons, Nazr Mohammed, Mark Pope, Walter McCarty, Antoine Walker, Jared Prickett, Ron Mercer, trainer Eddie Jamiel, assistant strength coach Layne Kaufman and strength coach Shaun Brown.

freshman class that included Wayne Turner, Oliver Simmons, Nazr Mohammed and prep All-American Ron Mercer.

One player who wouldn't return was Rhodes. After three turbulent years, Rhodes opted to leave UK. Such was the depth of UK's next team that a player who scored 1,208 points in three seasons wasn't missed.

Coming up: Another NCAA championship and one of UK's top-five greatest teams of all-time.

1995-96

Kentucky's five greatest teams? Certainly the 1947-48 "Fabulous Five" team makes the list. So does the 1950-51 team that had Spivey, Hagan and Ramsey. The unbeaten 1953-54 club led by Hagan, Ramsey and Tsioropoulos can't be overlooked. Nor can the 1977-78 Givens-Robey-Macy club that some say is the best of all-time.

Those four teams are non-negotiables.

Near-misses include the 1946-47 team that had enough talent to keep ex-All-Americans Bob Brannum and Jim Jordan off the postseason traveling squad; the 1948-49 team that had four of the Fabulous Five returning; the 1951-52 team, which probably would have been the school's greatest had Spivey been allowed to play; Rupp's 1965-66 band of

overachieving "Runts"; the 1969-70 team that went 26-2 despite the absence of Mike Casey; and the 1974-75 Kevin Grevey-led team that finished second to UCLA in the NCAA Tournament.

However, no list of UK's five greatest teams would be complete — or accurate — without the 1995-96 team. This club, Pitino's seventh at UK, had it all — experience, talent, smarts, size, strength, shooters, rebounders, quickness, excellent defenders and the ever-so-mysterious team chemistry that had been lacking in the two previous seasons.

More important, though, this team had everything in warehouse abundance. Few teams in UK history can come close to matching this one in terms of quality depth at all positions. Throughout the season, rival coaches and basketball commentators said that UK's second five could easily have been a Top 10 team, and they weren't joking. Just how rich in talent was this team? Enough so that the loss of Prickett was seen as a blessing rather than a blow to the team's chances of winning a national title. In fact, the UK coaches, concerned about having too many players and not enough minutes, actively pursued a medical redshirt for the senior forward, which was granted after only five games.

It's no surprise that this team went 34-2 overall, 16-0 in

the SEC and won the national title.

With Pope scoring 26 points and Delk adding 21, the top-ranked Cats opened the season with a 96-84 victory over Maryland. Starters for the Cats that night included Walker and Mercer at the forward spots, Pope in the middle, Anderson at shooting guard and Delk at the point. It was a lineup that only lasted two games. Following a 92-82 loss to UMass, Epps took over at the point, Delk went back to his natural two-guard position, Anderson moved into the small forward spot and Mercer became a valuable sixth man. McCarty also drew several starts, sharing post position duties with Pope.

Twenty-three turnovers and the inability to contain Marcus Camby doomed the Cats in their loss to UMass. Camby led all scorers with 32 points. Delk had 21 for the Cats, while McCarty added 17.

That would be the Cats' last loss until the championship game of the SEC Tournament. In between, the Cats left the basketball freeway scattered with the bones of 27 fallen opponents. Included in that stretch was a 16-0 SEC record, the first umblemished league record since Alabama turned the trick in 1956.

Inserting Epps at the point paid immediate dividends for the Cats, who began their 27-game streak with an 89-82 win over Indiana in Indianapolis. Walker had 24 for the Cats and Anderson added 18. Epps finished with

nine points and six assists. Brian Evans led IU with 26.

After a nonchalant 74-62 win over Wisconsin-Green Bay, the Cats gave a mighty effort in demolishing Georgia Tech 83-60. The unselfish Cats, who had 24 assists, broke the game open with a spectacular 29-8 second-half run. Their defense was also superb, holding Georgia Tech to 35 percent shooting while forcing 22 turnovers. Five Cats scored in double figures, led by Walker with 16. Others included Sheppard with 12 and Mercer, Pope and McCarty with 10 each.

Walker hit for 22 in a 96-32 win over Morehead State, then Pope scored 21 and Epps handed out 12 assists to lead the Cats past Marshall 118-99. In that game, the Cats were up 45-12 after 10 minutes and took a 70-49 lead into the locker room at intermission.

On the day Tim Couch committed to UK, the Cats, led by Delk's 30 points, smoked Louisville 89-66 in Rupp Arena. Delk scored his team's final 12 points of the first half, putting the Cats in front 36-24 at the break. Walker finished with 20 for UK, while Epps had 14 and McCarty 12. Alvin Sims topped the Cardinals with 23 points.

The Cats returned to New York to capture the ECAC

Rick Pitino chats it up with ESPN analyst Dick Vitale. Both men knew that the 1995-96 UK club had the talent, experience and depth to capture the national crown.

Holiday Festival championship for the second time in four years, beating Rider 90-65 and Iona 106-79. Walker and Delk had 27 and 24 points, respectively, against Rider. Delk, the tourney MVP, came back to score 29 points in the title game.

Delk's six treys and 28 points enabled the Cats to kick off SEC action with an 89-60 victory at South Carolina. That was followed by a 90-60 win over Ole Miss and a 74-56 win over 17th-ranked Mississippi State in Starkville. Delk had 14 in the win over Ole Miss, which shot just 26.6 percent and turned the ball over 24 times. Walker's 16 led the scoring against Mississippi State.

An easy 61-44 win over Tennessee (despite an uninspired performance) was quickly followed by a record-smashing 129-97 laugher against LSU. The Cats shot 67.3 percent en route to an 86-42 lead at intermission. The 86 points are the most-ever by a UK team in a single half. Walker was the prime destroyer, making good on 14 of 16 first-half shots and finishing with 32 points. Mercer had 15, Delk 14, Anderson 13, Sheppard 11 and Turner 10 for the Cats. Epps ended the night with 11 assists. Ronnie Henderson led LSU with 22 points.

Another record-shattering performance highlighted the Cats' 124-80 victory over Texas Christian University. Delk connected on a school-record nine treys in 12 attempts against a stunned TCU defense to finish with 27 points for the Cats.

In a hard-fought battle against Georgia, it took back-to-back buckets by Edwards to help the Cats escape with an 82-77 victory in Athens. The second of Edwards' two baskets gave UK a 76-72 lead and some breathing room against the

Derek Anderson's blend of quickness, athleticism, scoring ability and defensive daring made him the quintessential Pitino-type player. He came to UK after playing two seasons at Ohio State.

fast-charging Bulldogs. Delk again came up big, hitting for 29 to lead all scorers. Edwards, the hero, had five. Carlos Strong and Shandon Anderson each had 17 for Georgia.

Another highlight reel blitz (30-2) turned a precarious 46-45 UK lead into an easy 89-57 win over South Carolina. During that run, the Cats knocked down five treys. McCarty led UK with 20 points.

The Cats continued to roll, pounding Florida 77-63, Vanderbilt 120-81 (Vandy's worst home loss ever), Arkansas 88-73, Georgia 86-73 and Tennessee 90-50. There were tremendous individual performances in each of those five wins. Delk tallied 87 points, Pope had back-to-back double-doubles (11 points, 11 rebounds against Arkansas, 16 points, 11 rebounds against Georgia), McCarty had 16 points and 11 rebounds in the win over Vandy, Epps scored 17 points and nailed a critical three-pointer to quash an Arkansas comeback, and Edwards came off the bench to score 11 points in the win over Georgia.

With only four regular season games left, the Cats continued their march toward perfection by easily handling Alabama 84-65. Anderson led the way with 15 points, while Walker and Pope each contributed 13.

After learning that top-ranked UMass had been bumped off by George Washington University, the No. 2-ranked Cats, led by Walker's excellent 20-point, 11-rebound effort, crushed Florida 94-63 in Gainesville to reclaim the top spot in the national rankings. McCarty and Delk each scored 12, Mercer had 11 and Anderson and Turner 10 apiece.

The Cats beat Auburn 88-73, then put the finishing touch on their masterpiece SEC season by blasting Vander-

bilt 101-63 in the season finale. Delk led UK with 23.

The win gave the Cats a 16-0 league record, with an incredible average victory margin of 24.2 points. Overall, the Cats entered the SEC Tournament, which they had won every year since coming off probation in 1992, with a 26-1 record.

First up for the Cats was Florida, which shot a blistering 52.7 from the field yet still came up on the short end of a 100-76 score. The Cats' scoring balance (five players in double figures) and defense (forced 24 turnovers) were enough to offset Florida's hot shooting. Walker led the UK attack with 21 points. Others in double figures included Anderson (18), Mercer (17), McCarty (15) and Sheppard (10). Dametri Hill had 20 for the Gators.

Walker's 21-point, 14-rebound performance shot the Cats past Arkansas 95-75 and into the championship game for the fifth straight year. The Cats built a 43-29 halftime cushion, then cruised home with the easy win. McCarty also contributed 17 to the Cats' winning cause, while Delk and Mercer added 14 and 11, respectively. Darnell Robinson had 19 to lead Arkansas.

The final game, which UK was favored to win handily, turned out to be an unexpected shocker. Mississippi State, getting an All-World performance from Dontae Jones, upset the powerful Wildcats 84-73 to claim the SEC tourney title. Jones was magnificent, hitting 12 of 18 shots, scoring 28 points and grabbing 11 rebounds. With him paving the way, the Bulldogs shot 54.4 percent from the field (31 of 57) and won the rebounding battle 42-36. Delk's 16 led the Cats.

The humbled Cats unleashed the full wrath of their

Rick Pitino was all smiles at the post-game press conference following UK's semifinal win over UMass. Two nights later, the Cats beat Syracuse in the championship game.

fury (and Pitino's) in a 110-72 win over poor San Jose State in NCAA tourney opening-round action. The Cats, who registered 35 assists, got 24 points from McCarty and 22 from Delk.

A huge game by Walker (21 points, 11 rebounds) and nine second-half dunks carried the airborne Cats to an easy 84-60 victory over Virginia Tech in second-round action. UK's nine dunks were one shy of the total number of field goals scored by Virginia Tech in the final 20 minutes. McCarty had another big game, scoring 19 points.

Of this team's many blitzes throughout the season, none was more impressive or more overwhelming than the one against Utah in round three. Leading 11-5 early, the Cats buried 12th-ranked Utah under an avalanche of points, connecting on 13 straight shots to build an insurmountable 40-19 lead. Eight different Wildcats contributed during that dizzying run, led by Walker's three buckets and two each from Anderson, Edwards and Sheppard. It was a whirlwind of destruction that left the Utes battered and bewildered.

Walker paced the UK attack with 19 points. Anderson added 18, Delk and Epps 14 each. In all, 12 UK players cracked the scoring column. Keith Van Horn had 23 points and eight rebounds for Rick Majerus' club.

Against Wake Forest, the Cats shot out to a quick 13-3 lead, upped their advantage to 38-19 at the half, then went on to post an 83-63 win that earned them their second Final Four appearance during the Pitino Era. Delk did the most damage, lighting it up for 25 points. Epps and Anderson each had 12 and McCarty chipped in with 10. Tim Duncan led Wake Forest with 14 points and 16 rebounds.

Final Four MVP Tony Delk waves to the crowd during a celebration in Rupp Arena. Delk knocked down seven treys and scored 24 points in the championship win over Syracuse.

On deck: A rematch with UMass, an earlier 92-82 conquerer of the Wildcats.

In this semifinal showdown, the Cats forged a big second-half lead, only to see it shaved to three with less than four minutes to play. A 7-0 run to start the second half put the Cats on top 43-28. After UMass trimmed the difference to 63-60, the Cats went on an 8-1 run to extend their lead to 71-61. Pope started the run by dropping in a pair of free throws. Walker connected on one of two free throws, then Sheppard rammed down a dunk. Following a lone Camby free throw, Sheppard hit one of two free tosses and Walker sank a pair to give the Cats their 10-point advantage.

But UMass wouldn't fade away, again pulling to within three at 73-70. The Cats responded with six unanswered points, two each by Pope, Walker and Delk, to finally put the game in the win column.

Delk had 20 for the Cats, while Walker added 14. Camby was the game's top scorer with 25.

Two nights later, despite shooting just 38.4 percent from the field, the Cats beat Syracuse 76-67 to capture their sixth national championship and their first since 1978. UK's shooting percentage was the lowest by a tourney champ in 33 years.

The three-point shot (12 in all, a record-tying seven by Delk) and a superb 20-point performance by Mercer off the bench were the keys to this UK victory. Delk, the Final Four MVP, knocked down seven of 12 three-point attempts and scored 24 points in his final game as a Wildcat, while Mercer made good on eight of 12 shots in what was easily his finest effort of the season.

Although the Cats led by nine at the half (42-33) and by as many as 13 in the second half (59-46), poor shoot-

ing kept them from putting away the Orangemen. Midway through the final half, Syracuse outscored the Cats 16-5 to pull to within 64-62 with just under five minutes left. McCarty tipped in a Delk miss, then after the Cats shut down the Orangemen on their next possession, Anderson drained a three to make it 69-62. Jason Cipolla and Pope swapped 12-footers before Walker hit one of two free throws. A three-pointer by Todd Burgan pulled Syracuse to within 72-67, but two freebies by Pope and a Delk layup finalized the deal in UK's favor.

The Wildcats were national champions.

Almost immediately, rumors began to swirl that Pitino was leaving for the NBA. This was nothing new to UK fans, who had seen this Pitino-NBA dance in each of the two previous years. Several NBA teams, including Golden State, Philadelphia and Orlando, expressed an interest in luring Pitino back into the pro ranks. Many felt that this was the year he would leave. He had resurrected the UK program, he'd put fun back into it for Big Blue fans and he

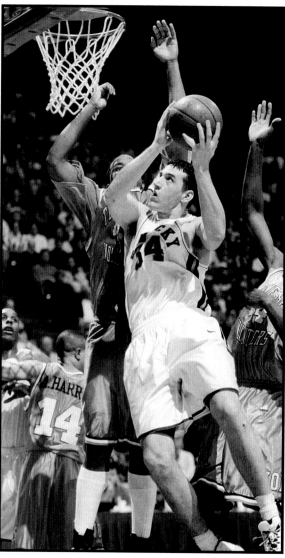

Ex-academic exile Scott Padgett brought a unique package of skills to the team. His ability to play inside or on the perimeter made him a tough player to defend.

Walker, McCarty and Pope would have left the basketball program in shambles. Maybe even years away from returning to the top. But not at Kentucky, which has, throughout the decades, consistently filled the holes, regardless of how deep or wide. The old phrase, "they don't rebuild, they reload," was probably first uttered by a jealous Wildcat opponent.

And with good reason. Few schools could have accomplished what UK did in 1996-97. Despite losing four players who accounted for more than 50 percent of the previous team's scoring and rebounding totals, this club, while a notch below its immediate predecessor, almost repeated as NCAA champs, losing an 84-79 overtime thriller to Arizona in the final game.

A 35-5 record, another SEC tourney title, second place in the NCAA Tournament, No. 2 in the final polls — monumental achievements for any team, much less one that played more than half the season without its best all-around player. Had Derek Anderson not gone down with a torn ACL midway

finally had that NCAA ring he could show off to the pope. In addition, next year's club would be without Delk, Pope and McCarty, who were graduating, and Walker, who had declared himself eligible for the NBA draft. Given that set of circumstances, no one would have been shocked to see Pitino leave.

But Pitino, always up for a challenge, opted to stay put. And in what was his final year at UK, he came within an injured knee of pulling off a second straight miracle.

1996-97

At most schools, losing four quality players like Delk,

through the campaign, it's probable that the Wildcats would have one more NCAA championship banner hanging from the rafters.

Given the circumstances, this team's accomplishments rival those of any previous team in UK history. And the coaching job by Pitino and his staff ranks as possibly his finest during his eight-year reign at UK.

Pitino knew going in that this could be a solid club. Anderson and Mercer had NBA talent, Turner and Epps were solid point guards, and a healthy Prickett added experience and toughness. Pitino had enough confidence in this team's

depth and talent, especially on the perimeter, to suggest that Sheppard consider redshirting. Sheppard, a senior, quickly agreed.

Pitino's chief concerns revolved around the pivot position, where untested sophomore Nazr Mohammed and freshman Jamaal Magloire were both unknown quantities.

For this team to succeed, there were two players who had to come through — Edwards and Padgett. Edwards, though talented, had essentially been little more than a spot player during his first two seasons at UK. Now Pitino was counting on the Miami native to provide strong play at the small forward position.

Padgett, the former academic exile, brought a unique package of skills to this team — rebounding, outside shooting, mental toughness, passing and excellent ball-handling. He had to sit out the first semester (eight games), but once he became eligible, he immediately made his presence felt. More than anything else, it was Padgett's emergence as a standout player that enabled this team to overcome the loss of Anderson and achieve its high level of success.

The Cats' opening-game performance was anything but an indicator of the success that lay waiting down the road. Clemson put the clamps on the cold-shooting Cats, winning 79-71 in overtime. Anderson had 22 for the Cats, who shot just 42.6 percent from the field. Harold Jamison led Clemson with 20 points, including eight in the overtime.

Thanks to Anderson, the Cats got hot in the cold of Alaska, easily win-

ning three games to claim the Great Alaska Shootout championship. Anderson tossed in 25 to lead the Cats past Syracuse 87-53, then came back with 30 in a 104-72 romp past host Alaska-Anchorage. Mercer finished with 20 in that win, while Epps added 15. In the 92-65 title-game win over College of Charleston, five Wildcats scored in double figures, led by Mercer's 22. Edwards had 17, Anderson 12 and centers Magloire and Mohammed 10 each.

Before returning to Lexington, the Cats, led by Mercer's 30-point performance, topped Purdue 101-87 in a Great Eight showdown. Mercer scorched the Purdue defense, making good on 13 of 16 field goal attempts. Prickett finished with 17 for the Cats.

Anderson and Mercer combined for 56 points and the UK defense forced Indiana into 28 miscues as the charging Cats humbled Bobby Knight's club 99-65 in Freedom Hall. Anderson and Mercer had 30 and 26, respectively, for the Cats. Jason Collier led IU with 21.

After easily beating Wright State 90-62, the third-ranked Cats rode an early 18-0 second-half blitz to an 80-56 win over Notre Dame. The Cats struggled in the opening half, shooting just 36 percent from the field. But with Mercer paving the way, the Cats blew it open with their second-half stampede. Mercer's 21 paced the UK scoring attack.

With Padgett scoring 12 points and pulling down seven rebounds in

The gifted Ron Mercer only played two seasons at UK, but he left his mark as one of the most explosive Wildcats of all-time.

Rick Pitino managed to laugh as superstar Ron Mercer announced his intention to enter the NBA draft after the 1997 season. As it turned out, this would also be Pitino's last season at UK. He left to take over the Boston Celtics.

his first game in 18 months, the Cats blistered Georgia Tech 88-59 in Atlanta. Anderson led UK with 21 points, while Mercer added 20.

Anderson hit for 23, Mercer had 18 and Edwards added 17 as the Cats continued to win with ease, ripping UNC-Ashville 105-51. Mercer then gave a 22-point, 13-rebound effort to lead UK to an 81-65 win over Ohio State. Anderson also scored 22 against his former Buckeye teammates.

After trailing for much of the game, the Cats rallied late, outscoring 14th-ranked Louisville 35-12 in the final 10 minutes, to come away with an impressive 74-54 road win. Anderson scored 19 to lead UK. Mercer finished with 16, Padgett 15 and Prickett and Mohammed 10 apiece. B.J. Flynn, son of ex-Cat Mike Flynn, led the Cards with 12.

The Cats began SEC action with a pair of easy wins, beating Tennessee 74-40 and Mississippi State 90-61. Magloire led the Cats with 13 against the Vols. Anderson scored 26 against Mississippi State, including 23 in the second half.

Anderson scored 17 points before leaving with a back injury and Prickett had 10 points and 11 rebounds as the Cats posted a 68-45 non-conference win over Canisius.

Anderson's injury, a pulled back muscle, limited him to just 10 minutes of action in the Cats' next outing, a 73-69 loss at Ole Miss. After trailing by as many as 13 points in the second half, the Cats closed to within 70-69 inside the last minute. But the courageous Rebels scored the game's final three points to hold on for the upset win. Joezon Darby led Ole Miss with 19 points. Ansu Sesay added 18. Prickett had his second straight double-double, finishing with 14 points and 10 rebounds.

In an ugly game that saw 59 fouls called and 90 free throws attempted, the Cats got the best of Georgia 86-65 in Athens. The Bulldogs made just 15 field goals during the game, but managed to stay within striking range by hitting 30 of 50 free throws. Anderson had 24 points to lead all scorers.

It was in the Cats' next game, a 77-53 win over Auburn, that Anderson went down with his injury. Anderson left the game thinking it was only a bruised knee. However, two days later, the injury was diagnosed as a torn ACL. Anderson, UK's leading scorer at the time with a 17.7 average, was finished for the season.

In their first post-Anderson game, the Cats used the

three-point shot to get past Vanderbilt 58-46. A 20-4 second-half run that featured five treys, including three by Padgett, was enough to put away the pesky Commodores. Padgett and Edwards each had 16 to lead UK. Billy DiSpaltro had 16 for Vandy.

Mills had his first big game of the season, coming off the bench to score 12 points and spark the Cats to an 83-73 win over Arkansas. UK also turned in a superb defensive effort, holding Arkansas to 40.6 percent shooting while causing 25 turnovers. Mohammed led the Cats with 18.

Mohammed and Mercer each scored 18 and Epps added 16 in a 92-65 win over Florida, then Mercer came through with 20 to help the Cats beat Tubby Smith's Georgia club 82-57. UK's six-game winning streak was snapped by South Carolina, which edged the Cats 84-79 in overtime. The Gamecocks scored the first bucket in the extra frame — a jumper by Melvin Watson — and never trailed again. BJ McKie led all scorers with 22 points. Mercer had 18 for the Cats.

The Cats got back on

Cameron Mills sizzled during postseason action, making good on 63 percent of his three-point attempts. His outside bombing helped the Wildcats make it to a second straight NCAA championship game.

By this stage of the season, it was clear that Mercer was on his way to earning All-America status. Despite being a marked man by opposing defenses, the gifted Mercer proved to be difficult to shut down. After Epps scored 18 in an 84-48 victory over LSU, Mercer pitched in 23 points in each of the Cats' next three games, wins over Florida (85-56), Alabama (75-61) and Vanderbilt (82-79). Mercer also contributed eight assists in the win over Florida. Against Vandy, Mercer scored 17 points after intermission to help the Cats wipe out a 22-point deficit and escape with the victory.

Padgett put the hammer to Tennessee, hitting for 24 points in a 74-64 Wildcat victory. Then in the season finale, South Carolina came into Rupp Arena and scored a 72-66 upset, snapping UK's 27-game home winning streak. It marked UK's first loss on Seniors' Night since 1964. One person who wasn't around to see the finish was Pitino. After voicing his displeasure with the officiating, and with the visitors' steady march to the charity stripe

the winning track, giving two brilliant performances in back-to-back non-conference wins over Western Carolina (82-55) and 16th-ranked Villanova (93-56). The wins also featured double-doubles by Padgett, 23 points, 13 rebounds against Western Carolina, and Mercer, 23 points, 11 rebounds against Villanova.

(South Carolina shot 44 free throws to UK's 15), Pitino was given the heave-ho. Mercer finished with 25 points to earn game-high honors. McKie and Larry Davis had 22 and 20, respectively, for South Carolina.

In that loss, Mills connected on two treys in three attempts. No one realized it at the time, but it was

the quiet beginning of an amazing display of long-range shooting accuracy. In postseason action, Mills, a walk-on, connected on 63 percent of his three-points attempts, making him one of the most valuable contributors during the Cats' run for a second straight national crown.

To everyone's surprise, the second-seeded Wildcats breezed through the SEC tourney, beating Auburn 92-50, Ole Miss 88-70 and Georgia 95-68 in the championship game. The Cats' path was made easier when top seeds South Carolina and Arkansas were both bounced from the tournament in early action. Mercer was named tourney MVP after scoring 60 points in UK's three wins. Epps also played terrific basketball, scoring 51 points, including 22 in the title game, despite having been replaced by Turner in the starting lineup. Turner, in only his second start, had 19 points and five assists in the win over Auburn. Mills continued to sizzle from downtown, making good on 10 of 16 three-point attempts.

The top-seeded Wildcats, sent to the West Region, opened defense of their national title by blasting Montana 92-54 in Salt Lake City. Once again, it was fast-closing newcomers Mills and Turner who led the way with 19 points each. Mills, now virtually automatic from the outside, connected on five of seven three-pointers. Mercer also hit double figures with 16, while Prickett chipped in with 14.

Two late buckets by Padgett, one a trey, and superb first-half performances by Prickett and Mills enabled foul-plagued UK to hold off Iowa 75-69 in a second-round thriller. With Mercer and Turner sidelined by early foul trouble, Prickett and Mills combined for 26 first-half

Nazr Mohammed developed into a solid inside player for Tubby Smith's first UK club. After helping lead that team to the NCAA championship, Mohammed spurned everyone's advice and entered the NBA draft.

points to keep the Cats in the game. Prickett scored all of his team-high 15 points prior to intermission. Turner had 13, Mills 11 and Mercer and Mohammed 10 each.

Mills buried five of six three-pointers and matched Mercer with 19 points as the Cats advanced to the Elite Eight with an 83-68 victory over St. Joseph's. Turner had 16 points for the Wildcats, who hit 29 of 52 from the field for 56 percent. Rashid Bey led St. Joseph's with 26 points.

Standing between the Wildcats and another trip to the Final Four was a familiar March opponent — Utah. This was the third time in six years that the two clubs crossed swords in NCAA tourney action. It wouldn't be the last.

With Mercer scoring 21 points and Padgett doing an outstanding defensive job against Keith Van Horn, the Cats clipped Utah 72-59 to once again earn a ticket to the Final Four. The two clubs were dead even at 43-43, but a Mercer 10-foot jumper ignited an 18-6 Wildcat run that finished off Utah. Mercer was UK's top scorer with 21 points. Epps finished with 15, Turner 12 and Padgett 11. Van Horn, the great Utah All-American, was held to 15.

In a semifinal matchup against third-ranked Minnesota, the Cats again proved to be superior in the clutch, using another late blitz to break open a close game and come away with a 78-69 victory. With the score knotted at 54-54, the Cats outscored Minnesota 11-2 during the

next two minutes to take control. Capping that drive was a three-pointer by Padgett. Mercer led UK with 19 points. Bobby Jackson had 23 for the Golden Gophers.

Another highlight in that Wildcat win was the appearance of Anderson, who came off the bench to hit a pair of free throws following a technical on Minnesota coach Clem Haskins.

The title game with Arizona was a white-knuckler from start to finish, with 11 lead changes and eight ties in the first half alone. It was also a tale of field goals versus free throws. For the game, UK had eight more buckets (30-22), but Arizona made up the difference by hitting 34 of 41 free throws to nine of 17 by the Cats. In the game-deciding overtime, all 10 Arizona points came at the charity stripe.

Arizona led 72-68 and appeared to have things under control when the Cats made one final drive. The weary Mercer connected on a three-pointer to make it 72-71 with 49 seconds remaining. Then after Arizona's Bennett Davison scored on a layup, the gutsy Epps stroked a trey with 13 seconds left to tie it at 74-74 and bring on the extra period.

Miles Simon hit 14 of 17 free throws and had a game-high 30 for Arizona. His backcourt mate Mike Bibby added 19. Padgett paced the Cats with 17, while Mercer, in his final game as a Wildcat, contributed 13. Mohammed and Mills each scored 12 and Epps had 11.

Less than two months later, Pitino announced that he was leaving UK and accepting the challenge of rebuilding the once-mighty Boston Celtics NBA franchise. With his decision to return to the pro ranks, Pitino closed the book on a truly remarkable eight-year reign in which he resurrected the fallen UK program and led it to a level of success unmatched since the "Glory Years" between 1946-54. Pitino's teams were 219-50 (20 of those losses came in the first two years), won a national title, made three Final Four appearances and captured the SEC tourney title five times in six tries.

C.M. Newton wasted no time filling the vacancy created by Pitino's departure. Newton had one man in mind for the job, and he

immediately went after him. Six days after Pitino's resignation, Newton got what he wanted: Orlando "Tubby" Smith agreed to leave Georgia and take over as UK's new coach.

By accepting the job, Smith became the first black head coach in UK basketball history. That fact was little noted among Big Blue fans, who saw Smith as not only a logical choice, but a good one as well.

And Smith more than proved it in his first year, leading the Wildcats to another NCAA championship, earning National Coach of the Year honors and setting a new record for most wins by a coach in his initial season at a school.

It was the finest start ever by a Wildcat coach.

1997-98

C.M. Newton had plenty of reasons for wanting Tubby Smith as his new coach. Smith had proved himself a winner at Tulsa and at Georgia. He was known for running clean, scandal-free programs. He ranked as a superb recruiter. Few men were more respected within the college coaching fraternity. Plus, Smith had been an assistant to Pitino, so he was familiar with the pressures that go along with being UK's coach.

Not surprisingly, Newton's choice met with universal approval from Wildcat fans. And by season's end, after the

C.M. Newton looks on as UK president Dr. Charles Wethington puts a UK pin on Tubby Smith's lapel. Smith was Newton's first and only choice to succeed Rick Pitino as UK's coach.

Cats had gone 35-4 and captured another NCAA crown, even those few skeptics who wondered if anyone could ever replace Pitino had been won over. Tubby Smith was now their guy.

Smith is the only UK coach to win a national title in his first year, and his 35 victories are the most-ever by a coach in his rookie season at a school.

Thanks to the good work by Pitino, Smith inherited a program that was now rock solid in every respect. The roster was flush with talented veterans, and the freshman class, which included Michael Bradley, Saul Smith, Ryan Hogan and Myron Anthony, was loaded with potential.

Smith also benefited from two crucial Pitino decisions — redshirting Jeff Sheppard and signing transfer Heshimu Evans. The talented Sheppard, now a fifth-year senior, brought experience, unselfishness and leadership to the team, while the hard-working Evans, a 6'6" transfer from Manhattan College, was quick, athletic and highly energetic.

Smith's lineup card for the opener against Morehead State

Jeff Sheppard launches a jumper from the corner. Sheppard redshirted after his junior season, then came back as a fifth-year senior to lead the Wildcats to another NCAA title.

featured Padgett and Edwards at the forward positions, Magloire in the middle, and Sheppard and Turner in the backcourt. With Edwards scoring 15 points, the ninth-ranked Cats made Smith's debut a success, easily beating ex-Cat Kyle Macy's club 88-49.

In the Maui Classic, Turner had 16 points and eight steals as the Cats ripped George Washington University 70-55. In a semifinal matchup against top-ranked Arizona, the cold-shooting Cats fell behind early and never caught up. Arizona, with guard Mike Bibby scoring 20 points, stung

the Cats 89-74. In that game, the Cats outrebounded Arizona 53-39, but shot just 38.8 percent from the field while committing 18 turnovers. Padgett paced the Cats with 16 points, while Mohammed pulled down 16 rebounds.

In the consolation game, Magloire had a double-double — 18 points, 17 rebounds — as the Cats rolled to a 77-55 win over Missouri.

Against 13th-ranked Clemson in Phoenix, the Cats, after falling behind 47-42, went on a 16-2 run that led to a 76-61 victory. Turner led the charge with 17 points. Other Cats in double digits included Padgett (15), Edwards (13) and Mohammed (10).

The Cats concluded a 9,700 mile trip (Lexington to Hawaii to Phoenix to Chicago) with an 89-75 win over fifth-ranked Purdue. Mohammed led the Cats with 19 points. Chad Austin had 24 for the Boilermakers.

Mohammed and Sheppard each scored 21 points and Mills knocked down four treys as the Cats edged past Indiana 75-72 in Indianapolis. The Hoosiers closed to within two late in the game, but a free throw by Turner sealed the win for UK. Mohammed also had 12 rebounds for the Cats. Rob Turner had a game-high 25 for IU.

Still on the road, the Cats, led by Sheppard's 21 points, had an easy time against outmanned Canisius, winning 81-54. Canisius stayed within striking distance for awhile, but eight points by Sheppard to start the second half broke the game open. Edwards chipped in 14 points for the Cats, who shot a blistering 69.2 percent in the second half.

After nearly three weeks on the road, the Cats returned

Heshimu Evans breaks up a pass intended for Duke's Trajan Langdon during action in the South Regional final. The Cats erased a 17-point deficit with less than 10 minutes remaining to beat Duke 86-84 and earn a third consecutive trip to the Final Four.

home to face yet another ranked foe, No. 24 Georgia Tech. The early going was all Georgia Tech, which used a 17-2 run to build a 27-16 lead. But the Cats, fueled by three Evans buckets, cut the difference to 35-34 by intermission. The Cats continued their red-hot pace after the break, outscoring the Yellow Jackets 28-9 in the first 10 minutes to put the game away. Evans led UK with 14 points and 10 rebounds. In all, UK's bench outscored Tech's reserves 30-4. Edwards, Magloire, Sheppard and Mohammed each finished with 12 points. Georgia Tech's Dion Glover had 27 points to lead all scorers.

Defense was the difference in the Cats' 74-53 win over Tulsa. After trailing 29-28 at the half, the stingy Cats held Tubby Smith's old team to just six second-half field goals.

Mohammed had 17 points for the Cats.

A late 10-0 run to close out the first half, followed by a 27-9 blitz to open the final 20 minutes resulted in an easy 75-52 victory over American. Once again, UK's bench came up big, racking up 32 points. Edwards led the Cats with 16 points.

Louisville turned the tables on UK, using the three-point shot to post a 79-76 win in Rupp Arena. The hot-shooting Cardinals hit 12 treys in 22 attempts, including three each by

Eric Johnson and Tony Williams. The Cats led 35-31 at the half, and were still clinging to a 61-59 advantage at the 8:18 mark when Johnson buried a trey to put Louisville in front for good. Johnson led all scorers with 20 points. Sheppard had 18 for the Cats, who shot a chilly 37.5 percent from the field (27 of 72).

With five players cracking double figures, the Cats bounced back to crush Ohio University 95-58. The pivot duo of Mohammed and Magloire led UK with 15 points each. Padgett finished with 13, while Evans and Mills had 11 and 10, respectively.

Thanks to a 57-18 rebounding advantage, the Cats began SEC play on a positive note by clipping Vanderbilt 71-62. Vandy led at the break, but a pair of UK runs — 11-2 to begin the second half, followed by a later 10-0 blitz — were enough to subdue the always-dangerous Commodores. Padgett and Mohammed each recorded double-doubles. Mohammed had 19 points and 12 rebounds, while Padgett had 13 points and 14 rebounds. Sheppard chipped in with 16 points.

In a game highlighted by all sorts of family ties (father vs. son, brother against brother, mom caught in the middle), Tubby Smith returned to his old haunts and guided the Cats to a 90-79 win over Georgia in Athens. Turner was outstanding for the Cats, scoring 20 points and handing out five assists. Ray Harrison led Georgia with 17 points. In the brother vs. brother matchup between G.G. and Saul Smith, elder brother G.G. came away with an 8-6 scoring edge.

Padgett tossed in 23 points in a 77-71 win over Mississippi State, then Sheppard came through with 16 and Turner added 15 as the Cats ripped 14th-ranked South Carolina 91-70. The Cats nailed their first seven shots against South Carolina to grab a lead they never relinquished. BJ McKie had 24 for the Gamecocks.

Evans scored his team's first seven points in overtime to lift the Cats to an 80-77 win over No. 22-ranked Arkansas. The Cats won despite hitting just two of 19 from behind the three-point line. Evans finished with 20 points to lead UK in scoring. Turner had 16, while Mohammed (14/13) and Padgett (11/12) again registered double-doubles.

It took a gutsy second-half performance by Padgett for the Cats to beat upset-minded Alabama 70-67 in Freedom Hall. With Alabama leading 47-37, Padgett, playing in his hometown, scored nine of UK's next 13 points to cut the difference to a single point. Later, Padgett, who finished with 24 points, canned a trey, a short jumper and a pair of free throws to finally calm the Tide. Mohammed also played well, finishing

with 22 points and 10 rebounds. Damon Bacote hit seven of nine three-pointers and finished with 25 points for Alabama.

Padgett tallied 20 points and Sheppard and Turner each contributed 17 in an impressive 85-67 UK win in Knoxville. The Cats dominated the inside, scoring 50 points in the paint. In addition to his 17 points, Turner also handed out 11 assists.

Only a miracle by Mohammed saved the Cats against Vanderbilt in the second meeting between the two clubs. With time running out and the score knotted at 61-61, Mohammed banked in a bizarre running one-hander from 10 feet away to give the Cats their ninth straight win. Sheppard led UK with 20 points. Drew Maddux had 19 for Vandy.

Jason Williams and Kenyan Weaks each scored 24 points to lead Florida past the Cats 86-78. The Gators won despite a 31-point performance by Mills, who hit 10 of 19 shots, including eight of 14 from three-point land. After Florida bolted to a 31-16 lead and threatened to turn the game into a blowout, Mills accounted for 14 points in six minutes to bring the Cats to within 40-34 at the half. But the Gators, behind the scoring of Williams and Weaks, answered every UK challenge and held on for the upset victory.

Solid second-half efforts by Turner and Sheppard were all that stood between the Cats and a second consecutive loss. The two veteran guards each scored 11 points after intermission to help the Cats escape with a 63-61 win over LSU. Trailing 49-47, the Cats went on a 12-2 run to reclaim the upper hand and secure the hard-earned win. Sheppard led UK with 12 points. Turner and Padgett each finished with 11.

Stepping outside of SEC play, the Cats scored a 79-63 win over Villanova in Philadelphia. Mohammed and Sheppard each scored 18 for UK, while Evans added 17. Mohammed also grabbed 11 rebounds.

Mohammed and Padgett gave dominating inside performances in the Cats' 80-74 victory over Tennessee. In one of his finest efforts as a Wildcat, Mohammed had 21 points, 16 rebounds, five blocked shots and three assists. The always-reliable Padgett scored 17 points and speared 10 rebounds.

In a real shocker, Ole Miss accomplished something it hadn't done since 1927 — beat the Cats in Lexington. The 18th-ranked Rebels overcame an 11-point halftime deficit to beat UK 73-64. Ole Miss took a 45-44 lead on a jumper by Rahim Lockhart with 11:39 left and never trailed again. Keith Carter had 21 points to lead the Rebels. Sheppard scored 15 for UK.

The Cats closed out their regular season (and began

Final Four MVP Jeff Sheppard and Tubby Smith acknowledge the UK faithful after the Cats'
78-69 win over Utah in the NCAA championship game. Smith became the only coach to win a
national title in his initial season at a school.

lines, the Cats connected on a season-high 13 three-pointers to easily put away South Carolina. Turner, the tourney MVP, led UK with 18 points. Edwards chipped in with 15 and Evans added 11.

The second-seeded Cats traveled to Atlanta to open NCAA tourney play, and by the time they departed three days later all that remained was the wreckage of South Carolina State and St. Louis. The Cats opened with an 82-67 win over South Carolina State, then followed that by smacking the Billikens 88-61. Mohammed scored 18 points, including 14 in the first half, to lead the way against South Carolina State. Padgett had 14, Edwards 13 and Evans 12 in that win. Five Wildcats hit for double figures against St. Louis, topped by Sheppard with 18.

their run to the national title) by beating Florida 79-54, Georgia 85-74, Auburn 83-58 and South Carolina 69-57. Mohammed scored 35 points in the first two of those four wins, then Sheppard, who had been mired in a shooting slump, came alive to score 25 in the win over Auburn and 24 against South Carolina.

The SEC Tournament once again turned out to be a showcase for the Wildcats. They beat Alabama 82-71, Arkansas 99-74 and South Carolina 86-56 to claim the title for the sixth time in seven years. Sheppard had 17 points and Bradley came off the bench to score 10 points and pull down six rebounds in the win over Alabama. Then in what Smith called "the best half of basketball we've played all season," the Cats, behind 25 first-half points from Sheppard and Padgett, built a 58-33 halftime lead and never looked back against Arkansas. Sheppard led the Cats with 17 points despite leaving the game early in the second half after suffering a sprained ankle.

In the title game, with Sheppard watching from the side-

In what figured to be a down-to-the-wire thriller between two of college basketball's most-honored programs, the Wildcats shot a hot 54.4 percent from the field and roasted 19th-ranked UCLA 94-68. The Cats owned this game from beginning to end, courtesy of an early 18-3 run that was highlighted by Edwards' reverse jam and a defense that held the Bruins to 29.1 percent shooting, came up with 10 steals and forced 19 miscues. Padgett had 19 for UK, followed by Sheppard with 16 and Mohammed with 15.

It was in the next game, the first meeting with Duke since the classic 1992 encounter, that the Cats began to earn their nickname as the "Comeback Cats." In what turned out to be one of the tournament's most-exciting games, the Cats roared back from a 17-point deficit with 9:38 remaining to nip third-ranked Duke 86-84 and earn a trip to the Final Four for the third straight year.

Treys by Evans and Padgett and a Turner jumper triggered a 17-1 spurt that put the Cats back into the hunt. Then with just 2:15 left, Mills, who hadn't scored a bucket during the

tournament, knocked down a three-pointer to give the Cats an 80-79 lead. After Roshown McLeod dropped in a pair of free throws to put Duke back in front, Padgett hit a free throw and a three-pointer to give the Cats an 84-81 lead. Turner and Edwards each hit a freebie inside the final 17 seconds to preserve the win.

Sheppard led the Cats with 18 points. Also in double figures were Turner (16), Evans (14), Padgett (12) and Edwards (11). McLeod had a game-best 19 for the Blue Devils.

Sheppard's career-high 27-point performance and another courageous second-half comeback keyed the Cats to an 86-85 overtime win over Stanford in semifinal action. With the win, UK became the first team since UCLA in 1973 to advance to three straight national championship games.

Stanford built a 46-36 cushion early in the second half, but the Cats, behind Sheppard's outside gunning, clawed back to take a 72-68 lead with 1:17 left in regulation. But Stanford wrapped a Mark Madsen bucket and an Arthur Lee trey around a Turner free throw to tie the score at 73-73 and bring on the extra frame. The Cats scored the first five points in OT, only to see their lead sliced to 79-78 with 2:05 left. But the Cats weren't about to cave in, and when Sheppard answered with a three-pointer from the top of the circle, the win belonged to them.

Mohammed had 18 for UK, Edwards had 11 and Padgett finished with 10. Lee led Stanford with 26.

In the championship game against Utah, with the NCAA title at stake, the Cats found themselves staring at a 41-31 deficit at the half. In the history of NCAA championship games, no team had ever recovered from a 10-point deficit and come back to win. But these "Comeback Cats" did just that.

Superior depth and improved rebounding (Utah outrebounded UK 24-6 in the first half) enabled the Cats to once again dig their way out of the graveyard. Evans canned a trey that ignited a UK run that didn't end until a Mills three-pointer and Sheppard's baseline jumper put the Cats on top 65-64 with 4:54 remaining. The Utes, worn down by UK's relentless onslaught, missed 11 straight field goal attempts inside the final five minutes. As Utah was falling apart, the Wildcats pulled away for a 78-69 win and a second national championship in three years.

Padgett led UK with 17 points, while Sheppard, the Final Four MVP, scored 16. Evans and Mohammed each contributed 10 and Mills added eight. Andre Miller had 16 for Utah.

UK finished the season with a 35-4 record, marking the

Despite a dismal 0-for-18 start from three-point range, Scott Padgett went on to have a superb senior season. He led the team in scoring and rebounding, and was voted MVP of the SEC tourney.

10th 30-win season in the school's history. For his efforts, Smith was voted National Coach of the Year by *Basketball Weekly*.

1998-99

Tubby Smith knew coming into the season that he would be without graduated veterans Sheppard, Edwards and Mills. What Smith hadn't counted on, however, was the absence of Mohammed, the 6'10 center who averaged 12 points, 7.2 rebounds and shot 59.7 percent from the field as a junior. Spurning virtually everyone's advice, Mohammed made himself available for the NBA draft and was the last player chosen in the first round.

Mohammed's defection to the pros upped the ante considerably for Magloire and Bradley, two talented yet very dfferent 6'10" post players. Magloire, a Canadian, was rugged and unpolished, a superb defender and shot-blocker. Bradley, who hailed from Worcester, Mass., was mobile, quick and an excellent shooter. Together the duo gave Smith a complete pivotman. Magloire could defend, Bradley could score. And, combined, they had 10 fouls to give.

Smith's second Wildcat team wasn't short on talent, experience or mental toughness. Returning were several old faces, including proven warriors like Turner, Padgett, Evans, Saul Smith, Hogan, Anthony (who would leave the team early in the season) and popular walk-on Steve Masiello. Joining them were freshmen Tayshaun Prince (6'9", Compton, Calif.), Desmond Allison (6'5", Tampa, Fla.), Souleymane "Jules" Camara (6'11", Dakar, Senegal), and Kentucky natives J.P. Blevins (6'2", Edmonton) and Todd Tackett (6'2", Paintsville).

It was an intriguing — and exceptionally athletic — rookie class, and one that was sure to be tested early against what has to rank as the most difficult pre-SEC schedule any UK team has ever faced. These Cats would take on UCLA, Pittsburgh, Kansas, Miami, Indiana, Maryland, Georgia Tech, Duke and Louisville — all before January.

With six players scoring in double figures, the fourth-ranked Cats opened the season with an easy 99-64 romp past Eastern Kentucky University. Starters that night were Padgett, Evans, Bradley, Smith and Turner. Padgett led the scoring parade with 21 points, while Evans had 15, Bradley 13, Turner 11 and freshmen Prince and Camara 10 each.

Wayne Turner always played his best in money situations. With three Final Four appearances, two NCAA titles and three SEC championships under his belt, Turner ranks as the winningest UK guard since the great Ralph Beard.

The Cats tuned up for their trip to San Juan by blistering Mercer 82-51 and Wright State 97-75. Turner and Camara topped the Cats with 15 points apiece in the win over Mercer. Evans had 18 and Bradley 14 against Wright State.

A splendid performance by Prince (15 points, six rebounds, three blocked shots) highlighted the Cats' 64-52 comeback win over Colorado in the Puerto Rico Shootout opener. Colorado raced to a quick 9-0 lead before a Prince bucket ended the bleeding. With Prince leading the charge,

Jamaal Magloire used excellent rebounding and shot-blocking abilities to overcome his sometimes shaky offensive skills. Magloire also had to overcome a temper that consistently kept him in foul trouble.

the Cats tied it at 11-11, then took the lead for good on a short jumper by Turner.

In a coaching matchup between ex-Pitino assistants Smith and Ralph Willard, the cold-shooting Cats dropped a 68-56 decision to Pittsburgh. For the game, the Cats made good on two of 22 three-point attempts and were a poor four of 12 from the charity stripe. Vonteego Cummings led Willard's Panthers with 20 points. Bradley

topped UK with 16.

Sixteen points by Evans and back-to-back treys by Prince to begin the second half enabled the Cats to slip by 10th-ranked UCLA 66-62 in the consolation game. The Bruins led 32-27 at the half, but a 13-0 run, sparked by Prince's two bombs, put the Cats on top for good. In all, the Cats connected on nine three-pointers. Turner also hit for double figures with 12 points, while Prince finished with nine.

The Cats used an overwhelming defense to beat seventh-ranked Kansas 63-45 in a Great Eight marquee matchup between two of college basketball's most-legendary programs. UK totally dominated the Jayhawks, who managed just 29.4 percent shooting from the field while registering their lowest scoring output since 1982. Turner paced UK with 14 points. Evans registered a double-double — 11 points and 11 rebounds.

Bradley scored a career-high 19 points and Padgett snapped out of a 0-for-18 three-point shooting slump as the Cats dusted off Miami 74-65 in Rupp Arena. Padgett knocked down three treys, all in the second half, and finished with 16 points. Tim James had 22 for ex-UK assistant Leonard Hamilton's Hurricanes.

Padgett came through with eight of his 17 points in overtime to lead the Cats past 11th-ranked Indiana 70-61 in Freedom Hall. Padgett's heroics nullified a magnificent comeback by Indiana, which overcame a nine-point deficit inside the final 1:21 to force the OT. Evans was UK's top scorer with 22 points. Luke Recker, architect of IU's comeback, led his club with 18.

All-America performances by seniors Padgett, Evans and Turner (73 points, 22 rebounds, 14 assists) lifted the Cats to a thrilling 103-91 upset win over No. 2-ranked Maryland. It was the Cats' fourth straight win over a ranked opponent, and their 11th straight dating back to last season. UK's three seniors couldn't have been more brilliant. Evans scored a career-high 31 points, Padgett accounted for 25 points and 13 rebounds, and Turner had 17 points and seven assists. Prince also played well, finishing with 13 points. Terrence Morris and Steve Francis led Maryland with 26 and 25 points, respectively.

In what had to be the worst rout since Sherman's bunch marched through, the Cats, after bolting to a 25-2 lead to start the game, went on to destroy Georgia Tech 80-39 in Atlanta. Georgia Tech, always a dangerous challenger, scored only 12 points in the first half and shot an Arctic-

like 24.2 percent from the field. Bradley paced the Cats with 16 points, while Magloire and Hogan each added 15.

The defensive tables turned in the Cats' next outing, a 70-61 loss to No. 2-ranked Duke in the Jimmy V Classic. The Blue Devils, who held UK to a season-low 34.9 percent shooting, used an 11-0 run early in the second half to break open what had been a tightly contested battle. Elton Brand scored 22 to lead Duke. Padgett and Evans each had 13 for the Cats.

Louisville made it two straight over the Cats, winning 83-74 in Freedom Hall. It marked the first time in five years that UK dropped back-to-back decisions. The Cardinals had no trouble solving UK's defense, making good on 25 of 48 shots for 52.1 percent. The Cats, meanwhile, struggled with their shooting, particularly from three-point range, where they made just two of 15. Marques Maybin led UL with 19 points. Padgett had 13 for the Cats.

In their final game before hitting the SEC trail, the Cats got a breather against Tennessee State, winning easily 97-47. All 12 Wildcat players scored, headed by Magloire with 15 and Turner and Hogan with 11 each.

The Cats thundered out of the gate once SEC action began, blasting Florida 93-58 in Rupp Arena, then beating South Carolina 68-61 and Vanderbilt 73-57 on the road. The Cats knocked down 11 treys in the win over Florida, now coached by ex-Pitino assistant Billy Donovan. Padgett led a balanced UK attack with 19 points. Bradley had 18, Hogan 11 and Camara 10. Brent Wright paced the Gators with 20.

Padgett scored 19, Bradley 14 and Magloire had a double-double (12/11) in the win at South Carolina. The Gamecocks' classy guard BJ McKie led all scorers with 31 points. Padgett had 12 points in the win over Vandy, but it was UK's depth that proved to be the difference. Wildcat subs, led by Hogan's 10 points, accounted for 40 points.

A three-pointer by Brandon Wharton with 1:09 left gave Tennessee a 47-46 win over the Cats. It was UT's first win in Lexington since 1979. Cold shooting (30.9 percent) contributed to UK's lowest point total since 1987. Turner led UK with 13 points. Wharton ended the night with 14.

Depth and defense were this club's salvation in wins over Ole Miss and sixth-ranked Auburn. Saul Smith came off the bench to score 17 points and Padgett added 13 (all in the second half) against an Ole Miss club that went 17 minutes in the second half without scoring a bucket. In the Cats' 72-62 victory over unbeaten Auburn, it was Allison

Tayshaun Prince flashed great promise during his rookie campaign. The long-armed California native had seven double-figure performances, including 12 points in UK's 73-66 NCAA tourney loss to Michigan State.

who provided the spark. Allison canned four of six shots and scored 10 points to help the Cats build a 31-22 lead by intermission. Evans paced UK with 20 points and nine rebounds. Chris Porter had 16 for Auburn.

After beating Mississippi State 76-49, the Cats came back to nip Georgia 91-83 in overtime. Once again, Padgett proved to be a tough cookie in crunch time, scoring 10 of his team-high 23 points in the extra period. Evans opened

the OT with an old-fashioned three-point play, then Padgett hit two treys, scored on a tip-in and dropped in a pair of freebies to clinch the win for UK. Georgia's Jumaine Jones topped all scorers with 34 points.

The Cats had no trouble polishing off LSU 86-62 in Rupp Arena. Turner led UK with 14 points, Allison had 11 and Magloire picked up another double-double (10/11). That win was followed by back-to-back road losses — 75-68 at Florida and 62-58 at Alabama. UK had seven more field goals than Florida, but the Gators overcame that difference by hitting 24 of 34 free throws to 10 of 19 by the Cats. Mike Miller paced Florida with 20 points. Turner led the Cats with 15.

In a game that featured nine ties and seven lead changes in the second half, Alabama prevailed by making more big plays down the stretch. With the Cats leading 58-57, Sam Haginas rammed home a dunk to give Alabama the lead for good. Bradley and Padgett each had 14 to lead UK. Doc Robinson tossed in 20 for the victorious Crimson Tide.

The Cats snapped their first two-game SEC losing skid since 1992 by spanking South Carolina 74-40 and Georgia 92-71. Against the Gamecocks, five Cats hit in double figures, led by Padgett with 13. In the win over Georgia, seven UK players cracked double digits, topped by Evans and Turner with 13 each.

Arkansas built a 67-54 lead then fought off a late UK charge to post a 74-70 win in Fayetteville. Treys

Sophomore Michael Bradley started every game during the 1998-99 season, averaging 9.8 points and setting a UK single-season record by hitting 65.7 percent of his field goal attempts. After the season, Bradley surprised everyone by announcing his decision to leave UK.

by Padgett and Hogan, a layup by Smith, a rebound bucket by Magloire, an Allison free throw and a Turner layup pulled the Cats to within 69-68 with just under three minutes left. After Arkansas' Chris Walker buried a three, Magloire scored on a tip-in to make it 72-70 with 2:25 left to play. That would be the Cats' last bucket. Magloire had 14 points and 11 rebounds for UK. Padgett also scored 14, while Allison and Smith finished with 12 and 10, respectively. Kareen Reid and Pat Bradley shared scoring honors for Arkansas with 17 points each.

The Cats split their final two regular season games, crushing Vanderbilt 88-63 and losing to Tennessee 68-61. Padgett led the Cats in the win over Vandy, racking up 16 points and 10 rebounds. At Knoxville, the Cats blew a nine-point second-half advantage, resulting in the Vols' first sweep of UK since 1979. Tony Harris had 18 for Tennessee. Padgett and Bradley each had 10 for the Cats, who were done in by sloppy ball-handling (20 turnovers) and poor shooting (44.8 percent).

As they had done so often in the past, seniors Padgett and Turner took their game to a higher level once postseason play began. Turner scored 21 of his career-high 24 points after intermission to propel the foul-plagued Cats to a tough 83-73 win over Ole Miss in SEC Tournament quarterfinal action. The score was knotted 31-31 at the half, but the Cats, sparked by Turner's second-half explosion, gained control early in the second stanza and slowly pulled away for the win. Evans finished with

16 points for the Cats, while Padgett chipped in with 10. Carter led Ole Miss with 23.

Next up for the Cats: fourth-ranked Auburn, the SEC's regular-season champs. The Cats, though a slight underdog, rocked Auburn early, bolting to a 26-9 lead less than 10 minutes into the game. Auburn made a late charge, pulling to within six, but clutch buckets down the stretch by rookies Prince and Allison enabled the Cats to hang on for the 69-57 victory and advance to their eighth consecutive SEC tourney final. Turner and Padgett each had 13 points to lead UK. Others in double figures included Evans with 11 and Allison and Magloire with 10 each. Jay Heard had 14 for the Tigers.

Tourney MVP Padgett scored 15 of his game-high 20 points in the second half, and reserves Smith and Hogan led a first-half comeback, as the Wildcats topped Arkansas 76-63 to capture their seventh SEC Tournament championship in eight years. The Razorbacks were sitting on a 19-6 advantage when Smith buried a three-pointer and Hogan added two more treys to kickstart UK's comeback. The Cats seized control early in the second half, going on an 8-0 run to take a 47-40 lead. It was a lead they never relinquished. Magloire also turned in a solid effort, finishing with 13 points. Padgett was joined on the all-tournament team by Turner, who had 11 points in the title game.

The Cats opened NCAA Tournament play with an 82-60 win over pesky New Mexico State in New Orleans. The win was expected but more difficult than anticipated. Leading 44-43, the Cats rattled off 21 unanswered points to break the game open. Once again, it was the UK seniors who delivered when things got nervy. Evans, Padgett and Turner combined for 40 points, 10 rebounds and 10 assists in leading the Cats to victory. Following the game, Smith informed his team that UK signee John Stewart had died earlier that evening while participating in an Indiana high school tournament game.

Reverting to classic "Comeback Cats" form of a year earlier, the Wildcats, behind Padgett's 29-point, 10-rebound performance, overcame a five-point deficit with 1:29 left in regulation to beat Kansas 92-88 in overtime. Down 79-74, the Cats forced the OT when Turner sank two free throws and Padgett drained a three-pointer from the top of the key. The overtime belonged to Padgett, who bagged a jumper and five free throws to secure the UK win. Turner had 19 points for the Cats, while Evans added 14. Kansas' Ryan Robertson claimed game-high honors with 31.

Another standout defensive effort resulted in a comfort-

able 58-43 Wildcat victory over tourney Cinderella Miami (Ohio) in Mideast Region semifinal action at St. Louis. The Cats held Miami to only 14 field goals, eight of which were scored by All-American Wally Szczerbiak. Padgett again paced the UK attack with 17 points. Szczerbiak finished with 23, but managed just eight in the second half.

With a fourth straight Final Four appearance at stake, the Cats squared off against Big Ten power Michigan State. In the early going, thanks to a blistering start by Evans, it appeared as if the Cats were on their way to St. Petersburg. Evans scored 12 quick points, enabling the Cats to open the game with a 17-4 run. But the gutsy Spartans refused to fold, and by the time All-American guard Mateen Cleaves hit a 30-footer just ahead of the halftime buzzer, they had cut UK's once-formidable lead

The insertion of talented freshman Keith Bogans into the starting lineup helped turn around UK's season. Bogans scored at a 12.5 clip, earning SEC All-Freshman honors.

to 36-35.

The Cats clung to the lead until a layup by Andre Hutson put Michigan State in front 55-54 with 7:30 left to play. While the Cats were misfiring on their next three shots, Michigan State was increasing its lead to six points. Padgett hit a pair of late three-pointers to keep the Cats close, but six free throws by Morris Peterson down the stretch sealed the outcome.

Final: Michigan State 73, UK 66.

Peterson had 19 points and 10 rebounds for the winners. Cleaves, the outstanding point guard, had 10 points and 11 assists. Prince and Evans, who was slowed by early foul troubles, finished with 12 points to lead UK. Padgett had 11 in his final game as a Wildcat.

The Cats had acquitted themselves well, ending with a 28-9 record against a brutal schedule. Padgett led the club in scoring with a 12.6 average, Turner ended his career as UK's all-time greatest thief with 238 steals and Bradley set a new UK single-season mark for field goal accuracy by making good on 65.7 percent of his shots.

Even though the talented trio of Turner, Padgett and Evans were graduating, the Cats had a solid core of players set to return next season. But that number was soon to shrink by two. Sophomores Bradley and Hogan, both unhappy with their situation at UK, announced their intention to transfer.

Suddenly, the UK roster looked much thinner and much younger.

Saul Smith puts up a jumper over a defender. Smith faced the dual challenge of being the club's point guard and the coach's son.

achieved numbers that surpassed virtually all of those accomplished by his predecessors. His Cats had captured the NCAA crown, two SEC tourney titles and one SEC regular-season title while fashioning an overall record of 63-13. Only Adolph Rupp's 85.7 winning percentage in his first two years topped Smith's 82.9 percent.

Smith's third season, unlike the first two, turned out to be anything but smooth. Despite finishing with a fine 23-10 record and a share of the SEC East Division championship, this was a season of struggle, turmoil, manpower shortage and an inability — almost painful at times — to put the ball in the basket. No UK team has ever had more sustained scoring droughts than this one.

By March, Smith had only nine players, his point guard — and son Saul — was a lightning rod for criticism and Wildcat fans, never known for patience, were beginning to howl.

What got lost in the midst of all the unhappiness is the fact that Smith and his coaching staff did a superb job under nearly impossible circumstances. Although the Cats shot just 42.3 percent from the field, an even colder 29.2 percent from beyond the three-point line and had 75 more turnovers than assists, they still put together a solid won-lost record against one of the nation's most-demanding schedules.

After a 4-4 start and a fall from the Top 20 for the first time in a decade, Smith and his coaches guided this young and undermanned team to 19 wins in its final 25 games, including one stretch in which the Cats won 13 of 14. Smith achieved

1999-00

In his first two seasons at UK, Tubby Smith had

this by masking the deficiencies (as best he could) while developing one of the best half-court defensive teams in UK history. Opponents managed just 39-percent shooting against a tall, long-armed Wildcat team that blocked 185 enemy shots.

Seldom were the wins easy or pretty. In fact, if winning ugly was artistry, this UK team was Barishnikov.

Smith knew going in that he had more holes to fill than a grave digger. Some were expected, some came as a surprise. Turner, Padgett and Evans were lost to graduation, but Bradley and Hogan, the team's two best shooters, pulled a shocker when they opted to leave. One UK signee, talented 6'9" Marquis Estill, was ineligible to play as a freshman, and another, 6'9" JUCO transfer Nate Knight, played nine games and then transferred. In March, the Cats' roster, now numbering 10, was cut by one when starter Desmond Allison was charged with a DUI. Further damaging UK's late-season hopes was an injury to Marvin Stone's hand that hampered his play.

Given the circumstances, for Smith and his staff to squeeze 23 wins out of this thin band of warriors was nothing less than a minor miracle.

At the core of this club's success was Magloire, the 6'10" senior center who tamed his WWF instincts, improved his offensive abilities and became a superb team leader. Magloire finished with a 13.2 scoring average, shot 50 percent from the field, pulled down 9.1 rebounds per game, had 15 double-doubles and blocked 57 shots, giving him a school-record 268 for his career. His efforts earned him first-team All-SEC recognition.

Joining Magloire was senior Masiello, juniors Smith and Knight, sophomores Prince, Camara, Allison, Camara, Blevins and Tackett, and talented rookies Stone and Keith Bogans.

Stone, a 6'10" Alabama native, came off the bench to score 12 points and spear six rebounds in the Cats' 67-50 win over Penn in the Preseason NIT. Magloire and Allison each added 11 points for the Cats in what proved to be a preview of what lay ahead. The Cats struggled from the field (24 of 59 for 40.7 percent), but came out on top by holding the opposition to 31 percent shooting and winning the rebounding wars 43-37.

Magloire scored 15 and Prince added 11 as the Cats beat old foe Utah 56-48 to earn a shot at 24th-ranked Maryland in semifinal action in Madison Square Garden. With Prince scoring 21 points and Bogans adding 17, the Cats built a 40-27 halftime lead and then managed to hang on for a 61-58 win. Stone again played well, pulling down 13

rebounds.

In the title game match up against eighth-ranked Arizona, it was the defense of Lute Olson's team that made the difference. Arizona held UK to 35.6 shooting, had 15 steals and forced 21 turnovers. The result was a 63-51 Arizona win. Prince paced the Cats with 16 points, while tourney MVP Gilbert Arenas had 20 for Arizona.

That defeat was quickly followed by back-to-back losses to Dayton (68-66) and Indiana (83-75). Camara's 12 points topped the Cats against Dayton, while Prince had 17 in the loss to Indiana. All-American guard A.J. Guyton led the Hoosiers with 21.

The Cats split their next two games, destroying UNC-Asheville 86-41, then dropping a 72-66 rematch decision to Maryland. Five Cats cracked double figures against UNC-Asheville, led by Allison with 15. Others included Magloire

Athletic sophomore Jules Camara showed flashes of brillance during the 1999-00 campaign. He cracked double figures nine times, and proved to be a superb passer from the top of the key.

with 14, Bogans and Stone with 12 each and Camara with 11.

Turnovers (20) again proved costly in the loss to Maryland. The Terps, led by Terence Morris' 22 points, held off a late charge by UK to claim the win. Smith had 15 points and Magloire recorded his first double-double with a 12-point, 16-rebound performance.

With his team struggling along at 4-4, Tubby Smith made the decision to insert Bogans into the starting quintet. It was a move that paid immediate dividends (six straight wins, 13 in UK's next 14 games), and, perhaps more than any other factor, was the reason why the Cats were able to turn a potential nightmare season into one that was more than respectable. Bogans possessed the ability to score from the outside or take it to the rack and score in close. He

Ex-Metcalfe County standout J.P. Blevins was the team's deadliest three-point shooter. He hit for a season-high 14 in a win over Georgia.

was also creative and audacious, ingredients that brought instant offense to a slumping team badly in need of a knockout punch.

Louisville was the first to feel the sting of UK's new lineup, losing 76-46 in Rupp Arena. After leading 35-34 at the half, the Cats outscored the stunned visitors 41-12 in the final 20 minutes to come away with the easy victory. It was one of UK's rare on-target shooting nights — 31 of 52 for 59.6 percent. Prince led a balanced UK attack with 20 points. Allison finished with 16, Magloire and Bogans each had 12.

Taking advantage of an absent Mateen Cleaves, the Cats overcame an early 26-11 first-half deficit then went on to edge Michigan State 60-58. The Cats, after trailing all the way, finally claimed a 50-49 lead when Blevins knocked down his third three-pointer. Magloire and Michigan State's Morris Peterson shared game-high honors with 18 points apiece. Prince had 17 points for the Cats and Blevins chipped in with nine.

The Cats continued their superb play, rolling to impres-

sive wins over Alaska-Anchorage (62-42), Missouri (70-53) and Georgia Tech (80-71) to close out their pre-SEC campaign with a 9-4 record. Prince, Magloire and Stone each had 10 points against Alaska-Anchorage, then Magloire followed that with a 21-point, 13-rebound effort against Missouri in the Sugar Bowl Classic. Against Georgia Tech, sophomores Prince and Camara fueled the Cats to their first win in the new millennium. Prince had 21 points and 10 rebounds, while Camara came off the bench to toss in a career-best 15 points. Jason Collier topped the Yellow Jackets with 21.

Prince gunned in five treys and scored 17 points to lead the Cats to a 72-52 pasting of Vanderbilt in the SEC opener. It was another superb effort by the Cats, and it kept Vandy winless in Rupp Arena. Magloire tossed in 15 for the Cats, while Bogans and Blevins each contributed 10.

Thanks to a combined 57 points from Chris Porter, Doc Robinson and Kentucky native Daymeon Fishback, fourth-ranked Auburn snapped the Cats' six-game winning streak, winning 66-63 at home. The Cats rallied from 14 down to grab a 55-50 advantage with less than eight minutes remaining. Then Porter and Robinson went to work, scoring 12 of their club's next 14 points. With the score knotted at 61-61, Robinson buried a three-pointer to put the Tigers in front for good. Porter led Auburn with 22 points and 13 rebounds. Robinson and Fishback finished with 18 and 17, respectively. Magloire had 16 to lead UK.

The Cats bounced back to rip South Carolina 64-48, using a stifling defense to hold the homestanding Gamecocks to 27-percent field goal shooting. Magloire again paced the Cats with 15 points, while Prince and Camara had 13 and 12, respectively.

In a game marred by four technical fouls, the Cats dug out of a 10-point halftime hole to edge Ole Miss 74-69. Magloire sparked the comeback win by turning in a ter-

rific 19-point, 14-rebound performance. He received solid support from Bogans with 12 points and Prince with 10. Ole Miss forward Marcus Hicks had 27 points to lead all scorers.

Allison and Magloire came up big in UK's next outing, an 81-73 overtime win at Vanderbilt. Another factor in the Cats' win was their outside shooting. In a rare display of long-range accuracy, they connected on 12 of 27 three-point attempts. Allison and Magloire each had 23 points for the Cats, while Smith added 12. Fifteen of Magloire's points came after the intermission, including four in the OT.

After Magloire scored 19 and Prince and Bogans each added 14 in a 75-69 win at Georgia, the Cats stepped away from SEC action for a match up against ex-UK assistant coach Leonard Hamilton's Miami Hurricanes. It was a hard-nosed defensive tussle,

Steady Desmond Allison's absence from the NCAA Tournament was the final blow for a Wildcat team that was already facing a manpower shortage.

and it wasn't decided until Prince hit a running one-hander that put the Cats ahead for good at 58-57. Two Magloire free throws with 3.4 seconds left sealed the win for UK. Bogans paced the Cats with 16 points.

Bogans erupted for 25 points and Prince added 17 as the Cats beat sixth-ranked Tennessee 81-68 for their sixth straight victory. Smith also gave a strong showing for UK, scoring 12 points and handing out five assists.

The Cats' win streak reached seven when Magloire and Bogans combined for 44 points in a 76-63 victory over South Carolina. Magloire had 23 and Bogans 21 to pace UK. Allison and Prince also cracked double digits with 11 and 10, respectively.

The thin Cats proved to be no match for deep and talented Florida, losing 90-73 in Gainesville. Billy Donovan's club pounded the Cats in every area, shooting 50 percent from the field and controlling the boards 49-36. Six Gators scored in double figures, led by Teddy Dupay with 14. Bogans led all scorers with 24.

LSU, taking advantage of UK's dismal 18-point first-half effort, built a 45-25 second-half lead, watched it trimmed to five with 4:21 left to play, then went on to post a 70-57 win in Baton Rouge. Stromile Swift keyed the LSU win with 26 points. Smith, who sparked UK's second-half surge, finished with 15 for the Cats.

Against Alabama, it was the Cats who built a big 18-point lead, saw it evaporate to five with less than three minutes remaining, then held on for a tough 66-54 win. After the Tide pulled to within 54-49, Prince scored on a layup and Magloire added four points to secure the win. Magloire had 16 for UK, Prince had 14 and Bogans and Camara 10 each.

With Prince, Bogans and Allison not in the starting lineup, Blevins picked up the slack, scoring 14 points and dishing out four assists, including one on a crowd-pleasing Chapmanesque behind-the-back pass to Camara, to help the Cats escape with a 70-64 win over Georgia. Bogans came in to score 13, Camara added 11 and Smith and Magloire finished with 11 each for the winning Wildcats.

Ignited by a 27-point performance by guard Tony Harris, Tennessee invaded Rupp Arena and conquered the Cats 74-67. Harris was splendid, hitting seven of 14 shots, including six of 11 from behind the three-point arc. Hopkinsville native Isiah Victor also put the hammer to UK, scoring 22 points and grabbing seven rebounds. Allison paced the Cats with 15.

Bogans scored 22 in a 60-55 win over Arkansas, then Magloire and Prince each had 16 as the Cats polished off Mississippi State 73-61. Then in the regular-season finale, the Cats turned in their finest performance of the season, hitting 53 percent from the field in a convincing 85-70 revenge win over Florida. Five Wildcats hit double figures, led by Prince with 19. Magloire, in his final home appearance, had 14 points and 13 rebounds.

The momentum from the Florida game failed to have a

long shelf-life. The Cats' post-season was anything but grand or threatening. Beginning with a sudden exit from the SEC Tournament, the Cats played hard but poorly, and hampered by lack of depth, were no longer able to mask or overcome such deficiencies as cold shooting and sloppy ball-handling.

Arkansas blistered the Cats in their SEC tourney opener, winning easily 86-72. The Cats committed 16 first-half turnovers and trailed 36-22 at the break. Bogans turned in the Cats' best effort, scoring a game-high 25 points. Magloire had 16 and Prince 15. Joe Johnson scored 21 for the winning Razorbacks.

Three days later, and only hours before opening against St. Bonaventure in the NCAA Tournament, the Cats got word that Allison had been suspended. It was the knockdown punch for a UK team that was already reeling unsteadily against the ropes. His absence cost the Cats size, defense, experience and manpower. With Allison out, Tubby Smith took a nine-man team to the Big Dance.

With only seven players seeing action, the gutsy Cats,

Junior Tayshaun Prince's brilliant play earned him SEC Player of the Year recognition for the 2000-01 season and the league tourney's MVP award.

points — three by Bogans, two by Prince — to finally pass this survival test.

Prince was the Cats' top gun, scoring a season-high 28 points. Bogans added 19 and Magloire finished with 11.

But once again, any hope that the ever-so-capricious momentum had landed in UK's corner turned out to be fool's gold. Facing Syracuse, in a game in which bad won out over worse, the Cats lost 52-50. Combined, the two teams shot 35.5 percent and committed 32 turnovers. Still, despite playing poorly, the Cats had their chances to pull it out. With the score knotted at 50-50, the Cats had the ball and were looking to score the go-ahead bucket. But Syracuse guard Jason Hart tied up Smith, giving the Orangemen the ball on the alternate-possession arrow. Moments later, freshman Preston Shumpert hit a 17-foot jumper from the right corner to give Syracuse a 52-50 lead with 36.8 seconds left. UK's hopes of snatching a win or forcing an overtime died when Bogans' seven-foot twisting leaner fell short of the basket.

Bogans and Magloire led the Cats with 12 points apiece. Prince and Camara each had 10.

thanks to a dramatic Prince three-pointer with seven seconds left in regulation, lived to see another day by squeaking to an 85-80 double-overtime victory. Prince gunned in his jumper with his team on the short end of a 63-60 score.

UK led by five in the first overtime, and was still in front 76-73 when Stone fouled the three-point shooting Messiah Capers with one tick remaining. The icy Capers drilled all three freebies to send the game into a second extra period. After Magloire and Stone sandwiched a bucket each around four points by Capers, the Cats scored five unanswered

Shumpert tied for game-high honors with 12.

Despite shooting just 42.3 percent, the lowest by a UK team since 1962-63, the Cats finished with a 23-10 record. Prince led the club in scoring with a 13.3 average, while Bogans, an SEC All-Freshman pick, finished with a 12.5 scoring clip.

2000-01

Few Wildcat clubs have gotten off to a shakier start than this one, and few have made a more-complete recovery. In every way, this was another test for Tubby Smith, who once

again proved that he has few equals when it comes to turning around a struggling team. In every way, Smith's coaching performance this season ranks among the best-ever in UK history.

Smith's calming presence was essential to this young, thin and inexperienced team's success. So was his patience. This was a team that had more new faces (seven) than a Beverly Hills plastic surgeon's office, began the season after just three weeks of practice and had to go up against the usual difficult Wildcat slate. Smith knew it was going to be a difficult challenge, and it was.

In many ways, this season closely mirrored the one that preceded it. For the second straight year, a key player fell victim to a DUI charge, a slow start was followed by a strong finish and a lineup change played a pivotal role in that turnaround. It also didn't hurt that junior Tayshaun Prince and sophomore Keith Bogans emerged as big-time players. Without their superb season-long efforts, this team couldn't have achieved what it did.

UK's first loss came long before the season began, coming in the court rather than on the court. Junior Jules Camara, one of the team's most-athletic players, was charged with a DUI and suspended for the season. Camara, unlike Desmond Allison, chose to remain at UK, sit out the season, then rejoin the club in 2001-02. Still, though, his absence clearly affected the team. The Cats missed his athleticism, shot-blocking and passing skills, and his experience.

But what the fates taketh away, they can also giveth. In this case, that gift was named Jason Parker, a 6'8", 255-pound prep All-American from Charlotte, N.C. The much-coveted Parker was ticketed to attend North

Carolina, only to see that dream evaporate when N.C. officials ruled that he was academically ineligible. When Parker expressed an interest in becoming a Wildcat, UK officials took a closer look at his transcript. What they found was that he hadn't been given credit for certain classes, and that he was immediately eligible to play. It was a huge bonus for the Wildcats. His strength and imposing presence provided solid inside play while also helping to offset the loss of Camara.

Veterans Prince, Bogans, Saul Smith, Marvin Stone and J.P. Blevins were surrounded by so many newcomers that they probably needed name tags to identify their teammates during the first weeks of practice. Joining the club were sophomore Marquis Estill and freshmen Parker, Cliff Hawkins, Gerald Fitch, Erik Daniels, Cory Sears and Matt Heissenbuttel. Another veteran, junior Todd Tackett, opted to redshirt after undergoing knee surgery.

The rookies were a diverse, intriguing group. Parker was clearly the centerpiece, having earned a national reputation as one of the top prep players in the country. But the others, although talented, weren't McDonald's All-Americans with big-time national press clippings. The 6'9" Estill, a Richmond Madison Central graduate, was coming back after sitting out his freshman year as a partial qualifier; Hawkins, a jet-quick 6'1" point guard, came from prestigious Oak Hill Academy; Fitch, a 6'3" guard/forward, came from Macon, Ga.; and Daniels, a 6'7" lefty, played

Saul Smith goes airborne to save the ball from going out of bounds. The hustling Smith finished his UK career with 363 assists.

for Princeton High School in Cincinnati. They were joined by Kentucky natives Sears, 6'6" from Corbin, and Heissenbuttal, 6'4" from Lexington Catholic.

With so much inexperience, and with so little preparation time, it was probably inevitable that this team would struggle coming out of the gate. And it did. Back-to-back losses in the Coaches vs. Cancer Classic had this club in an 0-2 hole for the first time since the 1975-76 season. Then, just a month later, after the Cats saw their record dip to 3-5, the Big Blue faithful, never known for *their* patience, began to howl their disenchantment, their primary targets being the Smiths — Tubby and Saul. However, by season's end, those jeers had become cheers, thanks to Tubby's excellent job of turning this club around and Saul's on-court effort and his grace under pressure.

But without question, it was the play of Prince and Bogans that keyed this club's resurrection. Both were steady and brilliant, giving the Cats a magnificent 1-2 knockout punch. Prince averaged 16.9 points, earned second-team All-America status and was named the SEC's MVP for the regular season and postseason tourney. Bogans, the team's leading scorer with a 17-point clip, was named to the SEC all-tournament team and was a second-team All-SEC selection for his play during the season.

Early on, after the rocky start, it looked as if this team's fate might be decided more by who wasn't in uniform rather than who was. Remember, this club could have had Camara, Allison, Michael Bradley, Ryan Hogan, Myron Anthony and John Stewart on its roster. Add those six, or even two or three, and this club would have been much bigger, stronger and experienced.

The Cats opened by giving two dreadful performances in Madison Square Garden, losing to St. John's 62-61 and UCLA 97-92 in overtime. Against the Red Storm, in a game that had 11 ties and seven lead changes, the Cats hit just two of 15 three-point attempts and blew a seven-point second-half lead. Despite their sloppy play, the Cats were done in by a questionable call at the end. With his team up by two, Prince had the ball knocked away and out of bounds. The official, however, awarded the ball to the Red Storm. On the ensuing in-bounds play, Anthony Glover scored, drew a foul from Parker and hit the game-deciding free throw. Estill had a strong debut effort, leading the Cats with 15 points. Bogans and Stone each added 14. Glover led all scorers with 21.

Against the Bruins in the consolation game, Bogans

The inclusion of Gerald Fitch into the starting lineup was a big reason why the Cats turned their season around.

came through with 25 points and Prince added 20, but it wasn't enough to get the win. The Cats led by three in the extra frame, only to watch the Bruins reel off 11 unanswered points to notch the victory. Smith also played well for UK, scoring 13 points and handing out eight assists. Jason Kapono paced the Bruins with 21, while Earl Watson and Ray Young each had 20.

Led by hometown hero Daniels, the Cats scorched outmanned Jacksonville State 91-48 in Cincinnati to snap their two-game skid. Daniels topped the Cats with a game-high 19 points. Also in double figures for UK were Bogans (14), Prince (14), Parker (13) and Stone (10). The Cats

connected on 31 of 51 shots (60.8 percent) while limiting the visitors to just 15 field goals. UK's defense also forced 33 turnovers.

Thanks to 57 points from brothers Joe and Jon Crispin, the Cats' first game in Rupp Arena turned out to be anything but a happy experience. With Joe scoring 31 and Jon adding 25, Penn State shocked the Cats 73-68. Combined, the Crispin brothers burned the Cats from long range, hitting 13 of 23 three-pointers. Daniels paced the Cats with 16, while Parker finished with 15 points and 15 rebounds.

If the Penn State loss was a home court shocker, then the Cats' easy 93-76 win over North Carolina in Chapel Hill was a road surprise of equal magnitude. The Cats broke away from a three-point halftime advantage to bury the Tar Heels during the final 20 minutes. It was a dazzling effort, especially by the UK reserves, who scored 38 points and hauled down 20 rebounds. Hawkins ignited the charge, scoring nine of his 11 points in a first-half explosion that enabled the Cats to overcome an early 21-11 deficit. Estill led UK with 19 points. Bogans finished with 18, Prince 15 and Smith 12. Joseph Forte topped the Tar Heels with 19 points.

Despite committing 29 turnovers, the Cats still had too much firepower for Eastern Kentucky, winning convincingly 94-79 in Rupp Arena. Bogans paced the Cats with 21 points, while Smith chipped in with 17. Prince and Daniels also cracked double digits with 15 and 14, respectively.

The Cats followed that win by dropping a pair of heartbreakers, losing to Georgia Tech 86-84 in Atlanta and to Michigan State 46-45 in East Lansing. Shaun Fein knocked down a baseline jumper with 1.3 seconds left to give the Yellow Jackets their victory. Fein's bucket offset a brilliant comeback effort by the Cats, who rallied from 13 points down to take an 84-83 lead with just over a minute remaining. Bogans again led UK with 22 points. Prince finished with 20. Halston Lane was the game's top scorer with 23.

Against the second-ranked Spartans, the Cats were brilliant on defense, holding the defending national champs to 18 first-half points and a cool 35.3 percent shooting from the field. But the Cats were equally cold, going almost seven minutes before scoring their first bucket in the second half. That allowed the Spartans to climb back in it, setting the stage for a thrilling finish. Andre Hutson scored the game-winning layup with 26.4 seconds left. The Cats had one final chance, but Bogans failed to connect as time ran down.

It was at this stage, with his team owning a 3-5 record,

that Tubby Smith made a move that proved to be brilliant and productive. He inserted Fitch into the starting quintet, replacing Stone. The move made the Cats smaller but much quicker. It also made the lanky, agile Prince, now the power forward, a much more difficult player to defend.

Smith's strategy paid immediate dividends, an impressive 88-74 win over tough Indiana in Freedom Hall. Bogans

Freshman Jason Parker provided the Cats with a powerful inside presence. He came to UK after earning prep All-America honors in North Carolina.

Keith Bogans discusses a Wildcat victory with ex-Cat Larry Conley. Bogans had a superb sophomore season, leading the club in scoring with a 17-point average.

keyed the Cats with 26 points, hitting nine of 13 from the field. Prince tossed in 20, Stone added 13 and Fitch registered 10 points and six rebounds in his debut start. No one realized it at the time, but this was the beginning of a seven-game UK winning streak.

The Cats closed out their pre-SEC schedule by blasting High Point 102-49 and edging Louisville 64-62 in Freedom Hall. All 12 Cats scored against Tubby Smith's alma mater, led by Parker with 16 and Daniels with 14. In the comeback win over Louisville, it was a pair of Prince freebies with 26.5 seconds left that was the difference. Bogans paced UK with 16. Prince chipped in with 13, while Parker and Stone each had 11. Reece Gaines was the lone Cardinal in doubles figures with 27.

In the league opener against Georgia, the Cats led by 15 in the first half and were on top by 11 with less than four minutes remaining, then had to hang on in the closing seconds to escape with 67-63 win. It was a nerve-wracking scenario that became all too familiar to Big Blue fans during the last half of the season. After Georgia closed to within 65-63 with 12 seconds left, Fitch hit one of two free tosses to make it 66-63. Following a D.A. Layne miss, the Cats added another freebie to account for the final margin. Prince and Estill each had a dozen points for the Cats, but it was eight points by Blevins off the bench that sparked this Wildcat win.

Balanced scoring enabled the Cats to top South Carolina 69-63 after again blowing a big advantage late in the game. After leading by 12 with less than 11 minutes left, the Cats needed back-to-back buckets by Prince and Bogans to break away from a 61-61 tie and earn the hard-fought win. Bogans and Estill each had 11 points to lead UK. Prince and Parker contributed 10 apiece. Marius Petravicius led all scorers with 13.

The Cats continued their winning ways, beating No. 25-ranked Notre Dame 82-71 and fourth-ranked Tennessee 84-74. Both wins came in Rupp Arena. Prince led four Cats in double figures against the Irish, scoring 19 points. Other double-digit scorers included Bogans (14), Fitch (13) and Daniels (10). Troy Murphy led the Irish with 14,

while Lexington Catholic grad David Graves added 13.

Four Cats also cracked double figures against the Volunteers, topped by Bogans with 21. Others included Prince with 16 and Parker and Fitch with 10 each. Vincent Yarbrough tossed in 21 to match Bogans for game-high honors.

UK's success against ranked teams came to an end with back-to-back losses to No. 21 Ole Miss (65-55) in Oxford and No. 18 Alabama (70-60) in Tuscaloosa. The surprising Rebels used a superb defensive effort to get this win, holding the Cats to 38.5 percent shooting while forcing 21 miscues. Jason Harrison led Ole Miss with 16 points. Estill's 13 topped UK.

At Alabama, the Cats were on top 54-47 when Rod Grizzard went to work, accounting for 11 of his 25 points in the final five minutes to lift the Crimson Tide to victory. Prince paced the Cats with 15 points.

Estill and Saul Smith combined for 37 points to help the Cats snap their two-game skid with an 86-75 win over Vanderbilt. Once again, the Cats had to hang on after building a huge second-half lead (49-29). A Prince dunk, followed by a Fitch trey enabled the Cats to escape disaster. Estill and Smith scored 19 and 18, respectively, while Prince had 15

Cincinnati native Erik Daniels was one of the few bright spots during the Cats' slow start. Daniels, a lefty, hit 57 percent from the field in his rookie season.

with 21 to lead all scorers.

In the Cats' next outing, at Georgia, Bogans and Prince each turned in brilliant double-double efforts in an 85-70 win. Bogans ended the night with 26 points and 11 rebounds, while Prince had 23 points and 10 boards. Estill also hit double

figures for UK with 16 points. Layne led the Bulldogs with 16.

Prince and Bogans stayed hot, hitting for 50 points in the Cats' 94-61 pasting of South Carolina in Columbia. Prince had 29 points and Bogans added 21. Combined, the duo made good on 20 of 26 field goal attempts.

Prince nailed one of his patented baby hooks with 3.3 ticks remaining to lift the Cats past No. 8 Florida 71-70 in Rupp Arena. Billy Donovan's club had battled back from a 45-31 halftime deficit to grab a 70-67 lead on a basket by Brett Nelson with 1:52 left. Following a Stone bucket and a key rebound by Fitch, Prince dropped in the game-clinching bucket. Prince had 19 points to lead UK. Nelson's 18 was tops for the Gators.

The Cats ripped Mississippi State 76-57, then rode a 30-point effort by Prince to a 103-95 win at Tennessee. Prince made good on nine of 13 shots, including six of seven from behind the three-point arc. Bogans offered solid support, scoring 22 points. The Cats also got strong efforts from Fitch (11 points, 11 rebounds) and Smith (nine points, eight assists). Yarbrough burned the Cats for 28 points.

Prince racked up 16 of his team's final 23 points as the Cats held on to beat Vanderbilt 79-74 on the road. Once again, the scenario was maddeningly familiar. The Cats led 45-29 at intermission, then fell behind 62-60. With Vandy clinging to a 67-65 advantage, Prince went to work, hitting three free throws, a rebound bucket and a short jump-hook inside the final three minutes to preserve the win.

The Cats split their next two games, ripping LSU 84-61, then losing 82-78 at Arkansas. Bogans had 40 points in

those two outings to lead the Cats, who, after their dismal start, now owned an 18-8 record overall and an 11-3 mark in SEC action.

With Parker scoring 19 points on nine of 12 shooting, the Cats clinched the regular-season SEC championship by beating Auburn 90-78. The win also secured a No. 1 seed in the upcoming SEC Tournament. Parker received plenty of support from his teammates. Prince tallied 12, Daniels and Fitch 11 each, and Bogans 10. The game was senior Saul Smith's final home appearance.

In the regular-season finale for both clubs, sixth-ranked Florida, behind Teddy Dupay's 28-point performance, bumped off the 15th-ranked Cats 94-86 in Gainesville. Bogans scored a career-high 29 points and the Cats scorched the nets for 59.5 percent second-half shooting, yet it wasn't enough to slip past the talented Gators. Prince finished with 18 and Smith 12 for the Cats, while Udonis

Haslem had 20 for Florida.

Led by an MVP performance by Prince, the Cats captured the SEC tourney crown for the third time during Tubby Smith's four-year tenure, beating South Carolina 78-65, Arkansas 87-78 and Ole Miss 77-55 to claim the hardware. The Cats, fueled by Bogans' 23 points, had little trouble in the win over South Carolina. Parker finished with 14, while Prince and Fitch chipped in with 12 and 10, respectively. Rolando Howell had 20 for Eddie Fogler's club.

The revenge win against Arkansas was anything but easy. The Cats had to battle back from a 40-25 deficit to secure a spot in the title game. Bogans (23/10) and Prince (19/10)

Newcomers Marquis Estill, left, and Cliff Hawkins made solid contributions during the 2000-01 season. Estill could score from inside or outside, while Hawkins added speed and quickness from his point-guard spot.

again rang up double-doubles for the Cats. Fitch scored a career-best 17 points and Stone added 11 points and eight rebounds. Joe Johnson had 24 points for the Hogs.

In the championship game, the Cats took the lead for good on a Hawkins layup, then raced to the 23rd SEC Tournament title in the school's history. The Cats led 36-19 at the break, upped that margin to 28 in the second half and never looked back. Prince led the charge with a 26-point, 12-rebound effort, earning him MVP honors. Bogans, who finished with 19 points, was also named to the All-SEC squad.

Pitted against ex-UK assistant Ralph Willard's Holy Cross club in first-round NCAA Tournament action, the Cats, a heavy favorite, used a late Prince-led rally to edge the Crusaders 72-68 and avoid disaster. With the score knotted at 58-58, and with the momentum clearly in the Holy Cross corner, Prince drained two clutch three-pointers to put the Cats on top by six. Seconds later, after Holy Cross closed to within 68-65, Prince waited as the shot clock ran down, then canned a 10-footer to seal the win. Prince paced UK with 27 points. Bogans scored 17 and Parker added 10. Jared Curry led Holy Cross with 16.

Thirty-one points from Prince, 22 from Estill and 58.5 percent shooting were enough to carry the Cats past Iowa 92-79 and into the Sweet 16. The Cats trailed early, then took the lead for good on a Fitch bucket. That lead swelled to a dozen by intermission, eventually extending to 18 in the final 20 minutes. Prince again blistered the nets, hitting nine of 14 shots, including six of eight three-pointers. Estill was equally hot, knocking down nine of his 11 field goal tries. Bogans had 12 and Fitch 10 for the Cats. Dean Oliver paced Iowa with 26 points.

The Cats' dream of an eighth national championship ended when Southern Cal posted a hard-earned 80-76 victory in Philadelphia. It was the story of two halves. USC owned the first 20 minutes, building a 43-24 lead over the lethargic Wild-

Jason Parker answered questions about his knee injury during a press conference. His absence was a big blow to the 2001-02 club.

cats, who played with little energy or enthusiasm. But in the second half, the Cats came alive, and by the time Bogans and Smith each buried a pair of treys, they had chiseled the USC lead to 61-60 with just over eight minutes left. The Trojans, led by the gutsy play of David Bluthenthal, managed to hang on for the win. After a Daniels bank shot made it 75-74, Bluthenthal, who led all scorers with 27 points, hit five of six free throws inside the final 32 seconds to put away the Cats. Bogans paced the Cats with 23, while Parker had 22 points and 13 rebounds. Smith, in the final game of his career, turned in a sparkling effort, hitting five treys and finishing with 17 points.

Despite the season-ending loss to USC, the Cats acquitted themselves well after stumbling so badly from the gate. They fashioned a 24-10 record overall, won the school's 41st SEC regular-season title and its 23rd SEC tourney title. They had been the recipients of all-everything performances from Prince and Bogans, received solid support from veterans Smith, Stone and Blevins, and been given a huge boost by the play of newcomers Parker, Fitch, Estill, Daniels and Hawkins.

In the end, a season that had all the makings of a disaster turned out to be another success.

2001-02

Injuries, transfers, fake IDs, suspensions, griping players, disgruntled parents — little wonder, then, that this club came to be known as "Team Turmoil."

From the opening tipoff to the final buzzer, this was a season in which controversy and unrest far exceeded excitement and accomplishment. There was little joy for the Wildcat faithful or for the players. Few seasons in UK's now 100-year-old history have been more disappointing and

After much controversy, Marvin Stone left UK in December and transferred to Louisville.

dispiriting than this one. With the exception of the classy and consistent play of the marvelous Tayshaun Prince, the 2001-02 campaign turned out to be a long, joyless and unsatisfying voyage.

Despite the Cats' final 22-10 record and a Top 20 ranking, such was the chaos surrounding this season that by the time the end came, Big Blue fans were openly questioning whether Tubby Smith had lost control of his program. It also didn't help that the 10 losses marked the first time in its storied basketball history that UK has lost 10 or more games three years in succession.

In truth, the Cats' decline began months before the season kicked off. Sophomore post player Jason Parker, counted on to provide inside strength and power, suffered a knee injury (twice) that required surgery. The injury sent him to the sidelines for the entire season, and although no one could have realized it at the time, his absence proved to be a severe blow for a team that lacked strength and power.

Despite Parker's absence, the Cats were ranked in everyone's preseason Top 10, with several prognosticators putting them as high as No. 2. Their reasoning was simple — the Cats returned a core group of veteran players, including Prince and Keith Bogans, both of whom flirted with the NBA draft before finally choosing to remain in school. Other veterans included Gerald Fitch, Cliff Hawkins, Marvin Stone, Erik Daniels, Marquis Estill, J.P. Blevins and Jules Camara, who was back after sitting out the 2000-01 season. Joining this mix were two highly recruited freshmen, Rashaad Carruth and Chuck Hayes, along with Kentucky's Mr. Basketball Josh Carrier and Louisville Ballard All-State standout Adam Chiles.

At the heart of this club's hopes were Prince and Bogans, two battle-tested warriors who had both been sensational in the previous season. Prince averaged 16. 9 points, was the SEC Player of the Year, the MVP of the SEC tourney and a second-team All-America selection, while Bogans, who led the team in scoring with a 17-point scoring clip, had been steady and dependable, earning second-team All-SEC recognition. Prince would go on to have a superb senior season, again earning All-America honors, but Bogans, the other half of UK's 1-2 punch, struggled through a disappointing, nightmare campaign.

The Cats' woes began with a season-opening 64-52 loss to Western Kentucky in the first round of the NABC Classic in Rupp Arena. The fired-up Hilltoppers shut down the UK offense and, in particular, Prince and Bogans. For the game, the UK duo made just seven of 24 field goal attempts. Prince and Stone each had 12 points for the Cats, while WKU's David Boyden led all scorers with 15.

The UK lineup for the opener consisted of Prince, Stone, Bogans, Fitch and Hawkins, who opened at point guard in place of the injured Blevins.

With Bogans tossing in 22 and Estill adding 21, the Cats bounced back to beat Marshall 90-73 in the consolation game. The Cats also got strong play from Daniels, who finished with 10 points, and Hayes, who had eight points and 10 rebounds.

Although the Cats made it two straight with a 94-75 victory over Kyle Macy's Morehead State club, Smith was less than pleased by his team's effort, calling it "horrible" and "just awful." In particular, Smith voiced his displeasure

Freshman Rashaad Carruth had the talent to become a great Wildcat, but unhappiness over lack of playing time led him to leave UK at season's end.

with the team's defense. Despite their poor play, the Cats simply had too much firepower for the Eagles. Prince topped the UK attack with 23 points. Bogans finished with 20 and Estill added 10.

Estill continued his hot scoring, hitting for 19 to tie Bogans for high-point honors in the Cats' 82-68 victory over Kent State. The win didn't come easily. It took a 14-2 run early in the second half to ensure the Cats' third win in a row. Prince and Hawkins also hit double figures with 17 and 12, respectively. Hawkins handed out six assists.

Prince registered his first double-double of the season, hitting for 21 points and raking in 10 rebounds, as the Cats blasted VMI 99-57 in Rupp Arena. Prince made good on nine of 16 shots, including two of five from three-point range. Bogans had 16, Stone 13 and Estill 11 for UK, which shot 55.7 percent from the field (39 of 70).

In a battle between the two most successful Division I programs of all-time, Prince turned in one of the greatest performances ever by a Wildcat, scoring 31 points, grabbing 11 rebounds, knocking down seven of 11 three-point attempts and handing out four assists to lead his club to an easy 79-59 win over North Carolina. Prince ended the drama early, hitting five treys in a span of just over two minutes, including one that ex-Cat Mike Pratt said was from "the suburbs of trey-ville." Thanks to Prince's kingly effort, the Cats built a 47-35 halftime lead and never looked back. Stone was the only other Cats to hit double figures, tossing in 11.

Estill scored 21 points, Prince had 18 and Bogans added 17 as UK showed little mercy to Winston Bennett's Kentucky State club, pounding the ex-Cats' team 118-63. Estill

Jules Camara's return helped the Cats offset the absence of Jason Parker and the early departure of Marvin Stone.

hit nine of 11 shots, while Prince made good on eight of nine attempts. Fitch and Daniels also hit double digits, finishing with 12 and 10, respectively.

It was in the Kentucky State game that the first rumblings of discontent were heard within the UK camp. Carruth, the prep All-American from Oak Hill Academy, in an apparent protest over lack of playing time, took no shots, refusing even to look at the bucket.

In yet another thriller with Duke, the Cats, despite giving what many considered their finest performance of the season, dropped a 95-92 overtime heartbreaker to the top-ranked Blue Devils in the Jimmy V Classic. The Cats had opportunities to win, both in regulation and in the OT, but those chances were consistently shot down by Duke guard Jason Williams, who accounted for 27 of his career-high 38 points after intermission. His three-point play with 1:39 left in overtime erased an 89-88 UK lead and put Duke on top for good. Mike Dunleavy had 21 points for the winners, while Carlos Boozer added 15.

Carruth ended his protest, connecting on seven of 10 shots and finishing the night with 19 points. Other Cats in double figures included Prince (17), Hawkins (15), Fitch (11) and Camara (10). Camara also led all rebounders with 11.

Hawkins turned in a superb 17-point, five-assist effort to help lead the Cats to a 66-52 win over Indiana in Indianapolis. Hawkins had five points and a pair of assists in a 17-6 first-half run that broke the game open. Prince recorded his second double-double, scoring 17 points and pulling down 11 rebounds.

In their highly anticipated showdown against Rick Pitino's Louisville club, the Cats assumed control early in the second half, then raced to a convincing 82-62 victory. UK's defense was instrumental to the outcome, holding the Cardinals to just 36.2 shooting from the field. Prince paced the Cats with 18 points. Bogans chipped in with 17, while Estill and Fitch each contributed 10.

By this point in the season, the status of Stone, the 6'10" junior from Huntsville, Ala., was in limbo. Unhappy over his lack of playing time, Stone would eventually be dismissed from the team, then opted to transfer to the University of Louisville. Initially, UK balked at granting Stone his release, but after Stone's attorney threatened to sue (and UK was slammed by a landslide of negative press), the decision was made to grant the unhappy Wildcat his request to join the Cardinals.

The off-court distractions never bothered the steady

Freshman Chuck Hayes turned out to be a steady, dependable rookie.

Prince, who canned 10 of 13 shots en route to a 22-point effort in the Cats' easy 101-67 romp past Tulane. Prince received solid support from Bogans and Fitch, each of whom scored 16 points. The 6'3" Fitch also led all rebounders with 10.

Mississippi State outscored the Cats 9-4 in overtime to pull off a 74-69 upset in Starkville. The loss was especially disappointing for the sixth-ranked Cats, who made good on 12 of their first 16 shots to grab a 30-10 lead. The Cats still owned a 16-point advantage with 13 minutes left in the

Marquis Estill slams down a dunk over a pair of Tennessee defenders. Estill scored 21 points in wins over Kentucky State and Auburn.

game, only to watch helplessly as things began to unravel. With just under a minute left in regulation, the Cats were clinging to a 65-61 lead after Daniels scored on a layup. But four straight points by MSU's Mario Austin sent the game into OT. Even in the extra frame, UK had a chance to escape with the win. With his team trailing 70-69, Bogans missed an unchallenged layup. After that it was all Mississippi State.

Prince led UK with 18 points. Austin, the talented sophomore center, was the game's top scorer with 32 points.

The Cats fell to 0-2 in SEC play when Georgia, fueled by Jarvis Hayes' 30-point outburst, waltzed into Rupp Arena and danced out with an 88-84 win. Hayes gunned down the Cats, hitting 12 of 18 field goal attempts, including four of eight from behind the three-point arc. Ezra Williams also blistered the Cats, knocking in six of 10 treys and finishing with 20 points.

Camara had 16 for UK. Prince and Carruth each chipped in with 15.

Thanks to a late bucket by Hawkins, the Cats avoided a third straight league setback by edging South Carolina 51-50 in Columbia. Hawkins saved the Cats by hitting a heavily contested leaner in the lane with 3.4 seconds remaining. The UK point guard finished with eight points, five rebounds and two assists. Fitch paced the struggling Cats with 11 points.

Solid defense and a rare hot-shooting night keyed the

Cats to an easy 87-64 pasting of Ole Miss. The Cats shot 52.6 percent from the field while limiting Ole Miss to just 33.3 percent. Prince led the Cats with 19 points. Fitch registered a double-double with 13 points and 11 rebounds.

Bogans snapped out of his scoring slump to toss in 23 points in a hard-fought 72-65 win at Notre Dame. Bogans, who had connected on just 11 of 33 shots in the previous four games, made good on eight of 12 against the Irish. Bogans also hit five of eight three-point attempts.

Twenty-one points by Estill off the bench and a clutch three-point bucket by Prince lifted the Cats to a 69-62 win at Auburn. The Cats led throughout, only to watch as Auburn whittled the difference to four late in the game. That's when Prince, who had made just one bucket in seven attempts, canned his crucial trey. Bogans finished the night with 13 points.

Alabama became the third team to bump off the Cats in Rupp Arena, winning a hard-fought 64-61 decision. The Crimson Tide took advantage of a UK team bent on launching from long range. In all, the Cats put up 30 three-pointers, making just seven. Alabama had four fewer buckets than UK (24-20), but more than made up the difference by hitting 21 free throws to UK's six.

Erwin Dudley led the Tide with 16 points. Prince topped the Cats with 14.

In a pivotal and much-needed win, the Cats went into Gainesville and knocked off No. 5-ranked Florida 70-68. The win gave the Cats a 4-3 SEC record, keeping alive their hopes of capturing the Eastern Division title. Bogans and

Prince were superb, scoring 20 and 19 points, respectively. But it was Hayes, making his first start, who pulled the Cats through, scoring 10 points and grabbing seven boards, including a key offensive rebound that resulted in a Bogans trey that put UK in front 67-63.

By February, the discontent had spread from the locker room to the living room. Chiles' mother publicly questioned her son's lack of playing time, then threatened to take him elsewhere at season's end if the situation didn't change. In addition, rumors began to swirl that Carrier was displeased and thinking of transferring. However, his father, ex-WKU/Kentucky Colonel great Darel Carrier, dismissed the rumors, saying that the family would "evaluate" the situation at the end of the season.

Seventeen points from Fitch, 16 from Prince and 15 from Hawkins catapulted the Cats to a runaway 91-74 win over South Carolina. The Cats sizzled from the field, making 35 of 60 shots for 58.3 percent. In all, 12 Wildcats

cracked the scoring column.

A bucket by Marcus Haislip with 18.3 seconds left lifted Tennessee to a come-from-behind 76-74 overtime win over the Cats in Knoxville. Haislip turned in an all-world performance, with 24 points, 12 rebounds and four blocked shots. After watching his team blow a nine-point halftime lead and then fail to make crucial plays down the stretch, Smith was left to admit that he was "perplexed" by his club. Prince led the Cats in scoring with 22 points. Hayes added 15.

A strong first-half performance was enough to carry the Cats to a 68-56 win over LSU in Baton Rouge. The Cats built a 42-28 advantage by the break, then held on for the victory. Prince again paced the Cats with 18 points.

During this game it once again became clear that all was

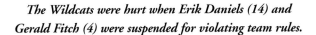

The Wildcats were hurt when Erik Daniels (14) and Gerald Fitch (4) were suspended for violating team rules.

not well inside the UK camp. Bogans, who drew Smith's ire for taking several ill-advised shots, was benched for the final 18 minutes, while Carruth saw no action at all.

Prince scored 20 points, Bogans 12 and Fitch and Camara 10 apiece as the Cats clipped Vanderbilt 67-59. The loss gave the Commodores a 0-25 record in Rupp Arena. The Cats won despite hitting just 39.2 percent from the field.

Sparked by 20 points from Ezra Williams and 19 from Jarvis Hayes, Georgia swept the regular-season series by bumping off the Cats 78-69 in Athens. In this outing, the Cats were clearly their own worst enemy, putting up 28 three-pointers against the smaller Bulldogs. Fitch and Prince led UK with 17 points each.

Fitch wasn't around to help the Cats in their 64-61 comeback win over Tennessee — the sophomore guard was serving a one-game suspension for violating a team rule. The Cats showed plenty of courage, overcoming a 16-point first-half deficit to come away with the win. Three points by Hawkins and a Carruth freebie broke a 59-59 tie and put UK on top for good. Camara gave a superb effort, scoring 17 points and grabbing eight rebounds. Prince finished with 15 points, while Hawkins and Hayes chipped in with 11 and 10, respectively. Tennessee's Vincent Yarbrough led all scorers with 27.

With Fitch and Daniels suspended indefinitely for using a fake ID to enter a local bar, the Cats, using just eight players, slapped Arkansas 71-58 in Rupp Arena. Five Wildcats hit double figures, led by Prince with 16. Others included Estill (12), Hayes (10), Bogans (10) and Carruth (10). Prince also had 10 rebounds.

Vanderbilt connected on 11 three-pointers and shot 53.6 percent from the field to beat the Wildcats 86-73. It was

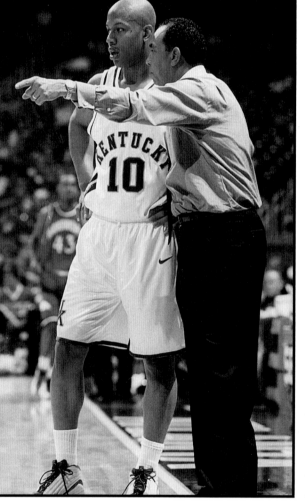

Keith Bogans listens as Tubby Smith makes a point

Vandy's first win over UK since 1993. Reserve point guard Brendan Plavich was the chief thorn in UK's side, hitting six of seven three-pointers and scoring 20 points. Prince and Carruth led the Cats with 24 and 22 points, respectively.

In the final home game for seniors Prince and Blevins, clutch play by Hawkins and a reinstated Fitch spurred the Cats to a thrilling 70-67 win over Florida and a share of the SEC Eastern Division title. With his club down 65-63, Hawkins nailed a 12-footer to knot the score with 1:37 left. Then with 33 seconds remaining, Fitch, playing for the first time in two weeks, buried a trey to put the Cats in front 68-65. Hawkins sealed the win by sinking a pair of freebies with 12.4 seconds left.

Prince led the Cats with 13 points. Fitch and Estill each had 10. Gator guard Brett Nelson claimed game-high honors with 23.

Thanks to poor shooting, more team discontent and an overall lethargic performance, the Cats' stay in the SEC Tournament was short and anything but sweet. The cold-shooting and uninspired Cats dropped a 70-57 decision to South Carolina. However, as poor as the Cats played, the big questions revolved around what was happening off the court with Smith's troubled team. Prior to the game, Smith suspended Chiles for violating a team rule. Then, after what Smith called a "difference of opinion," the UK coach benched Fitch for the entire game. Although the players and coaches did their best to put a positive spin on the situation, clearly the turmoil and unrest was affecting the on-court performance.

Six Gamecocks hit double figures against the Cats, led by Aaron Lucas with 12. The lone bright spot for UK was Hayes, who finished with 10 points and 13 rebounds.

Given the sad state of internal affairs, it's safe to conclude that few UK teams have gone into NCAA tourney action on shakier grounds. Even the most optimistic Big Blue fan had little confidence in this club's chances of advancing deep into the tournament draw. With this team, trouble always seemed to be bubbling just beneath the surface.

But with Bogans busting out of his slump to score 21 points, the Cats notched an 83-68 win over Valpariso in NCAA Tournament first-round action. Bogans, who had hit on just two of his last 24 three-point attempts, buried four of five against Valpo. Bogans keyed a strong first half effort that saw the Cats take an insurmountable 41-23 lead at the break. Prince scored 13, Estill 12 and Camara 11.

Giving the most-remarkable performance of his great career, Prince gunned in 41 points to lead the Cats to a hard-earned 87-82 second-round victory over Tulsa. Prince's effort was eerily similar to the one turned in by Jack "Goose" Givens in the 94-88 NCAA championship win over Duke in 1978. In that game, Givens, a southpaw who also wore No. 21, tallied 41 points.

Prince made good on 14 of 21 shots, including six of eight from beyond the three-point line. He accounted for 28 of UK's final 46 points. After UK took a 51-47 lead early in the second half, Prince scored 21 of the Cats' next 30 points. In addition, he also had nine rebounds.

Bogans turned in another solid effort, ending the night with 19 points.

Powerful Maryland ended UK's long, strange and unhappy season by posting a 78-68 win in Syracuse. The Cats acquitted themselves well, battling back from a 39-33 halftime deficit to even things at 45-45 on a Prince trey with 16:09 left. After the score was tied three more times during the next six minutes, the Terps turned to their inside attack, which proved to be deadly and virtu-

Tayshaun Prince earned All-America honors after his final season.

ally unstoppable. With the score tied at 53-53, the Terps reeled off 14 unanswered points to assume control. During the final 6:11, the Cats managed just one field goal.

All-American Juan Dixon led the Terps with 19 points and eight rebounds. Lonny Baxter finished with 16 points, 14 after intermission.

Prince topped the Cats with 17 points, giving him 1,775 for his career, good enough to pass Cotton Nash for seventh place on UK's list of all-time scorers. Bogans had 15, Estill 12 and Camara 10 for the Wildcats.

After the season, amid much speculation concerning the fate of several Wildcats, the UK roster went through some overhauling. Carruth and Chiles, two of the unhappiest Cats, departed, as did seldom-used Corbin native Cory Sears. Although there was talk that Fitch, Daniels and Carrier might not return, in fact all three will be in uniform for the 2002-2003 season.

With a host of talented veterans returning, joined by a solid crop of newcomers and a healthy Parker, the Cats figure to be a powerhouse again next year. If the chemistry and discipline are there, this could easily be a Final Four club.

2002-03

Given the disappointment and turmoil of the previous season, Big Blue fans were unsure of what to expect when the 2002-03 campaign rolled around. Few seasons had been so troubled and unhappy as the preceding one had been, and no one wanted to see that nightmare scenario play out again.

Weary Wildcat fans had their fingers crossed that this would not be another winter of discontent.

From a personnel standpoint, there was plenty of reason for optimism. The Cats had some big guns in their arsenal, including veterans Keith Bogans, Gerald Fitch, Marquis

Estill, Erik Daniels, Cliff Hawkins, Jules Camara and Chuck Hayes. Kelenna Azubuike and Antwain Barbour were being counted on for additional firepower, while Josh Carrier, Bernard Cote, Ravi Moss, Brandon Stockton, Preston LeMaster and Matt Heissenbuttel were also available.

That was the good news. The bad news was, this was essentially the same cast of characters responsible for Team Turmoil. Only the steady and dependable Tayshaun Prince was missing. Could this group, now a year older and wiser, and minus Prince's steadying influence, overcome personal differences and turn the negative into something positive? Could they regain the faith of disgruntled Big Blue fans?

Those questions hovered like a black cloud as the season rolled around, and no one, not even Tubby Smith, could predict what the answers might be.

As things turned out, no one could have expected — or predicted — the miracle this group of Wildcats managed to pull off. These Cats, so rocky and unsteady a year earlier, gave UK fans one of the greatest seasons in the school's illustrious history, finishing with a 32-4 record. This season saw the Wildcats fashion a 26-game winning streak, a perfect 19-0 mark against SEC competition and a No. 1 ranking in the final regular-season polls.

So steady, spectacular and team-oriented were these Cats that virtually all post-season hardware wound up in Big Blue territory. Smith became the first coach in 28 years to sweep all national Coach of the Year honors, while Bogans was named SEC Player of the Year and MVP of the SEC Tournament. The only thing missing from this club's final resume was a Final Four trip.

Ironically, this would be the last season of peaceful coexistence between Tubby Smith and many Big Blue fans. Despite leading his teams to outstanding won-loss records, especially over the next two seasons (55-11), Smith felt increasing heat as more and more Wildcat fans became disenchanted with the coach they snidely labeled "10-loss Tubby" and for what they perceived as a style of play that lacked tempo and excitement. Adding more fuel to the fire was the recruiting situation, where many UK fans questioned Smith's ability to land big-name high school prospects.

In a mere four years after this magical 32-4 season, Smith would leave UK for the head coaching job at the University of Minnesota.

However, during the winter of 2002-03, no one could doubt the accomplishments of Smith and his blue-and-white clad troops. This group, despite several early season

Keith Bogans helped lead the Cats to a surprising 32-4 record.

obstacles, was simply terrific in every way. Gone was the disarray and discontent that dampened the previous season. Gone were the players who put individual stats ahead of team goals. With Smith doing perhaps his finest coaching job, and with a rejuvenated Bogans rebounding from his disappointing junior season, these Cats quickly erased the memories of Team Turmoil.

What made this club's success even more impressive is that it happened despite the lack of a genuine superstar. True, Bogans had a beast of a season, earning All-America recognition, yet he only averaged 15.7 points per game, far below the numbers posted by top scorers in the past. No, the real strength of this team was its unselfishness and bal-

ance. Virtually every Wildcat was capable of having a big scoring night and, in fact, six different players led the team in scoring during the season.

But this season, great as it turned out to be, didn't begin smoothly. Jason Parker, a player many counted on for big scoring and rebounding numbers, opted to leave UK, transferring to South Carolina. Hawkins, a jet-quick point guard, was sidelined for the first seven games due to academic problems, while Daniels missed the first four games due to NCAA suspension for playing in a sanctioned summer league.

Despite the thin roster, Smith and the Wildcats headed to Hawaii for the season opener against Arizona State in the Maui Classic. With Daniels and Hawkins absent, Smith knew that players like Barbour, Hayes, Azubuike, Carrier and Camara would have to step up if the Cats hoped to succeed.

Led by Bogans' hot hand, UK opened with a solid 82-65 victory over the Sun Devils. Bogans hit seven of 10 shots, including three of four from three-point range, and finished with 20 points. He received strong support from Estill, who had 14 points, and Fitch and Barbour, both of whom had 13.

In all, the Cats connected on 29 of 57 shots for 51 percent.

One night later, against Virginia's zone defense, the Cats' hot hand turned icy cold. The result was a 75-61 loss. In this outing, the Cats shot just 37.3 percent from the field, while misfiring on their first 17 three-point attempts. Despite such poor shooting from the field, the Cats were able to build a nine-point first-half lead. That early firepower came from Estill, who scored 10 points in the game's first five minutes. However, foul trouble limited Estill's playing time to 13 minutes.

For the game, UK hit just two of 22 three-pointers. The Cats were also outrebounded 41-32. Estill, Bogans and Camara led UK with 12 points each.

In the consolation game, UK, sparked by Camara's 12 points off the bench, bounced back to beat 20th-ranked Gonzaga 80-72. The Cats trailed by six late in the opening half, but buckets by Barbour and Bogans, wrapped around a Cote trey, put them in front 33-32 at intermission. After the Zags scored the first five points of the second half, UK went on a 9-0 run to reclaim the lead for good.

Bogans paced UK with 18 points. Blake Stepp had 24 points to lead Gonzaga, which connected on 12 three-pointers for the game.

After Bogans tossed in 21 points and Fitch added 18 in an easy 84-64 romp past High Point, the Cats, now ranked No. 18, entertained 12th-ranked North Carolina. With just under 22,000 on hand in Rupp Arena, the Cats, down 43-40 at the break, smoked the Tar Heels with an 18-2 run early in the second half en route to an impressive 98-81 victory. The Cats outscored UNC 58-38 in those final 20 minutes.

Estill was the difference, scoring all 20 of his points after intermission, including back-to-back buckets that put UK on top 44-43 early in the second half. After a Tar Heel layup, Fitch nailed a jumper that gave UK a lead it would not give up. Hot shooting accounted for this big win. For the game, the Cats shot 60.2 percent from the field, and an even hotter 62.5 percent (10 of 16) from behind the three-point line. During one stretch, UK connected on eight consecutive field goal attempts.

Fitch led UK with 25 points, while Bogans had 20 and Hayes 16. Daniels had nine points and five rebounds in his first game back after serving his suspension.

The Cats split their next four games, topping Tulane 76-60 and Indiana 70-64, whole losing to Michigan State 71-67 and Louisville 81-63.

Bogans had 21 points in the win over Tulane, then came back with 23 in the loss to Michigan State in Rupp Arena. In that hotly contested battle, there were six ties and 10 lead changes, the last one coming when Tim Bograkos buried a three-pointer with 50 seconds remaining to give the Spartans a 69-67 lead. After Bogans missed a trey attempt, the Spartans hit two freebies to account for the final margin.

The Indiana game in Freedom Hall was a heart-stopper until the final seconds, when it suddenly became the Great Mike Davis Meltdown. In a game that was nip and tuck all the way — there were six lead changes in the final 2:19 — the Cats nudged ahead 65-64 when Estill took a Camara pass and laid in a contested layup with 13 ticks remaining.

After Estill's bucket, IU guard Bracey Wright missed a driving layup in heavy traffic. Convinced that Wright had been fouled, IU coach Davis exploded, charging onto the floor to protest the no-call. He was immediately hit with two technicals, resulting in his automatic ejection from the game. Bogans hit five of six free throws to account for the final score.

Bogans and Fitch led UK with 17 and 16 points, respectively. In his first game back, Hawkins had four points and five assists, including one on a lob pass to Camara that

Chuck Hayes did the dirty work for the Cats, like rebounding and playing solid defense.

resulted in a dunk that put UK on top 63-62.

The loss to Louisville, in which the Cats blew an early 20-9 lead, had a strangely familiar feel to it. Rick Pitino, once UK's coach, now called the shots for the Cardinals, while Marvin Stone, who led all scorers in this game with 16 points, was an ex-Cat. If that weren't enough, Lexington native Erik Brown had nine points, including a three-pointer that triggered a 17-4 second-half run that put the game away.

UK dominated early, hitting nine of its first 17 shots to take command. But following that hot start, the Cats cooled off, missing 19 of their next 24 shots. By that time, Pitino's Cardinals had caught up and surged ahead.

Bogans had 14 points to lead UK.

The Cats, after the loss to Louisville, now stood at 6-3 for the season. They would not lose again for three full months, reeling off 26 straight victories, becoming the first team since the 1951-52 Wildcats to go undefeated in SEC play and capture the SEC tourney.

That streak began with a trio of relatively easy non-conference wins — 115-87 over Tennessee State, 94-63 over Alcorn State and 83-75 over Ohio. Bogans finished with 26 against Tennessee State, while Hayes had 15 and Daniels 12 in the win over Alcorn State. Bogans came back with 21 points as the Cats squandered a big lead against Ohio, then held on for the win. Hayes had a double-double with 11 points and 12 rebounds.

UK's run through the SEC began with a predictably tough encounter with Tennessee in Knoxville. After the Vols erased a five-point deficit to take the lead on a C.J. Watson layup with 1:21 remaining, Camara buried a jumper from the free throw line to give UK a one-point lead with 53 seconds left. Inside that final minute, the Cats were able to hang on for a 74-71 win.

Bogans topped UK with 20 points and nine rebounds despite not starting. Fitch had 17 points and Camara 12 for the Cats. Ron Slay paced the Vols with 22 points.

Daniels had 19 points in a comfortable 62-55 win over visiting South Carolina, then Fitch had 18 to lead the Cats to a surprisingly easy 74-52 win over Vanderbilt in traditionally tough Memorial Gym. Fitch received strong support against the Commodores. In all, four Cats cracked double figures — Bogans (16), Estill (15) and Hayes (11).

Balanced scoring was again the key as four Cats hit double figures in an 88-73 win over longtime non-SEC rival Notre Dame. Estill led the way with 18 points, while Hayes had a monster game with 17 points and 16 rebounds. Daniels and Bogans finished with 15 and 13 points, respectively.

It was at this stage of the season that the Cats went from hot to scorching, winning their next six games by an average margin of 17 points. It was during this stretch that the Cats rose from 10th in the national polls to third.

Five Cats hit double figures, led by Estill and Fitch with 16 apiece, in a 67-51 win over No. 24 Auburn. Camara and Bogans each had 13 against the Tigers, and Hawkins added 10.

Defense was the key in a 63-46 win at Alabama. For the game, UK held the Tide to just 10 field goals and 23.8 percent shooting from the field. Fitch paced UK with 16 points.

Estill's 18 points keyed UK's 87-69 win at South Carolina, as once again five Cats hit double figures. Others besides Estill included Bogans (16), Daniels (14), Hayes (12) and Hawkins (10). Hayes also pulled down 10 rebounds.

UK blasted Florida 70-55 after using a stifling defense to build a 45-22 halftime cushion. In those opening 20 minutes, the Cats limited Florida to six field goals and 20 percent shooting.

Bogans led UK with 15 points. The Gators' Anthony Roberson claimed high-point honors with 18.

UK's Sherman-like march through the SEC continued with an 80-62 romp past Ole Miss and an 87-67 pasting of Georgia. Daniels tossed in 20 against the Rebels, then was one of six Cats in double figures against Georgia. Estill had 16, Fitch 14, Daniels and Bogans 12, and Hayes and Hawkins 11.

Despite shooting a chilly 39.3 percent, the Cats managed to hang a 68-57 defeat on pesky LSU in Rupp Arena. The Cats led just 35-30 early in the second half, but a 20-5 run gave the Cats plenty of breathing room. They needed it, as the Tigers chopped the difference to just five with less than a minute remaining. The Cats used the free throw stripe to put away the win.

Bogans topped UK's scoring with 20 points.

The Cats, now ranked No. 2 in the country, went into Bud Walton Arena and smoked Arkansas 66-50 for their 15th straight win. Once again, the Cats parlayed a strong defensive effort, especially in the second half, to an impressive victory. Leading 36-29 at intermission, the Cats limited Arkansas to a lone bucket in the first 10 minutes while padding their lead to as many as 21 points.

Fitch had 17 points and Daniels 10 to lead UK.

Bogans racked up 18 points in a 70-62 win against Mississippi State, then came back to score 15 to lead a balanced attack in an 80-68 win over Tennessee. Estill scored 16 as the Cats topped Georgia 74-66 to clinch at least a share of the SEC championship.

In a 106-44 laugher against Vanderbilt, every Wildcat put points on the board. Daniels led the way with 20, while Estill had 17 and Azubuike, in his best outing, finished with 16.

The Cats closed out a perfect 16-0 SEC record by managing to escape a furious late Florida rally for a 69-67 win. The Cats led by 12 at the break, and upped their advantage to 60-46 after Bogans hit a trey with 11:40 left to play. But with Matt Bonner scoring on the inside and Roberson

doing damage from outside, the Gators clawed back, cutting the difference to seven.

After Fitch and Daniels accounted for five unanswered points to give UK some room, the Gators went on an 11-3 run inside the final five minutes to make things interesting. But when Roberson's three-point attempt at the buzzer was off the mark, the Cats had their win and their flawless SEC record.

The Cats opened play in SEC tourney action with a sluggish start against Vanderbilt, a club they were meeting for the second time in 10 days. Vandy quickly jumped in front 17-8, but a 9-0 run by the Cats evened things up. A Camara dunk put the Cats on top 28-26, and from that point on, the game belonged to the men in blue. The Cats won 81-63.

Bogans had 16 points for UK, which placed four players in double figures. Others included Camara (13), Estill (11) and Daniels (10). Hawkins made his first start of the season, taking over for Fitch, who was benched for violating a team rule. Hawkins made the most of his opportunity by dishing out nine assists.

Next up for the Cats was a semifinal matchup against Auburn. With Daniels tossing in 17 points on eight of 11 shooting, the Cats broke away from a 36-36 halftime deadlock to post a 78-58 win. A 15-6 spurt early in the second half propelled the Cats past Auburn and into a title-game showdown with Mississippi State.

In that championship-game tussle, the Bulldogs proved to be a difficult club to subdue. The Cats trailed 31-30 at intermission, but just moments into the second half, following a Bogans three-pointer that squared things at 33-33, the Cats grabbed the advantage and never looked back, winning 64-57.

It marked the Cats' fourth tourney title in six tries under Smith's guidance.

But on this occasion, the Cats were fortunate to escape the upset. Inside the final two minutes, MSU's Derrick Zimmerman missed a layup and teammate Mario Austin misfired on two free throws that would have given his team the lead.

Bogans finished with 22 points, earning the tourney MVP award for his efforts. Estill, who had 13 points, joined Bogans on the all-tourney squad.

The Cats began their quest for a national title by blasting IUPUI 95-64 in Nashville's Gaylord Entertainment Center for their 30th victory. It marked the 11th time a UK team had won 30 games in a season.

The outcome was never in doubt, thanks to UK's hot

Tubby Smith maps his strategy. Smith swept all Coach-of-the -Year honors after guiding the Cats to a 32-4 record.

points, and with the defense holding Utah to under 40 percent shooting accuracy, the Cats rolled into the Sweet 16 on the strength of an easy 74-54 victory. On the flip side, the Cats shot 47.3 percent from the field while making good on all 18 free throw attempts.

The Cats were next pitted against Wisconsin, and, thanks to a huge 28-point performance by Estill, they managed to slip away with a hard-earned 63-57 win. Estill made 12 of 18 shots, and were it not for poor effort at the charity stripe (four of 10), his numbers would have been even more impressive.

Estill's career-best effort couldn't have come at a more crucial time. Bogans, UK's leading scorer, suffered an ankle sprain late in the first half that sidelined him for the remainder of the game.

Hayes was another hero in this victory. After the Badgers' Kirk Penney accounted for 17 first-half points, Hayes was handed the task of shutting down the red-hot All-Big Ten standout, which he did, holding Penney to one field goal and three points in the final 20 minutes.

But UK's dream of a Final Four appearance and an eighth NCAA title was dashed by Marquette, which took full advantage of a superhuman performance by Dwayne Wade to post an 83-69 upset of the top-ranked Cats. Wade gave one of the greatest individual performances ever by a UK foe, registering a rare triple-double (29 points, 11 rebounds, 11 assists) that proved to be more than the Cats could overcome.

Wade wasn't the lone thorn in UK's side. Teammate Robert Jackson added 24 points and 15 rebounds to Marquette's ledger sheet.

The Cats trailed 45-26 at the half, only to close the gap to 59-47 following a layup by Barbour. Seconds later, on what was a controversial call, another Barbour bucket was negated by a charging call. That bucket would have pulled UK to within single digits. Instead, Marquette went on an 8-2 run to put the game away.

Bogans, who played despite his sore ankle, and Fitch led UK with 15 points each. Estill finished with 10.

Although the Cats came up short in their NCAA championship run, there was no shortage of post-season accolades, especially for Smith, who topped every Coach of the Year poll.

Bogans led the club in scoring with a 15.7 average, finishing his superb career with 1,923 points, fourth-best in UK history. Fitch averaged 12.3 points, while Estill scored at an 11.6 clip.

Bogans, Estill and Camara would be the only departing

shooting (61.5 percent) and a career-best 25-point effort from Fitch. The junior guard connected on 10 of 13 shots from the field, including five of seven from beyond the three-point arc.

Estill, Bogans and Hawkins each chipped in with 13 points apiece.

Perennial NCAA foe Utah was the Cats' next victim, but unlike years past, this game was a no-doubter from beginning to end. With Estill and Bogans each contributing 18

seniors from this outstanding club, leaving Smith with the nucleus of another strong title-contending outfit. Joining the returning players in 2003-04 would be UK's tallest players ever, imports from Canada and Poland, a player who grew up in the shadow of Duke University and a walk-on from Hopkinsville.

In every regard, Smith had a roster that was loaded from top to bottom.

2003-04

There were enough familiar names on the roster to virtually guarantee that the Wildcats would follow last season's magical ride with another successful campaign. And they didn't disappoint, ending up with an outstanding 27-5 record, capturing another SEC Tournament championship (the school's 25th) and claiming the SEC Eastern Division title.

Yet, this club, like last year's, would come up short in NCAA tourney action, suffering a stunning one-point loss to UAB in the second round. It was following this unexpected setback that the anti-Tubby Smith drumbeat began to be heard in earnest. The volume would only increase over the next three years.

But during this season, Big Blue fans had little reason to complain. This club was, in many ways, even more impressive and dominant than last year's club. Proof of that can be found in a single statistic: the Cats held double digit leads in 27 of 32 games.

There was no reason for this club to not be superb. Stalwards Fitch, Daniels, Hawkins, Hayes and Barbour were returning. So was Azubuike, now a sophomore, who was being counted on to show off the offensive skills that enabled him to lead Oklahoma high school scorers in each of his final three prep seasons.

Other returning veterans included Carrier, Cote, Stockton, Heissenbuttel and LeMaster.

If there was a question surrounding this group it revolved around the middle. There was no true pivot player on the team. Daniels, the tallest of the returning starters at 6'8", was a natural forward. Cote, at 6'9", had size but was still an uneven, unproven player at this level. The 6'6" Hayes was tough and rugged, but could he successfully defend against players 6'9" or 6'10"?

Despite those concerns — and they were legitimate — this was the "tallest" team in UK history, and the first to feature a pair of 7-footers. Unfortunately for Smith, neither of the rookie giants — 7'4" New York native Shagari

Alleyne or 7'1" Polish-born Lukasz Obrzut — was even close to being ready to step in and offer immediate help with post play.

The other three incoming freshmen had potential, although none had the size to solve the pivot problem. Bobby Perry, the 6'7" Durham, N.C., native, and Canadian Sheray Thomas, also 6'7", came in with solid skills, while walk-on Ravi Moss, a graduate of University Heights in Hopkinsville, was a standout long-range shooter.

Smith solved this potentially troubling dilemma by going with a three-guard, two-forward starting quintet for much of the season, utilizing Fitch, Hawkins and Azubuike in the backcourt, with Daniels and Hayes handling the chores down low. Those five, along with timely help from fellow teammates, proved to be more than adequate, eventually winning the battle of the boards by more than 150 rebounds.

These Cats picked up where they left off last season, winning their first seven games and 11 of their first 12. Included among their early victims were 21st-ranked Michigan State, No. 9 North Carolina, 20th-ranked Vanderbilt and 20th-ranked Mississippi State.

The Cats barely broke a sweat winning their first three games, blasting Winthrop 65-44, Tennessee Tech 108-81 and Marshall 89-76. Fitch was the Cat who made the most noise, scoring 12 points in the opener against Winthrop, then following that effort with a 36-point explosion against Tennessee Tech and another 24 points in the win over Marshall. In those last two outings, Fitch made good on 24 of 39 field goal attempts, including nine of 21 from three-point range.

Azubuike also flashed his offensive potential, ringing up 43 points in those three victories.

The Cats' first real test came against UCLA in the John Wooden Classic, a game that turned out to be the kind of nip-and-tuck thriller one would expect from two schools that had a combined 18 NCAA title trophies between them.

Defense dominated this struggle, with the Cats able to squeak out a 52-50 win despite shooting a miserable 27 percent from the field (16 of 59). UCLA, which managed just 17 first-half points, fared little better, connecting on 17 of 50 for 34 percent. UK, despite being the smaller team, won the battle of the boards 41-39.

The Cats, who never trailed, built a 17-point first half lead, only to watch as the Bruins whittled the difference to three — 36-33 — with just under eight minutes remaining. But a bucket by Daniels and a trey by Fitch

provided the Cats with some breathing room at 41-33. Down the stretch, Hawkins accounted for his club's final seven points, enough to give the Cats their sixth win in nine meetings against UCLA.

Daniels had 14 points to lead UK, while Hawkins finished with 12. Dijon Thompson had 14 for UCLA to tie Daniels for top honors.

With a basketball world-record crowd of 78,129 in attendance, the eighth-ranked Cats bumped off 21st-ranked Michigan State 79-74 in Detroit's Ford Field. The Cats turned in their most solid effort thus far in the campaign, hitting 60 percent from the field, winning the rebounding wars 28-26 and placing four players in double figures, led by Fitch with 25.

For the second straight outing, the Cats built a comfortable advantage, only to see that lead virtually disappear down the stretch. The Cats were up by 15 in the first half, but the Spartans roared back to within 62-61 with eight minutes remaining. And yet, for the second straight game, the Cats didn't cave in to the pressure, eventually upping the lead to six with a little more than a minute left. After Shannon Brown's two free throws brought the Spartans to within two, UK, thanks to a pair of late Fitch freebies, managed to hang on for the big win.

Hayes finished with 17 points and 12 rebounds in a superb effort for UK. Daniels and Hawkins finished with 16 and 13 points, respectively, for the Cats. Paul Davis, who connected on all 14 free throw attempts, paced the Spartans with 24 points.

On the heels of that victory, the Cats jumped to No. 1 in the ESPN/USA Today's poll and No.2 in the AP poll. Those lofty rankings only seemed to energize the Cats, who quickly flexed their muscles by humbling Indiana 80-41 in a Rupp Arena romp.

It was a dazzling display of basketball by the Wildcats,

Kelenna Azubuike came to UK with the reputation of a big-time offensive threat.

especially on the defensive end, where they limited IU to 15 second-half points and just 24 percent shooting overall. After leading 32-26 at intermission, the Cats, sparked by quick back-to-back buckets by Hayes, went on a 9-0 run that broke the game open. From that point on, it was all UK.

Hayes fashioned his second consecutive double-double (17 points, 12 rebounds), with Daniels chipping in with 19 points and 10 rebounds. Azubuike tossed in 11 points, while Hawkins had 10 points and seven assists.

IU's Bracey Wright led all scorers with 23.

After Fitch scored 26 points and Hawkins added 16 in an easy 101-72 win over Eastern Kentucky, the Cats squared off against Rick Pitino's Louisville Cardinals in Rupp Arena. The unbeaten and second-ranked Cats, playing on the home front, were favored to revenge last season's loss in Freedom Hall. But things didn't go according to the script. Louisville topped the Cats 65-56.

The Cardinals, after trailing 31-26 at the break, owned the second half, shooting a blistering 54.2 during those 20 minutes. UK, meanwhile, shot just 33.3 percent after intermission.

A pair of Azubuike free tosses put UK on top 51-50 with 4:12 left to play. That would be the last time the Cats held the upper hand. A basket by Kendall Dartez and a three-pointer by Taquan Dean put an end to any dream the Cats had of avoiding their first regular-season setback in a year.

Azubuike and Hawkins each had 12 points to lead UK. Otis George topped the Cardinals with 13 points, while Luke Whitehead and Larry O'Bannon each contributed 11.

UK's final two pre-SEC outings resulted in a pair of tight victories — 61-53 against upstart Austin Peay and 61-56 against No. 9-ranked North Carolina. The two wins put the Cats' record at 9-1 heading into rugged conference action.

Facing Austin Peay in Freedom Hall, the Cats were solid in the opening half, building a safe enough lead to withstand a furious second-half surge by the Governors. UK led 26-12 at the break, and was in front 41-24 midway through the second half. It was then that the Cats went on cruise control, thus allowing the scrappy Governors to carve the difference to 56-53 with under three minutes left.

But the Cats were able to hang on, thanks to five of six free throw shooting during crunch time.

Fitch paced UK with 14 points. Hayes had 12 points, while Daniels continued his strong play, scoring 11 points and snaring 10 rebounds.

Against No. 9-ranked North Carolina, Fitch scored 21 points, including a game-clinching trey, to help the Cats beat the Tar Heels for the fourth straight season. To escape with the victory, the Cats had to rally from a 10-point second-half deficit, eventually taking the lead for good at 43-41 on a Daniels bucket with 10:53 left.

The Heels twice closed to within a single point, the last time at 57-56 on a three-pointer by Raymond Felton with 56 seconds left. The Cats ran the shot clock down to three seconds before Fitch connected on his fifth trey of the game, putting his club in front by four. Following a UNC

turnover, Hawkins made one of two free throws to account for the final margin.

Fitch led UK with 21 points. Daniels had another double-double (18 points, 10 rebounds) and Hayes added 10 points.

Melvin Scott topped UNC with 16 points.

The Cats opened SEC action by coming away victorious in a pair of difficult, tense thrillers, topping Vanderbilt 75-63 and Mississippi State 67-66. Against the 20th-ranked Commodores, the Cats got 16-point performances from Azubuike, Fitch and Daniels. Azubuike also claimed 11 rebounds.

At Mississippi State, Daniels grabbed a desperation pass and laid in the game-winner as time expired. The Bulldogs rallied from 16 points down to take a 66-65 lead before Daniels dropped in the deciding bucket. The Cats also benefited from shoddy free throw shooting by the previously unbeaten Bulldogs, who twice missed the front end on bonus situations that could have preserved the win.

Fitch paced UK with 23 points, while hero Daniels finished with 16. Timmy Bowers led the Bulldogs with 20.

Georgia, led by Rashad Wright's 20 points, marched into Rupp Arena and stunned the Cats 65-57. Georgia completely dominated the Cats, defensively and offensively. Georgia shot 39 percent from the field (50 percent from three-point range), while decisively whipping the Cats on the boards 36-23.

Daniels had 15 points for UK.

The Cats, after building a 41-28 halftime advantage, needed a rebound bucket by Hayes to hold on for a 69-68 overtime win over Tennessee in Knoxville. It marked the 300th career win for Tubby Smith.

The Vols actually took a 64-61 on two freebies by C.J. Watson with 22 seconds remaining. But a three-pointer by Hawkins was enough to send the game into the extra frame.

Scooter McFadgon, who led all scorers with 33 points, scored all four Volunteer points in the OT. UK won it, thanks to a Daniels trey and Hayes' last-second bucket. Daniels led UK with 19 points, with Hayes adding 18 points and 16 rebounds.

The Cats stepped away from league play with a 71-63 victory over Notre Dame in the Joyce Center. Hayes had 21 points in that UK win.

Daniels erupted for 24 points, and Hawkins and Barbour added 14 and 12, respectively, in a hard-earned 71-61 win over Ole Miss. The two clubs were knotted at 29-29 at

Erik Daniels and Gerald Fitch celebrate another UK win. Both players scored more than 1,000 points as Wildcats.

intermission, but the Cats, courtesy of Barbour's four treys, managed to break it open in the final 20 minutes.

Memorial Gym in Nashville once again proved to be a death trap for the Wildcats. Vanderbilt, always tough at home, rode a 20-point, 11-rebound effort by Matt Freije to a 66-60 upset win. After the Commodores opened on fire, making their first eight shots to take an early lead, the Cats roared back in the second half to go in front 58-52 with 4:29 remaining. Then it was time for another Vandy run, and when Dan Cage buried a three-pointer with 2:18 left, the Commodores went in front for good at 61-60.

Daniels and Fitch each had 13 points for UK, which had five more field goals than the Commodores.

Thanks to a big effort by Daniels and a clutch steal and bucket by Hawkins, the Cats bounced back to beat young and talented Florida 68-65 in the O'Connell Center. To win, the Cats had to overcome a 65-57 deficit inside the game's final minutes. They did so by holding the Gators scoreless down the stretch.

After battling back to within a single point, the Cats claimed the win when Hawkins intercepted a pass and scored on an easy layup that put UK on top for good at 66-65.

Daniels finished with 22 points for the Cats. Florida was led by Anthony Roberson's 19 points.

It took four Cats scoring in double-digits to beat South Carolina 65-64 in yet another down-to-the-wire thriller. This one featured 11 lead changes, including six in the final eight minutes. In addition, neither team led by more than six points.

It was the Cats' third one-point win in SEC action this season.

Daniels once again was the top-scoring Wildcat with 17 points. Hayes had 15, Azubuike 11 and Barbour, making his first start of the season, finished with 10.

The Cats split their next two games, topping Alabama 66-55 before losing 74-68 at Georgia. Barbour broke loose for 23 points in the win over Alabama, while Azubuike scored 23 in the loss to Georgia. Jonas Hayes' 19-point effort was instrumental in helping the Bulldogs complete a season sweep of the highly ranked Cats.

It would be the Cats' last loss in SEC action this season. Beginning with a 73-56 win over Arkansas, the Cats reeled off nine straight league wins, including three in the SEC Tournament. During this run, the Cats played perhaps their finest basketball of the campaign.

Daniels had 21 points in the win over Arkansas, then

Fitch followed with an 18-point effort in a 68-59 win at Auburn. Five Cats, headed by Azubuike's 17 points, cracked double figures in a surprisingly easy 92-60 romp past Tennessee. Other Cats in double digits included Barbour (16), Hawkins (15), Hayes (14) and Daniels (12).

Fitch had 23 points in a 70-64 win at LSU, then Hawkins finished with 21 points and Fitch added 16 as the Cats ripped South Carolina 84-65. In the regular-season finale, Fitch accounted for 21 points to lead UK to a convincing 82-62 win over Florida.

First up for the Cats in SEC tourney action was a third meeting against dangerous Georgia. This game, like the first two, was a bitter war from start to finish. However, this time, the Cats, with Hawkins leading the way, were able to come out on top, claiming a 69-60 win.

Hawkins had 23 for the Cats. Georgia's Wright shared game-high honors with 23.

In semifinal action, Fitch scored 24 points and Daniels added 21 as the Cats beat South Carolina 78-63. Azubuike chipped in 14 points for the winners.

Matched against Florida in the title game, the Cats used a blistering first half to build a big lead, then fought off every challenge down the stretch to post an 89-73 victory. It marked the 25th time that UK had won the SEC tourney championship.

Hayes was brilliant for the Cats, scoring 23 points on 10-of-14 shooting. Fitch, the tourney MVP, and Azubuike each added 18.

Matt Walsh paced the Gators with 17 points.

UK headed into NCAA action with a 26-4 record and a No. 2 national ranking. Waiting for the Cats was Florida A&M, which despite a 15-16 record, proved to be a difficult foe to put away. But in the end, UK simply had too much of everything for the upset-minded Rattlers, eventually notching a 96-76 victory.

Defense was a no-show in the opening half, which ended with UK on top 60-52. The Cats did tighten the screws considerably in the second stanza, limiting the Rattlers to 24 points.

Still, it took a late 15-2 run for the Cats to secure the win. That came after the Rattlers closed to within 77-67 with under 10 minutes left.

Fitch continued his hot hand, scoring 26 points on 10-of-17 shooting. Daniels ended the night with 18 points, while Hawkins and Azubuike each had 14.

UK's hopes for another NCAA crown were quickly

Cliff Hawkins is honored on UK Ssnior Night.

dashed, thanks to a stunning 76-75 loss to ninth-seeded UAB. It was a devastating loss for an overachieving Wildcat team that had been amazingly solid and consistent during the entire season.

UAB won it on a Mo Finley 17-foot jumper with 12.2 seconds remaining. Fitch misfired on a potential game-winning trey with 2.2 ticks left, then a follow-up tip-in attempt by Hayes rolled off the rim as the final horn sounded.

After falling behind early, the Cats came back to grab a 75-74 lead on an Azubuike dunk. Following a timeout, UAB worked the ball to Finley, who launched the game-deciding shot.

Finley finished with 17 points, a total matched by UK's Fitch.

The disappointed Cats ended the season with a marvelous 27-5 record. They were the 49th Wildcat club to register 20 wins in a season, and they won both the SEC Eastern Division and SEC Tournament titles.

Five players averaged in double figures, headed by Fitch's 16.2 clip. Others included Daniels (14.5), Azubuike (11.1), Hayes (10.7) and Hawkins (10.3).

Hayes was the top rebounder with 260, while Hawkins dished out 166 assists.

UK said goodbye to three big-gun seniors Fitch, Daniels

and Hawkins, who had accounted for 3,283 career points. Also departing were fellow seniors Barbour and Heissenbuttel.

Despite losing such experience and firepower, Smith still had a solid group of returning veterans, highlighted by the tough Hayes and the explosive Azubuike. Other returning players included Perry, Thomas, Carrier, Stockton, Moss, LeMaster and the two seven-footers, Obrzut and Alleyne.

However, without question, it was the incoming class of new faces that caused the most excitement and anticipation in the Big Blue Nation. It was a class that featured a trio of McDonald's All-Americans (Randolph Morris, Joe Crawford and Rajon Rondo), a speedy backcourt player from New York (Ramel Bradley) and a much-heralded transfer from Western Kentucky University (Patrick Sparks).

It was enough to make Big Blue fans dream big.

2004-05

Tubby Smith knew he had a loaded deck of cards when he brought this group together for the start of the season. The talent level was off the charts, easily UK's best group of skilled, highly regarded players in years. The trick, for Smith, would be blending his talented newcomers in with the returning veterans, not always an easy task for any coach.

Morris, at 6'11", gave the Cats an imposing presence in the middle, both offensively and defensively, given his ability to score, defend and block shots. Most observers agreed that Morris had the potential to be UK's best true pivotman since Sam Bowie.

Flanking Morris down low would be Azubuike and Hayes, both of whom figured to be even better and more productive than they had been the previous season.

With that trio, Smith certainly had one of college basketball's premier frontlines. And with the always hustling Perry, Thomas and the two seven-footers as backup, Smith had plenty of depth at his disposal.

However, it was the backcourt, with its vast talent level, that generated the most excitement, and without question, much of that excitement centered around Sparks. The Muhlenberg North All-State standout had spent his first two seasons at WKU, scoring 783 points while earning the reputation as a fierce competitor and a late-game shotmaker. During his redshirt season on the sidelines, his play in practice was of such intensity and so impressive that it was often said by his teammates that the best player on the 2003-04 club wasn't even eligible to play.

But Sparks wasn't the only UK guard causing excite-

ment. Rondo, with his huge hands and jet-quick speed, was viewed by many as the most naturally gifted player on the club. It wouldn't take long for Rondo to flash his brilliant ability.

Crawford and Bradley also came to UK with a scrapbook full of magnificent press clippings. The 6'4" Crawford was blessed with outside shooting range and the strength to beat defenders to the bucket, while the 6'1" Bradley was a slick passer, hard-nose competitor and superb at breaking down opposing defenses.

In virtually every crucial area, this was a most-formidable Wildcat team.

With Hayes, Azubuike, Morris, Rondo and Sparks as the starting quintet, the Cats opened strong, smashing overmatched Coppin State 77-46, Ball State 73-53, Georgia State 77-59 and Tennessee Tech 92-63.

The scoring in those four easy wins was balanced, as it would be throughout the season. Hayes and Sparks each scored 12 in the opener, then Sparks came back with 20 in the win over Ball State. Azubuike and Hayes were the leading point producers in the next two games. After each player scored 16 against Georgia State, Azubuike had 21 and Hayes 17 against Tennessee Tech. In addition, Hayes registered double-doubles in three of those four outings.

The unbeaten and eighth-ranked Cats next squared off against ninth-ranked North Carolina in Chapel Hill. It was never a contest, with the Tar Heels riding a blazing first-half performance by Rashad McCants to a convincing 91-78 victory.

McCants scored 20 of his game-high 28 points in the opening half, which helped the Heels build a 47-32 lead at the break. The Cats, behind solid play by Azubuike, Crawford and Bradley, managed to pull to within 79-72 before a final late push by the Tar Heels sealed the win.

McCants had solid support from Jawad Williams with 19 points and Sean May with 14 points and 19 rebounds.

Azubuike topped the Cats with 24 points, while Crawford and Bradley finished with 11 and 10, respectively.

Azubuike continued his hot shooting, knocking down 21 points in an easy 71-40 Wildcat win over Morehead State. Alleyne came off the bench to contribute 11 points and eight rebounds. Sparks and Hayes also hit double-digits with 10 points apiece.

A tremendous effort by a trio of big men, along with another excellent performance by Sparks, was more than enough for UK to continue its dominance over Indiana by

Big Randolph Morris was an imposing presence in the middle. He could score, rebound, defend and block shots.

posting a 73-58 win in Louisville's Freedom Hall.

Sparks topped UK with 16 points and six assists, with the threesome of Hayes, Morris and Alleyne combining for 35 points on 14-of-20 shooting. Hayes had 14 points, Morris 11 and Alleyne 10.

It was UK's fifth consecutive win over the Hoosiers, and its 12th in the last 14 meetings.

The Cats made a second straight Freedom Hall appear-

ance, and it was in this thrilling 60-58 rise-from-the-grave win over Louisville that Sparks forever etched his name alongside a string of past late-game Big Blue heroes. And he did so amid a swirl of controversy, a time-consuming series of TV replays and a hostile crowd that did everything in its power to rattle his nerves.

Nothing seemed to bother Sparks, who, after being fouled while attempting a trey with less than a second remaining, calmly sank three free throws to give the Cats an improbable 60-58 win over Rick Pitino's talented Cardinals.

Sparks would finish with 25 points, hitting five of eight three-pointers.

During the early moments of the game, no one in Freedom Hall would have dared to think this one would be close. Or that Louisville would lose. The Cards bolted to a quick lead, and owned a 32-16 advantage at intermission. Larry O'Bannon did the most damage, leading UL with 16 points.

But the Cats, keyed by Sparks' long-range bombing and a more tenacious defense, slowly clawed back into contention, finally taking a 55-54 lead on a pair of Azubuike freebies. The Cards came back, going on top 58-57 when O'Bannon dropped in two free throws.

That set the stage for Sparks' game-deciding heroics. Following a UK timeout with 4.8 ticks remaining, Sparks inbounded the ball, took a quick return pass, did a pump fake, then went airborne with his three-point attempt, drawing a foul from Ellis Myles as time expired.

While the three referees convened to check the instant replay to see if time had expired prior to the foul being committed, veteran TV analyst Billy Packer argued that it was all moot, that Sparks had traveled before shooting.

After what seemed like an eternity, it was decided that six-tenths of a second should be put back on the clock, and that Sparks would be awarded three free tosses, which he calmly made to settle the issue.

It was one of the most memorable comebacks in UK's long and storied basketball history.

Azubuike added 12 points to UK's tally, while Juan Palacios finished with 11 for the Cards.

After escaping Louisville, the Cats readied for SEC action by easily polishing off a pair of overmatched foes — William & Mary 92-47 and Campbell 82-50. Those two victories gave the Cats a 9-1 record heading into league play.

Hayes had 18 points, Azubuike 17 and Crawford 12 in the win over William & Mary. Morris erupted for 25 points on 11-of-14 shooting to lead the win over Campbell. Azu-

buike chipped in with 14.

Azubuike pitched in 21 points as five Cats cracked double figures in a tough 79-75 win over South Carolina in the SEC opener. After trailing 41-35 at intermission, the Cats, thanks to four Azubuike treys, were able to take charge midway through the final 20 minutes, then hang on for the win. Sparks and Moss combined for four key free throws during the stretch run.

Hayes had 15 points and 10 rebounds, while Rondo finished with 11 points and Sparks and Morris 10 each.

Tre Kelley led the Gamecocks with 19.

Unbeaten Kansas, despite playing without pre-season All-America candidate Wayne Simien, came into Rupp Arena and bumped off the Cats 65-59. Kansas led 52-44 at the 6:12 mark, but a 9-0 Wildcat run, capped off by a driving Sparks bucket, put the home club in front 53-52 with just under four minutes left. But the Jayhawks regained the lead, thanks to Aaron Miles' only basket of the night. And once in front, the Jayhawks refused to yield the upper hand.

Azubuike led UK with a dozen points. Sparks and Perry each contributed 10.

Rondo's 18 points on eight-of-11 shooting keyed the Cats to a 69-54 win over Vanderbilt. Rondo also finished with four rebounds, four assists and three steals in his finest effort of the young season.

The Cats led by just three — 33-30 — at the break, and the game stayed close until a Rondo basket triggered a game-breaking 17-3 spurt.

Azubuike chipped in with 16 points, Hayes had 14 and Sparks 11 for the winners.

Corey Smith paced the Commodores with 16.

Sparks scored 15, Bradley 14 off the bench and Hayes had 13 points and 11 rebounds to lead the Cats past home-standing Georgia 76-55. The Cats were in complete control from start to finish, building their biggest advantage at 68-38 with less than three minutes left.

The Cats' next road trip, to Ole Miss, was anything but a breather. In fact, the Cats, after falling behind early, erased a 15-point first-half deficit to come away with a 53-50 victory.

Rondo keyed the comeback, accounting for 11 of his 13 points after intermission. It was a Rondo basket with 3:02 left that pushed the Cats in front for the first time at 49-48. Ole Miss, down 51-50, had a chance to regain the lead, but Kendrick Fox missed a three-point attempt. Sparks accounted for the final margin by dropping in a pair of freebies.

Azubuike had 11 points to support Rondo, while Hayes fashioned another double-double with 10 points and 10 rebounds.

Sparks buried five of seven three-points attempts for 15 points as the Cats smashed LSU 89-58 in Rupp Arena. Azubuike had 16 points to pace UK, with Hayes and Bradley each racking up 10.

Sparks stayed hot, scoring 19 points in a surprisingly easy 84-62 victory over Tennessee in Thompson-Boling Arena. Azubuike also put together another big game, finishing with 17 points.

Mason County graduate Chris Lofton led the Vols with 17 points.

Perry came off the bench to score nine critical points as the Cats escaped with a 68-67 win at Arkansas. Perry connected on four of five field goal attempts, including a basket that put UK on top 66-61 with a minute remaining.

Jonathan Modica answered with a three-point play to make it 66-64, but Sparks sealed it for the Cats by knocking down a jumper with 24.2 seconds left.

Azubuike led UK with 13 points, with Rondo adding 12.

The Cats built a 46-29 halftime advantage, increased their lead to 71-47 midway through the second half, then coasted to a rare easy 84-70 win over Vandy in Memorial Gym.

Azubuike, Hayes and Sparks each tallied 15 points for the Cats. Rondo added 12.

The win gave the Cats a 17-2 record overall and a flawless 8-0 mark in SEC play.

The Cats upped their league record to 10-0 by topping Florida 69-66 and Georgia 60-51. Azubuike had 18 points and Rondo 14 in the win over Florida, while Hayes and Sparks each had 14 in the win over Georgia.

But the Cats' dream of another unbeaten run through SEC action was shattered by South Carolina, which claimed a 73-61 upset win at home. It was the Cats' first loss after 19 straight wins against SEC foes.

The Gamecocks used a stingy defense, combined with a superb second half from Carlos Powell to pick up the win. South Carolina held UK to just 35 percent shooting from the field. The Gamecocks also won the rebounding battle 37-35 while forcing the Cats into 21 turnovers.

Tarence Kinsey led the winners with 17 points. Powell ended the night with 14, including 12 in the second half.

Azubuike had 16 to lead UK. Moss came off the bench to add 12.

The Cats returned to Rupp Arena, where they picked

up a pair of victories, beating Mississippi State 94-78 and Auburn 81-73. Both of those wins came courtesy of strong second-half efforts.

The Cats led by three (46-43) against Mississippi State at the half, and by four (36-32) against Auburn. However, in each game, the Cats were able to pull away by controlling the second half.

Seven Cats scored in double figures against Mississippi State, headed by Morris and Hayes with 17 points apiece. Others in double digits included Azubuike (15), Sparks (14), Rondo (11), Moss (10) and Bradley (10).

It was the Kelenna Azubuike show in the win over Auburn. UK's splendid junior forward erupted for a career-high 31 points, hitting nine of 17 field goal attempts and nine of 11 free throws. In addition, Azubuike claimed 11 rebounds.

Saprks owned the hot hand in the next outing, torching Alabama for 26 points in a 78-71 UK win on the road. Sparks connected on eight of 14 shots from the field, and was on fire from beyond the three-point arc, hitting seven of 10.

Azubuike had 15 points in that win, with Moss adding 10.

The Cats closed out their regular season by splitting the final two games. With Sparks scoring 14, Hayes 13 and Azubuike 10, the Cats had enough firepower to offset a 19-point effort by Chris Lofton and beat Tennessee 73-61. In his final home game, the steady and solid Hayes had 13 points and four rebounds.

Florida, led by Anthony Roberson's 21 points, upset the third-ranked Cats 53-52 in the O'Connell Center. Roberson was the hero, stripping the ball from Sparks, drawing a foul, then burying a pair of free throws to seal the victory.

Matt Walsh also came up big for the Gators, knocking down two key baskets and a free throw late in the game.

Rajon Rondo goes to the bucket despite heavy defensive pressure. Rondo was a superb defensive player and an excellent passer.

With UK on top 49-45, Walsh registered an old-fashion three-point play to make it 49-48. After a Sparks trey made it 52-48, Walsh answered with a three-pointer to close the gap to 52-51, setting the stage for Roberson's heroics.

The Cats had one final chance to pull out the win, but came up empty when Azubuike's last-second three-point attempt rattled harmlessly off the rim and into the hands

of Walsh.

Roberson received solid support from Walsh and David Lee with 11 points each.

Hayes, with 11 points, was the only Wildcat to hit double figures.

In the SEC Tournament opener, the Cats squared off against dangerous Tennessee and its high-scoring guard Chris Lofton, who had scored 36 points in the teams' two regular-season meetings. But in this critical battle, which UK won convincingly 76-62, the Cats' defense limited Lofton to just 10 points on four-of-13 shooting.

Azubuike keyed a lightning start that saw the Cats take control early, building a 47-29 advantage by intermission. Azubuike accounted for 10 of UK's first 13 points, hitting a pair of treys in that explosion. He finished with 18 points to lead the Cats.

Sparks contributed 16, while Hayes had 14 points and 11 rebounds. Morris also hit double figures with 11 points.

The Vols' C.J. Watson claimed high-scoring honors with 26 points.

A spinning basket in the lane by Hayes with 7.9 seconds remaining lifted the Cats to a 79-78 overtime win over LSU in semifinal action. Hayes banked in the game-winner with his left hand despite being guarded by LSU's Glen Davis.

Hayes late game heroics ended a back-and-forth tussle that saw each team consistently come up with big-time plays. Brandon Bass hit a miracle shot at the end of regulation to force the OT.

After LSU built a five-point lead in the extra frame, Sparks nailed a trey to narrow the gap. Davis missed a pair of free tosses with 39 ticks left to give UK an opening. Azubuike hit one of two free throws to make it 78-77. He missed his second attempt, but Hayes managed to snare the rebound.

Following a timeout, the Cats worked the ball to Hayes, who spun in the lane and banked in the winner. It was only his third bucket of the night in 10 tries.

Azubuike led UK with 19 points. Sparks and Crawford finished with 17 and 14, respectively.

Antonio Hudson topped the Tigers with 21 points. Bass ended the night with 16 points and 13 rebounds.

The Cats' hopes for a third straight SEC tourney title were dashed by hot-shooting Matt Walsh and his talented Florida teammates. Walsh, a player UK fans loved to hate, was brilliant, finishing with 26 points.

The win marked the first time Florida laid claim to the SEC tourney trophy.

The Gators seized control early, eventually building a 34-27 lead at the break. But the Cats battled back, taking the lead at 42-40 on a Morris bucket with just under 13 minutes left. After a Gator turnover, Sparks scored on a driving layup to push the Cats in front by four. That would turn out to be the Cats' last hoorah.

Two Walsh treys and a basket by Roberson shifted the momentum back to the Gators, and once in front, they never looked back. Walsh, Roberson and Corey Brewer led a late assault that put the Gators on top 61-46 with less than four minutes remaining.

The Cats' cold shooting from the field proved to be too much to overcome. For the game, the Cats shot 35 percent, and an even more frosty two of 19 from behind the three-point line.

Walsh got plenty of help from Roberson with 10 points and David Lee with 17 rebounds.

Azubuike was the lone Cat in double figures with 17.

For their NCAA Tournament opener, the Cats traveled to Indianapolis to face a team located a mere 20 miles from Lexington — the Eastern Kentucky Colonels. The pairing also meant the Cats would be going up against a very familiar coach — ex-UK standout Travis Ford.

This may have been a pairing the NCAA brain trust loved, but that feeling was not shared by anyone in Kentucky.

The fifth-ranked Cats, though heavily favored, found themselves in real dogfight against a fearless EKU club eyeing the big upset. But size made the difference, especially in the paint, where the Cats' big men had a 42-24 scoring advantage.

The final: UK won 72-64.

Both clubs finished with 26 field goals, but UK had a big advantage at the charity stripe, connecting on 18 of 26 to just six of 11 by the Colonels.

Hayes and Azubuike led UK with 16 points each. Rondo added 12.

EKU's Matt Witt led all scorers with 21.

The Cats continued to own the paint area in their next outing, a 69-60 victory over Cincinnati. In this game, UK's big men outscored their opponents 34-12.

This game, like so many others this season, saw the Cats trailing at the half, only to battle back in the final 20 minutes to claim the win. Cincinnati led 35-33 at the half, but the Cats, fueled by a 9-2 run, took the lead at 42-37. The Bearcats twice closed the gap to a single point, but late

Patrick Sparks is one of the most intense, competitive Wildcats ever. He also had a knack for knocking down big-time shots.

baskets by Hayes, Azubuike and Morris were enough to give UK the win.

Azubuike paced the Cats with 19 points. Others in double figures included Rondo (16), Morris (11), Sparks (11) and Hayes (10).

Next up for the Cats was a meeting against another familiar NCAA tourney foe — Utah. This marked the sixth time since 1993 that the two teams collided in NCAA Tournament action. The outcome of this game was no different than the other five.

UK won 62-52.

Ironically, it was an early exit by Morris that may have been the difference. After committing his second foul just 90 seconds into the game, Morris went to the bench. His replacements, seven-footers Alleyne and Obrzut, both turned in superb efforts, especially on the defensive end, where their task was to contain Utah All-American Andrew Bogut.

Bogut, who finished with 20 points, misfired on eight of his first 10 shots against the two UK giants. He also struggled at the charity stripe, hitting just four of 11.

The Cats, meanwhile, had one of their best shooting performances, connecting on 24 of 39 shots for 62 percent.

Hayes had 12 points to lead UK. Rondo ended the night with 10.

With a Final Four berth on the line, the Cats faced off against Big Ten powerhouse Michigan State. The game turned out to have more twists and turns than Route 66, a see-saw affair the Spartans eventually won 94-88 in double overtime.

Each team had its chances, and neither team backed off an inch. It was thrilling, gut-wrenching college basketball at its finest.

It also provided Sparks with another shot destined to go down in Wildcat lore. After battling back from an eight-point deficit, yet still trailing by three, the Cats got the ball to Sparks with barely a second remaining. He launched a three-point attempt as the buzzer sounded. The ball bounced around the rim four times before dropping through the nets, trying the game at 75-75.

The referees, like those in the Louisville game, weren't convinced that Sparks got his shot off in time. They went to the replay, and after what seemed like an eternity decided that Sparks did shoot before the clock ran out. The Cats were still alive.

The Cats scored the first four points in OT, but couldn't maintain their lead. Michigan State fought back to tie it at 81-81, sending the game into a second extra frame.

Kelvin Torbert sank a free throw to open the second OT and the Spartans never trailed again. They made 11 straight

free throws to seal the victory.

Morris topped UK with 20 points. Hayes and Sparks had 16 and 15, respectively.

Sophomore Shannon Brown led the Spartans with 24 points.

The loss left the Cats with a 28-6 record. During the past two years, Smith's Cats fashioned a 55-11 mark. Despite those impressive numbers, grumblings about Smith's coaching were beginning to be heard within Big Blue Nation. Over the next two seasons, those grumblings would swell in volume and intensity.

2005-06

By any standard of measurement, this season should have turned out better than it did. The talent, depth and experience were certainly present in abundance. There was size, strength and quickness. On paper, this should have been a terrific Wildcat club, one much better than its final 22-13 record.

But something was amiss with this team from the beginning. That missing ingredient was chemistry. These Wildcats never seemed to be on the same page at the same time. They never clicked, never jelled, never became a cohesive unit. There was never an all-for-one, one-for-all attitude.

Given all that, it's not surprising that this was an unhappy, unsuccessful and unfulfilling campaign in virtually every way. It was also during this long winter that the anti-Tubby Smith crowd began to swell in numbers.

This season's woes began before the opening tip-off, thanks to Morris' on-again, off-again flirtation with the NBA. Morris was suspended for the first 14 games after it was discovered that he had dealings with a professional agent. That was a huge blow to a club that was counting on the big sophomore to provide big scoring and rebounding numbers.

Still, it appeared as though the Cats had a deadly enough arsenal to overcome Morris' absence. Returning veterans included Sparks, Rondo, Crawford, Bradley, Perry, Moss, Thomas, Obrzut, Stockton, Alleyne and LeMaster. New faces included Rekalin Sims, Jared Carter and Adam Williams.

With that roster, even minus Morris, the Cats should have been a dangerous, formidable team. Sadly, they were never better than ordinary.

For the opener, Smith's starting quintet featured Thomas, Crawford, Obrzut, Rondo and Sparks. In that game, and

Kelenna Azubuike scored a career-high 31 points in a win over Auburn.

the next one, it was the standout play by Rondo that enabled the Cats to open with a pair of easy wins.

Rondo had 17 points, 12 rebounds and six assists in a 71-54 romp past South Dakota State, then came back with a 19-point, seven-rebound, five-assist effort in a 67-49 win over Lipscomb in the first round of the Guardians Classic.

Rondo, not known as a deadly shooter, made good on 14 of 23 field goal attempts in those two contests, including three of five from beyond the three-point line.

Crawford chipped in with 10 points in the opener, then Moss and Bradley finished with 13 and 12, respectively, against Lipscomb.

In semifinal action, the seventh-ranked Cats' cold shooting, a plague that would haunt them throughout the campaign, led to a 67-63 loss to No. 18-ranked Iowa. For the game, the Cats shot just 33 percent from the field.

The game was tight from beginning to end, with neither team able to carve out more than a seven-point advantage. The Cats trailed 61-58, but tied it on a Perry trey with 1:12 remaining. But with the outcome in the balance, it was the Hawkeyes who made the big plays in crunch time.

Sims rebounded an Iowa miss, then threw an errant pass that Rondo couldn't handle. Iowa answered by hitting four straight freebies to take a 65-61 lead. After a Moss bucket pulled the Cats to within two, Adam Haluska buried two free throws with less than a second left to seal the win for Iowa.

Sims led UK with 22 points, while Rondo grabbed 19 rebounds from his guard position. Greg Brunner had 17 points and a dozen rebounds for the winners.

A slump-busting performance by Sparks, combined with a 20-0 first-half run, was enough the lift the Cats to an 80-66 victory over 13th-ranked West Virginia. The Mountaineers broke to a quick 9-2 lead before going icy cold from the field, misfiring on 13 consecutive shots.

Conversely, Sparks was white-hot from the outside, connecting on eight of 13 field goal attempts, including seven of 11 from three-point territory. For the game, Sparks finished with 25 points.

Rondo turned in another solid effort, scoring 15 points while snaring 10 rebounds.

Kevin Pittsnogle led all scorers with 27 points. He also claimed 10 rebounds.

The Cats did as expected, easily winning their next two outings against severely overmatched opponents — 81-51 over Liberty and 75-55 over High Point, Tubby Smith's

Joe Crawford had the ability to score in close or from long range.

alma mater.

Perry led the way with 22 points against Liberty. Rondo and Bradley each had 14 points and Sparks added 13 in the win over High Point.

North Carolina came into Rupp Arena and handed the Cats an 83-79 setback. To do so, the Tar Heels bucked some awfully big odds. For the game, UK shot 51 percent from the field, making this only the second time in Tubby Smith's tenure that the Cats shot 50 percent or better and lost. Until this setback, UK was 96-1 in such games.

Rebounding was a big reason why the Tar Heels won it. They won the board wars 37-30.

Reyshawn Terry burned the Cats with a career-best 25-point performance. David Noel offered strong support with 15 points.

Rondo scored 20 points on nine-of-11 shooting to lead the Cats. Moss finished with 17, Bradley 12 and Sparks 10.

With back-up center Alleyne scoring a career-high 16 points and Crawford chipping in with 14, the Cats got back on track with an 73-46 romp past Georgia State. Bradley and Sparks also cracked double digits with 12 and 10 points, respectively.

Rondo sat out the Georgia State game with strep throat.

The Cats' next outing turned out to be one of the worst and most embarrassing during Smith's years at the helm. In the Indianapolis RCA Dome, Indiana thoroughly outclassed the Cats in every way, easily winning 79-53.

It was, in every respect, a horrendous effort by the Cats, who fell to 6-3 with the loss. The Hoosiers, who led 35-19 at the half, shot 53 percent, UK 31 percent. Indiana's relentless defense forced 19 turnovers while holding the Cats to .074 shooting (two of 27) from three-point range.

The Hoosiers featured a balanced attack, placing four players in double figures, led by Marco Killingsworth with 23 and A.J. Ratliff with 21.

Rondo was the lone bright spot for the Cats, finishing with 21 points and nine rebounds. This marked the fifth time Rondo had led the Cats in scoring.

In their yearly tussle against arch-enemy Louisville, the Cats took advantage of early foul trouble by center David Padgett to build a lead too big for Rick Pitino's Cardinals to overcome. Padgett committed two fouls in the first 88 seconds, then spent the remainder of the half on the bench. Padgett could only look on as his team fell behind 39-24 by intermission. UK won 73-61.

Rondo was once again a difference-maker for the Cats,

ending the night with 25 points and seven assists. After Louisville pulled to within 17-13, Rondo scored six unanswered points, then lobbed to Alleyne for a dunk that made it 25-13 and gave the Cats all the momentum they needed for the win.

Thomas added 11 points to UK's coffers, while Obrzut grabbed nine rebounds.

Juan Palacios led the Cards with 15 points.

The Cats needed a solid 11-point, six-rebound off-the-bench effort from Sims to escape an upset bid by Iona, winning 73-67 in Freedom Hall. The Cats seized control early, breaking away from a 4-4 tie by reeling off eight straight points to take a lead they would never relinquish.

Rondo paced the Cats with 13 points. Crawford contributed 12.

Iona's Steve Burtt, the nation's No. 3 scorer, had 23 points, including 21 after intermission.

The Cats' next two games, expected to be breathers, turned out to be heart-stopping thrillers. Bradley's late-game fireworks provided the difference in a 71-63 win over Ohio, then Rondo bailed out his teammates by sinking a last-second turnaround jumper that beat Central Florida 59-57.

To survive the Ohio scare, the Cats had to fight back from a nine-point deficit, finally going on top 60-59 on a Sims tip-in and three-pointer. A late Bradley trey sealed the win for UK.

Crawford paced the Cats with 23 points. Bradley ended the game with 18, Sims with 11.

Against Central Florida, the Cats built a 33-26 halftime lead, thanks to 14 first-half points by Bradley. Central Florida kept hanging tough, and eventually knotted the score at 57-57 on a Mike O'Donnell three-pointer.

With the clock winding down, Rondo, who had 13 points, knocked down the game-winning bucket.

Bradley led UK with 16 points, hitting three of four three-point attempts.

The Cats' final pre-SEC tune up turned out to be a humbling, humiliating experience, one that rivaled — and perhaps surpassed — the Indiana debacle.

Kansas, led by freshman Brandon Rush's 24 points, completely dismantled the Cats, cruising to a 73-46 victory. The Cats dug their own grave, missing 17 of their first 20 shots. At intermission, Kansas owned an insurmountable 41-19 advantage.

The Jayhawks' defense was especially dominating, lim-

iting UK to 24-percent shooting (15 of 62). Kansas also controlled the boards, winning that battle 46-38.

UK was led by Crawford and Rondo with nine points apiece.

As SEC action began, there was good news and bad news within the UK camp. The good news — Morris was now eligible to play. The bad news — Sparks, the Cats' outside scoring ace, was mired in a horrible shooting slump, having connected on just seven of his last 31 attempts.

It didn't take long for Big Blue fans to discover that this wasn't going to be business as usual for the Wildcats in SEC play. The Cats had virtually owned the SEC for the past decade, and with back-to-back league games in friendly Rupp Arena, there was no reason to believe that their domination wouldn't continue.

But in this case, the past was anything but a bright light shining through to the present.

Before you could say "what's going on here?" the Cats were 0-2 in SEC play and staring up from the bottom of the pack. The double setbacks came courtesy of Vanderbilt and Alabama, two clubs not known for successful forays into Rupp Arena. In fact, Vandy had never won in Rupp Arena, and had not posted a victory in Lexington since 1974.

This was the beginning of an SEC journey that saw the Cats eventually finish with a 9-7 league record.

Vandy topped the Cats 57-52 despite making just 15 field goals. As always, though, the Commodores were lethal from the charity stripe, hitting 21 of 25. That accuracy, coupled with a solid 16-point performance by Shan Foster, was enough to offset Morris' return to action.

Vandy built a 14-point second-half lead, but the Cats, fueled by four Moss treys, came back to take a 42-41 lead on a Thomas dunk. Seconds later, Julian Terrell canned a pair of free throws to give Vandy the lead for good.

Moss paced UK with 16 points. Morris, in his long-awaited season debut, finished with 10 points and seven rebounds.

Alabama knocked off the Cats 68-64 thanks to a monster 28-point outburst by Jermareo Davidson, who blistered the nets for 10 field goals in 14 attempts. Davidson got strong support from Ronald Steele with 14 points and Brandon Hollinger with 10.

After the Cats grabbed a 64-63 lead on consecutive treys by Bradley and Moss, and a Rondo layup, Davidson connected on a three-point bomb that put Alabama back on

Dependable Bobby Perry was an unsung player who quietly went about getting the job done.

top while effectively closing the lid on UK's coffin.

Morris, making his first start of the season, had 19 points to lead the Cats. Bradley added 14 and Crawford 11.

The Cats, now desperately in need of a win, ventured to Athens, where a solid second-half performance, especially by the slumping Sparks, was enough to earn a 69-55 win.

Sparks, who had scored just 14 points in the last six games, scored all 12 of his points after intermission to lead the Cats to victory. Morris led the Cats with 14 points, while Bradley had 13 and Rondo matched Sparks with 12.

With members of the fabled "Rupp's Runts" looking on, Rondo, for the second time this season, played the role of hero, hitting a three-pointer with a single second remaining

to left the Cats to a stirring 80-78 comeback victory over South Carolina.

The Cats trailed 58-46 before beginning their comeback run, which saw them take a 77-76 lead on a Sparks three-pointer. Following a pair of Antoine Tisby free tosses with 10 seconds left that gave South Carolina a 78-77 advantage, Rondo barely beat the buzzer with his game-deciding bucket.

Crawford paced a balanced scoring attack with 15 points. Other Cats in double figures included Sparks (14), Perry (13) and Morris (12). Rondo, the hero, ended the night with nine points.

Tarence Kinsey led all scorers with 21 points.

The Cats pushed their winning streak to five by claiming three more victims — Auburn 71-62, Arkansas 78-76 and Mississippi State 81-66.

Crawford came up big in the win over Auburn, burning the nets for 23 points. To beat Arkansas in Rupp Arena, the Cats had to claw their way back from an 18-point deficit. Morris was the key to this win, scoring 19 points and spearing eight rebounds.

Sparks did the main damage in the win over Mississippi State, finishing with 25 points. The Cats buried 13 treys, with Sparks and Crawford combining for nine in 16 attempts.

Now riding the crest of a five-game winning streak that had them poised to grab the SEC Eastern Division lead, the Cats journeyed to Gainesville for a showdown with talent-rich Florida. For a half, it appeared as though the Cats might make it six wins in a row. After a superb first-half effort, the Cats led 41-39.

Then, in a flash, it was over. Billy Donovan's powerful Gators, who would go on to claim the national title, went on an 18-1 run early in the second half to easily trounce the Cats 95-80.

Taurean Green and Joakim Noah combined for 54 points to lead the Florida rampage. Green had 29, Noah 26. Corey Brewer added 16.

Rondo and Crawford led UK with 22 and 19, respectively.

Tennessee marched into town and became the third SEC club to beat UK in Rupp Arena this season. And they did it thanks to Chris Lofton, who proved to be the hottest thing to come out of Maysville since George Clooney. Lofton scored 31 points, connecting 11 of 18 from the field and seven of 11 behind the three-point line.

Lofton's long-range bombing keyed the Vols to a 75-67

win, their first after eight straight losses to the Cats.

Morris had 20 points to top UK's scoring.

Vanderbilt kept the Cats spiraling downward, claiming an 84-81 win in Nashville. It marked the first time since the 1973-74 campaign that the Commodores swept the season series.

Once again, the Cats overcame a late deficit to put themselves in position to win. But inside the final minute, with Vandy ahead by three, Rondo missed two free throws and a three-point attempt, and Bradley misfired on a trey that could have sent the game into overtime.

Sparks led the Cats with 17 points. Bradley finished with 14 and Moss added 12.

DeMarre Carroll scored a career-high 22 points to pace Vandy. Derrick Byars chipped in with 17.

Displeased with his team's effort, Smith rattled a few cages when the Cats met Georgia, benching starters Morris, Rondo and Crawford in favor of Obrzut, Moss and little-used Brandon Stockton.

While the new trio offered little more than splendid effort, the cage rattling did manage to get the attention of the benched starters, especially Morris and Crawford, who combined for 18 points and 12 rebounds.

Their play, along with 13 points from Thomas and 11 from Sparks, was enough to propel the Cats to a 68-61 victory.

In UK's next game, Sparks connected on six treys and scored 26 points to key the Cats past home-standing South Carolina 79-66. Sparks was white-hot, hitting eight of 11 field goal attempts, including six of eight from three-point land.

Morris also turned in an outstanding effort, accounting for 13 points and 11 rebounds. Other Cats to crack double digits included Crawford with 12 and Perry with 11.

Kinsey led the Gamecocks with 21 points.

Thirteen Wildcats scored in an easy 80-40 romp past Ole Miss. Crawford led the way with 17 points. LeMaster had his best game, ending with 12 points. Rondo handed out 12 assists.

In Baton Rouge, Glen Davis proved to be too much for the Cats to handle. His 28-point, 15-rebound performance was good enough to lift LSU to a 71-67 win over the inconsistent Wildcats.

Although Davis did the most damage, he received plenty of help from Darrel Mitchell, who finished with 13 points and eight assists.

Despite the strong play by Davis and Mitchell, the

Cats had a chance to escape with the win. But once again, it was the opponent who made the clutch plays in gut-check time.

Sparks buried a trey to tie the score at 67-67 with 27 seconds left to play. On LSU's next possession, Mitchell went to the bucket, drawing a foul on Moss. Mitchell swished both freebies to put LSU back on top 69-67.

The Cats tried to answer, but a short baseline jumper by Thomas was off the mark. Davis rebounded, drew a foul and dropped in two free tosses to account for the final score.

Morris had 17 for UK, while Sparks ended the night with 13.

Next, the Cats traveled to Knoxville, where they managed to pull off another comeback win, edging the Vols 80-78. It was a genuine nail-biter, and a game in which neither club was exactly

Ramel Bradley's late-game heroics helped the Cats slip past Ohio.

dynamite down the stretch. In fact, it often appeared as if neither team wanted the win.

With the score tied at 76-76, UK ran off four unanswered points, the last two courtesy of a Rondo layup, to go on top 80-76. Dane Bradshaw scored for the Vols with 1:46 remaining to make it 80-78.

After that, it was the Keystone Kops against the Little Rascals.

C.J. Watson missed a trey, then JaJuan Smith missed the front end of a bonus after Rondo grabbed Smith's jersey. Moments later, Smith lost possession of the ball when he

slipped and fell. Stockton came up with the loose ball and got it to Crawford, who was fouled intentionally. Crawford missed, then Watson missed a potential game-winning three at the buzzer.

Morris led the Cats with 22 points. Rondo had 16 points and eight assists.

Lofton, Watson and Smith all had 15 points each for the Vols.

Florida completed a rare season sweep of the Wildcats, winning 79-64 in Rupp Arena. After a close first half that ended with the visitors leading 34-33, it was all Florida in the final 20 minutes. Back-to-back three-pointers by Lee Humphrey keyed a run that saw the Gators build their advantage to 17 points.

Humphrey led Florida with 17 points. Crawford paced the Cats with a game-best 21 points.

This would be the final home appearance for seniors Sparks, Moss, Stockton and LeMaster, all of whom were homegrown Kentucky products. It would also turn out to be Rondo's swan song as well. At the end of this season, Rondo departed for the NBA.

With their 9-7 league record, the Cats found themselves having to play on opening night of the SEC Tournament in Nashville. This was the first time that had happened since 1979.

For awhile, it appeared as though the Cats' stay in Nashville would be shorter than a Country-Western ballad. Facing Ole Miss, the Cats trailed 29-26 at the break. But with the score tied at 46-46, a 13-2 run spearheaded by Rondo

and Morris was enough to send the Cats to a 71-57 win, their 20th of the season. It was the 16th straight year UK reached the 20-win plateau.

Morris led UK with 17 points. Sparks ended the night with 14, while Crawford and Bradley each contributed 11.

Next up was Alabama, a club that whipped the Cats 68-64 in their only regular-season confrontation. This time around, with a possible NCAA berth still an uncertainty, the Cats, thanks to a balanced scoring attack, were able to get revenge with a 68-61 victory.

The outcome of this battle was as uncertain as UK's tournament status, and it wouldn't be until the final minute that the Cats put the Tide away for good. The Cats wiped out an 11-point deficit in the final seven minutes to notch the win. A Perry layup at the 1:15 mark broke a 61-61 tie and gave UK the lead for good.

The Cats won despite making just four of their first 23 shots. For the game, they shot just under 40 percent from the field.

Crawford, one of four Cats in double figures, led UK with 14 points. Perry and Sparks each had 13, while Morris had 11.

Alabama's Alonzo Gee claimed high-point honors with 18.

The win advanced the Cats to a semifinal pairing against South Carolina, a club they had beaten twice during regular-season action. This time, however, the Gamecocks turned the tables, upsetting the Cats 65-61.

Once again, it was the opposition that performed better when the outcome was on the line. Trailing 50-45 in the second half, South Carolina went on a 14-3 run, highlighted by a string of three-point buckets, to take control of the game.

Bryce Sheldon hit a three to even things at 50-50, then he and Tarence Kinsey wrapped a pair of treys around one by Crawford to make it 56-53. Kinsey then dropped in another three-point bomb to up the Gamecocks' lead to 59-53. UK would pull to within three but could never regain the upper hand.

Kinsey was the game's leading scorer with 18. Crawford's 13 led UK.

With their 21-12 record, the Cats were seeded eighth by the NCAA Tournament Selection Committee. Their first-round opponent was not only a familiar team, it was also one that had given Big Blue fans two of the most painful tourney losses in the school's glorious history.

When it was announced that UAB was the opening-round foe, Cat fans could only cringe, recalling those past nightmare tournament losses — 69-62 in 1982 and 76-75 in 2003.

But this time it was the Cats who prevailed, winning 69-64 thanks to a brilliant effort by Perry and some uncanny accuracy at the charity stripe.

Perry finished with 25 points, making good on all 10 of his free throw attempts. For the game, UK sank 26 of 30 free tosses.

Perry scored 19 of his points in the second half, including nine straight during one stretch, to help the Cats overcome a three-point half-time deficit and walk away with the win.

No other Wildcat scored in double figures. Rondo had 10 rebounds to lead UK in that category.

The Cats' win earned them a shot at No. 1 seeded Connecticut, owner of a glittering 28-3 record. This was the first-ever meeting between the two schools, and it was one for the ages.

The Huskies dominated the early going, leading 43-31 at intermission. They were still in control at the 13:37 mark, sitting on a 13-point advantage. It was then that things began to get interesting.

Still trailing 66-57, the Cats clawed to within four on a Thomas baseline jumper and a Perry three-pointer. The Huskies pushed their lead back to eight before treys by Thomas and Rondo keyed a 10-4 run that brought UK to within 74-72 with 3:16 remaining.

The Huskies again stretched their lead back to eight, only to see Sparks bury a trey that helped UK fight back to within two with 53 ticks left. After Marcus Williams made two foul shots, Perry scored on a layup to make it 83-81. Two more Williams freebies were matched by a Perry putback before Rudy Gay iced it for Connecticut by sinking two free throws with 3.3 seconds left. Final: UConn 87, UK 83.

The loss left the Cats with a final 22-13 record.

Sparks was brilliant in his final game, wracking up 28 points on 10 of 16 shooting from the field. He also made four of nine three-pointers.

Perry also turned in an excellent effort, ending the game with 20 points. Others in double figures included Morris (14), Rondo (11) and Thomas (10).

Williams and Gay had 20 and 19 points, respectively, to lead the Huskies.

The Cats' final record and their early exit from the NCAA tourney only seemed to provide additional ammu-

nition for the ever-increasing number of disgruntled Big Blue fans who wanted Tubby Smith gone. If their voices had been loud before, after this season they rose like constant blasts of thunder.

Outside observers were baffled as to why a coach who had won a national title, 76 percent of his games and dominated SEC regular-season and tournament action would be the center of such a firestorm of criticism. In their eyes (and opinion), Big Blue fans were longing for a level of past glory that simply was not attainable in today's college basketball world.

What Smith needed to silence the critics (if that was possible at this point) was nothing less than increased success on the recruiting trail and another Final Four appearance.

Neither happened, and in just one short year, Smith would be gone.

2006-07

In many ways, Tubby Smith's final UK team bore an eerie similarity to last year's club. Although this team had far better on-court team chemistry than its immediate predecessor, the final season record of 22-12 and yet another early exit from the NCAA Tournament did nothing to dissuade the growing multitude of Big Blue Nation fans from clamoring for a change. It didn't help that this team, which had such a promising start, ended by losing seven of its last 11 games. The way UK fans saw it, the time for Smith to be gone had clearly arrived.

And in four short months, those fans would get what they asked for — Smith said so long to UK, then signed on as the head coach at the University of Minnesota. However, the joy expressed by those fans who wanted Smith gone didn't last too long, proving once again that the devil you know just might be superior to the devil you get.

In truth, Smith's final team only had the ingredients to be an average team at best. Morris and Crawford possessed big-time potential, but neither had really demonstrated an ability to consistently dominate. The remaining veterans

Patrick Sparks shook off a mid-season slump to finish strong, scoring 28 points in an NCAA tourney loss to UConn.

included Perry, Thomas, Obrzut, Bradley and Carter, the 7'2" center from Georgetown. This group was solid and steady but not spectacular or dominating.

A quintet of incoming freshmen was added to the mix, and if this team had any chance of being successful, these rookies would have to produce. The new guys were Perry Stevenson, a 6'9" stingbean inside player, Michael Porter, a tough-minded 6'3" guard, 6'7" forward Ramon Harris and a pair of backcourt standouts who did possess tremendous potential — 6'6" point guard Derrick Jasper and 6'4" Jodie Meeks, a long-range marksman who would etch his name in the UK record books before his playing days were over. Also on the club was 6'9" walk-on Mark Coury.

Perry, Stevenson, Morris, Bradley and Crawford were

the starters for the season opener, a sluggish 57-46 win over Miami (Ohio). The Cats struggled to a 31-27 half-time lead, then managed to put the game away in the final 20 minutes.

Crawford led the Cats with 18 points. Bradley and Morris each finished with 12, while Meeks tossed in seven. Morris also had 10 rebounds.

With Bradley, Morris and Meeks combining for 52 points, the Cats notched an easy 79-56 win over Mississippi Valley State. In that win, in which the Cats held the visitors to 18 first-half points, Bradley led the way with 21 points, while Morris had 18 and Meeks had 13.

The Cats next faced DePaul in the opening round of the Maui Classic. It took the Cats' best performance to date in order to claim a hard-earned 87-81 victory. Hot shooting was the key to victory. For the game, the Cats shot 53 percent from the field, making good on 32 of 56 attempts.

Morris had 20 points, including nine of the club's final 11, to lead the Cats. Others in double figures included Bradley (16), Crawford (13) and Perry (11).

UCLA, thanks to an 18-point performance from Luc Richard Mbah A Moute, handed the Cats their first loss of the season, claiming a 73-68 win. Mbah A Moute accounted for six points down the stretch to help the Bruins hold off a last-ditch effort by the Cats.

After trailing 26-9 early and 38-30 at the break, the Cats managed to even the score at 48-all on a Crawford three-pointer with 11:46 to play. Following three lead changes and four ties, the Bruins assumed control and pulled away for the win.

Crawford paced UK with 16 points. Jasper, giving his best performance of the early season, finished with 12 points and nine rebounds. Morris and Stevenson also cracked double figures with 11 and 10, respectively.

The consolation game against Memphis saw the Cats play a solid opening half, only to be blown away during the final 20 minutes. Memphis, leading 43-40 at the half, went on a 14-0 run to claim an easy 80-63 win. Robert Dozier had 15 points to lead Memphis. Chris Douglas-Roberts and Jeremy Hunt each had 13.

Morris scored 18 to top UK's scoring. Crawford ended the night with 15, while Perry added 10.

Little did anyone realize at the time that the man guiding Memphis — John Calipari — would be sitting on the UK bench three years down the road.

With Morris scoring 17 points, Crawford adding 15 and

Randolph Morris was the leading scorer and rebounder on Tubby Smith's last UK team.

Joe Crawford scored 29 points in a tough overtime loss to Georgia.

lina's heralded star Tyler Hansbrough. Morris also claimed seven rebounds and blocked three shots.

Bradley tossed in 23 points to get UK back on track by registering a 79-63 win over UT-Chattanooga. This would prove to be the first win in an impressive 11-game winning streak. It was also the first game in which Smith opted for a three-guard lineup, with Jasper joining Bradley and Crawford on the perimeter.

Crawford provided solid support with 19 points, while Perry and Morris each contributed 17. Jasper, now UK's starting point guard, scored only one point but pulled down a team-best 10 rebounds.

Thanks to double-double efforts by Morris and Perry, the Cats managed to post a 59-54 win over Indiana in Rupp Arena. Morris had 16 points and Perry had 11. Both players grabbed 10 rebounds.

A thundering dunk by Morris, followed by a Jasper steal and dunk, turned things in the Cats' favor after there had been 14 lead changes in the tightly contested battle, the 50th meeting between these long-time border rivals.

D.J. White led Indiana with a game-high 23 points.

Stevenson 14 off the bench, the Cats rebounded with an easy 77-61 win over College of Charleston.

In yet another matchup between college basketball's two winningest programs, No.7-ranked North Carolina snapped a two-game losing streak against UK by posting a 75-63 win in Chapel Hill. Wayne Ellington led the Heels with 17 points, while teammates Brandan Wright and Reyshawn Terry each finished with 16.

Morris had a monster game for UK, scoring 23 points on 11-of-12 shooting, completing outplaying North Caro-

Behind the deadeye Meeks' 18-point performance, the Cats made it three in a row against Rick Pitino's Louisville Cardinals, carving out a 61-49 victory. In that win, the UK rookie came off the bench to bury four of five three-point attempts.

While Meeks was on fire from long-range, the Cardinals made good on just three of 24 from beyond the arc.

A bucket by Brandon Jenkins put UL on top 41-40 with just under 11 minutes to play. Then Meeks took over, knocking down back-to-back treys and then hitting three straight free throws to give the Cats a lead they would never relinquish.

For his efforts, Meeks was named SEC Freshman of the Week, the first of three times he would earn this honor.

Bradley was on the only other Cat in double figures with 15. David Padgett led UL with 16 points and 10 rebounds.

Morris' 23-point, 13-rebound effort, combined with a strong second-half performance, was enough to give UK a 74-60 victory over Santa Clara. After leading 30-28 at the half, UK outscored the visitors 44-32 in the second frame to win going away.

Bradley and Jasper also hit double digits with 14 and 10 points, respectively.

Hot shooting and a balanced scoring attack were key factors in UK's impressive 82-68 win over a UMass squad now coached by ex-Cat standout Travis Ford. For the game, the Cats shot 57-percent from the field (30 of 51), including seven of 11 from three-point land.

Ford's club made it interesting early, taking a 19-16 lead midway through the first half. But a 23-3 run by the Cats dashed any hope that Ford would earn his first win in four tries against his alma mater. Ford was 0-3 against UK while coaching at EKU.

Morris, Bradley and Crawford each had 14 points for UK. Meeks added 10 in another strong effort off the bench.

Morris scored 25 points and yanked down 10 rebounds to lead the Cats to a 78-65 win over scrappy EKU. Bradley ended the night with 20 points, while Crawford chipped in 13.

Adam Leonard led the Colonels with 20 points.

Morris continued his superb play, posting another double-double (20,10) in a 77-70 win over Houston. This was the Cats' final tune-up before venturing into the always-treacherous SEC waters.

Jasper also turned in a strong effort, scoring 12 points and handing out six assists. Bradley finished with 11 points, Crawford with 10, and Thomas with five points and seven rebounds.

In what Smith called "our best defensive effort of the year," the Cats opened SEC play by knocking off Ole Miss 68-58 in Oxford. It was UK's defense during the final 12 minutes that turned defeat into victory.

Ole Miss led 37-35 at the half, and following a see-saw battle that saw 19 lead changes, the Rebels were back in front 53-51 with 12:02 remaining. That's when UK's defense clamped down, limiting the Rebels to just a pair of

field goals in 13 tries down the stretch.

Meeks buried a trey — his only bucket of the night — to put UK in front for good at 56-53 with just under nine minutes remaining.

Crawford led UK with 23 points on eight-of-10 shooting. He also hit four of five three-point attempts. Morris registered another double-double (14,10) and Bradley chipped in with 13 points.

Crawford stayed hot, scoring 21 points, and Bradley recorded his first double-double (18 points, 12 rebounds) as the Cats waltzed past Auburn 84-57. Perry and Morris each contributed 12 points in the win.

UK ran its winning streak to 10 by easing past pesky Mississippi State 64-60 in Rupp Arena. The victory put the Cats' overall record at 14-3.

It was another game that saw plenty of lead changes (10) and yet another gutsy late-game effort by the Cats. After Charles Rhodes scored on a tip-in to tie it at 57-57, the Cats took the lead for good courtesy of a Morris layup.

Morris had 17 points to lead UK's scoring. Crawford and Bradley ended the night with 14 and 11, respectively.

Thanks to a 23-point effort by Crawford and another double-double by Morris, the Cats stormed past South Carolina 87-49 in an impressive road victory. For the game, UK shot 58 percent from the field, while limiting to South Carolina to just 15 field goals.

Morris finished with 17 points and 11 rebounds. Bradley had 15 points and Meeks added 12.

Riding the crest of an 11-game winning streak, the Cats, now ranked No. 25 in the latest polls, hosted Vanderbilt, a team that already owned three wins over ranked opponents this season.

The Commodores, thanks to a 23-point performance from Derrick Byars, made UK its fourth highly ranked victim, upsetting the Cats 72-67. This marked Vandy's third straight win over UK, and its second in a row in Rupp Arena.

UK led 33-32 at the half, and was still on top 59-58 after a Bradley bucket with three minutes remaining. But Vandy's Shan Foster answered with a layup, then came up with a steal and assist that led to a Byars basket that sealed the deal.

Five Cats scored in double figures, headed by Perry with 13. Others included Crawford (12), Thomas (12), Morris (11) and Bradley (10).

Georgia overcame a 17-point deficit to hand the Wildcats a disappointing 78-69 overtime loss in Athens. After leading 43-26 late in the opening half, and still on top

50-38 following a Meeks trey, the Cats were outscored 19-5 to fall behind 57-55. The final score at the end of regulation was 65-65.

Crawford opened the OT with a bucket, but a short jumper by Takais Brown and a three-pointer by Terrance Woodbury put the Bulldogs in front for good.

Crawford turned in a brilliant effort, finishing with 29 points.

Brown paced Georgia with 20.

Behind Bradley's 21-point performance, the Cats bounced back to defeat Tennessee 76-57. After trailing 32-31 at intermission, the Cats outscored UT 45-25 in the second half to win easily.

Meeks gave Big Blue fans — and Tennessee — a preview of coming attractions by knocking in 16 points in this win. Crawford continued his fine play by tossing in 15 points.

The Cats improved to 6-2 in league play by posting an impressive 82-74 win at Arkansas. For the second straight outing, the Cats won despite trailing at intermission. In fact, the Cats had to erase a 14-point deficit in order to walk away with the win.

Trailing 45-31 in the second half, the Cats, riding Bradley's hot hand, managed to fight back and take a 54-53 lead on a Meeks layup. The Cats never trailed after that.

Bradley scored 22 of his career-high 24 points in the second half. He also had six rebounds and five assists. Meeks continued to sizzle, scoring 15 points on six of seven shooting.

A huge first-half advantage proved to be enough for the Cats to hang on for a 95-89 win over South Carolina. In the second half, with UK apparently on cruise control, the Gamecocks, fueled by Tre' Kelley, outscored the Cats 61-45 to make it interesting.

Kelley burned the Cats for 36 points.

Bradley paced UK with 21 points, while Perry had a season-high 18. Morris, benched by Smith, finished 17 points and eight rebounds.

It was at this point, with UK sporting an 18-5 record overall and a 7-2 mark in SEC play, that the season began to unravel. Seven losses in their final 11 games turned a potentially great season into another year of disappointment. It also laid to rest any hope that disgruntled UK fans might lightened their criticism of Tubby Smith.

The long slide into darkness began with a 64-61 home-court loss to top-ranked Florida. (In truth, the darkness was only beginning, and would not lift for another two full

Rookie Jodie Meeks buried four treys to help lift the Cats past Louisville.

years.) This marked the fifth straight Florida win over UK, which was looking to claim its 400th win in Rupp Arena.

Despite trailing the entire game, including a 16-point deficit at one point, the Cats made a late charge, closing to within three only seconds ahead of the final buzzer. As time expired, Bradley misfired on a trey attempt that would have sent the game into overtime.

Bradley led UK with 20 points. Morris added 18.

Corey Brewer and Taurean Green paced Billy Donovan's Gators with 16 and 13 points, respectively.

Tennessee added to the Cats' woes with an 89-85 win in Knoxville. Former Mason County standout Chris Lofton burned UK with 23 points. Duke Crews had 18 and Wayne Chism 16 for the Vols.

Crawford's 24 points led the UK attack.

Home-standing 25th-ranked Alabama used a huge advantage at the charity stripe to hand stumbling UK a 72-61 setback. Bama had 22 field goals to UK's 21, but made good on 20 of 28 free throws compared to the Cats' 14 of 21.

Richard Hendrix topped Bama's scoring with 16 points. Crawford had 17 to lead UK.

UK snapped its losing streak by edging past LSU 70-63, thanks to a double-double by Morris and hot outside shooting by Meeks. Morris finished with 20 points and 10 rebounds, while Meeks tallied 18 points.

At Vanderbilt, after leading the entire game, the Cats' inability to hang on down the stretch resulted in a tough 67-65 loss. Vandy never led in the game until there were just 25.5 seconds remaining. That's when the alert Byars rebounded his own missed free throw and scored a bucket to give the Commodores the lead.

The Cats had one final chance to pull out the win, but their hopes ended when the triple-teamed Bradley drove the lane and fired up a shot that missed.

Byars ended with 26 points, while Foster had 21.

Perry's 18 points topped UK's scoring.

In an 82-70 win over Georgia, Perry continued his strong play, scoring 22 points and grabbing five rebounds. He received solid support from Bradley with 18 points, Morris with 17 and Meeks with 11.

Joakim Noah and Taurean Green each tossed in 17 points to lead fifth-ranked Florida to a convincing 85-72 thumping of the Cats, thus becoming the first SEC team to ever beat UK six times in a row.

The game was knotted 43-43 at the half, but the final 20 minutes belonged to the talented Gators, who shot 69.6

percent from the field during the second half and 64 percent for the game.

Perry led the Cats with 20 points.

With a final regular-season record of 21-10 and a 9-7 mark in league play, the Cats once again had to play on opening night of the SEC Tournament. As the fourth seed in the Eastern Division, they would face Alabama, the fifth seed in the Western Division.

The Tide won the only regular-season meeting between the two clubs, but in the SEC tourney, with any hope of an NCAA Tournament bid on the line, the Cats prevailed 79-67, thanks to another huge effort by Morris, who scored 17 points and snared 11 rebounds.

Bradley also had 17 points, as five UK players cracked double figures. Others included Crawford (16), Meeks (12) and Perry (10).

One day later, Mississippi State ended any hope UK had of capturing another SEC crown by outlasting the Cats 84-82 in overtime. Adding insult to injury was a bone-head violation that wiped out a free throw attempt that had it been made would have sealed the win for the Cats.

After overcoming a 14-point deficit, the Cats were in front 75-73 with 5.1 seconds left and Meeks at the charity stripe to shoot a pair. He made the first and was preparing to launch the second free toss when Thomas backed out of the lane. The officials caught the violation, which deprived Meeks of his second shot and gave possession to the Bulldogs.

Jamont Gordon then buried a three-pointer as the horn sounded, sending the game into OT. Gordon led the Bulldogs with 26 points and 11 rebounds.

Morris had a game-best 29 points and 15 rebounds to lead all scorers. Crawford finished with 20.

By now, Smith's critics had become so vocal that UK athletics director Mitch Barnhart was moved to give the embattled coach a vote of confidence. It did little to silence the naysayers.

Despite an early exit from the SEC tourney, the Cats were invited to the Big Party, earning an eight seed in the West Regional. Their first-round foe would be ninth-seeded Villanova, which posted a 22-10 season mark.

The Cats won 67-58 on the strength of a strong second-half effort in which they outscored and thoroughly outplayed Nova. Morris provided most of the muscle, scoring 19 points while picking off 11 rebounds.

Meeks ended the night with 12 points. Bradley and Craw-

ford also hit double figures with 11 and 10, respectively.

UK's season ended two days later when top-seeded Kansas handed the Cats an 88-76 loss. Julian Wright, playing in his hometown Chicago, scored 21 points, including 15 in the second half, to lead the Jayhawks to victory.

The Cats stayed close until Morris committed his third foul early in the second half. With Morris sidelined, the Jayhawks had little trouble steamrolling past the Cats.

Morris finished with 22 points to lead UK. Perry added 21.

For the season, Morris led the team with a 16.1 scoring average. His 7.8 rebounds per game also topped the team in that category. Crawford averaged 14 points per game and Bradley 13.4 points per game.

Within four days after the Cats lost to Kansas, Smith announced his resignation as UK's coach. The man who carved out a 263-83 win-loss record (76 percent) during his 10-year stint as head coach, and who led the school to the 1998 NCAA title was leaving to take a similar post at the University of Minnesota.

Following Smith's departure, several prominent names were floated as possible replacements. Heading that list were, as expected, Florida's Donovan, a former UK assistant, and Calipari, who had been wildly successful at UMass and Memphis.

But on April 6, with more than 4,000 fans on hand, Barnhart announced that Billy Gillispie would become the 21st head coach in UK's long and illustrious basketball history. Barnhart said Gillispie agreed to a seven-year contract.

Considered "an up and comer" within the coaching community, Gillispie was fresh from leading Texas A&M to a 27-7 record, earning him Big 12 Conference Coach of the Year accolades for the third straight year. Prior to his time at Texas A&M, he had been head coach at UTEP.

But this was different. Now he was taking over the most storied and tradition rich basketball program in all of college hoops.

A new man was now in charge.

Big Blue Nation got what it wished for.

And then it got much less than it hoped for.

2007-08

It took 10 years for the marriage between Tubby Smith and UK fans to go sour; it took just two games before the Gillispie-Big Blue Nation relationship hit rocky shores. And it would take only two years for the marriage to be dissolved.

From the beginning, Gillispie proved to be a different sort of cat. He possessed an inward personality and a leave-me-alone-just-let-me-coach-basketball attitude. That attitude might work at every other college in the country, but it won't fly at UK, where the basketball coach is arguably the most recognizable person in the commonwealth. This is what Gillispie never seemed to grasp: the simple fact that the UK coach is public property.

Gillispie also seemed to lack any willingness to compromise or be flexible. Like his role model, Bobby Knight, Gillispie wanted to strictly play man-to-man defense. Zones are for sissies. He was tough on his players, with criticism far outdistancing praise in most cases. He had no great love for the media. Nor did he have much affinity for the fans, all of whom desperately wanted him to succeed.

Even more puzzling were some of the decisions he made, many of which were truly bizarre. He never signed his legal contract to coach UK despite endless pleadings from Barnhart and UK president Dr. Lee Todd. He opted out of traditional speaking engagements in front of UK alumni groups. He put his players through game-day practices that were lengthy and physical. He continued to start Mark Coury, who ended up averaging two points and 1.7 rebounds per game. And, perhaps most bizarre of all, he offered future scholarships to players who had just entered high school.

Hindsight may be 20-20, but it didn't take a soothsayer to know that Gillispie's future as UK coach likely would be short-lived.

Gillispie did have some successes during his two-year stint. He managed to sign West Virginia blue-chip star Patrick Patterson, who would go on to prove himself to be one of the classiest Wildcats of all-time. Gillispie talked Jasper into staying at UK, after Jasper talked of transferring to a school closer to home. And Gillispie did earn co-SEC Coach of the Year honors after leading the Cats to a 12-4 conference mark.

But that 18-13 overall mark, including four losses in Rupp Arena and first-round losses in the SEC and NCAA tournaments, did not endear him to Big Blue Nation fans hungry for the glory that once was.

Members of Gillispie's first team included Crawford, Bradley, Meeks, Jasper, Stevenson, Coury, Harris, Carter, Patterson, Michael Porter, A.J. Stewart, Mark Krebs, Alex Legion, Dwight Perry, Kerry Benson, Matt Scherbenske, Dusty Mills and Morakinyo Williams.

Gillispie did face his share of tough breaks during his

Billy Gillispie came to UK from Texas A&M. His stint as UK coach was not successful. Was the sign a hint of things to come?

first season. Meeks, who scored 34 points in a preseason win over Pikeville, played only 11 games after suffering an injury. Jasper, injured during the summer, played just 20 games. And most devastating of all, Patterson, who was averaging 16.4 points and 7.7 rebounds, suffered an injury that forced him to miss the last five games.

The era of "Billy Ball" officially began with a 67-40 thumping of Central Arkansas in the opening round of the 2K Sports College Hoops Classic in Rupp Arena. The Cats led 34-20 at the half, and held their opponents to 20-percent shooting from the field. Starters for UK were Bradley, Porter, Meeks, Coury and Patterson.

Crawford, a senior, paced 20th-ranked UK with 20 points, despite being one of the last players to enter the game. In yet another bizarre Gillispie move, Crawford did not see action until around the seven-minute mark of the first half.

Coury also played well, scoring 13 points while grabbing 10 rebounds.

Game two, a stunning and decisive 84-68 loss to

unheard of, unheralded Gardner-Webb, can be seen in hindsight as the earliest event to foreshadow Gillispie's quick exit as head coach.

Gillispie's Cats were outplayed in every aspect of the game. Gardner-Webb took command early, led 38-27 at the break, and was never seriously threatened. Bradley had 24 points to lead UK. Legion came off the bench to score 13, and Patterson rang up his first career double-double with 12 points and 12 rebounds.

Patterson tossed in 23 points and Crawford added 22 as the Cats bounced back with an 80-54 win over Liberty. Bradley and Stewart each contributed 10 points to the winning cause.

Crawford, finally inserted into the starting lineup, erupted for a career-high 32 points on 12 of 17 shooting to lead UK to an easy 83-35 romp past Texas Southern. Patterson and Bradley finished with 21 and 17 points, respectively.

Patrick Patterson was a blue-chip prep standout from West Virginia. He would distinguish himself as one of the classiest Wildcats of all-time.

In what turned out to be another difficult struggle against an unheralded foe, the Cats managed to hang on to defeat Stony Brook 62-52. The Cats led by 19 in the second half, only to see the visitors slice the difference to 43-37 with seven minutes left. But strong play down the stretch, especially by Stevenson, enabled UK to avoid a second embarrassing setback.

Stevenson had 18 points, 10 rebounds and four blocked shots for the Cats, who misfired on 12 of their first 13 shots. Patterson led UK with 19 points. Crawford added 11.

early in the second half killed any hope of a UK upset. At the time, UK trailed by five at 44-39.

Free throws were the difference in this battle. Both teams had 26 field goals, but the Tar Heels made good on 27 of 34 free throw attempts to UK's 18 of 22.

Danny Green led UNC with 20 points. Wayne Ellington had 18 points, while Tyler Hansbrough finished with 14 points and 11 rebounds.

Crawford topped UK with 21 points. Patterson and Bradley, who did not start, each had 19.

With Jordan Crawford outplaying brother Joe, 15th-ranked Indiana easily outgunned the Cats 70-51 in Bloomington. Jordan Crawford led a balanced IU attack with 20 points, while D.J. White had 16.

Patterson led UK with 15 points. Joe

Two days later, on Nov. 29, former Wildcat standouts Ralph Beard and Tommy Kron passed away. Beard, UK's only consensus three-time first-team All-American, is still regarded by many as the finest guard to ever wear the blue and white. Kron was one of the key ingredients on the 1965-66 Rupp's Runts club that lost to Texas Western in the NCAA title game.

The Cats next took on top-ranked North Carolina, and despite giving their best effort of the young season, dropped an 86-77 decision in Rupp Arena. A 13-0 Tar Heel run

Crawford, now a member of UK's 1,000-point club, finished with 10.

The game was close early, but a 15-5 run put IU on top 29-15. After UK closed to within 31-23 on a Crawford bucket, IU pushed its advantage to 37-25 by intermission. IU then scored the first nine points of the second half to break the game open.

Misery continued for the Cats, who dropped back-to-back games against UAB and Houston, running their losing streak to four and giving them a 4-5 overall season

record. It made UK's first four-game losing skid since 1989-90, when Pitino's first club lost five in a row. This was definitely not what UK fans wanted — or expected — when they demanded Tubby Smith's head on a platter.

Making the 79-76 loss to UAB even more stinging was that it happened during UK's annual visit to its second home — Freedom Hall. The Cats had now lost three times in friendly environments.

Robert Vaden single-handedly destroyed UK, giving a 33-point performance that included a crucial three-pointer with 1:15 left that put UAB on top for good. Vaden hit 10 of 18 shots, and was seven for 11 from behind the three-point line.

Bradley had 23 points to lead UK. Patterson had 18, while Crawford, who didn't start, finished with 16.

Gillispie continued to play around with his starting five. For the UAB game, Porter, Harris and Coury started alongside Bradley and Patterson.

In the 83-69 loss at Houston, the Cats had Meeks back but were without Patterson, who was sidelined with a sprained ankle. Meeks made his presence felt, coming off the bench to score 21 points, second only to Crawford's game-best 28.

Without Patterson, the Cats were outrebounded 38-33. They also coughed up the ball on 18 occasions. But once again, free throws made the difference. UK had three more field goals than Houston (25-22), but the Cougars hit 28 free tosses to the Cats' 11.

A strong second-half effort, combined with a 24-point, 15-rebound performance by Patterson, was more than enough to lift the Cats past Tennessee Tech 69-47. After leading 29-21 at intermission, the Cats, who shot 53 percent from the field, pulled away for the win.

Bradley and Crawford, neither of whom was in the starting lineup, combined for 17 second-half points to ignite the runaway.

Meeks sat out this game with a hip injury.

San Diego came to town and handed the Cats yet another home-court loss — 81-72. Brandon Johnson did the most damage to UK, scoring 27 points, 22 of which came in the second half.

Bradley and Patterson led UK with 20 points each.

In this game, UK's starting quintet included Stewart, who was fresh off of a nine-point effort against Tennessee Tech. He had two points against San Diego.

When asked what he had to say to Big Blue fans who don't think this club is any good, Gillispie said, "I couldn't disagree with them very much with the way we're playing."

There was some good news within the UK camp. Meeks and Jasper were back and healthy. Meeks was needed for his offense, Jasper for his cool team leadership.

Bradley scored 22, Meeks 21 and Patterson 20 as the Cats pounded Florida International 92-49. Crawford, still not a starter, added 11.

Jasper scored only four points, but had 10 rebounds and five assists in 28 minutes of playing time.

Rick Pitino's Louisville Cardinals silenced a wild Rupp Arena crowd by handing the Cats an 89-75 loss, thus snapping a three-game losing streak against the school he once led to a national title. The Cardinals trailed 31-30 at halftime, but rattled off eight unanswered points at the start of the second stanza to take control, eventually pushing their advantage to 62-40 with nine minutes remaining.

Juan Palacios and Jerry Smith topped the Cardinals with 17 points apiece.

Bradley had 27 points to lead UK. Crawford, again coming off the bench, scored 19.

It took two overtimes and another double-double by Patterson to lift the Cats to a 79-73 victory over No. 13-ranked Vanderbilt. Patterson ended the long night with 23 points and 12 rebounds.

Bradley and Crawford, a starter in this game, had 20 and 17 points, respectively.

Shan Foster had 20 points for Vandy.

Following a see-saw struggle, Vandy came back from a 10-point halftime deficit to tie it at 65-65 at the end of regulation. UK appeared to have the game won in the first OT, only to see Vandy's A.J. Ogilvy knot it again at 72-72 by scoring on a put-back with 1.8 seconds left. But it was all UK in the second overtime, thus giving Gillispie his first win against a ranked opponent.

After beating Vandy, the Cats fell to 1-2 in SEC play, suffering road losses to Mississippi State (69-64) and Florida (81-70). This marked Florida's seventh straight win over UK, a feat accomplished by only one other team — Notre Dame.

Against Mississippi State, UK had no answer for Jamont Gordon, who scored 24 points, making good on five of seven three-point attempts.

Bradley paced UK with 22 points. Crawford had 20. Neither Meeks not Jasper played in this game.

Florida outscored the Cats 20-9 in overtime to claim its win. Nick Calathes, Marreese Speights and Walter

Hodge all came up big for the Gators in OT. Calathes scored five straight points to put Florida in front 68-67, then Speights and Hodge rattled in back-to-back buckets to seal the win.

A trey by UK's Bradley with 2.5 seconds left sent the game into the extra frame. Florida allowed the Cats to get back in the game by misfiring on seven of nine free throws during the final four minutes of regulation.

Calathes had 24 points and Speights 20 for Florida. Bradley (23), Crawford (16) and Patterson (15) led UK's attack. Jasper's 10 rebounds led UK in that category.

It was at this stage that the Cats began to turn things around, winning five straight and nine of their next 10. In the process of going from an also-ran to a league contender, the Cats gave some of their finest and most-consistent efforts of the season. This was the stretch that earned Gillispie post-season coaching honors.

The streak began with an impressive 72-66 win over third-ranked Tennessee in Rupp Arena. UK's defense was the difference. After trailing for much of the game, the Cats limited Tennessee to just three buckets during the final 10 minutes. Two late freebies each by Bradley and Meeks sealed the win for UK.

Patterson had 20 points to lead the Cats. Bradley (16), Stevenson (14) and Crawford (10) also hit double figures.

Lofton, the Mason County native, scored 22 for the Vols.

The Cats beat South Carolina 78-70 at home, then went on the road to post victories over Georgia (63-58) and Auburn (66-63). Bradley was the top gun against the Gamecocks, scoring 26 points, hitting all five of his three-point attempts and pulling down 10 rebounds. Patterson had 22 points, Meeks 13 and Stevenson 12.

Crawford led the way against Georgia and Auburn, combining for 46 points in those two wins. He had 26 against Georgia and 20 against Auburn. Patterson had 35 points in those two games.

Bradley scored 19 points, hitting three clutch treys, to help send the Cats past Alabama 62-52. The win pushed the Cats' record to 12-9 overall and 6-2 in SEC play, good enough for second place in the East behind Tennessee.

The Cats' five-game winning streak came to an inglorious end with one of the most humiliating, humbling, lopsided losses in the school's illustrious history. In the death valley known as Memorial Gym, Vanderbilt obliterated the Cats, winning 93-52. It was UK's worst loss since losing to Kansas by 55 in 1989.

Ramel Bradley fires from long distance. Bradley scored 27 points in a loss to Louisville.

Vandy controlled the game from the outset, limiting the Cats to just 11 points during the first 20 minutes. The Commodores held a 30-point advantage (41-11) at intermission.

Foster led a balanced Vandy attack with 20 points. Ogilvy finished with 19, while Kentucky native Ross Neltner added 15.

Bradley was the lone bright spot for UK, scoring 21 points, including 18 in the second half.

To his credit, Gillispie was able to rally his troops after the crushing defeat in Nashville, taking them on the road and guiding them to a character-building 67-63 win at LSU. For a while, after the Cats blew an eight-point lead, it looked as

if a second straight loss was in store. But a Bradley trey put the Cats in front for good at 54-51. Still, the Cats were not out of danger. It would take two Jasper free throws and four from Bradley inside the final minute to seal the win.

Crawford led the Cats with 21 points. Bradley finished with 16, Patterson with 14.

After playing four of their last five games on the road, the Cats came home to record hard-fought wins over Georgia (61-55), Arkansas (63-58) and Ole Miss (58-54). The trio of Crawford, Patterson and Bradley continued to sizzle, accounting for 145 points in those three wins.

Crawford's best game was a 23-point effort against Georgia. Patterson's best was 20 against Georgia. Bradley had 18 against Arkansas.

In the midst of the winning streak, there was bad news. Patterson suffered an ankle injury that would sideline him for the rest of the year.

Following a 63-60 loss at Tennessee, the Cats closed out the regular season on a high note, topping South Carolina 71-63 on the road, and then came home to upset Florida 75-70. The Cats desperately needed these two wins to have any chance of earning a spot in the NCAA Tournament.

At Tennessee, after a Jasper trey cut the lead to three, the Cats had their chances to win or send the game into OT. But the Vols survived when Jasper and Crawford both missed three-point attempts inside the final 20 seconds.

Tyler Smith led UT with 15 points. Lofton added 14.

Bradley led UK with 17.

Crawford's career-best 35-point performance catapulted the Cats past South Carolina. Crawford made 10 of 19 shots from the field and 11 of 12 free throw attempts.

Thanks to an 18-point, 10-rebound performance by Stevenson, the Cats ended a seven-game drought against Florida. Stevenson, who didn't start, connected on a pair of free tosses with 9.6 seconds remaining to clinch the win.

Crawford finished with 16 points. Jasper and Bradley each had 14.

Speights led the Gators with 20.

The Cats ended the regular season with an 18-11 record overall and a 12-4 mark in league play. Their first opponent in the SEC tourney was Georgia, a club they had whipped twice during the regular campaign. However, the third time wasn't charm for the Cats, who suffered a 60-56 overtime loss to the Bulldogs.

Because a tornado damaged the Georgia Dome during the Mississippi State-Alabama game, UK's game against Georgia was moved to the 1,500-seat Alexander Memorial Coliseum on the Georgia Tech campus.

Zac Swansey was Georgia's unlikely hero, scoring five points in OT, including a spinning three-pointer that put his team on top 57-56. Swansey's bucket came seconds after a Bradley jumper put UK in front 56-54 with 8.8 seconds left.

Crawford paced UK with 24 points. Terrance Woodbury had 17 to lead Georgia.

With a mediocre 18-12 record, and no guarantee that UK would receive an invitation to the Big Dance, Wildcat fans could only hold their collective breath when the seedings were unveiled. When it was announced that the Cats were an 11 seed and would square off against sixth-seeded Marquette, all Big Blue fans let out a sigh of relief.

But the Cats would last no longer in this tournament than they did in the SEC tourney. Marquette prevailed 74-66 against a UK club that simply could not overcome the absence of Patterson's scoring, rebounding and inside presence.

Crawford did everything in his power to pull the Cats through, giving a brilliant 35-point performance. With his team trailing 54-43, Crawford rattled off six unanswered points to pull the Cats to within five. But that would prove to be as close as the Cats would get.

Bradley also played well, scoring 19 points.

Jerel McNeal topped Marquette with 20 points.

Crawford led UK in scoring with a 17.9 average. Patterson scored at a 16.4 clip, while Bradley averaged 15.9 points per game. Patterson was also the top rebounder, pulling down just under eight caroms per outing.

Several Cats earned post-season recognition. Bradley was named to the Coaches' All-SEC first team. He was also named to the All-Defensive team. Crawford and Patterson were voted onto the second team. Patterson was chosen to the All-Freshman team.

Gillispie shared SEC coaching honors with Tennessee's Bruce Pearl.

On March 31, it was announced that Bill Keightley had passed away. His death brought an end to an era. He was the last connecting link to a coaching chain that ran all the way back to the days when Adolph Rupp patrolled the sidelines in his famous brown suit. Every UK coach since the "Baron" — Joe B. Hall, Eddie Sutton, Rick Pitino, Tubby Smith and Gillispie — and every Wildcat player could count on support, friendship, humor and counsel from the man everyone knew as "Mr. Wildcat."

With high scorers Crawford and Bradley gone, and with Jasper finally following through on his desire to transfer, UK fans had to wonder where the firepower would come from in 2008-09. Patterson and Meeks, if he could stay healthy, were the two absolutes. But in order for the Cats to improve on this season's mediocre mark, others would have to step up.

If they didn't, it could be another long, cold winter for Big Blue Nation. And as things turned out, it was.

2008-09

For his second season at the helm, Gillispie felt confident that he could count on the inside-outside tandem of Patterson and Meeks. And those two players would not disappoint. In the end, their final combined scoring averages would amount to more than 50 percent of the team's total.

To improve from last season, though, others would have to step up. Some did, but not with enough consistency to make a real difference. As a result, this UK team would finish with a 22-14 record, lose six times at home, come unglued during the final weeks of the campaign and fail to make it into the NCAA Tournament for the first time since 1991.

Among those players being counted to support Patterson and Meeks were Stevenson, Harris, Stewart, Porter, Carter, Krebs, Slone and Perry. New faces included Darius Miller, DeAndre Liggins, Kevin Galloway, Josh Harrellson and Mark Halsell.

Any hope that this team would be superior to last year's club melted away faster than ice in a microwave. Back-to-back losses out of the starting game, including an embarrassing opening-night home-court loss to VMI, sent this team crashing off the rails in a hurry.

VMI came into Rupp Arena and upset the Cats 111-103 despite a 39-point performance by Meeks. Stevenson had 20 points and 14 rebounds, Harris had 16 points and the rookie Miller added 12 in his debut effort.

For the opener, in which UK trailed by as many as 23 points, Gillispie's starting five consisted of Patterson, Meeks, Stevenson, Harris and Porter.

Game two turned out to be another nightmare for the Cats, who were soundly drubbed by North Carolina 77-58. The Tar Heels led from the start, winning handily despite the absence of Hansbrough.

Deon Thompson paced the Tar Heels with 20 points. Patterson and Meeks each had 19 for UK.

The Cats finally dented the win column by blasting Delaware State 71-42. Meeks had 22 points and Miller 13 in this easy romp, the first in what would be a five-game winning streak.

Patterson scored a career-best 28 points in another easy win, 91-57 over Longwood. Meeks chipped in with 17 and Harrellson added 12.

UK's next two wins came against quality opponents in the Las Vegas Invitational. The Cats edged Kansas State 74-72, thanks to a 37-point effort from Meeks. Meeks had 24 points at intermission, one more than the entire Kansas State team.

In the championship game, Meeks scored 19, Patterson 15 and Harrellson 12 as the Cats knocked off unbeaten West Virginia 54-43. Patterson and Harrellson each pulled down 10 rebounds.

For his efforts, Meeks was named the tourney MVP.

Patterson scored 31 points on 11 of 12 shooting to lead the Cats past Lamar 103-61. Meeks (19), Liggins (16) and Harrellson (12) also hit double figures.

Miami (Fla.) took advantage of UK's ice-cold shooting (36 percent) to hand the Cats a 73-67 setback in Rupp Arena. The Hurricanes, ranked No. 21 in the polls, led 49-28 before the Cats went on a 12-1 run to slice the deficit to 10 at 50-40. The Cats later closed to within four on the heels of buckets by Meeks and Liggins, but two long jump shots by Miami's Brian Asbury preserved the win for the visitors.

Patterson and Liggins led UK with 19 and 18 points, respectively. Miami's Jack McClinton led all scorers with 23.

Following the Miami loss, the Cats reeled off six consecutive wins in what was arguably their finest stretch this season, although with the exception of Indiana, the list of victims did not include top quality opposition. Those wins came at the expense of Mississippi Valley State (88-65), Indiana (72-54), Appalachian State (93-69), Tennessee State (102-58), Florida Atlantic (76-69) and Central Michigan (84-52).

Meeks (24) and Patterson (21) combined for 45 points in the win over Mississippi Valley State. Harrellson had 15 off the bench against a mediocre Indiana club, then Meeks erupted for 46 points against outmanned Appalachian State. Patterson had 33 and Meeks 32 against Tennessee State. Patterson also had 11 rebounds in that win.

Patterson rang up a second straight double-double, scoring 27 points and grabbing 14 rebounds against a Florida Atlantic club that battled the Cats down to the wire. This

game featured nine ties and 19 lead changes, and wasn't decided in UK's favor until Patterson scored four straight points inside the final minute to ice the win.

Meeks had 23 points, Patterson 15 and Porter 12 in the win over Central Michigan. This victory pushed UK's season record to 11-3.

Edgar Sosa brought UK's winning streak to an abrupt halt by nailing a 30-foot jumper with 2.8 seconds left to give Rick Pitino's 18th-ranked Louisville Cardinals a hard-earned 74-71 victory in Freedom Hall.

After Sosa dropped in a pair of free tosses, the Cardinals held a 71-64 advantage and appeared to have things under control. But Meeks wasn't about to let his club go down without a fight. The brilliant junior guard scored seven unanswered points on five free throws and a bucket to knot the score at 71-71, thus setting the stage for Sosa's game-deciding jumper.

Meeks ended the game with 28 points, while Patterson had 22 points and 15 rebounds. Terrence Williams led UL with 19. Sosa, the hero, had 18.

With four players cracking double digits, topped by Meeks' 21, the Cats opened SEC action on a positive note by beating Vanderbilt 70-60 in Rupp Arena. Other Cats in double figures included Harris (12), Patterson (11) and Stevenson (10).

The Cats, after leading by only four (31-27) at the break, broke the game open by going on a 21-4 run early in the second half.

In the Cats' next outing, a 72-66 win at 24th-ranked Tennessee, Meeks shattered not only the Vols' defense, he also broke the most sacred individual record in UK hoops history — Dan Issel's 39-year-old single-game mark of 53 points.

Meeks scored 54, making good on 15 of 22 shots from the field, including 10 of 15 from behind the three-point line, and all 14 of his free throws. It was in every way a remarkable performance, and the fact that it happened in the enemy's nest against a quality opponent made it all the more remarkable.

Staying on the road, the Cats posted another impressive win, pounding Georgia 68-45. Meeks again led UK with 22 points.

The Cats came home to beat Auburn 73-64, then went on the road to clip Alabama 61-51. Those two wins pushed UK's SEC mark to 5-0.

Meeks and Patterson did the damage against Auburn,

Patrick Patterson combined with Jodie Meeks to give the Wildcats one of their greatest 1-2 tandems.

combining for 52 points. Meeks had 31, while Patterson had 21 points and 18 rebounds. Stevenson also had a double-double with 13 points and 12 rebounds.

The scariest moments in the come-from-behind win at Alabama came off the court, when Harris collapsed outside the locker room prior to the start of the second half. Harris was immediately taken to the hospital, accompanied by Gillispie, who missed the opening minutes of the second half in order to remain with his fallen player. The medical report on Harris, who missed five games after suffering a neck injury against Lamar, was all good news. He returned to action in UK's next game.

Jodie Meeks scored 54 points against Tennessee to shatter Dan Issel's single-game school record.

To beat Bama, the Cats, with Patterson sidelined due to early foul trouble, had to overcome a six-point halftime deficit. Meeks again paced the Cats with 27 points. Stevenson and Liggins had 16 and 11, respectively.

At this stage of the season, UK was the SEC's only undefeated team. The win also earned them a No. 24 rank-

ing in the latest polls. Unfortunately, those accomplishments only proved to be fool's gold. During the next week, the Cats were bounced from the top and sent crashing straight into the middle of the pack.

A three-game skid, including back-to-back losses at home, did the trick, beginning with a tough 85-80 setback at Ole Miss. The Rebels won despite the absence of a trio of starters, all of whom were out with season-ending knee injuries.

UK led 39-37 at intermission, even though Meeks was without a field goal. Ole Miss opened the second half by going on a 16-4 run to seize command, handing the Cats their first conference loss.

Patterson paced the Cats with 24 points. Despite going only four of 15 from the field, Meeks tallied 21. Miller had 12 points and a team-best nine rebounds.

Terrico White and David Huertas led Ole Miss with 21 points apiece.

This would be the start of a downward spiral that saw the Cats drop eight of their next 11 games. It would also be the beginning of the end for Gillispie.

The Cats' dream of remaining atop the SEC standings came to a sudden end when South Carolina and Mississippi State waltzed into Rupp Arena and walked away victorious. South Carolina, coached by Lexington native Darrin Horn, prevailed 78-77, Mississippi State 66-57.

Devan Downey's turnaround jumper with three seconds remaining was the difference in UK's loss to the Gamecocks. Downey's heroics came on the heels of two missed free tosses by Stevenson. Downey finished with 23 points, one less than teammate Zam Fredrick.

Patterson's 28 led UK. Meeks added 20.

Mississippi State's first-half dominance was too much for the Cats to overcome. After building a 37-24 advantage at the break, the Bulldogs saw their lead sliced to 45-42 after a Stevenson dunk with just over 10 minutes left. But a dunk by Jarvis Varnado keyed a 10-3 spurt that put the game away.

Four Bulldogs scored in double figures, headed by Phil Turner's 18. The high-flying Varnardo had 12 rebounds and seven blocked shots.

Meeks and Patterson each had 15 to lead UK, now 16-7 overall and 5-3 in league play.

The Cats snapped out of the doldrums to post much-needed wins over Florida (68-65) and Arkansas (79-63). Meeks was the difference-maker in both of those victories, scoring 23 points and rattling in a three-pointer with five seconds left to knock off Florida, then coming back with another monster 45-point performance against the Razorbacks. In that game, Meeks connected on 17 of 24 field goal attempts.

The Cats were without Patterson in the win at Arkansas. He was sidelined with a sprained ankle.

With Patterson still out of action, the Cats fell at Vanderbilt 77-64. The game was knotted 30-30 at intermission, but the Commodores quickly assumed control by scoring the first nine points after the break.

Vandy was led by Jermaine Beal and Lance Goulbourne with 17 points each. Meeks had 26 and Stewart 11 for UK.

Patterson returned to score 19 points and Miller added 17 as the Cats topped Tennessee 77-58. Hopkinsville native Scotty Hopson paced the Vols with 14 points.

That would prove to be the Cats' last win in regular-season play. They would drop their next four games, leaving them with an 8-8 record in SEC action.

The first of those four setbacks came at South Carolina. The Gamecocks built a 48-28 first-half margin, then coasted to an easy 77-59 win. The backcourt duo of Downey and Fredrick once again did the primary damage, combining for 36 points.

Patterson acquitted himself in exemplary fashion, scoring 28 points and snaring 12 rebounds.

The next two losses occurred in Rupp Arena — 73-70 to LSU and 90-85 to Georgia. These two setbacks likely sealed UK's fate concerning a possible NCAA Tournament bid. It would take winning the SEC tourney for the Cats to get their ticket punched to the Big Dance.

Marcus Thornton had 23 points and Tasmin Mitchell added 21 in LSU's win over the Cats. After Miller tied it at 70-70 by knocking down a trey, Mitchell answered by connecting on a three-pointer that decided the outcome.

Patterson and Meeks had 28 and 24 points, respectively, to lead the Cats.

Georgia, which came into Rupp Arena with a 12-17

record overall and a 2-12 mark in SEC play, overcame a two-point halftime deficit to hang the loss on UK. To achieve only their fourth win in Rupp Arena, the Bulldogs shot 50 percent from the field (27 of 54), while dominating the boards (38-27).

Terrance Woodbury buried the Cats by giving a 30-point performance. In all, four Bulldogs scored in double figures.

Meeks led UK with 23 points. Porter contributed 15.

In the regular-season finale, the Cats dropped a 60-53 decision to home-standing Florida. Walter Hodge scored 18 points to lead the Gators.

Patterson had 16 points and 13 rebounds for UK.

By now, it was clear to everyone that the Cats had to win the SEC tourney if they hoped to compete for a national title. Otherwise, the NIT would be the Cats' next stop.

The Cats opened tourney play by topping Ole Miss 71-58, thanks to 25 points from Meeks and yet another double-double by Patterson (15/14). Ole Miss led 38-36 at the half, but the Cats, behind strong play by Meeks, Patterson, Stevenson and Miller, were able to safely pull away during the final 20 minutes.

Stevenson had 13 points and Miller 12 to provide solid support for UK's two superstars.

UK's hope for an NCAA bid ended one night later with a 67-58 quarterfinal loss to LSU. Once again, Marcus Thornton, the SEC Player of the Year, did the most damage, scoring 21 points.

Patterson had 15 points and 10 rebounds for the Cats. Meeks was limited to a season-low eight points.

Passed over by the NCAA tourney selection committee, UK did accept a bid to participate in the NIT. This was not what Big Blue Nation fans wanted or expected. Nor was it what the UK hierarchy wanted or expected.

The Cats, playing in Memorial Coliseum for the first time since 1976, opened with a solid 70-60 win over UNLV. With Rupp Arena unavailable due to a scheduling conflict, more than 8,000 fans packed the old gym to see the Cats post this win.

Meeks topped the Cats' scoring with 19 points. Patterson and Stevenson finished the night with 16 and 10, respectively.

A three-point play by Meeks with just under 11 ticks remaining lifted the Cats to a 65-63 win over Creighton in Omaha. The Cats, who trailed for most of the game, took advantage of Creighton's horrible free throw shooting to register the come-back win. Creighton misfired on five

of seven free throws inside the final four minutes.

The Cats, down 63-62, won it when Meeks scored on a layup, drew a foul and sank the freebie to account for the final margin.

Moving on to South Bend, the Cats had no answers for burly Luke Harangody, who had 30 points and 11 rebounds to lead Notre Dame to a 77-67 victory. The Cats also failed to contain the Irish's long-range bombers. For the game, the Irish connected on a dozen three-pointers.

Meeks had 21 points in his final game as a Wildcat. His next stop would be the NBA. He finished his final season at UK with a 23.7 scoring average, earning All-America and All-SEC recognition.

Patterson had 18 points for UK. His final season scoring average was 17.9. He also averaged 9.3 rebounds per game.

On March 27, at a press conference in Memorial Coliseum, Barnhart and Dr. Todd announced that Gillispie would not be retained as UK's coach, and that they would begin an immediate search for a replacement. That search would not be long or drawn out. The two men had one name on their list, and they would get him.

On April 1, John Calipari, one of the most successful college coaches ever, agreed to take over the UK reins, inking an eight-year contract worth $31.65 million plus incentives.

During coaching stints at UMass and Memphis, Calipari had carved out a 445-140 won-loss record for a 76.1 winning percentage. He had earned Coach of the Year honors in 2009 after leading Memphis to a 33-4 record, the fourth straight year his Memphis clubs won 30 or more games. His 2008 team advanced to the NCAA title game.

While Calipari was undoubtedly a successful on-court basketball coach, a strong case could be made that he was

Billy Gillispie was fired as UK coach after failing to lead the Cats into the NCAA Tournament.

an even better recruiter. His ability to bring in blue-chip prospects was nothing less than staggering. And it didn't take him long to showcase that ability. Within days of taking the UK job, he signed prep All-Americans John Wall and DeMarcus Cousins, two of the most highly coveted recruits in the nation. Those two standouts would be joined by an incoming group that included Eric Bledsoe, Daniel Orton, Kentucky's Mr. Basketball Jon Hood and junior college transfer Darnell Dodson.

So talented were these rookies that ex-starters Stevenson and Harris would be relegated to the bench.

Calipari received a bit of good luck when Patterson removed his name from the NBA draft in favor of returning to UK for his junior season. His steady, unselfish play would serve as the anchor on a team that immediately put UK hoops back on top.

Calipari was exactly what Big Blue Nation fans wanted and needed — a charismatic leader who could coach and recruit, a man who embraced rather than ran away from the challenges inherent in the UK job. Through him, the bright spotlight would once again shine brightly on Wildcat basketball.

2009-10

If John Calipari coaches at the collegiate level for another 25 years, it is doubtful that he will ever again coach a team as talented as this one. So rich in raw athletic ability and basketball skills was this team that when the season concluded five players were chosen in the first round of the NBA draft, including Wall, the number one pick.

While the gifted 6'4" Wall was the crown jewel in this recruiting class, Cousins, a 6'11", 260-pound behemoth, was a close second. Blessed with great strength, soft hands and terrific footwork, Cousins was viewed by some as an even better NBA prospect than Wall.

Bledsoe was a quiet player with excellent overall skills, while the 6'10" Orton, who missed most of his senior year in high school due to an injury, was a work in progress. Dodson, a 6'7" shooting guard, was on board to supply outside firepower.

But for all the talk about the newcomers, it was Patterson's return that was critical. Like all great team leaders, he provided steadiness to his younger cohorts and was a calming influence as the season wore on. And, of course, his on-court performances were consistently excellent.

Despite the wealth of talent, for this team to succeed, Calipari had to achieve several goals. First, he had to blend those newcomers in with veterans Patterson, Miller, Stevenson, Harris, Harrellson, Liggins and Krebs. Second, he had to handle Cousins, whose mercurial personality could go from boyish to angry to fun-loving to sullen in a split-second. Third, he had to infuse in his rookies, all of whom were high scorers as prep All-Americans, a team-first attitude.

None of this was easy, but Calipari pulled it off magnificently, giving UK fans one of the greatest, most memorable seasons in school history. With Calipari brilliantly directing the action, these Cats went 35-3, winning their first 19 games out of the gate, became the first school to record 2,000 wins, won the SEC regular-season title, captured the SEC tourney crown, earned a No. 1 ranking in the polls, and advanced to the Elite Eight in the NCAA Tournament.

(One can only ponder what might have been had Meeks returned to UK rather than take his game to the NBA. His presence would have eliminated this team's Achilles' heel — lack of consistent outside shooting. Indeed, it was this weakness that cost the Cats a trip to the Final Four and a possible NCAA championship.)

The Calipari Era began with a 75-59 win over Morehead State. The fourth-ranked Cats won the opener without Wall, whose much-anticipated debut was put on hold due

John Calipari's ability to sign exceptionally gifted players like John Wall is a key reason why UK quickly regained its place of prominence in college hoops.

to a one-game suspension handed down by the NCAA.

Bledsoe, inserted into the starting lineup, made the most of his opportunity, leading the Cats with 24 points. Patterson had 20 points and 12 rebounds, while Dodson chipped in with 15 points.

Miller and Cousins rounded out the starting five in Calipari's first game at the helm.

John Wall is without question one of the most gifted UK players ever. His one season as a Wildcat was a continuous highlight reel.

Wall flashed his brilliance and his cool-under-pressure demeanor in the Cats' hard-earned 72-70 victory over Miami (Ohio). It was his 15-foot jumper as time expired that proved to be the difference. Wall finished the night with 19 points.

Early on, it appeared as if the Cats were going to suffer another embarrassing home-court loss. Miami, one of only four teams able to stay within five points of the Cats during their 19-game winning streak, raced to an 18-point first-half lead, and were on top 39-36 at the break. But UK's inside power was more than Miami could handle. Thanks to double-doubles by Patterson (17/10) and Cousins (10/10), the Cats won the rebounding battle 37-25. They also outscored Miami 32-12 in the paint.

The Cats next four games came in the Cancun Challenge, the first two in Rupp Arena, the final two in Mexico. Behind Cousins' 27-point, 18-rebound effort the Cats opened tourney play by defeating Sam Houston 102-92. All five UK starters cracked double figures. Wall had 21, Patterson 20, Bledsoe 19 and Miller 15.

Wall scored 21 points and handed out 11 assists, while Patterson had 19 points and a career-best 18 rebounds as the Cats routed Rider 92-63 to advance to the semifinal round in Cancun. Cousins also had another big night, scoring 18 points.

The Cats advanced to the championship game by topping Cleveland State 73-49 in a game that was fairly competitive until Wall found his footing in the second half. Wall accounted for 11 of his team-high 15 points after intermission, at which point the Cats were only holding a 35-27 advantage.

Cousins ended the night with 14 points.

Wall was once again the hero in UK's 73-65 overtime win over Stanford in the title game. Wall knotted the score at 61-61 by sinking a 12-foot jumper with 30 ticks remaining, then calmly swished two free throws with 2.4 seconds left to send the game into OT. In the extra period, a long three-pointer by Bledsoe gave the Cats a lead they would not relinquish.

Wall led the Cats with 23 points. Cousins and Miller each had 13, while Patterson finished with 12 points and 11 rebounds.

In a stuff-your-stat-line 94-57 laugher against UNC-Asheville in Freedom Hall, Cousins led the way with 24

points and 10 rebounds. Patterson had 17 points, Dodson added 15, and Wall ended the night with 12 points and 14 assists.

UK's next three games were anything but easy. That trio of close encounters began with a 68-66 win over 10th-ranked North Carolina in Rupp Arena. The game was tight even though the Cats went on a 28-2 run in the first half, and were ahead 43-28 at the break.

Down the stretch, it would take clutch free throw shooting by Wall and Bledsoe to ice the win. After the Tar Heels closed to within 63-61, the two rookie guards hit five of six free throw attempts inside the final 30 seconds to lift UK to victory.

Patterson and Wall had 19 and 16 points, respectively, for UK. Deon Thompson paced UNC with 14 points.

Giving his best performance thus far, Wall scored a career-best 25 points, including 12 of his club's final 15, to lead the Cats to a 64-61 win over 12th-ranked UConn in Madison Square Garden. Wall made good on 10 of 16 shots from the field.

Patterson tallied 16 points, while Cousins had 10 points and 10 rebounds.

A blistering second half that featured an 18-0 run broke open a close game and sent the Cats past Indiana 90-73, their first win in Bloomington since 1981. UK, which led just 42-41 at the half, shot 53 percent from the field and 50 percent from three-point range.

Five Cats scored in double figures, headed by Bledsoe's 23 points. Others included Patterson (19), Cousins (14), Wall (11) and Dodson (10). Patterson also had 11 rebounds.

Patterson had 21 points and Cousins added 19 as UK crushed Austin Peay 90-69 for win number 1,999. The win gave UK (and Calipari) an 11-0 season mark, the best-ever start by a first-year UK coach. The previous best was 10-0 by legendary Adolph Rupp in 1930-31.

In what Calipari accurately termed "a special moment for this program and this state," UK became the first school to win 2,000 games by pounding Drexel 88-44 in Rupp Arena. Cousins and Patterson came up big in this win, scoring 18 points apiece. Wall scored 16. In all, 11 different Wildcats dented the scoring column.

The Cats bounced back from a lethargic first half effort to beat Long Beach State 86-73, then trounced Hartford 104-61 to extend their unbeaten record to 14-0. Against Long Beach State, the Cats pulled away in the second half, after being tied 37-37 at intermission. Wall paced UK with

19 points. Patterson (15/11) and Cousins (15/10) had double-doubles to help the Cats escape disaster.

Wall's record-breaking 16 assists performance was the highlight of UK's win over Hartford. Wall shattered the previous record of 15 held by Travis Ford.

Cousins and Dodson led UK with 19 points each. Miller finished with 16, Patterson 11 and Orton, in his best outing to date, had 10.

A monster 18-point, 18-rebound effort from Cousins was enough to lift the Cats to a 71-62 win over arch-rival Louisville. The win snapped a two-game losing streak to the Cardinals.

Wall and Patterson each contributed 17 points for UK. Edgar Sosa and Jerry Smith paced UL with 11 points apiece.

The Cats opened SEC play by reeling off four straight wins, pushing their season mark to 19-0. Those wins — two at home, two on the road — came at the expense of Georgia (76-68), Florida (89-77), Auburn (72-67) and Arkansas (101-70).

How balanced was the UK attack during these wins? A different player was high-point scorer in each game, beginning with 17 points each by Patterson and Wall in the win over Georgia. Bledsoe was the top Cat against Florida, knocking in 25 points. Cousins had 16 against Auburn, then it was an 18-point effort from Miller that led the way against Arkansas.

The Cats, now ranked No. 1 in the latest polls, saw their dream of a perfect season come to an end with a disappointing 68-62 setback at South Carolina. The Cats had no answers for Devan Downey, who scored 30 points. The Gamecocks trailed 47-42 before Downey sparked a late run that enabled them to come back and hand UK its first loss.

Cousins had 27 points and 12 rebounds for UK.

Following that loss, the Cats responded by going on an eight-game winning streak, beginning with an 85-72 victory over Vanderbilt. Cousins had another double-double, finishing with 21 points and 10 rebounds. Dodson contributed 16, Wall and Bledsoe 13 apiece, and Patterson 12.

UK continued to steamroll past opponents, beating Ole Miss 85-75, LSU 81-55 and Alabama 66-55. Cousins was scary good in those three wins, combining for 53 points and 40 rebounds. UK's big center had now registered seven consecutive double-doubles, three shy of Jim Andrews' mark of 10 straight.

DeMarcus Cousins may have been moody, but he could also play. He was a beast on the boards and a superb scorer.

Once again, Wall proved tough in the clutch, scoring 18 points, including five in overtime, to help the Cats ease past Mississippi State 81-75. Wall also had 10 rebounds and eight assists.

The Cats rose from the grave to get this win. Trailing 67-60 with three minutes remaining, they rattled off seven unanswered points, the final two coming on a Patterson jumper, to send the game into OT. Given new life, Wall took charge, sinking a jumper and three free tosses to give the Cats a tough road win.

Continuing to play the role of super hero, Wall knocked down a pair of free throws with 20 seconds left to help the Cats squeeze past Vanderbilt 58-56 in Nashville. After Wall's freebies put UK in front 57-53, Vandy's John Jenkins buried a trey to pull his team to within a single point. Bledsoe missed two free throws, giving Vandy a chance to pull off the upset. But Wall wasn't about to let that happen, blocking a three-point attempt by Jenkins, then hitting one of two free throws with 2.5 seconds left.

Cousins had 19 points to pace the Cats. Wall and Patterson each had 13 points.

With Hall of Fame legend Magic Johnson looking on, Patterson scored 23 points and Cousins added 19 as the Cats gained a measure of revenge by spanking South Carolina 82-61. Wall chipped in with 12.

Downey led all scorers with 26.

Thanks to a standout performance by J.P. Prince, 17th-ranked Tennessee handed second-ranked UK a 74-65 loss in Thompson-Boling Arena. After the Cats overcame a 19-point second half deficit to tie it at 65-65 with two minutes left, Prince scored six points in the final 90 seconds to give his team the win. The Vols also got a three-pointer by Hopson during that decisive 9-0 run.

Prince topped all scorers with 20 points. Wall had 19 for the Cats, now 27-2 overall and 12-2 in league play.

This would be the Cats' last loss until the Elite Eight matchup against West Virginia in the NCAA Tournament.

The Cats' 73-62 win against Tennessee didn't come without a struggle. In fact, the Cats trailed 52-50 following a three-point play by J.P. Prince with just under 10 minutes remaining. But with the game on the line, the Cats scored 10 unanswered points, six coming from Wall, to pull away for the win.

Wall paced the Cats with 24 points. Bledsoe had 16. Cousins managed 12 rebounds, but scored only four points to snap his streak of double-doubles.

The Cats closed out the regular season with wins over Georgia (80-68) and Florida (74-66). Wall scored 24 in the win over Georgia. Patterson had 17 and Dodson 11.

Solid performances by Miller and Bledsoe keyed the Cats past Billy Donovan's Gators. Miller and Bledsoe each scored 14 points to lead UK's balanced attack. Patterson had 13, Wall 11 and Dodson 10 for the Cats.

Opening SEC tourney action, the Cats rallied from a 35-30 halftime deficit to post a 73-67 quarterfinal win over gutsy Alabama. The Cats trailed by as many as 11 points during the opening 20 minutes.

Wall had 23 points for the Cats, with Patterson adding 20. Bledsoe ended the night with 10.

This win gave UK its 12th 30-win season, and its first since going 32-4 in 2003. It also marked the fifth straight season — and seventh overall — that a Calpari-coached team has won 30 games.

The semifinal clash with Tennessee was expected to be another down-to-the-wire thriller. It turned out to be anything but. With Cousins recording another double-double — 19 points, 15 rebounds — and with Wall dishing out 14 assists, the Cats rolled to a convincing 74-45 victory.

Bledsoe continued his strong play, scoring 17 points.

One day later, the championship game with Mississippi State did turn out to be a down-to-the-wire thriller, with the Cats managing to prevail 75-74 in overtime. This was the 26th time UK captured the SEC Tournament title.

To win the crown, the Cats had to come from five points down with 2.28 left in regulation. The comeback ended with a Cousins rebound bucket that tied the score at 64-64 as the final horn sounded. Not surprisingly, the OT belonged to Wall, who scored seven of his 15 points in that extra frame. Bledsoe also came up big, knocking down a jump shot that put UK on top for good.

Bledsoe led UK's attack with 18 points. Patterson and Cousins had 15 and 10, respectively.

Wall was voted the tourney's MVP. Cousins and Bledsoe were also selected to the all-tournament team.

The second-ranked Cats, seeded No. 1 in the East Regional, blistered their first two opponents, rapping East Tennessee State 100-71 and Wake Forest 90-60. Bledsoe gave a record-breaking performance against ETSU, hitting eight three-pointers en route to a 29-point effort. His eight treys were the most ever by a UK player in NCAA tourney play, breaking the previous record of seven set by Tony Delk against Syracuse in the 1996 title game.

Patterson had 22 points in that win, while Wall had 17 points and 11 assists.

Miller tossed in 20 points and Cousins added 19 as the hot-shooting Cats stormed past Wake Forest. For the game, the Cats connected on 38 of 63 shots for 60 percent.

The backcourt duo of Wall and Bledsoe also hit double figures with 14 and 13 points, respectively.

Next up for the Cats was Cornell, a deliberate team with an impressive 29-4 record. Pace would be the key to

Eric Bledsoe scored 24 points in his first game as a Wildcat.

Patrick Patterson was an anchor on John Calipari's young and wildly talented first UK team.

the outcome of this battle. UK wanted to play lightning fast, Cornell molasses slow.

Initially, after Cornell took a 10-2 lead, it looked like the Cats might be in for a long night. But in the end, the Cats simply had too much of everything for the upstart Ivy Leaguers to handle, going on to post a 65-42 win.

Cousins had 16 points to lead UK. Bledsoe added 12. Patterson pulled down 12 rebounds.

The Elite Eight matchup against West Virginia pitted Calipari against his good pal Bob Huggins, who just happened to own a 7-1 won-loss record in head-to-head pairings between two of the most successful coaches in the business.

Huggins made it 8-1 by directing his Mountaineers to a 73-66 win and a berth in the Final Four. Da'Sean Butler led the winners with 18 points, while Joe Mazzulla, making his first start of the season, had 17.

There was no mystery why the Cats lost this game. Ice cold shooting, especially from three-point range, was the killer. The Cats, who missed their first 20 three-point attempts, made good on just four of 32 for the game.

West Virginia, meanwhile, connected on 10 of 23.

Wall finished with 19 points in what would be his final game in a UK uniform. Cousins, in his swan song, had 15. The two standouts would later be named first-team All-America by the Associated Press. Wall was also voted SEC Player of the Year.

When the NBA held its annual draft several months later, Wall was the first player chosen. Before the first round was concluded, Cousins, Patterson, Bledsoe and Orton would all hear their names called as well.

Losing so much firepower at once would likely send most coaches into a deep, dark state of depression. Not so

for Calipari, who simply went out and recruited yet another group that possessed staggering amounts of talent and skill. The era of "one-and-done" players, so despised by purists, was proving to be no hurdle for the man Big Blue Nation fans call "Coach Cal."

Calipari landed prep All-Americans Brandon Knight and Terrence Jones, along with Doron Lamb, Eloy Vargas, Stacey Poole and Jessamine County standout Jarrod Polson.

This bunch, along with veterans Miller, Liggins, Harrellson and Hood, would give UK fans another terrific season, one remembered for three things: a trip to the Final Four, the disappointing Enes Kanter affair, and the surprising emergence of Harrellson as a solid player and folk hero.

2010-11

UK's long basketball history has been littered with many "what-if" moments. Situations held hostage by facts both fair and unfair that, had factors been altered slightly, might have resulted in drastically different outcomes.

What if Bill Spivey, the best big man in the game at the time, pro or college, had played his senior season? Had he done so, that 1951-52 club, which went 29-3 without him, would have gone undefeated, won the NCAA championship and gone down as the greatest UK team of all-time. What if the unbeaten 1953-54 team, led by Cliff Hagan and Frank Ramsey, had participated in the NCAA tourney? No one was going to beat that bunch. What if Mike Casey had not been injured prior to the 1969-70 season? That injury probably cost the Cats another national title? What if Dwight Anderson had stayed three or four years? What if Shawn Kemp, maybe the most-gifted UK recruit ever, had worn the blue and white? What if Derek Anderson had been healthy for UK's title game battle against Arizona? And, more recently, what if Jodie Meeks had stayed for his senior campaign?

Change any of those "what-ifs" and the UK history books would have to be rewritten.

Calipari's second season at UK was clouded over from start to finish by another huge "what-if." In this instance, it involved Enes Kanter, the talented 6'11" center from Turkey. Had he been allowed to play, this team, which advanced to the Final Four without him, likely would have claimed another title. His commanding inside presence would have made the difference.

UK fought hard for Kanter, but the NCAA brain trust ruled him permanently ineligible, saying he had received $33,000 in excess benefits while playing pro ball overseas. Not surprisingly, it was a ruling Big Blue Nation fans didn't much care for.

Even without Kanter, there was no question that this was going to be another terrific team. However, this team, talented as it was, differed greatly from its immediate predecessor. The Wall-Cousins team came out of the gate fully formed, ready to win from the beginning. They were adults at birth. Calipari's second team wasn't like that; it had to learn how to win. It would take time for this team to grow its wings.

Fortunately for Calipari, this was an intelligent team, headed by Knight, the talented and brainy point guard, Jones, a strong, gifted inside player, and Lamb, the team's most-consistent long-range threat. It also helped to have

Wildcat fans can only wonder what might have been had Enes Kanter been allowed to play.

battle-tested veterans like Miller, Liggins and Harrellson to add into the mix with the rookies.

As events unfolded, it was this "Super 6" that carried much of the load for UK this season. The big question was, could six players get the job done over the course of a long season?

With Jones scoring 25 points and pulling down 12 rebounds, the Cats opened the season by posting an easy 88-65 win over East Tennessee State. Lamb added 20 and Knight 17 to UK's coffers.

In that win, the Cats connected on 13 of 26 three-point attempts.

Knight scored 21 and Miller added 15 as the Cats beat Portland 79-48. Jones, playing in his hometown, finished with 12 points.

Playing in the Maui Invitational, the Cats, led by Jones' 29-point,13-rebound effort, topped Oklahoma 76-64.

The youthful Cats hung on despite blowing an 18-point advantage.

Despite poor shooting (39 percent) and a 4.7 magnitude earthquake that rattled tables and chairs, the Cats managed to advance to the finals by edging past Washington 74-67. Knight led the way with 24 points, while Jones had 16 points and 17 rebounds.

In the title matchup against UConn, the Cats had no answer for tourney MVP Kemba Walker, who scored 29 points to lead his team to a convincing 84-67 win. A 21-2 run to close out the first half put UConn firmly in control. This would not be the last time the Cats crossed swords with the Huskies. They would square off again in three months.

Jones, who sat out much of the first half with foul problems, led UK with 24 points. Miller chipped in with 15.

The Cats split their next two games, beating Boston University 91-57, then falling to North Carolina 75-73 in Chapel Hill. After leading by only seven at intermission, the Cats opened the second half by going on an 18-3 run that crushed any hopes the visitors from Boston might have had of pulling off the upset.

Knight paced UK with 23 points. Jones had 18 points and 10 rebounds.

In a tense struggle that featured five lead changes in the final three minutes, the Tar Heels, thanks to a career-best 27-point effort from Tyler Zeller, were able to edge past the 10th-ranked Cats. Zeller scored 12 of his team's final 16 points, including the go-ahead free throws with 47 seconds remaining.

UK had one final chance to pull out the win, but Lamb

Brandon Knight became the latest in a long line of great point guards coached by John Calipari. His short jumper beat Ohio State in the NCAA tourney.

misfired on a three-pointer as time expired. Lamb was superb for the Cats, scoring 24 points on seven-of-12 shooting from the floor.

Knight, one of four Cats to foul out, ended the game with 15 points.

Following that setback, the Cats reeled off seven consecutive wins, a streak that included Notre Dame, Indiana and Louisville as victims. In those wins, four different Cats led the scoring parade.

Jones had 27 points and 17 rebounds in a solid 72-58 win over Notre Dame in Freedom Hall. Knight had 20 points in the win. Liggins had a career-best 19 points in UK's 81-62 win over Indiana in Rupp Arena. Liggins also had nine rebounds and two steals.

The next three games, against Mississippi Valley State, Winthrop and Coppin State, were predictably easy. The Cats won those three games by a total of 92 points.

Jones had 19 points, Lamb and Liggins 16 each, Miller and Knight 14 apiece in the Cats' 85-60 romp past Mississippi Valley State. The most entertaining moment in this game came when Calipari was tossed with 6:26 remaining.

Lamb came off the bench to score a record-shattering 32 points in the Cats' 89-52 win over Winthrop. Lamb's total broke the freshman record of 31 held by Jamal Mashburn. To achieve his total, Lamb blistered the nets, hitting 11 of 12 shots, including seven of eight from three-point land.

Knight finished with 21 points.

Jones had 18 points as UK ripped Coppin State 91-61.

Lamb and Knight each scored 17 points, while Liggins had 10 points, eight rebounds and six assists.

It was in UK's next game, an impressive 78-63 victory over Louisville in Freedom Hall, that Harrellson began to carve out his legacy as a folk hero. The burly 6'10", 275-pound center scored 23 points and snared 14 rebounds in what was easily his best performance in a UK uniform. Harrellson, who had been in Calipari's doghouse following what could be called "Twitter-gate," hit 10 of 12 field goal attempts, including one three-pointer.

Knight led UK with 25 points. Preston Knowles topped UL with 22.

The Cats closed out their pre-SEC slate by blasting Penn 88-62. The win wasn't as easy as the final margin indicates. In fact, the Cats trailed by 12 points during the early going, and were only on top 33-32 at intermission. The turnaround came when Calipari assigned Liggins to guard Tyler Bernardini, who had scored 16 points in the opening 15 minutes. Liggins did the job, holding Bernardini to only six points the rest of the way.

Knight led the Cats with 22 points. Harrellson, giving another solid effort, finished with 12 points and 11 rebounds. Miller also played well, scoring 11 points, grabbing seven rebounds and handing out six assists.

Riding the crest of a seven-game winning streak, the 10th-ranked Cats opened SEC action at Georgia. And were soundly defeated, dropping a 77-70 decision. The win was the ninth straight for the Bulldogs, who led 41-30 at the half, then had to come back after a Jones three-point play gave the Cats a 56-55 lead with just over 10 minutes left. Down the stretch, the Bulldogs made good on 11 of 12 free throws to clinch the upset.

Trey Thompkins led the winners with 25 points. Jones had 24 to lead UK.

The Cats bounced back by posting easy wins over Auburn (78-54) and LSU (82-44). Against Auburn, Jones, coming off the bench for the first time, scored 35 points, breaking Lamb's month-old record for most points by a freshman. Jones made 11 of 17 shots, and hit four treys.

Knight had 19 points in the win over LSU. Other Cats in double figures included Jones (17), Liggins (15), Miller (15) and Lamb (10). Harrellson had 14 rebounds.

If there was one trend that marked the difference between last year's club and this one, it was this bunch's inability to win SEC games on the road. During the regular season, these Cats would lose six of eight league road games, all of which were by margins of seven points or less.

Alabama won a 68-66 thriller, hanging on after the valiant Cats rallied from 20 points down to give themselves a chance at winning. JaMychal Green led the Tide with 18 points and 11 rebounds.

Jones had 17 points and nine rebounds for the Cats, who hurt their chances of winning by missing seven of 14 second-half free throws.

Knight's 23 points keyed the Cats to one their two SEC

Wide-body Terrence Jones came out of the gate strong, scoring 29 points and grabbing 13 rebounds in a win over Oklahoma in the Maui Invitational.

road wins — 67-58 at South Carolina. After the Cats saw a 16-point lead slip to 61-56 with 1:16 left, Lamb connected on four straight free tosses to help seal UK's first win at South Carolina in three years.

Miller finished with a career-high 18 points.

With Hall of Fame coach Larry Brown in attendance, Lamb scored 19 points as the Cats avenged an earlier loss to Georgia with a 66-60 win in Rupp Arena. It was a pair of buckets by Lamb that stymied a late Bulldog rally.

Miller continued his strong play, tallying 14 points,

With road woes continuing, the Cats would drop three of their next four games by a total of eight points, losing at Ole Miss (71-69), Florida (70-68) and Vanderbilt (81-77). Sandwiched in between was a 73-61 home-court win over Tennessee. At the end of this four-game set, the Cats were 17-7 overall, 5-5 in SEC play and in last place in the Eastern Division.

Maysville native Darius Miller finished the season strong, earning MVP honors after helping lead the Cats to another SEC tourney title.

Alex Tyus and Chandler Parsons enabled the Gators to escape with the win.

Parsons topped the Gators with 17 points. Knight and Jones had 24 and 18 points, respectively, for UK.

With their old teammate John Wall on hand to lend support, Liggins scored 19 points and Harrellson added 16 as the Cats beat Tennessee 73-61 to snap their two-game skid.

At Vandy, John Jenkins erupted for a career-high 32 points to help his team claim an 81-77 victory. In this game, Vandy hit 11 treys and were 20 of 23 from the charity stripe.

Jones had 25 points for UK, while Knight added 20.

Clearly, at this stage, UK's prospects for postseason action were iffy at best. With six SEC games remaining — two on the road — the Cats needed to finish strong in order to secure a spot in the NCAA Tournament. They did — in a big way.

But it was also at the end of this difficult stretch that these young Cats morphed into a tough, gritty and mature basketball team. They would lose only two more times the rest of the way. Under Calipari's guidance, they learned what it took to win.

Ole Miss beat the Cats 71-69 courtesy of a Chris Warren 25-footer with 2.9 seconds remaining. Down 64-55, UK clawed back, taking a 69-68 lead on a pair of Jones free throws, thus setting the stage for Warren's game-winner.

Warren had 22 points for the Rebels. Jones scored 22 and Lamb had 20 for the Cats.

In another heart-breaking loss, the Cats, after overcoming a 13-point deficit to take a 64-63 lead, fell to Florida 70-68. Key plays inside the final minute by Erving Walker,

The Cats kicked off the crucial final surge by beating Mississippi State 85-79 and South Carolina 90-59. A full-court press and a costly technical foul on Bulldog coach Rick Stansbury provided the momentum for the Cats. With his team trailing 40-35, Knight drew a foul from Brian Bryant. When the officials awarded Knight three free throws, Stansbury stormed after the officials, earning a T. Knight made four of five freebies to make it 40-39. Later, with his team down 50-47, Calipari called for the press, which resulted in an 11-0 run that put the Cats in front for good.

Knight scored 24 and Lamb 20 for the Cats.

In the easy 90-59 romp past South Carolina, the Cats made good on 11 of 20 three-point attempts. Miller led the way, sinking six treys en route to a 22-point performance.

Facing John Pelphrey's Arkansas club on the road, the Cats dropped a tough 77-76 overtime decision. It marked the popular ex-Cat's first win against his alma mater. It also marked the last time these Cats would be on the short end of the score until the Final Four.

The Cats led 76-75, but a costly turnover resulted in the game-deciding bucket by Marcus Britt with 17 ticks remaining. The Cats had several shots in the final seconds, none of which found the mark.

Rotnei Clarke paced the Razorbacks with 26 points. Knight matched Clarke's 26 points for high-scoring honors.

A standout 24-point performance by Miller was the highlight of UK's 76-68 victory over Florida. Knight had 16 points and six assists in this win, which was Calipari's 500th as a college coach.

The Cats closed out regular-season play by edging No. 21-ranked Vanderbilt 68-66 at home, and then going on the road to knock off Tennessee 64-58. Against Vandy, the Cats were up 40-29 at intermission, then had to fight for their lives during the final minutes in order to avoid another close loss.

Knight paced the Cats with 17 points. Jones and Miller added 15 and 12, respectively.

If there was a time when these young Cats showed their new-found grit and determination, it was in their 64-58 win at Tennessee. Down 29-22 at the break, the Cats, propelled by 17 second-half points by Knight, roared back to claim the win. The gifted Knight finished with 19 points. Miller and Jones each had 15 points. Jones also pulled down 12 rebounds.

The win gave the Cats a final record of 22-8 overall and 10-6 in SEC play, good enough for second place in the Eastern Division. The win also secured them a first-round bye in the SEC tourney.

Any lingering questions about this group's toughness or its will to win were washed away during the SEC Tournament, which the Cats won by giving three solid performances highlighted by a balanced scoring attack. In all three wins, at least four Cats scored in double digits.

UK opened tourney play by limiting Ole Miss to 33 percent shooting en route to a 75-66 win. The Cats never trailed in this game, although it was close at the end. The Rebels pulled to within 68-66, but five Knight free throws

Doron Lamb was one of UK's most-reliable outside shooters. He scored 32 point in an easy victory over Winthrop University.

in the final 41 seconds were enough to fend off the upset.

Lamb led the Cats with 19 points. Others in double figures were Knight (17), Miller (15) and Harrellson (13).

In semifinal action, five Cats hit double figures in a surprisingly easy 72-58 win over dangerous Alabama. The Cats stormed to a 37-21 lead by the half and never looked back.

Lamb had 15 points to lead UK. Harrellson and Liggins each had 14, Knight 12 and Miller 10. Harrellson also had 10 rebounds.

Knight scored 17 points, Jones had 16 and Miller, the tourney MVP, added 15 as the Cats routed Florida 70-54 to claim the school's 27th tourney title. Liggins chipped in 10 points for the winners.

DeAndre Liggins brought an element of toughness to the team, especially on the defensive end.

Any hopes Florida had of coming back were ended when Miller connected on back-to-back treys with just over nine minutes remaining, giving the Cats a comfortable 14-point cushion.

When the NCAA pairings were announced, it was obvious that the Cats, seeded No. 4 in the East Regional, had been handed a nightmare challenge. In what was easily the toughest region, the Cats would run into the likes of West Virginia, Ohio State and North Carolina on their path to the Final Four. They would not only face them, they would have to beat them all. No easy task, by any stretch.

Forget those powerhouses looming ahead; the Cats were

lucky to make it past 13th-seeded Princeton 59-57 in the tourney opener. In a game that had upset written all over it, the Cats managed to avoid disaster when Knight scored on a layup with two seconds remaining. It was Knight's only basket in the game.

Miller topped the Cats with 17 points. Harrellson registered a double-double with 15 points and 10 rebounds.

On deck for the Cats was West Virginia, the team that bumped last year's club from the tournament. And for a while, it appeared as if the same scenario was going to play itself out. The Mountaineers led 41-33 at the half, and were seemingly in control.

But Knight, held to just two points against Princeton, scored a career-high 30 to help the Cats come back for a 71-63 win. Knight led an 11-0 run after the break that put the Cats in contention, and then he made six free throws in the final minute to seal the win.

Harrellson contributed 15 points, while Jones had 12 points and a dozen rebounds.

UK's next two wins, which earned them a trip to the Final Four, stand among the most-impressive in school history. With everything on the line, the Cats nipped top-seeded Ohio State 62-60, and then beat second-seeded North Carolina 76-69. Few UK teams have successfully scaled heights more demanding or intimidating than these.

Knight was the hero against Ohio State, knocking down a short jumper with five seconds left to play. Knight's bucket came after Ohio State's John Diebler sank a trey to tie the score at 60-60 with 21 seconds remaining.

Although Knight came through again in the clutch, it was the strong performance by Harrellson that helped the Cats pull off the upset. Harrellson, or "Jorts" to his ever-growing legion of fans, had 17 points and 10 rebounds, more than holding his own against the Buckeyes' super frosh Jared Sullinger, who had 21 points and 16 rebounds in a losing cause.

Having dispatched the top seed, the Cats were now pitted against the second-seeded North Carolina. The two teams had collided back in early December, a game won by the Tar Heels 75-73. But the Final Four hadn't been on the line then. This time it was.

Josh Harrellson, or "Jorts," emerged as a solid player and something of a Kentucky folk hero.

And this time it was the young Cats who came away victorious. Hitting 12 of 22 three-point attempts, the Cats punched their ticket to the Big Dance for the first time since 1998 by gaining revenge against the Tar Heels.

Five Wildcats hit double figures, topped by Knight's 22 points. Harrellson and Liggins each had 12, while Jones and Miller had 11 apiece.

In the semifinal game, the Cats were once again paired against another familiar foe — UConn. The two clubs met in Maui, where the Huskies drubbed the Cats 84-67.

This game was ugly from beginning to end, with neither team playing particularly well, especially offensively. In the end, however, UConn prevailed, eeking out a 56-55 win.

For the second straight year, poor shooting sounded the death knell for UK. Against the Huskies, the Cats made good on 21 of 62 shots (33.9 percent) from the field and nine of 27 (33 percent) from three-point range.

Despite the icy shooting, despite being down 31-21 at the half, the Cats had their chances to pull off the win. They came back to take the lead early in the second half, and the score was tied at 48-48 on a jumper by Lamb. But the Huskies reeled off six unanswered points to take a lead they would not relinquish.

UConn's Walker led all scorers with 18 points. Knight had 17 for the Cats. Lamb scored 13, and Jones had 11 points and 15 rebounds.

Although the ending wasn't what fans wanted, it was still another terrific season for UK hoops. In two years, Calipari's teams were 64-12, won two SEC regular-season titles, two SEC tourney titles and made a trip to the Final Four.

And as far as good times go, there appears to be no end in sight. Even though next year's club will be without Knight and Liggins (NBA) and Harrellson (graduated), the replacements set to arrive on the scene are more than adequate. In fact, UK signees Marquis Teague, Anthony Davis, Mike Gilchrist and Kyle Wiltjer were rated the No. 1 recruiting class.

Throw them in with Jones, Lamb and Miller and things could get real interesting in a hurry.

Michael Kidd-Gilchrist powers past a Kansas defender.

2011-12

Even though John Calipari's first two seasons had been incredibly successful, there had been no pot of gold at the end of the rainbow. A terrific won-loss record, SEC regular-season and tourney titles, a trip to the Final Four—those all look good on the resume, but for championship-starved fans in Big Blue Nation, only a national title would end their collective misery.

And Calipari's third team did just that, thanks to a player so unique and so gifted that many long-time UK observers will argue that he just might be the best Wildcat of all-time.

Anthony Davis.

With his dark eyebrow that stretched uninterrupted from east to west, the smile of an A-list Hollywood matinee idol, a winning personality and the unselfishness of a saint, Davis was not only a winner on the court but off the court as well. In his one season as a Wildcat, he averaged 14.2 points per game, 10.4 rebounds, blocked 186 shots, made good on 62 percent of his field goal attempts and registered 20 double-doubles. He was National Player of the Year, a first-team All-America selection and the Most Outstanding Player in the Final Four.

Even more important, though, it would be on the shoulders of the 6'10" Davis that this talented UK club would bring home the school's eighth national championship, ending a drought that extended back to 1998.

What made Davis so unique was his ability to dominate a game despite scoring few points. Nowhere was that more

on display than in the 67-59 NCAA title-game victory over Kansas. In that win, Davis scored just six points on 1 of 10 shooting, but came up with 16 rebounds, six blocked shots, five assists and three steals.

Little wonder, then, that he is ranked among the all-time greatest Wildcats. And it's scary to contemplate what he might have accomplished had he stayed at UK for three or four years.

Though Davis was clearly the engine that drove the machine, he was far from being the only important component on a club that fashioned a 38-2 record, went 16-0 in SEC action and put together a 24-game winning streak. He received plenty of support from a solid group that included Terrence Jones, Doron Lamb, Michael Kidd-Gilchrist, Marquis Teague, Darius Miller, Kyle Wiltjer, Eloy Vargas, Jarrod Polson, Sam Malone, Brian Long and Twany Beckham.

This was not a particularly deep team, but it was one that featured a balanced scoring attack. In all, five starters averaged in double figures, with sixth man Miller finishing just a shade below at 9.9 points per game. In addition to Davis, others in double digits included Lamb (13.7), Jones (12.3), Kidd-Gilchrist (11.9) and Teague (10.0).

For the second straight season, Calipari would essentially count on six players to do the heavy lifting.

With Davis scoring 23 points on 10 of 13 shooting and snaring 10 rebounds in his debut effort, the Cats began the campaign with a convincing 108-58 romp past Marist. Teague finished with 16 points, Lamb and Kidd-Gilchrist with 15 each, and Wiltjer 14 in this easy win.

Competition got stiffer when the Cats collided with Kansas in the season's second game. With five starters hitting for double figures, topped by Lamb's 17 points, the Cats broke away from a 28-28 halftime deadlock to notch a tough 75-65 win. Lamb got support from Jones with 15

points, Davis with 14, Teague and Kidd-Gilchrist 12 apiece.

Tyshawn Taylor made good on 15 of 17 free throws en route to a 22-point effort for the Jayhawks.

This would not be the last meeting between the two schools. They would face off against each other again in a game with the big hardware at stake.

Lamb racked up 26 points, Wiltjer had 19 and Jones 15 as the Cats cruised to an 85-47 win over Penn State.

Getting a strong effort from Miller, the Cats battled to a surprisingly tough 62-52 win over Old Dominion. Miller came off the bench to score 13 points, a total matched by Kidd-Gilchrist. Davis ended the night with 11 points. Kidd-

Terrence Jones joined the 1,000-point club during his sophomore season.

Anthony Davis had 18 points and 10 rebounds in a win over Louisville.

Gilchrist and Davis each had nine rebounds in this win.

Seventeen points from Jones, 15 from Kidd-Gilchrist, 13 from Teague, 12 from Davis and 10 from Lamb led to an 88-40 romp past outmanned Radford. In this win, Wiltjer had nine points, Miller six, Vargas four and Malone two.

Jones and Miller each scored 19 points as the Cats pushed their season record to 6-0 with another easy win, this time beating Portland 87-63. Other Cats in double figures included Teague (14), Davis (13) and Kidd-Gilchrist (11). Davis also pulled down a dozen rebounds.

Jones stayed hot, hitting for 26 points in an 81-59 victory over St. John's. To achieve his game-best total, the burly Jones hit on 7 of 12 field goal attempts, including one three-pointer, and 11 of 16 from the charity stripe. Jones also finished with nine rebounds.

In that win, Lamb had 16 points, while Davis registered another double-double (15/15).

The Cats' next two games, both against long-time rivals, were anything but easy. Both were decided by a single point—a 73-72 win over North Carolina and a 73-72 loss at Indiana.

Against the Tar Heels, the Cats had to overcome a 43-38 halftime deficit to sneak out with the win. The Cats trailed until Davis hit a short jumper to make it 61-60 with 7:32 remaining. After that, the Cats never trailed again despite repeated charges by the Tar Heels. A pair of Kidd-Gilchrist free throws with 1:33 left gave the Cats a four-point cushion, just enough to offset a three-point bucket by Reggie Bullock with 49 ticks remaining.

Kidd-Gilchrist paced the Cats with 17 points and 11 rebounds. Jones and Lamb each contributed 14 points, with Miller adding 12.

Harrison Barnes and Cody Zeller each had 14 points for North Carolina.

A dramatic three-point bucket by Christian Watford with one second remaining lifted the Hoosiers to their one-point win in Bloomington. Watford's killing shot came after the Cats took a 71-70 lead on a Teague layup, which was followed by a Lamb free throw at the five-second mark.

Watford finished with a game-best 20 points.

Lamb had 19 to lead the Cats. Kidd-Gilchrist and Teague added 18 and 15 points, respectively.

As with Kansas, this would be the first of two meetings between these powerful clubs.

That loss to Indiana would be Cats' last setback for the next 24 games.

The Cats rolled through their next four games, posting wins over Chattanooga 87-62, Samford 82-50, Loyola 87-63 and Lamar 86-64. Lamb was the big gun in the first two of those wins, torching Chattanooga for 24 points and Samford for 26. Against Loyola, it was Wiltjer's turn to take home scoring honors with 24 points. Kidd-Gilchrist led the way with 18 points against Lamar.

Against arch-rival Louisville, the Cats grabbed an early lead and never relinquished it on their way to a 69-62 victory. Kidd-Gilchrist and Davis both posted double-doubles for the winners. Kidd-Gilchrist had 24 points and 19 rebounds, while Davis had 18 points and 10 rebounds. Lamb also hit for double figures with 10 points, with Jones collaring 11 rebounds.

Russ Smith led the Cardinals with 30 points.

Louisville would be the third pre-conference foe the Cats would tangle with again in post-season action.

In a final tune-up prior to starting SEC play, the Cats, behind 22 points and 16 rebounds from Davis, topped Arkansas Little Rock 73-51. Miller chipped in with 15 points and Jones added 10.

The Cats began their perfect journey through SEC regular-season action by limiting South Carolina to 18 first-half points on their way to a solid 79-64 win. Jones paced the Cats with 20 points. Teague tossed in 17, Davis 12 and Lamb 10 in a winning effort.

At Auburn, the Cats found themselves in a struggle before finally pulling away for a 68-53 victory. The winners only led 32-28 at intermission. Lamb and Davis fueled the win with 14 points each. Teague and Jones each contributed 12.

After trailing much of the game at Tennessee, the Cats came back to post a 65-62 win. Davis's jump shot with 7:22 left to play put the Cats in front for good at 54-52. Davis led the Cats with 18 points. The always-tough Kidd-Gilchrist finished with 17 points and 12 rebounds.

A monster 27-point, 14-rebound performance by Davis was enough to drive the Cats past Arkansas 86-63. Davis made good on 10 of 12 shooting from the field and seven of eight from the charity stripe.

Others in double figures included Lamb (14), Jones (13), Miller (11) and Kidd-Gilchrist (10).

It took six Wildcats hitting for double digits to get past upset-minded Alabama 77-71 in Rupp Arena. Jones led the balanced attack with 15 points. Lamb had 14, Kidd-Gilchrist 13, Davis and Miller 11 each, and Teague 10.

Darius Miller played in more games than any Wildcat.

In an ugly game at Georgia, Miller came to the rescue, hitting for 19 points to lead the Cats to a 57-44 victory. Miller made good on seven of eight field goal attempts, including hitting all four three-point shots.

Kidd-Gilchrist put together another double-double with 14 points and 11 rebounds.

The Cats' next four games all resulted in easy wins, beginning with a 74-50 romp past LSU in Baton Rouge. That was followed by wins over Tennessee 69-44, South Carolina 86-52 and Florida 78-58. Jones scored 27 against LSU, Davis led with 18 against Tennessee and 22 at South Carolina, and Lamb topped the scoring with 18 against the Gators.

Teague handed out 10 assists in the win over Florida.

Thanks to a defense that held home-standing Vanderbilt to 36.5 percent shooting, the Cats claimed a tough road win 69-63. The Cats led 36-23 at the break, then had to hang on down the stretch in order to escape with the win.

Lamb paced the Cats with 16 points. Davis had 15, Jones 14 and Teague 13 for the winners.

Lamb came back with 16 points to lead the Cats past Ole Miss 77-62. Jones had 15 points and 11 rebounds, while Miller and Wiltjer finished with 14 and 13 points, respectively.

With five players again hitting in double figures, the Cats stormed back from a 41-28 halftime deficit to claim a 73-64 win at Mississippi State. Kidd-Gilchrist (18/10) and Davis (13/11) each posted double-doubles, with Miller scoring 12 points, Jones and Lamb 11 apiece.

Davis gave yet another one of those scary-good performance in an 83-74 win over Vanderbilt. The gifted freshman scored 28 points, pulled down 11 rebounds and blocked five Commodore shots. For the game, Davis hit 10 of 11 from the field, eight of nine from the free throw line.

Impressive wins over Georgia 79-49 and at Florida 74-59 ended a perfect 16-0 run through the SEC. Against Georgia, Miller led the scoring with 17 points. At Florida, Davis had 22 points and 12 rebounds, while Jones ended the night with 19 points and Teague with 12.

After playing so well during regular-season action, the Cats proved to be less than sharp during the three SEC tourney games. Despite not playing particularly well, they managed to get past LSU 60-51 in the opener before dispatching Billy Donovan's Florida Gators 74-71 in semifinal action.

Kidd-Gilchrist had 19 points in the win over LSU, with Jones and Davis each coming through with double-double efforts. Jones had 15 points and 11 rebounds, while Davis had 12 points and 14 rebounds. Lamb also tossed in 12 points.

The Cats trailed Florida until midway through the second half before finally taking a 57-56 lead when Jones came up with a steal and an assist that led to a layup by Lamb. After that, the Cats never trailed again.

Lamb led the Cats with 16 points. Jones, Davis and Teague each contributed 15, with Kidd-Gilchrist adding 10. Davis also snared 12 rebounds.

Erik Murphy had 24 points and Bradley Beal 20 for Florida.

In the title game, Vanderbilt took home the big trophy by proving to be tougher down the stretch. After the two clubs were knotted 38-38 at the half, the Cats took control early during the final 20 minutes, and were leading 62-55 with 5:23 remaining. Vandy reeled off seven unanswered points to tie it at 62-62 on a tip-in by Festus Ezeli with 1:55 left. Following a UK miss, Kedren Johnson came up with an old-fashion three-point play to give Vandy a 65-62

lead with 92 seconds left. It was a lead the Commodores wouldn't surrender.

Miller led the Cats, now 32-2 on the season, with 16 points. Jones and Davis each had 12, with Lamb adding 11.

Jeffery Taylor paced Vandy with 18 points. Ezeli and John Jenkins had 17 apiece.

The Cats opened NCAA tourney action by facing in-state rival Western Kentucky in Freedom Hall. With Jones scoring 22 points and hauling down 10 rebounds, the Cats cruised past the Hilltoppers 81-66. Davis and Lamb also played well, scoring 16 points each. Teague finished with 12 points and four assists.

Teague and Miller were the top guns in an 87-71 victory over Iowa State, a win that put the Cats in the Sweet 16. Teague ended with 24 points, while Miller had 19. Lamb chipped in with 16, with Davis registering another double-double—15 points, 12 rebounds.

In Atlanta, Indiana, one of the two teams to claim a win over the Cats, was the next hurdle to be cleared. In what turned out to be one of the Cats' finest performances of the season, they advanced to the Elite 8 by posting a solid 102-90 victory.

There were plenty of heroes in this Wildcat win, beginning with Kidd-Gilchrist, who had a 24-point, 10-rebound night. Lamb had 21 points, Miller had 19, Teague had 14 points and seven assists, Jones had 12 points, and Davis had nine points and 12 rebounds.

IU's Christian Watford, the first-game assassin, blistered the Cats with 27 points, while Cody Zeller added 20.

All that stood between the Cats and a second consecutive Final Four appearance was Baylor, and Calipari's club wasn't about to let the opportunity pass by. After jumping to a 42-22 halftime advantage, the Cats coasted to an 82-70 victory, thus punching their ticket to New Orleans.

Kidd-Gilchrist led the winners with 19 points. Davis had 18 points and 11 rebounds, Lamb had 14 points and Jones a dozen.

The Cats were in the Final Four, and Rick Pitino and his always-dangerous Louisville Cardinals were waiting for them. This was absolutely a showdown that had Big Blue Nation fans sweating bullets. A loss now would be a huge disappointment; losing to the Cardinals would have been devastating.

In this second battle between the two clubs, the Cats went in front 4-2 and, despite several challenges by the Cardinals, never trailed the rest of the way. When it was over, the Cats were on top 69-61 and all of Big Blue Nation breathed a collective sigh of relief.

Davis did the most damage to the Cardinals, accounting for 18 points, 14 rebounds and five blocked shots. Miller also had a nice game, finishing with 13 points.

A big key to this UK win was limiting high-scoring Russ Smith to nine points. Peyton Siva led the Cards with 11 points.

Now Kansas was all that stood between the Wildcats and their eighth national title.

Thanks to 53.3 percent first-half shooting, the Cats bolted in front early, leading by as many as 16 points on three occasions. Those first 20 minutes ended with the Cats on top 41-27.

The second half was a different story. In those 20 minutes, the Cats shot only 26.9 percent from the field. Despite going cold, they somehow managed to hang on for a 67-59 victory.

National championship number eight, and the first under John Calipari, was now officially in the record books.

Lamb paced the Cats with 22 points in the title game. Teague had 14 and Kidd-Gilchrist 11. But it was the magnificent Davis who was named Most Outstanding Player after scoring six points, grabbing 16 rebounds and blocking six shots.

Joining Davis on the all-tournament squad were Lamb and Kidd-Gilchrist.

Tyshawn Taylor led Kansas with 19 points, while teammate Thomas Robinson finished with 18 points and 17 rebounds in a losing cause.

In what was a spectacular season, these Wildcats finished with a 38-2 overall record. It also upped Calipari's three-year record at UK to 102-14 for an 87.9 winning percentage.

Although UK would say goodbye to Davis, Lamb, Jones, Kidd-Gilchrist, Teague and Miller, the UK coffers were quickly restocked, thanks to Calipari's genius for recruiting top-flight talent.

Among the new faces set to come on board for the 2012-13 season were Archie Goodwin, Alex Poythress, Nerlens Noel, Ryan Harrow, Willie Cauley-Stein and Julius Mays.

They would team up with Wiltjer, who was being counted on to help steady the rookies.

For fans of Big Blue Nation, the arrival of those talented newcomers brought with them the dream of another successful season. But it didn't take long for that dream to become a nightmare, one that dealt those lofty expectations a mighty blow.

Losing Nerlens Noel was a big blow to this UK team.

2012-13

Any school that follows a national championship season with one so mediocre that the NCAA selection committee fails to extend an invitation to the Big Dance is bound to be embarrassed. That it happened to mighty UK caused far more than mere embarrassment. In the words of John Calipari, "it was a humbling experience."

Failing to secure the chance to defend their title was only the first half of the humiliation. After accepting a bid to participate in the NIT, the Cats dropped a 59-57 decision to Robert Morris.

And if that wasn't enough, Rick Pitino's Louisville Cardinals would go on to win the national championship, adding

further insult to injury for Big Blue Nation fans.

Talk about an ignominious end to a season that began with such high expectations.

In retrospect, however, perhaps those expectations were simply too lofty to begin with. After all, those six departing Wildcats accounted for about 98 percent of points scored, rebounds, blocked shots and steals. Asking any group of newcomers to fill such a huge vacuum was placing them in a tough situation.

Not that the rookies weren't good; they most certainly were. But for whatever reason, this team didn't click the same way Calipari's first three clubs did. As a result, these Wildcats had a respectable 21-12 record overall. But it was the 12-6 mark in SEC play and a first-round loss in the SEC Tournament that helped seal their fate when it came time for NCAA tourney invitations to be handed out.

The rookies set to join sophomore Kyle Wiltjer included Nerlens Noel, Alex Poythress, Archie Goodwin, Ryan Harrow, Willie Cauley-Stein and Julius Mays. Other team members included Jarrod Polson, Jon Hood, Sam Malone, Twany Beckham and Brian Long.

But without question, misfortune played a key role in this club's failure to reach its full potential. Bad luck struck in the Cats' 24th game at Florida when the 6'10" Noel, the team's best player, tore his ACL, an injury that sidelined him for the remainder of the season. With Noel out, the Cats struggled home, losing five of their final eight games.

The opener against Maryland in Brooklyn's Barclays Center alerted Calipari (and Big Blue Nation) that this was destined to be a challenging season. After jumping to a 49-36 halftime advantage, the Cats fell behind 59-57 with just over eight minutes remaining, then had to battle back to earn a hard-fought 72-69 victory.

Wiltjer paced the Cats with 19 points. Goodwin, in his debut, added 16, but it was the gutsy play by Polson that enabled the Cats to avoid the loss. A crucial Polson field goal and a pair of late free tosses inside the final seconds sealed the victory.

Facing Duke in Atlanta, the Cats fell behind early and never caught up, eventually dropping a 75-68 decision.

Poythress had a big night for the Cats, finishing with 20 points. Noel and Goodwin each contributed 16.

Seth Curry led all scorers with 23 points, while teammate Mason Plumlee added 18.

After such a difficult start to the season, what the Cats needed was a breather, which they got with a 101-49 romp past Lafayette. Playing at home for the first time, the Cats got 23 points from Wiltjer and 22 from Poythress in this easy win. Also in double figures were Noel (15), Cauley-Stein (14) and Goodwin (13).

It took a huge 28-point performance from Goodwin for the Cats to get past stubborn Morehead State 81-70 in Rupp Arena. The Cats were in front by a single point (32-31) at the break before finally easing away for the win.

Goodwin, who hit 12 of 17 free throws, got strong support from Poythress with 20 points. Mays added 11 points, while Noel yanked down 11 rebounds.

Twenty-two points each from Poythress and Goodwin, 18 from Noel, 15 from Mays and 12 from Cauley-Stein enabled the Cats to claim a 104-75 home-court win over LIU Brooklyn. In this win, the red-hot Cats made good on 42 of 62 field goal attempts for a 67.7 shooting percentage.

That trio of impressive wins was followed by a pair of setbacks, one coming on the road and one in Rupp Arena. The Cats lost 64-60 to Notre Dame in South Bend, then came home, where they suffered a shocking 64-55 loss to Baylor.

Mays's 16 points topped the scoring against the Irish, with Goodwin leading the way with 17 in the Baylor loss. Noel claimed 16 rebounds against the Bears.

The Cats responded to those two losses by bouncing back to post runaway victories over Samford 88-56, Portland 74-46, Lipscomb 88-50 and Marshall 82-54. All four of those wins came in Rupp Arena.

Six Wildcats cracked double digits in the win over Samford—Goodwin (18),

Poythress (16), Noel (13), Cauley-Stein (12), Wiltjer (10) and Mays (10). For good measure, Madisonville native Jon Hood added six.

Poythress and Goodwin each had 15 against Portland, then Wiltjer snapped out of a minor slump by hitting for 23 against Lipscomb. Poythress posted a double-double in that win, scoring 11 points and grabbing 10 rebounds.

Harrow had his best game to date, knocking in 23 points and handing out four assists against Marshall. Goodwin ended the night with 18 points, while Noel had 11 points and 10 rebounds.

Facing powerful Louisville in the Yum Center, the Cats

Alex Poythress flashed tremendous potential as a freshman.

Archie Goodwin avoids pursuit from a pair of LSU defenders.

were handed a tough 80-77 defeat. The Cardinals took command early, and despite a late charge by the Cats, managed to hang on for the win. Russ Smith and Chane Behanan led the winners with 21 and 20 points, respectively, while Peyton Siva chipped in 19.

Goodwin had 22 points for the Cats, with Harrow adding 17 and Wiltjer 14.

In a final tune-up prior to kicking off SEC action, the Cats, with five players hitting for double figure, improved their season record to 9-4 by ripping Eastern Michigan 90-38. Wiltjer paced the scoring parade with 17 points. Others in double digits included Poythress (16), Harrow (15), Mays (13) and Cauley-Stein (11) Noel had 13

rebounds and Cauley-Stein 11 as the Cats dominated the boards 52-27.

It took a late bucket by Wiltjer, followed by a four straight points from Noel for the Cats to slip past Vanderbilt in Nashville. Wiltjer's jumper at the 1:58 mark gave the visitors a 56-54 lead. Noel sealed the victory with a dunk and a short jumper in the lane.

Harrow led the winners with 16 points. Noel added 13 and Goodwin 12.

For the second time this season, the Cats failed to survive at home, dropping an 83-71 decision to Texas A&M, thanks to an outrageous 40-point performance by Elston Turner, who made good on 14 of 19 field goal attempts, 6 of 10 from three-point range and a perfect six for six from the free throw stripe.

Goodwin had 17 points for the Cats, with Noel finishing with 15 points and 11 rebounds.

The Cats improved to 3-1 in SEC play by posting back-to-back victories, topping Tennessee 75-65 at home and Auburn 75-53 on the road. Wiltjer led the way with 17 points in each of those two wins.

After building a 33-24 first-half lead, the Cats watched as Alabama roared back to claim a 59-55 win in Tuscaloosa. In that second half, the cold Cats shot a frosty 29.6 percent from the field. Adding to their misery, they connected on just 6 of 11 free throw attempts.

Wiltjer again paced the Cats with 14 points.

Getting 20 points and 12 rebounds from Poythress, the Cats handled visiting LSU 75-70. Goodwin ended the game with 15 points, while Harrow and Noel had 11 and 10, respectively.

The Cats continued to give strong efforts, winning their next four games, beginning with an 87-74 victory at Ole Miss. Wiltjer and Goodwin were terrific, combining for 50 points. Wiltjer had 26, Goodwin 24.

Next, the Cats gained a measure of revenge by posting a 72-68 overtime win at Texas A&M. The Cats led 30-21 at intermission, but the Aggies stormed back to tie the score at 62-62 at the end of regulation. In the OT, Noel nailed a short jumper to put the Cats in front 64-62. It was a lead they would not relinquish.

Noel and Mays topped the scoring with 19 points apiece. Noel also claimed 14 rebounds.

Behind 15 points from Mays and 13 each from Goodwin and Cauley-Stein, the Cats had no trouble dispatching South Carolina 77-55 in the first of two straight home games. That was followed by a much-tougher 72-62 victory over stubborn Auburn. In that encounter, Wiltjer had 14 points, Harrow and Cauley-Stein 12 each, Noel and Mays 10 apiece.

Now sporting a 17-6 record and back in the Top 25 (ranked 25th), the Cats were no match for Billy Donovan's seventh-ranked Florida Gators, who scored an easy 69-52 win in Gainesville. The Gators jumped in front early and never looked back.

Scottie Wilbekin led the winners with 14 points. Mays and Cauley-Stein each had 10 points for the Cats.

It was in this game that Noel suffered his season-ending injury.

At Tennessee, with Polson and Cauley-Stein in the starting lineup, the Cats were smeared by the Vols 88-58. Trae

Golden had 24 points for the winners, who shot a blistering 58 percent from the field.

Wiltjer paced the Cats with 18 points, with Mays adding 12 and Polson 11 in his debut start.

Despite playing without Noel, the gutsy Cats reeled off three consecutive victories, beating Vanderbilt 74-70, Missouri 90-83 in OT and Mississippi State 85-55. All three wins came in Rupp Arena.

Cauley-Stein scored 20 against the Commodores, then Mays had 24 and Poythress 21 in the win over Missouri. Against Mississippi State, five Cats cracked double figures, led by Harrow with 19. Others included Poythress (16), Cauley-Stein (12), Goodwin (11) and Mays (11).

Kyle Wiltjer averaged 10.2 points per game as a sophomore.

After that trio of wins, it was all downhill for the Cats, who dropped two of their final three regular-season games. The lone win, however, was an impressive 61-57 upset of 11th-ranked Florida in Rupp Arena. Goodwin paced the Cats in that win with 16 points.

The two losses, both on the road, were administered by Arkansas 73-60 and Georgia 72-62. Goodwin was the Cats' leading scorer in both games, putting in 14 against the Razorbacks and 20 against Georgia.

With a 21-10 record overall and a 12-6 mark in SEC action, the Cats, clearly on the fence concerning an NCAA bid, needed a strong showing in the SEC Tournament to convince the powers that be that they were worthy of being given the opportunity to defend their national title. Most experts agreed that Calipari's wounded club needed to win at least one, possibly two games in order to receive a bid.

It didn't happen, thanks to a Vanderbilt team that shot 50 percent from the field and easily demolished the Cats 64-48 in the SEC tourney opener. This loss killed any hopes the Cats had of being invited to play in the NCAA Tournament.

This marked the second time in the past five seasons that UK was not an NCAA tourney participant.

Goodwin had 12 points and Wiltjer 10 in this disappointing setback.

Paired against Robert Morris in the NIT first round at Moon Township, Pennsylvania, the Cats gave an uninspired effort, dropping a 59-57 decision to finish the long campaign with a final 21-12 record.

In this nightmare outing, the Cats failed to score until Polson connected on a bucket with 15:17 left in the first half. By that time, Robert Morris had built a 10-0 advantage. The Cats fought back to take the upper hand, but were on the short end of a 28-27 halftime score.

Robert Morris seized control early in the second half, eventually extending its lead to 49-36. But the Cats fought their way back into contention, and when Goodwin knocked in a bucket, the score was knotted at 57-57.

With eight ticks remaining, Mike McFadden hit a pair of freebies to give Robert Morris its two-point lead. The Cats had one final chance to avoid the upset, but when a last-second three-point attempt by Wiltjer failed to connect, the door was slammed shut on this season.

Goodwin had 18 points and Polson 10 in the loss.

For the season, Goodwin was the top scorer with a 14.1 average. Poythress scored at an 11.2 clip, while Noel aver-

aged 10.5 and Wiltjer 10.2. Noel, despite missing those nine games, led the club with 227 rebounds and 106 blocked shots.

Noel and Goodwin would depart for the NBA, and Wiltjer would opt to transfer to Gonzaga, leaving some big shoes for Calipari to fill. And he did, bringing in the country's top-ranked freshman class, a superb group that included Julius Randle, James Young, Aaron Harrison, Andrew Harrison, Dakari Johnson, Marcus Lee and a pair of Kentucky natives, Derek Willis and Dominique Hawkins.

As always, Big Blue Nation could hardly wait for the new season to arrive.

2013-14

John Calipari had clearly established himself as the premier recruiter of blue-chip prospects, but with this latest group he took it to an entirely different level. In fact, this class, along with the next three, was loaded with a legion of players talented enough to have NBA owners and coaches paying close attention. Not surprisingly, these last four recruiting classes were ranked either one or two by all the experts.

It also came as no great shock that this talented bunch reclaimed UK's place among college basketball's elite programs, finishing with a 29-11 record and advancing to the Final Four before losing to UConn in the championship game.

James Young and the Harrison twins—Aaron and Andrew—were superb talents, but the centerpiece of this strong recruiting class was Julius Randle, the 6'9" lefty from Dallas. And Randle did not disappoint, earning a host of post-season honors, including All-America recognition.

This team featured a balanced scoring attack, with four players averaging in double figures, topped by Randle's 15 points per game clip. Young averaged 14.3, while Aaron Harrison and Andrew Harrison averaged 13.7 and 10.9 points, respectively.

Other strong contributors were returning veterans Alex Poythress and Willie Cauley-Stein. Rounding out the squad were Dakari Johnson, Marcus Lee, Derek Willis, Dominique Hawkins, Jarrod Polson, Jon Hood, E.J. Floreal, Sam Malone and Brian Long.

The top-ranked Cats opened with a pair of easy wins, crushing UNC-Asheville 89-57 and Northern Kentucky 93-63. Randle was a monster in both games, notching a

Julius Randle scored 45 points and pulled down 29 rebounds in his first two games as a Wildcat.

Facing Michigan State in the Champions Classic, the Cats fell behind 10-0 and were never able to catch up, despite closing to within a single point in the final minutes. In the end, the Spartans hung on for a 78-74 victory.

Randle had another huge game for the Cats, scoring 27 points and pulling down 13 rebounds. Young added 19 points in this losing effort.

After that loss, the Cats came back to notch five consecutive victories, all in relatively easy fashion. Those conquered foes included Robert Morris 87-49, UT-Arlington 105-76, Cleveland State 68-61, Eastern Michigan 81-63 and Providence 79-65.

Aaron Harrison led the charge with 28 points against Robert Morris, then Young had 26, Randle 22 and Cauley-Stein 14 against UT-Arlington. In the come-from-behind win over Cleveland State (the Cats trailed 31-27 at intermission), Randle had 15 points and 15 rebounds, with Aaron Harrison adding a dozen points.

Andrew Harrison, with 22 points, was the top scorer in the win over Eastern Michigan. Cauley-Stein finished with 15 points, while Johnson added 10 off the bench. Young scored 18 points, Cauley-Stein and Aaron Harrison 15 each, and Randle 12 against Providence.

Following that string of easy wins, the Cats dropped two of their next three games, managing to sandwich a 70-55 win over Boise State between a 67-62 loss to Baylor and an 82-77 setback at North Carolina. In the lone victory, Young had 21 points and Randle 17. Against Baylor, Randle was the Cats' leading scorer with 16. In the loss to the Tar Heels, Aaron Harrison had 20 points. But the big guns in this game were Tar Heels Marcus Paige and James McAdoo, who burned the Cats for 23 and 20 points, respectively.

With conference play looming around the corner, the Cats needed to get their act together, which they did by beating upset-minded Belmont 93-80 and the defending champion Louisville Cardinals 73-66. Belmont led the Cats 43-41 at halftime, but the visitors had no answer for Randle, who scored 29 points and claimed 10 rebounds. Aaron Harrison also came up big with 23 points.

In a tense struggle against Louisville, the Cats went in front 55-53 on a bucket by Young and then held on for the win. Young and Andrew Harrison paced the Cats with 18 points each. The Cards' Russ Smith was the game's top scorer with 19.

SEC action began with a pair of solid victories, an 85-63 win over visiting Mississippi State and a 71-62 win at

Andrew Harrison fires a jumper against South Carolina.

pair of double-doubles—23/15 and 22/14. In the opener, Lee accounted for 17 points, Young 11, Aaron Harrison and Poythress 10 each. Poythress also claimed 13 rebounds.

Against Northern Kentucky, Aaron Harrison scored 16 points, while brother Andrew chipped in with 13.

Vanderbilt. Young blistered Mississippi State for 26 points, with Cauley-Stein and Poythress finishing with 12 each. In the win at Vandy, Randle had 15 points, Aaron Harrison 14 and Andrew Harrison 10.

The Cats dropped their next game, losing to Arkansas 87-85 in overtime despite getting 23 points from Young and 20 from Randle, who also yanked down 14 rebounds.

Behind 26 points from Andrew Harrison and 18 from Randle, the Cats kicked off a three-game winning streak by topping Tennessee 74-66. Next, with Poythress giving a strong 16-point effort, the Cats beat Texas A&M 68-51. Then with four players hitting for double figures, the Cats destroyed Georgia 79-54. Aaron Harrison led the scoring with 15 points, followed by Randle with 14, Young with 13 and Poythress with 11.

That trio of wins, all of which came in Rupp Arena, pushed the Cats' season record to 15-4.

In Baton Rouge, LSU, getting a 29-point effort from Johnny O'Bryant, built a big early lead, then rode home for an 87-82 victory. O'Bryant made good on 12 of 20 field goal attempts for the Tigers, who shot 50 percent for the night.

Young paced the Cats with 23 points. Johnson, in a solid performance, came through with 15 points off the bench.

After the LSU setback, the Cats put together another winning streak, this one covering four games. It began with an 84-79 win at Missouri, and was followed by wins over Ole Miss 80-64, Mississippi State 69-59 and Auburn 64-56.

Aaron Harrison and Young scored 21 and 20 points, respectively, in the first of those wins, then Cauley-Stein had 18 against Ole Miss. Randle's 16 points fueled the ugly win at Mississippi State. Against Auburn, in yet another less-than-stellar Wildcat performance, Andrew Harrison scored 16 points and Randle 12.

The last month of the regular season proved to be a difficult time for the Cats, who would lose three of their final four SEC games, beginning with a 69-59 home loss to No. 3-ranked Florida. The Gators trailed 31-28 at the half, but roared back to dominate the final 20 minutes to get their 23rd win in 25 games while improving their league record to an unblemished 12-0.

The Cats were done in by Casey Prather and Scottie Wilbekin, who combined for 47 points. Prather had 24, Wilbekin 23.

Andrew Harrison paced the Cats with 20 points.

After a solid 84-70 road win against Ole Miss, the Cats split a pair of overtime thrillers, edging LSU 77-76 and then losing to Arkansas 71-67. Against the Rebels, Randle put together another supreme effort, scoring 25 points and snaring 13 rebounds.

Randle also proved to be the difference in the OT win over LSU. After a steal by Young, Randle scored in the paint with three seconds left to lift his club past the Tigers. Two pressure-packed free throws by Andrew Harrison with 10 seconds remaining tied the score at 65-65, sending the game into the extra frame.

Aaron Harrison and Young led the Cats with 21 and 20 points, respectively.

The home loss to Arkansas was especially disappointing. In this one, the Cats trailed by nine in the second half, then fought back to take a five-point lead, only to watch the Razorbacks come back to knot the count at 60-60 at the end of regulation. The OT belonged to the visitors, who assumed control early and never surrendered the upper hand.

Cauley-Stein posted a double-double for the Cats, with 16 points and 13 rebounds.

The Cats continued to struggle, losing two of their next three games, beginning with a 72-67 loss at South Carolina. Following a 55-48 Rupp Arena win over Alabama, the Cats traveled to Gainesville, where they were soundly thrashed by top-ranked Florida 84-65.

Aaron Harrison had 21 points and Young 19 in the South Carolina loss. In that low-scoring win over Alabama, in which the Cats shot a frosty 32.7 percent from the field, Randle was the leading scorer with 12. At Florida, Randle again led the way with 16 points and 10 rebounds.

Florida, which raced to a 49-28 first-half advantage, was paced by Patric Young with 18 points.

Now sporting a 22-9 record and clearly a struggling team, the prospects for post-season success were iffy at best. But this Wildcat squad, like so many before it, upped its level of play when it was needed the most. As a result, these Cats marched all the way to the NCAA title game.

However, before that NCAA journey began, the Cats had to deal with some familiar faces in the SEC Tournament in Atlanta. In the opener, a strong 85-67 win over LSU, the Cats placed four players in double figures, led by Young with 21. Others included Randle with 17 (he also had 16 rebounds), Aaron Harrison with 14 and Andrew Harrison with 11.

Georgia stayed close for a half, but the Cats pulled away in the final 20 minutes to post a 70-58 semifinal victory. Once again, four Cats cracked double digits, headed by Aaron Harrison's 22 points. Young finished with 14, while Randle and Andrew Harrison each contributed 12.

With the title at stake, the Cats squared off against Florida, and for the third time this season, they came out on the short end, losing 61-60. The Gators led by 10 at the half, then extended their lead to 16 midway through the second half. That's when the gutsy Cats began to chip away at the margin, eventually slicing the difference to a single point—54-53—with 6:16 remaining.

Florida eased back in front 59-55 before a layup by Aaron Harrison pulled the Cats to within a bucket with 2:16 left to play. After Florida's Patric Young put in a bucket that made it 61-57, the Cats' James Young buried a trey that made it 61-60 at the 1:31 mark. That would prove to be the final points scored, although the Cats did have a couple of chances to get the upset, but both shots failed to connect.

Aaron Harrison paced the Cats with 16 points. Young had 13, Andrew Harrison and Cauley-Stein had 10 apiece.

Patric Young and Michael Frazier led the winners with 14 points each.

Every path through the NCAA tourney is surrounded by landmines, and that was most assuredly the case for this Wildcat team. To reach the Final Four, these Cats had to come up with a poker hand strong enough to beat four of a kind—Kansas State, Wichita State, Louisville and Michigan. Three of those four clubs were ranked in the top seven. Only first-round foe Kansas State wasn't ranked.

In the opener, Randle came through with 19 points and 15 rebounds to lead his team to a low-scoring 56-49 victory. The Cats went on top early and never looked back, although their performance wasn't particularly compelling. Aaron Harrison chipped in with 18 points in the win.

Next up was No. 2-ranked Wichita State, and thanks to some courageous free throw shooting down the stretch, the Cats managed to pull off a big 78-76 upset that sent them to the Sweet 16.

This was tense battle from start to finish. The Cats trailed 37-31 at the break, then came back to snag to lead late in the game. Inside the final minute, four free tosses by Andrew Harrison and two by Randle gave the Cats their

Underrated James Young came up big against UConn in Final Four action.

two-point advantage. Wichita State had one last chance to avoid elimination, but a three-point attempt by Fred Van Vleet at the buzzer was off the mark.

The Harrison brothers were superb, with Andrew hitting for 20 points and Aaron 19. Young and Randle each had 13 points for the winners, who had to overcome a 31-point performance from Wichita State's Cleanthony Early.

That win earned the Cats a second meeting against Louisville, now ranked No. 5 in the country. As expected, this one went down to the wire, and once again the Cats survived 74-69 thanks to a big comeback effort and another gutsy performance at the charity stripe.

Louisville led from the opening tip until a Poythress three-point play tied it at 66-66 with 2:11 left. After Poythress connected on another freebie to put the Cats on top, Russ Smith nailed a bucket to give his club a 68-67 advantage. A trey by Aaron Harrison made it 70-68, then Wayne Blackshear hit one of two free tosses to pull the Cardinals to within one. That would be the last point scored by Louisville.

The Cats sealed the victory by sinking four straight free throws, two each by Randle and Aaron Harrison. Accuracy at the stripe was the difference in this game. The Cats connected on 22 of 27, while the Cards made good on just 13 of 23, with Russ Smith, the game's leading scorer (23 points) hitting just 4 of 10.

Randle, Johnson and Aaron Harrison all had 15 points each, while Andrew Harrison added 14.

It would be in the next two games that Aaron Harrison added his name to a select group of Wildcat players whose last-second heroics are the stuff of legend, a list that includes Vernon Hatton, Terry Mobley, Kyle Macy, Kenny Walker, Sean Woods, Anthony Epps, Scott Padgett, Patrick Sparks and Brandon Knight. But none of those guys ever performed such heroics on back-to-back occasions.

Last-second three-pointers by Aaron were the difference in a 75-72 win over Michigan and a 74-73 win over Wisconsin in the semifinal game. Those two buckets propelled the Cats into the Final Four and into the title tilt. The first killing shot came with four seconds left, the second with six ticks remaining.

In the win over Michigan, Randle had 16 points and 11 rebounds. Young finished with 13 points, while Aaron Harrison, the Big Blue hero, had 12, all coming from behind the three-point line.

Had Aaron Harrison misfired on that final shot against

Back-to-back late-game heroics by Aaron Harrison lifted the Cats to a pair of NCAA victories.

Michigan, the game would have gone into overtime. Not so in the Cats' game against Wisconsin. Miss this one and the Cats, who were down 73-71, head back to Lexington, their season ended.

Early on, it appeared to be 12th-ranked Wisconsin's night. The Cats trailed 40-36 at intermission, and didn't get the upper hand until a Johnson three-point play put them in front 45-43 with just over 17 minutes remaining. After that, it was a see-saw struggle until Aaron Harrison nailed the game-winner. It was the only three-point attempt he took all night. He accounted for eight points.

Young paced the Cats with 17 points. Randle finished with 16, while Johnson added 10.

A big key to the Cats' victory was holding Frank Kaminsky to eight points. Sam Dekker and Ben Brust had 15 points apiece for Wisconsin.

Now, one year after having been exiled to the NIT, Calipari had his Wildcats back in prime time, ready to do battle against a UConn team that was ranked 18th in the country. The Cats, after having dispatched Wichita State, Louisville, Michigan and Wisconsin, were favored by many experts to take home the big trophy. As they saw things, after back-to-back miracles by Aaron Harrison, these Cats were surely a team of destiny.

But there were no miracles on this night. Destiny, forever fickle, had simply moved on. UConn captured the title with a 60-54 victory.

The clear difference in this game was the free throw stripe, where UConn made good on all 10 attempts, while the Cats could do no better than 13 of 24. This was a disappointing statistic for a UK team that had won so many games this season by being accurate at the free throw line.

Young led the Cats with 20 points. UConn's Shabazz Napier had 22 points for the champs.

This Wildcat team, with its 29-11 record and runner-up finish, might have come up one victory short of achieving its goal of winning it all. But this club did what Big Blue Nation fans wanted—it put the program back in the spotlight.

Although Randle and Young would depart for the NBA, Wildcat fans had little cause for concern. After all, Calipari had inked yet another top-ranked recruiting class. In the eyes of everyone, UK's talent cup was full.

But for Calipari, there were probably moments when he had the feeling that his cup runneth over.

Many experts predicted John Calipari's sixth team would capture a national crown.

2014-15

Even before this season got underway the whispers had already begun: "Run the table," "40-0," "national championship."

"Perfection."

The dream of perfection was daring in every way, and it wasn't limited to Big Blue Nation fans; more than a few basketball experts also felt that this UK team had all the

ingredients necessary to go through a season undefeated, including capturing the NCAA championship, a feat that had not been accomplished since Bobby Knight's Indiana club did it in 1975-76.

Only one modern-era UK team—1953-54—finished with a perfect record (25-0), but that club refused to participate in the NCAA tourney when its three best players—Cliff Hagan, Frank Ramsey, Lou Tsioropoulos—were declared ineligible because they were fifth-year seniors attending graduate school.

There were plenty of reasons why the dream of perfection surrounded this team—talent, size and, unexpectedly, experience. Because NBA lights failed to shine on the Harrison twins, Willie Cauley-Stein, Alex Poythress and Marcus Lee, those five would return for a second reason, along with Kentucky natives Derek Willis and Dominique Hawkins.

Joining them was another world-class group of freshmen that included Karl-Anthony Towns, Devin Booker, Trey Lyles and Tyler Ulis.

So deep was this team that John Calipari had little choice but to use a platoon system, something he probably would have preferred not to do. For such a system to succeed meant that a group of high school All-Americans were being asked to make a huge sacrifice when it came to playing time. There were many who doubted that the platoon system could work, but the

UK players, to a man, proved to be unselfish, selfless and more than willing to put team goals ahead of individual statistics.

The proof: Aaron Harrison, the team's leading scorer, averaged just 11 points per game, the lowest since the great

Trey Lyles helped lead the Cats to an easy romp past Kansas.

Ralph Beard averaged 10.9 in 1946-47. During this entire campaign, only six times did a Wildcat score 20 or more points in a game.

The result: A perfect regular-season record, an SEC tournament title and a record-setting 38 straight victories. And yet, despite it all, this club came up short in the NCAA tourney, losing to Wisconsin in the Final Four semifinal round.

The Cats wasted no time demonstrating how overpowering they could be, winning their first seven games by a whopping average margin of 34 points. The conquered included Grand Canyon 85-45, Buffalo 71-52, Kansas 72-40, Boston University 89-65, Montana State 86-28, UT-Arlington 92-44 and Providence 58-38.

Andrew Harrison led with 16 points in the opener, then Lyles and Ulis each had 12 against Buffalo. Johnson topped the scoring against Kansas with 11 points, Aaron Harrison had 19 against Boston and Booker came through with 18 against Montana and 19 against UT-Arlington. Towns and Cauley-Stein each contributed 11 in the romp past Providence.

Unbeaten Texas played the top-ranked Cats to a 26-26 halftime standoff, but with Cauley-Stein scoring 21 points and snaring 12 rebounds, Calipari's club pulled away in the final 20 minutes to post a 63-51 victory.

After Towns tossed in 19 points in an easy 82-49 victory over Eastern Kentucky, the Cats turned in what was arguably their worst effort of the season, doing just enough to get past Columbia 56-46 after trailing 25-23 at intermission. In this miserable performance, the Cats shot just 37 percent from the field, made good on 2 of 17 three-point attempts and 10 of 17 from the charity stripe.

Willie Cauley-Stein throws down a dunk against LSU.

Aaron Harrison led the scoring with 14 points, while Lyles and Cauley-Stein each grabbed 10 rebounds. It was after this game that Poythress suffered a torn ACL during practice that sidelined him for the remainder of the season.

The Cats' next trio of games featured visits from North Carolina and UCLA followed by a visit to Louisville. With Booker and Cauley-Stein each scoring 15 points, Aaron Harrison 14 and Andrew Harrison 11, the Cats opened this difficult stretch by beating North Carolina 84-70.

In a battle between two schools with a combined 19 NCAA titles, the Cats roared to an incredible 41-7 half-

time advantage and then went on to pound UCLA 83-44. Although the Cats were heavily favored to win, no one expected such a massacre.

Booker and Aaron Harrison paced the winners with 19 and 15 points, respectively.

Playing in the Yum Center, the Cats, in a low-scoring defensive struggle between a pair of unbeaten clubs, managed to pull away in the final minutes to notch a 58-50 victory over Louisville. The win pushed the Cats' record to 13-0 heading into SEC action, while the loss dropped the Cards to 11-1.

Ulis was superb in this important outing, finishing with 14 points. Towns also cracked double digits with 10.

The Cats' road to perfection almost took a detour when upset-minded Ole Miss came to town. In what was a seesaw battle from start to finish, the Cats managed to get away with an 89-86 win in overtime.

Ole Miss led at the half—38-36—and was in front 77-76 when Andrew Harrison made one of two free tosses to knot the score and bring on the OT. With his team down 85-83, Andrew Harrison connected on a three-pointer to give his club an 86-85 advantage. After Ole Miss tied it at 86-86, three freebies, two by Aaron Harrison and one by Andrew inside the final 1:29 enabled the Cats to remain unbeaten.

Aaron Harrison led all scorers with 26 points. Booker tallied 13, Andrew Harrison 12, Towns 11 and Lyles 10. Stefan Moody led the Rebels with 25 points.

Following that narrow escape, the Cats found themselves in a second straight thriller, this one at Texas A&M. Once again, Calipari's Cats survived, edging the Aggies 70-64 in double overtime.

The score was tied 53-53 at the end of regulation, and it took a pair of Lyles free throws with six seconds left to knot the score at 57-57 and send the

game into the second OT. In that one, the Cats took the lead for good at the 1:26 mark when Ulis buried a three-pointer.

Booker paced the winners with 18 points, while Aaron Harrison added a dozen.

Having twice avoided disaster, the Cats got back in overpowering form in their next six games, destroying Missouri 86-37, Alabama 70-48, South Carolina 58-43, Missouri 69-53 and Alabama 70-55. Only visiting Vanderbilt put up a good fight before falling 65-57. Those six wins improved the Cats to 21-0 overall and 8-0 in league play.

Aaron Harrison topped the scoring with 16 against Missouri, with Towns adding a double-double (12/10). Booker led the way with 13 against Alabama, Aaron Harrison had 14 and Johnson 10 in the win over Vandy, Booker came back with 18 against South Carolina, Andrew Harrison scored 15 against Missouri, and Towns and Cauley-Stein

The Harrison twins combined for 25 points in a tough win over North Carolina. That's Aaron on the left, Andrew on the right.

each had 12 points in that second win over Alabama.

A surprisingly difficult 69-58 victory over Georgia was the first of three straight tough wins. Against the Bulldogs, Andrew Harrison had 23 points, with Towns recording another double-double (15/13).

At Florida, the Cats trailed 30-28 at intermission before taking charge in the final 20 minutes to earn a 68-61 win. Aaron Harrison led four Cats in double figures with 23 points. Others included Towns (19), Cauley-Stein (13) and Booker (12).

In their next outing, the visiting Cats pulled off another Houdini-like escape by edging past LSU 71-69. The Cats led 60-50 midway through the second half, only to watch LSU reel off 16 unanswered points to take a 66-60 advantage. A jumper by Towns put the Cats in front 70-69, then Booker dropped in a freebie with 15 seconds remaining to account for the final score.

Cauley-Stein paced the Cats with 15 points, while Booker added 14, Andrew Harrison 13 and Towns 12.

Win number 25 came courtesy of an easy 77-43 win over South Carolina. In this one, the Cats built a 43-18 lead at the half, then easily cruised home. Cauley-Stein had

Devin Booker and Alex Poythress celebrate another
SEC Tournament Championship.

14 points for the winners.

Against Tennessee, the Cats broke away from a close first-half struggle to put down the Vols 66-48 in Knoxville. The Cats led 35-31 at intermission. Booker was the top gun with 18 points.

With six players hitting for double figures, the Cats stormed past Auburn 110-75 in Rupp Arena. Towns led the scoring parade with 19 points, followed by Aaron Harrison (18), Johnson (13), Andrew Harrison (12), Booker (11) and Ulis (10).

With Lyles connecting for 18 points and Aaron Harrison 16, the Cats traveled to Starkville and posted a 74-56 win over Mississippi State. Booker tallied 14 points in this victory, with Towns scoring 12 points and grabbing 10 rebounds.

The Cats closed out their perfect run through the SEC regular season by posting three fairly easy wins, topping Arkansas 84-67, Georgia 72-64 and Florida 67-50. That trio of victories gave the top-ranked Cats a 31-0 record to take into post-season play.

In beating Arkansas, Lyles and Andrew Harrison led the way with 18 points apiece. Ulis and Booker also cracked double digits with 14 and 10 points, respectively.

The win at Georgia was the toughest of the three. The score was tied 32-32 at intermission before the Cats, fueled by Towns with 19 points and Aaron Harrison with 16, were able to pull away for the victory. Andrew Harrison finished with 12 points.

The season finale against Billy Donovan's always-dangerous Gators followed a script similar to the one at Georgia. The Cats, leading by three at the break, broke it open in the second half, ending with a 67-50 win. Lyles paced the Cats with 14 points, while Towns added 13.

As fate would have it, the Cats had to face Florida again in the SEC Tournament's quarterfinal round, and for the second straight time, the game had a familiar ring to it. The Cats were in front 31-27 after a hard-fought first 20 minutes, then slowly eased away in the second half to post a 64-49 win. Towns and Aaron Harrison topped the Cats with 13 points each in this low-scoring affair.

With five players scoring in double figures, the Cats pummeled Auburn 91-67 to advance to the championship game. This one was never in doubt, with the Cats blowing out to a 47-29 lead by intermission.

Cauley-Stein led the balanced attack with 18 points. Andrew Harrison finished with 15, while Lyles, Booker and Aaron Harrison accounted for 12 points apiece.

A strong first-half effort was instrumental in the Cats' claiming the title with a 78-63 win over Arkansas. In this game, the Cats dominated the opening 20 minutes, taking a 41-25 lead into the dressing room at the break. Arkansas actually outscored the Cats 38-37 in the second half, but it was too little, too late.

Cauley-Stein and Andrew Harrison were the Cats' top guns with 15 points each. Aaron Harrison chipped in with 11.

Undefeated, top-ranked and seeded No. 1 overall, the Cats began their quest for the school's ninth NCAA title by pounding overmatched Hampton 79-56. Towns was the dominant force for the winners, scoring 21 points and hauling down 11 rebounds. For the game, Towns made good on 8 of 12 shooting from the field and five of six from the free throw stripe.

Andrew Harrison finished with 14 points, Ulis had 11 and Lyles had 10, while Cauley-Stein matched Towns with 11 caroms.

Next up was Cincinnati, a team noted for toughness and strong defense. The game was close until midway through the second half, then the deeper and more-talented Cats finally began to assert their superiority, advancing to the Sweet 16 with a 64-51 victory.

Aaron Harrison and Lyles paced the winners with 13 and 11 points, respectively. Lyles also yanked down 11 rebounds.

No one expected the outcome of the Cats' Sweet 16 battle against West Virginia, a game most experts figured to be close. It wasn't. The Cats ran out to a 44-18 halftime lead, then went on to claim a 78-39 win.

It was after this easy win that many of those experts were ready to crown the unbeaten Cats as national champs.

The Cats shot 48 percent from the field while holding West Virginia to just 24.1 percent. The taller Cats also won the battle of the boards 44-32.

Lyles led five players in double figures with 14 points. Andrew Harrison had 13, with Johnson, Aaron Harrison and Booker each tossing in a dozen.

Now just one victory away from another trip to the Final Four, the Cats squared off against Notre Dame in what turned out to be a classic down-to-the-wire thriller. Any thoughts that the Cats would go unchallenged on their way to picking up the NCAA hardware were quickly dispelled by the Irish.

It took a pair of gutsy Andrew Harrison free throws with six seconds remaining, and a missed three-point attempt by Jerian Grant before Big Blue Nation fans could finally breathe a sigh of relief.

Final: Cats 68, Notre Dame 66.

Following a 31-31 deadlock at intermission, Notre Dame seized control in the second half, eventually building a 59-53 lead with 6:14 remaining. The Cats went in front 64-63 on an Aaron Harrison trey, but Grant then buried one to give the Irish a 66-64 advantage.

After a Towns layup tied it at 66-66 with 1:12 left, the Irish coughed up the ball on a turnover. With six seconds remaining, Andrew Harrison drew a foul on Demetrius Jackson. Harrison sank both free tosses to give the Cats their two-point win and a trip to the Final Four.

Towns turned in a huge 25-point effort for the Cats, who shot 53.2 percent from the field. For the game, Towns hit 10 of his 13 attempts.

Booker was the only other Cat in double figures with 10.

Zach Auguste led the Irish with 20 points.

Almost one year ago to the day, the Cats, courtesy of Aaron Harrison's last-second three-point bucket, slipped past Wisconsin 74-73 in Final Four semifinal action. Now,

for the second straight year, the Cats once again found themselves squaring off against the Badgers.

These two powerful clubs went into this tussle with a combined record of 73-3.

Defense against Frank Kaminsky played a key role in the Cats' win last year. In that game, the Cats held the big guy to just eight points. If there was one player on the court this time around with redemption in mind, it was Kaminsky. The All-American wasn't going to let his club down a second time, and he didn't.

Behind Kaminsky's 20-point, 11-rebound performance, Wisconsin ended the Cats' dream of perfection by scoring a 71-64 upset. Kaminsky received plenty of support from Sam Dekker, who ended the game with 16 points.

Towns again led the Cats with 16 points, while the Harrison twins combined for 25 points (Andrew 13, Aaron 12).

It was a disappointing end to what had been a record-breaking season. This club tied the school record for most games won in a season (38), and it became the first Division I team to win its first 38 games.

In the end, however, it might be argued that this club's greatest attribute was it unselfishness. During what has become known as the me-first era, when individual stats tend to overshadow team play, this classy group of Wildcats set aside personal glory for the good of the team. For that, they are winners who should be applauded.

But this team was so talented that no fewer than seven Wildcats headed off to the pro ranks, including Towns, Booker, Cauley-Stein, Lyles, Johnson and the Harrison twins.

But not to worry; once again Calipari inked another incredibly talented group of rookies, bringing in seven new faces, among them two from Canada (Jamal Murray, Mychal Mulder), one from Haiti (Skal Labissiere), one from Australia (Isaac Humphries), one from New Zealand (Tai Wynyard) and two from the U.S. (Isaiah Briscoe, Charles Matthews).

Tyler Ulis had arguably the greatest season ever by a Wildcat point guard.

If nothing else, this would surely be the United Nations of Wildcat teams.

2015-16

Any basketball program that waves goodbye to seven players of superior talent is bound to take a hit. There's simply no way it can't. But at the University of Kentucky, thanks to John Calipari's magical recruiting touch, the pain is much less considerable than it would be at most other schools.

Whether or not you agree with the so-called "one-and-done" scenario, there is no denying the fact that Calipari embraces it and, even more importantly, he makes it work. The truth is, he is taking advantage of a terrible situation whose fault lies not with college hoops but with the greedy NBA. If you want a villain to blame, look no farther than the NBA.

In a seven-for-seven trade, Calipari replaced the departed stars with a new crop of Wildcats. The two diamonds in this collection were 6'11" Skal Labissiere, from Port-au-Prince, Haiti, and 6'4" Jamal Murray, who hails from Kitchener, Canada.

Those two came to UK with starkly different backgrounds. Murray was extremely experienced, and had been a key player for Team Canada in the 2015 Pan Am Games. Conversely, Labissiere, who survived a devastating earthquake, had only been playing basketball for a short period

Skal Labissiere goes high to win the tip. The rookie got off to a fast start, then went through some rocky times.

of time and hadn't competed at all for the past two years.

Other newcomers on this team included Charles Matthews, Isaiah Briscoe, Isaac Humphries, Tai Wynyard and junior college transfer Mychal Mulder.

But fortunately for this team, there were several familiar faces set to return, among them senior Alex Poythress, juniors Marcus Lee, Dominique Hawkins and Derek Willis, and the tiny cat-quick sophomore point guard Tyler Ulis.

EJ Floreal, Johnny David and Dillon Pulliam rounded out the roster.

From the very beginning it was obvious that this club would never be as powerful or dominant as last year's club. This was a team destined to go through some difficult and stressful growing pains, at times playing well, while on other occasions, struggling to find its true identity.

With this team, no one dared dream of a perfect 40-0 season.

The Cats opened the long campaign by topping Albany 78-65. Murray, in his debut performance, led the winners with 19 points. Willis finished with 14, while Lee and Ulis each contributed 12.

Behind 26 points from Labissiere, the Cats crushed NJIT 87-57 in their second outing. Labissiere was spectacular, making good on 10 of 12 field goal attempts and all

Isaiah Briscoe passes to a teammate after slashing to the bucket.

six of his free throws. Afer this performance by Labissiere, UK fans were convinced they were witnessing the second coming of Anthony Davis or Karl-Anthony Towns. But that assessment proved to be premature. Unlike his predecessors, Labissiere was a work-in-progress.

In this win, Willis and Briscoe each had 11 points, while Lee added 10.

Now ranked second in the nation, the Cats, getting a solid 18-point, six-assist effort from Ulis, beat No. 5-ranked Duke 74-63 in the Champions Classic. Ulis received plenty of help from Murray with 16 points and Briscoe with 12. The always-dependable Lee registered a double-double with 10 points and 10 rebounds.

Having dispatched Duke, the Cats returned home for an encounter with Wright State, which they won handily 78-63. Ulis again paced the Cats with 21 points. Briscoe ended the night with 15, Murray and Labissiere 13 apiece, and Poythress with 10. Poythress also claimed 10 rebounds.

With five players cracking double figures, the Cats ran their record to 5-0 by pummeling Boston University 82-62.

Labissiere led the scoring parade with 16 points, followed by Ulis (15), Poythress (14), Murray (12) and Briscoe (11). Poythress had his second straight double-double, pulling down 10 rebounds.

Two more solid victories followed, with the Cats besting South Florida 84-63 and Illinois State 75-63. Murray had 21 points and Labissiere added 17 in the win over South Florida, then Briscoe was the key guy against Illinois State with 18 points. Murray and Lee finished with 16 and 13, respectively, in that win.

Traveling to Los Angeles for a game against UCLA, the Cats suffered their first defeat, dropping an 87-77 decision. Unlike the previous year's game in which the Cats embarrassed Steve Alford's club, this time around the revenge-minded Bruins grabbed the upper hand early and never relinquished it. Their 53 percent shooting from the field played a huge role in the outcome.

Briscoe paced the Cats with 20 points, while Murray had 17 and Willis 11. All five UCLA starters hit double figures, led by Thomas Welsh with 21. Welsh also collared 11 rebounds.

Eastern Kentucky paid a visit to Rupp Arena and was

promptly handed an 88-67 loss. Poythress turned in a big effort, scoring 21 points and snaring 13 rebounds. Murray tossed in 16 points, Lee had 11, Briscoe and Labissiere 10 apiece.

Facing a good Arizona State club, the Cats broke away from a tight 32-31 halftime score to earn a 72-58 victory. Red-hot second-half shooting (15 of 26 for 58 percent) was the difference in this one. Murray again led the Cats with 17 points. Also hitting double figures were Lee (14), Ulis (12) and Poythress (10).

It was in this game that Labissiere's struggles began. In this outing, he had no points and no rebounds.

Taking on Ohio State in Brooklyn's Barclays Center, the Cats, despite a brilliant 33-point performance by Murray, were handed their second setback of the season—74-67. The Buckeyes took control early and clearly outplayed the Wildcats from beginning to end.

Murray's 33 points are the second-most ever scored by a UK freshman, trailing only Terrence Jones's 35 against Auburn in 2011. This would not be the last time Murray cracked the 30-point mark this season.

In the annual in-state Armageddon between the Cats and Louisville, it was the game's smallest player who gave the biggest performance. Behind 21 points from Ulis, and thanks to several crucial buckets by Hawkins, the Cats were able to hang on down the stretch to sneak away with a 75-73 victory over Rick Pitino's Cardinals.

The Cats were sitting on a 52-36 lead early in the second half and seemed to be in control. But the Cardinals were far from finished. Led by Damion Lee, Pitino's club began to chip away at the deficit, closing to within 65-64 at the 5:34 mark.

After Ulis buried a trey to make it 68-64, Damion Lee wrapped a pair of buckets around a Marcus Lee dunk that made it 70-68. Then with 2:47 left, Hawkins hit what might have been the biggest shot of the game, a three-pointer that gave the Cats a 73-68 lead and some breathing room. Inside the final two minutes, Hawkins, who scored a career-best 13 points, canned a pair of free throws to seal the win.

Louisville's Damion Lee led all scorers with 27.

The Cats began their journey through the SEC jungle by entertaining Ole Miss. That journey began on solid footing, thanks to a double-double by Ulis. His 20-point, 10-assists performance propelled the Cats to an 83-61 victory.

A huge first-half proved to be the difference. In those 20 minutes, the Cats outscored the visitors 46-22.

Murray ended the evening with 18 points, while Lee added 13.

The journey didn't go so well at LSU, where the home-standing Tigers used a big rebounding advantage to pound the Cats 85-67. LSU won the battle of the boards by a decisive 46-32 margin.

Winning the rebounding war, coupled with 49.2 percent shooting from the field (to UK's 41.4), translated into this a relatively easy win for the home-standing Tigers. Another reason why the Cats stumbled in this outing was poor free throw shooting. For the game, they made good on 12 of 23.

Ulis and Lee again paced the Cats with 23 and 21 points, respectively.

LSU had a more balanced attack with three players posting double-doubles—Tim Quarterman (21/10), Craig Victor (15/12) and highly touted Ben Simmons (14/10).

At Alabama, the Cats bolted to a 38-28 lead at intermission, and then rolled to an impressive 77-61 victory.

Poythress broke out of a slump (he only had 10 points in the two previous games), scoring 25 points on 8 of 10 shooting from the field and 9 of 11 from the charity stripe. He also pulled down seven rebounds.

Murray continued his steady play, racking up 21 points. Briscoe also cracked double figures with 12.

Back home in Rupp Arena, the Cats found themselves in a real struggle before finally putting away Mississippi State 80-74. The Cats led by eight at the half (39-31), but red-hot shooting by Mississippi State kept things close. For the game, the Bulldogs hit 27 of 51 field goal attempts for 52.9 percent.

Once again, Murray and Ulis proved to be a lethal 1-2 punch, combining for 43 points. Murray had 22, Ulis 21. Briscoe finished with 14 points, with Willis offering a preview of coming attractions by tossing in eight.

For the 14th-ranked Cats, the next game, a humbling 75-70 setback at Auburn, had to be one of the most-disappointing losses during the John Calipari Era. In this one, the Cats led 35-30 at intermission, increased their advantage to a dozen and then promptly came unglued.

The loss also overshadowed a gutsy 12-point, 12-rebound effort by Willis.

Murray had 22 points for the Wildcats, while Ulis toyed with a rare triple-double—17 points, 10 rebounds and eight assists.

Auburn's Kareem Canty led all scorers with 26. Teammate Tyler Harris added 21.

Jamal Murray heads to the rim. Murray scored more points than any UK freshman.

Following that humbling experience, the Cats traveled to an even more treacherous venue for their next outing—Arkansas. But in what was a complete turnaround, by giving what was a superb all-around effort, the Cats dispatched the Razorbacks with an 80-66 win.

Ulis was spectacular in this victory, scoring 24 points and handing out five assists. For the game, the tiny point guard connected on 14 of 15 free throw attempts.

Murray turned in another strong performance, finishing with 19 points, while Willis, making the most of his first start, had 12 points and seven rebounds. Labissiere posted his best scoring output in a while, coming through with 11 points.

Back home, the 23rd-ranked Cats raced to a quick early advantage, then went on to beat Vanderbilt 76-57. Ulis, Murray and Poythress put the big hurt on the Commodores, combining for 55 points. Ulis led the way with 21 (hitting 9 of 13 from the field), Murray had 18 and Poythress 16.

Willis led the rebounding with nine.

At this stage it had become clear that the insertion of Willis into the starting five made this a better Wildcat club. The 6'9" ex-Bullitt East High School standout had always been recognized as a superb athlete and an excellent outside shooter. His ability to burn opponents from long range forced opposing coaches to stretch their defense, which opened things up for UK's trio of guards to have a clear pathway to the bucket.

The big questions surrounding Willis were his intensity level (not always high), his confidence (often somewhat shaky) and his willingness to rebound (also on the low side.) However, after a chat with his father, all those negatives seemed to melt away and he suddenly emerged as a terrific player.

All the stars aligned perfectly in the Cats' next game, an 88-54 blowout of Missouri. In that game, Willis, sinking six of nine shots from the field, posted a double-double, scoring 18 points and spearing 12 rebounds. It was his best performance in a UK uniform.

Ulis topped a balanced scoring attack with 20 points. After Willis's 18, Briscoe had 15, Labissiere had 12 and Murray had 11.

Taking a break from league play, the Cats traveled to Lawrence, Kansas, for a battle against No.4-ranked Kansas in Allen Fieldhouse. And it was a battle. In what was a super-hyped made-for-TV showdown between two of college basketball's true blue bloods, this game more than lived up to all the hoopla that surrounded it.

With both teams firing on all cylinders, especially in the first half (UK shot 63 percent, Kansas 55.6 percent), this was an old-fashioned shootout that certainly pleased the fans even as the opposing coaches lamented the lack of defense.

The Cats led 46-40 at intermission, and after a see-saw second half, took a 74-72 lead when Poythress slammed down a dunk with 1:11 remaining. But the Jayhawks fought back to tie it at 76-76 and send the game into overtime.

Two free throws by Wayne Selden put the home club in front 78-76, but Labissiere followed by knocking down a jumper to even the score at 78-78. At the 3:11 mark, Selden scored on a dunk to give the Jayhawks the lead for good.

The final: Kansas won it 90-84.

The difference in this one was the charity stripe. For the game, the Cats had seven more buckets (33-26), but Kansas hit 30 of 47 freebies compared to 13 of 22 by the visitors.

Losing four inside players to foul problems also played a role in this loss. Lee, Poythress, Willis and Labissiere were all tagged with five fouls.

Kansas also clearly won the battle of the boards 42-31.

Selden was the gunslinger who couldn't be handled in this game. He burned the Cats for 33 points.

The tireless Ulis, who played all 45 minutes, paced the Cats with 26 points and eight assists. Murray had 15 points, Poythress 13 and Briscoe had 12, despite missing 6of his 12 free throw attempts.

Despite losing at Kansas, the consensus among most experts (and UK fans) was that the Cats had turned in yet another solid effort. Coaches invariably decry the notion of a moral victory, but the truth is there are losses and there are losses.

Translation: Some losses hurt much worse than others.

And what happened in the Cats' next outing at Tennessee clearly belongs in the "much worse" category. This loss really stung. It was the Cats' fifth loss to an unranked team.

After building a 21-point first-half lead, the Cats crumbled down the stretch, eventually dropping an 84-77 decision. What this means is that the Volunteers outscored the Cats by 28 points during the game's final 25 minutes.

Once again, the twin demons of too many fouls and the lack of an inside presence haunted the Cats. For the game, the Cats had more field goals (26-23), but Tennessee hit 30 of 34 freebies to 18 of 23 by the visitors.

Marcus Lee could always be counted on to provide energy and rebounding.

With the scored tied at 70-70, the Vols reeled off six unanswered points to seize control. They finished it off by hitting five of six free throws in the final 40 seconds.

Poythress led the early charge, scoring 10 points to help the Cats build their huge advantage. But Poythress, who fouled out, only had four points the rest of the way. With him out, his inside brothers had little to offer. Lee and Labissiere each finished with two points.

Murray led the Cats with 21 points, while Ulis, who also fouled out, added 20. Briscoe hit for double figures with 10. Willis and Briscoe each picked up eight rebounds.

Kevin Punter was the game's top scorer, burning the Cats with 27 points. He got big help from Armani Moore, who had 18 points and 13 rebounds.

The loss dropped the Cats' record to 16-6 overall and 6-3 in SEC action.

The Cats' next two games—both easy victories—were dominated by the blistering-hot shooting of Murray, who combined for 59 points while making good on 21 of 35 field goal attempts, including 14 of 20 from three-point range.

Murray hit for 35 points in the Cats' 80-61 win against Florida. Those 35 points tied Terrence Jones for the most scored by a UK freshman. Against the Gators, Murray hit 13 of 21 shots, and was 8 for 10 from beyond the three-point line.

Ulis turned in another excellent effort, finishing with 18 points and 11 assists. Willis also cracked double figures with 12 points.

Murray continued to storm enemy beaches in his team's

next outing, this time pouring in 24 points as the Cats put away Georgia 82-48. In this easy romp, Murray hit 8 of 14 from the field, and was 6 of 10 from outside the three-point arc.

Ulis finished with 14 points, Willis had 11 and Hawkins added nine.

In what was easily their best performance to date, the Cats, minus Calipari, completely dismantled a strong South Carolina team on the road, winning 89-62. Calipari, violently objecting to a call, got the heave-ho less than three minutes into the game.

It didn't matter one iota. With Ulis directing the action on both ends of the floor, the Cats played brilliantly, once building a 34-point advantage—77-43—with just over seven minutes remaining.

The game was a showcase for Ulis's leadership skills, his scoring and his unselfish play. In one of the greatest performances ever by a Wildcat point guard, Ulis had 27 points, 12 assists and a single turnover. All this against a bully-type South Carolina team known for its stingy defense.

After this performance, Ulis saw his name move to the top of the list for SEC Player of the Year, and, in some quarters, a serious candidate for National Player of the Year.

Murray had another strong effort, torching the Gamecocks for 26 points. Briscoe had 10 points, but it was the play of Lee that enabled the Cats to handle South Carolina's tough inside players. For the game, Lee had 11 points and 13 rebounds.

Michael Carrera led South Carolina with 25 points and 10 rebounds.

Tying a UK record by knocking down 11 treys, the Cats beat Tennessee 80-70 in Rupp Arena. This marked the team's fourth straight victory, and the fourth consecutive time the team nailed 10 or more three-pointers, a record shared with three previous Wildcat teams.

The rampaging Murray burned the Vols for 28 points, but it was Willis who stole the show on this night, tossing in a career-best 25 points on 8 of 12 from the field, and 7 of 11 from three-point range.

After a tight first half—UK led 36-30—the Cats went on a 13-1 run early in the second half that broke the game open. When Ulis buried a trey, the Cats' advantage was 54-36.

Despite a poor shooting night (3 for 15), Ulis still managed to score 11 points and hand out nine assists. Briscoe led the Cats with 10 rebounds.

The win was the 20th for the Wildcats to go against six losses.

No loss is easy to bear, but the one at Texas A&M—79-77 in overtime—was a pill almost too bitter to swallow. A last-second rebound bucket and a questionable call by an official were at the forefront of the next-day morning headlines and the reason why phones were lighting up on the TV/radio call-in shows. To say Big Blue Nation fans disagreed with the official's call is putting it in the mildest terms possible.

The game was close throughout, with neither team able to establish a healthy advantage. The score was tied 68-68 at the end of regulation. That's when the real drama began. In the five-minute OT, the lead changed hands six times.

With the Cats on top 76-75, Humphries intercepted a Texas A&M pass and was fouled. In his excitement, the big freshman, who had given a splendid performance, slammed the ball to the floor. His show of exuberance was deemed egregious enough that referee Pat Adams blew his whistle and slapped Humphries with the technical.

Danuel House connected on two free throws to put the Aggies on top 77-76 with 9.4 seconds remaining. The technical against Humphries was his fifth foul, so Labissiere came in to attempt the two free throws for UK. He hit the first, missed the second, good enough to tie things up at 77-77.

The Aggies won it when Tyler Davis scored on a put-back with less than a second remaining.

Ulis and Murray paced the Wildcats with 22 and 21 points, respectively. Ulis also handed out 11 assists. Humphries, pressed into service due to the absence of Poythress and an injury to Willis, finished with six points and an all-important 12 rebounds. The Cats were being pounded on the glass until Humphries entered the battle.

Willis went down with a severely sprained ankle, making his status uncertain for upcoming games.

Texas A&M's Jalen Jones led all scorers with 24 points.

With Willis sidelined by his injury but Poythress healthy again, the Cats bounced back from their disheartening setback at Texas A&M by soundly thumping Alabama 78-53 for their 21st victory of the campaign. This win also put the Cats alone at the top of the SEC standings with an 11-4 league record.

Poythress, who had missed the previous five games, came off the bench to score 15 points, making good on five of six field goal attempts and four of six free throws.

The Cats' brilliant backcourt duo of Murray and Ulis continued their rampage, this time combining for 42 points. Murray had 23 and Ulis 19. Ulis also handed out 10 assists. Briscoe cracked double figures with 10 points, while Lee led all rebounders with 12.

Defense was a key in this Wildcat win. For the game, the Cats limited Alabama to 35 percent shooting from the field. The Cats led 33-21 at intermission, and had it not been for Bama's Retin Obasohan, that lead would have been much greater. Obasohan scored 15 of his team's 21 first-half points. He finished with a game-high 29.

In virtually every Wildcat loss this season, the team resembled a doughnut or a bagel—there was been a huge hole in the middle. That was certainly the case at Vanderbilt, a game the Cats lost 74-62.

Still minus the injured Willis, UK's "bigs," the fanciful term now used to describe those formerly known as post players or inside players, Poythress, Labissiere and Humphries combined for zero points and five rebounds.

To borrow a line from Adolph Rupp: "Fellas, you had exactly five more rebounds than a dead man."

The Cats' seventh setback of the season negated another outstanding offensive performance by Murray. The Canadian freshman finished with 33 points and nine rebounds. His hot shooting had the Cats on top 39-36 at intermission.

But the home-standing Commodores, led by Matthew Fisher-Davis, battled back to take control early in the final 20 minutes. Still, the Cats stayed in contention, and were trailing by a single bucket (58-56), only to go nearly four minutes without scoring. Vandy, meanwhile, rattled off seven unanswered to points to increase its lead to 65-56 at the 6:26 mark. The Cats made one last charge, narrowing the gap to six points (68-62), but they could never reclaim the upper hand.

Ulis, who connected on just 5 of 20 field goal attempts, ended the night with 12 points and six assists. Lee had nine points and Briscoe added eight for the Cats.

Fisher-Davis paced Vandy with 20 points, while Luke Kornet led all rebounders with 11.

Following a bit of "tweaking" by Calipari, the Cats, getting a solid effort from Labissiere, got back on the winning track by polishing off Florida 88-79 in Gainesville. Labissiere, inserted into the starting lineup, scored 11 points and had eight rebounds in 15 minutes of action.

What didn't need tweaking was the Cats' backcourt trio of Murray, Ulis and Briscoe, a threesome that combined for 53 points. Murray led the scoring with 21 points, while Ulis had 19 and Briscoe added 13. Ulis also doled out 11 assists.

Poythress bounced back from a scoreless performance against Vandy by posting a double-double—12 points, 10

rebounds. This marked just the fifth time all season that five Wildcats hit for double figures.

Florida's John Egbunu led all scorers with 27 points.

The Cats were once again without the services of Willis, who remained sidelined with a severely sprained ankle.

When this season began, the two most celebrated incoming freshmen were Labissiere and LSU's Ben Simmons. Before the first tip-off, they were projected as the top two picks in the 2016 NBA draft. Simmons, for his part, lived up to the hype, while Labissiere struggled to the point that at times he was practically irrelevant. He had become the poster child for unfulfilled expectations.

But a funny thing happened in the Cats' season finale against LSU in Rupp Arena. In this game, which the Cats won 94-77, Labissiere clearly outplayed his fellow freshman, giving a splendid performance in which he scored 18 points, grabbed nine rebounds and blocked six LSU shots. Labissiere made good on 8 of 10 field goal attempts, most coming on mid-range jumpers.

Along with helping his team get revenge against the Tigers, Labissiere, the quiet kid from Haiti, suddenly became relevant once again.

Labissiere wasn't the only Wildcat to play well, In all, five players hit for double figures, led once again by Murray, who finished with 22 points. This was his tenth consecutive game in which he scored 20 or more points.

Ulis posted another double-double, accounting for 14 points and 14 assists, while Poythress and Lee each had a dozen points. Briscoe ended the game with eight points, with Willis, now off the injured list, chipping in with six.

Tim Quarterman led LSU with a game-high 23 points. Despite being outplayed by Labissiere, Simmons acquitted himself well, ending with 17 points and 11 rebounds.

The win left the Cats with a 23-8 record overall and a 13-5 SEC mark, good enough for a first-place tie with Texas A&M. However, thanks to a questionable call against the Cats in their loss at Texas A&M, the Aggies were the top seed in the SEC Tournament.

With a full roster and everyone healthy (for the first time all season), the Cats opened defense of their SEC Tournament title by taking on Alabama in Nashville. And the unfolding of this game bore an eerily similar resemblance to the two regular-season matchups between the long-time league foes.

For the third time, the Cats won handily (85-59), and for the third time, it was Poythress who led the charge.

The gifted senior, playing in his final SEC tourney, connected on four of five three-point tries en route to an outstanding 20-point, seven-rebound performance.

In three games against Bama, Poythress made good on 20 of 24 field goal attempts.

The Cats' outside bombing was the difference in this win. For the game, the Cats hit 13 treys in 22 attempts. Murray led the way, hitting five of nine. He ended the game with 23 points.

Ulis was the third Cat in double figures, finishing with 17 points.

Bama stayed close until just past the halfway mark of the opening stanza. At that point, the Cats went on a 19-4 run that had them on top 37-27 at the break. Bama sliced the difference to 34-27, but back-to-back treys by Ulis propelled the Cats to their relatively easy victory.

Arthur Edwards paced the Crimson Tide with 20 points.

The win sent the Cats into the semifinal round tussle with Georgia, a 65-64 upset winner over South Carolina.

There are times when the final outcome is not indicative of the way the game unfolded. That was certainly the case in the Cats' 93-80 victory over gritty Georgia, a game in which the Bulldogs were in charge for the first 30 minutes.

It took a supreme effort by the Cats' backcourt trio of Murray, Ulis and, especially, Briscoe to survive and advance to the title game. Although Briscoe scored 12 points and had seven assists—fewer points than either Murray or Ulis—he was the one who twice came up with crucial plays that helped his club take command. His putback of a missed three by Ulis put the Cats on top 68-67 with 8:16 remaining. It marked the first time the Cats owned the lead since early in the second half.

The Bulldogs rode 61.3 percent first-half shooting to a 49-44 lead at intermission. But in the second half, the Cats upped their defensive intensity, limiting the Bulldogs to just 35 percent shooting (9 of 26).

Meanwhile the Cats, sparked by Murray, Ulis, Briscoe and Willis, were able to take control in the final 10 min-

Dominique Hawkins applies defensive pressure against Louisville.

utes. Murray had 26 points, Ulis 25 and Willis 14 for the winners. Poythress ended the game with 10 points.

Yante Maten led Georgia with 20 points, while teammate J. J. Frazier added 19.

With this victory, the Cats moved into the championship game against top-seeded Texas A&M, a 79-77 overtime winner in the regular-season contest between the two clubs.

Very few SEC championship games have been more exciting or played at a higher level than the one between the Cats and the Aggies. Players on both teams performed with sustained intensity, fearlessness and courage. This was a prime-time game in every respect.

As with the first meeting between the two teams, this game also went into an extra period. But this time around, the Cats prevailed 82-77.

Heroes for UK were plenty. Ulis scored a career-high 30 points and dished out five assists. Murray tallied 17 points, while Briscoe, Poythress and Willis each contributed 10.

After trailing 38-34 at intermission, the Cats battled back to take a 50-45 lead with 14:03 remaining. The Aggies, led by Danuel House, rattled off eight unanswered points to go on top 53-50. Then the Cats, riding Ulis's hot hand, charged back to grab a 67-60 lead with just over four minutes left.

The score was 71-71 at the end of regulation.

With 1:01 remaining and the score tied at 75-75, Willis nailed a three-pointer from deep in the corner to put his team in front for good. Moments later, after House missed a shot, Murray connected on a trey that gave the Cats an 81-75 lead.

The school's 29th SEC tourney title was in the record books.

House paced the Aggies with a game-best 32 points.

Ulis was voted the tourney's Most Valuable Player. Murray joined him on the all-tournament squad.

Winning the SEC Tournament didn't earn the Cats any big favors when it came time for NCAA tourney seeding. Although many experts predicted the Cats, by virtue of winning the SEC event and their strong finish would likely be a No. 3 seed. It didn't happen. The Cats were seeded fourth in the power-filled East Regional, where potential opponents Indiana and North Carolina stood in the way of a trip to the Final Four.

The Cats opened tourney action by taking on 13th-seeded Stony Brook in Des Moines, Iowa. In a surprisingly easy 85-57 victory fueled by a dominant defensive performance, the Cats advanced to a second-round meeting against Indiana.

For the game, the Cats held Stony Brook to 26.3 percent shooting (20 of 76), while blocking 15 shots, the most by the team this season and the most in NCAA tourney action. Labissiere led by smacking away six enemy attempts.

Offensively, the Cats placed five players in double figures, headed by Murray's 19 points. Others included Briscoe with 13, Labissiere and Poythress with 12 each, and Ulis with 10. Willis added eight points, connecting on all three of his shots, two of which were treys.

Briscoe also pulled down 11 rebounds, while Ulis handed out seven assists, giving him 243 for the season, two better than the school-record 241 set by John Wall during the 2009-10 campaign.

Derek Willis nailed the go-ahead jumper against Texas A&M in the SEC title game.

Strong play early by Labissiere helped set the tone for this win. He came out ready for action, taking five of the Cats' first 10 shots and blocking five shots in the game's first 10 minutes. The Cats, despite getting only four points from Murray, owned a 33-19 lead at intermission.

With Murray getting untracked—scoring 15 of his 19 points after the break—the Cats rolled on, doubling the score to 50-25 on a Murray trey, which continued his streak of hitting at least one three-pointer in each of UK's 35 games.

The win sent the Cats into a second-round battle against Indiana, an easy 99-74 winner over Chattanooga.

Jubilant Wildcats were all smiles after capturing the SEC tourney hardware.

Ferrell finished with 18 points.

Ulis did his best to bring his club back by rattling off eight straight points. First, he knocked down a trey, then scored on a layup, and after being fouled while attempting a three-pointer, he sank all three free tosses. His heroic effort pulled the Cats to within 68-65 with 36.4 seconds remaining.

But the Hoosiers

Throughout this long season, it had become clear to everyone that the Cats' backcourt duo of Ulis and Murray were something special. They were the glue that held this club together. Rarely has a UK backcourt tandem played with such consistency and such poise.

But it was equally clear that if this Wildcat team was going to be something special, then the inside players had to perform at a high level on a consistent basis. The Cats were at their best when the so-called "bigs" played well; the losses occurred when they failed to produce.

Against Indiana, the Cats' big men were essentially a no-show, combining for 14 points on 5 of 16 shooting. On a night when Murray struggled offensively—he scored 16 points but connected on just one of nine from behind the three-point line—the Cats needed big numbers from their post players if they hoped to get past the Hoosiers. On this night, however, none of the Cats' inside players stepped up enough to overcome Murray's rare off-night from three-point range.

Ulis, the smallest player on the court, did step up. Going head to head against IU's superb point guard Yogi Ferrell, Ulis finished with 27 points, three assists and two steals.

Indiana led 33-32 at the half, then upped the lead to 38-32 early in the second half before Murray's only trey keyed a Wildcat run that put them in front 42-40 with 14:55 left to play.

With the score knotted at 50-50, the Hoosiers, sparked by freshman Thomas Bryant and the senior Ferrell, went on a 10-2 run that had them on top 60-52. Bryant scored 11 of his 19 points inside the final eight minutes, while

sealed the win when Bryant hit a pair of freebies with 10.4 seconds left.

The loss left the Cats with a final 27-9 record. It also marked the first time a Calipari-coached Wildcat club failed to advance past the second round.

Ulis and Murray both wrote their names into the UK record books. Murray's 720 points are most ever by a Wildcat freshman, and his 20-point scoring average tops all UK rookies. In addition, he is the only Wildcat freshman to score 30 points on more than one occasion; he cracked that mark three times.

Ulis ended his sophomore year with 246 assists, the single-season UK record.

A major honor was bestowed on Poythress when he was named the 2016 Arthur Ashe Jr. Athlete of the Year. Poythress, who had to overcome a series of injuries, was a four-time member of the SEC Academic Honor Roll.

Even though this season ended sooner than Big Blue Nation fans expected it to, and although several key players departed for the NBA, they know that the outlook going forward is anything but bleak. Once again, Calipari has hauled in a freighter load of talent, which, according to some experts, just might be his most-talented group yet, which is saying a lot, given his past recruiting achievements.

The new Wildcats include Malik Monk, Edrice Adebayo, De'Aaron Fox, Wenyen Gabriel and Sacha Killeya-Jones.

With that talented bunch ready to wear the blue and white, UK's future looks extremely bright.

UK Championship Victories

UK 46, Rhode Island 45

National Invitation Final
March 20, 1946
Madison Square Garden

UK captured its first national championship when gum-chewing freshman guard Ralph Beard dropped in a free throw with 40 seconds remaining to send the top-seeded Wildcats past Rhode Island 46-45 in the 1946 NIT title game. Beard's freebie settled a nip-and-tuck thriller in which there were 12 ties and never more than four points separating the two clubs in the final 17 minutes.

The Cats, an eight-point favorite, were trailing 45-44 with less than two minutes left when Dutch Campbell made good on one of two free throws to knot the score. Following a Rhode Island miss, the Cats rebounded and got the ball to Beard, who was immediately fouled. With 18,000 charged-up fans making their presence felt, Beard calmly sank the game-deciding free throw. The Rams had several chances to win, but failed to connect as time ran out.

Fouls plagued the Wildcats throughout the contest, and had it not been for the sterling efforts by subs Campbell, Buddy Parker and Joe Holland, the outcome would have been different. Jack Tingle and Wah Wah Jones both fouled out inside the last seven minutes.

In the early going, it looked as if the oddsmakers were on the mark. With the score tied at 15-15, a bucket each by Jack Parkinson, Jones and Beard and two free throws by Wilbur Schu gave the Cats a 23-16 advantage with five minutes left before halftime. But the Rams, fueled by tourney MVP Ernie Calverley, battled back to grab a 27-26 lead at the break.

The first half, though certainly exciting, was a funeral compared to the heart-pounding final 20 minutes that lay ahead.

The score was tied at 30, 34, 36 and 38 before the Rams went up 39-38 on a free throw by Dick Hole. After Beard laid in a crip shot to give UK a 40-39 lead, Rhode Island's Robert Shea shoved in a bucket while drawing the fifth

foul on Jones. Shea hit the free toss to up the Rams' lead to 42-40. Campbell and Parker each connected on a free throw to even the score, but the Rams quickly regained the lead when Calverley hit one of two from the charity stripe. Holland and Jack Allen swapped baskets, then Campbell hit his free throw to account for the final tie at 45-45 and set the stage for Beard's game-winner.

Beard led all scorers with 13 points, while Jones, UK's other marvelous freshman, finished with 10 before fouling out. Schu chipped in with nine.

Hole had 12 to lead Rhode Island.

The win gave the Wildcats a final record of 28-2.

Kentucky (46)	FG	FT	PF	TP
Tingle	2	1	5	5
Holland	1	0	0	2
Schu	3	3	1	9
Jones	3	4	5	10
Campbell	0	2	3	2
Parkinson	1	0	0	2
Beard	5	3	4	13
Parker	1	1	0	3
Totals	**16**	**14**	**18**	**46**

Rhode Island (45)	FG	FT	PF	TP
Hole	5	2	3	12
Nichols	5	1	4	11
Palmieri	0	0	2	0
Calverley	2	4	5	8
Goodwin	0	0	0	0
Shea	1	2	2	4
Allen	3	4	3	10
Schlafani	0	0	2	0
Totals	**16**	**13**	**21**	**45**

Halftime: Rhode Island 27, UK 26

UK 58, Baylor 42
NCAA Championship
March 23, 1948
Madison Square Garden

In a text book performance on both ends of the court, the powerful Wildcats capped their magnificent season by ripping outmanned Baylor 58-42 to claim the first of UK's

seven NCAA championships. This "Fabulous Five" club, which many consider to be UK's best-ever, finished the season with a 34-2 record.

With this win, UK became the second school to win NIT and NCAA championships. In addition, the 194 points scored by the Cats in their three NCAA tourney wins easily surpassed the old record of 179 set by Oklahoma A&M in 1945.

The outcome of the championship game was never in doubt. With Alex Groza doing the early damage, the Cats bolted to a 7-0 lead, and were on top 13-1 before Baylor managed its first bucket. UK owned a 29-16 lead at the half.

Midway through the second half, two baskets each by Ralph Beard and lefty Jim Line increased the Cats' lead to 44-28. The Bears rallied to trim the difference to 11, but Wah Wah Jones scored four unanswered points to put the game out of reach.

Groza, the tourney MVP, scored 14 points to lead all scorers. Beard tossed in 12, while Jones and Kenny Rollins each had nine.

By virtue of this victory, the Cats earned the right to participate in the Olympic Trials, which were also held in New York. The Cats defeated Louisville 91-57 and Baylor 77-59 before dropping a 53-49 decision to the AAU champion Phillips Oilers in the final game.

UK's starting five—Groza, Beard, Jones, Rollins and Cliff Barker—were named to the 1948 U.S. Olympic team. Rupp was the assistant coach. Later that summer in London, the five Wildcats helped the U.S. capture the gold medal. Groza was the team's top scorer with 76 points.

Kentucky (58)	FG	FTA	FTM	PF	TP
Jones	4	1	1	3	9
Barker	2	3	1	4	5
Line	3	1	1	3	7
Groza	6	4	2	4	14
Holland	1	0	0	1	2
Beard	4	4	4	1	12
Rollins	3	5	3	3	9
Barnstable	0	1	0	0	0
Totals	**23**	**19**	**12**	**19**	**58**

Baylor (42)	FG	FTA	FTM	PF	TP
Owen	2	2	1	0	5
DeWitt	3	4	2	3	8
Hickman	1	0	0	0	2

Pulley	0	1	1	0	1
Heathington	3	4	2	5	8
Preston	0	2	0	2	0
Johnson	3	7	4	5	10
Robinson	3	4	2	4	8
Brack	0	0	0	0	0
Totals	**15**	**24**	**12**	**19**	**42**

Halftime: UK 29, Baylor 16

UK 46, Oklahoma A&M 36

NCAA Championship
March 26, 1949
Seattle, Wash.

Red-hot Alex Groza put the thaw on Oklahoma A&M's deep freeze.

Groza, the 6'7" All-American center, scored 25 points to lead the defending national champion Wildcats to a 46-36 victory over the Aggies in Seattle. Groza repeated as tourney MVP after amassing a record 82 points in UK's three tourney wins.

The Cats' defense was equally brilliant, holding Henry Iba's talented club to just nine field goals for the game and only two in the final 20 minutes, with the first of those two buckets coming 13 minutes into the half. Jack Shelton, who had 12 points, was the only Aggie to solve UK's defense.

Tempo-minded Oklahoma A&M, after jumping to a quick 5-2 lead, sought to slow down the run-and-gun Wildcats. But that plan was foiled when Groza reeled off five unanswered points to give the Cats a 7-5 lead. By the half, the Cats, behind Groza's 15 points, were in front 25-20.

The second half was all UK, thanks to more scoring from Groza and a defense that completely shut down the Aggies' offense. The Cats increased their margin to 31-21 early in the second half, then coasted to their third national title in four years. UK won the 1946 NIT prior to taking home the NCAA tourney's top prize in 1948 and 1949. The Cats also reached the championship game of the 1947 NIT, losing to Utah 49-45.

This game marked the final appearance for Groza, Wah Wah Jones, Ralph Beard and Cliff Barker. All four would later join together to form the successful Indianapolis Olympians franchise in the NBA.

Kentucky (46)	FG	FTA	FTM	PF	TP
Jones	1	3	1	3	3
Line	2	2	1	3	5
Groza	9	8	7	5	25
Beard	1	2	1	4	3
Barker	1	3	3	4	5
Barnstable	1	1	1	1	3
Hirsch	1	0	0	1	2
Totals	**16**	**19**	**14**	**21**	**46**

Okla. A&M (36)	FG	FTA	FTM	PF	TP
Yates	1	0	0	1	2
Bradley	0	5	3	3	3
Harris	3	1	1	5	7
Parks	2	4	3	5	7
Shelton	3	7	6	4	12
Jaquet	0	2	1	0	1
McArthur	0	2	2	1	2
Pilgrim	0	2	2	1	2
Smith	0	0	0	1	0
Totals	**9**	**23**	**18**	**21**	**36**

Halftime: UK 25, Oklahoma A&M 20

UK 68, Kansas State 58

NCAA Championship
March 27, 1951
Minneapolis, Minn.

Despite having just six healthy players, the Wildcats brushed off Kansas State 68-58 to win their third NCAA championship in the past four years. With this victory, Kentucky became the first school to claim the NCAA crown three times.

Although the Cats went into the game with a 31-2 record, the oddsmakers tabbed Kansas State as a three-point favorite. Early on, it looked as if those bettors backing the morning spread were in line to collect some cash. Kansas State bolted to a 20-12 lead and appeared to be on the verge of breaking the game open.

At that point, UK coach Adolph Rupp sent an ailing Cliff Hagan into the game, and Hagan, who was suffering from an infected throat and high fever, quickly helped the Cats turn things around. Hagan and Bill Spivey led a charge that pulled the Cats to within 29-27 by halftime.

Peck	2	1	0	1	4
Schuyler	1	1	0	1	2
Totals	**23**	**20**	**12**	**31**	**58**

Halftime: Kansas State 29, UK 27

The final 20 minutes belonged to the Cats, and once again it was the defense that made the difference. With only two minutes having elapsed in the second half, the Cats had forged ahead 35-29. Moments later, thanks to a defense that held Kansas State without a bucket for almost nine minutes, the Cats had boosted their lead to 56-40.

Desperate Kansas State used a frantic full-court press to slice UK's lead to 58-48 with 4:40 left to play. But the Cats refused to fold under pressure. Two buckets by Hagan, a Spivey free throw and a layup by Skippy Whitaker ended the Kansas State threat and locked up the crown for UK.

Spivey paced the balanced Wildcat attack with 22 points and 21 rebounds. Hagan, the brilliant sophomore, finished with 10, while Frank Ramsey and Whitaker each had nine. Bobby Watson and Shelby Linville contributed eight apiece. Linville also pulled down eight rebounds for the Cats, who won the rebounding battle 45-30.

Lew Hitch led Kansas State with 13 points.

In addition to being hard hit by illness, the Cats were also without veteran Walt Hirsch, the regular-season starting forward. Hirsch, who averaged 9.1 during the regular campaign, was ineligible to participate in postseason action because he was a fifth-year senior.

Kentucky (68)	FG	FTA	FTM	PF	TP
Whitaker	4	1	1	2	9
Linville	2	8	4	5	8
Spivey	9	6	4	2	22
Ramsey	4	3	1	5	9
Watson	3	4	2	3	8
Hagan	5	2	0	5	10
Tsioropoulos	1	0	0	1	2
Newton	0	0	0	0	0
Totals	**28**	**24**	**12**	**23**	**68**

Kansas State (58)	FG	FTA	FTM	PF	TP
Head	3	2	2	5	8
Stone	3	8	6	5	12
Hitch	6	1	1	5	13
Barrett	2	2	0	1	4
Iverson	3	2	1	3	7
Housey	2	0	0	3	4
Gibson	0	1	1	5	1
Upson	0	0	0	1	0
Knostman	1	2	1	1	3

UK 84, Seattle 72

NCAA Championship
March 22, 1958
Louisville, Ky.

Thanks to 54 points from Vernon Hatton and Johnny Cox, some clever drives to the bucket by John Crigler and a superb effort off the bench by Don Mills, Adolph Rupp's "barnyard fiddlers" gave a Carnegie Hall-type performance in their 84-72 championship-game victory over Seattle in Freedom Hall.

It was UK's fourth NCAA title in the past 11 years. It would also turn out to be Rupp's last.

To win, the Cats had to overcome two 11-point deficits and a terrific 25-point, 19-rebound performance by Seattle's great All-American Elgin Baylor. They did so by playing near-perfect basketball in the final 10 minutes, and by getting Baylor into early foul trouble. It was Crigler's drives to the hoop that drew three fouls on Baylor before the intermission and a fourth with 16:44 left to play and UK on the short end of a 44-38 score.

With Baylor forced to play cautiously, the Cats, after falling behind 29-18, battled back to take a 61-60 lead on a bucket by Mills with just over six minutes left. A short jumper by Cox was followed by an Adrian Smith free throw that made it 64-60. Moments later, Hatton hit a freebie, missed the second, then grabbed the rebound and scored to up the Cats' lead to 67-60 with 4:18 remaining.

Seattle mounted one final drive, closing to within 68-65 on a three-point play by Baylor. But a Hatton jumper and two free throws by Cox killed the Seattle threat and put the game out of reach.

The win fulfilled a promise made by Rupp after the NCAA had suspended UK for the 1952-53 season: That he would not rest until the man who pronounced judgment against UK handed over another NCAA championship trophy.

Hatton led UK with 30 points, while Cox had 24, including 16 in the game's final 15 minutes. Crigler fin-

ished with 14 and Mills, subbing for foul-plagued Ed Beck, chipped in with nine points and five rebounds.

The Cats outrebounded Seattle 55-46, with Cox yanking down 16 and Crigler 14.

It was a storybook finish for a UK team that finished with 23-6 record and a No. 9 ranking in the AP's final regular season poll. Even Rupp had his doubts about this team. Prior to the season, he said:

"We're fiddlers, that's all. They're pretty good fiddlers—be right entertaining at a barn dance. But I'll tell you, you need violinists to play at Carnegie Hall. We don't have any violinists."

In the end, the team known as the "Fiddlin' Five" proved him wrong.

Kentucky (84)	FGA	FGM	FTA	FTM	RB	PF	TP
Crigler	12	5	7	4	14	4	14
Cox	23	10	4	4	16	3	24
Beck	1	0	1	0	3	4	0
Smith	8	2	5	3	6	4	7
Hatton	20	9	15	12	3	3	30
Mills	9	4	4	1	5	3	9
Totals	73	30	36	24	47	21	84

Seattle (72)	FGA	FGM	FTA	FTM	RB	PF	TP
Frizzell	6	4	11	8	5	3	16
Brown	17	6	7	5	5	5	17
Baylor	32	9	9	7	19	4	25
Harney	5	2	1	0	1	1	4
Saunders	2	0	0	0	2	3	0
Ogorek	7	4	2	2	11	5	10
Piasecki	0	0	0	0	0	0	0
Totals	69	25	30	22	43	21	72

Halftime: Seattle 39, UK 36

UK 71, UNCC 67
National Invitation Final
March 21, 1976
Madison Square Garden

Unheralded senior guard Reggie Warford, who had scored just three free throws in three previous tournament games, came through with 10 clutch second-half points to lift the foul-plagued Wildcats to a 71-67 come-from-

behind victory over UNCC in the NIT title game.

The win was the Cats' 10th in succession, giving them a final record of 20-10. It was also UK's first NIT championship since 1946.

Warford's heroics, and those of teammate Mike Phillips, were only part of the reason why the Cats prevailed. A strategic mistake by UNCC coach Lee Rose also played a big role in the ultimate outcome of this thriller. At the 10-minute mark, with his team leading 54-47, and with the entire UK frontline saddled with foul problems, Rose ordered his club to slow things down. It was a ploy that had disastrous results for the 49ers.

On the other side, everything UK coach Joe B. Hall tried came up roses. His most-important move was switching to a 1-3-1 zone defense, which not only stymied the 49ers, but also allowed Phillips, Jack Givens and James Lee, all of whom had four fouls, to avoid that fifth and fatal foul.

Warford led the comeback, and, appropriately, it was his driving layup that put the Cats in front 60-59. Seconds later, after the 49ers had reclaimed the lead, Warford hit a 15-foot jumper to give the Cats a 64-63 advantage with 1:07 remaining. Phillips, fouled on the play, hit a pair of free tosses to make it 66-63. Following a bucket by 49ers guard Melvin Watkins that made it 66-65, two free throws by Larry Johnson and a three-point play by Phillips inside the final 22 seconds sealed the win for UK.

Phillips and Johnson each had 16 points to lead UK. Warford, in his final game, finished with 14. UNCC's Cedric "Cornbread" Maxwell, the tourney MVP, led all scorers with 24.

The Cats managed their strong finish despite the absence of sophomore center Rick Robey, who went down with an injury after playing just 12 games. Robey was averaging 15.6 points at the time of his injury.

Kentucky (71)	FGA	FGM	FTA	FTM	RB	PF	TP
Givens	8	3	0	0	4	4	6
Lee	8	4	0	0	4	4	8
Phillips	13	5	9	6	7	4	16
Johnson	18	7	3	2	3	2	16
Warford	10	7	0	0	1	4	14
Casey	4	3	0	0	0	0	6
Fowler	2	2	2	1	2	2	5
Totals	63	31	14	9	21	20	71

UNCC (67)	FGA	FGM	FTA	FTM	RB	PF	TP
King	6	3	4	3	7	3	9
Massey	13	5	8	6	6	4	16
Maxwell	14	8	10	8	11	3	24
Ball	6	3	0	0	1	3	6
Watkins	7	4	1	0	5	3	8
Gruber	1	1	0	0	1	2	2
Pearce	0	0	2	2	1	2	2
Totals	**47**	**24**	**25**	**19**	**32**	**20**	**67**

Halftime: UNCC 37, UK 34

UK 94, Duke 88

NCAA Championship
March 27, 1978
St. Louis, Mo.

Sports Illustrated said it best: The Goose was Golden.

The Goose, in this instance, was Jack Givens, whose towering 41-point performance led the top-ranked Wildcats to a 94-88 victory over Duke in the NCAA championship game. It gave UK its fifth national title, and its first since the "Fiddlin' Five" club won it all in 1958.

This Wildcat team, unlike the famed Fiddlers, went into the season as heavy favorites to capture the crown. With the added weight of high expectations on their shoulders, this group of players lived an entire season inside a boiling pressure cooker. And at no time was that pressure greater than in the championship game against a young, upstart Blue Devil team that had the freedom to lose without feeling like failures.

It was Givens who gave the Cats some breathing room, scoring 16 of UK's final 18 points before the half to give his team a 45-38 lead at the break. The Blue Devils made just nine of 23 field goals in the first half, but managed to stay close by sinking 20 of 21 free throw attempts. The Cats, meanwhile, connected on 18 of 34 field goal attempts for 52.9 percent. Givens scored 23 points in the opening half.

Early in the second half, following a technical on Duke coach Bill Foster, two free throws by Kyle Macy and a Rick Robey dunk upped the Cats' advantage to 55-46. That lead swelled to 16 when a three-point play by Givens made it 66-50. The Cats continued to control the game, and were safely on top with just over a minute remaining when UK coach Joe B. Hall pulled his starters from the game. Almost immediately, the Blue Devils began to chop into UK's lead,

slicing the difference to 92-88 on a Mike Gminski jumper. Hall quickly inserted his starters back into the battle and the Cats were able to hang on for the victory.

The UK win was signed, sealed and delivered when James Lee took a long pass and slammed down one of his patented thunder dunks just ahead of the final horn.

Givens was simply unstoppable, hitting 18 of 27 from the field. His 41 points trail only Bill Walton (44) and Gail Goodrich (42) for the most scored in a championship game. To no one's surprise, Givens was voted MVP of the Final Four.

Robey also had a superb outing for the Cats, registering a double-double with 20 points and 11 rebounds. Macy helped spread the wealth around by dishing out eight assists.

Gene Banks had 22 to lead the Blue Devils. Jim Spanarkel and Gminski finished with 21 and 20, respectively.

The win left this UK team with a final record of 30-2.

Kentucky (94)	FGA	FGM	FTA	FTM	RB	PF	TP
Givens	27	18	8	5	8	4	41
Robey	11	8	6	4	11	2	20
Phillips	4	1	2	2	2	5	4
Macy	3	3	4	3	0	1	9
Claytor	5	3	4	2	0	2	8
Lee	8	4	0	0	4	4	8
Shidler	5	1	1	0	1	3	2
Aleksinas	0	0	0	0	0	1	0
Williams	3	1	0	0	4	2	2
Cowan	2	0	0	0	2	1	0
Stephens	0	0	0	0	0	0	0
Courts	0	0	0	0	0	0	0
Gettelfinger	0	0	0	0	0	0	0
Casey	0	0	0	0	0	1	0
Totals	**68**	**39**	**25**	**16**	**32**	**26**	**94**

Duke (88)	FGA	FGM	FTA	FTM	RB	PF	TP
Banks	12	6	12	10	8	2	22
Dennard	7	5	0	0	8	5	10
Gminski	16	6	8	8	12	3	20
Harrell	2	2	0	0	0	3	4
Spanarkel	16	8	6	5	2	4	21
Suddath	3	1	3	2	2	1	4
Bender	2	1	5	5	1	3	7
Goetsch	1	0	0	0	1	1	0
Totals	**59**	**29**	**34**	**30**	**34**	**22**	**88**

Halftime: UK 45, Duke 38

UK 76, Syracuse 67

NCAA Championship
April 1, 1996
East Rutherford, N.J.

With senior Tony Delk banging home a record-tying seven three-pointers and freshman Ron Mercer coming off the bench to score 20 points, the Wildcats captured the NCAA title with a 76-67 victory over Syracuse at the Meadowlands. The championship, UK's sixth, came just seven years after the proud basketball program had been leveled by NCAA sanctions and only five years since coming off probation.

It wasn't the prettiest win for a Wildcat team that had consistently played at the highest level throughout the season. The Cats shot poorly, hitting an uncharacteristically low 38.4 percent from the field. That's the worst accuracy by a champion since Loyola of Chicago hit a dismal 27.4 percent in its 1963 title win over Cincinnati.

After a close opening 10 minutes, the Cats took control when Mercer's three-point play broke a 28-28 tie and put the Cats on top 31-28. Two Delk treys, one by Mercer and a pair of free throws by Antoine Walker pushed the Cats to a 42-33 lead at the half. The Cats claimed the upper hand despite missing 12 of their first 15 shots.

Midway through the second half, the Cats reeled off 11 unanswered points to increase their lead to 59-46. Mercer started the run with a layup. That was followed by Walker's eight-footer, a trey by Mercer and a rare four-point play by Delk, who drained a three and was fouled on the play.

The Orangemen, led by John Wallace and Todd Burgan, chiseled into the UK lead, eventually pulling to within 64-62 with 4:46 remaining. But the gritty Cats responded with five straight points, a tip-in by Walter McCarty followed by a Derek Anderson trey, to go up 69-62. After Jason Cipolla and Mark Pope swapped 12-footers, a free throw by Walker, two more by Pope and a Delk layup sealed the win for UK.

Delk, the Final Four MVP, paced the Cats with 24 points, hitting on seven of 12 from three-point range. Mercer was the hottest Wildcat, connecting on eight of his 12 field goal attempts. Also in double figures for UK were Anderson and Walker with 11 each.

Wallace led all scorers with 29 points, while Burgan added 19.

Kentucky (76)	FGA	FGM	3FG	FTA	FTM	RB	PF	TP
Anderson	8	4	2-3	1	1	4	2	11
Walker	12	4	0-1	6	3	9	2	11
McCarty	6	2	0-0	0	0	7	3	4
Delk	20	8	7-12	2	1	7	2	24
Epps	6	0	0-3	0	0	4	1	0
Pope	6	1	0-2	2	2	3	3	4
Mercer	12	8	3-4	1	1	2	3	20
Sheppard	2	1	0-1	1	0	2	3	2
Edwards	1	0	0-1	0	0	0	0	0
Team			2					
Totals	**73**	**28**	**12-27**	**13**	**8**	**40**	**19**	**76**

Syracuse (67)	FGA	FGM	3FG	FTA	FTM	RB	PF	TP
Burgan	10	7	3-5	5	2	8	5	19
Wallace	19	11	2-3	5	5	10	5	29
Hill	9	3	0-0	1	1	10	2	7
Sims	5	2	1-4	2	1	2	2	6
Cipolla	8	3	0-3	0	0	1	1	6
Reafsnyder	1	0	0-0	0	0	4	0	0
Janulis	0	0	0-0	0	0	2	2	0
Nelson	0	0	0-0	0	0	0	0	0
Team			1					
Totals	**52**	**26**	**6-15**	**13**	**9**	**38**	**17**	**67**

Halftime: UK 42, Syracuse 33

UK 78, Utah 69

NCAA Championship
March 30, 1998
San Antonio, Texas

The "Comeback Cats" did something no team had ever done—rally from a 10-point halftime deficit in the final game to win the NCAA championship. The Cats clawed back from the grave for the third straight game, beating Utah 78-69 to take home the championship hardware for the second time in three years.

The win also made Tubby Smith the only UK coach to win a national championship in his first year on the job.

Utah used superior rebounding and a 10-0 run within the span of 90 seconds to build a 34-23 lead with 6:52 remaining before intermission. Andre Miller spearheaded the Utah drive, scoring a bucket and handing out assists to teammates Alex Jensen and Michael

Doleac. The Utes, who outrebounded UK 24-6 in the opening 20 minutes, held a 41-31 lead at the half. Only 12 Utah turnovers allowed the Cats to stay within striking distance.

Being behind at the half was nothing new to this UK club. Nine times during the season the Wildcats trailed at the break and came back to win. That's precisely what they had done in their two previous NCAA tourney games, beating Duke 86-84 and Stanford 86-85 in overtime.

The Cats still trailed 47-37 when Heshimu Evans scored eight quick points to spark the comeback rally. At the 7:49 mark, Cameron Mills drilled a three-pointer from the left corner to draw the Cats even at 58-58. Then, after making a steal, senior Jeff Sheppard, the Final Four MVP, scored on a dunk to give UK a two-point advantage. After Utah reeled off six straight points to reclaim a 64-60 lead, Mills knocked down another trey and Sheppard canned a short jumper from the right baseline to put the Cats back in front 65-64. They would never trail again, holding the weary Utes to only one bucket in the final 5:51. During one span, the Utes misfired on 11 straight shots.

Scott Padgett led UK with 17 points. Sheppard finished with 16, while Evans and Nazr Mohammed each contributed 10. Miller paced the Utes with 16 points.

The Cats ended the season with a final record of 35-4, marking the third consecutive 30-win season and the 10th overall.

Kentucky (78)	FGA	FGM	3FG	FTA	FTM	RB	PF	TP
Edwards	7	2	0-3	0	0	1	0	4
Padgett	11	6	1-5	4	4	5	4	17
Mohammed	9	5	0-0	0	0	2	4	10
Turner	5	2	0-1	4	2	2	0	6
Sheppard	14	7	0-2	2	2	4	1	16
Magloire	3	2	0-0	3	3	2	4	7
Evans	4	3	2-2	2	2	6	1	10
Mills	4	2	2-4	2	2	0	0	8
Smith	0	0	0-0	0	0	0	0	0
Bradley	0	0	0-0	0	0	1	1	0
Team			1					
Totals	**57**	**29**	**5-17**	**17**	**15**	**24**	**15**	**78**

Utah (69)	FGA	FGM	3FG	FTA	FTM	RB	PF	TP
Mottola	10	4	1-3	6	6	8	4	15
Jensen	6	5	1-1	3	3	2	2	14
Doleac	12	5	1-1	6	4	10	2	15
Miller	15	6	0-3	7	4	6	5	16
Hansen	6	1	0-2	0	0	5	2	2
Johnsen	4	3	1-2	0	0	4	0	7
McTavish	0	0	0-0	0	0	0	1	0
Jackson	1	0	0-1	0	0	0	2	0
Caton	1	0	0-1	0	0	0	0	0
Team			4					
Totals	**55**	**24**	**4-14**	**22**	**17**	**39**	**18**	**69**

Halftime: Utah 41, UK 31

Jeff Sheppard tossed in 16 points to help the Wildcats beat Utah 78-69 in the 1998 NCAA championship game. Sheppard's outstanding play earned him the MVP trophy.

UK 67, Kansas 59

NCAA Championship
April 2, 2012
New Orleans, La.

Behind 22 points from Doron Lamb and 16 rebounds, six points and six blocked shots by the marvelous Anthony Davis, Kentucky claimed its eighth national championship by beating Kansas 67-59 in New Orleans.

This marked UK first national title since 1998, and the first for head coach John Calipari.

The Cats won it, thanks to a strong first-half performance in which they rode 53 percent shooting (16 of 30) to a 41-27 advantage at intermission. At one point the Cats led by 18 (39-21) before Kansas managed to whittle the difference to 14 at the break.

But Kansas was too good to simply toss in the towel and head for the exit. Led by Tyshawn Taylor and Thomas Robinson, the Jayhawks fought back, eventually slicing the difference to 62-57 with 1:37 remaining.

Davis connected on one of two free tosses to make it 63-57, then following a Kansas miss, Marquis Teague dropped in a pair of freebies to give the Cats an eight-point cushion (65-57).

With 40 ticks remaining, Taylor buried a jumper to cut the margin to 65-59. But Lamb sealed it for the Cats by sinking two free throws with 17 seconds left the play.

Davis, despite scoring only six points on 1 of 10 shooting, was named the Final Four MVP.

Along with Lamb's 22 points, other Cats in double figures included Teague with 14 and Michael Kidd-Gilchrist with 11. Terrence Jones finished with nine points and seven rebounds.

Taylor and Robinson led Kansas with 19 and 18 points, respectively. Robinson also yanked down 17 rebounds.

It was a Jones dunk that triggered the Cats' big first-half surge. With his team in front 19-14, Jones slammed down his dunk, igniting a 20-7 run that upped the Cats' advantage to 39-21.

Shooting-wise, the game was a tale of two very different halves for the Cats. After registering that 53 percent number during the opening half, they managed to shoot just 26.9 percent (7 of 26) during the second half. For the game, that computes to 41.1 percent.

Thanks to Davis, the Cats won the rebounding war 43-35.

Kentucky (67)	FGA	FGM	3FG	FTA	FTM	RB	PF	TP
Jones	7	4	0-1	2	1	7	4	9
Davis	10	1	0-0	6	4	16	2	6
Kidd-Gilchrist	7	4	0-1	4	3	6	2	11
Lamb	12	7	3-6	6	5	2	2	22
Teague	14	5	2-3	3	2	2	2	14
Miller	5	2	1-2	0	0	6	2	5
Vargas	0	0	0-0	0	0	0	1	0
Wiltjer	1	0	0-1	0	0	0	0	0
Totals	**56**	**23**	**6-14**	**21**	**15**	**43**	**15**	**67**

Kansas (59)	FGA	FGM	3FG	FTA	FTM	RB	PF	TP
Robinson	17	6	0-0	7	6	17	2	18
Withey	8	2	0-0	1	1	7	2	5
Taylor	17	8	1-1	3	2	4	1	19
Johnson	13	5	3-7	0	0	2	1	13
Releford	6	1	1-2	2	1	1	5	4
Teahan	1	0	0-1	0	0	0	1	0
Wesley	0	0	0-0	0	0	0	0	0
Young	0	0	0-0	2	0	3	4	0
Totals	**62**	**22**	**5-11**	**15**	**10**	**35**	**16**	**59**

Halftime: UK 41, Kansas 27

John Calipari holds UK's eighth national championship trophy.

Anthony Davis was named Final Four MVP after leading UK to the title.

UK's Greatest Games

UK 20, Georgia 19

SIAA Championship
March 1, 1921
Atlanta, Ga.

Bill King's free throw after the timer's gun had sounded gave the Wildcats a 20-19 victory over Georgia in the championship game of the Southern Intercollegiate Athletic Association Tournament. The Cats easily advanced through the tourney draw, beating Tulane 50-28, Mercer 49-25 and Mississippi A&M 28-13 to set up the championship battle against Georgia.

The final was a tense, close struggle from beginning to end, with the two clubs never separated by more than three points. The Cats led 8-7 at the half.

After a see-saw second half, the Bulldogs claimed a 19-17 lead with a minute remaining. UK's Basil Hayden got free and scored a bucket to even the count at 19-19 with 45 ticks left on the clock. On the ensuing center jump, UK's Bobby Lavin came up with the ball, then fired a pass to teammate Paul Adkins near the bucket. As Adkins went up for a sure basket, he was fouled hard by a Georgia player.

Back then, one player was usually designated to shoot all of his team's free throws. King was UK's man. Also, in those days the clock didn't stop while free throws were being shot. However, a game could not end until the player had finished shooting.

As King lifted his arms to shoot, the timer's pistol was discharged. With the crowd now deathly silent, King calmly fired his free toss. The ball hit the rim, eased slightly to the right, then fell through, giving the Wildcats a 20-19 win and the tourney title.

The Wildcats finished the season with a record of 13-1.

Hundreds of adoring fans were on hand to meet the triumphant Wildcats when they arrived back in Lexington. This was the first time UK fans celebrated a championship with their conquering Big Blue heroes. It would not be the last.

UK 60, Notre Dame 55

Jan. 23, 1943
Louisville, Ky.

After seven unsuccessful tries, Adolph Rupp finally got his first win over Notre Dame.

With more than 6,000 fans looking on in the Jefferson County Armory, the Wildcats, led by Marvin "Big Train" Akers, wiped out a 10-point second-half deficit and went on to upset the unbeaten Irish 60-55.

The Cats survived despite losing Akers, Milt Ticco and Kenny Rollins to fouls. Superb play by reserves Ed Lander, Paul Noel, Bill Barlow and Clyde Parker enabled the Cats to hang on for the victory.

After six first-half ties, the Irish finally managed to ease ahead 33-27 by intermission. That lead ballooned to 37-27 early in the second stanza before Akers and the Wildcats began to crank up the intensity. The Cats shaved the difference to 49-47, then grabbed the upper hand when Akers converted on a three-point play to make it 50-49. Moments later, after Akers had been whistled to the sidelines, the Irish once again evened the count at 52-52. That would be Notre Dame's final hurrah. On UK's next possession, a magnificent pivot shot by Mel Brewer ignited a 6-0 run that put the Wildcats in front for good.

The Cats had five more buckets than Notre Dame (25-20), but the Irish stayed in contention by hitting 15 free throws to UK's 10.

Akers paced the Cats with 17 points. Ticco finished with 10, while Mulford "Muff" Davis added 12. Bob Rensberger led the Irish with 17.

Following the game, a jubilant Akers said, "It was a great game for Adolph Rupp. He is now thoroughly convinced that all things come to those who wait."

Kentucky (60)	FG	FT	PF	TP
Ticco	7	2	4	16
Davis	6	0	1	12
Brewer	3	3	2	9
Akers	8	1	4	17
Rollins	0	0	4	0
Noel	0	2	1	2
Lander	1	0	0	2
Parker	0	1	1	1
Barlow	0	1	0	1
Totals	**25**	**10**	**17**	**60**

Notre Dame (55)	FG	FT	PF	TP
Butler	2	2	0	6
Nemeira	1	1	4	3
Faught	6	4	2	16
Rensberger	6	5	2	17
Kuka	4	2	2	10
Curran	1	1	4	3
Brennan	0	0	3	0
Davis	0	0	1	0
Bonnicelli	0	0	0	0
Klier	0	0	0	0
Totals	**20**	**15**	**18**	**55**

Halftime: Notre Dame 33, UK 27

Utah 49, UK 45

NIT Championship
March 24, 1947
New York, N.Y.

In a stunning upset, unheralded Utah bumped off the heavily favored Wildcats 49-45 to win the 1947 NIT title. Going into the game, virtually no one gave the Utes a chance against a powerful UK club that had put together a 34-2 record.

But on this night, with a record crowd of 18,493 looking on, Utah outplayed and outscrapped the mighty Wildcats, who were defending the crown they won a year earlier. The Utes also put the clamps on UK's great Ralph Beard, holding the fiery guard to a single free throw. Many years later, Beard would say, "I still have nightmares about this game."

The game was a battle of wills, with each club looking to impose its style of play on the opposition. The Cats looked to run at every opportunity, the Utes wanted to play at a more deliberate pace. Utah bucked the odds by controlling the tempo, seldom allowing the run-oriented Wildcats to get untracked.

Utah led all the way, eventually building a lead of seven points late in the game. After the Cats rallied to within 45-44 with three minutes left, Utah standouts Arnie Ferrin and Vern Gardner wrapped a bucket apiece around a single free throw by Wah Wah Jones to account for the final score.

Ferrin and Gardner shared game-high scoring honors with 15 points each. Alex Groza and Jim Line led UK with 12 points apiece.

Another hero for the winning Utes was diminutive guard Wat Misaka, who spent the night making life miserable for

Beard. Beard went into the game averaging 11 points, and had earlier been voted the most outstanding visiting player to perform in Madison Square Garden that season by the New York sportswriters.

Kentucky (45)	FG	FT	PF	TP
Holland	1	0	3	2
Jones	2	4	4	8
Groza	5	2	4	12
Tingle	0	0	1	0
Barker	1	0	0	2
Rollins	2	0	2	4
Line	6	0	5	12
Beard	0	1	0	1
Jordan	1	2	4	4
Totals	**18**	**9**	**23**	**45**

Utah (49)	FG	FT	PF	TP
Watson	3	7	4	13
Misaka	0	2	2	2
Gardner	5	5	4	15
Ferrin	6	3	4	15
Weidner	1	2	1	4
Clark	0	0	1	0
Totals	**15**	**19**	**16**	**49**

Halftime: Utah 27, UK 21

UK 60, Holy Cross 52

NIT Semifinal
March 20, 1948
New York, N.Y.

Alex Groza may have provided the big scoring numbers, but it was Kenny Rollins who stole the show in the Cats' impressive 60-52 NCAA tourney semifinal win over Holy Cross in Madison Square Garden. Rollins, UK's Minister of Defense, with occasional relief from Dale Barnstable, held Holy Cross All-American Bob Cousy to a lone field goal and six points overall, nearly 15 below his season average.

Holy Cross came in with a 25-3 record, a 19-game winning streak and an unbeaten mark in Madison Square Garden. But the Cats, a five-point favorite, rode an early scoring burst by Ralph Beard to break away from a 7-7 deadlock and seize control of the game.

The Cats owned a 36-28 lead at the half, and were in front

by 14 when the Crusaders made a run, pulling to within four points. Following a timeout, the Cats reeled off seven unanswered points—five by Wah Wah Jones and two by Groza—to put the game away. Jones keyed the run with a one-hander from the side, then immediately followed that by knocking down a shot from the top of the key. After Groza scored in close, Jones ended the 7-0 blitz by sinking a free throw.

Groza led the Cats with 23 points, while the duo of Beard and Jones finished with 13 and 12, respectively. Rollins, the defensive ace, also chipped in with eight points.

George Kaftan had 15 to lead the Crusaders.

Three nights later, UK beat Baylor 58-42 to win the school's first NCAA championship.

Kentucky (60)	FG	FT	PF	TP
Jones	4	4	3	12
Barker	2	0	4	4
Line	0	0	1	0
Groza	10	3	4	23
Holland	0	0	0	0
Beard	6	1	1	13
Rollins	3	2	3	8
Barnstable	0	0	2	0
Totals	**25**	**10**	**18**	**60**

Holy Cross (52)	FG	FT	PF	TP
Oftring	4	4	2	12
McMullan	0	0	3	0
Cousy	1	4	5	6
O'Connell	3	3	2	9
Kaftan	6	3	2	15
Bollinger	1	0	0	2
Curran	3	0	5	6
Forman	0	0	1	0
Mullaney	0	0	0	0
Laska	1	0	1	2
Totals	**19**	**14**	**21**	**52**

Halftime: UK 36, Holy Cross 28

Phillips 66ers 53, UK 49

Olympic Trials Championship
March 31, 1948
New York, N.Y.

Decades before the UK-Duke classic in 1992, this was

labeled "the greatest game of all-time."

In a thrilling matchup between the AAU and NCAA championship clubs, the Phillips 66ers edged past UK 53-49 in front of 18,475 fans in New York's famed Madison Square Garden. By virtue of his team's victory, 66ers coach Bud Browning was named head coach of the 1948 U.S. Olympic team. UK's Adolph Rupp was named Browning's assistant.

To win, the 66ers had to overcome a marvelous 23-point performance by UK guard Ralph Beard. The great Wildcat backcourt ace carried a UK team that was hampered by the early departure of starters Cliff Barker (broken nose) and Wah Wah Jones (fouls). Barker suffered his injury midway through the first half, while Jones, the Cats' main combatant in the rebounding wars, fouled out in the final 20 minutes.

With Beard leading the charge, UK bolted to a 20-13 lead with eight minutes left in the first half. The 66ers, sparked by seven-foot center Bob Kurland, answered with an 11-0 run that put them in front 24-20. The two clubs battled to a 26-26 standstill by the half.

The second half featured more of the same, with the lead bouncing back and forth like a tennis ball. With just over six minutes remaining, Beard racked up a three-point play to give UK a 47-45 lead. That would be the last time the Cats held the upper hand.

A bucket in close by Kurland, a free throw apiece by Gerald Tucker and Jesse Renick, and a short jumper by Kurland pushed the 66ers in front 51-47. After Kurland rebounded a Wildcat miss, the 66ers put the ball in the deep freeze, killing the clock until Kurland scored with 43 ticks left to play. Seconds later, UK's Dale Barnstable banked in a short shot to account for the final 53-49 score.

Kurland paced the 66ers with 20 points. He also held UK's high-scoring center Alex Groza to one field goal and four points.

The five starters from both clubs, along with four other players, were chosen to represent the U.S. in the 1948 Olympic Games in London. Five months later, the U.S. team blasted France 65-21 to capture the gold medal. Groza led the U.S. team in scoring with 76 points.

Kentucky (49)	FG	FT	PF	TP
Barker	1	2	1	4
Holland	2	1	5	5
Rollins	2	2	4	6
Groza	1	2	3	4
Jones	1	3	5	5
Line	0	0	1	0
Barnstable	1	0	0	2
Beard	11	1	3	23
Totals	**19**	**11**	**22**	**49**

Phillips 66ers (53)	FG	FT	PF	TP
Beck	2	0	1	4
Jones	0	0	0	0
Pitts	0	1	1	1
Renick	4	3	2	11
Kurland	9	2	3	20
Carpenter	1	1	4	3
Beisner	0	0	0	0
Nash	0	2	2	2
Tucker	3	3	3	9
Reich	1	1	1	3
Totals	**20**	**13**	**17**	**53**

Halftime: UK 26, 66ers 26

UK 68, Kansas 39

Dec. 16, 1950
Lexington, Ky.

It was billed as a "battle of the giants."

It turned out to be a giant mismatch.

Bill Spivey, UK's 7'1" center, completely dominated his counterpart, Kansas' 6'9" Clyde Lovellette, winning their personal scoring duel 22-10. The result was an easy 68-39 UK victory over the fourth-ranked Jayhawks in Memorial Coliseum.

The final numbers don't accurately reflect the totality of Spivey's personal triumph in his head-to-head battle with Lovellette. Only the (rare) kindness of Rupp kept the destruction from being even more complete. When Lovellette was sent to the sidelines after committing his fifth foul, Rupp removed Spivey from the game for good. There was still 13:33 left to play.

When asked why he lifted Spivey with so much time still remaining, Rupp said, "We wanted the playing time to be exactly even. We wanted it just that way. We had a commanding lead, too."

The Cats got off to a ragged start, and were leading 8-5 midway through the first half. Then Spivey and Frank

Ramsey caught fire, rattling off 12 straight points to give the Cats a 20-6 lead. Ramsey started the run by sinking back-to-back buckets. Spivey followed with three straight baskets, the first coming after a steal, a coast-to-coast dribble and a dunk. Ramsey ended the UK surge by laying in an easy crip shot.

The Cats led 28-12 at the half, with Spivey and Ramsey having accounted for 22 of their team's points.

The second half was all UK. Spivey and Walt Hirsch opened the final frame by hitting a bucket each to increase the margin to 20—32-12. After the Jayhawks closed to within 36-21, Ramsey and Shelby Linville each scored a basket and Spivey added two more buckets to make it 44-21. That's when Lovellette fouled out and Rupp pulled Spivey.

Spivey made good on nine of 16 field goal attempts before leaving. Lovellette connected on just four of 17.

With Ramsey and Bobby Watson burning from long range, the Cats pushed their lead 64-33 before Rupp began clearing the bench.

Ramsey finished with 19 points and Hirsch added 10.

Kentucky (68)	FG	FT	PF	TP
Hirsch	5	0	2	10
Linville	4	0	1	8
Price	0	0	1	0
Newton	0	0	1	0
Spivey	9	4	3	22
Tsioropoulos	1	0	4	2
Ramsey	8	3	4	19
Watson	3	0	1	6
Whitaker	0	2	1	2
Castle	0	0	0	0
Totals	**30**	**8**	**18**	**68**

Kansas (39)	FG	FT	PF	TP
Linehard	3	0	2	6
Kenney	1	2	0	4
Beck	0	1	0	1
Bull	1	2	0	4
Hoag	1	0	0	2
Enns	0	0	0	0
Lovellette	4	2	5	10
Houghland	2	3	0	7
Waugh	0	0	0	0
Schaake	1	1	1	3
Engel	1	0	0	2
Wells	0	0	1	0
Totals	**14**	**11**	**9**	**39**

Halftime: UK 28, Kansas 12

UK 86, Temple 59

Dec. 5, 1953
Lexington, Ky.

With 13,000 screaming fans on hand, senior pivotman Cliff Hagan shattered UK's single-game scoring mark by tossing in 51 points in an easy 86-59 romp past Temple in the season opener. It marked the Cats' first outing in almost two years, having spent the 1952-53 campaign on the sidelines due to NCAA sanctions.

The silky-smooth Hagan was splendid, making good on 17 field goals and 17 free tosses en route to his record-breaking performance. So dominant was Hagan that he equaled Temple's first-half output of 20 points. However, it wasn't until he scored 13 points in the third quarter that fans began to sense that something special was in the works.

But getting there turned out to be anything but easy for the exhausted Hagan. With just over three minutes left, Hagan's total stood at 45. After missing several shots, Hagan knocked down two buckets to push his output to 49. No Wildcat player or SEC player had ever cracked the half-century mark, and by now his teammates were bent on seeing Hagan become the first to do so. With 43 seconds remaining, Hagan drew a foul and stepped to the charity stripe for a pair of freebies. He missed both attempts. The Memorial Coliseum crowd let out a collective groan, thinking that history wasn't destined to be made on this night. But just moments later, sophomore guard Linville Puckett grabbed a rebound and fired a perfect length-of-the-floor pass to Hagan, who calmly dropped in the easy crip shot for his 50th and 51st points.

Thanks to Hagan's hot hand, the Cats controlled the game from the start, jumping out to an 18-11 advantage after one quarter. That lead swelled to 37-20 by the halfway mark. After that, the only excitement remaining was generated by Hagan's quest for the record.

Frank Ramsey, the Cats' other great senior, hit for 10 points, while Lou Tsioropoulos and Billy Evans each scored seven.

Al Didriksen paced the Owls with 15 points.

Kentucky (86)	FG	FT	PF	TP

Smith	1	0	2	2
Dankes	0	0	2	0
Mohr	0	0	2	0
Miller	2	2	1	6
Didriksen	5	5	1	15
Lear	3	7	1	13
Totals	**19**	**21**	**24**	**59**

Score by quarters

Kentucky	18	19	22	27	86
Temple	11	9	18	21	59

UK 73, La Salle 60

UKIT Championship
Dec. 22, 1953
Lexington, Ky.

This game may have only been for the championship of the inaugural UKIT, but it ended up being something much more important.

The Cats beat La Salle 73-60 for their sixth win in as many outings. They would go on to win all 25 games this season, then pass on the chance to play for the NCAA championship after learning that the club's three best players—Cliff Hagan, Frank Ramsey and Lou Tsioropoulos—were declared ineligible for postseason action because they were graduate students.

The 1954 NCAA tourney champ: La Salle.

In a game highlighted by the long-awaited meeting between Hagan and Tom Gola, it was La Salle that took control early, jumping to a 13-4 lead midway through the first quarter. But the Cats dug in, scoring 12 unanswered points to grab a 16-13 lead at the end of the first stanza. Ramsey's three-point play keyed UK's spurt. Hagan followed with two free throws and a layup, Phil Grawemeyer scored on a tip-in, Tsioropoulos hit one of two free throws and Hagan cashed in another pair of freebies with one second left in the period.

La Salle reclaimed a 21-18 lead, but a tip-in by Tsioropoulos and a pair of Hagan buckets put the Cats on top for good. They led 32-27 at the half and 45-38 at the end of three quarters. The Cats steadily increased their lead in the final frame, eventually leading by as many as 15 on three occasions.

Hagan easily won his individual showdown with Gola, leading all scorers with 28 points. But Hagan wasn't the lone Wildcat hero. Tsioropoulos was brilliant on both ends of the court, scoring 18 points while holding the high-scoring Gola to five points through three quarters and 16

Cliff Hagan soars up for two of his 51 points in the Cats' easy 1953-54 season-opening romp past Temple.

Tsioropoulos	3	1	5	7
Grawemeyer	1	0	0	2
Evans	3	1	3	7
Bird	0	0	2	0
Bibb	0	0	1	0
Hagan	17	17	2	51
Ramsey	4	2	5	10
Rose	1	2	5	4
C. Evans	0	0	0	0
Puckett	2	0	3	4
Coy	0	0	1	0
Curry	0	1	0	1
Totals	**31**	**24**	**27**	**86**

Temple (59)	**FG**	**FT**	**PF**	**TP**
Silcox	2	4	5	8
Sylvester	1	0	5	2
Reinfeld	5	2	0	12
Kane	0	1	5	1

overall. Grawemeyer also turned in a superb effort, coming off the bench to score 13 points for the Wildcats.

Kentucky (73)	FG	FT	PF	TP
Tsioropoulos	6	6	4	18
Evans	2	1	2	5
Grawemeyer	6	1	2	13
Hagan	10	8	0	28
Ramsey	3	3	4	9
Rose	0	0	1	0
Totals	**27**	**19**	**13**	**73**

La Salle (60)	FG	FT	PF	TP
O'Malley	1	2	3	4
Singley	3	1	1	7
Blatcher	2	1	2	5
Ames	0	2	0	2
Greenberg	0	0	0	0
Yodsnukis	4	1	4	9
Gola	6	4	2	16
Maples	3	1	4	7
O'Hara	4	2	1	10
Totals	**23**	**14**	**17**	**60**

Score by quarters

Kentucky	16	16	13	28	73
La Salle	13	14	11	22	60

UK 63, LSU 56

SEC Playoff
March 9, 1954
Nashville, Tenn.

Frank Ramsey scored 30 points and Cliff Hagan added 17 as the Wildcats defeated LSU 63-56 in a one-game playoff to decide the SEC championship. Because of a scheduling conflict, the two teams, both unbeaten in league play, had not met during the regular season, thus forcing a head-to-head battle for all the marbles.

Moments after the victory was secured, UK officials announced that the Wildcats, although owning a 25-0 record, would not participate in the NCAA Tournament. UK made the decision after learning that fifth-year seniors Hagan, Ramsey and Lou Tsioropoulos were ineligible because they were graduate students.

For a while it appeared that the academic status of "The

Big Three" wasn't going to matter. After the Cats took an early 25-14 advantage, LSU slowly began chipping into the lead, closing to within 32-28 at the half. Then in the third period, with UK on top 36-32, the Tigers scored eight straight points, four each by Ned Clark and Don Sebastian, to take a 40-36 lead. It marked the only time all season that the Wildcats trailed in the second half.

After Ramsey stopped the bleeding by coming through with a three-point play, LSU All-American Bob Pettit nailed a jumper to give the Tigers a 42-39 lead. Tsioropoulos tied it with a three-point play, then the two teams traded a pair of buckets each to make it 46-46 heading into the final quarter.

In that tense, frantic fourth period, it was Ramsey who stood the tallest. The Madisonville native scored 10 crucial points to help the Cats survive their toughest struggle all season. It was a Ramsey jumper with eight minutes remaining that put UK in front for good at 50-49.

Following a bucket each by Ramsey and Pettit, it was Hagan's time to take over. Hagan hit a free throw, then knocked down one of his patented hook shots to give the Cats a 55-51 lead and some breathing room. A minute later, Ramsey sliced through the LSU defense to lay in a crip shot

Frank Ramsey's 30-point performance lifted the Wildcats to a tough SEC-clinching 63-56 victory over LSU.

that made it 57-51. In the final moments, clever dribbling by Gayle Rose and Willie Rouse, along with deadly free throw accuracy, enabled the Cats to put away LSU and close out their season with an unblemished record.

It was a fitting yet unsatisfying end to the careers of Ramsey, Hagan and Tsioropoulos, who were, in essence, punished for having succeeded in the classroom. All three were superb against the Tigers—Ramsey led all scorers with 30 points, Hagan finished with 17 and Tsioropoulos held Pettit to 17 points, 15 below his season average.

Pettit pulled down 21 rebounds for the Tigers.

Kentucky (63)	FG	FT	PF	TP
Tsioropoulos	1	1	3	3
Evans	1	1	5	3
Grawemeyer	0	0	0	0
Hagan	7	3	4	17
Ramsey	13	4	3	30
Puckett	1	1	2	3
Rose	1	5	0	7
Rouse	0	0	1	0
Totals	**24**	**15**	**18**	**63**

LSU	FG	FT	PF	TP
Clark	6	2	2	14
McNeilly	1	0	0	2
Belcher	3	3	1	9
Pettit	6	5	4	17
Magee	0	1	2	1
Sebastian	4	0	1	8
McArdle	1	3	3	5
Jones	0	0	0	0
Zinser	0	0	1	0
Totals	**21**	**14**	**14**	**56**

Score by quarters

UK	18	14	14	17	63
LSU	11	17	18	10	56

Georgia Tech 59, UK 58

Jan. 8, 1955
Lexington, Ky.

The silence was deafening, the realization of what just happened almost impossible to believe. Or accept.

Georgia Tech 59, UK 58.

In Memorial Coliseum, no less. An NCAA-record 129-game home-court winning streak, dating back to Jan. 2, 1943, had just come to a sudden and unexpected end. When the final horn sounded, most Wildcat fans, the majority of whom had never seen UK lose in person, sat in stunned silence. Only after a few minutes did they slowly begin to make their way out of the Coliseum.

Georgia Tech won it on a 12-foot jump shot by Joe Helms with 12 seconds left to play. The Cats had two chances to avoid the upset, but when both shots—a jumper by Linville Puckett and Phil Grawemeyer's tip-in attempt—missed their mark, it was celebration time for the visitors.

In every way, this was a shocker of major proportions. The Cats, 7-0 at the time, had already chalked up impressive wins over Xavier, La Salle and St. Louis. Georgia Tech, on the other hand, came in with a 2-4 record. The UK coaches were so confident of victory that they didn't even bother to scout the lightly regarded Yellow Jackets.

Many years later, Adolph Rupp told Cawood Ledford that the two worst disasters of his lifetime were Pearl Harbor and this loss to Georgia Tech.

The Cats trailed 26-23 at the intermission, then fell behind 38-30 early in the second half. At the 10-minute mark, a bucket by Grawemeyer keyed an 8-0 run that put the Cats on top 52-46. Georgial Tech rallied, hitting four free throws and a field goal to draw even with just under five minutes left.

After Puckett scored for the Cats, Helms hit one of two free throws and Dick Lenholt added two more freebies to give Georgia Tech a 55-54 lead. Bob Burrow and Grawemeyer combined for four unanswered points to make it 58-55 before Tech's Bobby Kimmel dropped in a pair of free throws to cut the difference to a single point with 1:12 remaining.

With 24 ticks left, following a jump ball, Helms moved in, swiped the ball from Billy Evans and put up the game-winning jumper.

Georgia Tech, which used only five players, was led by Helms with 23 points. Kimmel had 18 and Lenny Cohen added 10.

Grawemeyer topped the UK attack with 19, while Burrow and Puckett scored 16 and 10, respectively.

The Yellow Jackets did it again less than a month later, stinging UK 65-59 in Atlanta.

Kentucky (58)	FG	FT	PF	TP

Bird	3	1	1	7
Grawemeyer	8	3	4	19
Burrow	7	2	4	16
Mills	0	0	3	0
Puckett	5	0	3	10
Evans	1	3	4	5
Rose	0	1	1	1
Totals	**24**	**10**	**20**	**58**

Georgia Tech (59)	FG	FT	PF	TP
L. Cohen	5	0	4	10
Lenholt	0	4	4	4
B. Cohen	2	0	1	4
Helms	7	9	1	23
Kimmel	4	10	2	18
Totals	**18**	**23**	**12**	**59**

Halftime: Georgia Tech 26, UK 23

UK 85, Temple 83 (3OT)

Dec. 7, 1957
Lexington, Ky.

Vernon Hatton simply refused to let the Wildcats lose.

In one of the most unforgettable games in UK history, Hatton's heroics, including a desperation 47-foot bucket at the end of the first overtime, lifted the Wildcats to a thrilling 85-83 triple-overtime victory over Temple in Memorial Coliseum.

After saving the Cats with his monster heave in the first OT, Hatton, a senior guard from Lexington, scored six of his team's 10 points in the decisive final five-minute extra period. Earlier in regulation play, it was a Hatton free throw with 49 seconds left that tied the score at 65-65 and set the stage for his subsequent heroics.

The Cats fought an uphill battle throughout most of the fiercely contested struggle. They trailed 21-13 midway through the opening half but managed to pull to within 35-34 at the break. Temple pushed ahead 47-42 in the second half before the Cats again began a comeback charge that ended when Hatton dropped in his free throw to send the game into overtime.

The Owls appeared to have the game won when Guy Rodgers broke a 69-69 deadlock by sinking a 15-foot jumper with three seconds left in the first OT. Follow-ing a UK timeout, John Crigler inbounded the ball to Hatton, who then launched his desperation shot. It was dead center, tying the score and bringing on a second overtime.

Now it was Temple's turn to escape the grave. With his team down 75-73, Mel Brodsky canned two free throws with 53 seconds remaining to even the score once again. The Cats failed to break the deadlock, sending the game into yet another five-minute period.

Two freebies each by Crigler and Adrian Smith were offset by Jay Norman and Brodsky field goals. With the score now knotted at 79-79, Hatton took control, hitting a 20-footer to give the Cats an 81-79 lead. After Temple's Bill Kennedy nailed a jumper from the corner to account for the game's final tie, Hatton answered with a 20-foot jump shot and two free throws to provide a successful conclusion to the longest game in UK basketball history.

Johnny Cox paced a balanced Wildcat attack with 22 points. Hatton, Crigler and Smith all tallied 17 points apiece. Rodgers and Brodsky shared game-high honors with 24 points each.

Kentucky (85)	FGA	FGM	FTA	FTM	RB	PF	TP
Cox	24	10	4	2	16	2	22
Crigler	17	6	6	5	17	3	17
Beck	17	2	5	3	20	4	7
Smith	15	6	9	6	5	1	18
Hatton	14	5	9	7	5	2	17
Adkins	3	2	0	0	0	3	4
Totals	**90**	**31**	**33**	**23**	**63**	**15**	**85**

Temple (83)	FGA	FGM	FTA	FTM	RB	PF	TP
Brodsky	21	9	8	6	9	3	24
Norman	19	5	4	2	23	4	12
Fleming	1	0	1	0	0	0	0
Franklin	2	1	0	0	0	2	2
Van Patton	7	1	0	0	12	4	2
Kennedy	14	8	5	3	5	5	19
Rodgers	27	11	3	2	9	5	24
Peppe	0	0	0	0	0	0	0
Totals	**91**	**35**	**21**	**13**	**58**	**23**	**83**

Halftime: Temple 35, UK 34
Regulation: 65-65, 1OT: 71-71, 2OT: 75-75

UK 61, Temple 60

NCAA Semifinal
March 21, 1958
Louisville, Ky.

If Philadelphia judges meted out punishment for shooting down Owls, Vernon Hatton would have been given a life sentence.

For the second time in just over three months, Hatton came up big in the clutch against Temple, scoring the game-deciding bucket with 16 seconds left to give the Wildcats a 61-60 NCAA Tournament semifinal win in Freedom Hall. Less than 24 hours later, UK topped Seattle 84-72 in the title match to give veteran coach Adolph Rupp his fourth and final NCAA championship.

This second UK-Temple clash was every bit as tense and exciting as the triple-overtime classic won by the Cats 85-83 in early December. There was, however, one major difference between that earlier meeting and the encore showdown—this one had far more riding on the outcome.

Each team put together an early run—Temple raced to a 7-2 lead only to watch the Wildcats come back to grab a 23-16 advantage—before finally settling on a 33-33 tie at the half. In all, there were eight ties and 10 lead changes before Hatton's bucket settled the issue. But that didn't come until these two gritty warrior foes had played a frantic, spine-tingling 20 minutes of splendid basketball.

The Owls, led by the great Guy Rodgers, threatened to break the game open midway through the second half. With the score tied at 42-42, Rodgers went on a rampage, scoring four quick buckets to give Temple a lead and control of the momentum. Then, with his team still leading 59-55, Temple coach Harry Litwack ordered his players to put the ball in the deep freeze. It was a piece of strategy that was soon to backfire.

Temple guard Bill Kennedy was whistled for a charging foul against Adrian Smith. Smith hit both free throws to make it 59-57 with 1:30 left to play. Following a free throw by Dan Fleming with 55 seconds remaining, Smith again hit a pair of freebies that pulled the Cats to within a single point—60-59—with just 29 seconds left.

UK's Lincoln Collinsworth then fouled Rodgers, who misfired on his free throw attempt. After Smith came up with the rebound, UK called a timeout to set up the final play. The Cats worked the ball to Hatton, and the senior guard laid in the go-ahead basket at the 16-second mark.

Temple had one final chance to pull out the win, but that opportunity was lost when Kennedy bobbled a pass and lost the ball out of bounds.

Cox once again led the UK scoring with 22 points. The pressure-proof backcourt duo of Hatton and Smith finished with 13 and 12, respectively. Rodgers topped the Owls with 22 points.

Kentucky (61)	FGA	FGM	FTA	FTM	RB	PF	TP
Crigler	11	3	2	0	9	4	6
Cox	17	6	11	10	12	4	22
Collinsworth	0	0	0	0	0	1	0
Beck	9	3	2	2	15	2	8
Hatton	16	5	4	3	3	3	13
Smith	10	2	9	8	5	3	12
Totals	**63**	**19**	**28**	**23**	**44**	**17**	**61**

Temple (60)	FGA	FGM	FTA	FTM	RB	PF	TP
Norman	17	7	2	2	6	3	16
Brodsky	5	2	2	0	16	3	4
Van Patton	1	1	3	1	3	4	3
Fleming	7	3	6	3	3	1	9
Rodgers	24	9	6	4	5	4	22
Kennedy	7	3	1	0	3	4	6
Totals	**61**	**25**	**20**	**10**	**36**	**19**	**60**

Halftime: UK 33, Temple 33

UK 58, Maryland 56 (OT)

Dec. 15, 1958
Lexington, Ky.

There was no way the Wildcats could win this game. A rare home-court loss was inevitable.

The Memorial Coliseum scoreboard told the story: Maryland 54, UK 51. Ten seconds remaining. Local sportswriters were already busy composing UK's obituary.

During a timeout, the two coaches—one desperate, the other virtually certain of victory—mapped out completely different strategies.

UK's Adolph Rupp: "I told them we had to drive for a basket, and had to get fouled at the same time. One basket wouldn't do us any good. It was to be either (Bennie) Coffman or (Dickie) Parsons."

Maryland's Bud Millikan: "I told the boys to let Kentucky pass the ball in and go ahead and score. We'd still have possession of the ball and time would run out before we would have had to put it in play."

Bennie Coffman's memorable last-second three-point play enabled the Cats to slip past Maryland 58-56 in overtime.

Rupp's prayer for a miracle was heard; Millikan's call for common sense fell on deaf ears.

As planned, Coffman ended up with the ball. He drove through the middle of Maryland's defense, laid in a bucket and, incredibly, drew a foul from Al Bunge, who, for some unknown reason, attempted to block the shot. Coffman converted the free throw to send the game into overtime and give the Wildcats new life.

After Johnny Cox canned a one-hander from the side to give UK a 56-54 lead, the two teams went scoreless for the next three minutes. Following a Maryland miss, the Cats froze the ball until Parsons drew a foul with 34 seconds left. He hit both freebies to put the Cats on top 58-54.

Maryland's Jim Halleck sank a pair of free throws, but it was too little, too late.

The Wildcats escaped with a 58-56 victory.

"I told them not to foul, but to get out of the way if Kentucky drove," Millikan lamented. "They did just the opposite."

The Cats came out shooting blanks, going more than six minutes before registering their first field goal. Despite their cold shooting, the Cats held a 25-22 lead at the half. A 6-0 run inside the final minute put the Cats in front. Two free throws each by Sid Cohen and Coffman and a Billy Ray Lickert rebound bucket accounted for those six points.

UK built a 45-39 lead with just under 10 minutes left, but the Terps battled back to take a 49-47 lead on two freebies by Jim Bechtle. Cox answered with two free throws before Bechtle got free and scored an easy layup to make it 51-49. After Cohen missed a free throw attempt, Bill Murphy cashed in on one of two free tosses to give Maryland a 52-49 lead. Seconds later, UK's Don Mills scored on a tip-in to cut the difference to a single point. Bunge drew a foul but missed two free throws, opening the door for a UK win. But when Parsons missed a jumper from the side and Maryland's Murphy sank two free throws, it appeared as if the door had been slammed.

Then Coffman came through with his miraculous three-point play that sent the game into overtime.

Cox paced the Wildcats with 18 points and 14 rebounds. Lickert finished with 16 points, while Coffman chipped in with 10. Maryland's Charles McNeil led all scorers with 21 points.

Kentucky (58)	FG	FT	RB	PF	TP
Cox	6	6	14	5	18
Lickert	6	4	6	1	16
Mills	1	1	6	3	3
Cohen	2	4	3	5	8
Parsons	0	3	3	1	3
Coffman	2	6	3	2	10
Johnson	0	0	6	2	0
Totals	**17**	**24**	**41**	**19**	**58**

Maryland (56)	FG	FT	RB	PF	TP
McDonald	1	0	9	4	2
McNeil	9	3	15	0	21
Bunge	3	3	10	5	9
Danko	4	1	7	4	9
Bechtle	4	2	1	5	10

Murphy	0	3	2	3	3
Halleck	0	2	1	1	2
Wilson	0	0	0	0	0
Totals	**21**	**14**	**45**	**22**	**56**

Halftime: UK 25, Maryland 22
Regulation: UK 54, Maryland 54

UK 97, West Virginia 91

UKIT Championship
Dec. 20, 1958
Lexington, Ky.

Even a record-shattering performance by Jerry West couldn't derail the unbeaten Wildcats.

West gunned in 36 points (a UKIT best), but it wasn't enough to knock off the Cats, who edged past West Virginia 97-91 to win their own Christmas tournament. The Wildcats won despite playing without Billy Ray Lickert, the team's second-leading scorer. Lickert was hospitalized with an intestinal virus.

Balanced scoring was the key to UK's victory. In all, four Wildcats cracked double figures, led by Sid Cohen with 23 points. Other Cats in double digits included Bobby Slusher (19), Don Mills (17) and Johnny Cox (16).

Both teams torched the basket in a sizzling first half that ended with UK leading 54-50. The Cats connected on 23 of 38 shots for 60.5 percent, while West Virginia, led by West's 26 points, hit on 19 of 36 for 52.8 percent.

West single-handedly kept his team in the game during those first 20 minutes. At one stage, after a crip shot by Cohen, two Slusher buckets, a Bennie Coffman layup and a jumper by Cox from the corner, the Cats were on top 48-34. But West responded with three baskets and Willie Akers added a bucket and two free throws to shave UK's advantage to four by intermission.

The Cats opened strong in the second half, scoring five quick points on a Slusher crip, a free toss by Dickie Parsons and a Cohen set shot. UK's lead see-sawed between nine and 11 points for much of the second half as the two teams matched bucket for bucket. The Mountaineers did pull to within 78-73 with 6:59 remaining, but Parsons hit two free throws and Slusher followed with another jumper to pull the Cats out of danger.

Slusher turned in a superb effort filling in for Lickert. Another Wildcat who stood tall was Mills, who missed the

UKIT opener after being hit with the same virus that side-lined Lickert. Mills yanked down 11 rebounds to go along with his 17 points.

But no one could match the great West. He hit 15 of 25 shots and had 16 rebounds for West Virginia. One year later, West, despite playing with a broken nose, returned to the UKIT, breaking his own record by scoring 37 points in a 79-70 win over UK in the championship game.

Kentucky (97)	FGA	FGM	FTA	FTM	RB	PF	TP
Cox	14	6	4	4	12	4	16
Slusher	15	8	3	3	6	5	19
Jennings	1	1	0	0	2	2	2
Cohen	17	8	13	7	3	3	23
Coffman	5	3	3	3	1	0	9
Mills	8	3	11	11	11	3	17
Parsons	6	2	6	5	1	2	9
Johnson	1	1	0	0	2	4	2
Totals	**67**	**32**	**40**	**33**	**38**	**23**	**97**

West Va. (91)	FGA	FGM	FTA	FTM	RB	PF	TP
West	25	15	8	6	16	3	36
Smith	19	8	2	1	6	1	17
Clousson	11	5	9	5	8	4	15
Retton	2	1	2	2	0	5	4
Bolyard	4	3	0	0	2	5	6
Patrone	4	0	4	3	4	3	3
Goode	0	0	0	0	0	0	0
Akers	4	1	11	8	12	2	10
Ritchie	0	0	0	0	3	2	0
Totals	**69**	**33**	**36**	**25**	**51**	**25**	**91**

Halftime: UK 54, West Virginia 50

UK 96, Ohio State 93

Dec. 28, 1959
Lexington, Ky.

Billy Ray Lickert scored 29 points and Bennie Coffman added 26 as the Wildcats overcame a 15-point deficit to beat young and powerful Ohio State 96-93 in one of the greatest games ever played in Memorial Coliseum. The Buckeyes, led by the trio of Jerry Lucas, Larry Siegfried and John Havlicek, would go on to win the NCAA championship later that season.

The Cats fell behind early, and were trailing 57-42 with

less than two minutes left in the opening half. With Lucas proving to be unstoppable in close, it began to look like a Buckeye blowout. Despite a late UK rally, Ohio State still owned a comfortable 59-49 lead at the break.

Then the Cats caught fire, burning the nets from all over the court. In the second half, the Cats, ignited by Lickert and Coffman, connected on 61.5 percent of their field goal attempts. Ohio State, after a red-hot first half, shot just 34.2 percent during the final 20 minutes.

With just over six minutes gone in the second half, the Cats had pulled to within 67-66 and seemed to have the visitors on the ropes. But Ohio State quickly regained control, bumping its advantage to 80-72 at the 9:07 mark. The Buckeyes had avoided UK's knockout punch.

Now it was gut-check time for the Cats. With their backs squarely against the wall, the Cats stormed back to take an 85-84 lead on a Coffman 14-footer with 5:13 left. After Ohio State recaptured an 86-85 lead, Don Mills scored three straight points to put UK in front 88-86. That was the 10th and last lead change in this classic thriller.

UK led 90-86, then went cold at the free throw stripe, twice missing the front end of a one-and-one bonus situation. Those misses allowed the Buckeyes to creep to within 90-89 with only 45 seconds left to play.

But the Cats stiffened, hitting six straight free throws in the final 35 seconds to seal the victory. Cohen connected on four of those clutch freebies and Carroll Burchett added two more.

Lickert had one of his finest games in a UK uniform, making good on 12 of 23 shots from the field. Coffman, despite playing with a broken nose, was equally brilliant, hitting 10 of 15. Mills and Burchett also hit double figures with 13 points each.

Lucas led all scorers with 34 points. Havlicek and Siegfried finished with 16 and 15, respectively.

Kentucky (96)	FGA	FGM	FTA	FTM	RB	PF	TP
Mills	9	5	4	3	11	4	13
Burchett	6	5	3	3	11	0	13
Jennings	8	3	3	2	3	5	8
Coffman	15	10	6	6	4	2	26
Lickert	23	12	6	5	4	3	29
Feldhaus	3	1	2	1	3	0	3
Pursiful	1	0	0	0	0	0	0
Cohen	0	0	5	4	0	1	4
Totals	**65**	**36**	**29**	**24**	**35**	**15**	**96**

Ohio State (93)	FGA	FGM	FTA	FTM	RB	PF	TP
Havlicek	10	6	4	4	7	2	16
Roberts	15	7	1	0	15	2	14
Lucas	22	13	10	8	11	3	34
Nowell	14	5	2	2	3	5	12
Siegfried	12	6	4	3	4	4	15
Hoyt	4	1	0	0	3	2	2
Gearhart	0	0	0	0	0	2	0
Furry	0	0	0	0	0	1	0
Totals	**77**	**38**	**21**	**17**	**43**	**21**	**93**

Halftime: Ohio State 59, UK 49

UK 88, Vanderbilt 67

SEC Playoff
March 9, 1961
Knoxville, Tenn.

In a one-game shootout to decide the SEC representative to the NCAA Tournament, the Wildcats turned in their finest performance of the season, blasting Vanderbilt 88-67 to earn a tourney berth. Mississippi State captured the regular-season title, but elected to pass on participating in the Big Show.

The two clubs split a pair of heart-stoppers during the season, with Vandy winning 64-62 in Nashville and UK getting revenge with a 60-59 squeaker in Memorial Coliseum. The rubber game was expected to be another down-to-the-wire battle, but that battle never materialized. After a see-saw first six minutes, the hot-shooting Cats assumed command and never looked back.

With the score knotted at 13-13, a steal and layup by Billy Ray Lickert put the Cats in front for good. Ned Jennings followed by hitting a jumper and two free throws to extend UK's lead to 21-15 with 11 minutes left before intermission. After a pair of free tosses by Vandy's Bill Depp, two buckets by Jennings and one by Roger Newman increased the Cats' lead to 27-17. Thanks to five quick points by Newman inside the final minute, the Cats built a 44-30 lead at the break.

The Cats were in front 53-34, but Vandy, getting a superb effort from Kentucky native Don Ringstaff, managed to pull to within 12 points. But that would be as close as the Commodores would get. A late spurt, fueled by Larry Pursiful, Lickert and Newman, put the game out of reach.

All five Wildcat starters cracked double digits, led by Pur-

siful with 21. Newman finished with 18, while Lickert and Jennings each had 14. Dick Parson contributed 13. Jennings also led all rebounders with 12 before fouling out. In all, 52 fouls were whistled against the two clubs, with a total of five players being sent to the sidelines. The two teams combined to shoot 80 free throws.

Ringstaff, who played his prep ball at Livingston Central High School, matched Pursiful for high-point honors with 21 despite not entering the game until the five-minute mark of the opening half.

For the game, UK connected on 28 of 61 from the field for 46 percent, while holding Vandy to just 18 of 59 for a frosty 30.5 percent.

Kentucky (88)	FGA	FGM	FTA	FTM	RB	PF	TP
Lickert	14	6	2	2	3	1	14
Newman	10	4	11	10	7	5	18
Jennings	8	4	7	6	12	5	14
Parsons	10	5	5	3	1	4	13
Pursiful	12	6	11	9	3	4	21
Feldhaus	2	1	1	0	2	1	2
Burchett	5	2	3	2	6	5	6
McDonald	0	0	0	0	1	0	0
Totals	**61**	**28**	**40**	**32**	**35**	**25**	**88**

Vanderbilt (67)	FGA	FGM	FTA	FTM	RB	PF	TP
Banks	6	0	4	3	6	3	3
Depp	9	3	9	7	8	3	13
Griffiths	5	1	2	1	4	5	3
Bland	11	3	6	5	3	5	11
Russell	5	1	5	4	4	2	6
Ringstaff	10	7	8	7	5	3	21
Johnson	9	2	3	2	1	3	6
Doninger	2	1	0	0	1	0	2
Scott	1	0	1	0	2	3	0
Gish	0	0	0	0	1	0	0
Clark	1	0	2	2	0	0	2
Hosbach	0	0	0	0	0	0	0
Totals	**59**	**18**	**40**	**31**	**35**	**27**	**67**

Halftime: UK 44, Vanderbilt 30

Mississippi State 49, UK 44

Feb. 12, 1962
Lexington, Ky.

Visiting Mississippi State parlayed a deliberate, surgically

precise offense and some dazzling shooting into a stunning 49-44 victory over the Wildcats in Memorial Coliseum. The loss knocked the Cats out of first place in the SEC race, leaving them tied for the top spot with Mississippi State. The two clubs finished with identical 13-1 league records.

The Bulldogs did the one crucial thing necessary to winning this game—grab the early lead. Once in front, they were able to control the tempo, slowing the game to a crawl and frustrating the run-oriented Wildcats. It also didn't hurt that State sizzled from the field. In all, the visitors made good on 18 of 26 shots. In the final 20 minutes, they took only eight shots, making seven. For the game, State shot 69.2 percent from the field.

Conversely, the Cats, normally a deadeye group of gunners, connected on just 15 of 45 shots for 33 percent. Larry Pursiful, UK's ace long-range bomber, suffered through a nightmare outing, hitting just one bucket in 10 attempts. Scotty Baesler, Pursiful's backcourt mate, was equally ineffective, missing all six of his field goal attempts.

Cotton Nash, UK's great sophomore, was the lone standout for the Cats, finishing with 23 points and seven rebounds despite being surrounded by a host of Mississippi State defenders. On the night, Nash made good on nine of 15 field goal attempts.

After trailing 28-22 at the half, the Cats managed to claw to within a bucket on several occasions during the gut-wrenching final 20 minutes. But each UK challenge was met by the talented, veteran Mississippi State club. Down the stretch, clutch points from Leland Mitchell, Bobby Hutton and W.D. "Red" Stroud kept the Bulldogs in front.

UK was down 45-42 with 45 seconds remaining, but a pair of Stroud freebies iced the game for Mississippi State.

Stroud paced the Bulldogs with 17 points. Mitchell finished with 13 and Hutton chipped in with 10.

Roy Roberts was the only other Wildcat to hit double figures with 11 points. He also yanked down 11 rebounds.

When the final horn sounded, Mississippi State coach Babe McCarthy added insult to injury by giving a wreath to the team manager, who promptly laid it on the UK goal.

Miss. State (49)	FGA	FGM	FTA	FTM	RB	PF	TP
Mitchell	8	6	2	1	4	3	13
Gold	3	3	1	1	1	3	7
Shows	0	0	0	0	2	1	0
Berkshire	1	1	1	0	3	0	2
Stroud	7	5	10	7	3	0	17

Hutton	7	3	4	4	1	3	10
Totals	**26**	**18**	**18**	**13**	**14**	**10**	**49**

Kentucky (44)	FGA	FGM	FTA	FTM	RB	PF	TP
Roberts	8	4	4	3	11	3	11
Burchett	2	0	1	1	1	3	1
Nash	15	9	6	5	7	4	23
Baesler	6	0	0	0	0	3	0
Pursiful	10	1	3	3	2	0	5
Feldhaus	4	1	2	2	5	1	4
Totals	**45**	**15**	**16**	**14**	**26**	**14**	**44**

Halftime: Miss. State 28, UK 22

UK 100, North Carolina 80

Dec. 9, 1963
Lexington, Ky.

Clutch play by Terry Mobley, Larry Conley and Charlie Ishmael helped offset a gigantic 32-point, 20-rebound performance by Billy Cunningham and drive the Wildcats to a 100-80 victory over North Carolina in Memorial Coliseum.

The Cats, who led by just four at intermission, sizzled in the final 20 minutes, outscoring the Tar Heels 60-44 to win going away. The Cats were on top 75-64 with 6:22 remaining when the All-American Cunningham was hit with his fifth foul. With his departure, any hopes of a Tar Heel comeback quickly crashed and burned.

Mobley, who was celebrating his 20th birthday, was brilliant, canning eight of 10 field goal attempts and finishing with 21 points. Conley also played well, with 15 points, nine rebounds and four assists, while Ishmael came off the bench to score 17 points on eight-of-12 shooting.

All-American Cotton Nash had 23 points and nine rebounds for the victorious Wildcats. Ted Deeken turned in a strong double-double effort, finishing with 22 points and 13 rebounds.

With the Cats in front 20-15, North Carolina, sparked by 14 first-half points each from Cunningham and Ray Respess, reeled off 11 unanswered points to take a 26-20 lead. Still down 34-30, the Cats got consecutive buckets from Deeken, Mobley and Ishmael to take a 36-34 lead. After two free throws by UNC's Charlie Shaffer knotted the count for the seventh and final time, back-to-back buckets by Ishmael gave the Cats a 40-36 lead at the half.

Thanks to 58 percent shooting (23 of 40), the second half

belonged to the Cats. They immediately upped their lead to 58-48, and despite one final run by the Tar Heels, which Mobley shut down by scoring three straight points, the Cats managed to slowly pull away from Dean Smith's club.

The Cats won despite being whipped on the boards 46-43.

Nash's 23-point effort was his lowest output through the first four games of the season, but it was enough to send him past Bill Spivey and into sixth place on UK's all-time scoring list. By season's end, Nash would pass Alex Groza as the school's all-time leading scorer.

Cunningham connected on 11 of 28 field goal attempts and 10 of 15 free tosses to reach his game-high total. Mike Cooke and Respess finished with 18 and 16 points, respectively.

N. Carolina (80)	FGA	FGM	FTA	FTM	RB	PF	TP
Respess	9	5	6	6	10	2	16
McSweeny	3	0	3	2	6	2	2
Cunningham	28	11	15	10	20	5	32
Cooke	14	8	2	2	4	3	18
Shaffer	11	3	5	4	5	5	10
Bennett	0	0	0	0	0	3	0
Galantal	0	0	2	2	0	0	2
Yokley	0	0	0	0	0	0	0
Hassell	0	0	0	0	0	1	0
Katz	2	0	0	0	0	1	0
Smithwick	0	0	0	0	1	1	0
Iannarella	0	0	0	0	0	0	0
Brown	0	0	0	0	0	0	0
Totals	**67**	**27**	**33**	**26**	**46**	**23**	**80**

Kentucky (100)	FGA	FGM	FTA	FTM	RB	PF	TP
Deeken	20	9	6	4	13	4	22
Conley	13	6	8	3	9	4	15
Nash	23	9	6	5	9	4	23
Embry	3	1	0	0	0	2	2
Mobley	10	8	6	5	6	3	21
Ishmael	12	8	2	1	3	2	17
Adams	0	0	0	0	1	2	0
Kron	1	0	0	0	2	0	0
S. Harper	0	0	0	0	0	0	0
Kennett	0	0	0	0	0	0	0
Totals	**82**	**41**	**28**	**18**	**43**	**21**	**100**

Halftime: UK 40, UNC 36

UK 81, Duke 79

Sugar Bowl Championship
Dec. 31, 1963
New Orleans, La.

Terry Mobley buried a 15-foot jump shot with four seconds left to give the Wildcats a come-from-behind 81-79 victory over Duke in the championship game of the Sugar Bowl tournament.

Mobley wasn't the first—or obvious—choice to take UK's final shot. All-American Cotton Nash was. But when Mobley saw that Nash was being blanketed by the towering Duke frontline, he drove down the left side of the foul lane, pulled up and fired the winning jumper. With no timeouts left, all the Blue Devils could do was watch helplessly as the final four seconds ticked off.

Duke steamrolled the Cats early, forging a 47-37 lead by intermission. The big thorn is UK's side was Lexington Layfayette graduate Jeff Mullins. It was his first-half scoring that helped the Blue Devils build their huge advantage. Another factor was rebounding. Duke, with a frontline that featured the 6'10" tandem of Jay Buckley and Hack Tison, whipped the Cats on the boards 43-22.

But the Cats turned things around midway through the second half, thanks to Nash's hot hand and some splendid defensive work by sophomore Tommy Kron. Kron, who didn't make his first appearance until the 13:25 mark of the second half, held Mullins to a single field goal the rest of the way.

A long Nash bomb pulled the Cats even at 70-70 with 7:07 remaining. Moments later, a Ted Deeken hook shot put the Cats on top for the first time since the opening minutes of play. After Duke's Buckley hit one of two free throws, Deeken countered again to keep the Cats' lead at three—74-71. Tison retaliated for the Blue Devils, but Nash answered with a driving layup. Following another Tison basket, Randy Embry hit one of two free throws to give the Cats a 77-75 lead.

The Blue Devils made one final charge, getting back-to-back baskets from Buckley and Tison to go on top 79-77 with just under two minutes left to play. But Mobley, who had scored but one bucket through the first 38 minutes, connected on a short jumper to draw the Cats even at 79-79.

Duke tried to hold for the last shot, but that plan was foiled when Deeken swatted away a pass and Kron came up with the loose ball, thus setting the stage for Mobley's game-winning jumper.

Nash led all scorers with 30 points. His effort earned him tourney MVP honors. Deeken finished with 18 points, while Embry, also named to the all-tourney team, pitched in 15. Tison had 27 and Mullins 26 for the Blue Devils.

Kentucky (81)	FGA	FGM	FTA	FTM	RB	PF	TP
Deeken	16	9	1	0	2	3	18
Conley	7	2	5	3	3	5	7
Nash	29	13	8	4	5	3	30
Embry	11	7	1	1	5	1	15
Mobley	9	3	3	3	3	2	9
Gibson	4	1	0	0	2	0	2
Kron	0	0	0	0	2	0	0
Totals	**76**	**35**	**18**	**11**	**22**	**14**	**81**

Duke (79)	FGA	FGM	FTA	FTM	RB	PF	TP
Tison	14	10	11	7	7	3	27
Mullins	20	11	4	4	14	3	26
Buckley	11	5	3	2	9	4	12
Ferguson	3	1	0	0	4	2	2
Harrison	3	2	0	0	3	3	4
Kitching	2	0	2	2	4	0	2
Marin	6	3	0	0	2	0	6
Herbster	0	0	0	0	0	0	0
Totals	**59**	**32**	**20**	**15**	**43**	**15**	**79**

Halftime: Duke 47, UK 37

UK 83, Duke 79

NCAA Semifinal
March 18, 1966
College Park, Md.

Sparked by a courageous performance from flu-stricken Larry Conley, the Cats battled their way to a thrilling 83-79 semifinal victory over Duke in NCAA tourney action. The win put the Cats into the title game against Texas Western, which they lost 72-65.

Most experts figured that the survivor of this game would go on to capture the crown. That thinking was only logical, given that UK and Duke were ranked 1-2 in the AP poll.

The game was everything it was projected to be, a nip-

and-tuck thriller played at a championship-caliber level. Each team battled from behind, and neither team caved under the intense pressure of the moment. It was a superb 40 minutes of basketball and a worthy predecessor to the classic NCAA struggle these two clubs would wage 26 years later.

Conley only managed 10 points on the night, but his presence in the lineup was crucial. When he went out early in the first half (followed moments later by foul-plagued Thad Jaracz), the Cats watched a seven-point advantage become a five-point deficit.

Duke led 40-35 late in the opening half, but back-to-back jumpers by Pat Riley and Tommy Kron narrowed the difference to one. In the final minute, Mike Lewis scored on a hook shot and Kron knocked down a pair of free tosses to give the Blue Devils a 42-41 halftime lead.

The two clubs played on even terms throughout the second half, with the Cats finally taking the lead for good at 73-71 on a pair of Conley free throws with 3:55 remaining. UK's lead grew when Louie Dampier came up with a steal, then hit Riley for an easy layup.

After Duke failed to answer on its next trip down the floor, Riley drew a foul from Steve Vacendak. Riley missed the freebie, but Kron rebounded and got the ball to Dampier, who laid in an easy bucket that made it 77-71.

Jack Marin canned two free throws for Duke to cut the difference to four. Following a timeout, Conley got loose and scored a bunny to again push the Cats ahead by six. Inside the final 45 seconds, backup center Cliff Berger converted four straight free throws to seal the big win for UK.

Dampier paced the Cats with 23 points. Riley finished with 19, while Kron added 12. Kron was also the game's top rebounder with 10.

Marin, the deadly Duke lefty, took home game-high honors with 29. Lewis had 21 and Vacendak 17 before fouling out.

Both clubs made 32 buckets in 66 attempts for an identical field goal percentage of 48.5.

Kentucky (83)	FGA	FGM	FTA	FTM	RB	PF	TP
Dampier	20	11	2	1	4	3	23
Kron	13	5	2	2	10	1	12
Conley	5	3	4	4	1	0	10
Riley	17	8	4	3	8	5	19
Jaracz	5	3	3	2	4	5	8
Tallent	2	1	2	2	1	0	4
Berger	4	1	6	5	5	1	7
Gamble	0	0	1	0	0	1	0
Team					8		
Totals	**66**	**32**	**24**	**19**	**41**	**16**	**83**

Duke (79)	FGA	FGM	FTA	FTM	RB	PF	TP
Verga	7	2	0	0	3	1	4
Riedy	7	2	2	2	8	3	6
Marin	18	11	10	7	7	2	29
Vacendak	16	7	3	3	3	5	17
Lewis	13	9	3	3	6	3	21
Wendelin	4	1	1	0	2	4	2
Liccardo	1	0	0	0	0	0	0
Barone	0	0	0	0	0	1	0
Team					7		
Totals	**66**	**32**	**19**	**15**	**36**	**19**	**79**

Halftime: Duke 42, UK 41

Texas Western 72, UK 65

NCAA Championship
March 19, 1966
College Park, Md.

Bobby Joe Hill sent out an early message to the college basketball world: We don't care if Kentucky is top-ranked and favored to win—we've come to play.

The cat-quick Hill, a repeat offender for larceny within a span of 12 seconds, literally stole the thunder from the Wildcats, leading his Texas Western club to a 72-65 victory and the NCAA championship.

For the Wildcats, the beloved "Rupp's Runts" team, it was a disappointing end to what had been a magical season. Unheralded and unranked in December, the Wildcats won 23 straight before losing, easily captured the SEC title, finished with a 27-2 record and a No. 1 ranking in the final polls. Along the way, this team, like few others before or since, won the hearts and minds of all Big Blue fans.

But none of that mattered to a Texas Western team that outgunned, outquicked and simply outplayed the Wildcats on both ends of the court. In particular, it was the Miners' defense and rebounding that made the difference. They held the Cats to a season-low 38.6 percent shooting from the field (27 of 70), while winning the battle of the boards 35-33. During a critical stretch early in the game, the Cats went seven minutes without scoring a field goal.

The tone of the game was set by the larcenous Hill, who

converted back-to-back midcourt steals into easy layups, turning a 7-3 deficit into a 13-8 Texas Western lead. The gutsy Miners, though repeatedly challenged, never relinquished the upper hand. They led 31-28 at the break.

Thanks to buckets by Louie Dampier, Larry Conley and Thad Jaracz, the Cats were able to stay within striking distance during the early minutes of the second half. Three times they closed to within a single point, yet were never able to connect on the go-ahead bucket.

Then Texas Western took charge. With Orsten Artis, Hill, Nevil Shed and Willie Worsley doing most of the damage, the Miners increased their lead to 52-43 midway through the second half. The Cats, despite their poor shooting, refused to surrender, and by the time Pat Riley, Dampier and Tommy Kron had accounted for eight quick points, they had pulled to within 54-51.

But this group of Cats had finally run out of lives, and when Texas Western responded with a game-breaking 14-6 spurt that made it 68-57 with just over three minutes remaining, the outcome was decided.

Hill was the game's top scorer with 20 points. David "Big Daddy" Lattin chipped in with 16 and Artis added 15. UK's All-American duo of Dampier and Riley each had 19 for the Cats, while Conley finished with 10.

Kentucky (65)	FGA	FGM	FTA	FTM	RB	PF	TP
Dampier	18	7	5	5	9	4	19
Kron	6	3	0	0	7	2	6
Conley	9	4	2	2	8	5	10
Riley	22	8	4	3	4	4	19
Jaracz	8	3	2	1	5	5	7
Berger	3	2	0	0	0	0	4
Gamble	0	0	0	0	0	1	0
LeMaster	1	0	0	0	0	1	0
Tallent	3	0	0	0	0	1	0
Totals	70	27	13	11	33	23	65

Texas West. (72)	FGA	FGM	FTA	FTM	RB	PF	TP
Hill	17	7	9	6	3	3	20
Artis	13	5	5	5	8	1	15
Shed	1	1	1	1	3	1	3
Lattin	10	5	6	6	9	4	16
Worsley	4	2	6	4	4	0	8
Flourney	1	1	0	0	0	0	2
Cager	3	1	7	6	6	3	8

Team				2			
Totals	49	22	34	28	35	12	72

Halftime: Texas Western 31, UK 28

UK 102, Notre Dame 100

Dec. 27, 1969
Louisville, Ky.

Mike Pratt erupted for a career-best 42 points to lead the Wildcats past Notre Dame 102-100 in a classic Freedom Hall war between these two ancient rivals. It was during this game that veteran UK broadcaster Cawood Ledford declared that "Pratt has picked up the banner and gone to war for the Wildcats."

Indeed, it took all of Pratt's 42 points and 35 from Dan Issel to offset a 43-point performance by All-American Irish guard Austin Carr. Carr, red-hot from start to finish, made good on 20 of 27 field goal attempts against the Wildcat defense.

Both clubs scorched the nets—Notre Dame hitting 44 of 79 shots for 55.7 percent and UK knocking down 37 of 72 for 51.4 percent. The Cats won it at the charity stripe, making 28 to Notre Dame's 12.

The Cats led 55-47 at the half, increased that to a 15-point advantage early in the second half, then had to fight off a spirited Notre Dame comeback down the stretch. The Irish, sparked by Carr's seemingly unstoppable drives to the hoop, sliced the difference to 68-64 with 12:30 remaining. During the next four minutes, the Irish repeatedly charged at the Cats, only to be brushed back by Pratt's heroics. In that critical span, Pratt hit a jumper, a driving layup and five free throws to help the Cats keep their nose in front.

Then with the score standing at 83-79, Pratt received some help from Jim Dinwiddie and Bob McCowan, both of whom nailed critical buckets. Also, Issel, who had missed four free throws in the second half, dropped in four straight.

Still, the Irish refused to fold, slicing UK's 99-91 lead to 100-98 by sandwiching two buckets by Carr, one by Jim Hinga and a free toss by Sid Catlett around a lone Issel freebie.

After Pratt and Collis Jones swapped buckets to make it 102-100, the Cats coughed up the ball with 18 ticks remaining, giving the Irish a chance to tie things

up. But Jones, closely guarded by Issel, missed a short jumper, which the scrappy McCowan rebounded. McCowan was fouled on the play but missed his free throw. However, UK's Larry Steele managed to tap the ball away from the desperate Irish as time finally expired.

McCowan was the third Wildcat in double figures, finishing with 14. Issel picked off 16 rebounds to top the Cats in that category.

Catlett also had a big night for the Irish, scoring 17 points and grabbing 14 rebounds. Jones chipped in with 16 points.

N. Dame (100)	FGA	FGM	FTA	FTM	RB	PF	TP
Jones	16	8	2	0	9	3	16
Catlett	15	7	7	3	14	4	17
Pleick	3	2	0	0	1	5	4
O'Connell	12	6	2	2	8	4	14
Carr	27	20	4	3	4	4	43
Hinga	5	1	5	4	3	4	6
Zinezwski	1	0	0	0	1	2	0
Totals	**79**	**44**	**20**	**12**	**40**	**26**	**100**

Kentucky (102)	FGA	FGM	FTA	FTM	RB	PF	TP
Pratt	26	16	10	10	8	3	42
Steele	9	0	2	2	2	4	2
Issel	16	11	20	13	16	3	35
Dinwiddie	7	4	2	1	4	3	9
McCowan	14	6	3	2	5	2	14
Totals	**72**	**37**	**37**	**28**	**35**	**15**	**102**

Halftime: UK 55, Notre Dame 47

UK 121, LSU 105

Feb. 21, 1970
Baton Rouge, La.

Pistol Pete Maravich was hotter than ever, dumping in a record-breaking 64 points, but it wasn't enough to avoid a sound 121-105 thumping from the powerful Wildcats.

This marked the sixth and final time that Maravich faced the Cats during his magnificent career at LSU. Despite torching the Cats for 312 points in those games, Maravich and his Tigers lost all six times. In each of those six games, UK cracked the century mark.

The difference, of course, was depth. While Maravich was

forced to single-handedly carry the Tigers on his back, the talent-rich Cats spread the wealth around, led by Dan Issel with 51 points and Mike Pratt with 27. Other Cats in double digits included Tom Parker (18) and Terry Mills (14).

In their high-octane head-to-head duel, Maravich and Issel each scored 33 points in the second half. Maravich's 64 points and LSU's 105 were the most-ever against the Wildcats.

Although the final margin was relatively safe, the game had its tense moments for the Cats. After building a 74-64 lead midway through the second half, four points each by Maravich and Danny Hester trimed the difference to 74-72. With the Cats still ahead by just a single bucket (80-78), Mills canned two straight baskets to give the Cats some breathing room. Then Issel took over, scoring 16 points in the next five minutes to push UK's advantage to 14.

UK's biggest lead of the night was 111-91.

Issel was brilliant for the Cats, connecting on 19 of 33 field goal attempts and 13 of 17 free throws. He also pulled down a game-best 17 rebounds.

Pratt was the game's hottest shooter, hitting 11 of his 15 field goal attempts. Parker hit nine of 18, while Mills made good on six of 11. Parker also claimed 11 rebounds.

Maravich launched 42 shots, hitting 23. He was 18 of 22 at the charity stripe.

Hester had 17 points and 10 rebounds for the Tigers.

"If we could have tied the score, I think we might have gone on to win," LSU coach Press Maravich said. "But when they pulled away again by 10 I knew we couldn't make it. They are too strong and have great depth."

Kentucky (121)	FGA	FGM	FTA	FTM	RB	PF	TP
Dinwiddie	1	1	2	2	5	3	4
Parker	18	9	0	0	11	3	18
Pratt	15	11	8	5	4	3	27
Key	4	1	7	5	2	4	7
Issel	33	19	17	13	17	3	51
Mills	11	6	3	2	4	2	14
Hollenbeck	0	0	0	0	0	3	0
Totals	**82**	**47**	**37**	**27**	**43**	**21**	**121**

LSU (105)	FGA	FGM	FTA	FTM	RB	PF	TP
Maravich	42	23	22	18	4	4	64
Sanders	6	5	3	1	15	4	11
Tribbett	1	0	3	2	2	4	2
Hester	20	8	2	1	10	2	17

Newton	4	4	1	1	8	5	9
Hickman	3	1	0	0	0	3	2
Lang	1	0	0	0	1	2	0
Totals	**44**	**41**	**31**	**23**	**40**	**24**	**105**

Halftime: UK 56, LSU 48

Western Kentucky 107, UK 83

NCAA Mideast Regional
March 18, 1971
Athens, Ga.

The highly anticipated first meeting between two of college basketball's all-time winningest programs—and in-state rivals—turned out to be a laugher.

Red-hot Western Kentucky, led by All-American center Jim McDaniels, bolted from the gate with a vengeance, built a huge early lead, then went on to blast the Wildcats 107-83 in NCAA Tournament Mideast Regional action.

Western so dominated the Wildcats that the outcome was a virtual certainty less than five minutes after the opening tipoff. After Tom Parker canned a jumper to put UK ahead 2-1 (the Cats' only lead of the game), McDaniels rattled off eight quick points to help the Hilltoppers build a 24-12 advantage with 12 minutes left in the half. The Cats, sparked by reserves Kent Hollenbeck and Jim Andrews, did make a brief run, trimming the difference to 30-23. But that was as close as they would get. By intermission, Western, which shot 55 percent in the opening 20 minutes, held a commanding 51-38 lead.

Western flexed even more muscle in the second half. With McDaniels and teammate Jim Rose seemingly able to score at will against a variety of UK defenses, the Hilltoppers upped their lead to 68-47 with 13 minutes left. Later, when McDaniels hit a free throw to make it 100-79, UK's humiliation was total and complete.

Defense and rebounding were big factors in this easy WKU victory. The much-quicker Hilltoppers held UK to 44.6 percent shooting (six percent below its average) and won the board battle 50-45.

McDaniels gave a magnificent performance, scoring 35 points. Rose finished with 25 points, while forward Clarence Glover had 18 points and 17 rebounds.

Parker led the Wildcats with 23. Tom Payne and Mike Casey chipped in with 15 and 12, respectively.

Kentucky (83)	FGA	FGM	FTA	FTM	RB	PF	TP
Parker	18	11	1	1	5	4	23
Steele	5	1	3	2	1	5	4
Payne	18	7	3	1	10	2	15
Dinwiddie	7	2	0	0	2	2	4
Casey	11	4	5	4	6	2	12
Hollenbeck	2	2	4	3	0	5	7
Andrews	5	3	4	2	6	0	8
Mills	2	0	5	4	1	1	4
Key	4	3	0	0	3	2	6
Stamper	2	0	0	0	2	0	0
Team					9		
Totals	**74**	**33**	**25**	**17**	**45**	**23**	**83**

WKU (107)	FGA	FGM	FTA	FTM	RB	PF	TP
Dunn	8	3	5	3	7	4	9
Glover	16	8	5	2	17	2	18
McDaniels	21	12	11	11	11	4	35
Rose	21	12	1	1	3	3	25
Bailey	10	3	4	3	2	2	9
Sundmacker	2	2	2	1	1	3	5
Witt	4	2	0	0	1	0	4
Johnson	0	0	2	2	0	1	2
Kleycamp	0	0	0	0	0	0	0
Davis	0	0	0	0	0	0	0
Eaton	1	0	0	0	0	0	0
Team					8		
Totals	**83**	**42**	**30**	**23**	**50**	**19**	**107**

Halftime: WKU 51, UK 38

UK 92, Indiana 90

NCAA Mideast Regional Final
March 22, 1975
Dayton, Ohio

In one of the greatest performances ever given by a UK team, the Wildcats upset unbeaten and top-ranked Indiana 92-90 to earn a ticket to the 1975 Final Four in San Diego. The win also gave the Cats sweet revenge for an earlier 98-74 shelling at the hands of Bobby Knight's powerful IU club, which entered the game with a 34-0 record.

While the road to victory was paved by a host of Big Blue heroes, the clear standout for UK was senior guard Mike Flynn. Although known more as a defensive ace, Flynn, Indiana's 1971 prep Mr. Basketball, led the UK

scoring attack with 22 points, including 14 in the second half.

The two teams exchanged early leads before Indiana went on an 18-5 run to go on top 36-29. The Cats reclaimed the lead with a 9-0 spurt, then settled for a 44-44 tie at the half.

With IU minus its All-American forward Scott May, the Wildcats, sparked by deadly shooting from Flynn and Jimmy Dan Conner, used an 18-7 blitz to forge an 85-75 lead with four minutes remaining. Conner, who connected just two of eight first-half shots, scored 12 crucial points in the second half.

Despite having a broken wrist, May started the game for IU, but played only seven minutes in the first half and even less after intermission. With their leading scorer sidelined, the Hoosiers turned to center Kent Benson for offense, and the big guy responded with 33 points and 23 rebounds.

The Hoosiers closed the gap to 90-88, but two Kevin Grevey free throws with 20 seconds left gave the Cats enough breathing room to withstand a late bucket by John Laskowski that accounted for the final score.

Conner and Grevey each tallied 17 points, while freshmen centers Rick Robey and Mike Phillips, both of whom played superbly down the stretch, came through with 10 each. All of Phillips' points came in the second half.

Steve Green had 21 points for Indiana.

IU outrebounded UK 50-37, but committed 20 turnovers to only 14 by the Wildcats.

Kentucky (92)	FGA	FGM	FTA	FTM	RB	PF	TP
Grevey	19	6	6	5	3	4	17
Guyette	1	0	4	2	7	4	2
Robey	6	3	4	4	4	5	10
Conner	20	8	3	1	5	0	17
Flynn	13	9	5	4	3	4	22
Givens	7	4	0	0	6	0	8
Phillips	4	4	2	2	4	5	10
Johnson	5	3	1	0	1	0	6
Hall	0	0	0	0	1	0	0
Haskins	0	0	0	0	0	0	0
Team					3		
Totals	**75**	**37**	**25**	**18**	**37**	**22**	**92**

Indiana (90)	FGA	FGM	FTA	FTM	RB	PF	TP
Green	17	10	1	1	4	4	21
May	4	1	0	0	0	2	2
Benson	18	13	9	7	23	3	33
Buckner	11	3	2	2	7	5	8
Wilkerson	15	6	2	2	11	3	14
Laskowski	13	4	6	4	3	3	12
Abernethy	1	0	0	0	0	0	0
Radford	0	0	0	0	0	1	0
Team					2		
Totals	**79**	**37**	**20**	**16**	**50**	**21**	**90**

Halftime: UK 44, Indiana 44

UCLA 92, UK 85

NCAA Championship
March 31, 1975
San Diego, Calif.

UCLA gave John Wooden the perfect going-away present, beating the Wildcats 92-85 for their 10th national championship in the last 12 years. Wooden, the celebrated "Wizard of Westwood," announced his decision to call it quits on the day before the title game.

For the Wildcats, it was a disappointing and frustrating 40 minutes. Despite shooting poorly (38.4 percent) and being whipped on the boards (55-49), they still managed to put themselves into a winning position. But when the usually accurate Kevin Grevey missed a pair of crucial free throws following a UCLA technical, the momentum that had belonged to UK shifted back to the Bruins' corner.

With Grevey and Bob Guyette providing the heavy fireworks, the Cats trimmed a 10-point UCLA lead to 76-75 with seven minutes left. That's when UCLA opened the door and gave the Cats a golden opportunity to take control of the game. UCLA's Dave Meyers, after being called for a charging foul, was slapped with a technical for pounding his fist on the court. But Grevey, a 79-percent free throw shooter, missed the technical and the front end of the bonus. On the next possession, James Lee was called for an offensive foul, sending Meyers to the charity stripe. When the Bruin forward hit both freebies, UK's potential four-point lead was instead a 78-75 deficit.

Guyette rifled in a short jumper to make it 78-77, but that was as close as the Cats would get. The Bruins, having avoided disaster, slowly eased away in the final five minutes to give Wooden his championship sendoff.

Grevey paced the Wildcats with 34 points despite an off night from the field (13 of 30). Guyette gave a superb

effort, scoring 16 points, including 14 in the second half. Mike Flynn also hit double figures with 10.

Richard Washington had 28 points and 12 rebounds, while Meyers ended the night with 24 points and 11 boards. The Bruins also benefited from strong defensive efforts by Pete Trgovich and 7'1" Ralph Drollinger. Trgovich held Jimmy Dan Conner to just nine points. Drollinger, along with Washington, limited UK centers Rick Robey, Mike Phillips and Dan Hall to a combined total of eight points.

Kentucky (85)	FGA	FGM	FTA	FTM	RB	PF	TP
Grevey	30	13	10	8	5	4	34
Guyette	11	7	2	2	7	3	16
Robey	3	1	0	0	9	5	2
Conner	12	4	2	1	5	1	9
Flynn	9	3	5	4	3	4	10
Givens	10	3	3	2	6	3	8
Johnson	3	0	0	0	3	3	0
Phillips	7	1	3	2	6	4	4
Hall	1	1	0	0	1	0	2
Lee	0	0	0	0	0	1	0
Team					4		
Totals	**86**	**33**	**25**	**19**	**49**	**28**	**85**

UCLA (92)	FGA	FGM	FTA	FTM	RB	PF	TP
Meyers	18	9	7	6	11	4	24
Johnson	9	3	1	0	7	2	6
Washington	23	12	5	4	12	4	28
Trgovich	16	7	4	2	5	4	16
McCarter	6	3	3	2	2	1	8
Drollinger	6	4	5	2	13	4	10
Team					5		
Totals	**78**	**38**	**25**	**16**	**55**	**19**	**92**

Halftime: UCLA 43, UK 40

UK 67, Kansas 66 (OT)

Dec. 9, 1978
Lexington, Ky.

The great Houdini never pulled off a better bit of magic than the Wildcats did in this game against fifth-ranked Kansas.

Down by six with 31 seconds left in overtime, the Wildcats scored seven straight points, including the game-winning free throw by Kyle Macy after a Kansas technical, to come away with a climb-out-of-the-grave 67-66 victory.

It was one of the most improbable and unforgettable wins in UK's illustrious basketball history. Many of the 23,472 fans were on their way out of Rupp Arena when Macy and his teammates performed their own bit of Houdini-like magic.

Here's how the dramatic finish unfolded:

With 31 seconds remaining, Darnell Valentine canned two free throws to give Kansas its 66-60 lead and send Big Blue fans heading for the exits.

Nine seconds later, Dwight Anderson drove the lane and scored to cut the Kansas lead to four. On the ensuing in-bounds pass, Valentine was whistled for a foul, sending Anderson to the charity stripe. The precocious Wildcat freshman missed the front end of the bonus, then waded in, claimed the rebound and drew another foul. This time, he was on target with both free tosses to make it 66-64 with 10 seconds left.

As Kansas attempted to in-bounds the ball, Anderson knocked it away from Mac Stallcup, then somehow managed to slap it across court to Macy, who calmly swished a 15-footer with four seconds remaining.

Instinctively, Valentine signaled for a timeout. It was a fatal mistake—the Jayhawks were out of timeouts. Valentine's error resulted in a technical, sending Macy to the foul line. His free throw hit the front of the rim, then rolled in for the deciding point.

After the game, Vernon Hatton, another Wildcat famous for performing plenty of magic during his playing days, was asked if he was among those fans who had thrown in the towel.

"Almost," a grinning Hatton said. "No, not really. Ever since that Temple game, I don't leave my seat anymore until a game's over."

Then Hatton added: "They can forget all about me now and talk about this one for the next 20 years."

Macy led UK with 15 points. The unfortunate Valentine was the game's top scorer with 27 points.

Kentucky (67)	FGA	FGM	FTA	FTM	RB	PF	TP
Stephens	6	2	0	0	0	1	4
Cowan	9	4	2	0	7	4	8
Williams	4	2	6	6	9	4	10
Aleksinas	7	3	3	2	1	2	8
Macy	11	6	3	3	2	1	15
Claytor	9	3	0	0	0	5	6
Anderson	2	1	3	2	1	2	4

Shidler	9	4	0	0	0	5	8
Verderber	2	0	0	0	1	1	0
Tillman	6	2	0	0	6	0	4
Team					2		
Totals	**65**	**27**	**17**	**13**	**29**	**25**	**67**

Kansas (66)	FGA	FGM	FTA	FTM	RB	PF	TP
Guy	8	4	8	5	5	3	13
Crawford	8	5	2	1	6	4	11
Mokeski	11	4	0	0	8	5	8
Fowler	3	0	6	5	2	2	5
Valentine	15	9	11	9	6	4	27
Stallcup	1	1	0	0	1	0	2
Neal	0	0	0	0	0	0	0
Team					4		
Totals	**46**	**23**	**27**	**20**	**32**	**18**	**66**

Halftime: Kansas 35, UK 28
Regulation: UK 56, Kansas 56

UK 52, Michigan State 49

NCAA Mideast Region Final
March 18, 1978
Dayton, Ohio

Kyle Macy's six pressure-packed free throws inside the final three minutes enabled the Wildcats to hold off Michigan State 52-49 and earn a berth in the Final Four. In St. Louis a week later, these Cats would beat Arkansas and Duke to capture the school's fifth NCAA title and first since the Fiddlin' Five did the trick in 1958.

Another crucial key to this win was Joe B. Hall's decision to switch from a man-to-man defense to a 1-3-1 zone. That move stymied the Spartan offense, and in particular shut down Earvin "Magic" Johnson, who finished with just two field goals in 10 attempts and six points.

But it was Macy, cool and icy under pressure, who played the biggest role in helping the Cats secure the victory. After his three-point play snapped a 41-41 deadlock and gave the Cats their biggest lead of the second half, Macy went to the line three times with his club clinging to a one-point lead, making good on the one-plus-one each time. The final two came with 31 seconds remaining and UK on top 50-49. They also came after Spartan coach Jud Heathcote called a timeout, hoping to ice Macy. But Heathcote's gambit failed—all the ice was in Macy's veins.

"The timeouts didn't bother me," Macy later said. "In fact, I used them to get my breath back. I tried to do the reverse of what they were trying to do to me."

Michigan State, led by Greg Kelser, owned the opening half, taking a 27-22 lead into the dressing room at the break. The Spartans still held a 31-24 lead when the Cats began to make their move, eventually catching up at 35-35 on a James Lee dunk. Michigan State went ahead at 37-35 and 39-37, but each time the Cats managed to even things up, first on two freebies by Macy and later on a Jack Givens layup.

The Cats claimed their first lead since early in the game when Mike Phillips hit two free tosses to make it 41-39 with just over seven minutes remaining. After Johnson tied it with one of his two field goals, Macy's three-point play put UK on top for good.

And once the Cats were on top, Cool Kyle made sure they stayed there.

The Cats hit just 10 of 25 shots in the opening half, then picked it up in the final 20 minutes, shooting 57 percent. In all the Cats hit 18 of 39 for 46 percent. Michigan State hit 22 of 41 for 53.7 percent.

Macy paced the Cats with 18 points. Givens finished with 14, while Phillips added 10. Phillips also led the Cats with eight rebounds.

Kelser topped the Spartans with 19 points and 13 rebounds. Bob Chapman chipped in with 10 points.

Following the game, Spartan coach Heathcote proved himself to be something of a prophet.

"We told our kids whoever won this game would win the national championship," he said. "Maybe we're stupid, but we included ourselves in that. We could have won it. Now I believe Kentucky will win the national championship."

A week later, Hall's Cats turned that prophecy into reality.

Kentucky (52)	FGA	FGM	FTA	FTM	RB	PF	TP
Givens	12	6	3	2	7	3	14
Robey	4	3	0	0	4	1	6
Phillips	5	3	4	4	8	1	10
Macy	10	4	11	10	1	2	18
Claytor	5	0	0	0	0	2	0
Lee	1	1	0	0	1	4	2
Shidler	2	1	0	0	1	2	2
Williams	0	0	0	0	1	1	0
Totals	**39**	**18**	**18**	**16**	**23**	**16**	**52**
Mich. State (49)	**FGA**	**FGM**	**FTA**	**FTM**	**RB**	**PF**	**TP**

Joe B. Hall got together with All-American guard Kyle Macy prior to a UK practice. Macy's pressure-packed free throws beat Michigan State 52-49 and kept the Cats alive in their march to the 1978 NCAA title.

Johnson	10	2	2	2	4	4	6
Kelser	12	9	3	1	13	3	19
Vincent	7	4	0	0	1	1	8
Donnelly	0	0	2	2	0	5	2
Chapman	9	5	0	0	1	5	10
Charles	3	2	0	0	0	0	4
Brkovich	0	0	0	0	0	0	0
Totals	**41**	**22**	**7**	**5**	**19**	**18**	**49**

Halftime: MSU 27, UK 22

Louisville 80, UK 68 (OT)

NCAA Mideast Regional Final
March 26, 1983
Knoxville, Tenn.

For 40 minutes, the long-awaited "Dream Game" between UK and Louisville was a classic.

For five minutes, it was no contest.

Using a relentless full-court press, the Cardinals reeled off the first 14 points in overtime to turn a heart-in-the-throat thriller into a convincing 80-68 victory in the NCAA Mideast Regional final. It was the first meeting between the two schools since 1959.

The Cards upped the intensity level in the OT and the Cats withered under the pressure, coughing up the ball five times on their first seven possessions.

The Louisville press, said UK's Jim Master, "was like a calvary charge."

Each team had its run during the game's first 30 minutes. The Cats struck early, forging a 37-30 lead by the half. The Cardinals responded with a 20-8 run midway through the second half to take a 58-53 advantage, setting the stage for a wild final eight minutes of intense, emotional basketball.

Master banged home a 20-footer, Melvin Turpin and Derrick Hord combined for three free throws and Charles Hurt

scored on a rebound to even the score at 60-60 with 3:18 left in regulation. Following a Louisville turnover, the Cats worked the clock down to 16 seconds before Dirk Minniefield eased along the baseline for a layup. But Minniefield's shot was blocked by Charles Jones and rebounded by Scooter McCray. McCray fired a pass to brother Rodney, who then passed ahead to Lancaster Gordon. Gordon angled to the right and banked in a nine-foot jumper to give his team a 62-60 lead.

With time running out, a wide-open Master rescued the Cats by calmly swishing a 12-foot baseline jumper just as the final buzzer sounded.

But the euphoria was short-lived, thanks to Louisville's relentless press and 10 points by guard Milt Wagner. The Cards opened the OT with two quick buckets—both by Gordon—then went on to score 10 more before the Cats finally broke the ice. But by then the outcome had already been settled.

Gordon had 24 points to lead the Louisville attack. Wagner finished with 18 and Rodney McCray added 15.

Master and Turpin each scored 18 for the Cats, while Minniefield finished with 12.

Kentucky (68)	FGA	FGM	FTA	FTM	RB	PF	TP
Hord	9	4	2	1	2	1	9
Hurt	5	3	2	1	6	3	7
Turpin	13	8	2	2	9	4	18
Minniefield	13	6	0	0	3	4	12
Master	13	9	0	0	2	4	18
Beal	0	0	0	0	0	3	0
Harden	0	0	0	0	0	0	0
Bearup	1	1	2	0	3	0	2
Walker	3	1	0	0	1	1	2
Team					1		
Team	57	32	8	4	27	20	68

Louisville (80)	FGA	FGM	FTA	FTM	RB	PF	TP
S. McCray	6	3	1	1	7	3	7
R. McCray	7	7	2	1	8	3	15
Jones	9	4	6	4	7	1	12
Gordon	21	11	3	2	1	1	24
Wagner	10	7	4	4	2	2	18
Valentine	0	0	0	0	0	0	0
West	0	0	0	0	0	0	0
Hall	0	0	0	0	0	0	0
Thompson	4	2	1	0	2	1	4
Team					1		

| Totals | 57 | 34 | 17 | 12 | 28 | 12 | 80 |

Halftime: UK 37, Louisville 30
Regulation: UK 62, Louisville 62

Georgetown 53, UK 40

NCAA Semifinal
March 31, 1984
Seattle, Wash.

Three-for-33, 9.1 percent—numbers no Wildcat fan will ever forget.

After playing superbly in the opening half, building a 29-22 lead by intermission, the Wildcats suddenly turned colder than an Antarctic winter, hitting on just three of 33 second-half shots.

The outcome: Georgetown 53, UK 40.

Initially, the Cats' cold shooting was seen as a temporary slump. They would, everyone knew, regain their composure, solve the agressive Hoya man-to-man defense and find the shooting touch that had enabled them to control the first half. But as time passed, and as more and more shots continued to miss their mark, UK's futility level reached epic proportions. By the time a frazzled Joe B. Hall tossed his rolled-up program over his shoulder with four minutes remaining, UK's shooting woes had become almost comic.

What made it even more mystifying is that there was no hint of the disaster that lay ahead. The Cats shot 50 percent (10 of 20) in the first half. They handled the rugged, intimidating Hoya defense. They rebounded well. All of that, combined with Patrick Ewing's foul troubles, led to a 27-15 Wildcat lead with just over three minutes left in the first half. Ewing, the Hoyas' All-American center, sat out almost nine minutes after being hit with his third personal foul.

The Cats, making their first Final Four appearance since 1978, had the championship game well within their sights.

Then the second half began. One by one, the Wildcat players launched shots that failed to find the mark. The poor shooting had suddenly become contagious. It took almost 10 minutes before Winston Bennett scored to finally break the ice. By then, the Hoyas, keyed by Michael Jackson and David Wingate, were in complete control.

For the game, UK hit 13 of 53 shots for 24.5 percent. They also lost the rebounding battle 43-33.

Jackson led the Hoyas with 12 points and 10 rebounds. Bowie had 10 points and 11 rebounds for the Cats.

The day after watching his team's frustrating performance, Hall was asked how he slept during the night. "Like a baby," Hall replied. "I was up every two hours, crying."

Kentucky (40)	FGA	FGM	FTA	FTM	RB	PF	TP
Bowie	10	3	4	4	11	3	10
Walker	3	1	2	2	3	3	4
Turpin	11	2	2	1	5	2	5
Beal	8	2	2	2	1	4	6
Master	7	2	2	2	1	1	6
Bennett	8	1	0	0	7	5	2
Blackmon	5	2	2	1	1	3	5
Bearup	0	0	2	2	0	0	2
Harden	1	0	0	0	2	1	0
Team					2		
Totals	**53**	**13**	**16**	**14**	**33**	**22**	**40**

Georgetown (53)	FGA	FGM	FTA	FTM	RB	PF	TP
Wingate	8	5	2	1	3	0	11
Dalton	1	0	0	0	4	1	0
Ewing	6	4	0	0	9	3	8
Brown	1	0	1	0	2	4	0
Jackson	9	4	6	4	10	2	12
Smith	4	2	2	1	2	2	5
Martin	4	1	0	0	1	1	2
Graham	6	4	2	0	6	3	8
Williams	7	1	0	0	3	3	2
Broadnax	4	2	2	1	1	0	5
Team					2		
Totals	**50**	**23**	**15**	**7**	**43**	**19**	**53**

Halftime: UK 29, Georgetown 22

UK 85, Louisville 51

Dec. 27, 1986
Louisville, Ky.

Freshman Rex Chapman electrified a national television audience, knocking down five three-pointers and scoring 26 points to lead the Wildcats to an 85-51 win over Louisville in Freedom Hall.

It was a dazzling performance by a UK team that took charge early and never let up. The Cats shot 54.2 percent from the field (32 of 59), hit 11 of 17 three-point attempts and out-rebounded the Cardinals 41-33.

Chapman led the UK romp, scoring in every conceivable

manner—long-range bombs, in-close jumpers, dunks and tricky finger-rolls. His acrobatic layup through the teeth of Louisville's defense put an exclamation mark on a first half that ended with UK leading 38-28.

The Cards opened fast, going on top 4-0 on back-to-back baskets by Kenny Payne and Tony Kimbro. But that would be the Cards' one moment of glory. With Chapman dropping in three treys, the Cats quickly assumed command, going up 28-17 before settling on their 10-point halftime margin.

The issue was settled for good in the opening minutes of the second half, thanks to a 10-0 run that gave the Cats a 48-28 lead with 15:33 still left to play. From there, it only got worse for Louisville, which suffered its worst loss during the Denny Crum era. By the time James Blackmon buried two three-pointers in a span of 86 seconds and Rob Lock delivered a baseline dunk, the Cats' destruction of "Little Brother" (Eddie Sutton's term) was complete.

While Chapman was clearly the game's brightest star, he wasn't the only Wildcat to shine. Ed Davender finished with 16 points, eight rebounds and five assists, Blackmon had 11 points and was a perfect three-for-three from behind the three-point line, and Richard Madison scored nine points and pulled down 17 rebounds.

Kimbro and Felton Spencer led the Cardinals with 10 points each.

Kentucky (85)	FGA	FGM	3FG	FTA	FTM	RB	PF	TP
Thomas	3	2	0-0	2	2	5	4	6
Lock	5	4	0-0	1	1	7	4	9
Blackmon	7	4	3-3	2	0	1	2	11
Davender	13	5	1-3	7	5	8	1	16
Chapman	20	10	5-8	3	1	0	2	26
Madison	7	4	0-0	1	1	17	3	9
Miller	4	3	2-3	0	0	3	3	8
Jenkins	0	0	0-0	0	0	0	0	0
Bruce	0	0	0-0	0	0	0	0	0
Shigg	0	0	0-0	0	0	0	0	0
Team						0		
Totals	**59**	**32**	**11-17**	**16**	**10**	**41**	**19**	**85**

Louisville (51)	FGA	FGM	3FG	FTA	FTM	RB	PF	TP
Payne	8	3	1-4	0	0	1	2	7
Crook	5	1	0-0	6	4	7	2	6
Ellison	8	2	0-0	0	0	4	0	4
Hawley	3	1	0-1	0	0	2	1	2
Kimbro	9	4	0-0	2	2	3	3	10

Williams	2	0	0-2	0	0	0	0	0
McSwain	2	1	0-0	1	0	4	0	2
West	2	0	0-1	0	0	2	2	0
Marshall	2	1	0-0	0	0	1	1	2
Abram	10	4	0-0	0	0	3	2	8
Spencer	7	4	0-0	6	2	5	0	10
Team						1		
Totals	**58**	**21**	**1-8**	**15**	**8**	**33**	**13**	**51**

Halftime: UK 38, Louisville 28

UK 100, LSU 95

Feb. 15, 1990
Lexington, Ky.

With a record Rupp Arena crowd of 24,301 looking on, cool and calm Richie Farmer hit six free throws in the final 65 seconds to help the Wildcats hold on for a stunning 100-95 victory over fast-charging LSU.

This win, perhaps more than any other, set the tone for the Rick Pitino Era at UK. It also announced to the college basketball world that the Wildcats, despite being hammered by NCAA sanctions, were not to be taken lightly.

To knock off ninth-ranked LSU, the Cats had to overcome a sizzling 41-point performance by Chris Jackson and a Tiger frontline that featured seven-footers Shaquille O'Neal and Stanley Roberts.

The fearless Widcats struck hard and often in the early going, riding Derrick Miller's hot hand to a 41-18 lead with 6:24 left in the first half. LSU responded with a 14-0 run before Miller came through with another trey for the Wildcats. At the break, UK held a 48-36 advantage.

The Cats maintained a lead of 12 to 17 points throughout most of the second half, and were ahead 88-74 with five minutes left. Then Jackson took charge, hitting three-pointers from all over the court despite being double- and triple-teamed by the Cats. When he buried his sixth trey of the night, UK's once-formidable lead had been shaved to 94-92. The upset that appeared all but certain was now very much in doubt.

It was left to Farmer to slam the door shut on LSU's comeback bid. Farmer, the Clay County schoolboy legend, hit two free throws on each of the Wildcats' next three possessions to secure the upset.

Miller and Deron Feldhaus paced the UK scoring attack with 29 and 24 points, respectively. Sean Woods had 12,

Richie Farmer may have lost this rebound to massive Shaquille O'Neal, but his six late free throws were enough to help UK score a shocker over LSU.

Reggie Hanson 11 and Farmer and John Pelphrey 10 apiece.

O'Neal finished with 14 points, 21 rebounds and six blocked shots before fouling out with 6:52 left in the game.

Kentucky (100)	FGA	FGM	3FG	FTA	FTM	RB	PF	TP
Pelphrey	10	3	1-4	5	3	6	5	10
Feldhaus	18	9	1-3	6	5	9	2	24
Hanson	13	4	1-3	5	2	12	3	11
Miller	27	10	5-16	4	4	4	0	29
Woods	5	4	0-0	4	4	2	3	12
Brassow	4	1	1-2	2	1	6	5	4
Farmer	7	1	0-5	8	8	2	3	10
Team						8		

Totals	84	32	9-33	34	27	49	21	100

LSU (95)	FGA	FGM	3FG	FTA	FTM	RB	PF	TP
Singleton	1	0	0-0	0	0	3	3	0
O'Neal	8	6	0-0	5	2	21	5	14
Sims	6	2	0-1	3	3	3	0	7
Williamson	9	3	1-3	5	2	0	4	9
Jackson	29	13	7-18	9	8	3	3	41
Roberts	15	6	0-0	2	1	14	3	13
Devall	6	3	0-0	3	3	7	4	9
Boudreaux	0	0	0-0	0	0	3	1	0
Krajewski	1	1	0-0	0	0	0	0	2
Team						6		
Totals	75	34	8-22	27	19	60	23	95

Halftime: UK 48, LSU 36

Duke 104, UK 103 (OT)

NCAA East Regional Final
March 28, 1992
Philadelphia, Pa.

It has been called the greatest game ever played, and, perhaps fittingly, it took nothing less than perfection to decide the outcome.

Christian Laettner capped a perfect shooting night by hitting a turnaround jumper from 17 feet away as time expired to give Duke a 104-103 overtime victory against a Wildcat team that came within 2.1 seconds of earning a spot in the Final Four. Laettner caught Grant Hill's 75-foot pass, turned and fired the game-winner over Deron Feldhaus and John Pelphrey. For the game, Laettner was 10-for-10 from the field and 10-for-10 from the charity stripe, finishing with 31 points.

In a game marked by a succession of brilliant and remarkable plays, the gutsy Cats, although hampered by foul problems, overcame a 12-point second-half deficit to grab a 103-102 lead on Sean Woods' high-arcing shot over Laettner. Following a Duke timeout, Hill, unguarded at the baseline, rifled his pass to Laettner, who whirled and fired. The shot was dead center.

The final three minutes of regulation and the five-minute overtime period saw basketball—and the human spirit—raised to the highest level. Neither team backed down, neither team choked. Instead, it was almost as if the players were saying, "OK, that was a great play. Now let me show you a greater one."

It was terrific stuff.

The real fireworks began after Woods rattled home a three-pointer to tie it at 81-81. The two clubs continued to trade leads for the next two minutes, with the Cats going in front 89-87, only to see the Blue Devils fight back to regain a 93-91 advantage on a leaner by Thomas Hill with 1:03 left. The Cats answered when Feldhaus put in a Pelphrey miss to make it 93-93 and force the overtime.

With score knotted at 96-96, Pelphrey wormed his way between Grant Hill and Laettner to score on a short jumper. After Laettner tied it again by hitting two free throws, Woods missed a jumper and Duke rebounded. At the 32-second mark, Laettner knocked down an off-balance jump shot to give Duke a 100-98 lead. But once again the Cats were not to be denied. Mashburn took a pass from Pelphrey, drove the baseline, scored and drew a foul from Antonio Lang. Mashburn hit the free throw to make 101-100.

On Duke's next possession, Mashburn was whistled for his fifth foul while trying to steal the ball from Laettner. Once again, Laettner came through, hitting both free tosses to give Duke a 102-101 lead. Following a UK timeout with 7.8 seconds, Woods drove down the floor and laid in his driving shot over the 6'11" Laettner.

Duke called timeout with 2.1 seconds left.

The rest is history.

Mashburn led the Cats with 28 points and 10 rebounds. Woods finished with 21, while Dale Brown and Pelphrey had 18 and 16, respectively.

Bobby Hurley provided solid support for Laettner, scoring 22 points and handing out 10 assists. Thomas Hill chipped in 19 points for the winning Blue Devils, who would go on to repeat as national champions.

Kentucky (103)	FGA	FGM	3FG	FTA	FTM	RB	PF	TP
Mashburn	16	11	3-4	3	3	10	5	28
Pelphrey	7	5	3-4	3	3	1	4	16
Martinez	4	2	1-2	0	0	0	5	5
Woods	15	9	1-1	2	2	2	4	21
Farmer	3	2	1-2	6	4	1	2	9
Feldhaus	6	2	0-2	2	1	1	1	5
Brown	11	6	3-5	5	3	3	4	18
Ford	2	0	0-1	0	0	1	0	0
Timberlake	0	0	0-0	2	1	0	2	1
Riddick	0	0	0-0	0	0	0	1	0
Braddy	1	0	0-1	0	0	0	0	0
Team						2		
Totals	65	37	12-22	23	17	21	28	103

Duke (104)	FGA	FGM	3FG	FTA	FTM	RB	PF	TP
Lang	2	2	0-0	1	0	3	4	4
Davis	6	3	0-2	10	7	5	5	13
Laettner	10	10	1-1	10	10	7	4	31
Hurley	12	6	5-10	6	5	3	3	22
T. Hill	10	6	2-3	5	5	3	3	19
G. Hill	10	5	0-0	2	1	10	2	11
Parks	2	2	0-0	0	0	0	2	4
Clark	0	0	0-0	0	0	0	0	0
Totals	52	34	8-16	34	28	31	23	104

Halftime: Duke 50, UK 45
Regulation: UK 93, Duke 93

Michigan 81, UK 78 (OT)

NCAA Semifinal
April 3, 1993
New Orleans, La.

Michigan scored six unanswered points in the final 56 seconds to hang a bitter and disappointing 81-78 overtime loss on the Wildcats in NCAA Tournament semifinal action. It was the second straight year in which the Cats' championship hopes ended with an overtime defeat.

After building a 76-72 lead in the extra period, the Cats, hurt by the absence of three key players, managed to score just two points in the final 3:48. The most-noticeable Wildcat missing in action was Jamal Mashburn, who fouled out with more than three minutes remaining after scoring 26 points.

With Mashburn watching from the sidelines, Michigan charged back to take a 79-78 lead on a Chris Webber bucket in the low post. The Cats then squandered a chance to reclaim the lead when Rodney Dent mishandled the ball on a layup attempt. Jalen Rose, fouled during the scramble for the rebound, upped the Wolverines' lead to 81-78 by sinking a pair of free throws with 21 seconds left. The Cats twice looked for a three-point shot that would tie the game, but on each occasion Webber was there to swat the ball away.

Given the circumstances, the Cats were fortunate to still be breathing at the end of regulation. They trailed 40-35 at the half, and would have been further behind had it not been for Mashburn. The junior forward, playing in what would be his last game in a UK uniform, scored 17 of his team's final 28 points before intermission to keep the Cats close.

In the second half, trailing 54-44, the Cats rallied to

draw even by scoring 10 unanswered points in the next 82 seconds. But with 6:13 left in regulation, the Cats suffered their first crippling blow—senior guard Dale Brown was forced to leave the game after injuring his right shoulder. Brown had 16 points at the time of his injury.

The Cats also benefited from a controversial call with 10 seconds remaining in regulation. Down 71-69, the Cats set up a three-point shot for Travis Ford. But Ford, trapped by a swarm of Michigan defenders, lost the ball. As Webber picked up the loose ball, Jimmy King was called for fouling Ford. Ford made both free throws to send the game into OT.

The Cats quickly took their four-point lead, but any hope of holding off talent-rich Michigan was lost when Jared Prickett and Mashburn fouled out less than two minutes into the extra period.

Webber had a monster game for the Wolverines, scoring 27 points and spearing 13 rebounds. Rose and Juwan Howard racked up 18 and 17 points, respectively.

Ford chipped in with 12 for the Cats.

Kentucky (78)	FGA	FGM	3FG	FTA	FTM	RB	PF	TP
Mashburn	18	10	1-3	9	5	6	5	26
Prickett	6	1	0-1	7	7	7	5	9
Dent	6	2	0-0	2	2	3	4	6
Ford	10	3	2-6	4	4	5	2	12
Brown	10	6	4-6	0	0	1	2	16
Rhodes	1	0	0-1	2	1	1	4	1
Riddick	4	2	0-0	0	0	2	2	4
Martinez	3	0	0-2	0	0	1	3	0
Brassow	0	0	0-0	0	0	0	0	0
Delk	3	1	0-2	2	2	3	0	4
Braddy	0	0	0-0	0	0	0	0	0
Team						5		
Totals	61	25	7-21	26	21	34	27	78

Michigan (81)	FGA	FGM	3FG	FTA	FTM	RB	PF	TP
Webber	17	10	0-1	9	7	13	3	27
Jackson	7	4	0-0	5	3	8	4	11
Howard	12	6	0-0	7	5	3	4	17
Rose	16	6	0-2	7	6	6	3	18
King	3	1	0-0	0	0	3	5	2
Riley	4	2	0-0	0	0	4	2	4
Pelinka	1	0	0-1	2	2	1	3	2
Voskull	1	0	0-0	0	0	0	0	0
Team						2		
Totals	61	29	0-4	30	23	40	24	81

Halftime: Michigan 40, UK 35
Regulation: UK 71, Michigan 71

UK 99, LSU 95

Feb. 15, 1994
Baton Rouge, La.

In what will forever been remembered as the "Mardi Gras Miracle," the never-give-up Wildcats roared back from a 31-point deficit in the final 16 minutes to beat home-standing LSU 99-95. When the final buzzer sounded, and as the Cats celebrated the greatest comeback in school history, 11,253 LSU fans sat in stunned disbelief.

They had every right to be stunned. Only minutes earlier, after watching the Tigers build a 68-37 lead with just under 16 minutes remaining, the celebration and noise level inside the Maravich Assembly Center easily rivaled the party atmosphere out on Bourbon Street. The red-hot Tigers were unstoppable, racking up points in bunches, while the frustrated Cats were rapidly disintegrating. Ronnie Henderson led the assault, connecting on five treys, including three within a 61-second span. Later, when Clarence Ceasar scored nine points in an 18-0 run that separated the two teams by 31 points, the LSU faithful went into A-1 party mode.

But the celebration was premature. The Cats, thought to be down for the count, suddenly began to light up the joint with three-pointers. A trio of reserves—Chris Harrison, Walter McCarty and Jeff Brassow—were at the center of UK's comeback. Harrison accounted for eight points and Rodrick Rhodes added seven in a 24-4 UK spurt that whittled the LSU lead to 72-61 with 9:52 left. Brassow nailed four three-pointers during the Cats' comeback, including two that helped stymie LSU uprisings.

As the Cats continued to turn the party into a wake, LSU began to resemble the Keystone Kops. The Tigers fired up poor shots (hitting just six of 18 in the final 15:06), missed nine of 16 free throws during a crucial eight-minute period and generally handled the basketball like it was a blazing cinder.

The Cats kept closing the gap until a McCarty three-pointer put them in front 96-95 with 19 seconds remaining. The Tigers had two opportunities to avoid embarrassment, but failed to cash in on either chance. The door was left open for the Cats to finalized this historic comeback, which they did by sinking three of four free throws.

McCarty was UK's top gun with 23 points. Other Cats in double figures included Brassow (14), Gimel Martinez (13), Rhodes (11) and Travis Ford (10).

LSU was led by the 1-2 punch of Henderson and Ceasar, who scored 36 and 32 points, respectively.

"I've coached 200 NBA games and about 16 years of college," UK coach Rick Pitino said. "I've never, ever seen a comeback—on the road—like that in my life."

Kentucky (99)	FGA	FGM	3FG	FTA	FTM	RB	PF	TP
Rhodes	9	3	1-6	6	4	3	5	11
Prickett	4	1	0-0	2	0	0	1	2
Riddick	6	4	0-0	2	1	5	4	9
Delk	8	3	2-7	2	1	7	4	9
Ford	8	3	2-6	2	2	2	3	10
Martinez	10	6	0-3	2	1	3	2	13
Brassow	7	5	4-5	2	0	1	4	14
McCarty	14	9	4-7	2	1	8	3	23
Sheppard	1	0	0-0	0	0	1	0	0
Epps	0	0	0-0	0	0	0	1	0
Harrison	4	3	2-3	1	0	2	2	8
Team						1		
Totals	**71**	**37**	**15-37**	**21**	**10**	**33**	**29**	**99**
LSU (95)	FGA	FGM	3FG	FTA	FTM	RB	PF	TP
Ceasar	18	10	4-7	11	8	10	4	32
Brandon	10	3	1-3	8	6	8	2	13
Burns	4	1	0-0	1	0	7	5	2
Owens	2	1	0-1	2	2	1	0	4
Gipson	2	0	0-0	0	0	4	3	0
Henderson	19	12	8-13	4	4	2	1	36
Titus	1	1	0-0	9	3	2	3	5
Roubtchenko	4	1	0-0	2	1	4	5	3
Team						2		
Totals	**60**	**29**	**13-24**	**37**	**24**	**40**	**23**	**95**

Halftime: LSU 48, UK 32

UK 95, Arkansas 93

SEC Tournament Championship
March 12, 1995
Atlanta, Ga.

Talk about a double feature. On this afternoon, 30,067 fans got to see "Night of the Living Dead I and II."

Twice, the Wildcats clawed their way out of the grave, first by rallying from 19 points down in regulation, then by overcom-

ing a nine-point deficit in overtime to beat defending national champion Arkansas 95-93 and claim the SEC tourney title.

At the beginning, with Arkansas hitting 14 of its first 22 shots (including six treys), Big Blue fans must have thought they were watching "Slaughterhouse Five." With Scotty Thurman doing the main damage, the Razorbacks raced to a 35-16 lead with just under 10 minutes left before intermission. Thurman scored 15 of his 17 points before the break.

Then the Cats began one of their classic comebacks, hitting 11 of their final 16 shots to close the margin to 50-44 at the half. Antoine Walker led the charge with eight points.

Arkansas regained the upper hand in the second half, pushing its lead to 72-60 on a Corliss Williamson dunk. But a three-pointer by Anthony Epps sparked a 20-8 UK run that ended when Mark Pope dropped in a pair of free throws to make it 80-80 with 22 seconds left. After the Cats came up with a steal, Rodrick Rhodes drew a foul with just over one second remaining. Rhodes, a 78-percent free throw shooter, missed both shots, sending the game into overtime.

The Razorbacks crashed out of the gate, scoring on their first five possessions in the OT to take a 91-82 lead with 1:39 remaining. But once again, the Cats refused to surrender. McCarty converted a three-point play, and after two free throws by Clint McDaniel, Tony Delk knocked down a trey to make it 93-88. Moments later, after a Walker layup made it 93-92, Epps stole a pass and drew a foul with 19 seconds left. The sophomore guard swished both freebies to put the Cats in front 94-93.

Arkansas had one final chance to survive, but Thurman's 22-footer was off the mark. Delk rebounded, then hit one of two free throws with six seconds left to give the Wildcats their fourth straight SEC Tournament championship.

Walker was brilliant for the winning Cats, scoring 23 points and grabbing seven rebounds. For his efforts, he was voted the tourney MVP. Delk finished with 15 points, while Pope and McCarty added 12 and 11, respectively. Pope was the game's top rebounder with 10.

Williamson led the Razorbacks with 22 points.

Kentucky (95)	FGA	FGM	3FG	FTA	FTM	RB	PF	TP
Rhodes	4	2	0-1	8	5	3	3	9
McCarty	10	5	0-1	1	1	5	3	11
Riddick	2	0	0-0	2	2	1	4	2
Delk	13	6	1-7	4	2	4	1	15
Sheppard	6	3	0-0	0	0	1	5	6
Pope	7	4	1-1	6	3	10	3	12
Epps	7	2	1-5	3	3	1	0	8
Walker	17	9	0-2	5	5	7	1	23
Prickett	2	2	0-0	3	3	6	1	7
Harrison	2	1	0-1	0	0	1	0	2
Team						1		
Totals	**70**	**34**	**3-18**	**32**	**24**	**40**	**21**	**95**

Arkansas (93)	FGA	FGM	3FG	FTA	FTM	RB	PF	TP
Thurman	15	7	3-8	0	0	8	3	17
Williamson	18	9	0-0	5	4	7	5	22
Robinson	10	5	1-2	4	3	9	3	14
McDaniel	11	5	3-6	6	3	4	5	16
Beck	5	4	0-0	4	2	5	3	10
Wilson	2	1	0-3	0	0	1	1	2
Stewart	4	0	0-0	0	0	0	3	0
Dillard	2	1	1-2	0	0	0	0	3
Rimac	5	3	3-3	0	0	0	0	9
Martin	1	0	0-1	0	0	0	0	0
Team						8		
Totals	**73**	**35**	**11-25**	**19**	**12**	**42**	**23**	**93**

Halftime: Arkansas 50, UK 44

Regulation: UK 80, Arkansas 80

Arizona 84, UK 79 (OT)

NCAA Championship
March 31, 1997
Indianapolis, Ind.

Arizona ended the Cats' dream of a second straight NCAA championship, winning an 84-79 overtime thriller in the RCA Dome. It was the first time since 1989 that the final game went into overtime, and only the sixth time in NCAA tourney history.

This game also turned out to be Rick Pitino's last as UK coach. Six weeks later, Pitino announced that he was leaving his UK post to take over the Boston Celtics.

Pitino's Cats came close to becoming the first repeat champions since Duke did it in 1991 and 1992, and just the seventh in NCAA history. But in the end, after another intense nail-biter, it was Arizona that had more gas left in the tank.

Arizona, led by its marvelous backcourt duo of Miles Simon and Mike Bibby, used a huge advantage at the free throw line to hang on for the victory. Arizona made good on 34 of 41 freebies to nine of 17 by the Cats.

In all, four Wildcats fouled out of the game.

The game was close all the way, with 15 ties and 19 lead changes. No more than six points ever separated the two clubs. Arizona grabbed control early, jumping to a 19-13 lead. But five straight points by Cameron Mills and two by Wayne Turner sent the Cats back in front 20-19. It was a back-and-forth scenario that would be played out until the end.

Arizona led 33-32 at the half, and extended that advantage to 44-38 when Bibby canned a 15-foot jumper with 14 minutes left. After Nazr Mohammed scored on a layup, Turner and Ron Mercer followed with back-to-back buckets to draw the Cats even at 44-44. Simon laid in a crip to push Arizona back in front, but Mercer answered with a three-point play to give the Cats a 47-46 lead. That would be the weary Mercer's last basket for the next 10 minutes.

Arizona threatened to break away in the final two minutes of regulation. Following a four-footer by Turner and a pair of Scott Padgett free throws that gave UK a 68-67 lead, Simon scored four points and Bibby added two to put Arizona ahead 72-68 with 1:01 remaining. The Cats' situation grew even more dire when Turner was tagged with his fifth foul.

But Mercer, silent for 10 minutes, came off a curl and knocked down a trey to close the margin to 72-71 with 51 seconds left. After Bennett Davison scored on a layup with 18 seconds remaining, Anthony Epps found the mark with a three-pointer to tie the game and force an extra five minutes.

Davison opened the OT by hitting two free throws, giving Arizona a lead it would never relinquish. Arizona outscored the Cats 10-5 in the extra period to claim the win. All 10 Arizona points came at the charity stripe.

Simon led all scorers with 30 points, making good on 14 of 17 free throws. Bibby finished with 19.

Padgett paced UK with 17 points. Mercer scored 13, Mohammed and Mills had 12 each and Epps chipped in with 11. Mohammed was the game's top rebounder with 11.

Kentucky (79)	FGA	FGM	3FG	FTA	FTM	RB	PF	TP
Mercer	9	5	2-4	1	1	9	5	13
Padgett	16	5	3-12	4	4	1	5	17
Magloire	1	0	0-0	0	0	4	4	0
Turner	9	4	0-0	1	0	4	5	8
Epps	13	4	3-8	0	0	5	0	11
Edwards	0	0	0-0	0	0	0	0	0
Prickett	4	1	0-0	5	4	5	5	6
Mohammed	11	6	0-0	6	0	11	3	12
Mills	9	5	2-6	0	0	1	2	12
Masiello	0	0	0-0	0	0	0	0	0
Totals	**72**	**30**	**10-30**	**17**	**9**	**40**	**29**	**79**

Arizona (84)	FGA	FGM	3FG	FTA	FTM	RB	PF	TP
Davison	9	3	0-0	3	3	7	2	9
Dickerson	8	1	1-3	2	2	4	0	5
Bramlett	3	1	0-0	1	1	6	5	3
Bibby	12	5	3-5	6	6	9	1	19
Simon	18	8	0-2	17	14	3	1	30
Terry	6	2	2-3	2	2	2	1	8
Edgerson	0	0	0-0	2	2	5	2	2
Harris	2	2	0-0	8	4	7	4	8
Team						2		
Totals	**58**	**22**	**6-13**	**41**	**34**	**45**	**16**	**84**

Halftime: Arizona 33, UK 32
Regulation: UK 74, Arizona 74

UK 86, Duke 84

NCAA South Regional Final
March 22, 1998
St. Petersburg, Fla.

Seldom has revenge ever tasted sweeter.

With the memory of that epic 1992 UK-Duke battle hovering like the ghost of Hamlet's father, the Wildcats came from 17 points down in the second half to beat the Blue Devils 86-84 and earn their third straight trip to the Final Four.

For first-year coach Tubby Smith's club, soon to be christened the "Comeback Cats," this was the first of three straight miracle wins that resulted in UK's second NCAA title in three years and its seventh overall. It was also a victory that went a long way toward laying to rest the haunting memory of that 104-103 loss in 1992. The evil spirit of Christian Laettner had finally been exorcised.

But with just under 10 minutes remaining, the probablility of UK reaching the Final Four was virtually non-existent. Duke led 71-54 and appeared to be flying in cruise control. With Trajan Langdon hitting a pair of three-pointers, the Blue Devils went on a 17-0 first-half

run to pull ahead 38-30. UK rallied to within six near the end of the first half, but still trailed by 10—49-39—at the break.

Duke's lead stayed between eight and 10 points until Mike Chappell and Steve Wojciechowski buried back-to-back three-pointers to make it 67-51. Moments later, following a tip-in by Chris Carrawell, the Blue Devils had upped their lead to 71-54.

Payback for 1992 suddenly seemed out of the question.

But the Cats dug in. Lightning-like three-pointers by Heshimu Evans and Scott Padgett and a three-point play by Wayne Turner pulled the Cats to within 71-63. After Wojciechowski made one of two free throws, Allen Edwards canned a 20-footer, Jeff Sheppard hit three free throws and Turner laid in a six-footer to make it 72-71 with six minutes remaining. In that spurt, the Cats scored on seven straight possessions.

After two Shane Battier freebies were offset by another Turner bucket, the Blue Devils gained some daylight by wrapping five points around an Evans follow shot to push their lead to 79-75.

Turner cut the difference in half with an 11-footer, then with 2:15 left Cameron Mills drained a three-pointer, his first field goal of the tournament, to give the Cats their first lead of the game at 80-79.

Roshown McLeod put the Blue Devils back in front with a pair of free throws, but Padgett knotted the score by hitting one of two free throws, then hit a three-pointer with 39.4 seconds left to put the Cats in front for good.

Inside the final 17 seconds, Turner and Edwards each hit a free throw to help the Cats preserve their victory.

The Cats placed five players in double figures, led by Sheppard with 18. Turner had 16, Evans 14, Padgett 12 and Edwards 11. Sheppard and Evans also grabbed 11 rebounds each.

McLeod topped the Blue Devils with 19, while Langdon added 18.

This marked the 11th time that these two old foes have done battle in which the outcome was decided by five points or less.

Kentucky (86)	FGA	FGM	3FG	FTA	FTM	RB	PF	TP
Edwards	8	4	2-5	2	1	2	4	11
Padgett	10	4	3-5	2	1	6	3	12
Mohammed	10	4	0-0	2	0	5	2	8
Turner	14	5	0-1	8	6	5	1	16
Sheppard	11	5	1-3	9	7	11	4	18
Smith	0	0	0-0	0	0	0	1	0
Evans	8	5	2-2	2	2	11	3	14
Mills	1	1	1-1	2	2	3	1	5
Magloire	1	1	0-0	0	0	1	2	2
Team						1		
Totals	**63**	**29**	**9-17**	**27**	**19**	**45**	**21**	**86**

Duke (84)	FGA	FGM	3FG	FTA	FTM	RB	PF	TP
McLeod	20	7	2-7	7	3	8	4	19
Carrawell	11	5	0-2	2	2	5	1	12
Brand	4	1	0-0	4	2	2	5	4
Wojciechowski	5	3	3-5	3	1	3	4	10
Langdon	14	6	3-8	4	3	5	2	18
Avery	4	2	0-1	0	0	4	1	4
Chappell	2	2	2-2	0	0	0	0	6
Battier	6	3	0-0	6	5	8	3	11
Burgess	1	0	0-0	0	0	0	2	0
Team						4		
Totals	**67**	**29**	**10-25**	**26**	**16**	**39**	**22**	**84**

Halftime: Duke 49, UK 39

UK 86, Stanford 85 (OT)

NCAA Semifinal
March 28, 1998
San Antonio, Texas

Led by Jeff Sheppard's career-high 27 points, the "Comeback Cats" did their thing once again, erasing a 10-point second-half deficit to beat Stanford 86-85 in a semifinal overtime thriller. With this win, UK became the first school since UCLA in 1973 to advance to three straight national championship games.

Stanford wasted no time doubling its 37-32 halftime advange, outscoring the Cats 9-4 in the opening minutes of the second half to go on top 46-36. Then Nazr Mohammed went to work for the Cats, accounting for six points in a 12-3 run that closed the gap to 49-48. Allen Edwards and Sheppard each contributed three points in that rally.

Trailing 53-48, the Cats strung together eight straight points to claim a 56-53 lead. Wayne Turner triggered the run with a 12-footer, then Mohammed sandwiched a pair of dunks around two Scott Padgett free throws to give the Cats their three-point lead.

After a three-point play by Mark Madsen put Stanford

in front 68-66, Sheppard hit back-to-back three-pointers to give UK a 72-68 lead with 1:17 left in regulation. Madsen scored on a layup, then after Turner hit one of two free throws, Stanford guard Arthur Lee came through with a clutch three-pointer to send the game into overtime.

Mohammed opened the OT by hitting one of two free throws. Sheppard followed with a four-foot jumper, then Mohammed laid in an eight-footer to give the Cats a 78-73 lead. Stanford closed to within 83-82, but two free throws by Turner and one by Sheppard were enough to withstand a final three-pointer by Peter Sauer.

Sheppard, the Final Four MVP, connected on nine of 15 shots from the field, including four of eight from three-point range. Mohammed, held to only a single point in the first half, scored 17 after intermission to finish with 18. Edwards and Padgett scored 11 and 10, respectively.

Lee had 26 points to lead Stanford.

Halftime: Stanford 37, UK 32
Regulation: UK 73, Stanford 73

Kentucky (86)	FGA	FGM	3FG	FTA	FTM	RB	PF	TP
Edwards	10	4	1-2	3	2	3	1	11
Padgett	8	2	0-3	6	6	6	3	10
Mohammed	14	7	0-0	6	4	5	4	18
Turner	8	2	0-0	9	4	2	2	8
Sheppard	15	9	4-8	7	5	6	3	27
Evans	7	2	0-2	0	0	6	2	4
Magloire	3	2	0-0	2	2	4	2	6
Smith	1	0	0-0	0	0	2	2	0
Mills	1	1	0-0	0	0	2	2	2
Bradley	0	0	0-0	0	0	0	1	0
Team						4		
Totals	**67**	**29**	**5-15**	**33**	**23**	**40**	**22**	**86**

Stanford (85)	FGA	FGM	3FG	FTA	FTM	RB	PF	TP
Sauer	4	3	2-3	0	0	7	2	8
Madsen	6	5	0-0	1	1	16	5	11
Young	11	5	0-0	0	0	7	5	10
Weems	23	6	3-11	3	2	1	1	17
Lee	12	6	5-8	9	9	3	4	26
Moseley	3	0	0-2	2	2	1	1	2
Mendez	4	1	1-4	0	0	1	1	3
Collins	3	1	0-0	7	5	5	3	7
McDonald	1	0	0-0	0	0	1	0	0
Van Elswyk	1	0	0-0	2	1	0	1	1
Seaton	0	0	0-0	0	0	2	0	0
Team						1		
Totals	**68**	**27**	**11-28**	**24**	**20**	**45**	**23**	**85**

Tubby Smith relied on Cameron Mills to supply outside scoring during the 1998 team's run to the NCAA title. Mills came through with a crucial three-pointer in the Cats' 86-84 win over Duke in the South Regional final.

UK 69, Louisville 61

NCAA Semifinal
March 31, 2012
New Orleans, La.

Standing between the Cats and a spot in the championship game was their arch-enemy—Louisville. This was the second time the two clubs clashed this season, and it would be a game that followed a similar course as the first one, which the Cats won 69-62. But that initial meeting, though important (every UK-Louisville meeting is viewed as Armageddon), this one had much more riding on the outcome.

Simply stated: The winner moves on, the loser heads home.

In this one, the Cats seized control early, saw that lead quickly evaporate, then managed to come up big enough down the stretch to walk away with a 69-61 victory. The win sent them into the title-game matchup against Kansas.

The Cats led by as many as 10 points on several occasions in the opening half, and were on top 35-28 at the break. Their lead swelled to 13 points (45-32) with 16:14 left to play. That's when the Cardinals began their comeback surge.

Led by Peyton Siva, who scored all 11 of his points after intermission, the Cards fought back to tie the score at 49-49 with 9:12 still remaining. It was a Siva trey that knotted the score.

Back-to-back buckets by Michael Kidd-Gilchrist put the Cats back in front 53-49. It was a lead they would not surrender.

After Siva canned a pair of free tosses to make it 53-51, the Cardinals went scoreless for the next five minutes. While the Cards were unable to buy a bucket, the Cats went to work. First, Terrence Jones scored on a jumper, then Darius Miller buried a trey and two free throws to extend the Cats' lead to 60-51 at the 4:29 mark.

Moments later, the Cardinals closed the gap to 63-58 following a Siva dunk and a Russ Smith free throw. But Anthony Davis and Kidd-Gilchrist answered with consecutive dunks that sealed it for the Cats. Inside the final minute, Wayne Blackshear and Kidd-Gilchrist swapped buckets to account for the final score.

Davis led the Cats with 18 points, 14 rebounds and five blocked shots. Miller finished with 13 points and Doron Lamb added 10. Kidd-Gilchrist, so big down the stretch, had nine points, while point guard Marquis Teague ended the game with eight points and five assists.

Siva's 11 points topped the Cards' scoring. Chane Behanan had 10 points and Gorgui Dieng pulled down a dozen rebounds.

This was the Cats' fifth straight challenging encounter. Previously, they defeated Western Kentucky University, Iowa State, No. 4-seed Indiana and No. 3-seed Baylor.

Kentucky (69)	FGA	FGM	3FG	FTA	FTM	RB	PF	TP
Davis	8	7	0-0	6	4	14	2	18
Miller	7	4	1-4	4	4	3	2	13
Lamb	9	4	0-2	3	2	1	1	10
Kidd-Gilchrist	6	4	0-0	4	1	4	3	9
Teague	8	4	0-0	0	0	2	4	8
Jones	8	3	0-0	3	0	7	2	6
Wiltjer	3	2	1-1	0	0	1	0	5
Vargas	0	0	0-0	0	0	0	0	0
Totals	**49**	**28**	**2-7**	**20**	**11**	**32**	**14**	**69**

Louisville (61)	FGA	FGM	3FG	FTA	FTM	RB	PF	TP
Siva	11	4	1-2	2	2	3	2	11
Behanan	9	4	0-2	2	2	9	1	10
R. Smith	15	4	0-1	2	1	3	2	9
Blackshear	5	3	1-2	3	2	4	4	9
C. Smith	11	3	1-2	2	1	1	1	8
Kuric	8	3	1-2	1	0	5	3	7
Dieng	10	3	0-0	1	1	12	2	7
Swopshire	0	0	0-0	0	0	0	1	0
Justice	0	0	0-0	0	0	0	0	0
Totals	**69**	**24**	**4-11**	**13**	**9**	**37**	**16**	**61**

Halftime: UK 35, Louisville 28

UConn 60, UK 54

NCAA Championship
April 7, 2014
Arlington, Texas

With the national championship on the line, the Cats, a team many considered something of a disappointment during the regular season, suffered a tough 60-54 loss to UConn. Cold shooting, particularly in the second half, was the key factor in this loss. In those final 20 minutes, the Cats connected on 7 of 21 shots for a frosty 33.3 percent. For the game, they shot just 39.1 percent.

UConn wasn't much better, especially in a second half that saw defense clearly upstage offense. The Huskies were

even colder in the second half than UK, making good on just 8 of 25 shots. But they were superior in the opening half, hitting for 50 percent (14 of 28).

The Huskies started strong, building a 30-15 advantage with just under six minutes left in the opening half. They were still on top 33-20 when the Cats began to cut into the margin. Back-to-back three-pointers by James Young and Andrew Harrison, followed by a Dakari Johnson free throw sliced the difference to 33-27.

After Shabazz Napier knocked in a bucket, Julius Randle scored twice in the lane to make it 35-31 at intermission.

The second half was an uphill, frustrating struggle for the Cats, who were able to close the difference to a single point (48-47), but their poor shooting kept them from ever taking control. And to the Huskies' credit, when things got dicey, they refused to buckle under the pressure.

After two Young free throws made it 48-47, Napier answered by sinking a three-pointer. Randle scored for the Cats, but UConn's Niels Giffey canned another trey to put his club in front 54-49. After that, the Cats could get no closer than four points.

This UK club, which finished with a 29-11 record overall and 12-6 mark in SEC action, had to travel a nearly impossible road to get to the championship game. Granted no favors by the selection committee, the Cats took on—and defeated—Kansas State, Wichita State, Louisville, Michigan and Wisconsin prior to squaring off against UConn in the title tilt. No UK team has ever been asked to wade through such a dangerous NCAA tourney minefield.

Young paced the Cats in the final game with 20 points. Randle finished with 10 points.

Napier led all scorers with 22 points.

Randle and Young were named to the All-Final Four squad.

Julius Randle scored 10 points in a losing cause against UConn.

Kentucky (54)	FGA	FGM	3FG	FTA	FTM	RB	PF	TP
Young	13	5	2-5	9	8	7	0	20
Randle	7	3	0-0	7	4	6	0	10
Johnson	5	2	0-0	4	1	4	1	5
Harrison, Aaron	7	3	1-5	1	0	4	2	7
Harrison, Andrew	9	3	2-4	0	0	5	2	8
Lee	0	0	0-0	0	0	0	1	0
Poythress	5	2	0-2	1	0	5	4	4
Hawkins	0	0	0-0	2	0	1	0	0
Totals	**46**	**18**	**5-16**	**24**	**13**	**32**	**10**	**54**
UConn (60)	**FGA**	**FGM**	**3FG**	**FTA**	**FTM**	**RB**	**PF**	**TP**
Nolan	3	0	0-0	0	0	1	4	0
Daniels	14	4	0-4	0	0	6	3	8
Giffey	7	3	2-4	2	2	5	2	10
Boatright	6	5	0-1	4	4	4	2	14
Napier	16	8	4-9	2	2	6	1	22
Samuel	1	1	0-0	0	0	1	0	2
Kromah	4	1	0-1	2	2	6	1	4
Brimah	2	0	0-0	0	0	4	4	0
Totals	**53**	**22**	**6-19**	**10**	**10**	**33**	**17**	**60**

Halftime: UConn 35, UK 31

Famous Head-to-Head Showdowns

Down through the years, Wildcats fans have been treated to many terrific head-to-head showdowns between some of the greatest players (and teams) that ever stepped onto a basketball court. More often than not, UK prevailed, both individual-wise and team-wise. Here's a brief look at some of the top matchups, from Adolph Rupp's earliest years at the helm through 1980.

Adolph Rupp vs. Notre Dame

During those early years, when Rupp was forging the UK empire, the one team that consistently mystified the Cats was Notre Dame. The Irish won the first seven outings against the Rupp-coached Cats, and it wasn't until the 1942-43 campaign that UK finally prevailed, winning 60-55, thanks to a 17-point effort from Marvin "Big Train" Akers. Milt Ticco also came up big in that win, knocking in 16 points.

The Irish then went on to win four of the next six meetings, including victories over the 1945-46 NIT championship team, the 1947-48 Fabulous Five NCAA title team and the 1949-50 club that finished with a 25-5 record. However, after that, it was pretty much all UK. The Cats won nine straight, and 16 of the next 18 under Rupp's guidance.

Rupp vs. John Wooden

These two coaching giants only met three times, with UK winning on every occasion. Led by Cliff Hagan's 34 points, UK ripped UCLA 84-53 during the 1951-52 season. Almost a decade later, during the 1959-60 season, UK rode a 23-point performance by Billy Ray Lickert to a hard-earned 68-66 win in Los Angeles. One year later, Roger Newman's 26-point, 18-rebound effort enabled the Cats to nip the visiting Bruins 77-76. Larry Pursiful chipped in with 21 points for UK.

Rupp vs. Al McGuire

McGuire may have morphed into a lovable, slightly eccentric sage during his later years, but in his heyday as

Marquette coach he was no favorite of Rupp's or of Big Blue fans. In fact, he was despised by both. The iconoclastic McGuire loved nothing better than to get his digs in against the god-like Rupp. For instance, when the two teams met in Memorial Coliseum in a Mideast Region game, McGuire demanded that his team dress in the home team's dressing room and sit on the home team's bench. He also balked at playing the game with a basketball that had Rupp's name on it, which prompted this classic Rupp response, "Find a ball with your name on it, Al, and that's the one we'll use." The two coaches faced off four times during a five-year span, all in NCAA tourney play, with each coach claiming two victories.

Alex Groza vs. Bob Brannum

Easily the strangest matchup in UK history, namely because it paired two Wildcat All-Americans against each other. Brannum earned that distinction when, as a 17-year-old freshman, he averaged 12.1 points for the surprising 1943-44 club that went 19-2. Brannum then went into the military, and upon his return to UK found that Groza had replaced him in the pivot. Brannum stayed at UK, but was so upset by his lack of playing time that he transferred to Michigan State. As fate would have it, UK met the Spartans during the 1947-48 season. In that game, which UK won 47-45, Brannum extracted a measure of personal revenge by outscoring Groza 23-10.

Ralph Beard vs. Bob Cousy

These two backcourt greats met twice during their college days. In the first meeting, UK beat Holy Cross 60-52. Beard finished with 13 points, while Cousy, who was shut down by Kenny Rollins and Dale Barnstable, finished with six. In their second meeting, Beard and Cousy fought to a standstill, with each accounting for 11 points. UK won the game 51-48.

Groza vs. Paul Arizin

This turned out to be another dead heat between two terrific offensive terrors. UK clipped Villanova 85-72, with Groza and Arizin both racking up 30 points each.

Bill Spivey vs. Clyde Lovellette

This "Battle of the Giants" is arguably the most-celebrated of all the early individual matchups. As it turned out, it was a no-contest all the way. Spivey outscored

Lovellette 22-10, and it could have been worse had Rupp not removed Spivey from the game when Big Clyde fouled out with 12 minutes remaining. With Spivey and Frank Ramsey (19 points) leading the way, UK rolled to an easy 68-39 victory over Kansas.

Cliff Hagan vs. Bob Pettit

These two hardwood legends (and future St. Louis Hawks teammates) met three times in what proved to be a trio of the most bitterly contested games in UK history. The first two of those meetings with LSU came during the 1951-52 season, with UK winning both games—57-47 and 44-43. Pettit had 22 points in the first game and 25 in the second. Hagan was held under double figures in the first game, but came back to score 19 in the second outing. The final meeting, for the SEC title during the 1953-54 season, saw UK come from behind to claim a 63-56 victory. While Hagan and Pettit each accounted for 17 points, it was Ramsey who stole the show, scoring 30 points, including 10 in the tension-filled final quarter. Rupp would say of Ramsey, "If we win by 30 points, Frank gets three; if we win by three, Frank gets 30."

Hagan vs. Tom Gola

The magnificent Hagan dominated his only meeting against the La Salle All-American, outscoring Gola 28-16. UK easily dispatched La Salle 73-60 in the UKIT title game. Of course, this was the season (1953-54) in which UK went 25-0, then passed on the chance to participate in the NCAA tourney when Hagan, Ramsey and Lou Tsioropoulos were declared ineligible because they were fifth-year seniors. As all UK fans know, La Salle would go on to capture the NCAA championship.

Johnny Cox vs. Bailey Howell

These two first-team All-Americans clashed three times, with Howell and Mississippi State clearly getting the better of things. The Maroons won two of the three meetings (89-81 and 66-58), with UK winning once (72-62). In the first game, Howell had a monster effort, scoring 37 points and yanking down 20 rebounds. Cox also played well, scoring 28 points in a losing cause. In UK's lone win during the three years, Cox had 22 points for the Cats. Howell topped that by chalking up 28. During Mississippi State's rubber-game win in the 1958-59 season, Howell turned in a 27-point, 17-rebound effort, while Cox was held below double digits.

UK vs. Jerry West

Rupp always included this West Virginia great among the best players UK ever faced. And no wonder. West led the Mountaineers to two wins in three tries against UK, all in Memorial Coliseum. He scored 15 points in the first meeting, which West Virginia won 77-70. UK won 97-91 the next year, despite a 36-point performance by West. In the final meeting, West accounted for 33 points in West Virginia's 79-70 win. Many years later, when recalling the difficult task of guarding West, Billy Ray Lickert said, "I think the guy scored six points during the National Anthem."

Lickert vs. Tom Hawkins

In this game, which UK won 71-52, Lickert turned in one of the greatest individual performances ever by a Wildcat. The 6'3" sophomore from Lexington Lafayette scored 24 points and grabbed 17 rebounds, while holding Hawkins, the Notre Dame All-American, to 13 points, 11 below his average.

Cotton Nash vs. Billy Cunningham:

In the only meeting between these two exciting All-Americans, UK won the game, beating North Carolina 100-80, but Billy C got the better of Nash in their head-to-head duel. Cunningham, the "Kangaroo Kid," finished with 32 points and 20 rebounds, while Nash accounted for 23 points and nine rebounds.

Nash vs. Jeff Mullins

UK against Duke in the 1963 Sugar Bowl title game paired the great Nash against the talented Mullins, the Lexington Lafayette grad who was Kentucky's Mr. Basketball in 1960. The Cats edged Duke 81-79 on Terry Mobley's last-second jumper. Nash also got the best of Mullins, outscoring him 30 to 26.

Dan Issel vs. Pete Maravich

In this age of coach-controlled offenses, defense-oriented teams and players who flat out can't shoot the rock, it's hard to believe that individual players—and Pistol Pete, in particular—could post such off-the-chart numbers. Maravich played UK six times in three years, scoring a whopping total of 312 points. His 64 points in a 1970 game remain the most ever scored by a UK opponent. Despite his efforts, Maravich and his LSU teammates lost all six games to UK. Although Issel's numbers pale in comparison to Pistol Pete's, they are still more than impressive. Big Dan tallied 189 points in

those six wins over LSU, including 51 in the game in which Maravich had 64. Think about that: Maravich 64, Issel 51. In one game. No shot clock, no three-point bucket. These days, teams don't score that many points in an entire 40 minutes.

Issel vs. Artis Gilmore

This NCAA game, which paired the future Louisville Colonel teammates against each other, is another one Big Blue fans remember with great pain. Jacksonville upset the Cats 106-100, a win that was helped immeasurably when Issel fouled out with just under nine minutes remaining. Still, Issel, in his final UK performance, finished with 28 points and 10 rebounds, while Gilmore had 24 points and 20 rebounds.

Kevin Grevey vs. Adrian Dantley

These two offensive-minded players clashed three times, with UK winning twice and Notre Dame once. Individually, Dantley came out on top. In the first meeting, which Notre Dame won 94-79, Grevey outscored Dantley 25-22. One year later, UK blasted the Irish 113-96 despite Dantley's 39-point effort. Grevey had 28 in that UK romp. In the final meeting, which UK won 79-77, Dantley had 28 points, while Grevey failed to hit double figures.

Kyle Macy vs. Magic Johnson

Cool Kyle was the clear victor in this classic matchup, scoring 18 points, including six pressure-packed free throws in the final three minutes, to lead the Cats to a 52-49 win over Michigan State in NCAA tourney Mideast Region action. Johnson was limited to just six points. UK would go on to claim the 1977-78 NCAA title. One year later, Magic would lead the Spartans to the crown.

Kyle Macy against Michigan State.

Bill Spivey easily outclassed Clyde Lovellette in what was billed as a "Battle of the Giants."

Wildcat VIPs

The University of Kentucky basketball program rose to the top—and remains there today—because of almost a century's worth of hard work, dedication and sacrifice by the players and coaches. That has been, and will always remain, at the heart of UK's success. However, no program can reach—and sustain—such a high level of excellence and success without the presence of a strong support system. Throughout the years, UK has been fortunate to have a host of people who played fundamental roles in helping shape the direction of the program and in bringing UK basketball to the fans. That list includes UK presidents, athletic directors, announcers, sportswriters and various other VIPs. Here are but a few of those who had the strongest impact.

LARRY BOECK

Former sportswriter with both Louisville newspapers and the man reputed to have been the first to label the 1947-48 Wildcat starters as the "Fabulous Five." He initially worked for The *Times* prior to serving in the U.S. Army Air Force dur-

ing World War II, then went to work for *The Courier-Journal* after his discharge in 1946. In 1954, he broke the news that fifth-year seniors Cliff Hagan, Frank Ramsey and Lou Tsioropoulos were ineligible to participate in postseason play. That led to harsh words and a near-altercation between Boeck and UK assistant coach Harry Lancaster. The 52-year-old Boeck was working for the University of Louisville at the time of his death in 1972.

S.A. "DADDY" BOLES

The man who hired Adolph Rupp and Bernie Shively, two of the giant figures in UK basketball. Came to UK as a physical education instructor and assistant football coach. One year later, he took over as athletics director and head football coach. In 1918, he coached the men's basketball team. Retired as AD in 1933, but remained with the University for many years. He is also credited with helping bring about the Kentucky State High School basketball tournament.

Former Kentucky governor Happy Chandler accepts a gift from Fiddlin' Five starters Ed Beck, Johnny Cox, Vernon Hatton, John Crigler and Adrian Smith. Chandler was a big supporter of UK basketball, and one of Adolph Rupp's closest friends.

JOHN Y. BROWN JR.

Charismatic ex-governor and former owner of the Kentucky Colonels in the old American Basketball Association. He made a fortune with the Kentucky Fried Chicken Corporation prior to running for governor. As governor, he was very involved with athletics, and was among the strongest voices in favor of an annual UK-Louisville basketball series. He was also squarely in the Adolph Rupp camp during the debate over whether the Baron should be allowed to continue coaching past the mandatory retirement age of 70. His father, John Y. Brown Sr., was another longtime close friend of Rupp's.

HAPPY CHANDLER

The ex-Kentucky governor and former baseball commissioner who had the courage to go against the grain and allow the Brooklyn Dodgers to sign Jackie Robinson. One of the most-colorful men to ever grace the Kentucky stage, political or otherwise. A longtime close friend and confidant to Rupp. Despite their friendship, Chandler was no different from anyone else at a UK practice, which was noted for its silence. Once, after Chandler, a non-stop talker, made the mistake of breeching the silence, Rupp turned to his buddy and said, "Be quiet, or get out." Chandler was silent for the remainder of practice. He often sang *My Old Kentucky Home* prior to UK home games, and only those with a heart of stone could hold back the tears.

OSCAR COMBS

Left Hazard in 1975, moved to Lexington and started *The Cats' Pause*, the first publication of its kind in college sports. Got the idea after talking with three fans at a UK road game. The three had never seen UK play until that day, but had become fans by listening to Cawood Ledford. Combs was convinced that there were UK fans across the country who craved information about the Wildcats. Joe B. Hall was an early supporter of Combs' plan, but football coach Fran Curci was less enthusiastic. He wanted to approve every article before it was printed. Athletics director Cliff Hagan initially straddled the fence, then finally went along with the idea. At the height of its popularity, *The Cats' Pause* had a circulation of 22,000. Combs, who sold the paper in 1997, was inducted into the Kentucky Journalism Hall of Fame in 2000.

EARL COX

Veteran sportswriter who spent 33 years at *The Courier-Journal*, including 18 as Executive Sports Editor. An Irvine, Ky., native, he went to the C-J after returning from the service in 1955. Prior to entering the army, he worked his way through college at the Lexington *Herald*, where he was assistant sports editor. Cox had an extremely close relationship with Rupp, and was one of the few people allowed to attend UK's highly secretive—and always closed—practices. He was part of a task force that included Rupp and then AD Cliff Hagan that met with NCAA officials in St. Louis in an attempt to bring the Final Four to Lexington. Until his retirement in 2014 Cox wrote a syndicated column that was read throughout the commonwealth.

HERMAN L. DONOVAN

UK's president from 1941-56. His tenure saw great on-campus growth, including the construction of Memorial Coliseum and the Fine Arts Building. He and Gov. Chandler fought the battle to bring a medical school to UK. During the scandals that rocked college basketball in the late 1940s and early 1950s, he stood by Rupp when many were calling for the Baron to step down or be fired.

NEVILLE DUNN

Started as a sportswriter for the Lexington *Leader* in the early 1930s, then later became the sports editor for the Lexington *Herald*. He was the first to call Rupp "Baron" and "the man in the brown suit." The territorial Rupp, once angered by a Dunn column, suspected Dunn of "being a football man." Dunn went on to become a successful turf writer, publisher and thoroughbred breeder. He died in 1957 at the age of 52.

J.B. FAULCONER

A former team manager for Rupp's Wildcats, he went on to have a long and successful career in broadcasting and public relations. A superb announcer, Faulconer called UK games and thoroughbred racing for the Ashland Oil Network, which at one time was the biggest. He left the broadcasting booth, went to work at the Keeneland Race Track and headed the Thoroughbred Racing Association. He started the Eclipse Awards. Faulconer died in December of 2000.

RALPH HACKER

He probably knows how Joe B. Hall and Gene Bartow felt after following legends Adolph Rupp and John Wooden. Had the difficult task of taking over for Cawood Ledford, one of the true institutions in Kentucky. Assumed the play-by-play duties in 1992 after serving as Cawood's sidekick for 20 years. Began his broadcasting career at age 15, doing high school games. One year later, he was calling Eastern Kentucky University football and basketball. Moved to Lexington and spent many years at WVLK, which was the flagship station for UK sports. Has also done national broadcasts with ESPN and CBS-TV. He later owned WVLK.

CLIFF HAGAN

An ex-Wildcat All-American and a former All-NBA player, he assumed the athletics director duties after Harry Lancaster retired. Served as AD from 1975-88. Oversaw the growth of UK athletics from a relatively small endeavor to a multi-million dollar business. Played a big role in getting women's sports started at UK. His tenure ended on a sour note, getting crushed in the scandal that hit during Eddie Sutton's reign as head coach.

JIM HOST

A former Wildcat hurler, he did some broadcasting and made a run for lieutenant governor before he was 35 years old. However, he made his biggest mark when he won the broadcast rights to UK basketball and football in the mid-1970s, which he has held for the majority of the past quarter-century. Under his Host Communications banner, the UK Radio Network grew into one of the biggest and most-successful in the country, with nearly 100 stations across the commonwealth

Cawood Ledford chats with Rick Pitino during their highly popular courtside post-game show. In his 39 years as the "Voice of the Wildcats," Cawood became one of the most-respected and most-admired figures in UK sports history.

and adjoining states carrying Wildcat games live. He has also made a lot of money for UK and for the basketball and football coaches. Host held the broadcast and publishing rights for many colleges, and also held the radio broadcast rights to the Final Four for more than 25 years.

BILL KEIGHTLEY

The man known as "Mr. Wildcat" was a friend to UK coaches and a father confessor to Wildcat players since the 1950s. Began working part-time as equipment manager while still working his regular job as a mail carrier at the post office. He would often get home from the post office, then head out on a trip with the UK team. It was Joe B. Hall who tagged Keightley as "Mr. Wildcat." With the retirement of C.M. Newton, Keightley was the the last link to the days when Adolph Rupp was at the helm. Was a

favorite of all Big Blue fans.

HARRY LANCASTER

Known more for his work as Rupp's able assistant from 1947-69. Together, he and Rupp were a formidable coaching duo in every respect. Played football and basketball at Paris High and for Georgetown (Ky.) College in the first game Rupp coached at UK. Took over as AD after Shively passed away, thus putting himself in the awkward position of being Rupp's boss. Their relationship became strained during that period, but they did reconcile their differences before Rupp died. Considered tough but fair, Lancaster is, along with Rupp, Shively and Paul McBrayer, one of the key figures in UK hoops history.

CAWOOD LEDFORD

The legendary "Voice of the Wildcats" for 39 years and one of the most-beloved figures in UK history. Moved from Harlan to Lexington in 1953 and began calling games for WLEX. Later moved to Louisville and WHAS, where he stayed until 1979. During that time, UK went

to a single network and he was tabbed to handle the play-by-play duties. Few announcers have ever developed a more loyal following. And few have ever been better. It was once said that the lights weren't turned off in a Big Blue fan's house until Cawood signed off. When the Cats were on TV, UK fans turned down the volume and listened to Cawood instead. He also called football, pro baseball, and was widely considered one of the finest horse racing announcers in the country. Named Kentucky Sportscaster of the Year 22 times. Elected to the Kentucky Athletic Hall of Fame and the Kentucky Journalism Hall of Fame. Had an honorary jersey retired in Rupp Arena in 1991. Retired after the 1991-92 season.

FRANK McVEY

UK's president from 1917-40. Known for his fairness and integrity. Oversaw the growth of UK as a small school to one that was on its way to becoming a major institution. He was at the helm when Adolph Rupp was hired. He once scolded Rupp for blaming a loss on the officials.

C.M. NEWTON

Although recognized as a Hall of Fame coach following stints at Transylvania, Alabama and Vanderbilt, he will forever be remembered by Big Blue fans as the man who engineered UK's remarkable comeback after those dark days in the late 1980s. He brought instant integrity and respect to a program that was reeling from scandal and NCAA sanctions. His first move after taking over in 1989 was to hire Rick Pitino, a move that turned out to be a stroke of genius. He also hired Bernadette Mattox to rebuild the women's program, and later went after and hired Tubby Smith to replace Pitino. If Rupp is the man who built UK's basketball program, then Newton is the man who saved it.

JOHN W. OSWALD

Held the top spot from 1963-68. Came in with big ideas and bold initiatives. He was popular with many students during the turbulent '60s, but not so popular with certain activist students and some faculty. He consistently pressured Rupp to integrate the basketball program. Resigned on Sept. 1, 1968.

BILLY REED

Arguably the most widely recognized writer covering UK

C.M Newton and Adolph Rupp prior to a UK-Alabama game. Although Newton had a Hall-of-Fame coaching career, he will best be remembered for saving the UK program after the scandal of the late 1980s.

today. Began covering UK sports in 1959, seven years before graduating from Translyvania University. Spent many years writing for *The Courier-Journal*, then switched to the Lexington *Herald-Leader*, where he continued his outstanding work. Has also worked as a senior writer for *Sports Illustrated*. Co-authored books with Cawood Ledford, Denny Crum and C.M. Newton.

RUSSELL RICE

Without question, the pre-eminent historian of UK basketball and football. Served as the sports editor for the Lexington *Leader* before becoming the sports information director at UK. It was under his watch that the sports information department became one of the country's best. He was a longtime columnist for *The Cats' Pause*. He has also written several books about UK basketball, including a biography of Adolph Rupp, *The Wildcat Legacy, Joe B. Hall: My Own Kentucky Home* and the classic *Big Blue Machine*.

DAVID ROSELLE

Took over the reins on July 1, 1987. Less than a year into his tenure, he was faced with a major scandal within the basketball program. He not only cooperated fully with the NCAA, he also hired Lexington attorney James Park Jr. to conduct an investigation on behalf of UK. The results of the probes resulted in the firing of Eddie Sutton and his staff, the resignation of athletics director Cliff Hagan and severe sanctions meted out by the NCAA. At the time, many Big Blue fans considered Roselle to be something of a Judas. Subsequent events, however, have lessened their harsh judgment of Roselle. His hiring of C.M. Newton as athletics director began the chain of events that led to a decade of success unrivaled since the "Glory Decade" of 1945-54. Resigned from UK in 1989.

EARL RUBY

Spent nearly half a century at *The Courier-Journal* and was, at one time, the most widely read, most powerful and influential sportswriter in Kentucky. In those days, *The Courier-Journal* was the Bible and Ruby's word was the law. Began at the C-J as an office boy in 1921, and by 1936 he was writing a daily column called "Ruby's Report." He was a man who got things done. Ruby was chiefly responsible for the State Fairgrounds being built, the creation of the Kentucky Athletic Hall of Fame and the Derby Festival. He accompanied Rupp and the 1948 Wildcat players to the Olympic Games in London, and later served as Kentucky's goodwill ambassador to the Olympic Games in Rome and Mexico City. His daughter, Joan, married the late Jack Tingle, a four-time All-SEC performer during his days as a Wildcat. Ruby retired as sports editor of the C-J in 1968 but continued as outdoor editor until 1989. During his long and distinguished career, he had more stories published in "Best Sports Stories" than any other sports reporter. Ruby passed away at age 96 in 2000, two days after the Derby.

BERNIE SHIVELY

Known to everyone simply as "Shive," he is one of key figures in UK sports history. Served as AD from 1938 until his death in 1967. He was an outstanding football player at the University of Illinois, where one of his teammates was Red Grange. Came to UK in 1927 as an assistant football coach. After becoming the AD in 1938, he continued to coach football, baseball and track. In 1946, he hired Bear Bryant as UK's football coach. In 1953, he was the driving force behind the creation of the UKIT, which was for many years the premier holiday tournament. He is also the man who made the decision to create a single UK Basketball Network, which resulted in Cawood Ledford becoming the lone "Voice of the Wildcats." As chairman of the Division I basketball committee, he brought Final Fours to Louisville's Freedom Hall.

OTIS SINGLETARY

Named president on May 27, 1969 and held the position until 1987. A historian and publishing scholar, he led the school through some difficult and stormy times. But there was never any doubt about his support for UK athletics. Despite a swirl of controversy and campaigning on both sides, he held his ground and refused to bend the rules when Rupp reached the mandatory retirement age of 70, thus bringing to an end the coaching career of UK's most-revered figure.

CLAUDE SULLIVAN

Another world-class announcer and the number one guy on the scene during those days when the Memorial Coliseum court side was ringed with broadcast crews. Did his first broadcast when he was only 17, and called his first UK game in 1945. His first job was with WCMI in Ashland. Also worked for WAVE, WKLN and WVLK. In 1951, he organized the Standard Oil Sports Network. Joined the Cincinnati Reds broadcast team in 1964, serving as second man to Waite Hoyt. He later became the No. 1 man when Hoyt retired. He was named Kentucky's Outstanding Sportscaster eight times. Also called the races at Keeneland. Died of throat cancer on Dec. 6, 1967 at the age of 42.

CHARLES WETHINGTON

Became interim president upon Roselle resignation, then took over the job permanently on Sept. 18, 1990. He had been an administrator in UK's community college system for 22 years and its chancellor since 1982. Prior to leaving UK, he was a strong supporter of the basketball program, and the man who gave his blessings to the hiring of Tubby Smith.

UK in the NCAA

NCAA Championships

UCLA	11
Kentucky	8
Indiana	5
North Carolina	5
Duke	5
Connecticut	4
Kansas	3
Louisville	3
Cincinnati	2
Florida	2
Michigan State	2
N.C. State	2
Oklahoma State	2
San Francisco	2
Villanova	2

NCAA Tournament Appearances

Kentucky	55
North Carolina	47
UCLA	45
Kansas	45
Louisville	41
Duke	40
Indiana	39
Villanova	35
Notre Dame	35
Syracuse	34
Texas	33
Connecticut	32
Temple	32

Wayne Turner played on three Final Four teams during his UK career.

UK NCAA Records

Fewest Points Allowed (single game)
6 — Kentucky (75) vs. Arkansas State, Jan. 8, 1945

Fewest Field Goals (single game)
2 — Arkansas State vs. Kentucky, Jan. 8, 1945

Most Rebounds (single game)
108 — Kentucky vs. Ole Miss, Feb. 8, 1964

Most Consecutive Home-Court Victories
129 — Kentucky, Jan. 4, 1943 to Jan. 8, 1955

30-Game Winners

1947 — 34-3	1986 — 32-4	2003 — 32-4
1948 — 36-3	1993 — 30-4	2010 — 35-3
1949 — 32-2	1996 — 34-2	2012 — 38-2
1951 — 32-2	1997 — 35-5	2015 — 38-1
1978 — 30-2	1998 — 35-4	

Most Wins By A Coach In His First Year At A School:
35 — Tubby Smith, Kentucky, 1998
35 — John Calipari, Kentucky, 2010

Most Career Games Played — Individual
152 — Darius Miller, Kentucky, 2008-2012

UK NCAA Tournament Records

All-Time

Most Tournament Appearances	55
Most Tournament Games	170
Most Tournament Wins	121

Series

Most Assists in a Tournament	143 (1996, 6 games)
Most Blocks in a Tournament	48 (1998, 6 games)

Team

Fewest Points in a Final Four Game — 28
UK vs. Dartmouth, 1942

Most Blocks in a Tournament Game — 14
UK vs. UCLA, 1998

Most Personal Fouls by Two Teams — 61
UK vs. Syracuse, 1975

Individual

Highest Field Goal Percentage — 100.0%
Kenny Walker, 11-11 vs. Western Kentucky, 1986

Team — Championship Game

Largest Halftime Deficit Overcome — 10
Kentucky 31 vs. Utah 41, 1998

Most Points Scored by Two Teams — 182
Kentucky 94 vs. Duke 88, 1978

Most Field Goals Made by Two Teams — 71
UCLA 38 vs. Kentucky 33, 1975

Lowest Field Goal Percentage by Winner — 38.4
Kentucky vs. Syracuse, 1996

Most Three-Point Field Goals — 12
Kentucky vs. Syracuse, 1996

Most Three-Point Field Goals by Two Teams — 18
Kentucky vs. Syracuse, 1996

Most Disqualifications — 4
Kentucky vs. Arizona, 1997

Individual – Championship Game
Most Three-Point Field Goals — 7 (tied)
Tony Delk vs. Syracuse, 1996

Most Blocked Shots — 6
Anthony Davis vs. Kansas, 2012

All-NCAA Tournament (Final Four)

Alex Groza	1948,1949
Bill Spivey	1951
Shelby Linville	1951
Vernon Hatton	1958
Johnny Cox	1958
Pat Riley	1966
Louie Dampier	1966
Kevin Grevey	1975
Jack Givens	1978
Rick Robey	1978
Jamal Mashburn	1993
Tony Delk	1996
Ron Mercer	1996,1997
Scott Padgett	1997,1998
Jeff Sheppard	1998
Anthony Davis	2012
Michael Kidd-Gilchrist	2012
Doron Lamb	2012
Julius Randle	2014
James Young	2014

Final Four MVP

Alex Groza	1948,1949
Jack Givens	1978
Tony Delk	1996
Jeff Sheppard	1998
Anthony Davis	2012

Top 10 All-Time Winningest Division I Teams

School	Won	Lost	Tied	Pct.
Kentucky	2205	682	1	.764
Kansas	2186	836	0	.723
North Carolina	2173	774	0	.737
Duke	2085	863	0	.707
Syracuse	1943	865	0	.692
Temple	1870	1037	0	.643
UCLA	1818	819	0	.689
St. John's	1803	980	0	.648
Notre Dame	1819	984	0	.648
Indiana	1783	1003	0	.640

Top 10 All-Time Winningest Percentage

School	Won	Lost	Tied	Pct.
Kentucky	2205	682	1	.764
North Carolina	2173	774	0	.737
Kansas	2186	836	0	.723
Duke	2085	866	0	.707
Syracuse	1943	865	0	.692
UCLA	1818	819	0	.689
Louisville	1778	892	0	.666
Western Kentucky	1733	884	0	.662
Arizona	1762	927	0	.655
Notre Dame	1819	984	0	.648

Consecutive NCAA Tournament Appearances

Team	Appearances	Years
North Carolina	27	1975-2001
Kansas	27	1990-2016
Duke	21	1996-2016
Michigan State	19	1998-2016
Gonzaga	18	1999-2016
Wisconsin	18	1999-2016
Indiana	18	1986-2003
Kentucky	17	1992-2008
UCLA	15	1967-1981
Arizona	14	1985-1998
Cincinnati	14	1992-2005
Georgetown	14	1979-1992
Texas	14	1999-2012

Most Weeks at No. 1 All-Time

School	Weeks
1. UCLA	134
2. Duke	127
3. Kentucky	120
4. North Carolina	111
5. Kansas	57

Jack Givens blistered Duke for 41 points in the 1978 NCAA title game.

UK in the SEC

SEC Championships

Kentucky...48

LSU...11

Tennessee 8

Alabama..7

Florida..7

Miss. State...6

Vanderbilt..3

Arkansas...2

Auburn...2

Georgia 1

South Carolina.......................................1

Georgia Tech..1

Texas A&M...1

SEC Tournament Championships

Kentucky...29

Alabama..6

Tennessee 4

Florida..4

Miss. State...3

Georgia 2

Ole Miss...2

Vanderbilt..2

Arkansas...1

Auburn...1

LSU...1

Georgia Tech..1

SEC All-Time Standings
(Regular Season Games Only)

Team	Years	Won	Lost	Pct.	Championships
Kentucky	83	956	266	.782	48
Texas A&M	4	49	36	.576	1
Alabama	83	774	591	.567	6
Tennessee	83	715	560	.561	8
Vanderbilt	84	683	618	.525	3
Arkansas	25	220	201	.523	2
LSU	84	669	650	.507	11
Florida	83	616	636	.492	7
Auburn	83	585	725	.447	2
Miss. State	83	578	754	.434	6
Missouri	3	23	31	.426	0
Georgia	84	538	757	.415	1
South Carolina	25	168	253	.399	1
Ole Miss	83	507	805	.386	0

Former Members

Team	Years	Won	Lost	Pct.	Championships
Georgia Tech	32	201	207	.493	1
Tulane	34	195	252	.436	0
Sewanee	8	3	76	.038	0

SEC Player of the Year
All-Southeastern Conference

Associated Press

Pat Riley 1966
Tom Parker 1972
Kevin Grevey (1) 1973, 1975
Kyle Macy 1980
Kenny Walker 1985, 1986
Jamal Mashburn (2) 1993
Tony Delk 1996
Ron Mercer 1997
Tayshaun Prince 2001

John Wall 2010
Anthony Davis 2012
Tyler Ulis 2016

Coaches

Jamal Mashburn 1993
Tony Delk 1996
Ron Mercer 1997
Tayshaun Prince 2001
John Calipari 2010
Anthony Davis 2012
Tyler Ulis 2016

| *Pat Riley* | *Tom Parker* | *Kevin Grevey* | *Kyle Macy* | *Kenny Walker* | *Jamal Mashburn* | *Tayshaun Prince* |

All-Southeastern Conference

Ellis Johnson	1933
Forest Sale	1933
John DeMoisey	1933,1934
Bill Davis	1934
Leroy Edwards	1935
Dave Lawrence	1935
Ralph Carlisle	1936,1937
Warfield Donohue	1937
Bernie Opper	1938,1939
Layton Rouse	1940
Lee Huber	1941
James King	1941
Marvin Akers	1941,1943
Ermal Allen	1942
Melvin Brewer	1943
Bob Brannum	1944
Jack Parkinson	1944,1945,1946
Jack Tingle	1944, 1945, 1946, 1947
Kenton Campbell	1945
Ralph Beard	1946,1947,1948,1949
Wallace Jones	1946,1947,1948,1949
Joe Holland	1947
Alex Groza	1948,1949
Kenny Rollins	1947,1948
Jim Line	1950
Bill Spivey	1950,1951
Walt Hirsch	1951
Shelby Linville	1951
Bobby Watson	1951,1952
Frank Ramsey	1951,1952,1954
Cliff Hagan	1952,1954
Bill Evans	1955
Bob Burrow	1955,1956
Johnny Cox	1957,1958,1959
Vernon Hatton	1958
Don Mills	1960
Bill Lickert	1959,1960,1961
Larry Pursiful	1962
Cotton Nash	1962,1963,1964
Ted Deeken	1964
Tommy Kron	1965,1966
Pat Riley	1965,1966
Thad Jaracz	1966
Larry Conley	1966
Louie Dampier	1965,1966,1967

Mike Casey	1968,1969,1971
Dan Issel	1968,1969,1970
Mike Pratt	1969,1970
Larry Steele	1971
Tom Parker	1971,1972
Tom Payne	1971
Jim Andrews	1972,1973
Kevin Grevey	1973,1974,1975
Jack Givens	1976,1977,1978
Rick Robey	1977,1978
Kyle Macy	1978,1979,1980
Sam Bowie	1980,1981
Derrick Hord	1982
Melvin Turpin	1983,1984
Kenny Walker	1985,1986
Winston Bennett	1986,1988
Rex Chapman	1987,1988
Ed Davender	1987,1988
LeRon Ellis	1989
Chris Mills	1989
Reggie Hanson	1990,1991
Derrick Miller	1990
John Pelphrey	1991
Jamal Mashburn	1991,1992,1993
Travis Ford	1993
Tony Delk	1995,1996
Antoine Walker	1996
Ron Mercer	1997
Nazr Mohammed	1998
Scott Padgett	1999
Jamaal Magloire	2000
Tayshaun Prince	2001, 2002
Keith Bogans	2001
Erik Daniels	2004
Gerald Fitch	2004
Chuck Hayes	2005
Ramel Bradley	2008
Jodie Meeks	2009
Patrick Patterson	2009, 2010
DeMarcus Cousins	2010
John Wall	2010
Terrence Jones	2011, 2012
Brandon Knight	2011
Anthony Davis	2012
Michael Kidd-Gilchrist	2012
Doron Lamb	2012

Nerlens Noel 2013
Julius Randle 2014
James Young 2014
Willie Cauley-Stein 2015
Karl-Anthony Towns 2015
Devin Booker` 2015
Aaron Harrison 2015
Tyler Ulis 2016
Jamal Murray 2016

All-SEC TOURNAMENT

John DeMoisey 1933,1934
Aggie Sale 1933
Bill Davis 1933,1934
Ralph Carlisle 1936,1937
Whitey Anderson 1936
Warfield Donohue 1937
Rice Walker 1937
Walter Hodge 1937
Bernie Opper 1938,1939
Joe Hagan 1938
Keith Farnsley 1939,1940,1941
Layton Rouse 1940
Marvin Akers 1941,1942,1943
Lee Huber 1941
James King 1941,1942
Ermal Allen 1942
Melvin Brewer 1943
Milt Ticco 1943
Bob Brannum 1944
Jack Tingle 1944,1945,1946,1947
Jack Parkinson 1944,1945,1946
Wilbur Schu 1944,1946
Kenton Campbell 1945
Wallace Jones 1946,1947,1948,1949
Ralph Beard 1946,1947,1948,1949
Joe Holland 1947
Kenny Rollins 1947,1948
Alex Groza 1947,1948,1949
Cliff Barker 1948,1949
Jim Line 1950
Bill Spivey 1950,1951
Walt Hirsch 1951
Frank Ramsey 1951,1952
Cliff Hagan 1951,1952
Bobby Watson 1952

Truman Claytor 1979
Kyle Macy 1979,1980
Sam Bowie 1980
Dirk Minniefield 1982
Melvin Turpin 1984
Roger Harden 1986
Rex Chapman 1988
Winston Bennett 1988
Jamal Mashburn 1992
John Pelphrey 1992
Travis Ford 1993,1994
Andre Riddick 1993
Tony Delk 1994
Jeff Brassow 1994
Mark Pope 1995
Antoine Walker 1995,1996
Walter McCarty 1996
Anthony Epps 1997
Ron Mercer 1997
Jared Prickett 1997
Heshimu Evans 1998
Nazr Mohammed 1998
Scott Padgett 1998,1999
Wayne Turner 1998,1999
Tayshaun Prince 2001
Keith Bogans 2001, 2003
Marquis Estill 2003
Gerald Fitch 2004
Chuck Hayes 2004
Kelenna Azubuike 2004, 2005
Eric Bledsoe 2010
DeMarcus Cousins 2010
John Wall 2010
Josh Harrellson 2011
Brandon Knight 2011
Darius Miller 2011
Anthony Davis 2012
Terrence Jones 2012
Aaron Harrison 2014
Julius Randle 2014
Willie Cauley-Stein 2015
Aaron Harrison 2015
Andrew Harrison 2015
Tyler Ulis 2016
Jamal Murray 2016

SEC Tournament MVP

Bill Davis 1933
Whitey Anderson 1936
Rice Walker 1937
Walter Hodge.. 1937
Joe Hagan 1938
Keith Farnsley 1940, 1941
James King.. 1941
Marvin Akers 1942
Milt Ticco 1943
Wilbur Schu... 1944,1946
Alex Groza 1948
Cliff Barker 1948
Kyle Macy... 1979
Dirk Minniefield 1982
Rex Chapman 1988
Jamal Mashburn.. 1992
Travis Ford 1993,1994
Antoine Walker 1995
Ron Mercer 1997
Wayne Turner.. 1998
Scott Padgett 1999
Tayshaun Prince 2001
Keith Bogans... 2003
Gerald Fitch 2004
John Wall 2010
Darius Miller... 2011
Willie Cauley-Stein 2015
Tyler Ulis 2016

Kentucky vs. SEC Tournament Field

Team	All	1st Rd.	Quarters	Semis	Finals
Alabama	14-2	1-0	5-1	5-0	3-1
Arkansas	8-1	0-0	0-1	5-0	3-0
Auburn	13-1	1-0	7-1	4-0	1-0
Florida	13-4	4-1	4-1	2-0	3-2
Georgia	10-1	0-0	4-1	3-0	3-0
LSU	16-2	0-0	5-1	8-0	3-1
Ole Miss	15-0	5-0	6-0	3-0	1-0
Miss. State	8-2	1-0	3-1	1-0	3-1
Missouri	0-0	0-0	0-0	0-0	0-0
South Carolina	3-2	0-0	1-1	1-1	1-0
Tennessee	11-4	0-0	2-0	5-1	4-3
Texas A&M	1-0	0-0	0-0	0-0	1-0
Vanderbilt	4-5	1-1	3-2	0-0	0-2
Ex-Members	11-1	2-0	2-1	3-0	4-0
Totals	**127-25**	**15-2**	**42-11**	**40-2**	**30-10**

SEC Tournament Record

Team	Years	Won	Lost	Pct.	Titles
Kentucky	55	127	25	.738	29
Alabama	57	60	47	.561	6
Tennessee	56	62	48	.564	4
Arkansas	25	20	20	.500	1
LSU	57	44	52	.458	1
Florida	51	36	44	.450	3
South Carolina	25	16	21	.432	0
Georgia	56	41	50	.451	2
Vanderbilt	55	32	50	.390	1
Miss. State	56	27	49	.355	3
Auburn	54	27	49	.355	1
Ole Miss	54	24	49	.329	1
Texas A&M	4	3	4	.428	0
Missouri	3	2	3	.400	0

UK SEC Champions

Year	Won	Lost	SEC	
1933	21	3	8-0	
1935	19	2	11-0	(LSU Co-Champs)
1937	17	5	5-3	
1939	16	4	5-2	
1940	15	6	4-4	
1942	19	6	6-2	
1944	19	2	0-0	
1945	22	4	4-1	
1946	28	2	6-0	
1947	34	3	11-0	
1948	36	3	9-0	
1949	32	2	13-0	
1950	25	5	11-2	
1951	32	2	14-0	
1952	29	3	14-0	
1954	25	0	14-0	(LSU Co-Champs)
1955	23	3	12-2	
1957	23	5	12-2	
1958	23	6	12-2	
1962	23	3	13-1	(Miss. State Co-Champs)
1964	21	6	11-3	
1966	27	2	15-1	
1968	22	5	15-3	
1969	23	5	16-2	

1970	26	2	17-1	
1971	22	6	16-2	
1972	21	7	14-4	(Tennessee Co-Champs)
1973	20	8	14-4	
1975	26	5	15-3	(Alabama Co-Champs)
1977	26	4	16-2	(Tennessee Co-Champs)
1978	30	2	16-2	
1980	29	6	15-3	
1982	22	8	13-5	(Tennessee Co-Champs)
1983	23	8	13-5	
1984	29	5	14-4	
1986	32	4	17-1	
1995	28	5	14-2	
1996	34	2	16-0	
1998	35	4	14-2	
2000	23	10	12-4	(Fla., Tenn., LSU Co-Champs)
2001	24	10	12-4	(Florida Co-Champs)
2003	32	4	16-0	
2005	28	6	14-2	
2010	35	3	14-2	
2012	38	2	16-0	
2015	38	1	18-0	
2016	27	9	13-5	(Texas A&M Co-Champs)

UK in Invitational Tournaments

National Invitation Tournament (NIT)

1944
UK 46, Utah 38
St. John's 48, UK 45
UK 45, Oklahoma A&M 29 (consolation)

1946
UK 77, Arizona 53
UK 59, West Virginia 51
UK 46, Rhode Island 45 (final)

1947
UK 66, Long Island 62
UK 60, N.C. State 42
Utah 49, UK 45 (final)

1949
Loyola Chicago 67, UK 56

1950
CCNY 89, UK 50

1976
UK 67, Niagara 61
UK 81, Kansas State 78
UK 79, Providence 78
UK 71, UNCC 67 (final)

1979
Clemson 68, UK 67 (overtime)

Preseason NIT

1992
UK 106, West Virginia 80
Pittsburgh 85, UK 67

1999
UK 67, Penn 50
UK 56, Utah 48
UK 61, Maryland 58
Arizona 63, UK 51 (final)

Great Alaska Shootout

1979
UK 79, Bradley 58
UK 97, Alaska 68
UK 57, Iona 50 (final)

1988
UK 56, Iona 54
Seton Hall 63, UK 60
UK 89, California 71 (consolation)

1996
UK 87, Syracuse 53
UK 104, Alaska Anchorage 72
UK 92, College of Charleston 65 (final)

Maui Invitational

1993
UK 86, Texas 61
UK 100, Ohio State 88
UK 93, Arizona 92 (final)

1997
UK 70, George Washington 55
Arizona 89, UK 74
UK 77, Missouri 55 (consolation)

2002
UK 82, Arizona State 65
Virginia, 75, UK 61
UK 80, Gonzaga 72

2006
UK 87, DePaul 81
UCLA 73, UK 68
Memphis 80, UK 63

2010
UK 76, Oklahoma 64
UK 74, Washington 67
UConn 84, UK 67

Olympic Games*

1948
USA 86, Switzerland 21
USA 53, Czechoslovkia 28
USA 59, Argentina 57
USA 66, Egypt 28
USA 61, Peru 33
USA 63, Uruguay 28
USA 71, Mexico 40
USA 65, France 21 (final)

• UK players Kenny Rollins, Cliff Barker, Wah Wah Jones, Ralph Beard and Alex Groza won gold medals as members of the 1948 United States Olympic team.

UK's All-Time Leading Scorers

Player	Years	Points	Games	Average
1. Dan Issel	1968-70	2,138	83	25.8
2. Kenny Walker	1983-86	2,080	132	15.8
3. Jack Givens	1975-78	2,038	123	16.6
4. Keith Bogans	2000-03	1,923	135	14.2
5. Tony Delk	1993-96	1,890	133	14.2
6. Jamal Mashburn	1991-93	1,843	98	18.8
7. Kevin Grevey	1973-75	1,801	84	21.4
8. Tayshaun Prince	1999-02	1,775	135	13.1
9. Cotton Nash	1962-64	1,770	78	22.7
10. Alex Groza	1945-49	1,744	120	14.5
11. Ed Davender	1985-88	1,637	129	12.7
12. Louie Dampier	1965-67	1,575	80	19.7
13. Patrick Patterson	2008-10	1,564	97	16.1
14. Mike Casey	1968-71	1,535	82	18.7
15. Ralph Beard	1946-49	1,517	139	10.9
16. Melvin Turpin	1981-84	1,509	123	12.3
17. Cliff Hagan	1951-54	1,475	77	19.2
18. Pat Riley	1965-67	1,464	80	18.3

19.	Johnny Cox	1957-59	1,461	84	17.4
20.	Joe Crawford	2005-08	1,438	127	11.3
21.	Kyle Macy	1978-80	1,411	98	14.4
22.	Winston Bennett	1984-88	1,399	133	10.5
23.	Rick Robey	1975-78	1,395	105	13.3
24.	Gerald Fitch	2001-04	1,391	127	11.0
25.	Mike Phillips	1975-78	1,367	120	11.4
26.	Mike Pratt	1968-70	1,359	81	16.8
27.	Frank Ramsey	1951-54	1,344	91	14.8
28.	Ramel Bradley	2005-08	1,326	128	10.4
29.	Jim Andrews	1971-73	1,320	80	16.5
30.	Sam Bowie	1980-84	1,285	96	13.4
31.	Jim Master	1981-84	1,283	121	10.6
32.	John Pelphrey	1989-92	1,257	114	11.0
33.	Scott Padgett	1995-99	1,252	122	10.3
34.	Darius Miller	2008-2012	1,248	152	8.2
35.	Jodie Meeks	2007-09	1,246	81	15.4
36.	Tom Parker	1970-72	1,238	80	15.5
37.	Deron Feldhaus	1989-92	1,231	124	9.6
38.	Derrick Hord	1980-83	1,220	124	9.8
39.	Bill Spivey	1950-51	1,213	63	19.3
40.	Chuck Hayes	2002-05	1,211	134	9.0
41.	Rodrick Rhodes	1993-95	1,209	99	12.2
42.	Wayne Turner	1996-99	1,170	151	7.7
43.	Reggie Hanson	1988-91	1,167	101	11.6
44.	Derrick Miller	1987-90	1,156	105	11.0
45.	Vernon Hatton	1956-58	1,153	76	15.2
46.	Wallace Jones	1946-49	1,151	127	9.1
47.	Randolph Morris	2005-07	1,123	89	12.6
48.	Jeff Sheppard	1994-98	1,091	134	8.1
49.	Billy Ray Lickert	1959-61	1,076	73	14.7
50.	Rex Chapman	1987-88	1,073	61	17.6
51.	Dirk Minniefield	1980-83	1,069	123	8.7
52.	Terrence Jones	2010-12	1,064	76	14.0
53.	Jamaal Magloire	1997-00	1,064	145	7.3
54.	Erik Daniels	2001-04	1,053	127	8.3
55.	Jim Line	1947-50	1,041	135	7.7
56.	Bob Burrow	1955-56	1,023	51	20.1
57.	Doron Lamb	2010-12	1,018	78	13.1
58.	Ron Mercer	1996-97	1,013	76	13.3
59.	Jimmy Dan Conner	1973-75	1,009	85	11.9
60.	Bobby Watson	1950-52	1,001	96	10.4

Quickest 1,000 Points (Games Played)

Player	Games	Date	Opponent	Points
Cotton Nash	45	2/2/63	Florida	1,770
Dan Issel	49	2/22/69	LSU	2,138
Bob Burrow	51	3/17/56	Iowa	1,023
Mike Casey	51	3/1/69	Vanderbilt	1,535
Kevin Grevey	51	2/25/74	Florida	1,801
Bill Spivey	52	2/17/51	Tennessee	1,213
Louie Dampier	53	3/18/66	Duke	1,575
Pat Riley	54	3/19/66	Texas Western	1,464
Cliff Hagan	57	12/21/53	Duke	1,475
Jamal Mashburn	59	3/14/92	LSU	1,843
Patrick Patterson	59	3/23/09	Creighton	1,564

Most Points in First Varsity Game (Since 1947)

Player	Class	Points	Date	Opponent
Mike Casey	SO	28	12/2/67	Michigan
Cotton Nash	SO	25	12/2/61	Miami (Ohio)
Terrence Jones	FR	25	11/12/10	East Tennessee State
Eric Bledsoe	FR	24	11/13/09	Morehead State
Anthony Davis	FR	23	11/11/11	Marist
Julius Randle	FR	23	11/8/13	UNC-Asheville
Sam Bowie	FR	22	11/17/79	Duke
Roger Newman	SR	20	12/1/60	VMI
Doron Lamb	FR	20	11/12/10	E. Tennessee St.
John Wall	FR	19	11/16/09	Ohio
Jamal Murray	FR	19	11/13/15	Albany
Rex Chapman	FR	18	11/29/86	Austin Peay
Louie Dampier	SO	18	12/4/64	Iowa
Dan Issel	SO	18	12/2/67	Michigan

Highest Scoring Average (Career)

Player	Games	Points	Average	Years
Dan Issel	83	2,138	25.8	1968-70
Cotton Nash	78	1,770	22.7	1962-64
Kevin Grevey	84	1,801	21.4	1973-75
Bob Burrow	51	1,023	20.1	1955-56
Louie Dampier	80	1,575	19.7	1965-67
Bill Spivey	63	1,213	19.3	1950-51
Cliff Hagan	77	1,475	19.2	1951-52,54
Jamal Mashburn	98	1,843	18.8	1990-93
Mike Casey	82	1,535	18.7	1968-70
Pat Riley	80	1,464	18.3	1967-69
Rex Chapman	61	1,073	17.6	1986-88
Johnny Cox	84	1,461	17.3	1957-59

Highest Scoring Average (Single Season)

Player	Games	Points	Average	Year
Dan Issel	28	948	33.9	1970
Dan Issel	28	746	26.6	1969
Cliff Hagan	25	600	24.0	1954
Cotton Nash	27	648	24.0	1964
Jodie Meeks	36	854	23.7	2009
Kevin Grevey	31	730	23.6	1976
Cotton Nash	26	608	23.4	1962
Kenny Walker	31	710	22.9	1985
Pat Riley	29	637	22.0	1966
Kevin Grevey	29	547	21.9	1974

Most Points (Single Season)

Player	Year	Points
Dan Issel	1970	948
Jodie Meeks	2009	854
Jamal Mashburn	1992	767
Dan Issel	1969	746
Kevin Grevey	1975	730
Ron Mercer	1997	725
Kenny Walker	1986	721
Jamal Murray	2016	720
Jamal Mashburn	1993	714
Kenny Walker	1985	710
Alex Groza	1949	698
Cliff Hagan	1952	692
Brandon Knight	2011	657
Cotton Nash	1964	648
Tony Delk	1996	639
Pat Riley	1966	635
Bill Spivey	1951	635
John Wall	2010	616
Rex Chapman	1988	609

By a Freshman
Jamal Murray ... 2016 ... 720

By a Sophomore
Jamal Mashburn ... 1992 ... 767

By a Junior
Jodie Meeks ... 2009 ... 854

By a Senior
Dan Issel ... 1970 ... 948

Most Points Scored (Game)

54	Jodie Meeks, UK vs. Tennessee	2009
53	Dan Issel, UK vs. Ole Miss	1970
51	Cliff Hagan, UK vs. Temple	1953
51	Dan Issel, UK vs. LSU	1970
50	Bob Burrow, UK vs. LSU	1956
47	Dan Issel, UK vs. Alabama	1970
46	Jodie Meeks, UK vs. Appalachian St.	2008
45	Jodie Meeks, UK vs. Arkansas	2009
44	Dan Issel, UK vs. Notre Dame	1970
42	Cliff Hagan, UK vs. Tennessee	1952
42	Louie Dampier, UK vs. Vanderbilt	1966
42	Mike Pratt, UK vs. Notre Dame	1969
42	Dan Issel, UK vs. Auburn	1970
42	Melvin Turpin, UK vs. Tennessee	1983
42	Melvin Turpin, UK vs. Georgia	1984
41	Dan Issel, UK vs. Vanderbilt	1969
41	Dan Issel, UK vs. North Carolina	1970
41	Jack Givens, UK vs. Duke	1978
41	Tayshaun Prince, UK vs. Tulsa	2002
40	Louie Dampier, UK vs. Illinois	1967
40	Dan Issel, UK vs. Georgia	1970
40	Dan Issel, UK vs. Navy	1970
40	Kevin Grevey, UK vs. Georgia	1973
40	Bill Spivey, UK vs. Georgia Tech	1950
40	Bill Spivey, UK vs. Xavier	1951
40	Bob Burrow, UK vs. St. Louis	1956
40	Derrick Miller, UK vs. Vanderbilt	1990

UK All-Freshman Team Selections

Rex Chapman 1987	Rajon Rondo........................... 2005	Archie Goodwin..................... 2013
Eric Manuel 1988	Patrick Patterson 2008	Nerlens Noel 2013
Chris Mills.............................. 1989	DeMarcus Cousins 2010	Alex Poythress 2013
Jamal Mashburn...................... 1991	Eric Bledsoe 2010	Julius Randle........................... 2014
Rodrick Rhodes....................... 1993	John Wall 2010	James Young............................ 2014
Ron Mercer............................. 1996	Doron Lamb 2011	Devin Booker.......................... 2015
Jamaal Magloire 1997	Brandon Knight 2011	Trey Lyles 2015
Keith Bogans........................... 2000	Terrence Jones 2011	Karl-Anthony Towns............... 2015
Gerald Fitch 2001	Anthony Davis......................... 2012	Tyler Ulis 2016
Jason Parker 2001	Michael Kidd-Gilchrist 2012	Jamal Murray 2016
Chuck Hayes............................ 2002	Willie Cauley-Stein 2013	

Basketball Hall Of Fame
Enshrined in Springfield, Massachusetts

Adolph Rupp ....Inducted 1969
Cliff Hagan ....Inducted 1977
Frank Ramsey ....Inducted 1981
Dan Issel ....Inducted 1993
Cawood Ledford ....Inducted 1994
C.M. Newton ....Inducted 2000
Pat Riley..Inducted 2008
Adrian Smith..Inducted 2010
Louie Dampier...Inducted 2015
John Calipari..Inducted 2015

Other Wildcat All-Americans

Player	Year	Source
Louis McGinniss	1930	Helms Foundation
William Davis	1934	Converse Yearbook
Milt Ticco	1943	Pic Magazine
Wilber Schu	1945	Don Dunphy
Jim Line	1950	UPI
Bobby Watson	1952	Athletic Publications
Billy Ray Lickert	1961	Helms Foundation
Thad Jaracz	1966	AP
Mike Pratt	1970	Converse Yearbook
Rex Chapman	1988	NABC; Basketball Times
Scott Padgett	1999	John R. Wooden Award
Keith Bogans	2003	AP; NABC; The Sporting News; Basketball Times
Terrence Jones	2011	Yahoo

Year-by-Year Scoring Leaders (Total Points)

Year	Player	Games	Points	Average
1922-23	Carl Riefkin	13	133	10.2
1923-24	Jim McFarland	16	157	9.8
1924-25	Jim McFarland	20	143	7.2
1925-26	Gayle Mohney	18	200	11.1
1926-27	Paul Jenkins	16	98	6.1
1927-28	Cecil Combs	18	186	10.3
1928-29	Stan Milward	17	116	6.8
1929-30	Cecil Combs	19	125	6.6
1930-31	Carey Spicer	18	190	10.6
1931-32	Aggie Sale	17	235	13.8
1932-33	Aggie Sale	24	324	13.5
1933-34	John DeMoisey	17	212	12.5
1934-35	Leroy Edwards	21	343	16.3
1935-36	Ralph Carlisle	21	241	11.5
1936-37	Ralph Carlisle	21	208	9.9
1937-38	Joe Hagan	18	184	10.2
1938-39	Fred Curtis	20	183	9.2
1939-40	Mickey Rouse	21	175	8.3
1940-41	Jim King	25	151	6.0
1941-42	Marvin Akers	25	190	7.6
1942-43	Milt Ticco	23	233	10.1
1943-44	Bob Brannum	21	254	12.1
1944-45	Jack Tingle	26	293	11.3
1945-46	Jack Parkinson	30	339	11.3
1946-47	Alex Groza	37	393	10.6
1947-48	Alex Groza	39	488	12.5
1948-49	Alex Groza	34	698	20.5
1949-50	Bill Spivey	30	578	19.3
1950-51	Bill Spivey	33	635	19.2
1951-52	Cliff Hagan	32	692	21.6
1953-54	Cliff Hagan	25	600	24.0
1954-55	Bob Burrow	26	495	19.0
1955-56	Bob Burrow	25	528	21.1
1956-57	Johnny Cox	28	544	19.4
1957-58	Vernon Hatton	29	496	17.1
1958-59	Johnny Cox	27	485	17.9
1959-60	Billy Lickert	20	288	14.4
1960-61	Billy Lickert	28	450	16.0
1961-62	Cotton Nash	26	608	23.4
1962-63	Cotton Nash	25	514	20.6
1963-64	Cotton Nash	27	648	24.0
1964-65	Louie Dampier	25	426	17.0
1965-66	Pat Riley	29	637	22.0

1966-67	Louie Dampier	26	537	20.6
1967-68	Mike Casey	27	541	20.1
1968-69	Dan Issel	28	746	26.6
1969-70	Dan Issel	28	948	33.9
1970-71	Tom Parker	28	492	17.6
1971-72	Jim Andrews	28	602	21.5
1972-73	Jim Andrews	28	562	20.1
1973-74	Kevin Grevey	25	547	21.9
1974-75	Kevin Grevey	31	730	23.6
1975-76	Jack Givens	30	602	20.1
1976-77	Jack Givens	30	566	18.9
1977-78	Jack Givens	32	578	18.1
1978-79	Kyle Macy	31	470	15.2
1979-80	Kyle Macy	35	540	15.4
1980-81	Sam Bowie	28	488	17.4
1981-82	Derrick Hord	30	490	16.3
1982-83	Melvin Turpin	31	468	15.1
1983-84	Melvin Turpin	34	518	15.2
1984-85	Kenny Walker	31	710	22.9
1985-86	Kenny Walker	36	721	20.0
1986-87	Rex Chapman	29	464	16.0
1987-88	Rex Chapman	32	609	19.0
1988-89	LeRon Ellis	32	511	16.0
1989-90	Derrick Miller	28	538	19.2
1990-91	John Pelphrey	28	404	14.4
1991-92	Jamal Mashburn	36	767	21.3
1992-93	Jamal Mashburn	34	714	21.0
1993-94	Tony Delk	34	564	16.6
1994-95	Tony Delk	33	551	16.7
1995-96	Tony Delk	36	639	17.8
1996-97	Ron Mercer	40	725	18.1
1997-98	Jeff Sheppard	39	521	13.7
1998-99	Scott Padgett	37	467	12.6
1999-00	Jamaal Magloire	33	435	13.2
2000-01	Keith Bogans	34	577	17.0
2001-02	Tayshaun Prince	32	560	17.5
2002-03	Keith Bogans	36	564	15.7
2003-04	Gerald Fitch	29	470	16.2
2004-05	Kelenna Azubuike	34	499	14.7
2005-06	Rajon Rondo	34	380	11.2
2006-07	Randolph Morris	34	546	16.1
2007-08	Joe Crawford	30	538	17.9
2008-09	Jodie Meeks	36	854	23.7
2009-10	John Wall	37	616	16.6
2010-11	Brandon Knight	38	657	17.3
2011-12	Anthony Davis	40	567	14.2

2012-13	Archie Goodwin	33	466	14.1
2013-14	Julius Randle	40	599	15.0
2014-15	Aaron Harrison	39	430	11.0
2015-16	Jamal Murray	36	720	20.0

Jamal Murray set scoring records by a Wildcat freshman for most points scored and highest scoring average.

Records

Field Goals

Team Records
Field Goals Made
Game: 60 vs. Georgia Tech (2-27-56)
Season: 1,238 (1996-97)

Field Goals Attempted
Game: 125 vs. Ole Miss (2-8-64)
Season: 3,465 (1947-48)

Highest Field Goal Percentage
First Half: .786 vs. Ole Miss (1-14-81) [11-of-14]
Second Half: .875 at Alabama (2-9-80) [14-of-16]
Game: .765 vs. Notre Dame (12-29-81) [13-of-17]
Season: .556 (1982-83)

Individual Records
Field Goals Made
Game: 23, Dan Issel at Ole Miss (2-7-70)
Season: 369, Dan Issel (1969-70)
Career: 843, Jack Givens (1975-78)

Field Goals Attempted
Game: 42, Bill Spivey (2-18-50)

Season: 667, Dan Issel (1969-70)
Career: 1,638, Jack Givens (1975-78)

Highest Field Goal Percentage
Game (min. 10 made):
1.000, Rodney Dent vs. Morehead State (12-17-93) [12-of-12];
Kenny Walker vs. Western Kentucky (3-16-86) [11-of-11]
Season (min. 100 att.): .657, Michael Bradley (1998-99) [157-of-239]
Career (min. 400 att.): .602, Marquis Estill (2001-03) [365-of-606]

Longest Field Goal Made
Game: 63 feet, 7 inches, Cliff Barker vs. Vanderbilt (2- 26-49 in Alumn Gym). (Other long shots on record include 53 ft. 9 in., Ralph Beard vs. Tennessee in 1947- 48; 53 ft. 6 in., Linville Puckett vs. Mississippi State in 1953-54; 48 ft. 2 in., Red Hagan vs. Marquette in 1937- 38; and 47-feet, Vernon Hatton vs. Temple [12-7-57] that tied the score at the end of the first overtime. UK later won the game in 3 overtimes, 85-83).

Career Leaders
Field Goals Made

	Player	Seasons	G	FGA	FGM
1.	Jack Givens	1975-78	123	1,683	843
2.	Dan Issel	1968-70	83	1,591	825
3.	Kevin Grevey	1973-75	84	1,490	771
4.	Kenny Walker	1983-86	132	1,339	765

5.	Tony Delk	1993-96	133	1,441	683
6.	Jamal Mashburn	1990-93	98	1,307	675
7.	Keith Bogans	2000-03	135	1,535	671
8.	Alex Groza	1947-49	120	1,514	667
9.	Tayshaun Prince	1999-02	135	1,419	648
10.	Mike Casey	1968-69, 71	82	1,341	647

Field Goals Attempted

	Player	Seasons	G	FGM	FGA
1.	Jack Givens	1975-78	123	843	1,683
2.	Ralph Beard	1946-49	139	606	1,597
3.	Dan Issel	1968-70	83	825	1,591
4.	Alex Groza	1947-49	120	667	1,514
5.	Cotton Nash	1962-64	78	645	1,548
6.	Keith Bogans	2000-03	135	671	1,535
7.	Kevin Grevey	1973-75	84	771	1,490
9.	Johnny Cox	1957-59	84	564	1,425
10.	Tayshaun Prince	1999-02	135	648	1,419

Jack Givens holds the UK record for most field goals with 843.

Field Goal Percentage (min. 400 att.)

	Player	Seasons	FGM	FGA	Pct
1.	Marquis Estill	2001-03	365	607	.6013
2.	Willie Cauley-Stein	2013-15	346	583	.5935
3.	Charles Hurt	1980-83	303	511	.5930
4.	Melvin Turpin	1981-84	626	1,059	.5911
5.	Patrick Patterson	2008-10	617	1,054	.5854
6.	Rick Robey	1975-78	533	917	.5812
7.	Kenny Walker	1983-86	765	1,339	.5713
8.	Andre Riddick	1992-95	265	465	.5699
9.	Jim Andrews	1971-73	543	965	.5627
10.	Nazr Mohammed	1996-98	335	606	.5528

Single-Season Leaders

Field Goals Made

	Player	Season	G	FGA	FGM
1.	Dan Issel	1969-70	28	667	369
2.	Kevin Grevey	1974-75	31	592	303
3.	Ron Mercer	1996-97	40	603	297
4.	Dan Issel	1968-69	28	534	285
5.	Jamal Mashburn	1991-92	36	492	279
6.	Pat Riley	1965-66	29	514	265
7.	Cliff Hagan	1951-52	32	633	264
8.	Jodie Meeks	2008-09	36	568	263
9.	Kenny Walker	1985-86	36	447	260
10.	Jamal Mashburn	1992-93	34	526	259
	Alex Groza	1948-49	34	612	259

By a Freshman —

	Player	Season	G	FGA	FGM
1.	Jamal Murray	2015-16	36	538	244
2.	Brandon Knight	2010-11	38	513	217
3.	DeMarcus Cousins	2009-10	38	369	206
4.	John Wall	2009-10	37	438	202
5.	Chris Mills	1988-89	32	372	180

By a Sophomore —

	Player	Season	G	FGA	FGM
1.	Ron Mercer	1996-97	40	603	297
2.	Jamal Mashburn	1991-92	36	492	279
3.	Jack Givens	1975-76	30	494	243
4.	Patrick Patterson	2008-09	34	398	240
5.	Kevin Grevey	1972-73	28	441	236

By a Junior —

	Player	Season	G	FGA	FGM
1.	Dan Issel	1968-69	28	534	285
2.	Pat Riley	1965-66	29	514	265
3.	Cliff Hagan	1951-52	32	633	264
4.	Jodie Meeks	2008-09	36	568	263
5.	Jamal Mashburn	1992-93	34	526	259

By a Senior —

	Player	Season	G	FGA	FGM
1.	Dan Issel	1969-70	28	667	369
2.	Kevin Grevey	1974-75	31	592	303
3.	Kenny Walker	1985-86	36	447	260
4.	Alex Groza	1948-49	34	612	259
5.	Cotton Nash	1963-64	27	588	248

Records – 1903-2016

Field Goals Attempted

	Player	Season	G	FGM	FGA
1.	Dan Issel	1969-70	28	369	667
2.	Cliff Hagan	1951-52	32	264	633
3.	Bill Spivey	1950-51	33	252	632
4.	Bill Spivey	1949-50	30	225	619
5.	Alex Groza	1948-49	34	259	612
6.	Ron Mercer	1996-97	40	297	603
7.	Kevin Grevey	1974-75	31	303	592
8.	Cotton Nash	1963-64	27	248	588
9.	Jodie Meeks	2008-09	36	263	568
10.	Jamal Murray	2015-16	38	244	538

By a Freshman —

	Player	Season	G	FGM	FGA
1.	Jamal Murray	2015-16	38	244	538
2.	Brandon Knight	2010-11	38	217	513
3.	Terrence Jones	2010-11	38	206	466
4.	James Young	2013-14	40	183	450
5.	John Wall	2009-10	37	202	438

By a Sophomore —

	Player	Season	G	FGM	FGA
1.	Bill Spivey	1949-50	30	225	619
2.	Ron Mercer	1996-97	40	297	603
3.	Jack Givens	1975-76	30	243	494
4.	Jamal Mashburn	1991-92	36	279	492
5.	Antoine Walker	1995-96	36	228	492

By a Junior —

	Player	Season	G	FGM	FGA
1.	Cliff Hagan	1951-52	32	264	633
2.	Bill Spivey	1950-51	33	252	632
3.	Jodie Meeks	2008-09	36	263	568
4.	Ralph Beard	1947-48	38	194	536
5.	Dan Issel	1968-69	28	285	534

By a Senior —

	Player	Season	G	FGM	FGA
1.	Dan Issel	1969-70	28	369	667
2.	Alex Groza	1948-49	34	259	612
3.	Kevin Grevey	1974-75	31	303	592
4.	Cotton Nash	1963-64	27	248	588
5.	Bobby Watson	1951-52	32	184	517

Field Goal Percentage (min. 150 attempts)

	Player	Season	FGM	FGA	Pct
1.	Marcus Lee	2015-16	102	150	.680
2.	Michael Bradley	1998-99	157	239	.657
3.	Rick Robey	1977-78	167	263	.635
4.	Charles Hurt	1982-83	102	162	.630
5.	Marquis Estill	2001-02	111	178	.624
6.	Anthony Davis	2011-12	210	337	.623
7.	Willie Cauley-Stein	2012-13	105	169	.621
8.	Melvin Turpin	1982-83	192	311	.617
9.	Josh Harrellson	2010-11	127	208	.611
10.	Randolph Morris	2005-06	110	181	.608

By a Freshman —

62.3		Anthony Davis (210-337)	2012

By a Sophomore —

65.7		Michael Bradley (157-239)	1999

By a Junior —

68.0		Marcus Lee (102-150)	2016

By a Senior —

63.5		Rick Robey (167-363)	1978

Single-Game Leaders

Field Goals Made

	Player, Opponent (Date)	FGM
1.	Dan Issel at Ole Miss (2-7-70)	23
2.	Dan Issel at Alabama (2-23-70)	19
	Dan Issel at LSU (2-21-70)	19
	Bob Burrow vs. LSU (1-14-56)	19
5.	Melvin Turpin vs. Georgia (3-8-84)	18
	Melvin Turpin at Tennessee (1-31-84)	18
	Jack Givens vs. Duke (3-27-78)	18
	Dan Issel at Vanderbilt (3-1-69)	18
	Louie Dampier at Vanderbilt (2-2-66)	18
10.	10 players with	17

Field Goals Attempted

	Player, Opponent (Date)	FGA
1.	Bill Spivey vs. Georgia Tech (2-18-50)	42
2.	Bill Spivey vs. Xavier (2-13-51)	41

Field Goal Percentage (min. 10 attempts]

	Player, Opponent (Date)	FGM
1.	Rodney Dent vs. Morehead St. (12-17-93) [12-of-12]	1.000
	Kenny Walker vs. Western Ky. (3-16-86) 11-of-11]	1.000
3.	Jack Givens at Mississippi State (1-31-77) [11-of-12]	.917
	Rick Robey vs. Miami, Ohio (12-10-75) [11-of-12]	.917
5.	Jared Prickett vs. UT-Martin (11-26-94) [10-of-11]	.909
	Travis Ford vs. Wake Forest (3-25-93) [10-of-11]	.909
	LeRon Ellis vs. Austin Peay (12-27-88) [10-of-11]	.909
	Bob Guyette at LSU (1-5-74) [10-of-11]	.909
9.	Scott Padgett vs. Western Carolina (2-6-97) [9-of-10]	.900
	Jack Givens vs. Alabama (2-20-78) [9-of-10]	.900
	Mike Phillips vs. LSU (1-14-78) [9-of-10]	.900
	Larry Johnson at Florida (1-24-76) [9-of-10]	.900
	DeMarcus Cousins vs. Wake Forest (3-201-10) [9-of-10]	.900

Year-By-Year Field Goal Percentage

Year	Player	Class	FGM	FGA	Pct.
1946-47	James Line	Fr.	86	209	.411
1947-48	Alex Groza	Jr.	200	530	.377
1948-49	Alex Groza	Sr.	259	612	.423
1949-50	James Line	Sr.	155	369	.420
1950-51	Bill Spivey	Jr.	252	632	.399
1951-52	Cliff Hagan	Jr.	264	633	.417
1953-54	Cliff Hagan	Sr.	234	514	.455
1954-55	Bob Burrow	Jr.	198	473	.419
1955-56	Vernon Hatton	So.	123	249	.494
1956-57	Vernon Hatton	Jr.	112	255	.439

1957-58	Vernon Hatton	Sr.	192	458	.419
1958-59	Bennie Coffman	Jr.	110	216	.509
1959-60	Billy Ray Lickert	Jr.	110	274	.401
1960-61	Billy Ray Lickert	Sr.	166	395	.420
1961-62	Larry Pursiful	Sr.	204	400	.510
1962-63	Don Rolfes	So.	68	134	.507
1963-64	Larry Conley	So.	114	231	.493
1964-65	Louie Dampier	So.	171	334	.512
1965-66	Louie Dampier	Jr.	249	482	.516
1966-67	Cliff Berger	Jr.	98	176	.556
1967-68	Mike Casey	So.	231	474	.489
1968-69	Mike Pratt	Jr.	173	321	.539
1969-70	Dan Issel	Sr.	369	667	.553
1970-71	Kent Hollenbeck	Jr.	113	212	.533
1971-72	Jim Andrews	Jr.	236	409	.577
1972-73	Jim Andrews	Sr.	243	434	.560
1973-74	Bob Guyette	Jr.	138	248	.557
1974-75	Rick Robey	Fr.	135	248	.544
1975-76	Mike Phillips	So.	199	367	.542
1976-77	Rick Robey	Jr.	158	276	.573
1977-78	Rick Robey	Sr.	167	263	.635
1978-79	LaVon Williams	Jr.	119	219	.543
1979-80	Sam Bowie	Fr.	165	311	.531
1980-81	Dirk Minniefield	So.	118	213	.554
1981-82	Melvin Turpin	So.	160	275	.582
1982-83	Charles Hurt	Sr.	102	162	.630
1983-84	Melvin Turpin	Sr.	224	378	.593
1984-85	Kenny Walker	Jr.	246	440	.559
1985-86	Kenny Walker	Sr.	260	447	.582
1986-87	Rob Lock	Jr.	91	161	.565
1987-88	Rob Lock	Sr.	123	219	.562
1988-89	LeRon Ellis	So.	200	385	.519
1989-90	Reggie Hanson	Jr.	165	332	.497
1990-91	Deron Feldhaus	Jr.	106	203	.522
1991-92	Jamal Mashburn	So.	279	492	.567
1992-93	Travis Ford	Jr.	129	245	.527
1993-94	Andre Riddick	Jr.	117	207	.565
1994-95	Andre Riddick	Sr.	68	123	.553
1995-96	Walter McCarty	Sr.	152	280	.543
1996-97	Jared Prickett	Sr.	116	211	.550
1997-98	Nazr Mohammed	Jr.	190	318	.597
1998-99	Michael Bradley	So.	157	239	.657
1999-00	Jamaal Magloire	Sr.	148	296	.500
2000-01	Marquis Estill	So.	85	141	.603
2001-02	Marquis Estill	Jr.	111	178	.624
2002-03	Marquis Estill	Sr.	169	288	.587
2003-04	Erik Daniels	Sr.	201	346	.581
2004-05	Randolph Morris	Fr.	105	199	.528
2005-06	Randolph Morris	So.	110	181	.608
2006-07	Randolph Morris	Jr.	202	341	.592
2007-08	Perry Stevenson	So.	69	120	.575
2008-09	Patrick Patterson	So.	240	398	.603
2009-10	Patrick Patterson	Jr.	215	374	.575
2010-11	Josh Harrellson	Sr.	127	208	.611
2011-12	Anthony Davis	Fr.	210	337	.623
2012-13	Willie Cauley-Stein	Fr.	105	169	.621
2013-14	Willie Cauley-Stein	So.	106	178	.596
2014-15	Willie Cauley-Stein	Jr.	135	236	.572
2015-16	Marcus Lee	Jr.	102	150	.680

Free Throws

Team Records
Most Free Throws Made
Game: 46 at Vanderbilt (1-7-63)
Season: 666 (1978-79)

Most Free Throws Attempted
Game: 56 vs. Mississippi State (2-12-79)
Season: 971 (2009-10)

Highest Free Throw Percentage
Game (min. 10 att.): 1.000 vs. Mississippi State (2-8-83)
[19-of-19]; vs. Duke (3-3-30) [19-of-19]; at Ole Miss (1- 28-89)
[13-of-13]; vs. Georgia (3-13-88) [12-of-12];
vs. Auburn (2-27-93) [11-of-11]; at Vanderbilt (3-2-74) [11- of-11];
vs. Alabama (2-1-34) [11-of-11]; at Alabama (1-18-89) [10-of-10];
vs. Austin Peay (12-19-09) [18-18]
Season: .776 (1978-79) [666-of-858]

Fewest Free Throws Attempted
Game: 1 vs. Auburn (3-10-84); at Tennessee (1-5-80);
vs. Georgia (2-8-75)

Individual Records
Free Throws Made
Game: 18, Dwight Anderson vs. Miss.   State (1-15-79)
Season: 218, Kenny Walker (1984-85)
Career: 550, Kenny Walker (1983-86)

Free Throws Attempted
Game: 24, Cliff Hagan vs. Temple (12-18-54)
Season: 284, Kenny Walker (1984-85)
Career: 733, Kenny Walker (1983-86)

Highest Free Throw Percentage
Game (min. 10 att.): 1.000, (35 times),
most by Louie Dampier vs. Oregon State (12-22-66);
last by Jamal Murray vs. Wright State (11/20/15)
Game (min. 15 att.): .944, Cliff Hagan vs. Ole Miss (1- 2-52) [17-of-18]
Season (min. 50 att.): .912, Kyle Macy (1979-80) [104- of-114]
Career (min. 200 att.): .890, Jodie Meeks (2007-09) [299-336];
Kyle Macy (1978-80) [331-of-372]

Career Leaders
Free Throws Made

	Player	Seasons	G	FTA	FTM
1.	Kenny Walker	1983-86	132	733	550
2.	Dan Issel	1968-70	83	661	488
3.	Cotton Nash	1962-64	78	652	480
4.	Ed Davender	1985-88	129	553	438
5.	Alex Groza	1947-49	120	548	410
6.	Winston Bennett	1984-86, 88	133	516	368
7.	Rodrick Rhodes	1993-95	99	480	365
8.	Jack Givens	1975-78	132	441	352
9.	Frank Ramsey	1951-52, 54	91	518	346
10.	Jamal Mashburn	1991-93	98	495	345

Free Throws Attempted

	Player	Seasons	G	FTM	FTA
1.	Kenny Walker	1983-86	132	550	733
2.	Dan Issel	1968-70	83	488	661
3.	Cotton Nash	1962-64	78	480	652
4.	Alex Groza	1947-49	120	410	548
5.	Ed Davender	1985-88	129	438	553
6.	Frank Ramsey	1951-52, 54	91	346	518
7.	Winston Bennett	1984-86, 88	133	368	516
8.	Jamal Mashburn	1991-93	98	345	495
9.	Ralph Beard	1946-49	139	305	489
10.	Cliff Hagan	1951-52, 54	77	341	487

Free Throw Percentage (min. 200 att.)

	Player	Seasons	FTM	FTA	Pct
1.	Jodie Meeks	2007-09	299	336	.890
2.	Kyle Macy	1978-80	331	372	.890
3.	Travis Ford	1993-94	239	271	.882
4.	Jim Master	1981-84	259	305	.849
5.	Tyler Ulis	2015-16	209	247	.846
6.	Richie Farmer	1989-92	207	247	.838
7.	Louie Dampier	1965-67	297	356	.834
8.	Anthony Epps	1994-97	208	254	.819
9.	Larry Pursiful	1960-62	214	263	.814
10.	Doron Lamb	2011-12	202	249	.811

Single-Season Leaders

Free Throws Made

	Player	Season	G	FTA	FTM
1.	Kenny Walker	1984-85	31	284	218
2.	Jodie Meeks	2008-09	36	234	211
3.	Dan Issel	1969-70	28	275	210
4.	Julius Randle	2013-14	40	289	204
5.	Kenny Walker	1985-86	36	263	201
6.	Alex Groza	1948-49	34	248	180
7.	Dan Issel	1968-69	28	232	176
8.	John Wall	2009-10	37	232	175
9.	Rodrick Rhodes	1993-94	33	215	167
	Tyler Ulis	2015-16	34	195	167

Free Throws Attempted

	Player	Season	G	FTM	FTA
1.	Julius Randle	2013-14	40	204	289
2.	Kenny Walker	1984-85	31	218	284
3.	Dan Issel	1969-70	28	210	275
4.	DeMarcus Cousins	2009-10	38	162	268
5.	Kenny Walker	1985-86	36	201	263
6.	Alex Groza	1948-49	34	180	248
7.	Terrence Jones	2010-11	38	157	243
8.	Cotton Nash	1962-63	25	162	236
9.	Cliff Hagan	1951-52	32	164	235
10.	Jodie Meeks	2008-09	36	211	234

Free Throw Percentage (min. 50 att.)

	Player	Season	FTM	FTA	Pct
1.	Kyle Macy	1980	104	114	.912
2.	Travis Ford	1994	103	113	.912
3.	Jodie Meeks	2009	211	234	.902
4.	Jodie Meeks	2007	61	68	.897
5.	Jim Master	1982	95	106	.896
6.	Kyle Macy	1978	115	129	.892
7.	Gimel Martinez	1992	68	77	.883
8.	Kent Hollenbeck	1971	82	93	.882
9.	Bennie Coffman	1960	67	76	.882
10.	Travis Ford	1993	104	118	.881

Consecutive Free Throws Made

	Player (Seasons)	FT
1.	Travis Ford (1992-93 to 1993-94)	50
2.	Jim Master (1981-82)	40
3.	Jodie Meeks (2008-09)	36
4.	Ed Davender (1987-88)	33
5.	Kyle Macy (1978-79 to 1979-80)	32

Single-Game Leaders

Free Throws Made

	Player, Opponent (Date)	FTM
1.	Dwight Anderson vs. Mississippi State (2-12-79)	18
2.	Cotton Nash at Vanderbilt (1-8-62)	17
	Roger Newman vs. Ohio State (3-18-61)	17
	Cliff Hagan vs. Temple (12-5-53)	17
	Cliff Hagan vs. Ole Miss (1-3-52)	17
6.	Rodrick Rhodes vs. Ole Miss (1-18-95)	16
	Jamal Mashburn vs. Eastern Kentucky (12-8-92)	16
	Kenny Walker vs. Alabama (3-8-86)	16
	Scotty Baesler at Vanderbilt (1-7-63)	16
10.	nine players with	14

Free Throws Attempted

	Player, Opponent (Date)	FTA
1.	Cliff Hagan vs. Temple (12-5-53)	24
2.	Dwight Anderson vs. Mississippi State (2-12-79)	23
3.	Roger Newman vs. Ohio State (3-18-61)	22
4.	Alex Groza vs. Tulane (3-5-49)	21
5.	Heshimu Evans vs. Ole Miss (3-5-99)	20
	Rodrick Rhodes vs. Ole Miss (1-18-95)	20
	Kenny Walker vs. Kansas (12-31-84)	20
	Jim Andrews vs. Kentucky (1-10-72)	20
	Dan Issel vs. Notre Dame (12-27-69)	20
	Dan Issel vs. Navy (12-19-69)	20

Free Throw Percentage (min. 12 attempts]

	Player, Opponent (Date)	Pct
1.	Jodie Meeks at Tennessee (1-13-09) [14-of-14]	1.000
	Ramel Bradley vs. Gardner-Webb (11-7-07) [14-of-14]	1.000
	Louie Dampier vs. Oregon St. (12-22-66) [14-of-14]	1.000
	Travis Ford vs. Ohio State (12-22-93) [13-of-13]	1.000
	Louie Dampier vs. Florida (1-30-65) [13-of-13]	1.000
	Jodie Meeks vs. West Virginia (11-29-08) [12-of-12]	1.000
	Kyle Macy vs. Vanderbilt (1-19-80) [12-of-12]	1.000
	Rick Robey vs. Vanderbilt (3-1-75) [12-of-12]	1.000
	Kevin Grevey at Georgia (2-19-73) [12-of-12]	1.000
	Dan Issel vs. Miami, Ohio (3-15-69) [12-of-12]	1.000
	Cotton Nash vs. Notre Dame (12-29-62) [12-of-12]	1.000
	Larry Pursiful vs. Kansas St. (12-23-61) [12-of-12]	1.000
	Johnny Cox vs. Maryland (12-15-56) [12-of-12]	1.000
	Phil Grawemeyer vs. Florida (2-3-55) [12-of-12]	1.000

Yearly Leaders

Free Throw Percentage (min. 50 att.)

Year	Player	CL	FT	FTA	Pct
1945-46	Wilbur Schu	Sr.	58	82	.707
1946-47	Kenneth Rollins	Jr.	86	107	.803
1947-48	Kenneth Rollins	Jr.	67	92	.728
1948-49	Alex Groza	Sr.	180	248	.725
1949-50	Bill Spivey	So.	128	176	.727
1950-51	Shelby Linville	Jr.	53	70	.757
1951-52	Cliff Hagan	Jr.	164	235	.697
1953-54	Bill Evans	Jr.	49	63	.778
1954-55	Bill Evans	Sr.	81	109	.743
1955-56	Bob Burrow	Sr.	114	171	.667
	Vernon Hatton	So.	100	150	.667
1956-57	Johnny Cox	So.	138	180	.766
1957-58	Vernon Hatton	Sr.	112	144	.777
1958-59	Don Mills	Jr.	101	122	.827
1959-60	Bennie Coffman	Sr.	67	76	.882
1960-61	Larry Pursiful	Jr.	99	118	.838
1961-62	Larry Pursiful	Sr.	89	109	.816
1962-63	Scotty Baesler	Sr.	59	69	.855
1963-64	Terry Mobley	Jr.	43	56	.767
1964-65	Louie Dampier	So.	84	100	.840
1965-66	Tommy Kron	Sr.	57	67	.851
1966-67	Louie Dampier	Sr.	99	119	.831
1967-68	Mike Casey	So.	79	96	.823
1968-69	Dan Issel	Jr.	176	232	.759
1969-70	Dan Issel	Sr.	210	275	.764
1970-71	Kent Hollenbeck	Jr.	82	93	.882
1971-72	Ronnie Lyons	So.	70	80	.875
1972-73	Mike Flynn	So.	55	75	.733
1973-74	Kevin Grevey	Jr.	83	100	.830
1974-75	Rick Robey	Fr.	51	63	.810
1975-76	Jack Givens	So.	116	140	.829
1976-77	Jack Givens	Jr.	94	113	.832
1977-78	Kyle Macy	So.	115	129	.892
1978-79	Kyle Macy	Jr.	112	129	.868
1979-80	Kyle Macy	Sr.	104	114	.912
1980-81	Dirk Minniefield	So.	55	63	.873
1981-82	Jim Master	So.	95	106	.896
1982-83	Derrick Hord	Sr.	65	79	.823
1983-84	Jim Master	Sr.	60	74	.811
1984-85	Kenny Walker	Jr.	218	284	.768
1985-86	Ed Davender	So.	104	131	.794
1986-87	Ed Davender	Jr.	107	145	.738
1987-88	Ed Davender	Sr.	149	171	.871
1988-89	Reggie Hanson	So.	57	76	.750
1989-90	Richie Farmer	So.	50	59	.847
1990-91	Richie Farmer	Jr.	64	76	.842
1991-92	Gimel Martinez	So.	68	77	.883
1992-93	Travis Ford	Jr.	104	118	.881
1993-94	Travis Ford	Sr.	103	113	.912
1994-95	Anthony Epps	So.	58	80	.850
1995-96	Tony Delk	Sr.	88	110	.800
1996-97	Anthony Epps	Sr.	75	90	.833
1997-98	Scott Padgett	Jr.	87	102	.853
1998-99	Heshimu Evans	Sr.	94	128	.734
1999-00	Desmond Allison	So.	53	68	.779
2000-01	Tayshaun Prince	Jr.	97	115	.843
2001-02	Chuck Hayes	Fr.	48	65	.738
2002-03	Chuck Hayes	So.	82	104	.788
2003-04	Kelenna Azubuike	So.	58	76	.763
2004-05	Chuck Hayes	Sr.	81	111	.730
2005-06	Ramel Bradley	So.	46	59	.780
2006-07	Jodie Meeks	Fr.	61	68	.897
2007-08	Ramel Bradley	Sr.	142	171	.830
2008-09	Jodie Meeks	Jr.	211	234	.902
2009-10	John Wall	Fr.	175	232	.754
2010-11	Darius Miller	Jr.	58	68	.853
2011-12	Doron Lamb	So.	123	149	.826
2012-13	Julius Mays	Sr.	55	65	.846
2013-14	Aaron Harrison	Fr.	139	176	.790
2014-15	Devin Booker	Fr.	53	64	.828
2015-16	Tyler Ulis	So.	167	195	.856

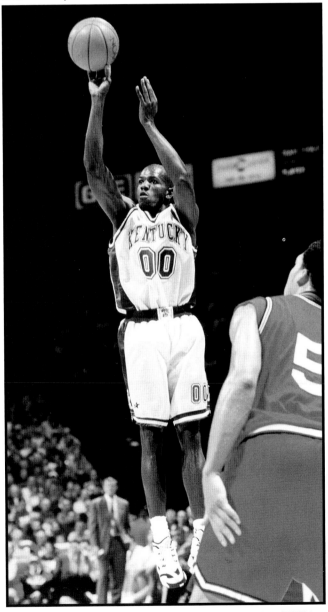

Tony Delk nailed a UK-best nine three-pointers against TCU in 1996. Delk also owns the mark for most career treys with 283.

Records – 1903-2016

Three-Point Field Goals

Team Records

Most 3-point Field Goals Made
Game: 21 vs. North Carolina (12-27-89) [21-of-48]
Season: 340, 1992-93 [340-of-862 in 34 games]

Most 3-point Field Goals Attempted
Game: 53 vs. UL Lafayette (12-23-89) [15-of-53]
Season: 888, 1991-92 [317-of-888 in 36 games]

Highest 3-point Field Goal Pct.
Game (min. 10 made): .667 vs. Wake Forest (3-25-93) [16- of-24]
Game (min. 20 made): .571 vs. LSU (3-4-95) [20-of-35]
Season: .397, 1995-96 [317-of-888 in 36 games]

Individual Records

Most 3-point Field Goals Made
Half: 7, Jodie Meeks at Tennessee (1/13/09); Tayshaun Prince vs. North Carolina (12-8-01); Derrick Miller vs. Kansas (12-9-89)
Game: 10, Jodie Meeks at Tennessee (1/13/09) [10-of-15]
Season: 117, Jodie Meeks (2008-09) [117-of-288]
Career: 283, Tony Delk (1993-96) [283-of-712]

Most 3-point Field Goals Attempted
Game: 19, Derrick Miller vs. Kansas (12-8-90) [8-of-19]
Season: 289, Derrick Miller (1989-90) [99-of-289]
Career: 712, Tony Delk (1993-96) [283-of-712]

Highest 3-point Field Goal Pct.
Game (min. 5 made): 1.000, Ramel Bradley vs. South Carolina (1-26-08) [5-of-5]; Keith Bogans vs. Tulane (12-10-02) [5-of-5]; Tayshaun Prince vs. South Carolina (2-3-01) [5-of-5]; Jamal Mashburn vs. Wake Forest (3-25-93) [5-of-5]
Season (min. 75 att.): .532, Cameron Mills (1996-97) [42-of-79]
Season (min. 100 att.): .529, Travis Ford (1992-93) [101-of-191]
Career (min. 150 att.): .474, Cameron Mills (1995-98) [81-of-171]

Career Leaders

3-point Field Goals Made
	Player	Years	Pct	3FGA	3FG
1.	Tony Delk	1993-96	.398	712	283
2.	Keith Bogans	2000-03	.342	743	254
3.	Tayshaun Prince	1999-02	.329	621	204
4.	Gerald Fitch	2001-04	.396	502	199
5.	Derrick Miller	1986-90	.358	533	191
6.	Travis Ford	1992-94	.445	427	190
7.	Joe Crawford	2004-08	.350	532	186
8.	Jodie Meeks	2007-09	.386	459	177
	Ramel Bradley	2004-08	.355	499	177
10.	Darius Miller	2008-12	.379	462	175

3-point Field Goals Attempted
	Player	Years	Pct	3FG	3FGA
1.	Keith Bogans	2000-03	.342	254	743
2.	Tony Delk	1993-96	.398	283	712
3.	Tayshaun Prince	1999-02	.329	204	621
4.	Derrick Miller	1986-90	.358	191	533
5.	Joe Crawford	2004-08	.350	186	532
6.	Gerald Fitch	2001-04	.396	199	502
7.	Ramel Bradley	2004-08	.355	177	499
8.	Jodie Meeks	2007-09	.386	177	459
9.	John Pelphrey	1989-92	.370	160	433
10.	Jeff Brassow	1990-94	.357	153	428

3-point Field Goals Percentage (min. 150 att.)
	Player	Years	3FG	3FGA	Pct
1.	Doron Lamb	2011-12	144	303	.4752
2.	Cameron Mills	1995-98	81	171	.4737
3.	Travis Ford	1992-94	190	427	.4450
4.	Jamal Murray	2015-16	113	277	.4079
5.	Walter McCarty	1994-96	75	187	.4011
6.	Rex Chapman	1987-88	134	335	.4000
7.	Derek Anderson	1994-96	61	153	.3987
8.	Tony Delk	1993-96	283	712	.3975
9.	Gerald Fitch	2001-04	199	502	.3964
	Anthony Epps	1994-97	155	391	.3964

Single-Season Leaders

3-point Field Goals Made
	Player	Year	Pct	3FGA	3FG
1.	Jodie Meeks	2008-09	.406	288	117
2.	Jamal Murray	2015-16	.408	277	113
3.	Travis Ford	1992-93	.529	191	101
4.	Derrick Miller	1989-90	.332	298	99
5.	Tony Delk	1993-94	.374	254	95
6.	Tony Delk	1995-96	.443	210	93
7.	Brandon Knight	2010-11	.377	231	87
8.	Patrick Sparks	2004-05	.376	218	82
	James Young	2013-14	.349	235	82
10.	Keith Bogans	2002-03	.383	209	80
11.	Gerald Fitch	2003-04	.401	197	79
12.	Tony Delk	1994-95	.391	197	77
13.	Doron Lamb	2011-12	.466	163	76
14.	Keith Bogans	2000-01	.361	205	74
15.	Jeff Sheppard	1997-98	.376	189	71

3-point Field Goals Attempted
	Player	Year	Pct	3FG	3FGA
1.	Derrick Miller	1989-90	.332	99	298
2.	Jodie Meeks	2008-09	.406	117	288
3.	Jamal Murray	2015-16	.408	113	277
4.	Tony Delk	1993-94	.374	95	254
5.	James Young	2013-14	.349	82	235
6.	Brandon Knight	2010-11	.377	87	231
7.	Patrick Sparks	2004-05	.376	82	218
8.	Tony Delk	1995-96	.443	93	210
9.	Keith Bogans	2002-03	.383	80	209
10.	Keith Bogans	2000-01	.361	74	205
11.	Gerald Fitch	2003-04	.401	79	197
	Tony Delk	1994-95	.391	77	197
13.	Travis Ford	1992-93	.529	101	191
	Tayshaun Prince	2001-02	.340	65	191
15.	Jeff Sheppard	1997-98	.376	71	189

Highest 3-point Field Goal Percentage (min. 100 att.)

	Player	Year	3FG	3FGA	Pct
1.	Travis Ford	1992-93	101	191	.529
2.	Doron Lamb	2010-11	68	140	.486
3.	Doron Lamb	2011-12	76	163	.466
4.	Tony Delk	1995-96	93	210	.443
	Darius Miller	2010-11	58	131	.443
6.	Derek Willis	2015-16	53	120	.442
7.	Jamal Mashburn	1991-92	58	132	.439
8.	Rex Chapman	1987-88	66	159	.415
9.	Devin Booker	2014-15	58	141	.411
	Jeff Brassow	1993-94	46	112	.411

Single-Game Highs

3-point Field Goals Made

	Player	Opp (Date)	3FGA	3FG
1.	Jodie Meeks	at Tennessee (1-13-09)	15	10
2.	Tony Delk	TCU (1-20-96)	12	9
3.	Jodi Meeks	App. State (12-20-08)	14	9
	Eric Bledsoe	E. Tennessee St (3-18-10)	11	9
4.	Cameron Mills	Florida (2-1-98)	14	8
	Derrick Miller	Tennessee (1-20-90)	13	8
	Derrick Miller	N. Carolina (12-27-89)	16	8
	Derrick Miller	Kansas (12-9-89)	19	8

3-Point Field Goals Attempted

	Player	Opp (Date)	3FG	3FGA
1.	Derrick Miller	Kansas (12-9-89)	8	19
2.	Derrick Miller	Tenn. Tech (12-6-89)	7	18
3.	Derrick Miller	LSU (2-15-90)	7	16
	Derrick Miller	N. Carolina (12-27-89)	7	16
	Derrick Miller	UL Lafayette (12-23-89)	7	16
6.	Jodie Meeks	at Tennessee (1/13/09)	10	15
	Jodie Meeks	Tennessee St. (12/22/09)	8	15
	Jamal Mashburn	S. Carolina (1-4-92)	5	15
	Derrick Miller	Vanderbilt (2-7-90)	6	15
	Derrick Miller	Ole Miss (1-27-90)	4	15

Consecutive Games with 3-point Field Goal

	Player	Streak
1.	Jamal Murray	36 (2015-16)
2.	Tony Delk	34 (32 in 1993-94, 2 in 1994-95)
3.	Travis Ford	32 (27 in 1992-93, 5 in 1993-94)
4.	Keith Bogans	29 (3 in 2001-02, 27 in 2002-03)
5.	Jodie Meeks	27 (1 in 2007-08, 26 in 2008-09)

Yearly Leaders

3-point Field Goals Made

Year	Player	CL	3FG	3FGA	Pct
1986-87	Derrick Miller	Fr.	35	81	.432
1987-88	Rex Chapman	So.	66	159	.415
1988-89	Derrick Miller	Jr.	54	139	.388
1989-90	John Pelphrey	So.	44	120	.367
1990-91	John Pelphrey	Jr.	62	164	.378
1991-92	Jamal Mashburn	So.	58	132	.439
1992-93	Travis Ford	Jr.	101	191	.529
1993-94	Jeff Brassow	Sr.	46	112	.411
1994-95	Tony Delk	Jr.	77	197	.391
1995-96	Tony Delk	Sr.	93	210	.443
1996-97	Cameron Mills	Jr.	42	79	.532
1997-98	Cameron Mills	Sr.	38	87	.437
1998-99	Scott Padgett	Sr.	61	160	.381
1999-00	Tayshaun Prince	So.	46	150	.307
2000-01	Keith Bogans	So.	74	205	.361
2001-02	Tayshaun Prince	Sr.	65	191	.340
2002-03	Gerald Fitch	Jr.	61	147	.415
2003-04	Gerald Fitch	Sr.	79	197	.401
2004-05	Patrick Sparks	Jr.	82	218	.376
2005-06	Patrick Sparks	Sr.	69	179	.385
2006-07	Ramel Bradley	Jr.	69	188	.367
2007-08	Ramel Bradley	Sr.	58	153	.379
2008-09	Jodie Meeks	Jr.	117	288	.406
2009-10	Darnell Dodson	So.	50	144	.347
2010-11	Brandon Knight	Fr.	87	231	.377
2011-12	Doron Lamb	So.	76	163	.466
2012-13	Julius Mays	Sr.	65	175	.371
2013-14	James Young	Fr.	83	235	.349
2014-15	Aaron Harrison	So.	59	159	.316
2015-16	Jamal Murray	Fr.	113	277	.408

Rebounding

Team Records

Most Rebounds
Game: 108 vs. Ole Miss (2-8-64)
Season: 2,109 (1950-51)

Highest Rebounding Average
Season: 64.6 (1955-56) [1,680 in 26 games]

Highest Rebounding Margin
Season: 21.5 (1955-56)

Individual Records

Most Rebounds
Game: 34, Bob Burrow vs. Temple (12-10-55);
Bill Spivey vs. Xavier (2-13-51)
Season: 567, Bill Spivey (1950-51)
Career: 1,078, Dan Issel (1968-70)

Highest Rebounding Average
Season: 17.7, Bob Burrow (1954-55) [459 in 26 games]
Career: 16.1, Bob Burrow (1955-56) [823 in 51 games]

Career Leaders

Rebounds

	Player	Seasons	G	Avg	Reb
1.	Dan Issel	1968-70	83	12.9	1,078
2.	Frank Ramsey	1951-52, 54	91	11.4	1,038
3.	Cliff Hagan	1951-52, 54	77	13.4	1,035
4.	Johnny Cox	1957-59	84	12.0	1,004
5.	Cotton Nash	1962-64	78	12.3	962
6.	Kenny Walker	1983-86	132	7.1	942
7.	Chuck Hayes	2002-05	134	6.8	910
8.	Sam Bowie	1980-81, 84	96	8.8	843
9.	Rick Robey	1975-78	105	8.0	838
10.	Bob Burrow	1955-56	51	16.1	823

Records – 1903-2016

Rebounding Average

	Player	Seasons	G	Reb	Avg
1.	Bob Burrow	1955-56	51	823	16.1
2.	Cliff Hagan	1951-52, 54	77	1,035	13.4
3.	Dan Issel	1968-70	83	1,078	12.9
4.	Cotton Nash	1962-64	78	962	12.3
5.	Johnny Cox	1957-59	84	1,004	12.0
6.	Frank Ramsey	1951-52, 54	91	1,038	11.4
7.	Don Mills	1957-59	71	669	10.3
8.	Ed Beck	1956-58	78	783	10.0
9.	DeMarcus Cousins	2009-10	38	374	9.8
	Jim Andrews	1971-73	80	783	9.8

Single-Season Leaders

Rebounds

	Player	Season	G	Reb	Avg
1.	Bill Spivey	1950-51	33	567	17.2
2.	Cliff Hagan	1951-52	32	528	16.5
3.	Bob Burrow	1954-55	26	459	17.7
4.	Frank Ramsey	1950-51	34	434	12.8
5.	Julius Randle	2013-14	40	417	10.4
6.	Anthony Davis	2011-12	40	415	10.4
7.	Frank Ramsey	1951-52	32	383	12.0
8.	Dan Issel	1968-69	28	381	13.6
9.	Ed Beck	1956-57	27	380	14.1
10.	DeMarcus Cousins	2009-10	38	374	9.8

Rebounding Average

	Player	Season	G	Reb	Avg
1.	Bob Burrow	1954-55	26	459	17.7
2.	Bill Spivey	1950-51	33	567	17.2
3.	Cliff Hagan	1951-52	32	528	16.5
4.	Bob Burrow	1955-56	25	364	14.6
5.	Ed Beck	1956-57	27	380	14.1
6.	Dan Issel	1968-69	28	381	13.6
7.	Cliff Hagan	1953-54	25	338	13.5
8.	Cotton Nash	1961-62	26	345	13.3
9.	Dan Issel	1969-70	28	369	13.2
10.	Don Mills	1959-60	25	323	12.9

Single-Game Highs

Rebounds

	Player	Opp (Date)	Reb
1.	Bob Burrow	Temple (12-10-55)	34
	Bill Spivey	Xavier (2-13-51)	34
3.	Cotton Nash	Ole Miss (2-8-64); Temple (12-18-61)	30
5.	Dan Issel	LSU (2-22-69)	29
6.	Mike Phillips	Tennessee (1-10-76)	28
7.	Dan Issel	Xavier (11-30-68)	24
	Dan Issel	Florida (12-4-67)	24
	Don Mills	Southern California (12-5-59)	24

Yearly Leaders

Rebounding

Year	Player	CL	G	Reb	Avg
1950-51	Bill Spivey	Jr.	33	567	17.2
1951-52	Cliff Hagan	Jr.	32	528	16.5
1953-54	Cliff Hagan	Sr.	25	338	13.5
1954-55	Bob Burrow	Jr.	26	459	17.7
1955-56	Bob Burrow	Sr.	25	364	14.6
1956-57	Ed Beck	Jr.	27	380	14.1
1957-58	Johnny Cox	Jr.	29	365	12.6
1958-59	Johnny Cox	Sr.	27	329	12.2
1959-60	Don Mills	Sr.	25	323	12.9
1960-61	Roger Newman	Sr.	28	265	9.5
1961-62	Cotton Nash	So.	26	345	13.2
1962-63	Cotton Nash	Jr.	25	300	12.0
1963-64	Cotton Nash	Sr.	27	317	11.7
1964-65	John Adams	Sr.	25	214	8.6
1965-66	Pat Riley	Jr.	29	259	8.9
1966-67	Thad Jaracz	Jr.	26	215	8.3
1967-68	Dan Issel	So.	27	328	12.1
1968-69	Dan Issel	Jr.	28	381	13.6
1969-70	Dan Issel	Sr.	28	369	13.2
1970-71	Tom Payne	So.	28	283	10.1
1971-72	Jim Andrews	Jr.	28	315	11.3
1972-73	Jim Andrews	Sr.	28	348	12.4
1973-74	Bob Guyette	Jr.	26	205	7.9
1974-75	Rick Robey	Fr.	31	214	6.9
1975-76	Mike Phillips	So.	30	295	9.8
1976-77	Rick Robey	Jr.	30	273	9.1
1977-78	Rick Robey	Sr.	32	261	8.2
1978-79	LaVon Williams	Jr.	31	213	6.9
1979-80	Sam Bowie	Fr.	34	276	8.1
1980-81	Sam Bowie	So.	28	254	9.1
1981-82	Melvin Turpin	So.	30	212	7.1
1982-83	Melvin Turpin	Jr.	31	195	6.3
1983-84	Sam Bowie	Sr.	34	313	9.2
1984-85	Kenny Walker	Jr.	31	315	10.2
1985-86	Kenny Walker	Sr.	36	276	7.7
1986-87	Richard Madison	Jr.	29	216	7.4
1987-88	Winston Bennett	Sr.	33	258	7.8
1988-89	Chris Mills	Fr.	32	277	8.7
1989-90	Reggie Hanson	Jr.	28	200	7.1
1990-91	Reggie Hanson	Sr.	28	201	7.2
1991-92	Jamal Mashburn	So.	36	281	7.8
1992-93	Jamal Mashburn	Jr.	34	284	8.3
1993-94	Jared Prickett	So.	33	232	7.0
1994-95	Mark Pope	Jr.	33	271	6.3
1995-96	Antoine Walker	So.	36	302	8.4
1996-97	Jared Prickett	Sr.	38	225	5.9
1997-98	Nazr Mohammed	Jr.	39	282	7.2
1998-99	Scott Padgett	Sr.	37	217	5.9
1999-00	Jamaal Magloire	Sr.	33	300	9.1
2000-01	Tayshaun Prince	Jr.	34	221	6.5
2001-02	Tayshaun Prince	Sr.	32	202	6.3
2002-03	Chuck Hayes	So.	36	244	6.8
2003-04	Chuck Hayes	Jr.	32	260	8.1
2004-05	Chuck Hayes	Sr.	34	263	7.7
2005-06	Rajon Rondo	So.	34	209	6.1
2006-07	Randolph Morris	Jr.	34	264	7.8

2007-08	Patrick Patterson	Fr.	25	192	7.7
2008-09	Patrick Patterson	So.	34	316	9.3
2009-10	DeMarcus Cousins	Fr.	38	374	9.8
2010-11	Terrence Jones	Fr.	38	336	8.8
2011-12	Anthony Davis	Fr.	40	415	10.4
2012-13	Nerlens Noel	Fr.	24	227	9.5
2013-14	Julius Randle	Fr.	40	417	10.4
2014-15	Karl-Anthony Towns	Fr.	39	261	6.7
2015-16	Marcus Lee	Jr.	36	216	6.0

Assists

Team Records

Most Assists
Game: 35 vs. San Jose State (3-14-96)
Season: 783 (1995-96)

Individual Records

Most Assists
Game: 16, John Wall vs. Hartford (12-29-09)
Season: 241, John Wall (2009-10)
Career: 646, Dirk Minniefield (1980-83)

Most Assists Per Game
Season: 6.4, Roger Harden (1985-86) [282 in 36 games]
Career: 5.3, Sean Woods (1990-92) [482 in 91 games]

Career Leaders

Assists

	Player	Seasons	G	Avg	Asst
1.	Dirk Minniefield	1980-83	123	5.3	646
2.	Anthony Epps	1994-97	141	3.9	544
3.	Roger Harden	1983-86	122	4.1	498
4.	Wayne Turner	1996-99	151	3.3	494
5.	Sean Woods	1990-92	91	5.3	482
6.	Kyle Macy	1978-80	98	4.8	470
7.	Cliff Hawkins	2001-04	126	3.7	468
8.	Ed Davender	1985-88	129	3.4	436
9.	Travis Ford	1992-94	100	4.3	428
10.	Tyler Ulis	2015-16	72	5.3	381
11.	Saul Smith	1998-01	143	2.5	363
12.	John Pelphrey	1989-92	114	2.9	327
13.	Larry Johnson	1974-77	112	2.8	319
14.	Ramel Bradley	2004-08	128	2.5	316
15.	Keith Bogans	2000-03	135	2.3	314

Assists Per Game

	Player	Seasons	G	Asst	Avg.
1.	Sean Woods	1990-92	91	482	5.30
2.	Tyler Ulis	2015-16	72	381	5.29
3.	Dirk Minniefield	1980-83	123	646	5.25
4.	Kyle Macy	1978-80	98	470	4.80
5.	Travis Ford	1992-94	100	428	4.28
6.	Rajon Rondo	2005-06	68	285	4.19
7.	Roger Harden	1983-86	122	498	4.08
8.	Anthony Epps	1994-97	141	544	3.86
9.	Cliff Hawkins	2001-04	126	468	3.71
10.	Larry Conley	1964-66	81	293	3.62

Single-Season Leaders

Assists

	Player	Season	G	Avg	Asst
1.	Tyler Ulis	2015-16	35	7.0	246
2.	John Wall	2009-10	37	6.50	241
3.	Roger Harden	1985-86	36	6.4	232
4.	Anthony Epps	1996-97	40	4.8	193
	Travis Ford	1993-94	33	5.9	193
6.	Dirk Minniefield	1981-82	30	6.3	188
7.	Dirk Minniefield	1982-83	31	5.8	181
8.	Kyle Macy	1977-78	32	5.6	178
9.	Anthony Epps	1995-96	36	4.9	175
10.	Wayne Turner	1997-98	39	4.4	173
11.	Rajon Rondo	2005-06	34	4.9	167
	Sean Woods	1991-92	36	4.6	167
13.	Cliff Hawkins	2003-04	32	5.2	166
	Travis Ford	1992-93	34	4.9	166
15.	Sean Woods	1989-90	28	5.9	164
16.	Kyle Macy	1979-80	35	4.7	163
17.	Sean Woods	1990-91	27	5.6	151
	Dirk Minniefield	1980-81	28	5.4	151
19.	Sean Sutton	1988-89	31	4.6	146
20.	John Pelphrey	1991-92	36	4.0	145
	Wayne Turner	1998-99	37	3.9	145

Assists Per Game

	Player	Seasons	G	Asst	Avg
1.	Tyler Ulis	2015-16	35	246	7.03
2.	John Wall	2009-10	37	241	6.50
3.	Roger Harden	1985-86	36	232	6.44
4.	Dirk Minniefield	1981-82	30	188	6.27
5.	Sean Woods	1989-90	28	164	5.86
6.	Travis Ford	1993-94	33	193	5.85
7.	Dirk Minniefield	1982-83	31	181	5.84
8.	Sean Woods	1990-91	27	151	5.59
9.	Kyle Macy	1977-78	32	178	5.56
10.	Dirk Minniefield	1980-81	28	151	5.39

Single-Game Highs

Assists

	Player	Opp (Date)	Asst
1.	John Wall	Hartford (12-29-09)	16
2.	Travis Ford	Eastern Kentucky (12-8-93)	15
3.	John Wall	UNC-Asheville (11-30-09)	14
	Dickey Beal	BYU (3-17-84)	14
	Dirk Minniefield	Villanova (12-4-82)	14
	Tyler Ulis	LSU (3-5-16)	14
7.	Anthony Epps	LSU (3-4-95)	13
	Rodrick Rhodes	Morehead State (12-19-92)	13
	Dirk Minniefield	Auburn (2-3-82)	13
	Dirk Minniefield	Mississippi State (1-23-80)	13

Single-Season Leaders

Assists

Year	Player	CL	G	Asst	Avg
1961-62	Scotty Baesler	Jr.	26	112	4.3
1962-63	Cotton Nash	Jr.	25	66	2.6
1963-64	Larry Conley	So.	27	112	4.2
1964-65	Larry Conley	Jr.	25	81	3.2

Records – 1903-2016

1965-66	Larry Conley	Sr.	29	100	3.4
1966-67	Pat Riley	Sr.	26	68	2.6
1967-68	Mike Pratt	So.	27	82	3.0
1968-69	Mike Casey	Jr.	28	129	4.6
1969-70	Mike Pratt	Sr.	28	99	3.5
1970-71	Larry Steele	Sr.	24	93	3.9
1971-72	Stan Key	Sr.	28	89	3.2
1972-73	Jimmy Dan Conner	So.	28	83	3.0
1973-74	Mike Flynn	Jr.	26	83	3.2
1974-75	Jimmy Dan Conner	Sr.	31	106	3.4
	Mike Flynn	Sr.	31	106	3.4
1975-76	Larry Johnson	Jr.	30	98	3.3
1976-77	Larry Johnson	Sr.	30	143	4.8
1977-78	Kyle Macy	So.	32	178	5.6
1978-79	Kyle Macy	Jr.	31	129	4.2
1979-80	Kyle Macy	Sr.	35	163	4.7
1980-81	Dirk Minniefield	So.	28	151	5.4
1981-82	Dirk Minniefield	Jr.	30	188	6.3
1982-83	Dirk Minniefield	Sr.	31	181	5.8
1983-84	Dickey Beal	Sr.	30	133	4.4
1984-85	Roger Harden	Jr.	30	142	4.7
1985-86	Roger Harden	Sr.	36	232	6.4
1986-87	Rex Chapman	Fr.	29	103	3.6
1987-88	Ed Davender	Sr.	33	131	4.0
1988-89	Sean Sutton	So.	31	146	4.7
1989-90	Sean Woods	So.	28	164	5.9
1990-91	Sean Woods	Jr.	27	151	5.6
1991-92	Sean Woods	Sr.	36	167	4.6
1992-93	Travis Ford	Jr.	34	166	4.9
1993-94	Travis Ford	Sr.	33	193	5.8
1994-95	Anthony Epps	So.	33	138	4.2
1995-96	Anthony Epps	Jr.	36	175	4.9
1996-97	Anthony Epps	Sr.	40	193	4.8
1997-98	Wayne Turner	Jr.	39	173	4.4
1998-99	Wayne Turner	Sr.	37	145	3.9
1999-00	Saul Smith	Jr.	33	115	3.5
2000-01	Saul Smith	Sr.	34	134	3.9
2001-02	Cliff Hawkins	So.	32	136	4.3

2002-03	Cliff Hawkins	Jr.	29	111	3.8
2003-04	Cliff Hawkins	Sr.	32	166	5.2
2004-05	Patrick Sparks	Jr.	34	122	3.6
2005-06	Rajon Rondo	So.	34	167	4.9
2006-07	Ramel Bradley	Jr.	34	129	3.8
2007-08	Ramel Bradley	Sr.	30	101	3.7
2008-09	DeAndre Liggins	Fr.	33	92	2.8
	Michael Porter	Jr.	36	92	2.6
2009-10	John Wall	Fr.	37	241	6.5
2010-11	Brandon Knight	Fr.	38	159	4.2
2011-12	Marquis Teague	Fr.	40	191	4.8
2012-13	Julius Mays	Sr.	33	63	2.9
2013-14	Andrew Harrison	Fr.	40	159	4.0
2014-15	Andrew Harrison	So.	39	139	3.6
2015-16	Tyler Ulis	So.	35	246	7.0

Blocks

Team Records

Most Blocks

Game: 17 vs. Morehead State (11-20-97)
Season: 273 (2009-10)

Individual Records

Most Blocks

Game: 12, Nerlens Noel vs. Ole Miss (1-29-13)
Season: 186, Anthony Davis (2011-12)
Career: 268, Jamaal Magloire (1997-00)

Most Blocks Per Game

Season: 4.65, Anthony Davis (2011-12) [186 in 40 games]
Career: 4.65, Anthony Davis (2011-12) [186 in 40 games]

Career Leaders

Blocks

	Player	Seasons	G	Avg	Blks
1.	Jamaal Magloire	1997-00	145	1.8	268
2.	Willie Cauley-Stein	2013-15	105	2.2	233
3.	Melvin Turpin	1981-84	123	1.8	226
4.	Sam Bowie	1980-81, 84	96	2.3	218
5.	Andre Riddick	1992-95	126	1.7	212
6.	Anthony Davis	2011-12	40	4.7	186
7.	Perry Stevenson	2007-10	134	1.2	159
8.	Jules Camara	1999-00, 02-03	136	1.1	155
9.	Patrick Patterson	2008-10	97	1.6	152
10.	Marquis Estill	2001-03	100	1.4	143

Blocks Per Game (min. 75 blocks)

	Player	Seasons	G	Blks	Avg
1.	Anthony Davis	2011-12	40	186	4.65
2.	Nerlens Noel	2012-13	24	106	4.42
3.	Sam Bowie	1980-81, 84	96	218	2.27
4.	Karl-Anthony Towns	2014-15	39	88	2.27
5.	Willie Cauley-Stein	2013-15	105	233	2.22
6.	Jamaal Magloire	1997-00	145	268	1.85
7.	Melvin Turpin	1981-84	123	226	1.84
8.	Andre Riddick	1992-95	126	212	1.68
9.	Patrick Patterson	2008-10	97	152	1.57
10.	Nazr Mohammed	1996-98	94	135	1.44

Tyler Ulis challenges a Kansas defender.

Single-Season Leaders
Blocks

	Player	Season	G	Blks	Avg
1.	Anthony Davis	2011-12	40	186	4.65
2.	Nerlens Noel	2012-13	24	106	4.42
	Willie Cauley-Stein	2013-14	37	106	4.42
4.	Karl-Anthony Towns	2014-15	39	88	2.27
5.	Andre Riddick	1993-94	34	83	2.4
	Melvin Turpin	1982-83	31	83	2.7
7.	Sam Bowie	1980-81	28	80	2.9
8.	Jamaal Magloire	1996-97	40	79	2.0
9.	Nazr Mohammed	1997-98	39	75	1.9
10.	Sam Bowie	1979-80	34	73	2.1

Single-Game Highs
Blocks

	Player	Opp (Date)	Blks
1.	Nerlens Noel	Ole Miss (1-29-13)	12
2.	Willie Cauley-Stein	Providence (12-1-13)	9
	Willie Cauley-Stein	Boise Statev(12-10-13)	9
	Andre Riddick	LSU (3-14-93)	9
	Sam Bowie	Vanderbilt (2-21-81)	9
6.	Anthony Davis	Tennessee (1-31-12)	8
	Anthony Davis	St. John's (12-1-11)	8
	Nerlens Noel	Alabama (1-22-13)	8
	Patrick Patterson	Georgia (3-4-09)	8
	Andre Riddick	Morehead State (12-17-93)	8
11.	Perry Stevenson	Miami (OH) (11-15-06)	7
	Andre Riddick	Arkansas (3-12-94)	7
	Andre Riddick	Ole Miss (1-29-92)	7
	Andre Riddick	Eastern Kentucky (1-18-92)	7

Single-Season Leaders
Blocks

Year	Player	CL	G	Blks	Avg
1978-79	Freddie Cowan	So.	31	36	1.2
1979-80	Sam Bowie	Fr.	34	73	2.1
1980-81	Sam Bowie	So.	28	80	2.9
1981-82	Melvin Turpin	So.	30	67	2.2
1982-83	Melvin Turpin	Jr.	31	83	2.7
1983-84	Sam Bowie	Sr.	34	65	1.9
1984-85	Kenny Walker	Jr.	31	37	1.2
1985-86	Kenny Walker	Sr.	36	43	1.2
1986-87	Rob Lock	Jr.	29	31	1.1
1987-88	Rob Lock	Sr.	33	32	1.0
1988-89	LeRon Ellis	So.	32	35	1.1
1989-90	Reggie Hanson	Jr.	28	40	1.4
1990-91	Reggie Hanson	Sr.	28	53	1.9
1991-92	Andre Riddick	Fr.	28	33	1.2
1992-93	Andre Riddick	So.	31	52	1.7
1993-94	Andre Riddick	Jr.	34	83	2.4
1994-95	Andre Riddick	Sr.	33	44	1.3
1995-96	Walter McCarty	Sr.	36	51	1.4
1996-97	Jamaal Magloire	Fr.	40	79	2.0
1997-98	Nazr Mohammed	Jr.	39	75	1.9
1998-99	Jamaal Magloire	Jr.	34	66	1.9
1999-00	Jamaal Magloire	Sr.	33	57	1.7
2000-01	Tayshaun Prince	Jr.	34	37	1.1
2001-02	Marquis Estill	Jr.	32	43	1.3
2002-03	Tayshaun Prince	Sr.	32	43	1.3
	Marquis Estill	Sr.	36	64	1.8
	Tayshaun Prince	Sr.	32	43	1.3
2003-04	Chuck Hayes	Jr.	32	45	1.4
2004-05	Shagari Alleyne	So.	29	44	1.5
2005-06	Randolph Morris	So.	21	24	1.1
2006-07	Randolph Morris	Jr.	34	70	2.1
2007-08	Perry Stevenson	So.	31	46	1.5
2008-09	Patrick Patterson	So.	34	70	2.1
2009-10	DeMarcus Cousins	Fr.	38	67	1.8
2010-11	Terrence Jones	Fr.	38	72	1.9
2011-12	Anthony Davis	Fr.	40	186	4.7
2012-13	Nerlens Noel	Fr.	24	106	4.4
2013-14	Willie Cauley-Stein	So.	37	106	2.9
2014-15	Karl-Anthony Towns	Fr.	39	88	2.3
2015-16	Skal Labissiere	Fr.	36	59	1.6
	Marcus Lee	Jr.	36	59	1.6

Steals

Team Records
Most Steals
Game: 23 vs. Tennessee-Martin (11-26-94); vs. Mississippi State (1-9-91)
Season: 480 (1996-97)

Individual Records
Most Steals
Game: 8, Rajon Rondo vs. Mississippi State (2-19-05);
Wayne Turner vs. George Washington (11-24-97)
Season: 87, Rajon Rondo (2004-05)
Career: 238, Wayne Turner (1996-99)

Most Steals Per Game
Season: 2.56, Rajon Rondo (2004-05) [87 in 34 games]
Career: 2.29, Rajon Rondo (2005-06) [156 in 68 games]

Career Leaders
Steals

	Player	Seasons	G	Avg	Stls
1.	Wayne Turner	1996-99	151	1.6	238
2.	Tony Delk	1993-96	133	1.5	201
3.	Cliff Hawkins	2001-04	126	1.6	199
4.	Ed Davender	1985-88	129	1.5	191
5.	Jared Prickett	1993-97	143	1.3	187
6.	Anthony Epps	1994-97	141	1.3	184
7.	John Pelphrey	1989-92	114	1.5	173
8.	Chuck Hayes	2002-05	134	1.3	170
9.	Rodrick Rhodes	1993-95	99	1.6	163
10.	Rajon Rondo	2005-06	68	2.3	156
	Dirk Minniefield	1980-83	123	1.3	156

Steals Per Game (Min. 75 Steals)

	Player	Seasons	G	Stls	Avg
1.	Rajon Rondo	2005-06	68	156	2.294
2.	Derek Anderson	1996-97	55	98	1.782
3.	Rodrick Rhodes	1993-95	99	163	1.646
4.	Sean Woods	1990-92	91	144	1.582
5.	Cliff Hawkins	2001-04	126	199	1.579
6.	Wayne Turner	1996-99	151	238	1.576

Records – 1903-2016

	Player			G		Stls
7.	Jamal Mashburn	1991-93		98	153	1.561
8.	John Pelphrey	1989-92		114	173	1.518
9.	Reggie Hanson	1988-91		101	153	1.515
10.	Tony Delk	1993-96		133	201	1.511

Single-Season Leaders

Steals

	Player	Season	G	Avg	Stls
1.	Rajon Rondo	2004-05	34	2.6	87
2.	Wayne Turner	1996-97	40	2.0	79
3.	Rodrick Rhodes	1993-94	33	2.3	76
4.	Cliff Hawkins	2003-04	32	2.3	74
5.	Rajon Rondo	2005-06	34	2.0	69
	Kyle Macy	1978-79	31	2.2	69
7.	Anthony Epps	1996-97	40	1.7	68
8.	Tony Delk	1995-96	36	1.9	67
9.	Jared Prickett	1996-97	38	1.7	66
	Ron Mercer	1996-97	40	1.7	66
	John Wall	2009-10	38	1.8	66

Steals Per Game (Min. 30 Steals)

	Player	Season	G	Stls	Avg
1.	Rajon Rondo	2004-05	34	87	2.559
2.	Cliff Hawkins	2003-04	32	74	2.313
3.	Rodrick Rhodes	1993-94	33	76	2.303
4.	Kyle Macy	1978-79	31	69	2.226
5.	Reggie Hanson	1989-90	28	61	2.179
	John Pelphrey	1991-92	28	61	2.179
7.	Nerlens Noel	2012-13	24	50	2.083
8.	Rajon Rondo	2005-06	34	69	2.029
9.	Wayne Turner	1996-97	40	79	1.975
10.	Tony Delk	1993-94	34	64	1.882

Single-Game Highs

Steals

	Player	Opp (Date)	Stls
1.	Rajon Rondo	Mississippi State (2-19-05)	8
	Wayne Turner	George Washington (11-24-97)	8
3.	Jared Prickett	Tennessee (3-12-93)	7
	Reggie Hanson	Ole Miss (2-16-91)	7
	John Pelphrey	LSU (2-15-90)	7
	Winston Bennett	Mississippi State (1-16-85)	7

Single-Season Leaders

Steals

Year	Player	CL	G	Stls	Avg
1978-79	Kyle Macy	Jr.	31	69	2.2
1979-80	Kyle Macy	Sr.	35	58	1.7
1980-81	Dirk Minniefield	So.	28	35	1.3
1981-82	Dirk Minniefield	Jr.	30	42	1.4
1982-83	Dirk Minniefield	Sr.	31	45	1.5
1983-84	Kenny Walker	So.	34	31	0.9
1984-85	Ed Davender	Fr.	31	33	1.1
1985-86	Ed Davender	So.	36	59	1.6
1986-87	James Blackmon	Sr.	29	50	1.7
1987-88	Rex Chapman	So.	32	53	1.7
1988-89	Reggie Hanson	So.	29	47	1.6
1989-90	Reggie Hanson	Jr.	28	61	2.2
	John Pelphrey	So.	28	61	2.2

Year	Player	CL	G	Stls	Avg
1990-91	Sean Woods	Jr.	27	50	1.9
1991-92	Jamal Mashburn	So.	36	61	1.7
	John Pelphrey	Sr.	36	61	1.7
1992-93	Travis Ford	Jr.	34	56	1.6
1993-94	Rodrick Rhodes	So.	33	76	2.3
1994-95	Tony Delk	Jr.	33	53	1.6
1995-96	Tony Delk	Sr.	36	67	1.9
1996-97	Wayne Turner	So.	40	79	2.0
1997-98	Wayne Turner	Jr.	39	62	1.6
1998-99	Wayne Turner	Sr.	37	57	1.5
1999-00	Keith Bogans	Fr.	33	47	1.4
2000-01	Saul Smith	Sr.	34	51	1.5
2001-02	Cliff Hawkins	So.	32	48	1.5
2002-03	Keith Bogans	Sr.	36	42	1.2
	Chuck Hayes	So.	36	42	1.2
	Cliff Hawkins	Jr.	29	42	1.4
2003-04	Cliff Hawkins	Sr.	32	74	2.3
2004-05	Rajon Rondo	Fr.	34	87	2.6
2005-06	Rajon Rondo	So.	34	69	2.0
2006-07	Ramel Bradley	Jr.	34	44	1.3
2007-08	Ramel Bradley	Sr.	31	48	1.5
2008-09	Jodie Meeks	Jr.	36	48	1.3
2009-10	John Wall	Fr.	38	66	1.8
2010-11	DeAndre Liggins	Jr.	38	46	1.2
2011-12	Anthony Davis	Fr.	40	54	1.4
2012-13	Nerlens Noel	Fr.	24	50	2.1
2013-14	Willie Cauley-Stein	So.	37	44	1.2
2014-15	Willie Cauley-Stein	Jr.	39	47	1.2
2015-16	Tyler Ulis	So.	35	51	1.5

Miscellaneous

Team Records

Most games Played
Season: 40 (1996-97, 2011-12)

Most Wins
Season: 38 (2011-12, 2014-15)

Fewest Wins
Season (20 or more games): 13
(1966-67, 1973-74 and 1988-89)

Longest Win Streak
Overall: 38 (Nov. 11 , 2014 to April 4, 20155)
SEC: 51 (Jan. 28, 1950 to Jan. 8, 1955)

Longest Home Win Streak
Overall: 129 (Jan. 4, 1943 to Jan. 8, 1955)
SEC: 70 (Jan. 21, 1939 to Jan. 8, 1955)

Most Losses
Season: 19 (1988-89) [13-19]

Fewest Losses
Season: 0, 1911-12 [9-0] and 1953-54 [25-0]

Longest Losing Streak
Overall: 9 (1922-23) **SEC:** 6 (1988-89)

Most Personal Fouls

Game: 41 vs. Tennessee (1-21-92); vs. Ohio (1-12-48)
Season: 837 (1991-92)

Fewest Personal Fouls

Season: 307 (1944-45)

Individual Records
Most Games Played

Season: 40, Anthony Epps, Jamaal Magloire, Ron Mercer
and Wayne Turner (1996-97)
Anthony Davis, Micheal Kidd-Gilchrist, Doron Lamb, Terrence Jones,
Marquis Teague and Darrius Miller (2011-12)
Career: 152, Darius Miller (2008-12)
Career (SEC): 72, Kenny Walker (1983-86)

Most Games Started

Season: 40, Ron Mercer (1996-97)
Career: 136, Ralph Beard (1946-49)

Most Consecutive Games Started

Career: 110, Chuck Hayes (Feb. 19, 2002 to Mar. 27, 2005);
Alex Groza (Nov. 28, 1946 to Mar. 26, 1949)
Career (SEC): 54, Dan Issel (1968-70); Mike Pratt (1968-70);
Jack Givens (1975-78)

Most Wins

Career: 132, Wayne Turner (1996-99)

Career Leaders
Double-Doubles

	Player	Seasons	G	DD
1.	Dan Issel	1968-70	83	64
2.	Cotton Nash	1962-64	78	44
3.	Jim Andrews	1971-73	80	43
4.	Kenny Walker	1983-86	132	31
	Tom Parker	1970-72	80	31
6.	Patrick Patterson	2008-10	97	30
	Rick Robey	1975-78	105	30
8.	Mike Pratt	1968-70	81	29
9.	Sam Bowie	1980-81, 84	96	27
10.	Jamal Mashburn	1991-93	98	26

30-Point games

	Player	Seasons	G	30+
1.	Dan Issel	1968-70	83	31
2.	Cotton Nash	1962-64	78	21
3.	Louie Dampier	1965-67	80	12
4.	Kevin Grevey	1973-75	84	11
5.	Kenny Walker	1983-86	132	9
6.	Cliff Hagan	1951-54	77	8
7.	Jodie Meeks	2007-09	81	7
	Jamal Mashburn	1991-93	98	7
	Jim Andrews	1971-73	80	7
	Bob Burrow	1955-56	51	7
	Alex Groza	1945-49	120	7

Games Played

	Player	Seasons	G
1.	Darius Miller	2008-12	152
2.	Wayne Turner	1996-99	151
3.	Jamaal Magloire	1997-00	145
4.	Saul Smith	1998-01	143
	Jared Prickett	1993-97	143
6.	Anthony Epps	1994-97	141
7.	Ralph Beard	1946-49	139
8.	Jules Camara	1999-00, 02-03	136

Games Started

	Player	Seasons	GS
1.	Ralph Beard	1946-49	136
2.	Keith Bogans	2000-03	122
3.	Chuck Hayes	2002-05	111
4.	Alex Groza	1947-49	110
5.	Ed Davender	1985-88	109
	Tayshaun Prince	1999-02	109
7.	Gerald Fitch	2000-03	107
	Dirk Minniefield	1980-83	107
9.	Tony Delk	1993-96	103
	Kenny Walker	1983-86	103

Single-Season Leaders
Double-Doubles

	Player	Season	G	DD
1.	Dan Issel	1969-70	28	26
2.	Dan Issel	1968-69	28	22
3.	Jim Andrews	1972-73	28	21
4.	DeMarcus Cousins	2009-10	38	20
5.	Jim Andrews	1971-72	28	19
6.	Cotton Nash	1961-62	26	18
7.	Dan Issel	1967-68	27	16
8.	Patrick Patterson	2008-09	34	15
	Jamaal Magloire	2099-00	33	15
	Tom Parker	1971-72	27	15

30-Point games

	Player	Season	G	30+
1.	Dan Issel	1969-70	28	19
2.	Dan Issel	1968-69	28	10
3.	Cotton Nash	1963-64	27	9
	Cotton Nash	1961-62	26	9
5.	Jodie Meeks	2008-09	36	7
6.	Louie Dampier	1966-67	26	6
	Bob Burrow	1955-56	25	6
	Alex Groza	1948-49	34	6
9.	Kenny Walker	1984-85	31	5
	Kevin Grevey	1974-75	31	5
	Jim Andrews	1971-72	28	5
	Cliff Hagan	1951-52	32	5

Single-Game Highs
Triple-Doubles

	Player	Opp (Date)	P	R	A
1.	Chris Mills	Austin Peay (12-27-88)	19	10	10

*A quartet of outstanding Wildcats.
Mike Casey (34), Mike Pratt (22),
Larry Steele (25) and Dan Issel
(44) were at the heart of some
great UK teams.*

All-Time Results – 1903-2016

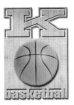

1903 — Won 1, Lost 2

Coach: Unnamed
Starters: (J. White Guyn & R.H. Arnett, G; Joe Coons, C; H.J. Wurtele & Lee Andrews, F)

Feb. 6	Georgetown	H	6	15
Feb. 18	Lex. YMCA	H	11	10
Feb. 20	Kentucky U.	H	2	42
			19	67

1904 — Won 1, Lost 4

Coach: Leander E. Andrus, Mgr.
Captain: St. John (Guyn, Arnett, St. John, Wurtele, Coons)

Feb. 4	Georgetown	A	11	26
Feb. 11	Kentucky U.	A	5	12
Feb. 13	Georgetown	H	10	22
Feb. 26	Kentucky U.	A	12	14
Mar. 4	Cincinnati	H	25	21
			63	95

*Kentucky University (Transylvania and Georgetown game at UK was called off because of failure to agree on a referee. State College (University of Kentucky) team was present and agreed to play. The offer was accepted and KU won 12-5.

1905 — Won 1, Lost 4

Coach: NA
Captain: J.M.Coons

Jan. 13	Georgetown	H	9	14
Jan. 21	Cincinnati YMCA	H	22	43
Jan. 27	Kentucky U.	H	30	29
Feb. 4	Kentucky U.	H	1	22
Feb. 22	Kentucky U.	H	23	33
			85	141

1906 — Won 5, Lost 9

Coach: W.B. Wendt (Mgr.)
Captain: D.P. Branson (Baer, Donan, Barbee, Wilson, Herman)

Jan. 11	Lexington YMCA[1]	H		
Jan. 12	Miami (Ohio)	H	10	15
Jan. 19	Central U.	H	15	14
Jan. 20	Georgetown	A	9	34
Jan. 26	Central U.	A	17	15
Jan. 27	Cincinnati	H	16	29
Feb. 3	Christ Church, Cin.	H	24	38
Feb. 9	Georgetown	H	22	28
Feb. 12	New Albany YMCA	A	12	29
Feb. 13	Vernon College	A	34	14
Feb. 14	Moores Hill	A	32	11
Feb. 15	Christ Church, Cin.	A	17	54
Feb. 16	Cincinnati YMCA	A	9	38
Feb. 17	Miami (Ohio)	A	19	29
			236	348

[1]W.B. Wendt on Jan. 9, 1969 verified that State College opened the 1906 season against Kentucky U. in the YMCA. Athletic committees of the two schools had cancelled all games after a fight at a football game in November 1905. Wendt and the Kentucky U. manager agreed to play at the YMCA and list the State College foe as YMCA instead of Kentucky U. State College won but Mr. Wendt didn't remember the score, which he hadn't listed.

1907 — Won 3, Lost 6

Coach: A.M. Kirby (Mgr.)
Captain: J.M. Wilson (Shanklin, Baer, Bryant, Barbee)

Jan. 16	Lexington YMCA	H	17	25
Jan. 19	Georgetown	H	16	15
Jan. 25	Central U.	H	22	9
Feb. 12	Central U.	A	23	*25
Feb. 15	Kentucky U.	H	16	14
Feb. 21	Georgetown	A	8	19
Mar. 1	Lexington YMCA	A	22	41
Mar. 7	Kentucky U.	A	5	19
Mar. 9	Central U.	H	13	15
			142	182

1907-08 — Won 5, Lost 6

Coach: J.S. Chambers (Mgr.)
Captain: Richard Barbee

Jan. 10	Lexington YMCA	A	19	29
Jan. 21	Kentucky U.	H	20	15
Jan. 25	Central U.	A	21	32
Feb. 4	Kentucky U.	A	20	15
Feb. 8	Louisville Coliseum	H	29	28
Feb. 10	Georgetown	A	22	30
Feb. 13	Central U.	H	31	20
Feb. 15	Lexington YMCA	H	19	23
Feb. 22	Louisville Coliseum	A	18	30
Mar. 3	Georgetown	H	18	13
Mar. 7	Central U.	A	10	29
			227	264

1908-09 — Won 5, Lost 4

Mgr: J.S. Chambers
Captain: W.C. Fox

Jan. 9	Lexington High	H	28	9
Jan. 18	Advent Mem. Club	A	27	41
Jan. 19	Cincinnati	A	25	41
Jan. 27	Central U.	H	24	23
Feb. 6	Central U.	A	20	35
Feb. 8	Georgetown	H	43	32
Feb. 15	Georgetown	A	48	19
Feb. 18	Cincinnati	H	28	23
Feb. 26	Central U.	H	20	26
			263	249

1909-10 — Won 4, Lost 8

Coach: R.E. Spahr and E.R. Sweetland
Captain: Bill Rodes

Jan. 8	Ky. Wesleyan	A	14	*12
Jan. 22	Georgetown	H	31	11
Jan. 24	DePauw	H	11	24
Jan. 28	Central	A	17	87
Feb. 4	Georgetown	A	16	34
Feb. 7	Cincinnati	A	17	47
Feb. 9	DePauw	A	16	28
Feb. 10	Rose Poly Technic	A	11	52
Feb. 16	Tennessee	H	26	5
Mar. 5	Central U.	H	13	31
Mar. 8	Georgetown	H	24	23
Mar. 11	Central	A	9	51
			205	405

1910-11 — Won 5, Lost 6

Coach: H.J. Iddings
Captain: J.H. Gaiser

Jan. 13	Lexington High	H	29	36
Jan. 20	Transylvania	H	18	23
Jan. 27	Ky. Wesleyan	A	19	25
Feb. 4	Bethany	H	24	11
Feb. 9	Ohio Wesleyan	A	19	37
Feb. 10	Otterbein	A	27	41
Feb. 11	Christ Church, Cin.	A	21	32
Feb. 17	Georgetown	A	47	22
Feb. 23	Butler	H	21	16
Feb. 27	Transylvania	A	22	19
Mar. 3	Transylvania	H	30	24
			277	286

1911-12 — Won 9, Lost 0

Southern Champions

Coach: E.R. Sweetland
Captain: W.C. Harrison

Jan. 5	Georgetown	H	38	9
Jan. 12	Central U.	A	32	13
Jan. 19	Miami (Ohio)	H	31	14
Jan. 27	Lexington YMCA	H	32	20
Feb. 1	Central U.	H	52	10
Feb. 7	Tennessee	H	27	15
Feb. 22	Vanderbilt	H	28	17
Feb. 23	Vanderbilt	H	22	18
Mar. 1	Georgetown	A	19	18
			281	134

— Leading Scorers —
Binkley Barnett (Jr. F)....7.1
D.W. Hart (Jr. F)....5.4
W.C. Harrison (Sr. C)....4.0
Jake Gaiser (Sr. G)....3.9
R.C. Preston (So. G)....2.7
H.L. Farmer (Jr. F)....2.2

1912-13 — Won 5, Lost 3

Coach: J.J. Tigert
Captain: B. Barnett

Jan. 24	Lexington YMCA	H	25	27
Feb. 8	Cincinnati	H	20	18
Feb. 13	Marietta	H	42	16
Feb. 15	Louisville	H	34	10
Feb. 19	Vanderbilt	H	17	24
Feb. 20	Vanderbilt	H	42	29
Feb. 27	Miami (Ohio)	H	24	16
Mar. 1	Christ Church, Cin.	H	19	30
			223	170

— Leading Scorers —
R.C. Preston (Jr. C)....9.1
Binkley Barnett (Sr. F)....8.4
Ralph Morgan (So. F)....4.0
H.L. Farmer (Sr. F)....3.9
William Tuttle (So. F)....1.0

1913-14 — Won 12, Lost 2

Coach: Alpha Brumage
Captain: William Tuttle

Jan. 10	Ashland YMCA	H	28	15
Jan. 17	Louisville YMCA	H	30	21
Jan. 20	Ashland YMCA	A	30	19
Jan. 21	Marshall	A	46	6
Jan. 22	Virginia U	A	23	39
Jan. 24	Va. Military Inst.	A	18	32
Jan. 31	Louisville YMHA	H	59	12
Feb. 7	Louisville	H	22	17
Feb. 11	Tennessee	H	21	14
Feb. 12	Tennessee	H	20	18
Feb. 21	Cincinnati	H	20	18
Feb. 23	Chattanooga	H	40	7
Feb. 28	Marietta	H	19	17
Mar. 3	Louisville	A	26	13
			402	248

— Leading Scorers —
R.C. Preston (Sr. F)....6.1
*Tom Zerfoss (Sr. F)....6.0
Karl Zerfoss (So. G)....4.7
William Tuttle (Jr. F)....3.9
Herschel Scott (Jr. G)....3.2
* Only played in first six games.

1914-15 — Won 7, Lost 5

Coach: Alpha Brumage
Captain: Ralph Morgan

Jan. 16	Maryville	H	37	17
Jan. 23	Louisville	H	18	14
Jan. 30	St. Andrews	H	32	15
Feb. 4	Maryville	A	23	22
Feb. 5	Tennessee	A	21	36
Feb. 6	Tennessee	A	22	27
Feb. 12	Vanderbilt	H	34	39
Feb. 13	Vanderbilt	H	36	24
Feb. 17	Tennessee	H	22	13
Feb. 18	Tennessee	H	20	18
Feb. 26	St. Andrews	A	25	50
Feb. 27	Louisville	A	15	26
			305	301

— Leading Scorers —
Ralph Morgan (Sr. F)....8.3
Jim Server (Jr. C)....5.3
William Tuttle (Sr. F)....3.8
Karl Zerfoss (Jr. F)....3.7
Herschel Scott (Sr. G)....2.9

1915-16 — Won 8, Lost 6

Coach: James Park
Captain: K.P. Zerfoss

Jan. 14	Cincinnati	A	39	24
Jan. 18	Georgetown	A	29	22
Jan. 31	Georgetown	H	30	22
Feb. 4	Vanderbilt	H	25	39
Feb. 5	Vanderbilt	H	20	23
Feb. 12	Louisville	H	22	28
Feb. 15	Centre	A	38	5
Feb. 19	Cincinnati	H	34	10
Feb. 22	Louisville	A	32	24
Feb. 23	Tennessee	H	17	28
Feb. 26	Maryville	H	36	25
Feb. 29	Centre	H	38	14
Mar. 3	Marietta	H	22	27
Mar. 4	Marietta	H	23	27
			405	318

— Leading Scorers —
Derrill Hart (Sr. F)....13.3
Jim Server (Sr. C)....5.7
Robert Ireland (Jr. F)....5.6
Karl Zerfoss (Sr. F)....3.3
George Gumbert (Sr. G)....2.4

1916-17 — Won 4, Lost 6

Coach: W.P. Tuttle
Captain: Robert Y. Ireland

Jan. 17	Centre	H	31	21
Jan. 27	Georgetown	A	19	22
Jan. 30	Rose Poly Technic	H	33	12
Feb. 9	Tennessee	H	20	23
Feb. 10	Tennessee	H	19	22
Feb. 16	Centre	A	24	28
Feb. 21	Georgetown	H	32	18
Mar. 1	Cumberland	A	48	20
Mar. 2	Tennessee	A	26	27
Mar. 3	Tennessee	A	10	30
			262	223

— Leading Scorers —
C.C. Shrader (Sr. F)....7.1
Robert Ireland (Sr. F)....5.4
"Dutch" Longworth (Sr. C-F)....4.4
Pat Campbell (Jr. F)....4.2
William Rodes (Sr. G)....1.3

1917-18 — Won 9, Lost 2, Tie 1

Coach: S.A. Boles
Captain: Patrick Campbell

Jan. 9	Ky. Wesleyan	H	23	13
Jan. 17	Centre	A	21	29
Jan. 24	Georgetown	H	22	18
Feb. 7	Tennessee	H	33	26
Feb. 8	Tennessee	H	40	12
Feb. 9	Ky. Wesleyan	A	21	21
(This unique tie game resulted from scorer's error which was not discovered until after the teams' departures. The contest was rescheduled, but never played for unknown reasons.)				
Feb. 14	Georgetown	A	25	16
Feb. 21	Centre	H	22	***20
Feb. 28	Cumberland	A	42	21
Mar. 1	Tennessee	A	29	18
Mar. 2	Tennessee	A	32	20
Postseason Game (For State Championship)				
Mar. 9	Centre	N-Lou.	12	24
			322	238

— Leading Scorers —
H.C. Thomas (Jr. C-F)....10.8
Arthur Bastin (Jr. G)....4.0
A.P. Shanklin (Sr. F)....3.5
Pat Campbell (Sr. F)....3.2
Goerge Zerfoss (Jr. F)....2.8

1918-19 — Won 6, Lost 8

Coach: Andrew Gill
Captain: J.A. Dishman

Jan. 13	Ky. Wesleyan	H	46	5
Jan. 18	Georgetown	H	30	32
Jan. 25	Centre	A	30	38
Jan. 31	Cincinnati	A	18	28
Feb. 6	Chattanooga	A	28	25
Feb. 7	Tennessee	A	22	40
Feb. 8	Cumberland	A	22	21
Feb. 14	Vanderbilt	H	26	36
Feb. 15	Georgetown	A	18	22
Feb. 21	Cincinnati	H	34	21
Feb. 22	Ky. Wesleyan	A	18	13
Feb. 24	Centre	H	10	21
Feb. 28	Tennessee	H	30	14
Mar. 8	Miami (Ohio)	H	14	38
			346	354

— Leading Scorers —
H.C. Thomas (Sr. F)....7.1
J.C. Everett (Jr. F)....6.6
Bob Lavin (Fr. G)....5.0
Tony Dishman (Sr. G)....3.3
Ed Parker (Sr. F)....3.3

1919-20 — Won 5, Lost 7

Coach: George C. Buchheit
Captain: J.C. Everett

Jan. 17	Cincinnati	A	11	13
Jan. 22	Maryville	H	27	13
Jan. 31	Georgetown	H	25	14
Feb. 5	Tennessee	H	24	29
Feb. 7	Tennessee	H	26	27
Feb. 14	Centre	A	15	44
Feb. 17	Georgetown	A	28	16
Feb. 21	Ky. Wesleyan	H	43	13
Feb. 26	Cumberland	A	21	30
Feb. 27	Tennessee	A	25	28
Feb. 28	Tennessee	A	34	26
Mar. 6	Centre	A	18	*20
			297	273

— Leading Scorers —
Basil Hayden (So. F)....10.8
William Blakely (Sr. G)....7.0
J.C. Everett (Sr. C)....5.5
Bob Lavin (So. F)....4.1
Jim Wilhelm (Jr. F)....3.6

1920-21 — Won 13, Lost 1

Southern Intercollegiate Champions

Coach: George C. Buchheit
Captain: Basil Hayden

Jan. 12	Ky. Wesleyan	H	38	13
Jan. 15	Cumberland	H	37	21
Jan. 18	Georgetown	H	38	23
Jan. 21	Chattanooga	H	42	10
Jan. 26	Cincinnati	A	26	19
Jan. 29	Auburn	H	40	25
Feb. 8	Centre	A	27	29
Feb. 15	Georgetown	A	56	11
Feb. 18	Centre	H	20	13
Feb. 22	Vanderbilt	H	37	18
			361	182

All-Time Results – 1903-2016

	SIAA Tournament (Atlanta, Ga.)			
Feb. 25	Tulane		50	28
Feb. 26	Mercer		49	25
Feb. 28	Mississippi A & M		28	13
Mar. 1	Georgia (finals)		20	19
			508	267

— Leading Scorers —
William King (Fr. F)....11.4
Basil Hayden (Jr. F)....9.6
Paul Adkins (Jr. C)....6.5
Bob Lavin (Jr. G)....2.5
Fred Fest (So. C)....1.3

1921-22 — Won 10, Lost 6

Coach: George C. Buchheit
Captain: R.E. Lavin

Jan. 14	Georgetown	H	17	26
Jan. 17	Louisville	A	38	14
Jan. 18	Vanderbilt	A	12	22
Jan. 21	Louisville	H	29	22
Jan. 26	Mississippi A & M	H	28	21
Jan. 27	Marshall	H	34	12
Feb. 4	Centre	A	28	21
Feb. 6	Georgetown	A	26	17
Feb. 8	Washington & Lee	A	21	20
Feb. 9	Va. Military Inst.	A	32	37
Feb. 11	Georgetown U.	A	23	28
Feb. 13	Virginia	A	30	*32
Feb. 16	Clemson	H	38	14
Feb. 20	Centre	H	40	23
	SIAA Tournament (Atlanta, Ga.)			
Feb. 24	Georgetown		41	21
Feb. 25	Mercer		22	35
			459	365

— Leading Scorers —
Paul Adkins (Sr. C)....8.8
William King (So. F)....8.3
Bob Lavin (Sr. F)....5.2
Basil Hayden (Sr. F)....5.0
William Poynz (Jr. F)....2.9

1922-23 — Won 3, Lost 10

Coach: George C. Buchheit
Captain: Fred Fest

Jan. 13	Georgetown	A	24	13
Jan. 20	Tennessee	A	26	30
Jan. 22	Chattanooga	H	25	18
Jan. 25	Alabama	H	35	45
Jan. 27	Centre	H	14	21
Feb. 3	Georgia	H	19	23
Feb. 5	Cincinnati	A	24	33
Feb. 7	Centenary	H	21	29
Feb. 10	Tennessee	H	23	28
Feb. 14	Centre	A	10	17
Feb. 15	Clemson	H	13	30
Feb. 19	Georgetown	H	21	48
Feb. 23	Sewanee	H	30	14
			285	349

— Leading Scorers —
Carl Riefkin (Jr. F)....10.2
Fred Fest (Sr. C)....7.2
William Poynz (Sr. G)....3.3
Gilbert Smith (Sr. G)....1.5
W.G. Wilkinson (Sr. F)....1.2

1923-24 — Won 13, Lost 3

Coach: G.C. Buchheit
Captain: A.T. Rice

Jan. 1	Vanderbilt	H	33	13
Jan. 8	Mexico YMCA	H	25	14
Jan. 12	Georgetown	A	32	24
Jan. 14	Mississippi A & M	H	16	17
Jan. 15	Sewanee	H	50	15
Jan. 18	Tennessee	A	13	20
Jan. 19	Chattanooga	A	24	23
Feb. 4	West Virginia	H	24	21
Feb. 9	Centre	A	27	18
Feb. 11	Georgetown	H	39	35
Feb. 13	Clemson	H	38	13
Feb. 14	Virginia	H	29	16
Feb. 19	Virginia Tech	H	36	14
Feb. 21	Centre	H	38	24
Feb. 23	Georgia Tech	H	33	27
	SIAA Tournament (Atlanta, Ga.)			
Feb. 29	North Carolina		20	41
			477	335

— Leading Scorers —
Jim McFarland (So. F)....9.9
Will Milward (Jr. C)....5.3
Lowell Underwood (So. C)....4.9
Carl Riefkin (Sr. F)....4.3
Bill King (Sr. F)....2.9

ALUMNI GYM ERA (1924-50)

1924-25 — Won 13, Lost 8

Coach: C.O. Applegran
Captain: James McFarland

Dec. 13	Cincinnati	H	28	23
Dec. 18	Indiana	H	18	20
Dec. 20	Michigan	H	11	21
Jan. 3	Cincinnati	A	20	24
Jan. 5	Illinois	A	26	36
Jan. 6	Wabash	A	10	57
Jan. 9	Mississippi	H	26	23
Jan. 10	Georgetown	H	25	17
Jan. 17	Centre	A	33	26
Jan. 30	Washington & Lee	H	28	22
Feb. 2	West Virginia	H	29	19
Feb. 5	Alabama	A	15	24
Feb. 6	Georgia Tech	A	18	16
Feb. 7	Georgia	A	24	28
Feb. 9	Tennessee	A	35	22
Feb. 12	Tulane	H	29	22
Feb. 14	Georgetown	A	36	21
Feb. 18	Tennessee	H	26	21
Feb. 21	Centre	H	39	10
	Southern Conference Tournament (Atlanta, Ga.)			
Feb. 27	Mississippi A & M		31	26
Feb. 28	Georgia		31	32
			538	510

— Leading Scorers —
Jim McFarland (Jr. F)....7.1
Lowell Underwood (Jr. F)....6.3
Will Milward (Sr. C)....6.2
Foster Helm (So. F)....3.7
Charles Alberts (Jr. G)....2.5

1925-26 — Won 15, Lost 3

Coach: Ray Eklund
Captain: Burgess Carey

Dec. 19	DePauw	H	29	38
Jan. 5	Indiana	A	23	34
Jan. 9	Berea	H	37	23
Jan. 12	Georgetown	A	36	21
Jan. 16	Georgia Tech	H	25	24
Jan. 21	Centre	H	45	25
Jan. 30	Georgetown	H	25	20
Feb. 1	Alabama	H	27	16
Feb. 4	Centre	A	46	19
Feb. 5	Washington & Lee	H	44	34
Feb. 8	Auburn	H	35	26
Feb. 12	Tennessee	A	51	17
Feb. 15	Georgia	A	22	18
Feb. 18	Tennessee	H	27	21
Feb. 20	Vanderbilt	H	30	20
	Southern Conference Tournament (Atlanta, Ga.)			
Feb. 26	Va. Military Inst.		32	25
Feb. 27	Georgia		39	34
Mar. 1	Mississippi A & M		26	31
			599	446

— Leading Scorers —
Gayle Mohney (Jr. G)....11.1
Paul Jenkins (So. F)....7.3
Jim McFarland (Sr. F)....5.6
Lowell Underwood (Sr. C)....3.7
Henry Besuden (Sr. C)....2.1

1926-27 — Won 3, Lost 13

Coach: Basil Hayden
Captain: Paul Jenkins

Dec. 18	Cincinnati	H	10	48
Dec. 21	Indiana	H	19	38
Dec. 27	Cincinnati	A	22	51
Dec. 31	Princeton	H	26	30
Jan. 3	Florida	H	44	36
Jan. 10	Ky. Wesleyan	A	24	31
Jan. 15	Vanderbilt	H	32	48
Jan. 21	Tennessee	A	14	19
Jan. 22	Georgia Tech	A	16	48
Jan. 29	Centre	H	27	25
Feb. 1	Georgetown	A	19	26
Feb. 4	Washington & Lee	H	34	36
Feb. 7	West Virginia	H	26	44
Feb. 11	Mississippi	H	17	37
Feb. 12	Centre	A	22	16
Feb. 19	Tennessee	H	21	30
			373	563

— Leading Scorers —
Paul Jenkins (Jr. F)....6.1
Edwin Knadler (Sr. F)....4.4
Van Buren Ropke (Sr. F-C)....4.2
Frank Phipps (Jr. F)....3.4
Foster Helm (Sr. C)....2.5

1927-28 — Won 12, Lost 6

Coach: John Mauer
Captain: Paul Jenkins

Dec. 16	Clemson	H	33	17
Dec. 20	Miami (Ohio)	H	31	36
Jan. 4	Berea	H	37	16
Jan. 9	Centre	A	36	23
Jan. 14	Vanderbilt	H	43	23
Jan. 16	Virginia	A	31	28
Jan. 18	Naval Academy	A	26	32
Jan. 19	Maryland	A	7	37
Jan. 28	Tennessee	H	48	18
Feb. 3	Washington & Lee	H	34	28
Feb. 4	Indiana	A	29	48
Feb. 8	Vanderbilt	A	54	29
Feb. 9	Tennessee	A	43	16
Feb. 11	Georgia Tech	H	31	35
Feb. 18	Centre	H	30	20
	Southern Conference Tournament (Atlanta, Ga.)			
Feb 24	South Carolina		56	40
Feb. 25	Georgia		33	16
Feb. 27	Mississippi		28	41
			630	503

— Leading Scorers —
Irvine Jeffries (Sr. G)....11.5
Cecil Combs (So. F)....10.3
Paul McBrayer (So. G-C)....5.5
Hays Owens (So. F)....3.8
Paul Jenkins (Sr. F)....3.3

1928-29 — Won 12, Lost 5

Coach: John Mauer
Captain: Lawrence McGinnis

Dec. 15	Eastern Normal	H	35	10
Dec. 21	Miami (Ohio)	H	43	***42
Jan. 4	North Carolina	H	15	25
Jan. 12	Notre Dame	A	19	16
Jan. 16	Georgia Tech	A	19	33
Jan. 17	Tennessee	A	35	29
Jan. 19	Tennessee	H	27	22
Jan. 26	Alabama	H	26	27
Feb. 1	Mississippi A & M	A	25	*23
Feb. 2	Mississippi A & M	A	32	14
Feb. 3	Tulane	A	22	34
Feb. 8	Washington & Lee	H	31	30
Feb. 13	Centre	H	47	11
Feb. 22	Mississippi	H	35	30
Feb. 23	Mississippi	H	32	24
	Southern Conference Tournament (Atlanta, Ga.)			
Mar. 1	Tulane		29	15
Mar. 2	Georgia		24	26
			496	411

— Leading Scorers —
Stan Milward (So. C)....6.8
Louis McGinnis (So. F)....5.8
Cecil Combs (Jr. G)....5.8
Carey Spicer (So. F)....5.7
Paul McBrayer (Jr. G)....2.9

1929-30 — Won 16, Lost 3

Coach: John Mauer
Captain: Paul McBrayer

Dec. 14	Georgetown	H	46	9
Dec. 20	Miami (Ohio)	H	35	20
Dec. 31	Berea	H	29	26
Jan. 3	Clemson	H	31	15
Jan. 10	Creighton	H	27	28
Jan. 11	Creighton	H	25	21
Jan. 18	Tennessee	H	23	20
Jan. 24	Mississippi A & M	H	38	17
Jan. 25	Mississippi A & M	H	20	14
Jan. 31	Tennessee	A	24	*29
Feb. 1	Georgia	A	22	*21
Feb. 3	Clemson	A	34	20
Feb. 8	Georgia Tech	H	39	19
Feb. 14	Georgia	H	36	23
Feb. 18	Ky. Wesleyan	H	32	20
Feb. 22	Washington & Lee	H	28	*26
	Southern Conference Tournament (Atlanta, Ga.)			
Feb. 28	Maryland		26	21
Mar. 1	Sewanee		44	22
Mar. 3	Duke		32	37
			591	408

— Leading Scorers —
Cecil Combs (Sr. F)....6.6
Carey Spicer (Jr. F)....6.5
Stan Milward (Sr. C)....5.9
Louis McGinnis (So. F)....5.4
Paul McBrayer (Sr. G)....4.8

ADOLPH RUPP ERA

1930-31 — Won 15, Lost 3

Coach: Adolph Rupp
Captain: Carey Spicer

Dec. 18	Georgetown	H	67	19
Dec. 27	Marshall	H	42	26
Dec. 31	Berea	H	41	25
Jan. 3	Clemson	H	33	21
Jan. 10	Tennessee	H	31	23
Jan. 16	Chattanooga	H	55	18
Jan. 21	Vanderbilt	A	42	37
Jan. 31	Tennessee	A	36	*32
Feb. 6	Washington & Lee	H	23	18
Feb. 9	Georgia Tech	H	38	34
Feb. 13	Georgia	A	16	25
Feb. 14	Clemson	A	26	29
Feb. 16	Georgia Tech	A	35	16
Feb. 20	Vanderbilt	H	43	23
	Southern Conference Tournament (Atlanta, Ga.)			
Feb. 27	North Carolina State		33	28
Feb. 28	Duke		35	30
Mar. 2	Florida		56	36
Mar. 3	Maryland (finals)		27	29
			679	469

— Leading Scorers —
Carey Spicer (Sr. F)....10.6
Louis McGinnis(Sr. F)....9.6
George Yates (Jr. C)....7.0
Aggie Sale (So. C-F)....5.6
Jake Bronston (Jr. G)....3.9

1931-32 — Won 15, Lost 2

Coach: Adolph Rupp
Captain: Ellis Johnson

Dec. 15	Georgetown	H	66	24
Dec. 18	Carnegie Tech	H	36	34
Dec. 23	Berea	H	52	27
Dec. 30	Marshall	H	46	16
Jan. 2	Clemson	H	43	24
Jan. 14	Clemson	A	30	17
Jan. 15	Sewanee	A	30	20
Jan. 16	Tennessee	A	29	28
Jan. 21	Chattanooga	H	51	17
Jan. 30	Washington & Lee	H	48	28
Feb. 3	Vanderbilt	A	61	37
Feb. 6	Duke	H	37	30
Feb. 8	Alabama	H	50	22
Feb 13	Tennessee	H	41	27
Feb. 20	Vanderbilt	H	31	32
	Southern Conference Tournament (Atlanta, Ga.)			
Feb. 26	Tulane		50	30
Feb. 27	North Carolina		42	43
			743	456

— Leading Scorers —
Aggie Sale (Jr. F)....13.6
John "Frenchy" DeMoisey (So. C-F)....10.0
Darrell Darby (Jr. F)....8.4
Howard Kreuter (Jr. F)....3.9
Ellis Johnson (Jr. G)....3.6

1932-33 — Won 21, Lost 3

SEC Champions (Tournament)

Coach: Adolph Rupp
Captain: Forest Sale

Dec. 9	Alumni	H	52	17
Dec. 12	Georgetown	H	62	21
Dec. 17	Marshall	N1	57	23
Dec. 20	Tulane	H	53	17
Dec. 21	Tulane	H	42	11
Dec. 30	Chicago	A	58	26
Jan. 2	Ohio State	H	30	46
Jan. 6	Creighton	A	32	26
Jan. 7	Creighton	A	22	34
Jan. 10	South Carolina	H	44	36
Jan. 14	Tennessee	A	42	21
Jan. 16	Clemson	H	67	18
Jan. 28	Tennessee	H	44	23
Jan. 31	Vanderbilt	A	40	29
Feb. 1	Clemson	A	42	32
Feb. 2	South Carolina	A	38	44
Feb. 6	Mexico U.	H	81	22
Feb. 11	Georgia Tech	H	45	22
Feb. 13	Alabama	N2	35	31
Feb. 18	Vanderbilt	H	45	28
	SEC Tournament (Atlanta, Ga.)			
Feb. 24	Mississippi		49	31
Feb. 25	Florida		48	24
Feb. 27	LSU		51	38
Feb. 28	Mississippi State (finals)		46	27
			1125	647

(N1) Ashland (N2) Birmingham, Ala.

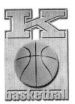

— Leading Scorers —

Aggie Sale (Sr. C-F) 13.8
John "Frenchy" DeMoisey (Jr. C-F) 12.0
Bill Davis (Jr. G) 7.0
Darrell Darby (Sr. F) 4.0
Ellis Johnson (Sr. G) 3.8

1933-34 — Won 16, Lost 1

Coach: Adolph Rupp
Captain: John DeMoisey

Dec. 5	Alumni	H	53	20
Dec. 9	Georgetown	H	41	12
Dec. 14	Marshall	H	48	26
Dec. 16	Cincinnati	H	31	25
Dec. 21	Tulane	A	32	22
Dec. 22	Tulane	A	42	29
Jan. 12	Sewanee	A	55	16
Jan. 13	Tennessee	A	44	23
Jan. 20	Chattanooga	H	47	20
Jan. 27	Tennessee	H	53	26
Feb. 1	Alabama	N1	33	28
Feb. 3	Vanderbilt	A	48	26
Feb. 8	Alabama	H	26	21
Feb. 10	Georgia Tech	H	49	25
Feb. 15	Sewanee	H	60	15
Feb. 17	Vanderbilt	H	47	27
	SEC Tournament (Atlanta, Ga.)			
Feb. 24	Florida		32	38
			741	399

(N1) Birmingham, Ala.

— Leading Scorers —

John "Frenchy" DeMoisey (Sr. C) 12.5
Bill Davis (Sr. G) 8.3
Dave Lawrence (Jr. F) 7.9
Garland Lewis (So. C) 4.9
Jack Tucker (Jr. F) 3.0

1934-35 — Won 19, Lost 2

SEC Co-Champions

Coach: Adolph Rupp
Captain: Dave Lawrence and Jack Tucker

Dec. 10	Alumni	H	55	8
Dec. 13	Oglethorpe	H	81	12
Dec. 21	Tulane	A	38	9
Dec. 22	Tulane	A	52	12
Jan. 2	Chicago	H	42	16
Jan. 5	New York U.	A	22	23
Jan. 14	Chattanooga	H	66	19
Jan. 18	Tulane	H	63	22
Jan. 19	Tulane	H	55	12
Jan. 26	Tennessee	H	48	21
Feb. 1	Alabama	N1	33	26
Feb. 2	Vanderbilt	A	58	22
Feb. 5	Xavier	A	40	27
Feb. 9	Georgia Tech	H	57	30
Feb. 11	Alabama	H	25	16
Feb. 13	Michigan State	A	26	32
Feb. 16	Tennessee	A	38	36
Feb. 22	Creighton	H	63	42
Feb. 23	Creighton	H	24	13
Mar. 2	Vanderbilt	H	53	19
Mar. 7	Xavier	H	46	29
			985	446

(N1) Birmingham, Ala.

— Leading Scorers —

Leroy Edwards (So. C) 16.3
Dave Lawrence (Jr. F) 9.1
Garland Lewis (Jr. C-F) 5.8
Jack Tucker (Sr. F) 3.7
Warfield Donohue (So. G) 3.5

1935-36 — Won 15, Lost 6

Coach: Adolph Rupp
Captain: Milerd Anderson

Dec. 6	Georgetown	H	42	17
Dec. 17	Berea	H	58	30
Dec. 23	Pittsburgh	H	35	17
Jan. 8	New York U.	A	28	41
Jan. 14	Xavier	A	36	32
Jan. 17	Tulane	H	49	24
Jan. 18	Tulane	H	39	21
Jan. 21	Michigan State	H	27	19
Jan. 25	Tennessee	H	40	31
Feb. 1	Vanderbilt	A	24	33
Feb. 3	Alabama	A	32	30
Feb. 7	Alabama	H	40	34
Feb. 10	Notre Dame	A	20	41
Feb. 11	Butler	A	39	28
Feb. 15	Tennessee	A	28	39
Feb. 18	Xavier	H	49	40
Feb. 21	Creighton	H	68	38
Feb. 22	Creighton	H	29	31
Feb. 24	Vanderbilt	H	61	41
	SEC Tournament (Knoxville, Tenn.)			
Feb. 28	Mississippi State		41	39
Feb. 29	Tennessee		28	39
			813	587

— Leading Scorers —

Ralph Carlisle (So. F) 11.5
Joe Hagan (So. F) 8.0
Garland Lewis (Sr. C) 7.5
Warfield Donohue (Jr. G) 3.0
J. Rice Walker (So. C-F) 2.4

1936-37 — Won 17, Lost 5

SEC Champions (Tournament)

Coach: Adolph Rupp
Captain: Warfield Donohue

Dec. 9	Georgetown	H	46	21
Dec. 12	Berea	H	70	26
Dec. 15	Xavier	A	34	*28
Dec. 21	Centenary	H	37	19
Jan. 2	Michigan State	H	28	21
Jan. 5	Notre Dame	N1	28	41
Jan. 8	Creighton	H	59	36
Jan. 14	Michigan State	A	23	24
Jan. 16	Akron U.	N2	32	22
Jan. 23	Tennessee	H	43	26
Jan. 30	Vanderbilt	A	41	26
Feb. 1	Alabama	N3	38	27
Feb. 3	Tulane	A	28	35
Feb. 4	Tulane	A	28	25
Feb. 8	Mexico U.	H	58	30
Feb. 10	Alabama	H	31	34
Feb. 13	Tennessee	A	24	26
Feb. 20	Vanderbilt	H	51	19
Feb. 22	Xavier	H	23	15
	SEC Tournament (Knoxville, Tenn.)			
Feb. 26	Louisiana State		57	37
Feb. 27	Georgia Tech		40	30
Mar. 1	Tennessee (finals)		39	25
			858	593

(N1) Louisville (N2) Cincinnati (N3) Birmingham, Ala.

— Leading Scorers —

Ralph Carlisle (Jr. F) 9.9
Joe Hagan (Jr. F) 7.3
Homer Thompson (So. C) 4.9
Walter Hodge (Sr. G) 3.7
Bernie Opper (So. G) 3.5

1937-38 — Won 13, Lost 5

Coach: Adolph Rupp
Captain: J. Rice Walker

Dec. 15	Berea	H	69	35
Dec. 18	Cincinnati	H	38	21
Dec. 22	Centenary	H	35	25
	Sugar Bowl (New Orleans, La.)			
Dec. 29	Pittsburgh (finals)		40	29
Jan. 8	Michigan State	A	38	43
Jan. 10	Detroit	A	26	34
Jan. 15	Notre Dame	A	37	47
Jan. 22	Tennessee	H	52	27
Jan. 29	Vanderbilt	A	42	19
Jan. 31	Alabama	N1	57	31
Feb. 5	Xavier	A	32	39
Feb. 7	Michigan State	H	44	27
Feb. 12	Alabama	H	28	21
Feb. 14	Marquette	H	35	33
Feb. 17	Xavier	H	45	29
Feb. 21	Vanderbilt	H	48	24
Feb. 26	Tennessee	A	29	26
	SEC Tournament (Baton Rouge, La.)			
Mar. 3	Tulane		36	38
			731	512

(N1) Birmingham, Ala.

— Leading Scorers —

Joe Hagan (Sr. F) 10.1
Fred Curtis (Jr. F) 6.3
Bernie Opper (Jr. G) 5.6
Homer Thompson (Jr. C) 4.9
Mickey Rouse (So. G) 4.4

1938-39 — Won 16, Lost 4

SEC Champions (Tournament)

Coach: Adolph Rupp
Captain: Bernard Opper

Dec. 2	Georgetown	H	39	19
Dec. 10	Ky. Wesleyan	H	57	18
Dec. 17	Cincinnati	H	44	27
Dec. 21	Washington & Lee	H	67	47
Jan. 4	Long Island	A	34	52
Jan. 6	St. Joseph's	A	41	30
Jan. 14	Notre Dame	N1	37	42
Jan. 21	Tennessee	H	29	30
Jan. 28	Alabama	N2	38	41
Jan. 30	Vanderbilt	A	51	37
Feb. 4	Marquette	H	37	31
Feb. 8	Xavier	A	41	31
Feb. 11	Alabama	H	45	27
Feb. 13	Mississippi State	H	39	28
Feb. 18	Tennessee	A	36	**34
Feb. 21	Xavier	H	43	23
Feb. 25	Vanderbilt	H	52	27
	SEC Tournament (Knoxville, Tenn.)			
Mar. 2	Mississippi		49	30
Mar. 3	Louisiana State		53	34
Mar. 4	Tennessee (finals)		46	38
			878	646

(N1) Louisville (N2) Birmingham, Ala.

— Leading Scorers —

Fred Curtis (Sr. F) 9.2
Homer Thompson (Sr. C) 6.7
Keith Farnsley (So. F) 6.4
Mickey Rouse (Jr. G) 5.4
Marion Cluggish (Jr. C) 5.3

1939-40 — Won 15, Lost 6

SEC Champions (Tournament)
Sugar Bowl Champions

Coach: Adolph Rupp
Captain: Layton Rouse

Dec. 9	Berea	H	74	24
Dec. 16	Cincinnati	H	30	39
Dec. 21	Clemson	A	55	31
	Sugar Bowl (New Orleans, La.)			
Dec. 27	Ohio State (finals)		36	30
Jan. 1	Kansas State	H	53	26
Jan. 6	Xavier	A	42	41
Jan. 8	West Virginia	H	47	38
Jan. 13	Notre Dame	A	47	52
Jan. 20	Tennessee	H	35	26
Jan. 27	Alabama	N1	32	36
Jan. 29	Vanderbilt	A	32	40
Feb. 3	Marquette	A	51	45
Feb. 10	Alabama	H	46	18
Feb. 12	Xavier	H	37	29
Feb. 13	Mississippi State	H	45	37
Feb. 17	Tennessee	A	23	27
Feb. 19	Georgia Tech	A	39	44
Feb. 24	Vanderbilt	H	43	38
	SEC Tournament (Knoxville, Tenn.)			
Feb. 29	Vanderbilt		44	31
Mar. 1	Tennessee		30	*29
Mar. 2	Georgia (finals)		51	43
			892	724

(N1) Birmingham, Ala.

— Leading Scorers —

Mickey Rouse (Sr. G) 8.3
Keith Farnsley (Jr. F) 7.2
Marion Cluggish (Sr. C) 7.2
Lee Huber (Jr. G) 5.4
Jim King (So. C) 3.9
Carl Combs (Jr. G) 3.9

1940-41 — Won 17, Lost 8

Coach: Adolph Rupp
Captain: Lee Huber

Dec. 7	Alumni	H	62	25
Dec. 12	West Virginia	H	46	34
Dec. 13	Maryville	H	53	14
Dec. 18	Nebraska	A	39	40
Dec. 19	Creighton	A	45	54
Dec. 20	Kansas State	A	28	25
Dec. 27	Centenary	H	70	18
	Sugar Bowl (New Orleans, La.)			
Dec. 30	Indiana		45	48
Jan. 4	Notre Dame	N1	47	48
Jan. 9	Xavier	A	48	43
Jan. 11	West Virginia	A	43	56
Jan. 18	Tennessee	A	22	32
Jan. 20	Georgia Tech	A	47	37
Jan. 25	Xavier	H	44	49
Feb. 1	Vanderbilt	A	51	50
Feb. 3	Alabama	A	38	36
Feb. 8	Alabama	H	46	38
Feb. 10	Mississippi	H	60	41
Feb. 15	Tennessee	H	37	28
Feb. 17	Georgia Tech	H	60	41
Feb. 24	Vanderbilt	H	58	31
	SEC Tournament (Louisville, Ky.)			
Feb. 27	Mississippi		62	52
Feb. 28	Tulane		59	30
Mar. 1	Alabama		39	37
Mar. 1	Tennessee		33	36
			1182	943

(N1) Louisville

— Leading Scorers —

Jim King (Jr. C) 6.0
Lee Huber (Sr. G) 5.9
KeithFarnsley (Sr. F) 5.8
Mel Brewer (So. C) 5.1
Milt Ticco (So. C-F) 4.8

1941-42 — Won 19, Lost 6

SEC Champions (Tournament)

Coach: Adolph Rupp
Captain: Carl Staker

Dec. 6	Miami (Ohio)	H	35	21
Dec. 13	Ohio State	A	41	43
Dec. 16	Nebraska	H	42	27
Dec. 22	South Carolina	H	64	25
Dec. 30	Texas A & M	H	49	29
Jan. 2	Washington & Lee	H	62	32
Jan. 10	Xavier	A	40	39
Jan. 17	Tennessee	A	40	46
Jan. 19	Georgia	A	51	26
Jan. 20	Georgia Tech	A	63	53
Jan. 24	Mexico	H	56	26
Jan. 31	Georgia	H	55	38
Feb. 2	Alabama	A	35	41
Feb. 7	Notre Dame	A	43	46
Feb. 9	Alabama	H	50	34
Feb. 14	Tennessee	A	36	33
Feb. 16	Georgia Tech	H	57	51
Feb. 21	Xavier	H	44	36
	SEC Tournament (Louisville)			
Feb. 26	Florida		42	36
Feb. 27	Mississippi		59	32
Feb. 28	Auburn		40	31
Feb. 29	Alabama (finals)		36	34
	Postseason Game (Louisville)			
Mar. 14	Great Lakes Navy		47	58
	NCAA Tournament (New Orleans, La.)			
Mar. 20	Illinois		46	44
Mar. 21	Dartmouth		28	47
			1161	928

— Leading Scorers —

Marvin Akers (Jr. G) 7.6
Mel Brewer (Jr. C) 7.0
Milt Ticco (Jr. F) 5.8
Ermal Allen (Sr. F) 4.9
Ken England (Jr. G) 4.9

1942-43 — Won 17, Lost 6

Coach: Adolph Rupp
Co-Captains: Marvin Akers and Melvin Brewer

Dec. 12	Cincinnati	H	61	39
Dec. 19	Washington	H	45	38
Dec. 23	Indiana	N1	52	58
Jan. 2	Ohio State	H	40	45
Jan. 4	Ft. Knox	H	64	30
Jan. 9	Xavier	A	43	38
Jan. 16	Tennessee	A	30	28
Jan. 18	Georgia	A	60	28
Jan. 19	Georgia Tech	A	38	36
Jan. 23	Notre Dame	N1	60	55
Jan. 26	Vanderbilt	H	39	38
Jan. 30	Alabama	A	32	41
Feb. 1	Vanderbilt	A	54	43
Feb. 6	Alabama	H	67	41
Feb. 8	Xavier	H	48	36
Feb. 13	Tennessee	H	53	29
Feb. 15	Georgia Tech	H	58	31
Feb. 20	DePaul	A	44	53
	SEC Tournament (Louisville)			
Feb. 25	Tulane		48	31
Feb. 26	Georgia		59	30
Feb. 27	Mississippi State		52	43
Feb. 27	Tennessee		30	33
	Postseason Game (Louisville)			
Mar. 6	Great Lakes Navy		39	53
			1116	897

(N1) Louisville

— Leading Scorers —

Milt Ticco (Sr. F) 10.1
Mel Brewer (Sr. C) 8.3
Marvin Akers (Sr. G) 7.1
Mulford Davis (So. F) 7.1
Kenny Rollins (So. G) 5.3

1943-44 — Won 19, Lost 2

SEC Champions (Tournament)

Coach: Adolph Rupp
Captain: NA

Dec. 1	Ft. Knox	H	51	18
Dec. 4	Berea (Naval V-12)	H	54	40
Dec. 11	Indiana	N1	66	41
Dec. 13	Ohio State	A	40	28
Dec. 18	Cincinnati	H	58	30
Dec. 20	Illinois	A	41	43
Dec. 28	Carnegie Tech	N2	61	14
Dec. 30	St. John's	A	44	38
Jan. 8	Notre Dame	N1	55	54
Jan. 15	Wright Field	H	61	28
Jan. 31	Ft. Knox A.R.C.	H	76	48
Feb. 4	DePauw	H	38	35
Feb. 7	Illinois	H	51	40
Feb. 12	Cincinnati	A	38	34

Feb. 26	Ohio U.	H	51	35

SEC Tournament (Louisville)

Mar. 2	Georgia		57	29
Mar. 3	Louisiana State		55	28
Mar. 4	Tulane (finals)		62	46

National Invitation Tournament (New York)

Mar. 20	Utah		46	38
Mar. 22	St. John's		45	48
Mar. 24	Oklahoma A & M (cons.)		45	29
			1095	724

(N1) Louisville (N2) New York

— Leading Scorers —
Bob Brannum (Fr. C) 16.7
Jack Tingle (Fr. F) 8.4
Jack Parkinson (Fr. G) 7.0
Wilbur Schu (So. G) 6.2
Tom Moseley (So. G) 4.2

1944-45 — Won 22, Lost 4

SEC Champions (Tournament)
Coach: Adolph Rupp

Dec. 2	Ft. Knox	H	56	23
Dec. 4	Berea	H	56	32
Dec. 9	Cincinnati	H	66	24
Dec. 16	Indiana	N1	61	43
Dec. 23	Ohio State	H	53	*48
Dec. 26	Wyoming	N2	50	46
Dec. 30	Temple	A	45	44
Jan. 1	Long Island	A	62	*52
Jan. 6	Ohio U.	H	59	46
Jan. 8	Arkansas State	H	75	6
Jan. 13	Michigan State	H	66	35
Jan. 20	Tennessee	A	34	35
Jan. 22	Georgia Tech	A	64	58
Jan. 27	Notre Dame	N1	58	*59
Jan. 29	Georgia	H	73	37
Feb. 3	Georgia Tech	H	51	32
Feb. 5	Michigan State	A	50	66
Feb. 17	Tennessee	H	40	34
Feb. 19	Ohio U.	A	61	38
Feb. 24	Cincinnati	H	65	35

SEC Tournament (Louisville)

Mar. 1	Florida		57	35
Mar. 2	Louisiana State		68	37
Mar. 3	Alabama		52	41
Mar. 3	Tennessee (finals)		39	35

NCAA Tournament (New York)

Mar. 22	Ohio State		37	45
Mar. 24	Tufts (Consolation)		66	56
			1464	1042

(N1) Louisville (N2) Buffalo, N.Y.

— Leading Scorers —
Alex Groza (Fr. C) 16.5
Jack Tingle (So. F) 11.5
Jack Parkinson (So. G) 10.4
Wilbur Schue (Jr. F) 8.0
Kenton Campbell (Fr. C) 6.3

1945-46 — Won 28, Lost 2

NIT Champions
SEC Champions (Tournament)
Coach: Adolph Rupp
Captain: Jack Parkinson

Dec. 1	Ft. Knox	H	59	34
Dec. 7	Western Ontario	H	51	42
Dec. 8	Western Ontario	H	71	28
Dec. 15	Cincinnati	H	67	31
Dec. 18	Arkansas	H	67	42
Dec. 21	Oklahoma	H	43	33
Dec. 29	St. John's	A	73	59
Jan. 1	Temple	A	45	53
Jan. 5	Ohio U.	H	57	48
Jan. 7	Ft. Benning	H	81	25
Jan. 12	Michigan State	A	55	44
Jan. 14	Xavier	A	62	36
Jan. 19	Tennessee	A	50	32
Jan. 21	Georgia Tech	A	68	43
Jan. 26	Notre Dame	N1	47	56
Jan. 28	Georgia Tech	H	54	26
Feb. 5	Michigan State	H	59	51
Feb. 4	Vanderbilt	A	59	37
Feb. 9	Vanderbilt	N2	64	31
Feb. 16	Tennessee	H	54	34
Feb. 19	Ohio University	A	60	52
Feb. 23	Xavier	H	83	40

SEC Tournament (Louisville)

Feb. 28	Auburn		69	24
Mar. 1	Florida		69	32
Mar. 2	Alabama		59	30
Mar. 2	Louisiana State (finals)		59	36

Postseason Game (Louisville)

Mar. 9	Temple		54	43

National Invitation Tournament (New York)

Mar. 16	Arizona		77	53

Ralph Beard floats up for an easy two points in a UK victory over Tennessee.

Mar. 18	West Virginia		59	51
Mar. 20	Rhode Island (finals)		46	45
			1821	1194

(N1) Louisville (N2) Paducah, Ky.

NIT Champions

— Leading Scorers —
Jack Parkinson (6-0 Jr. G) 11.3
Wallace Jones (6-4 Fr. F) 9.7
Ralph Beard (5-10 Fr. G) 9.3
Jack Tingle (6-3 Jr. F) 9.2
Wilbur Schue (6-4 Sr. F) 7.7

1946-47 — Won 34, Lost 3

SEC Champions (Tournament)
Coach: Adolph Rupp
Captain: Ken Rollins

Nov. 28	Indiana Central	H	78	36
Nov. 30	Tulane	H	64	35
Dec. 2	Ft. Knox	H	68	31
Dec. 7	Cincinnati	A	80	49
Dec. 9	Idaho	H	65	35
Dec. 12	DePaul	N1	65	43
Dec. 14	Texas A & M	H	83	18
Dec. 16	Miami (Ohio) U.	H	62	49
Dec. 21	St. John's	N2	70	50
Dec. 23	Baylor	H	75	34
Dec. 28	Wabash	H	96	24

Sugar Bowl (New Orleans)

Dec. 30	Oklahoma A & M		31	37
Jan. 4	Ohio U.	H	46	36
Jan. 11	Dayton U.	H	70	29
Jan. 13	Vanderbilt	A	82	30
Jan. 18	Tennessee	A	54	39
Jan. 20	Georgia Tech	A	70	47
Jan. 21	Georgia	A	84	45
Jan. 25	Xavier	H	71	34
Jan. 27	Michigan State	H	86	36
Feb. 3	Notre Dame	N1	60	30
Feb. 8	Alabama	A	48	37
Feb. 8	DePaul	A	47	53
Feb. 10	Georgia	H	81	40
Feb. 15	Tennessee	H	61	46
Feb. 17	Alabama	H	63	33
Feb. 19	Xavier	A	58	31
Feb. 21	Vanderbilt	H	84	41

Feb. 22	Georgia Tech	H	83	46

SEC Tournament (Louisville)

Feb. 27	Vanderbilt		98	29
Feb. 28	Auburn		84	18
Mar. 1	Georgia Tech		75	53
Mar. 1	Tulane (finals)		55	38

Postseason Game (Louisville)

Mar. 8	Temple		68	29

National Invitation Tournament (New York)

Mar. 17	Long Island		66	62
Mar. 19	North Carolina State		60	42
Mar. 24	Utah#		45	49
			2536	1416

(N1) Louisville (N2) New York
#Madison Square Garden Record Crowd. 18,493

— Leading Scorers —
Ralph Beard (5-10 So. G) 10.9
Alex Groza (6-7 So. C-F) 10.6
Kenneth Rollins (6-0 Jr. G) 8.4
Joe Holland (6-4 Sr. F) 6.2
Wallace Jones (6-4 So. C) 5.9

1947-48 — Won 36, Lost 3

World Champions (Olympic Games)
National Champions (NCAA Tournament)
SEC Champions (Tournament)
Coach: Adolph Rupp
Captain: Kenneth Rollins

Nov. 29	Indiana Central	H	80	41
Dec. 1	Ft. Knox	H	80	41
Dec. 5	Tulsa U.	H	72	18
Dec. 6	Tulsa U.	H	71	22
Dec. 10	DePaul	N1	74	50
Dec. 13	Cincinnati	A	67	31
Dec. 17	Xavier	H	79	37
Dec. 20	Temple	A	59	60
Dec. 23	St. John's	A	52	40
Jan. 2	Creighton	A	65	23
Jan. 3	Western Ontario	H	98	41
Jan. 5	Miami (Ohio)	A	67	53
Jan. 10	Michigan State	A	47	45
Jan. 12	Ohio U.	A	79	57
Jan. 17	Tennessee	A	65	54
Jan. 19	Georgia Tech	A	71	56
Jan. 20	Georgia	A	88	51
Jan. 24	Cincinnati	H	70	43
Jan. 31	DePaul	A	68	51
Feb. 2	Notre Dame	A	55	64
Feb. 5	Alabama	A	41	31
Feb. 7	Washington U.	N2	69	39
Feb. 9	Vanderbilt	A	82	51
Feb. 14	Tennessee	H	69	42
Feb. 16	Alabama	H	63	33
Feb. 20	Vanderbilt	H	79	43
Feb. 21	Georgia Tech	H	78	54
Feb. 24	Temple	N1	58	38
Feb. 28	Xavier	A	59	37

SEC Tournament (Louisville)

Mar. 4	Florida		87	31
Mar. 5	Louisiana State		63	47
Mar. 6	Tennessee		70	47
Mar. 6	Georgia Tech (finals)		54	43

NCAA Tournament (New York)

Mar. 18	Columbia		76	53
Mar. 20	Holy Cross		60	52
Mar. 23	Baylor (finals)		58	42

NCAA CHAMPIONS FOR FIRST TIME
Olympic Trials (New York)

Mar. 27	Louisville		91	57
Mar. 29	Baylor		77	59

(Championship Collegiate Bracket)

Mar. 31	Phillips Oilers (AAU Champs)		49	53
			2690	1730

(N1) Louisville (N2) Memphis, Tenn.

Olympic Team Exhibition Games
Kentucky vs. Phillips Oilers

June 30	Tulsa, OK		52	60
July 2	Kansas City, MO		70	**69
July 7	Lexington, KY		50	56

@ Olympic Games (London, England)

July 30	Switzerland		86	21
Aug. 2	Czechoslovakia		53	28
Aug. 3	Argentina		59	57
Aug. 4	Egypt		66	28
Aug. 6	Peru		61	33
Aug. 9	Uruguay		63	28
Aug. 11	Mexico		71	40
Aug. 13	France (finals)		65	21

WORLD CHAMPIONS

— Leading Scorers —
Alex Groza (6-7 Jr. C) 12.5
(488 TP in 39 games)
Ralph Beard (5-10 Jr. G) 12.5
Wallace Jones (6-4 Jr. C-F) 9.3
James Line (6-2 So. F) 6.9
Kenneth Rollins (6-0 Sr. G) 6.6

1948-49 — Won 32, Lost 2

National Champions (NCAA Tournament)
SEC Champions (Tournament)
Ranked First AP
Runner-Up Sugar Bowl
Loser NIT in attempted "Grand Slam"

Coach: Adolph Rupp
Captain: NA

Nov. 29	Indiana Central	H	74	38
Dec. 8	DePaul	N1	67	36
Dec. 10	Tulsa U.	H	81	27
Dec. 13	Arkansas	H	76	39
Dec. 16	Holy Cross	A	51	48
Dec. 18	St. John's	A	57	30
Dec. 22	Tulane	N1	51	47

Sugar Bowl (New Orleans)

Dec. 29	Tulane		78	47
Dec. 30	St. Louis		40	42
Jan. 11	Bowling Green State	N2	63	61
Jan. 15	Tennessee	A	66	51
Jan. 17	Georgia Tech	A	56	45
Jan. 22	DePaul	A	56	45
Jan. 29	Notre Dame	N1	62	38
Jan. 31	Vanderbilt	A	72	50
Feb. 2	Alabama	A	56	40
Feb. 3	Mississippi	N3	75	45
Feb. 5	Bradley	N4	62	52
Feb. 8	Tennessee	H	71	56
Feb. 12	Xavier	H	96	50
Feb. 14	Alabama	H	74	32
Feb. 16	Mississippi	H	85	31
Feb. 19	Georgia Tech	H	78	32
Feb. 21	Georgia	H	95	40
Feb. 24	Xavier	A	51	40
Feb. 26	Vanderbilt	H	70	37

SEC Tournament (Louisville)

Mar. 3	Florida		73	36
Mar. 4	Auburn		70	39
Mar. 5	Tennessee		83	44
Mar. 5	Tulane (finals)		68	52

National Invitation Tournament (New York)

Mar. 14	Loyola of Chicago		56	67

NCAA Tournament
(Eastern Regional) (New York)

Mar. 21	Villanova		85	72
Mar. 22	Illinois		76	47

NCAA Finals
(Seattle, Wash.)

Mar. 26	Oklahoma A & M		46	36
			2320	1492

NCAA CHAMPIONS FOR SECOND TIME

(N1) Louisville   (N2) Cleveland, Ohio
(N3) Memphis, Tenn.
(N4) Owensboro, Ky.

— Leading Scorers —

Alex Groza (6-7 Sr. C) 20.5
Ralph Beard (5-10 Sr. G) 10.8
Wallace Jones (6-4 Sr. F-C) 8.6
Cliff Barker (6-2 Sr. G-F) 7.3
Dale Barnstable (6-3 Jr. F-G) 6.1

1949-50 — Won 25, Lost 5

SEC Champions (Tournament)
Sugar Bowl Champions
Ranked 3rd AP

Coach: Adolph Rupp
Captain: Dale Barnstable

Dec. 3	Indiana Central	H	84	61
Dec. 10	Western Ontario	H	90	18
Dec. 15	St. John's	A	58	69
Dec. 21	DePaul	N1	49	47
Dec. 23	Purdue	A	60	54

Sugar Bowl (New Orleans)

Dec. 29	Villanova		57	*56
Dec. 30	Bradley (finals)		71	66
Jan. 2	Arkansas	N2	57	53
Jan. 4	Mississippi State	N3	87	55
Jan. 9	N. Carolina U.	H	83	44
Jan. 14	Tennessee	A	53	66
Jan. 16	Georgia Tech	A	61	47
Jan. 17	Georgia	A	60	71
Jan. 21	DePaul	A	86	53
Jan. 23	Notre Dame	A	51	64
Jan. 26	Xavier	A	58	47
Jan. 28	Georgia	H	88	56
Jan. 30	Vanderbilt	A	58	54
Feb. 2	Alabama	A	66	64
Feb. 4	Mississippi	N4	61	55
Feb. 11	Tennessee	H	79	52
Feb. 13	Alabama	H	77	57
Feb. 15	Mississippi	H	90	50
Feb. 18	Georgia Tech	H	97	62
Feb. 23	Xavier	H	58	53
Feb. 25	Vanderbilt	H	70	66

SEC Tournament (Louisville)

Mar. 3	Mississippi State		56	46
Mar. 4	Georgia		79	63
Mar. 4	Tennessee (finals)		95	58

National Invitation Tournament (New York)

Mar. 14	City Col. of New York		50	89
			2089	1696

(N1) Louisville   (N2) Little Rock, Ark.
(N3) Owensboro, Ky.   (N4) Memphis, Tenn.

— Leading Scorers —

Bill Spivey (7-0 So. C) 19.3
Jim Line (6-2 Sr. F) 13.1
Walt Hirsch (6-4 Jr. F) 9.9
Bobby Watson (5-10 So. G) 7.5
Dale Barnstable (6-3 Sr. G) 5.9

MEMORIAL COLISEUM ERA

1950-51 — Won 32, Lost 2

National Champions (NCAA Tournament)
SEC Champions (14-0)
Ranked 1st AP-UPI

Coach: Adolph Rupp
Captain: Walt Hirsch
(Including exhibition games, Kentucky won 39 games and lost 2)

Dec. 1	W. Texas State	H	73	43
Dec. 9	Purdue	H	70	52
Dec. 12	Xavier	A	67	56
Dec. 14	Florida	H	85	37
Dec. 16	Kansas	H	68	39
Dec. 23	St. John's	A	43	37

Sugar Bowl (New Orleans)

Dec. 29	St. Louis		42	*43
Dec. 30	Syracuse (consolation)		69	59
Jan. 5	Auburn	H	79	35
Jan. 8	DePaul	H	63	55
Jan. 13	Alabama	H	65	48
Jan. 15	Notre Dame	H	69	44
Jan. 20	Tennessee	A	70	45
Jan. 22	Georgia Tech	A	82	61
Jan. 27	Vanderbilt	A	74	49
Jan. 29	Tulane	A	104	68
Jan. 31	Louisiana State	A	81	59
Feb. 2	Mississippi State	A	80	60
Feb. 3	Mississippi	N1	86	39
Feb. 9	Georgia Tech	H	75	42
Feb. 13	Xavier	H	78	51
Feb. 17	Tennessee	H	86	61
Feb. 19	DePaul	A	60	57
Feb. 23	Georgia	H	88	41
Feb. 24	Vanderbilt	H	89	57

SEC Tournament (Louisville)

Mar. 1	Mississippi State		92	70
Mar. 2	Auburn		84	54
Mar. 3	Georgia Tech		82	56
Mar. 3	Vanderbilt		57	61

Postseason Game

Mar. 13	Loyola of Chicago	H	97	61

NCAA Tournament
(First Round) (Raleigh, N.C.)

Mar. 20	Louisville		79	68

(Eastern Regional) (New York)

Mar. 22	St. John's		59	43
Mar. 24	Illinois		76	74

(National Finals) (Minneapolis, Minn.)

Mar. 27	Kansas State (finals)		68	58
			2540	1783

NCAA CHAMPIONS FOR THIRD TIME
Exhibition Game

Apr. 27	KY All-Stars	H	92	49

Puerto Rico Exhibition Tour

Aug. 25	San German Ath.		86	38
Aug. 26	Ponce Lions		83	43
Aug. 27	San Turce		93	40
Aug. 29	Univ. of Puerto Rico		91	44
Sept. 2	U.S. Navy		52	23

(Called at half on account of rain)

Sep. 3	Puerto Rico		75	46

(N1) Owensboro, Ky.

— Leading Scorers —

Bill Spivey (7-0 Jr. C) 19.2
Shelby Linville (6-5 Jr. F) 10.4
Bobby Watson (5-10 Jr. G) 10.4
Frank Ramsey (6-3 So. G) 10.1
Walt Hirsch (6-3 Sr. F) 9.1

1951-52 — Won 29, Lost 3

Ranked 1st AP, UPI
SEC Champions (14-0)
Runner-Up Sugar Bowl

Coach: Adolph Rupp
Captain: Robert Watson

Dec. 8	Washington & Lee	H	96	46
Dec. 10	Xavier	A	97	72
Dec. 13	Minnesota	A	57	61
Dec. 17	St. John's	H	81	40
Dec. 20	DePaul	H	98	60
Dec. 26	UCLA	H	84	53

Sugar Bowl (New Orleans)

Dec. 28	Brigham Young		84	64
Dec. 29	St. Louis		60	61
Jan. 2	Mississippi	N1	116	58
Jan. 5	Louisiana State	H	57	47
Jan. 7	Xavier	H	83	50
Jan. 12	Florida	A	99	52
Jan. 14	Georgia	N2	95	55
Jan. 19	Tennessee	A	65	56
Jan. 21	Georgia Tech	A	96	51
Jan. 26	Alabama	A	71	67
Jan. 28	Vanderbilt	A	88	51
Jan. 30	Auburn	A	88	48
Feb. 2	Notre Dame	N3	71	66
Feb. 4	Tulane	H	103	54
Feb. 6	Mississippi	H	81	61
Feb. 9	Georgia Tech	H	93	42
Feb. 11	Mississippi State	H	110	66
Feb. 16	Tennessee	H	95	40
Feb. 21	Vanderbilt	H	75	45
Feb. 23	DePaul	A	63	61

SEC Tournament (Louisville)

Feb. 28	Georgia Tech		80	59
Feb. 29	Tulane		85	61
Mar. 1	Tennessee		81	66
Mar. 1	Louisiana State (finals)		44	43

NCAA Tournament
(Eastern Regional) (Raleigh, NC)

Mar. 21	Penn. State		82	54
Mar. 22	St. John's		57	64
			2635	1774

(N1) Owensboro, Ky.
(N2) Louisville
(N3) Chicago

— Leading Scorers —

Cliff Hagan (6-4 Jr. C) 21.6
Frank Ramsey (6-3 Jr. G) 15.9
Bobby Watson (5-10 Sr. G) 13.1
Lou Tsioropoulos (6-5 Jr. F) 7.9
Lucian Whitaker (6-0 Sr. F) 7.8

Bill Spivey applies the defense as teammates Shelby Linville and Walt Hirsch close in.

All-Time Results – 1903-2016

1952-53 — No Schedule

(Under suspension by NCAA)
Intra Squad Scrimmage Result
Coach: Adolph Rupp
Co-Captains: Cliff Hagan and Frank Ramsey

Dec. 13	Varsity	76	Freshman 45
Jan. 19	Ramsey's	71	Hagan's 50
Feb. 4	Hagan's	68	Ramsey's 55
Feb. 28	Blues	49	Whites 47
		264	197

1953-54 — Won 25, Lost 0

Ranked 1st AP, 2nd UPI
UKIT Champions
SEC Champions (14-0)
Declined NCAA Berth
Coach: Adolph Rupp
Co-Captains: Cliff Hagan and Frank Ramsey

Dec. 5	Temple	H	86	59
Dec. 12	Xavier	A	81	66
Dec. 14	Wake Forest	H	101	69
Dec. 18	St. Louis	A	71	59

UK Invitation Tournament

Dec. 21	Duke		85	69
Dec. 22	La Salle (finals)		73	60
Dec. 28	Minnesota	H	74	59
Jan. 4	Xavier	H	77	71
Jan. 9	Georgia Tech	H	105	53
Jan. 11	DePaul	H	81	63
Jan. 16	Tulane	H	94	43
Jan. 23	Tennessee	A	97	71
Jan. 30	Vanderbilt	A	85	63
Feb. 2	Georgia Tech	N1	99	48
Feb. 4	Georgia	H	106	55
Feb. 6	Georgia	N2	100	68
Feb. 8	Florida	A	97	55
Feb. 13	Mississippi	H	88	62
Feb. 15	Mississippi State	H	81	49
Feb. 18	Tennessee	H	90	63
Feb. 20	DePaul	A	76	61
Feb. 22	Vanderbilt	H	100	64
Feb. 27	Auburn	N3	109	79
Mar. 1	Alabama	A	68	43

SEC Playoff
(Nashville, Tenn.)
(Playoff game to determine SEC Champion and representative in NCAA Tournament. Kentucky and LSU tied for league title due to a schedule disagreement. Kentucky won but declined NCAA.)

Mar. 9	Louisiana State		63	56
			2187	1508

(N1) Louisville (N2) Owensboro , Ky.
(N3) Montgomery, Ala.
— Leading Scorers —
Cliff Hagan (6-4 Sr. C)...........................24.0
Frank Ramsey (6-3 Sr. G)......................19.6
Lou Tsioropoulos (6-5 Sr. F)..................14.5
Billy Evans (6-1 Jr. G).............................8.4
Gayle Rose (6-0 Jr. G).............................6.7

1954-55 — Won 23, Lost 3

UKIT Champions
SEC Champions (12-2)
Ranked 2nd AP, UPI
Coach: Adolph Rupp
Captain: Bill Evans

Dec. 4	Louisiana State	H	74	58
Dec. 11	Xavier	A	73	69
Dec. 18	Temple	H	79	61

UK Invitation Tournament

Dec. 21	Utah		70	65
Dec. 22	La Salle (finals)		63	54
Dec. 30	St. Louis	H	82	65
Jan. 1	Temple	A	101	69
Jan. 8	Georgia Tech	H	58	59
Jan. 10	DePaul	H	92	59
Jan. 15	Tulane	A	58	44
Jan. 17	Louisiana State	A	64	62
Jan. 22	Tennessee	A	84	66
Jan. 29	Vanderbilt	A	75	71
Jan. 31	Georgia Tech	A	59	65
Feb. 3	Florida	H	87	63
Feb. 5	Mississippi	N1	84	66
Feb. 7	Mississippi State	A	61	56
Feb. 9	Georgia	H	86	40
Feb. 14	Xavier	H	66	55
Feb. 19	DePaul	A	76	72
Feb. 21	Vanderbilt	H	77	59
Feb. 26	Auburn	H	93	59
Feb. 28	Alabama	H	66	52
Mar. 5	Tennessee	A	104	61

NCAA Tournament
(Eastern Regional)
(Evanston, IL)

Mar. 11	Marquette		71	79

Mar. 12	Penn. State		84	59
			1987	1588

(N1) Memphis, Tenn.
— Leading Scorers —
Bob Burrow (6-7 Jr. C)...........................19.0
Billy Evans (6-1 Jr. F)............................13.9
Jerry Bird (6-6 Jr. F).............................10.7
Phil Grawemeyer (6-7 Jr. F).................*13.0
Gayle Rose (6-0 Sr. G)............................7.4
*Grawemeyer ranked 4th in total points with 260 in 20 games. Broke leg against DePaul and missed last six games.

1955-56 — Won 20, Lost 6

Ranked 9th AP
2nd SEC (12-2)
UKIT Runner-Up
Coach: Adolph Rupp
Captain: Phil Grawemeyer

Dec. 3	Louisiana State	A	62	52
Dec. 10	Temple	H	61	73
Dec. 12	DePaul	H	71	69
Dec. 15	Maryland	A	62	61
Dec. 17	Idaho	H	91	49

UK Invitation Tournament

Dec. 20	Minnesota		72	65
Dec. 21	Dayton (finals)		74	89
Dec. 28	St. Louis	A	101	80
Jan. 7	Georgia Tech	H	104	51
Jan. 12	Tulane	H	85	63
Jan. 14	Louisiana State	H	107	65
Jan. 21	Tennessee	A	95	68
Jan. 28	Vanderbilt	A	73	81
Jan. 30	Georgia Tech	A	84	62
Feb. 1	Duke	H	81	76
Feb. 4	Auburn	N1	82	81
Feb. 6	Florida	A	81	70
Feb. 11	Mississippi	H	88	49
Feb. 13	Mississippi State	H	86	65
Feb. 18	DePaul	A	79	81
Feb. 20	Vanderbilt	H	76	55
Feb. 25	Alabama	N1	77	101
Feb. 27	Georgia	N2	143	66
Mar. 3	Tennessee	H	101	77

NCAA Tournament
(Kentucky represented the SEC in NCAA when champion Alabama declined the bid.)
(Eastern Regional)
(Iowa City, Iowa)

Mar. 16	Wayne U.	A	84	64
Mar. 17	Iowa	A	77	89
			2197	1802

(N1) Montgomery, Ala.
(N2) Louisville
— Leading Scorers —
Bob Burrow (6-7 Sr. C)...........................21.1
Jerry Bird (6-6 Sr. F)............................16.2
Vernon Hatton (6-3 So. G)......................13.3
Gerry Calvert (5-11 Jr. G)......................11.2
Phil Grawemeyer (6-7 Sr. F).....................8.4

1956-57 — Won 23 Lost 5

Ranked 3rd AP, UPI
UKIT Champions
SEC Champions (12-2)
Sugar Bowl Champions
Coach: Adolph Rupp
Honorary Co-Captains: Ed Beck and Gerry Calvert

Dec. 1	Washington & Lee	H	94	66
Dec. 3	Miami (FL)	H	114	75
Dec. 8	Temple	A	73	58
Dec. 10	St. Louis	H	70	71
Dec. 15	Maryland	H	76	55
Dec. 18	Duke	A	84	85

UK Invitation Tournament

Dec. 21	Southern Methodist		73	67
Dec. 22	Illinois (finals)		91	70

Sugar Bowl (New Orleans)

Dec. 28	Virginia Tech		56	55
Dec. 29	Houston (finals)		111	76
Jan. 5	Georgia Tech	H	95	72
Jan. 7	Loyola (Chicago)	H	81	62
Jan. 12	Louisiana State	A	51	46
Jan. 14	Tulane	A	60	68
Jan. 19	Tennessee	A	97	72
Jan. 26	Vanderbilt	A	91	83
Jan. 28	Georgia Tech	A	76	65
Jan. 30	Georgia	H	84	53
Feb. 2	Florida	H	88	61
Feb. 8	Mississippi	N1	75	69
Feb. 11	Mississippi State	A	81	89
Feb. 15	Loyola (Chicago)	A	115	65
Feb. 18	Vanderbilt	H	80	78
Feb. 23	Alabama	H	79	60
Feb. 25	Auburn	H	103	85
Mar. 2	Tennessee	H	93	75

1957-58 — Won 23, Lost 6

National Champions (NCAA Tournament)
SEC Champions (12-2)
Ranked 9th AP, 14th UPI
UKIT Participant
Coach: Adolph Rupp
Honorary Captain: Ed Beck

Dec. 2	Duke	H	78	74
Dec. 4	Ohio State	A	61	54
Dec. 7	Temple	H	85	***83
Dec. 9	Maryland	A	62	71
Dec. 14	St. Louis	A	73	60
Dec. 16	Southern Methodist	A	64	65

UK Invitation Tournament

Dec. 20	West Virginia		70	77
Dec. 21	Minnesota		78	58
Dec. 23	Utah State	H	92	64
Dec. 30	Loyola (Chicago)	H	75	42

John Crigler goes above Guy Rodgers for an easy bucket in UK's 61-60 NCAA Tournament win over Temple in 1958.

SEC Champions
NCAA Tournament
(Midwest Regional)
(Lexington)

Mar. 15	Pittsburgh		98	92
Mar. 16	Michigan State		68	80
			2357	1953

(N1) Memphis, Tenn.
— Leading Scorers —
Johnny Cox (6-4 So. F)..........................19.4
Gerry Calvert (5-11 Sr. G).....................15.2
Vernon Hatton (6-3 Jr. G)......................14.8
John Crigler (6-3 Jr. F).........................10.3
Ed Beck (6-7 Jr. C)................................9.5

Jan. 4	Georgia Tech	H	76	60
Jan. 6	Vanderbilt	A	86	81
Jan. 11	Louisiana State	H	97	52
Jan. 13	Tulane	H	86	50
Jan. 18	Tennessee	H	77	68
Jan. 27	Georgia Tech	A	52	71
Jan. 29	Georgia	N1	74	55
Jan. 31	Florida	A	78	56
Feb. 8	Mississippi	H	96	65
Feb. 10	Mississippi State	H	72	62
Feb. 15	Loyola (Chicago)	A	56	57
Feb. 17	Vanderbilt	H	68	57
Feb. 22	Alabama	N2	45	*43
Feb. 24	Auburn	N3	63	64
Mar. 1	Tennessee	A	77	66

NCAA Tournament
(Mideast Regional)
(Lexington)

Mar. 14	Miami (Ohio)		94	70
Mar. 15	Notre Dame		89	56

Finals (Louisville)

Mar. 21	Temple		61	60
Mar. 22	Seattle (finals)		84	72
			2166	1817

NCAA CHAMPIONS
FOR RECORD FOURTH TIME
(N1) Atlanta (N2) Montgomery, Ala.
(N3) Birmingham, Ala.
— Leading Scorers —
Vernon Hatton (6-3 Sr. G)......................17.1
Johnny Cox (6-4 Jr. F)...........................14.9
John Crigler (6-3 Sr. F).........................13.6
Adrian Smith (6-0 Sr. G)........................12.4
Ed Beck (6-7 Sr. C)................................5.6

Cotton Nash is the only Wildcat to average
20 points for three seasons.

1958-59 — Won 24 Lost 3

UKIT Champions
2nd SEC (12-2)
Ranked 2nd in Polls
Coach: Adolph Rupp
Honorary Captain: Johnny Cox

Dec. 1	Florida State	H	91	68
Dec. 6	Temple	A	76	71
Dec. 8	Duke	A	78	64
Dec. 11	Southern Methodist	H	72	60
Dec. 13	St. Louis	H	76	57
Dec. 15	Maryland	H	58	*56

UK Invitation Tournament

Dec. 19	Ohio State		95	76
Dec. 20	West Virginia (finals)		97	91
Dec. 29	Navy	H	82	69
Dec. 30	Illinois	N1	76	75
Jan. 3	Georgia Tech	H	72	62
Jan. 6	Vanderbilt	A	66	75
Jan. 10	Louisiana State	A	76	61
Jan. 12	Tulane	A	85	68
Jan. 17	Tennessee	H	79	58
Jan. 26	Georgia Tech	A	94	70
Jan. 29	Georgia	H	108	55
Jan. 31	Florida	H	94	51
Feb. 7	Mississippi	N2	97	72
Feb. 9	Mississippi State	A	58	66
Feb. 14	Notre Dame	N3	71	52
Feb. 18	Vanderbilt	H	83	71
Feb. 21	Auburn	H	75	56
Feb. 23	Alabama	H	39	32
Feb. 28	Tennessee	A	69	56

NCAA Tournament
(Kentucky represented the SEC in NCAA when champion
Mississippi State declined the bid.)
(Mideast Regional)
(Evanston, Ill.)

Mar. 13	Louisville		61	76
Mar. 14	Marquette		98	69
			2126	1737

(N1) Louisville
(N2) Jackson, Miss.   (N3) Chicago
— Leading Scorers —
Johnny Cox (6-4 Sr. F) 17.9
Billy Ray Lickert (6-3 So. G) 13.5
Bennie Coffman (6-0 Jr. G) 10.7
Don Mills (6-6 Jr. C) 10.5
Sid Cohen (6-1 Jr. G) 8.1
Dickie Parsons (5-10 So. G) 8.0

1959-60 — Won 18 Lost 7

3rd SEC (10-4)
UKIT Runner Up
Coach: Adolph Rupp
Co-Captains: Bill Lickert and Don Mills

Dec. 1	Colorado State	H	106	73
Dec. 4	UCLA	A	68	66
Dec. 5	Southern California	A	73	87
Dec. 12	St. Louis	A	61	73
Dec. 14	Kansas	A	77	*72

UK Invitation Tournament

Dec. 18	North Carolina		76	70
Dec. 19	West Virginia (finals)		70	79
Dec. 20	Temple	N1	97	92
Dec. 28	Ohio State	H	96	93
Jan. 2	Georgia Tech	H	54	62
Jan. 5	Vanderbilt	A	76	59
Jan. 9	Louisiana State	H	77	45
Jan. 11	Tulane	H	68	42
Jan. 16	Tennessee	A	78	68
Jan. 25	Georgia Tech	A	44	65
Jan. 27	Georgia	N2	84	60
Jan. 29	Florida	A	75	62
Feb. 6	Mississippi	H	61	43
Feb. 8	Mississippi State	H	90	59
Feb. 13	Notre Dame	H	68	65
Feb. 16	Vanderbilt	H	68	60
Feb. 20	Auburn	A	60	61
Feb. 22	Alabama	N3	75	55
Feb. 27	Tennessee	H	63	65
Mar. 5	Pittsburgh	H	73	66
			1838	1642

(N1) Louisville
(N2) Columbus, Ga.   (N3) Montgomery, Ala.
— Leading Scorers —
Billy Ray Lickert (6-3 Jr. f-G) 14.4
Don Mills (6-6 Sr. C-F) 12.7
Sid Cohen (6-1 Sr. G) 10.7
Bennie Coffman (6-0 Sr. G) 10.2
Ned Jennings (6-9 Jr. C) 8.8

1960-61 — Won 19 Lost 9

UKIT Runner-Up
2nd SEC (10-4)
Ranked 18th UPI
Coach: Adolph Rupp
Captain: Dick Parsons

Dec. 1	Virginia Military Inst.	H	72	56
Dec. 3	Florida State	H	58	63
Dec. 7	Notre Dame	N1	68	62
Dec. 13	North Carolina	N2	70	65
Dec. 17	Temple	A	58	66

UK Invitation Tournament

Dec. 21	Illinois		83	78
Dec. 22	St. Louis (finals)		72	*74
Dec. 31	Missouri	H	81	69
Jan. 2	Miami (Ohio)	H	70	58
Jan. 7	Georgia Tech	H	89	79
Jan. 9	Vanderbilt	A	62	64
Jan. 13	Louisiana State	A	59	73
Jan. 14	Tulane	A	70	72
Jan. 21	Tennessee	H	83	54
Jan. 30	Georgia Tech	A	60	62
Feb. 4	Florida	H	89	68
Feb. 7	Georgia	H	74	67
Feb. 11	Mississippi	N3	74	60
Feb. 13	Mississippi State	A	68	62
Feb. 17	UCLA	H	77	76
Feb. 21	Vanderbilt	H	60	59
Feb. 25	Alabama	H	80	53
Feb. 27	Auburn	H	77	51
Mar. 4	Tennessee	A	68	61

SEC Playoff
(Knoxville, TN)
(To determine SEC representative in NCAA Tournament
after champion Mississippi State declined bid. Second place
Kentucky and Vanderbilt each had 10-4 records.)

Mar. 9	Vanderbilt		88	67
Mar. 11	Marquette	N4	72	88

NCAA Tournament
(Mideast Regional)
(Louisville)

Mar. 17	Morehead		71	64
Mar. 18	Ohio State		74	87
			2027	1858

(N1) Louisville
(N2) Greensboro, N.C.
(N3) Jackson, Miss.
(N4) Chicago
— Leading Scorers —
Billy Ray Lickert (6-3 Sr. F-G) 16.0
Roger Newman (6-4 Sr. F-G) 14.1
Larry Pursiful (6-1 Jr. G) 13.4
Ned Jennings (6-9 Sr. C) 11.5
Carroll Burchett (6-4 Jr. F-C) 5.1

1961-62 — Won 23 Lost 3

UKIT Champions
SEC Co-Champions (13-1)
Ranked 3rd AP, UPI
Coach: Adolph Rupp
Captain: Larry Pursiful

Dec. 2	Miami (Ohio)	H	93	61
Dec. 4	Southern California	H	77	79
Dec. 11	St. Louis	H	86	77
Dec. 16	Baylor	H	94	60
Dec. 18	Temple	H	78	55

UK Invitation Tournament

Dec. 22	Tennessee		96	69
Dec. 23	Kansas State (finals)		80	67
Dec. 27	Yale	H	79	58
Dec. 30	Notre Dame	N1	100	53
Jan. 2	Virginia	H	93	73
Jan. 6	Georgia Tech	H	89	70
Jan. 8	Vanderbilt	A	77	68
Jan. 12	Louisiana State	H	84	63
Jan. 15	Tennessee	A	95	82
Jan. 29	Georgia Tech	A	71	62
Jan. 31	Georgia	N2	86	59
Feb. 2	Florida	A	81	69
Feb. 10	Mississippi	H	83	60
Feb. 12	Mississippi State	H	44	49
Feb. 19	Vanderbilt	H	87	80
Feb. 24	Alabama	A	73	65
Feb. 26	Auburn	A	63	60
Mar. 5	Tulane	H	97	72
Mar. 10	Tennessee	H	90	59

NCAA Tournament

1962-63 — Won 16 Lost 9

5th SEC (8-6)
UKIT Champions
Coach: Adolph Rupp
Captain: Scotty Baesler

Dec. 1	Virginia Tech	H	77	80
Dec. 8	Temple	A	56	52
Dec. 12	Florida State	H	83	54
Dec. 15	Northwestern	H	71	60
Dec. 17	North Carolina	H	66	68

UK Invitation Tournament

Dec. 21	Iowa		94	69
Dec. 22	West Virginia (finals)		79	75
Dec. 27	Dartmouth	H	95	49
Dec. 29	Notre Dame	N1	78	70
Dec. 31	St. Louis	A	63	87
Jan. 5	Georgia Tech	H	85	**86
Jan. 7	Vanderbilt	A	106	82
Jan. 11	Louisiana State	A	63	56
Jan. 12	Tulane	A	81	72
Jan. 19	Tennessee	H	69	*78
Jan. 26	Xavier	H	90	76
Jan. 28	Georgia Tech	A	62	66
Jan. 31	Georgia	H	74	67
Feb. 2	Florida	H	94	71
Feb. 9	Mississippi	N2	75	69
Feb. 11	Mississippi State	A	52	56
Feb. 18	Vanderbilt	H	67	69
Feb. 23	Auburn	H	78	59
Feb. 25	Alabama	H	80	63
Mar. 2	Tennessee	A	55	63
			1893	1697

(N1) Louisville   (N2) Jackson, Miss.
— Leading Scorers —
Cotton Nash (6-5 Jr. F-C) 20.6
*Charles Ishmael (6-5 Jr. G) 11.1
Ted Deeken (6-3 Jr. F) 9.8
Scotty Baesler (6-0 Sr G) 9.7
Roy Roberts (6-4 Sr. F) 9.0
*Ineligible second semester

1963-64 — Won 21 Lost 6

UKIT and Sugar Bowl Champions
SEC Champions (11-3)
Ranked 3rd UPI, 4th AP
Coach: Adolph Rupp
Co-Captains: Cotton Nash and Ted Deeken

Nov. 30	Virginia	H	75	64
Dec. 2	Texas Tech	H	107	91
Dec. 7	Northwestern	A	95	63
Dec. 9	North Carolina	H	100	80
Dec. 14	Baylor	H	101	65

UK Invitation Tournament

Dec. 20	Wisconsin		108	85
Dec. 21	Wake Forest (finals)		98	75
Dec. 28	Notre Dame	N1	101	81

Sugar Bowl (New Orleans)

Dec. 30	Loyola (La.)		86	64
Dec. 31	Duke (finals)		81	79
Jan. 4	Georgia Tech	A	67	76
Jan. 6	Vanderbilt	A	83	85
Jan. 10	Louisiana State	H	103	84
Jan. 11	Tulane	H	105	63
Jan. 18	Tennessee	H	66	57
Jan. 25	Georgia Tech	H	79	62
Feb. 1	Florida	A	77	72
Feb. 3	Georgia	A	103	83
Feb. 8	Mississippi	H	102	59
Feb. 10	Mississippi State	H	65	59
Feb. 17	Vanderbilt	H	104	73
Feb. 23	Auburn	N2	99	79
Feb. 24	Alabama	A	59	65
Feb. 29	Tennessee	A	42	38
Mar. 2	St. Louis	H	60	67

NCAA Tournament
(Mideast Regional)
(Minneapolis)

Mar. 13	Ohio University		69	85
Mar. 14	Loyola (Chicago)		91	100
			2326	1954

(N1) Louisville   (N2) Montgomery, Ala.
— Leading Scorers —

(Mideast Regional)
(Iowa City, IA)

Mar. 16	Butler		81	60
Mar. 17	Ohio State		64	74
			2141	1704

(N1) Louisville
(N2) Atlanta
— Leading Scorers —
Cotton Nash (6-5 So. C-F) 23.4
Larry Pursiful (6-1 Sr. G) 19.1
Carroll Burchett (6-4 Sr. C-F) 11.2
Scotty Baesler (6-0 Jr. G) 10.9
Roy Roberts (6-4 Jr. F) 7.0

All-Time Results – 1903-2016

Cotton Nash (6-5 Sr. C-F)	24.0
Ted Deeken (6-3 Sr. F)	18.5
Larry Conley (6-3 So. F-C)	12.2
Terry Mobley (6-2 Jr. G)	9.4
Randy Embry (5-11 Jr. G)	7.2

1964-65 — Won 15 Lost 10

5th SEC (10-6)
UKIT Runner Up
Coach: Adolph Rupp
Captain: Randy Embry

Dec. 4	Iowa	H	85	77
Dec. 7	North Carolina	N1	67	82
Dec. 9	Iowa State	H	100	74
Dec. 12	Syracuse	H	110	77
UK Invitation Tournament				
Dec. 18	West Virginia		102	78
Dec. 19	Illinois (finals)		86	91
Dec. 22	St. Louis	A	75	80
Dec. 29	Notre Dame	N2	97	111
Jan. 2	Dartmouth	H	107	67
Jan. 5	Vanderbilt	H	79	97
Jan. 9	Louisiana State	H	79	66
Jan. 11	Tulane	A	102	72
Jan. 16	Tennessee	A	58	77
Jan. 18	Auburn	H	73	67
Jan. 23	Florida	A	68	84
Jan. 25	Georgia	A	102	82
Jan. 30	Florida	H	78	61
Feb. 1	Georgia	H	96	64
Feb. 6	Mississippi	H	102	65
Feb. 8	Mississippi State	H	74	56
Feb. 16	Vanderbilt	A	90	91
Feb. 20	Auburn	A	69	88
Feb. 22	Alabama	A	71	75
Feb. 27	Tennessee	H	61	60
Mar. 1	Alabama	H	78	72
			2109	1914

(N1) Charlotte, N.C.
(N2) Louisville

— Leading Scorers —

Louie Dampier (6-0 So. G)	17.0
Pat Riley (6-4 So. F)	15.0
Tommy Kron (6-5 Jr. G-F)	12.3
John Adams (6-7 Sr. C)	11.8
Larry Conley (6-3 Jr. F)	11.6

1965-66 — Won 27 Lost 2

National Runner-Up in NCAA
SEC Champions (15-1)
UKIT Champions
Ranked First in Polls
Coach: Adolph Rupp
Honorary Captain:

Dec. 1	Hardin-Simmons	H	83	55
Dec. 4	Virginia	A	99	73
Dec. 8	Illinois	A	86	68
Dec. 11	Northwestern	H	86	75
UK Invitation Tournament				
Dec. 17	Air Force		78	58
Dec. 18	Indiana (finals)		91	56
Dec. 22	Texas Tech	A	89	73
Dec. 29	Notre Dame	N1	103	69
Jan. 3	St. Louis	H	80	70
Jan. 8	Florida	A	78	64
Jan. 10	Georgia	A	69	**65
Jan. 15	Vanderbilt	H	96	83
Jan. 24	Louisiana State	H	111	85
Jan. 29	Auburn	H	115	78
Jan. 31	Alabama	H	82	62
Feb. 2	Vanderbilt	A	105	90
Feb. 5	Georgia	H	74	50
Feb. 7	Florida	H	85	75
Feb. 12	Auburn	A	77	64
Feb. 14	Alabama	A	90	67
Feb. 19	Mississippi State	A	73	69
Feb. 21	Mississippi	A	108	65
Feb. 26	Tennessee	H	78	64
Mar. 5	Tennessee	A	62	69
Mar. 7	Tulane	H	103	74
NCAA Tournament				
(Mideast Regional)				
(Iowa City, Iowa)				
Mar. 11	# Dayton		86	79
Mar. 12	Michigan		84	77
(Finals)				
(College Park, Md.)				
Mar. 18	Duke		83	79
Mar. 19	Texas Western		65	72
			2519	2028

International Universities Tournament
(Tel Aviv, Israel)
(Not counted in Won-Loss Record)

Aug. 3	Warsaw University		67	58
Aug. 4	Cambridge University		104	45
Aug. 6	Salonika University		91	60
Aug. 10	Istanbul University		82	36
Aug. 11	Warsaw University		87	57
			431	256

(N1) Louisville

— Leading Scorers —

Pat Riley (6-4 Jr. F)	22.0
Louie Dampier (6-0 Jr. G)	21.1
Thad Jaracz (6-5 So. C)	13.2
Larry Conley (6-3 Sr. F)	11.5
Tommy Kron (6-5 Sr. G)	10.2

#Adolph Rupp wins his 747th game to pass Phog Allen of Kansas.

1966-67 — Won 13 Lost 13

(Worst Record under Rupp)
Tied 5th SEC (8-10)
UKIT Champions
Coach: Adolph Rupp
Honorary Captain:

Dec. 3	Virginia	H	104	84
Dec. 5	Illinois	H	97	*98
Dec. 10	Northwestern	A	118	116
Dec. 13	North Carolina	H	55	64
Dec. 17	Florida	H	75	78
UK Invitation Tournament				
Dec. 22	Oregon State		96	66
Dec. 23	Kansas State (finals)		83	79
Dec. 28	Cornell	H	77	92
Dec. 31	Notre Dame	N1	96	85
Jan. 5	Vanderbilt	H	89	*91
Jan. 14	Florida	A	72	89
Jan. 16	Georgia	A	40	49
Jan. 21	Auburn	H	60	58
Jan. 23	Tennessee	H	50	**52
Jan. 28	Louisiana State	H	102	72
Jan. 30	Mississippi	H	96	53
Feb. 4	Louisiana State	A	105	84
Feb. 6	Mississippi	A	79	70
Feb. 11	Mississippi State	H	72	*77
Feb. 13	Tennessee	A	57	76
Feb. 18	#Mississippi State	A	103	74
Feb. 20	Georgia	H	101	76
Feb. 25	Alabama	A	71	81
Feb. 27	Auburn	A	49	60
Mar. 4	Vanderbilt	A	94	110
Mar. 6	Alabama	H	110	78
			2151	2012

(N1) Louisville

— Leading Scorers —

Louie Dampier (6-0 Sr. G)	20.6
Pat Riley (6-4 So. F)	17.4
Thad Jaracz (6-5 Jr. C-F)	11.3
Cliff Berger (6-8 Jr. C)	11.3
Phil Argento (6-0 So. G)	5.2

#Coach Rupp passes Western Kentucky's E.A. Diddle to become the all-time winningest coach with 760 victories.

1967-68 — Won 22 Lost 5

SEC Champions (15-3)
UKIT Champions
Ranked 4th in Polls
Coach: Adolph Rupp
Captain: Thad Jaracz

Dec. 2	Michigan	A	96	79
Dec. 4	Florida	H	99	76
Dec. 6	Xavier	H	111	76
Dec. 9	Pennsylvania	H	64	49
Dec. 12	North Carolina	N1	77	84
UK Invitation Tournament				
Dec. 22	Dayton		88	85
Dec. 23	South Carolina (finals)		55	66
Dec. 30	Notre Dame	N2	81	73
Jan. 6	Vanderbilt	A	94	78
Jan. 8	Alabama	H	84	76
Jan. 13	Florida	A	78	96
Jan. 15	Georgia	H	104	73
Jan. 20	Auburn	A	73	74
Jan. 22	Tennessee	A	59	87
Jan. 27	Louisiana State	A	121	95
Jan. 29	Mississippi	A	85	76

1968-69 — Won 23 Lost 5

SEC Champions (16-2)
UKIT Champions
Ranked 7th in Polls
Coach: Adolph Rupp
Captain: Phil Argento

Nov. 30	Xavier	H	115	77
Dec. 2	Miami	A	86	77
Dec. 7	North Carolina	H	77	87
Dec. 14	Pennsylvania	A	102	78
UK Invitation Tournament				
Dec. 20	Michigan		112	104
Dec. 21	Army (finals)		80	65
Dec. 28	Notre Dame	N1	110	90
Dec. 31	Wisconsin	N2	65	69
Jan. 4	Mississippi	A	69	59
Jan. 6	Mississippi State	A	91	72
Jan. 11	Florida	H	88	67

Feb. 3	Louisiana State	H	109	96
Feb. 5	Mississippi	H	78	62
Feb. 10	Mississippi State	A	92	84
Feb. 12	Tennessee	H	60	59
Feb. 17	Mississippi State	H	107	81
Feb. 19	Georgia	A	106	87
Feb. 24	Alabama	H	96	83
Feb. 26	Auburn	H	89	57
Mar. 2	Vanderbilt	H	85	80
NCAA Tournament				
(Mideast Regional)				
(Lexington)				
Mar. 15	Marquette		107	89
Mar. 16	Ohio State		81	82
			2400	2103

(N1) Greensboro, N.C. (N2) Louisville

— Leading Scorers —

Mike Casey (6-4 So. G)	20.1
Dan Issel (6-8 So. C)	16.4
Mike Pratt (6-4 So. F)	14.1
Phil Argento (6-2 Jr. G)	12.3
Thad Jaracz (6-5 Sr. F)	11.3

Louie Dampier races upcourt during action in the Cats' 83-79 victory over Duke in 1966 NCAA tourney action.

Jan. 13	Georgia	H	88	68
Jan. 18	Tennessee	A	69	66
Jan. 25	Louisiana State	A	108	96
Jan. 27	Alabama	A	83	*70
Feb. 1	Vanderbilt	H	103	89
Feb. 3	Auburn	H	105	93
Feb. 8	Mississippi	H	104	68
Feb. 10	Mississippi State	H	91	69
Feb. 15	Florida	A	81	82
Feb. 17	Georgia	A	85	77
Feb. 22	Louisiana State	H	103	89
Feb. 26	Alabama	H	108	79
Mar. 1	Vanderbilt	A	99	101
Mar. 3	Auburn	A	90	86
Mar. 8	Tennessee	H	84	69

NCAA Tournament
(Mideast Regional)
(Madison, Wisc.)

Mar. 13	Marquette	74	81
Mar. 15	Miami	72	71
		2542	2199

(N1) Louisville (N2) Chicago
— Leading Scorers —
Dan Issel (6-8 Jr. C)...............................26.6
Mike Casey (6-4 Jr. G)............................19.1
Mike Pratt (6-4 Jr. F).............................16.9
Phil Argento (6-2 Sr. G).........................10.0
Larry Steele (6-5 So. F)..........................8.6

1969-70 — Won 26, Lost 2

SEC Champions (17-1)
UKIT Champions
Ranked First in Polls
Coach: Adolph Rupp
Co-Captains: Dan Issel and Mike Pratt

Dec. 1	West Virginia	H	106	87
Dec. 6	Kansas	H	115	85
Dec. 8	North Carolina	N1	94	87
Dec. 13	Indiana	H	109	92

UK Invitation Tournament

Dec. 19	Navy		73	59
Dec. 20	Duke (finals)		98	76
Dec. 27	Notre Dame	N2	102	100
Dec. 29	Miami (Ohio)	H	80	58
Jan. 3	Mississippi	H	95	73
Jan. 5	Mississippi State	H	111	76
Jan. 10	Florida	A	88	69
Jan. 12	Georgia	A	72	71
Jan. 17	Tennessee	H	68	52

Jan. 24	Louisiana State	H	109	96
Jan. 26	Alabama	H	86	71
Jan. 31	Vanderbilt	A	81	89
Feb. 2	Auburn	A	84	83
Feb. 7	Mississippi	A	120	85
Feb. 9	Mississippi State	H	86	57
Feb. 14	Florida	H	110	66
Feb. 16	Georgia	H	116	86
Feb. 21	Louisiana State	A	121	105
Feb. 23	Alabama	A	98	89
Feb. 28	Vanderbilt	H	90	86
Mar. 2	Auburn	H	102	81
Mar. 7	Tennessee	A	86	69

NCAA Tournament
(Mideast Regional)
(Columbus, Ohio)

Mar. 12	Notre Dame	109	99
Mar. 14	Jacksonville	100	106
		2709	2253

(N1) Charlotte, N.C. (N2) Louisville
— Leading Scorers —
Dan Issel (6-8 Sr. C)...............................33.9
Mike Pratt (6-4 Sr. F).............................19.3
Tom Parker (6-6 So. F)..........................10.4
Larry Steele (6-5 Jr. F)............................8.8
Terry Mills (6-2 Jr. G)..............................8.1

1970-71 — Won 22 Lost 6

SEC Champions (16-2)
UKIT Runner Up
Ranked 10th AP
Coach: Adolph Rupp
Honorary Co-Captains: Mike Casey and Larry Steele

Dec. 1	Northwestern	A	115	100
Dec. 5	Michigan	H	104	93
Dec. 7	West Virginia	A	106	100
Dec. 12	Indiana	A	95	*93

UK Invitation Tournament

Dec. 18	DePaul		106	85
Dec. 19	Purdue (finals)		83	89
Dec. 22	Oregon State	H	84	78
Dec. 29	Notre Dame	N1	92	99
Jan. 2	Mississippi	A	103	95
Jan. 4	Mississippi State	A	79	71
Jan. 9	Florida	H	101	75
Jan. 11	Georgia	H	79	66
Jan. 16	Tennessee	A	71	75
Jan. 23	Louisiana State	A	82	79
Jan. 25	Alabama	A	86	73

Jan. 30	Vanderbilt	H	102	92
Feb. 1	Auburn	H	114	76
Feb. 6	Mississippi	H	121	86
Feb. 8	Mississippi State	H	102	83
Feb. 13	Florida	A	65	74
Feb. 15	Georgia	A	107	95
Feb. 20	Louisiana State	H	110	73
Feb. 22	Alabama	H	101	74
Feb. 27	Vanderbilt	A	119	90
Mar. 1	Auburn	A	102	83
Mar. 6	Tennessee	H	84	78

NCAA Tournament
(Mideast Regional)
(Athens, Ga.)

Mar. 18	Western Kentucky	83	107
Mar. 20	Marquette	74	91
		2670	2373

(N1) Louisville
— Leading Scorers —
Tom Parker (6-7 Jr. F)...........................17.6
Mike Casey (6-4 Sr. G)..........................17.0
Tom Payne (7-2 So. C)..........................16.9
Kent Hollenbeck (6-4 Jr. G)...................14.0
Larry Steele (6-5 Sr. F)..........................13.1

1971-72 — Won 21 Lost 7

SEC Champions (14-4)
UKIT Champions
Ranked 14th UPI and 18th AP
Coach: Adolph Rupp
Honorary Co-Captains: Stan Key and Tom Parker

Dec. 1	Northwestern	H	94	85
Dec. 4	Kansas	A	79	69
Dec. 6	Kansas State	A	71	64
Dec. 11	Indiana	N1	89	**90
Dec. 13	Michigan State	H	85	91

UK Invitation Tournament

Dec. 17	Missouri		83	79
Dec. 18	Princeton (finals)		96	82
Dec. 28	Notre Dame	N1	83	67
Jan. 8	Mississippi	H	93	82
Jan. 10	Mississippi State	H	104	76
Jan. 15	Florida	A	70	72
Jan. 17	Georgia	A	73	85
Jan. 22	Tennessee	H	72	70
Jan. 24	Vanderbilt	H	106	80
Jan. 29	Louisiana State	H	89	71
Jan. 31	Alabama	H	77	74
Feb. 5	Vanderbilt	A	85	*80

Feb. 7	Auburn	A	78	72
Feb. 12	Mississippi	A	90	82
Feb. 14	Mississippi State	A	63	55
Feb. 19	Florida	H	95	68
Feb. 21	Georgia	H	87	63
Feb. 26	Louisiana State	A	71	88
Feb. 28	Alabama	A	70	73
Mar. 6	Auburn	A	102	67
Mar. 9	Tennessee	A	67	66

(Earned NCAA bid by beating Tennessee twice.)
NCAA Tournament
(Mideast Regional)
(Dayton, Ohio)

Mar. 16	Marquette	85	69
Mar. 18	Florida State	54	73
		2311	2093

(N1) Louisville
— Leading Scorers —
Jim Andrews (6-11 Jr. C).......................21.5
Tom Parker (6-7 Sr. F)...........................18.0
Ronnie Lyons (5-10 So. G).....................13.2
Stan Key (6-3 Sr. G)..............................12.5
Larry Stamper (6-6 Jr. F).......................10.3

JOE B. HALL ERA

1972-73 — Won 20 Lost 8

SEC Champions (14-4)
UKIT Champions
Ranked 15th UPI and 17th AP
Coach: Joe B. Hall
Honorary Captain: Jim Andrews

Dec. 2	Michigan State	A	75	66
Dec. 4	Iowa	H	66	79
Dec. 9	Indiana	N1	58	64
Dec. 11	North Carolina	N1	70	78

UK Invitation Tournament

Dec. 15	Nebraska		85	60
Dec. 16	Oregon (finals)		95	68
Dec. 23	Kansas	H	77	71
Dec. 30	Notre Dame	N1	65	63
Jan. 6	Mississippi	A	58	61
Jan. 8	Mississippi State	A	90	81
Jan. 13	Florida	H	95	65
Jan. 15	Georgia	H	89	68
Jan. 20	Tennessee	A	64	65
Jan. 22	Vanderbilt	A	75	76
Jan. 27	Louisiana State	A	86	71
Jan. 29	Alabama	A	95	93

The powerful 1969-70 Wildcats included, front row, Adolph Rupp, Dan Issel, Tom Parker, Bob McCowan, Larry Steele, Mike Pratt, Randy Noll and Joe B. Hall. Back row, Dick Parsons, Claude Vaughan, Kent Hollenbeck, Jim Dinwiddie, Clint Wheeler, Art Laib, Randy Pool, Mark Soderberg, Stan Key, Terry Mills, Bill Busey, T.L. Plain and Doug Billips.

Feb. 3	Vanderbilt	H	76	83
Feb. 5	Auburn	H	88	57
Feb. 10	Mississippi	H	88	70
Feb. 12	Mississippi State	H	100	*87
Feb. 17	Florida	A	94	83
Feb. 19	Georgia	A	99	86
Feb. 24	Louisiana State	H	94	76
Feb. 26	Alabama	H	111	95
Mar. 3	Auburn	A	91	79
Mar. 8	Tennessee	H	86	81

NCAA Tournament (Mideast Regional) (Nashville, Tenn.)

Mar. 15	Austin Peay		106	*100
Mar. 17	Indiana		65	72
			2341	2098

(N1) Louisville

— Leading Scorers —

Jim Andrews (6-11 Sr. C) 20.1
Kevin Grevey (6-5 So. F) 18.7
Jimmy Dan Conner (6-4 So. G-F) 11.2
Ronnie Lyons (5-10 Jr. G) 9.2
Mike Flynn (6-3 So. G) 9.1

1973-74 — Won 13, Lost 13

UKIT Champions
Worst Under Hall
Tied 4th SEC (9-9)

Coach: Joe B. Hall
Captain: Ronnie Lyons

Dec. 1	Miami (Ohio)	H	81	68
Dec. 3	Kansas	A	63	71
Dec. 8	Indiana	N1	68	77
Dec. 10	North Carolina	N2	84	101
Dec. 14	Iowa	A	88	80

UK Invitation Tournament

Dec. 21	Dartmouth		102	77
Dec. 22	Stanford (finals)		78	77
Dec. 29	Notre Dame	N1	79	94
Jan. 5	Louisiana State	A	84	95
Jan. 7	Georgia	H	80	74
Jan. 12	Auburn	H	79	58
Jan. 14	Tennessee	A	54	67
Jan. 19	Mississippi	H	93	64
Jan. 21	Alabama	A	77	81
Jan. 26	Florida	A	91	82
Jan. 28	Vanderbilt	H	65	82
Feb. 2	Mississippi State	A	82	70
Feb. 4	Louisiana State	H	73	70
Feb. 9	Georgia	A	86	72
Feb. 11	Auburn	A	97	*99
Feb. 16	Tennessee	H	61	58
Feb. 18	Mississippi	A	60	61
Feb. 23	Alabama	H	71	94
Feb. 25	Florida	H	65	75
Mar. 2	Vanderbilt	A	69	71
Mar. 4	Mississippi State	H	108	69
			2038	1987

(N1) Louisville (N2) Greensboro, N.C.

— Leading Scorers —

Kevin Grevey (6-5 Jr. F) 21.9
Bob Guyette (6-9 Jr. C) 12.7
Jimmy Dan Conner (6-4 Jr. F-G) 12.0
Mike Flynn (6-3 Jr. G) 11.5
Ronnie Lyons (5-10 Sr. G) 7.8

1974 Australian Exhibition Tour
(Not counted in Won-Lost Record)

May 13	Tahitian National Team	116	62
May 17	Australia	87	97
May 18	Newcastle	90	78
May 19	N.S.W. All Stars	123	67
May 21	Illawaarra Hawks	115	57
May 22	N.S.W. All Stars	106	50
May 23	A.C.T.	96	69
May 25	Bulleen Heidelberg	88	83
May 26	St. Kilda Business House	80	67
May 27	Nunawading	99	82
May 28	Melbourne	79	86
May 30	Gippsland All Stars	127	74
May 31	Bulleen Heidelberg	72	71
June 1	Laker All Stars	111	83
June 3	South Australian All Stars	109	96
Jane 4	South Australian All Stars	110	81
June 5	South Australian All Stars	111	84
June 6	Coburg	108	82
June 7	St. Kilda Business House	96	85
		1923	1454

1974-75 — Won 26, Lost 5

National Runner-Up (NCAA Tournament)
SEC Co-Champions (15-3)
UKIT Champions
Ranked 2nd AP, 4th UPI

Coach: Joe B. Hall
Captain: Jimmy Dan Conner

Nov. 30	Northwestern	H	97	70
Dec. 2	Miami (Ohio)	A	80	73
Dec. 7	Indiana	A	74	98
Dec. 9	North Carolina	N1	90	78

UK Invitation Tournament

Dec. 20	Washington State		97	75
Dec. 21	Oklahoma State (finals)		90	65
Dec. 23	Kansas	N1	100	63
Dec. 28	Notre Dame	N1	113	96
Jan. 4	Louisiana State	H	115	80
Jan. 6	Georgia	A	96	77
Jan. 11	Auburn	A	85	90
Jan. 13	Tennessee	H	88	82
Jan. 18	Mississippi	A	85	82
Jan. 20	Alabama	H	74	69
Jan. 25	Florida	H	87	65
Jan. 27	Vanderbilt	A	91	90
Feb. 1	Mississippi State	H	112	79
Feb. 3	Louisiana State	A	77	76
Feb. 8	Georgia	H	75	61
Feb. 10	Auburn	H	119	76
Feb. 15	Tennessee	A	98	103
Feb. 17	Mississippi	H	108	89
Feb. 22	Alabama	A	84	79
Feb. 24	Florida	A	58	66
Mar. 1	Vanderbilt	H	109	84
Mar. 8	Mississippi State	A	118	80

NCAA Tournament (Mideast Regional) (Tuscaloosa, Ala. and Dayton, Ohio)

Mar. 15	Marquette	N2	76	54
Mar. 20	Central Michigan	N3	90	73
Mar. 22	Indiana	N3	92	90

NCAA Final Four (San Diego, Calif.)

Mar. 29	Syracuse		95	79
Mar. 31	UCLA		85	92
			2858	2434

(N1) Louisville
(N2) Tuscaloosa, Ala.
(N3) Dayton, Ohio

— Leading Scorers —

Kevin Grevey (6-5 Sr. F) 23.6
Jimmy Dan Conner (6-4 Sr. G) 12.4
Rick Robey (6-10 Fr. C) 10.4
Jack Givens (6-4 Fr. F) 9.4
Mike Flynn (6-3 Sr. G) 9.0
Bob Guyette (6-9 Sr. F) 8.6

1975-76 — Won 20, Lost 10

UKIT Champions
NIT Champions
Tied 4th SEC (11-7)

Coach: Joe B. Hall
Captain: Jack Givens

Dec. 1	Northwestern	A	77	89
Dec. 8	North Carolina	N1	77	90
Dec. 10	Miami	H	91	69
Dec. 13	Kansas	A	54	48
Dec. 15	Indiana	N2	68	*77

UK Invitation Tournament

Dec. 19	Georgia Tech		66	64
Dec. 20	Oregon State (finals)		82	74
Dec. 30	Notre Dame	N2	79	77
Jan. 3	Mississippi State	A	73	77
Jan. 5	Alabama	A	63	76
Jan. 10	Tennessee	H	88	*90
Jan. 12	Georgia	H	92	76
Jan. 17	Vanderbilt	H	77	76
Jan. 24	Florida	A	89	82
Jan. 26	Auburn	A	84	*91
Jan. 31	Mississippi	H	89	81
Feb. 2	Louisiana State	H	85	71
Feb. 7	Tennessee	A	85	92
Feb. 9	Georgia	A	81	86
Feb. 14	Vanderbilt	A	65	69
Feb. 21	Florida	H	96	89
Feb. 23	Auburn	H	93	82
Feb. 28	Mississippi	A	94	87
Mar. 1	Louisiana State	A	85	70
Mar. 6	Alabama	H	90	85
Mar. 8	Mississippi State	H	94	*93

National Invitation Tournament (New York)

Mar. 13	Niagara		67	61
Mar. 16	Kansas State		81	78
Mar. 18	Providence		79	78
Mar. 21	U.N.C. Charlotte (finals)		71	67
			2415	2345

(N1) Charlotte, N.C. (N2) Louisville

— Leading Scorers —

Jack Givens (6-4 So. F) 20.1
Mike Phillips (6-10 So. C) 15.6
Larry Johnson (6-2 Jr. G) 11.2
James Lee (6-5 So. F) 9.3
Rick Robey (6-10 So. C-F)* 15.6
Reggie Warford (6-1 Sr. G) 6.5
*Played in 12 games.

RUPP ARENA ERA

1976-77 — Won 26, Lost 4

SEC Co-Champions (16-2)
Ranked 6th AP, 5th UPI

Coach: Joe B. Hall
Captains: Larry Johnson and Merion Haskins

Nov. 27	Wisconsin	H	72	64
Dec. 2	Texas Christian	H	103	53
Dec. 6	Indiana	A	66	51
Dec. 11	Kansas	H	90	63
Dec. 13	South Carolina	A	98	67

UK Invitation Tournament

Dec. 17	Bowling Green State		77	59
Dec. 18	Utah (finals)		68	70
Dec. 30	Notre Dame	N1	102	78
Jan. 3	Georgia	H	64	*59
Jan. 8	Vanderbilt	A	64	62
Jan. 12	Tennessee	H	67	*71
Jan. 15	Auburn	A	75	68
Jan. 17	Florida	A	73	71
Jan. 22	Louisiana State	H	87	72
Jan. 24	Mississippi	H	100	73
Jan. 29	Alabama	A	87	85
Jan. 31	Mississippi State	A	92	85
Feb. 5	Vanderbilt	H	113	73
Feb. 7	Florida State	N1	97	57
Feb. 12	Auburn	H	89	82
Feb. 14	Florida	H	104	78
Feb. 19	Louisiana State	A	90	76
Feb. 21	Mississippi	A	81	69
Feb. 26	Alabama	H	85	70
Feb. 28	Mississippi State	H	77	64
Mar. 5	Tennessee	A	79	81
Mar. 1	Georgia	A	72	54

NCAA Tournament (East Regional) (Philadelphia, Pa. and College Park, Md.)

Mar. 12	Princeton	N2	72	58
Mar. 17	VMI	N3	93	78
Mar. 19	North Carolina	N3	72	79
			2509	2070

(N1) Louisville (N2) Philadelphia, Pa.
(N3) College Park, Md.

— Leading Scorers —

Jack Givens (6-4 Jr. F) 18.9
Rick Robey (6-10 Jr. F) 14.2
Mike Phillips (6-10 Jr. C) 12.2
Larry Johnson (6-3 Sr. G) 10.7
James Lee (6-5 Jr. F) 9.8
Jay Shidler (6-1 Fr. G) 7.8
Truman Claytor (6-1 So. G) 6.6

1977-78 — Won 30, Lost 2

National Champions (NCAA Tournament)
SEC Champions (16-2)
UKIT Champions
Ranked 1st AP and UPI

Coach: Joe B. Hall
Captains: Jack Givens and Rick Robey

Nov. 26	Southern Methodist	H	110	86
Dec. 5	Indiana	H	78	64
Dec. 10	Kansas	A	73	66
Dec. 12	South Carolina	H	84	65

UK Invitation Tournament

Dec. 16	Portland State		114	88
Dec. 17	St. John's (finals)		102	72
Dec. 23	Iona	H	104	65
Dec. 31	Notre Dame	N1	73	68
Jan. 2	Vanderbilt	H	72	59
Jan. 7	Florida	A	86	67
Jan. 9	Auburn	A	101	77
Jan. 14	Louisiana State	H	96	76
Jan. 16	Mississippi	H	76	56
Jan. 21	Mississippi State	A	75	65
Jan. 23	Alabama	A	62	78
Jan. 30	Georgia	H	90	73
Feb. 4	Florida	H	88	61
Feb. 6	Auburn	H	104	81
Feb. 11	Louisiana State	A	94	*95
Feb. 13	Mississippi	A	64	52
Feb. 15	Tennessee	H	90	77
Feb. 18	Mississippi State	H	58	56
Feb. 20	Alabama	H	97	84
Feb. 25	Tennessee	A	68	57
Feb. 27	Georgia	A	78	67
Mar. 4	Nevada-Las Vegas	H	92	70
Mar. 6	Vanderbilt	A	78	68

NCAA Tournament (Mideast Regional)
(Knoxville, Tenn. and Dayton, Ohio)

Mar. 11	Florida State	N2	85	76
Mar. 16	Miami (Ohio)	N3	91	69
Mar. 18	Michigan State	N3	52	49

Finals (St. Louis, Mo.)

Mar. 25	Arkansas		64	59
Mar. 27	Duke		94	88
			2693	2234

NCAA CHAMPIONS FOR FIFTH TIME

(N1) Louisville (N2) Knoxville, Tenn.
(N3) Dayton, Ohio

— Leading Scorers —

Jack Givens (6-4 Sr. F) 18.1
Rick Robey (6-10 Sr. F) 14.4
Kyle Macy (6-3 So. G) 12.5
James Lee (6-5 Sr. F) 11.3
Mike Phillips (6-10 Sr. C) 10.2
Truman Claytor (6-1 Jr. G) 6.9

1978 Japan Exhibition Tour
(All games vs. Japan National Team)
(Not counted in Win-Loss Record)

Jun. 13	at Tokyo	104	71
Jun. 15	at Niigata	102	89
June 18	at Nagoya	97	59
June 19	at Osaka	87	82
June 20	at Fukuoka	88	61
June 22	at Nagasaki	122	79
June 24	at Tokyo	125	57
		705	498

1978-79 — Won 19, Lost 12

6th in SEC (10-8)
SEC Tournament Runner-Up

Coach: Joe B. Hall
Captains: Dwane Casey and Truman Claytor

Dec. 2	La Salle	H	109	77
Dec. 4	West Texas	H	121	67
Dec. 9	Kansas	H	67	*66
Dec. 16	Indiana	A	67	*68

UK Invitation Tournament

Dec. 22	Texas A & M		69	73
Dec. 23	Syracuse		94	87
Dec. 30	Notre Dame	N1	81	76
Jan. 3	Florida	A	65	76
Jan. 6	Louisiana State	H	89	93
Jan. 8	Mississippi	H	90	64
Jan. 13	Alabama	A	52	55
Jan. 15	Mississippi State	A	61	63
Jan. 20	Tennessee	H	55	66
Jan. 22	Georgia	H	73	64
Jan. 25	Auburn	A	86	*83
Jan 27	Florida	H	87	81
Jan. 29	Auburn	H	66	59
Feb. 3	Louisiana State	A	61	70
Feb. 5	Mississippi	A	87	82
Feb. 7	Vanderbilt	A	58	68
Feb. 10	Alabama	H	80	71
Feb. 12	Mississippi State	H	80	65
Feb 17	Tennessee	A	84	101
Feb. 19	Georgia	A	90	74
Feb. 23	Vanderbilt	H	96	70
Feb. 25	South Carolina	A	79	74

SEC Tournament (Birmingham, Ala)

Feb. 28	Mississippi		82	77
Mar. 1	Alabama		101	100
Mar. 2	Louisiana State		80	67
Mar. 3	Tennessee		69	*75

National Invitation Tournament (Lexington)

Mar. 7	Clemson		67	*68
			2446	2280

(N1) Louisville

— Leading Scorers —

Kyle Macy (6-3 Jr. G) 15.2
Dwight Anderson (6-3 Fr. G) 13.3
LaVon Williams (6-6 So. F) 11.5
Fred Cowan (6-8 So. C-F) 9.4
Truman Claytor (6-1 Sr. G) 8.7

1979-80 — Won 29, Lost 6

SEC Champions (15-3)
SEC Tournament Runner-Up
UKIT Champions
Great Alaska Shootout Champions
Ranked 4th AP, 3rd UPI

Coach: Joe B. Hall
Captain: Kyle Macy

Nov. 17	Duke	N1	76	*82

Great Alaska Shootout

Nov. 30	Bradley	N2	79	58
Dec. 1	Alaska	N2	97	68
Dec. 2	Iona	N2	57	50
Dec. 8	Baylor	H	80	46
Dec. 10	South Carolina	H	126	81
Dec. 12	Kansas	A	57	56
Dec. 15	Indiana	H	69	58
Dec. 17	Georgia	N3	95	69

UK Invitation Tournament

Dec. 21	California		78	52
Dec. 22	Purdue (finals)		61	60
Dec. 29	Notre Dame	N4	86	80
Jan. 2	Auburn	H	67	65
Jan. 5	Tennessee	A	47	49

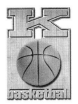

Jan. 9	Mississippi	A	79	73
Jan. 12	Alabama	H	64	78
Jan. 17	Florida	A	76	63
Jan. 19	Vanderbilt	H	106	90
Jan. 23	Mississippi State	A	89	67
Jan. 26	Georgia	H	56	49
Jan. 28	Louisiana State	H	60	65
Jan. 30	Auburn	A	64	62
Feb. 2	Tennessee	H	83	75
Feb. 6	Mississippi	H	86	72
Feb. 9	Alabama	A	72	63
Feb. 13	Florida	H	95	70
Feb. 15	Vanderbilt	A	91	73
Feb. 17	Nevada-Las Vegas	A	74	69
Feb. 20	Mississippi State	H	71	65
Feb. 24	Louisiana State	A	76	*74
	SEC Tournament (Birmingham, Ala.)			
Feb. 28	Auburn		69	61
Feb. 29	Mississippi		70	67
Mar. 1	Louisiana State		78	80
	NCAA Tournament (Mideast Regional) (Bowling Green and Lexington)			
Mar. 8	Florida State	N5	97	78
Mar. 13	Duke	H	54	55
			2685	2323

(N1) Springfield, Mass. (N2) Anchorage, Alaska
(N3) Atlanta, Ga. (N4) Louisville
(N5) Bowling Green

— Leading Scorers —

Kyle Macy (6-3 Sr. G) ... 15.4
Sam Bowie (7-1 Fr. C) ... 12.9
Fred Cowan (6-8 Jr. F) ... 12.5
LaVon Williams (6-7 Sr. F) ... 7.5
Jay Shidler (6-1 Sr. G) ... 6.2

1980-81 — Won 22 Lost 6

SEC Runner-Up (15-3)
UKIT Champions
Ranked 8th AP and UPI

Coach: Joe B. Hall
Captain: Chuck Verderber

Nov. 29	East Tennessee	H	62	57
Dec. 3	Ohio State	H	70	64
Dec. 6	Indiana	A	68	66
Dec. 13	Kansas	H	87	73
	UK Invitation Tournament			
Dec. 19	Alaska		91	56
Dec. 20	Alabama-Birmingham (finals)		61	53
Dec. 27	Notre Dame	N1	61	67
Dec. 30	Maine	H	100	54
Jan. 3	Georgia	H	76	62
Jan. 7	Auburn	A	79	66
Jan. 10	Tennessee	H	48	47
Jan. 14	Mississippi	H	64	55
Jan. 17	Alabama	A	55	59
Jan. 19	Louisiana State	A	67	81
Jan. 21	Florida	H	102	48
Jan. 24	Vanderbilt	A	78	64
Jan. 28	Mississippi State	H	71	64
Jan. 31	Georgia	A	71	**68
Feb. 4	Auburn	H	102	74
Feb. 7	Tennessee	A	71	87
Feb. 11	Mississippi	A	62	55
Feb 14	Alabama	H	77	62
Feb. 18	Florida	A	69	56
Feb. 21	Vanderbilt	H	80	48
Feb. 25	Mississippi State	A	78	74
Mar. 1	Louisiana State	H	73	71
	SEC Tournament (Birmingham, Ala.)			
Mar. 5	Vanderbilt		55	60
	NCAA Tournament (Mideast Regional) (Tuscaloosa, Ala.)			
Mar. 15	Alabama-Birmingham		62	69
			2040	1760

(N1) Louisville

— Leading Scorers —

Sam Bowie (7-1 So. C) ... 17.4
Dirk Minniefield (6-3 So. G) ... 10.4
Derrick Hord (6-6 So. G-F) ... 8.9
Fred Cowan (6-8 Sr. F) ... 8.2
Chuck Verderber (6-6 Jr. F) ... 7.5

1981-82 — Won 22, Lost 8

SEC Co-Champions (13-5)
UKIT Champions
Ranked 8th AP, 9th UPI

Coach: Joe B. Hall
Captain: Chuck Verderber

Nov. 28	Akron	H	83	64
Dec. 5	Ohio State	A	78	62
Dec. 8	Indiana	H	85	69
Dec. 12	Kansas	A	77	*74
	UK Invitation Tournament			
Dec. 18	Jacksonville		107	91
Dec. 19	Seton Hall (finals)		98	74
Dec. 26	North Carolina	N1	69	82
Dec. 29	Notre Dame	N2	34	*28
Jan. 2	Georgia	A	68	66
Jan. 6	Auburn	H	83	71
Jan. 9	Tennessee	A	66	70
Jan. 13	Mississippi	A	65	67
Jan. 16	Alabama	H	86	69
Jan. 20	Florida	A	91	76
Jan. 23	Vanderbilt	H	67	58
Jan. 25	Louisiana State	H	76	65
Jan. 27	Mississippi State	A	51	56
Jan. 30	Georgia	H	82	73
Feb. 3	Auburn	A	81	*83
Feb. 6	Tennessee	H	77	67
Feb. 10	Mississippi	H	56	49
Feb. 13	Alabama	A	72	62
Feb. 17	Florida	H	84	78
Feb. 20	Vanderbilt	A	73	69
Feb. 24	Mississippi State	H	71	54
Feb. 27	Louisiana State	A	78	94
	SEC Tournament (Lexington)			
Mar. 4	Auburn		89	66
Mar. 5	Mississippi		62	58
Mar. 6	Alabama		46	48
	NCAA Mideast Regional (Nashville, Tenn.)			
Mar. 4	Middle Tennessee		44	50
			2199	1993

(N1) East Rutherford, N.J.
(N2) Louisville

— Leading Scorers —

Derrick Hord (6-6 Jr. F) ... 16.3
Jim Master (6-5 So. G) ... 13.4
Melvin Turpin (6-10 So. C) ... 13.1
Dirk Minniefield (6-3 Jr. G) ... 11.3
Charles Hurt (6-6 Jr. F) ... 6.6

1982 Japan Exhibition Tour
(not Counted in Win-Loss Record)

July 1	W. Germany at Kariya	84	73
July 2	France at Kyotta	77	65
July 4	W. Germany at Sapporo	82	72
July 7	Japan Nat. at Akita	86	66
July 10	France at Moebashi	86	83
July 11	Japan at Tokyo	106	71

Note: the Wildcats also toured Taiwan and Hong Kong during the 1982 trip. The following are results of games played there:

July 12	China #2 at Taipei	86	63
July 15	China #1 at Hong Kong	119	48

1982-83 — Won 23, Lost 8

SEC Champions (13-5)
UKIT Champions
Ranked 12th AP and UPI

Coach: Joe B. Hall
Captain: Charles Hurt

Nov. 27	Butler	H	90	53
Dec. 1	Notre Dame	A	58	45
Dec. 4	Villanova	H	93	79
Dec. 7	Detroit	H	83	46
Dec. 11	Illinois	H	76	57
	UK Invitation Tournament			
Dec. 17	Duquesne		55	42
Dec. 18	Tulane (finals)		80	61
Dec. 22	Indiana	A	59	62
Dec. 29	Kansas	N1	83	62
Jan. 3	Mississippi	H	72	60
Jan. 5	Louisiana State	H	52	50
Jan. 8	Alabama	A	67	74
Jan. 10	Mississippi State	A	59	*53
Jan. 15	Auburn	H	67	75
Jan. 17	Florida	H	70	63
Jan. 22	Vanderbilt	A	82	*77
Jan. 29	Georgia	A	63	70
Jan. 31	Tennessee	A	63	65
Feb. 5	Alabama	H	76	70
Feb. 8	Mississippi State	H	88	67
Feb. 12	Auburn	A	71	69
Feb. 14	Florida	A	73	61
Feb. 19	Vanderbilt	H	82	63
Feb. 26	Georgia	H	81	72
Feb. 27	Tennessee	H	69	61
Mar. 3	Mississippi	A	61	58
Mar. 5	Louisiana State	A	60	74
	SEC Tournament (Birmingham, Ala.)			
Mar. 11	Alabama	N2	64	69
	NCAA Mideast Regional (First Round) (Tampa, Fla.)			
Mar. 19	Ohio		57	40
	NCAA Mideast Region (Knoxville, Tenn.)			
Mar. 24	Indiana		64	59
Mar. 26	Louisville		68	*80
			2186	1937

(N1) Louisville (N2) Birmingham, Ala.

— Leading Scorers —

Melvin Turpin (6-11 Jr. C) ... 15.1
Jim Master (6-5 Jr. G) ... 12.5
Derrick Hord (6-6 Sr. F) ... 8.9
Dirk Minniefield (6-3 Sr. G) ... 8.6
Charles Hurt (6-6 Sr. F) ... 8.2

1983-84 — Won 29, Lost 5

NCAA Mideast Region Champions
SEC Tournament Champions
SEC Champions (14-4)
UKIT Champions
Ranked 3rd AP and UPI

Coach: Joe B. Hall
Captain: Dickey Beal

Nov. 26	Louisville	H	65	44
Dec. 3	Indiana	H	59	54
Dec. 10	Kansas	A	72	50
	UK Invitation Tournament			
Dec. 16	Wyoming		66	40
Dec. 17	Brigham Young (finals)		93	59
Dec. 20	Cincinnati	A	24	11
Dec. 24	Illinois	A	56	54
Dec. 28	Purdue	N1	86	67
Jan. 2	Mississippi	A	68	55
Jan. 7	Louisiana State	A	96	80
Jan. 9	Alabama	H	76	66
Jan. 11	Mississippi State	H	51	42
Jan. 13	Auburn	A	63	82
Jan. 17	Florida	A	57	69
Jan. 20	Vanderbilt	H	67	46
Jan. 22	Houston	H	74	67
Jan. 28	Georgia	H	64	40
Jan. 30	Tennessee	H	93	74
Feb. 4	Alabama	A	62	69
Feb. 6	Mississippi State	A	77	58
Feb. 11	Auburn	H	84	64
Feb. 13	Florida	H	67	65
Feb. 19	Vanderbilt	A	58	54
Feb. 25	Georgia	A	66	64
Feb. 27	Tennessee	A	58	63
Mar. 1	Mississippi	H	76	57
Mar. 3	Louisiana State	H	90	68
	SEC Tournament (Nashville, Tenn.)			
Mar. 8	Georgia		92	79
Mar. 9	Alabama		48	46
Mar. 10	Auburn (finals)		51	49
	NCAA Mideast Regional (First Round) (Birmingham, Ala.)			
Mar. 17	Brigham Young		93	68
	NCAA Mideast Region (Lexington, Ky.)			
Mar. 22	Louisville		72	67
Mar. 24	Illinois		54	51
	NCAA Final Four (Seattle, Wash.)			
Mar. 31	Georgetown		40	53
			2318	1975

(N1) Louisville

— Leading Scorers —

Melvin Turpin (6-11 Sr. C) ... 15.2
Kenny Walker (6-8 So. F) ... 12.4
Sam Bowie (7-1 Sr. F) ... 10.5
Jim Master (6-5 Sr. G) ... 9.6
Winston Bennett (6-7 Fr. F) ... 6.5

1984-85 — Won 18, Lost 13

NCAA "Final 16"
Tied for Third in SEC (11-7)
UKIT Champions

Coach: Joe B. Hall
Captains: Winston Bennett and Kenny Walker

Nov. 27	Toledo	H	63	54
Dec. 1	Purdue	A	56	66
Dec. 4	Southern Methodist	H	54	56
Dec. 8	Indiana	A	68	81
Dec. 15	Louisville	A	64	71
	UK Invitation Tournament			
Dec. 21	East Tennessee State		69	54
Dec. 22	Cincinnati (finals)		66	55
Dec. 31	Kansas	N1	92	89
Jan. 2	Auburn	H	68	61
Jan. 5	North Carolina State	H	78	62
Jan. 7	Vanderbilt	H	75	58
Jan. 9	Mississippi	A	57	45
Jan. 12	Alabama	A	58	60
Jan. 16	Mississippi State	H	58	57
Jan. 19	Florida	H	55	67
Jan. 23	Georgia	A	73	81
Jan. 27	Tennessee	A	65	81
Jan. 31	Louisiana State	H	53	43
Feb. 2	Auburn	A	49	*47
Feb. 7	Vanderbilt	A	68	62
Feb. 9	Mississippi	H	67	52
Feb. 13	Alabama	H	51	48
Feb. 16	Mississippi State	A	69	82
Feb. 20	Florida	A	76	68
Feb. 24	Georgia	H	77	79
Feb. 28	Tennessee	H	92	67
Mar. 2	Louisiana State	A	61	67
	SEC Tournament (Birmingham, Ala.)			
Mar. 7	Florida		55	58
	NCAA West Regional (First Round) (Salt Lake City, Utah)			
Mar. 14	Washington		66	58
Mar. 16	Nevada-Las Vegas		64	61
	NCAA West Regional (Denver, Colo.)			
Mar. 22	St. John's		70	86
			2037	1976

(N1) Louisville

— Leading Scorers —

Kenny Walker (6-8 Jr. F) ... 22.9
Ed Davender (6-1 Fr. G) ... 8.5
Winston Bennett (6-7 So. F) ... 7.2
Bret Bearup (6-9 Sr. C) ... 6.3
James Blackmon (6-2 So. G) ... 5.4
Roger Harden (6-1 Jr. G) ... 5.3

EDDIE SUTTON ERA

1985-86 — Won 32, Lost 4

NCAA "Final 8"
SEC Champions (17-1)
SEC Tournament Champions
Ranked Third AP and UPI

Coach: Eddie Sutton
Captains: Kenny Walker, Roger Harden and Leroy Byrd

Nov. 22	Northwestern (LA) State	H	77	58
Nov. 26	Chaminade	A	89	57
Nov. 27	Hawaii	A	98	65
Dec. 3	Cincinnati	H	84	54
Dec. 7	Indiana	H	63	58
Dec. 14	Kansas	A	66	83
	UK Invitation Tournament			
Dec. 20	East Carolina		86	52
Dec. 21	Pepperdine (finals)		88	56
Dec. 28	Louisville	H	69	64
Dec. 30	Va. Military Institute	N1	93	55
Jan. 4	Vanderbilt	A	80	71
Jan. 6	Auburn	A	56	60
Jan. 8	Mississippi	H	75	58
Jan. 11	Alabama	H	76	52
Jan. 15	Mississippi State	A	64	52
Jan. 18	Florida	A	72	55
Jan. 23	Georgia	H	74	69
Jan. 25	Tennessee	H	74	57
Jan. 29	LSU	A	54	52
Jan. 31	Auburn	H	81	71
Feb. 2	North Carolina State	A	51	54
Feb. 5	Vanderbilt	H	73	65
Feb. 8	Mississippi	A	62	58
Feb. 13	Alabama	A	73	71
Feb. 15	Mississippi State	H	88	62
Feb. 19	Florida	H	80	69
Feb. 22	Georgia	A	80	75
Feb. 27	Tennessee	A	62	60
Mar. 1	LSU	H	68	57
	SEC Tournament (Lexington)			
Mar. 6	Mississippi		95	69
Mar. 7	Louisiana State		61	58
Mar. 8	Alabama		83	72
	NCAA Southeast Regional First/Second Round (Charlotte, N.C.)			
Mar. 14	Davidson		75	55
Mar. 16	Western Kentucky		71	64
	NCAA Southeast Regional (Atlanta)			
Mar. 20	Alabama		68	63
Mar. 22	Louisiana State		57	59
			2666	2210

(N1) Louisville

— Leading Scorers —

Kenny Walker (6-8 Sr. F) ... 20.0
Winston Bennett (6-7 Jr. F) ... 12.7
Ed Davender (6-2 So. G) ... 11.5
James Blackmon (6-3 Jr. G) ... 9.4
Roger Harden (6-1 Sr. G) ... 6.8

1986 Japan Tour
(Not counted in Won-Loss Record)

June 21*	Japan at Tokyo	80	55
Jun. 22*	Finland at Tokyo	87	67
June 24	Finland at Sendai	82	65

Ex-Cat John Pelphrey used his great intelligence and basketball savvy to get the best of players with better athletic ability. There was no doubt that he would one day become a coach.

Jun./ 26	Japan at Niigata		79	73
June 28	Finland at Ohtsu		80	56
June 29	Czechoslovakia at Sapporo		74	80
July 2	S. China		87	45

*Kirin World Tournament Hong Kong Game

1986-87 — Won 18, Lost 11
UKIT Champions
SEC Third Place (10-8)
Coach: Eddie Sutton
Captains: James Blackmon and Paul Andrews

Nov. 29	Austin Peay	H	71	69
Dec. 2	Texas Tech	H	66	60
Dec. 6	Indiana	A	66	71
Dec. 13	Lamar	H	71	56
UK Invitation Tournament				
Dec. 19	Iona		75	59
Dec. 20	Boston U. (finals)		81	69
Dec. 27	Louisville	A	85	51
Dec. 30	Georgia	N1	65	69
Jan. 3	Auburn	A	63	60
Jan. 7	Alabama	H	55	69
Jan. 10	Tennessee	A	68	75
Jan. 12	Mississippi State	A	57	49
Jan. 14	Florida	H	67	62
Jan. 18	LSU	H	41	76
Jan. 21	Vanderbilt	A	71	65
Jan. 25	Navy	H	80	69
Jan. 29	Ole Miss	A	65	76
Jan. 31	Mississippi State	H	50	36
Feb. 4	Auburn	H	75	71
Feb. 7	Alabama	A	70	69
Feb. 11	Tennessee	H	91	*84
Feb. 15	Florida	A	56	74
Feb. 19	Vanderbilt	H	65	54
Feb. 21	LSU	A	52	65
Feb. 25	Georgia	A	71	79
Feb. 28	Ole Miss	H	64	63
Mar. 1	Oklahoma	H	75	74
SEC Tournament				
(Atlanta)				
Mar. 6	Auburn		72	79
NCAA Southeast Regional				
First/Second Rounds				
(Atlanta)				
Mar. 13	Ohio State		77	91
			1965	1944

(N1) Louisville
— Leading Scorers —
Rex Chapman (6-4 Fr. G)..16.0
Ed Davender (6-3 Jr. G)...15.2
Richard Madison (6-7 Jr. F)..9.1
James Blackmon (6-3 Sr. G)..8.4
Robert Lock(6-11 Jr. C)...7.5

1987-88 — Won 25, Lost 5*
UKIT Champions
Best SEC Record (13-5)
Ranked 6th AP and UPI
Coach: Eddie Sutton
Captains: Winston Bennett, Ed Davender, Cedric Jenkins, Rob Lock, Richard Madison

Nov. 28	Hawaii	H	86	59
Dec. 1	Cincinnati	H	101	77
Dec. 5	Indiana	N1	82	*76
Dec. 12	Louisville	H	76	75
UK Invitation Tournament				
Dec. 18	Miami (Ohio)	H	85	71
Dec. 19	N.C. Charlotte (finals)	H	84	81
Dec. 28	Alaska	H	100	58
Dec. 31	Vanderbilt	H	81	74
Jan. 2	Georgia	A	84	77
Jan. 6	Mississippi State	H	93	52
Jan. 9	Auburn	H	52	53
Jan. 13	Alabama	A	63	55
Jan. 16	Tennessee	H	83	65
Jan. 20	Florida	H	56	58
Jan. 23	LSU	A	76	61
Jan. 27	Vanderbilt	A	66	83
Jan. 31	Notre Dame	N2	78	69
Feb. 3	Ole Miss	H	94	65
Feb. 6	Mississippi State	A	83	59
Feb. 10	Auburn	A	69	62
Feb. 13	Alabama	H	82	68
Feb. 17	Tennessee	A	70	72
Feb. 20	Florida	A	76	83
Feb. 24	LSU	H	95	69
Feb. 28	Syracuse	H	62	58
Mar. 2	Georgia	H	80	72
Mar. 5	Ole Miss	A	78	71
SEC Tournament				
(Baton Rouge, La.)				
Mar. 11	Ole Miss		82	64
Mar. 12	LSU		86	80
Mar. 13	Georgia		62	57
			2365	2024

(N1) Indianapolis
(N2) Louisville
— Leading Scorers —
Rex Chapman (6-4 So. G) 19.0
Ed Davender (6-3 Sr. G)...15.7
Winston Bennett (6-7 Sr. F) 15.3
Rob Lock (6-11 Sr. C) 10.9
Eric Manuel (6-6 Fr. F)..7.1

*As part of sanctions imposed upon the UK basketball program in 1989, the National Collegiate Athletic Association ordered Kentucky to erase from the record three NCAA tournament games from the 1987-88 season. Kentucky's 99-84 win over Southern, a 90-81 win over Maryland and an 80-74 loss to Villanova have been deleted from the records, thus changing the 1987-88 season record from 27-6 to 25-5.

#The presidents of the Southeastern Conference institutions voted to strip Kentucky of the 1987-88 SEC regular season and SEC Tournament championships. Kentucky was not forced to forfeit any of those regular season or tournament games.

1988-89 — Won 13, Lost 19
Tied for 6th in SEC (8-10)
Coach: Eddie Sutton
Captain: Mike Scott

Nov. 19	Duke	N1	55	80
Great Alaska Shootout				
Nov. 25	Iona	N2	56	54
Nov. 26	Seton Hall	N2	60	63
Nov. 28	California	N2	89	71
Dec. 3	Notre Dame	N3	65	81
Dec. 7	Northwestern State	H	82	85
Dec. 10	Western Carolina	H	78	60
UK Invitation Tournament				
Dec. 16	Bowling Green State		54	56
Dec. 17	Marshall		91	78
Dec. 20	Indiana	H	52	75
Dec. 27	Austin Peay	N4	85	77
Dec. 31	Louisville	A	75	97
Jan. 4	Georgia	H	76	65
Jan. 7	Vanderbilt	H	70	61
Jan. 9	Florida	A	69	56
Jan. 14	LSU	H	62	64
Jan. 18	Alabama	A	64	76
Jan. 21	Tennessee	A	66	65
Jan. 25	Auburn	H	86	76
Jan. 28	Ole Miss	A	65	70
Feb. 1	Mississippi State	H	73	61
Feb. 5	Georgia	A	72	84
Feb. 8	Vanderbilt	A	51	81
Feb. 11	Florida	H	53	59
Feb. 15	LSU	A	80	99
Feb. 18	Alabama	H	67	71
Feb. 20	Auburn	A	75	77
Feb. 22	Tennessee	H	76	71
Feb. 26	Syracuse	A	73	89
Mar. 1	Ole Miss	H	70	69
Mar. 4	Mississippi State	A	67	68
SEC Tournament (Knoxville, Tenn.)				
Mar. 10	Vanderbilt		63	77
			2220	2316

(N1) Springfield, Mass. (N2) Anchorage, Alaska
(N3) Indianapolis (N4) Louisville
— Leading Scorers —
LeRon Ellis (6-10 So. C)..16.0
Chris Mills (6-7 Fr. F)...14.3
Derrick Miller (6-5 Jr. G)..13.9
Reggie Hanson (6-7 So. F)...9.8
Sean Sutton (6-1 So. G)..5.9

RICK PITINO ERA

1989-90 — Won 14, Lost 14

SEC Record (10-8)

Coach: Rick Pitino
Captain: Derrick Miller

Nov. 28	Ohio	H	76	73
Dec. 2	Indiana	N1	69	71
Dec. 4	Mississippi State	H	102	97
Dec. 6	Tennessee Tech	H	111	75
Dec. 9	Kansas	A	95	150
Dec. 19	Furman	H	104	73

UK Invitation Tournament

Dec. 22	Portland		88	71
Dec. 23	Southwestern La. (finals)		113	*116
Dec. 27	North Carolina	N2	110	121
Dec. 30	Louisville	H	79	86
Jan. 3	Georgia	A	91	106
Jan. 6	Vanderbilt	A	85	92
Jan. 10	Florida	H	89	81
Jan. 13	LSU	A	81	94
Jan. 17	Alabama	H	82	65
Jan. 20	Tennessee	H	95	83
Jan. 24	Auburn	A	70	74
Jan. 27	Ole Miss	H	98	79
Jan. 31	Mississippi State	A	86	87
Feb. 3	Georgia	H	88	77
Feb. 7	Vanderbilt	H	100	73
Feb. 12	Florida	A	78	74
Feb. 15	LSU	H	100	95
Feb. 17	Alabama	A	58	83
Feb. 21	Tennessee	A	100	102
Feb. 24	Auburn	H	98	95
Feb. 28	Ole Miss	A	74	88
Mar. 5	Notre Dame	A	67	80
			2487	2461

(N1) Indianapolis
(N2) Louisville
— Leading Scorers —
Derrick Miller (6-5 Sr. G)..........................19.2
Reggie Hanson (6-7 Jr. C)..........................16.4
Deron Feldhaus (6-7 So. F)........................14.4
John Pelphrey (6-7 So. F)...........................13.0
Sean Woods (6-2 So. G)...............................9.1

1990-91 — Won 22 Lost 6

Best Record in SEC (14-4)
Ranked Ninth AP

Coach: Rick Pitino
Captains: Deron Feldhaus, Reggie Hanson, John Pelphrey

Nov. 24	Pennsylvania	H	85	62
Nov. 28	Cincinnati	A	75	71
Dec. 1	Notre Dame	N1	98	90
Dec. 8	Kansas	H	88	71
Dec. 10	North Carolina	A	81	84
Dec. 15	Tennessee-Chattanooga	H	86	70
Dec. 18	Indiana	A	84	87
Dec. 21	Western Kentucky	N2	84	70
Dec. 27	Eastern Kentucky	H	74	60
Dec. 29	Louisville	A	93	85
Jan. 2	Georgia	A	81	80
Jan. 5	LSU	H	93	80
Jan. 9	Mississippi State	H	89	70
Jan. 12	Tennessee	A	78	74
Jan. 16	Ole Miss	A	95	85
Jan. 19	Vanderbilt	H	58	50
Jan. 23	Florida	H	81	65
Jan. 26	Alabama	A	83	88
Jan. 29	Auburn	A	89	81
Feb. 3	Georgia	H	96	84
Feb. 5	LSU	A	88	107
Feb. 9	Mississippi State	A	82	83
Feb. 13	Tennessee	H	85	74
Feb. 16	Ole Miss	H	89	77
Feb. 20	Vanderbilt	A	87	98
Feb. 23	Florida	A	90	74
Feb. 26	Alabama	H	79	73
Mar. 2	Auburn	H	114	93
			2405	2186

(N1) Indianapolis
(N2) Louisville
— Leading Scorers —
John Pelphrey (6-7 Jr. F)...........................14.4
Reggie Hanson (6-8 Sr. C)..........................14.4
Jamal Mashburn (6-9 Fr. F).......................12.9
Deron Feldhaus (6-7 Jr. F)..........................10.8
Richie Farmer (6-0 Jr. G)............................10.1

1991-92 — Won 29, Lost 7

SEC East Champions (12-4)
SEC Tournament Champions
Ranked 6th AP and CNN/USA Today

Coach: Rick Pitino
Captains: Richie Farmer, Deron Feldhaus, John Pelphrey, Sean Woods

Preseason NIT

Nov. 20	West Virginia	H	106	80
Nov. 22	Pittsburgh	H	67	85
Dec. 4	Massachusetts	H	90	69
Dec. 7	Indiana	N1	76	74
Dec. 10	SW Texas State	H	82	36
Dec. 12	Morehead State	N2	101	84
Dec. 14	Arizona State	H	94	68
Dec. 21	Georgia Tech	A	80	81
Dec. 23	Ohio	N3	73	63
Dec. 28	Louisville	H	103	89
Jan. 2	Notre Dame	H	91	70
Jan. 4	South Carolina	A	80	63
Jan. 7	Georgia	H	78	66
Jan. 11	Florida	H	81	60
Jan. 15	Vanderbilt	A	84	71
Jan. 18	Eastern Kentucky	H	85	55
Jan. 21	Tennessee	A	85	107
Jan. 25	Arkansas	H	88	105
Jan. 29	Ole Miss	H	96	78
Feb. 2	LSU	A	53	74
Feb. 8	Auburn	A	85	67
Feb. 12	Alabama	H	107	83
Feb. 15	Western Kentucky	H	93	83
Feb. 19	Mississippi State	A	89	84
Feb. 23	Georgia	A	84	73
Feb. 26	South Carolina	H	74	56
Mar. 1	Vanderbilt	H	80	56
Mar. 4	Florida	A	62	79
Mar. 7	Tennessee	H	99	88

SEC Tournament
(Birmingham, Ala.)

Mar. 13	Vanderbilt		76	57
Mar. 14	LSU		80	74
Mar. 15	Alabama		80	54

NCAA East Regional
First/Second Rounds
(Worcester, Mass.)

Mar. 20	Old Dominion		88	69
Mar. 22	Iowa State		106	98

NCAA East Regional
(Philadelphia, Pa.)

Mar. 26	Massachusetts		87	77
Mar. 28	Duke		103	*104
			3086	2680

(N1) Indianapolis, Ind. (N2) Louisville
(N3) Cincinnati, Ohio

— Leading Scorers —
Jamal Mashburn (6-8 So. F).......................21.3
John Pelphrey (6-7 Sr. F)............................12.5
Deron Feldhaus (6-7 Sr. F)..........................11.4
Richie Farmer (6-0 Sr. G).............................9.6
Sean Woods (6-2 Sr. G)................................7.7

1992-93 — Won 30, Lost 4

NCAA "Final 4"
SEC Tournament Champions
2nd SEC East (13-3)
ECAC Holiday Festival Champions
Ranked 6th AP, 3rd CNN/USA Today

Coach: Rick Pitino
Captains: Junior Braddy, Dale Brown

Dec. 2	Wright State	H	81	65
Dec. 5	Georgia Tech	H	96	87
Dec. 8	Eastern Kentucky	H	82	73
Dec. 12	Louisville	A	88	68
Dec. 19	Morehead State	H	108	65
Dec. 22	Miami (Ohio)	H	65	49

ECAC Holiday Festival

Dec. 28	Rutgers	N1	89	67
Dec. 30	St. John's (finals)	N1	86	77
Jan. 3	Indiana	N2	81	78
Jan. 5	Georgia	A	74	59
Jan. 9	Tennessee	H	84	70
Jan. 13	Vanderbilt	A	86	101
Jan. 19	Alabama	A	73	59
Jan. 23	South Carolina	A	108	82
Jan. 26	LSU	H	105	67
Jan. 30	Florida	H	71	48
Feb. 3	Mississippi State	H	87	63
Feb. 6	Vanderbilt	H	82	67
Feb. 10	Arkansas	A	94	101
Feb. 13	Notre Dame	A	81	62
Feb. 17	South Carolina	H	87	66
Feb. 20	Georgia	H	86	70
Feb. 24	Tennessee	A	77	78
Feb. 27	Auburn	H	80	78
Mar. 3	Mississippi	A	98	66
Mar. 9	Florida	A	85	77

SEC Tournament (Lexington, Ky.)

Mar. 12	Tennessee		101	40
Mar. 13	Arkansas		92	81
Mar. 14	LSU		82	65

NCAA Southeast Regional
First/Second Rounds
(Nashville, Tenn.)

Mar. 19	Rider College		96	52
Mar. 21	Utah		83	62

NCAA Southeast Regional
(Charlotte, N.C.)

Mar. 25	Wake Forest		103	69
Mar. 27	Florida State		106	81

NCAA Final Four
(New Orleans, La.)

April 3	Michigan		78	*81
			2975	2374

(N1) New York (N2) Louisville
— Leading Scorers —
Jamal Mashburn (6-8 Jr. F)........................21.0
Travis Ford (5-9 Jr. G)................................13.6
Dale Brown (6-2 Sr. G).................................9.4
Rodrick Rhodes (6-6 Fr. F)..........................9.1
Rodney Dent (6-10 Jr. C).............................6.4

1993-94 — Won 27, Lost 7

SEC Tournament Champions
Tied for 1st SEC East (12-4)
Maui Invitational Champions
Ranked 7th AP, 8th CNN/USA Today

Coach: Rick Pitino
Captains: Travis Ford, Gimel Martinez, Jeff Brassow

Nov. 27	Louisville	H	78	70
Dec. 1	Tennessee Tech	H	115	77
Dec. 4	Indiana	N1	84	96
Dec. 8	Eastern Kentucky	H	107	78
Dec. 17	Morehead State	H	97	61

Maui Invitational

Dec. 21	Texas	N2	86	61
Dec. 22	Ohio State	N2	100	88
Dec. 23	Arizona (finals)	N2	93	92
Dec. 28	San Francisco	N2	110	83
Dec. 30	Robert Morris	H	92	67
Jan. 4	Vanderbilt	H	107	82
Jan. 6	Notre Dame	H	84	59
Jan. 8	Georgia	A	90	*94
Jan. 12	Mississippi	N3	98	64
Jan. 15	Tennessee	H	93	74
Jan. 18	Florida	A	57	59
Jan. 22	Mississippi State	A	86	70

Bill Keightley welcomes ex-Cat Jamal Mashburn back to Rupp Arena. Mashburn is the most-important Wildcat in the post-probation era.

Jan. 26	South Carolina	H	79	67
Jan. 30	Auburn	A	91	74
Feb. 2	Alabama	H	82	67
Feb. 6	Massachusetts	N4	67	64
Feb. 9	Arkansas	H	82	90
Feb. 12	Syracuse	A	85	93
Feb. 15	LSU	A	99	95
Feb. 19	Vanderbilt	A	77	69
Feb. 23	Tennessee	A	77	73
Feb. 27	Georgia	H	80	59
Mar. 2	Florida	H	80	77
Mar. 5	South Carolina	A	74	75

SEC Tournament
(Memphis, Tenn.)

Mar. 11	Mississippi State		95	76
Mar. 12	Arkansas		90	78
Mar. 13	Florida		73	60

NCAA Southeast Regional
First/Second Rounds
(St. Petersburg, Fla)

Mar. 18	Tennessee State		83	70
Mar. 20	Marquette		63	75
			2954	2537

(N1) Indianapolis, Ind. (N3) Louisville, Ky.
(N2) Maui, Hi. (N4) East Rutherford, N.J.
— Leading Scorers —
Tony Delk (6-1 So. G) 16.6
Rodrick Rhodes (6-7 So., F) 14.6
Travis Ford (5-9 Sr. G) 11.3
Jared Prickett (6-9 So. F) 8.2
Andre Riddick (6-9 Jr. C) 7.9

1994-95 — Won 28, Lost 5

SEC Champions (14-2)
SEC East Champions
SEC Tournament Champions
Ranked 2nd AP, 5th CNN/USA Today
Coach: Rick Pitino
Captains: Tony Delk, Mark Pope, Rodrick Rhodes

Nov. 26	Tennessee-Martin	H	124	50
Nov. 30	Ohio	H	79	74
Dec. 3	UCLA	N1	81	82
Dec. 7	Indiana	N2	73	70
Dec. 10	Boston University	H	90	49
Dec. 17	Texas Tech	N3	83	68
Dec. 27	Marshall	H	116	75
Jan. 1	Louisville	A	86	88
Jan. 4	Auburn	H	98	64
Jan. 7	South Carolina	A	80	55
Jan. 10	Florida	A	83	67
Jan. 14	Georgia	H	83	71
Jan. 18	Mississippi	N4	82	65
Jan. 21	Vanderbilt	H	81	68
Jan. 25	Tennessee	H	69	50
Jan. 29	Arkansas	A	92	94
Feb. 1	South Carolina	H	90	72
Feb. 5	Syracuse	H	77	71
Feb. 8	Tennessee	A	68	48
Feb. 12	Notre Dame	A	97	58
Feb. 14	Mississippi State	H	71	76
Feb. 18	Florida	H	87	77
Feb. 21	Alabama	A	72	52
Feb. 25	Vanderbilt	A	71	60
Mar. 1	Georgia	A	97	74
Mar. 4	LSU	H	127	80

SEC Tournament
(Atlanta, Ga.)

Mar. 10	Auburn		93	81
Mar. 11	Florida		86	72
Mar. 12	Arkansas (finals)		95	*93

NCAA Southeast Regional
First/Second Rounds
(Memphis, Tenn.)

Mar. 16	Mount St. Mary's		113	67
Mar. 18	Tulane		82	60

NCAA Southeast Regional
(Birmingham, Ala.)

Mar. 23	Arizona State		97	73
Mar. 25	North Carolina		61	74
			2884	2278

(N1) Anaheim, Calif.
(N2) Louisville
(N3) Cincinnati (N4) Memphis, Tenn.
— Leading Scorers —
Tony Delk (6-1 Jr. G) 16.7
Rodrick Rhodes (6-7 Jr., F) 12.9
Walter McCarty (6-9 Jr. F) 10.5
Jeff Sheppard (6-4 So. G) 8.3
Mark Pope (6-10 Jr. C) 8.2

1995 ITALY TOUR
(Not counted in Won-Loss Record)

Aug. 14	Cagiva Varese	A	123	114
Aug. 16	Venice Reyer	A	113	78
Aug. 17	Russia Dinamo	N5	116	81
Aug. 18	Montecatini	A	115	123
Aug. 21	Siena	N6	115	86

(N5) Venice, Italy (N6) Scauri, Italy

1995-96 — Won 34, Lost 2

National Champions (NCAA Tournament)
SEC Champions (16-0)#
SEC East Champions
ECAC Holiday Festival Champions
Ranked 1st CNN/USA Today, 2nd AP
Coach: Rick Pitino
Captains: Tony Delk, Walter McCarty, Mark Pope

Nov. 24	Maryland	N1	96	84
Nov. 28	Massachusetts	N2	82	92
Dec. 2	Indiana	N3	89	82
Dec. 6	Wisconsin-Green Bay	H	74	62
Dec. 9	Georgia Tech	H	83	60
Dec. 16	Morehead State	H	96	32
Dec. 19	Marshall	N4	118	99
Dec. 23	Louisville	H	89	66

ECAC Holiday Festival

Dec. 27	Rider	N5	90	65
Dec. 29	Iona (finals)	N5	106	79
Jan. 3	South Carolina	A	89	60
Jan. 6	Ole Miss	H	90	60
Jan. 9	Mississippi State	A	74	56
Jan. 13	Tennessee	H	61	44
Jan. 16	LSU	A	129	97
Jan. 20	Texas Christian	H	124	80
Jan. 24	Georgia	A	82	77
Jan. 27	South Carolina	H	89	57
Feb. 3	Florida	H	77	63
Feb. 7	Vanderbilt	A	120	81
Feb. 11	Arkansas	H	88	73
Feb. 14	Georgia	H	86	73
Feb. 17	Tennessee	A	90	50
Feb. 20	Alabama	H	84	65
Feb. 24	Florida	A	94	63
Feb. 27	Auburn	A	88	73
Mar. 2	Vanderbilt	H	101	63

SEC Tournament
(New Orleans, La.)

Mar. 8	Florida		100	76
Mar. 9	Arkansas		95	75
Mar. 10	Miss. State (finals)		73	84

NCAA Midwest Regional
First/Second Rounds
(Dallas, Texas)

Mar. 14	San Jose State		110	72
Mar. 16	Virginia Tech		84	60

NCAA Midwest Regional
(Minneapolis, Minn.)

Mar. 21	Utah		101	70
Mar. 23	Wake Forest		83	63

NCAA Final Four
(East Rutherford, N.J.)

Mar. 30	Massachusetts		81	74
Apr. 1	Syracuse (finals)		76	67
			3292	2497

NCAA CHAMPIONS FOR SIXTH TIME
(N1) Springfield, Mass. (N4) Louisville
(N2) Auburn Hills, Mich. (N5) New York
(N3) Indianapolis

UK's 16-0 regular season SEC record was the first perfect league slate since Alabama went 14-0 in 1956.
— Leading Scorers —
Tony Delk (6-1 Sr. G) 17.8
Antoine Walker (6-8 So. F) 15.2
Walter McCarty (6-10 Sr. F) 11.3
Derek Anderson (6-4 Jr. G-F) 9.4
Ron Mercer (6-7 Fr. F) 8.0

1996-97 — Won 35, Lost 5

NCAA Runner-up (NCAA Tournament)
SEC Tournament Champions
2nd SEC East (13-3)
Great Alaska Shootout Champions
Ranked 2nd CNN/USA Today, 5th AP
Coach: Rick Pitino
Captains: Derek Anderson, Anthony Epps, Jared Prickett

Nov. 15	Clemson	N1	71	*79

Great Alaska Shootout

Nov. 28	Syracuse	N2	87	53
Nov. 29	Alaska Anchorage	N2	104	72
Nov. 30	Coll. of Charleston (finals)	N2	92	65
Dec. 3	Purdue	N3	101	87
Dec. 7	Indiana	N4	99	65
Dec. 9	Wright State	H	90	62
Dec. 14	Notre Dame	H	80	56
Dec. 21	Georgia Tech	N5	88	59
Dec. 23	UNC Asheville	H	105	51
Dec. 28	Ohio State	N6	81	65
Dec. 31	Louisville	A	74	54
Jan. 4	Tennessee	H	74	40
Jan. 7	Mississippi State	H	90	61
Jan. 9	Canisius	H	68	45
Jan. 11	Ole Miss	A	69	73
Jan. 14	Georgia	A	86	65
Jan. 18	Auburn	H	77	53

Jan. 22	Vanderbilt	N7	58	46
Jan. 26	Arkansas	A	83	73
Jan. 29	Florida	A	92	65
Feb. 1	Georgia	H	82	57
Feb. 4	South Carolina	A	79	*84
Feb. 6	Western Carolina	H	82	55
Feb. 9	Villanova	H	93	56
Feb. 12	LSU	H	84	48
Feb. 15	Florida	H	85	56
Feb. 19	Alabama	A	75	61
Feb. 22	Vanderbilt	A	82	59
Feb. 25	Tennessee	A	74	64
Mar. 2	South Carolina	H	66	72

SEC Tournament
(Memphis, Tenn.)

Mar. 7	Auburn		92	50
Mar. 8	Ole Miss		88	70
Mar. 9	Georgia (finals)		95	68

NCAA West Regional
First/Second Round
(Salt Lake City, Utah)

Mar. 13	Montana		92	54
Mar. 15	Iowa		75	69

NCAA West Regional
(San Jose, Calif.)

Mar. 20	St. Joseph's		83	68
Mar. 22	Utah		72	59

NCAA Final Four
(Indianapolis, Ind.)

Mar. 29	Minnesota		78	69
Mar. 31	Arizona (finals)		79	*84
			3325	2512

(N1) Indianapolis (N6) Cleveland, Ohio
(N2) Anchorage, Alaska (N7) Cincinnati, Ohio
(N3) Chicago, Ill.
(N4) Louisville
(N5) Atlanta, Ga.

— Leading Scorers —
Ron Mercer (6-7 So. G-F) 18.1
Derek Anderson (6-5 Sr. G) 17.7
Scott Padgett (6-9 So. F) 9.6
Anthony Epps (6-2 Sr. G) 8.9
Allen Edwards (6-5 Jr. F) 8.6

ORLANDO "TUBBY" SMITH ERA

1997-98 — Won 35, Lost 4

National Champions (NCAA Tournament)
SEC Champions (14-2)
SEC East Champions
SEC Tournament Champions
Ranked 5th AP, 1st USA Today/ESPN
Coach: Tubby Smith
Captains: Allen Edwards, Cameron Mills, Jeff Sheppard

Nov. 20	Morehead State	H	88	49

Maui Invitational

Nov. 24	George Washington	N1	70	55
Nov. 25	Arizona	N1	74	89
Nov. 26	Missouri (Third Place)	N1	77	55
Nov. 29	Clemson	N2	76	61
Dec. 3	Purdue	N3	89	75
Dec. 6	Indiana	N4	75	72
Dec. 10	Canisius	A	81	54
Dec. 13	Georgia Tech	H	85	71
Dec. 20	Tulsa	H	74	53
Dec. 23	American	H	75	52
Dec. 27	Louisville	H	76	79
Dec. 30	Ohio	A	95	58
Jan. 3	Vanderbilt	H	71	62
Jan. 6	Georgia	A	90	79
Jan. 10	Mississippi State	A	77	71
Jan. 13	South Carolina	H	91	70
Jan. 17	Arkansas	H	80	*77

Tubby Smith led UK to the 1998 NCAA title, then helped guide the U.S. team to Olympic gold in 2000.

Jan. 21	Alabama	N5	70	67
Jan. 24	Tennessee	A	85	67
Jan. 27	Vanderbilt	A	63	61
Feb. 1	Florida	H	78	86
Feb. 4	LSU	A	63	61
Feb. 8	Villanova	A	79	63
Feb. 11	Tennessee	H	80	74
Feb. 14	Ole Miss	H	64	73
Feb. 18	Florida	A	79	54
Feb. 22	Georgia	H	85	74
Feb. 25	Auburn	A	83	58
Feb. 28	South Carolina	A	69	57

SEC Tournament
(Atlanta, Ga.)

Mar. 6	Alabama		82	71
Mar. 7	Arkansas		99	74
Mar. 8	South Carolina (finals)		86	56

NCAA South Regional
First/Second Rounds
(Atlanta, Ga.)

Mar. 13	South Carolina State		82	67
Mar. 15	Saint Louis		88	61

NCAA South Regional
(St. Petersburg, Fla.)

Mar. 20	UCLA		94	68
Mar. 22	Duke		86	84

NCAA Final Four
(San Antonio, Texas)

Mar. 28	Stanford		86	*85
Mar. 30	Utah (finals)		78	69
			3123	2612

NCAA CHAMPIONS
FOR SEVENTH TIME

(N1) Maui, Hi.	(N4) Indianapolis
(N2) Phoenix, Ariz.	(N5) Louisville
(N3) Chicago, Ill.	

— Leading Scorers —
Jeff Sheppard (6-3 Sr. G) 13.7
Nazr Mohammed (6-10 Jr. C) 12.0
Scott Padgett (6-9 Jr. F) 11.5
Wayne Turner (6-2 Jr. G) 9.3
Allen Edwards (6-5 Sr. F) 9.2

1998-99 — Won 28, Lost 9

SEC Tournament Champions
2nd SEC East (11-5)
Ranked 8th AP/t5th USA Today/ESPN
Coach: Tubby Smith
Captains: Heshimu Evans, Scott Padgett, Wayne Turner

Nov. 17	Eastern Kentucky	H	99	64
Nov. 19	Mercer	H	82	51
Nov. 23	Wright State	N1	97	75

Puerto Rico Shootout

Nov. 26	Colorado	N2	64	52
Nov. 27	Pittsburgh	N2	56	69
Nov. 28	UCLA	N2	66	62
Dec. 1	Kansas	N3	63	45
Dec. 5	Miami (Fla.)	H	74	65
Dec. 8	Indiana	N4	70	*61
Dec. 12	Maryland	H	103	91
Dec. 19	Georgia Tech	N5	80	39
Dec. 22	Duke	N6	60	71
Dec. 26	Louisville	A	74	83
Dec. 29	Tennessee State	H	97	47
Jan. 2	Florida	H	93	58
Jan. 5	South Carolina	A	68	61
Jan. 9	Vanderbilt	A	73	57
Jan. 12	Tennessee	H	46	47
Jan. 16	Ole Miss	A	63	57
Jan. 20	Auburn	H	72	62
Jan. 23	Mississippi State	H	76	49
Jan. 26	Georgia	A	91	*83
Jan. 30	LSU	H	86	62
Feb. 4	Florida	A	68	75
Feb. 6	Alabama	A	58	62
Feb. 13	South Carolina	H	74	40
Feb. 17	Georgia	H	92	71
Feb. 20	Arkansas	A	70	74
Feb. 24	Vanderbilt	H	88	63
Feb. 28	Tennessee	A	61	68

SEC Tournament
(Atlanta, Ga.)

Mar. 5	Ole Miss		83	73
Mar. 6	Auburn		69	57
Mar. 7	Arkansas (finals)		76	63

NCAA Midwest Regional
First/Second Rounds
(New Orleans, La.)

Mar. 12	New Mexico State		82	60
Mar. 14	Kansas		92	*88

NCAA Midwest Regional
(St. Louis, Mo.)

Mar. 19	Miami (Ohio)		58	43
Mar. 21	Michigan State		66	73
			2790	2320

(N1) Cincinnati, Ohio	(N2) Bayamone, Puerto Rico
(N3) Chicago, Ill.	(N4) Louisville, Ky.

Tayshaun Prince worked plenty of magic as a Wildcat, finishing as the school's
eighth all-time leading scorer with 1,775 points.

(N5) Atlanta, Ga.	(N6) East Rutherford, N.J.

— Leading Scorers —
Scott Padgett (6-9 Sr. F) 12.6
Heshimu Evans (6-6 Sr. F) 11.8
Wayne Turner (6-2 Sr. G) 10.5
Michael Bradley (6-10 So. C) 9.8
Jamaal Magloire (6-10 Jr. C)..7.0

1999-00 — Won 23, Lost 10

Tied for 1st SEC East (12-4)
Preseason NIT Runner-Up
Ranked 19th AP, 20th USA Today/ESPN
Coach Tubby Smith
Captains: Jamaal Magloire, Steve Masiello

Preseason NIT

Nov. 17	Pennsylvania	H	67	50
Nov. 19	Utah	H	56	48
Nov. 24	Maryland	N1	61	58
Nov. 26	Arizona(final)	N1	51	63
Nov. 29	Dayton	N2	66	68
Dec. 4	Indiana	N3	75	83
Dec. 7	UNC-Asheville	H	86	41
Dec. 11	Maryland	A	66	72
Dec. 18	Louisville	H	76	46
Dec. 23	Michigan State	A	60	58
Dec. 27	Alaska-Anchorage	H	62	42
Dec. 30	Missouri	N4	70	53
Jan. 5	Georgia Tech	N5	80	71
Jan. 8	Vanderbilt	H	72	52
Jan. 11	Auburn	A	63	66
Jan. 15	South Carolina	A	64	48
Jan. 19	Ole Miss	H	74	69
Jan. 22	Vanderbilt	A	81	*73
Jan. 26	Georgia	A	75	69
Jan. 29	Miami(Fla.)	A	60	57
Feb. 1	Tennessee	H	81	68
Feb. 5	South Carolina	H	76	63
Feb. 8	Florida	A	73	90
Feb. 13	LSU	A	57	70
Feb. 16	Alabama	H	66	54
Feb. 19	Georgia	H	70	64
Feb. 23	Tennessee	A	67	74
Feb. 26	Arkansas	H	60	55
Feb. 29	Mississippi State	A	73	61
Mar. 4	Florida	H	85	70

SEC Tournament
(Atlanta, Ga.)

Mar. 10	Arkansas		72	86

NCAA Midwest Regional
First/Second Rounds
(Cleveland, Ohio)

Mar. 16	St. Bonaventure		85	**80
Mar. 18	Syracuse		50	52
			2280	2074

(N1) New York
(N2) Cincinnati
(N3) Indianapolis
(N4) New Orleans
(N5) Louisville

— Leading Scorers —
Tayshaun Prince (6-9 So. F) 13.3
Jamaal Magloire 6-10 Sr. C) 13.2
Keith Bogans (6-5 Fr. G) 12.5
Desmond Allison (6-5 So F) 7.8
Jules Camara (6-11 So. F) 7.2

2000-01 — Won 24, Lost 10

Tied for 1st SEC East (12-4)
Ranked 9th AP, 8th USA Today/ESPN
Coach Tubby Smith
Captain: Saul Smith

Coaches vs. Cancer

Nov. 9	St. John's	N1	61	62
Nov. 10	UCLA	N1	92	*97
Nov. 21	Jacksonville State	N2	91	48
Nov. 25	Penn State	H	68	73
Dec. 2	North Carolina	A	93	76
Dec. 5	Eastern Kentucky	H	94	79
Dec. 9	Georgia Tech	H	84	86
Dec. 16	Michigan State	A	45	46
Dec. 22	Indiana	N3	88	74
Dec. 27	High Point	H	102	49
Jan. 2	Louisville	A	64	62
Jan. 6	Georgia	H	67	63
Jan. 10	South Carolina	H	69	63
Jan. 13	Notre Dame	H	82	71
Jan. 16	Tennessee	H	84	74
Jan. 20	Ole Miss	A	55	65

All-Time Results – 1903-2016

Keith Bogans is the fourth all-time leading scorer in UK history.

Jan. 23	Alabama	A	60	70
Jan. 27	Vanderbilt	H	86	75
Jan. 31	Georgia	H	85	70
Feb. 3	South Carolina	A	94	61
Feb. 6	Florida	H	71	70
Feb. 10	Mississippi State	H	76	57
Feb. 14	Tennessee	A	103	95
Feb. 17	Vanderbilt	A	79	74
Feb. 21	LSU	H	84	61
Feb. 25	Arkansas	A	78	82
Feb. 28	Auburn	H	90	78
Mar. 4	Florida	A	86	94

SEC Tournament
(Nashville, Tenn.)

Mar. 9	South Carolina	78	65
Mar. 10	Arkansas	87	78
Mar. 11	Ole Miss	77	55

NCAA East Regional First/Second Rounds
(Uniondale, N.Y.)

Mar. 15	Holy Cross	72	68
Mar. 17	Iowa	92	79

NCAA East Regional
(Philadelphia, Pa.)

Mar. 22	Southern Cal	76	80
		2713	2400

(N1) New York   (N2) Cincinnati   (N3) Louisville

— Leading Scorers —

Keith Bogans (6-5 So. G) 17.0
Tayshaun Prince (6-9 Jr.F) 16.9
Jason Parker (6-8 Fr. C) 8.6
Marquis Estill (6-10 So. C) 7.3
Saul Smith (6-2 Sr. G) 6.8
Gerald Fitch (6-3 Fr, G) 6.8

2001-02 — Won 22, Lost 10

Tied for 1st SEC East (10-6)
Ranked 16th AP, 13th USA Today/ESPN
Coach Tubby Smith
Captains: Tayshaun Prince, J.P. Blevins

NABC Classic

Nov. 15	Western Kentucky	H	52	64
Nov. 15	Marshall	H	90	73
Nov. 24	Morehead State	H	94	75
Nov. 28	Kent State	N1	82	68
Dec. 5	VMI	H	99	57
Dec. 8	North Carolina	H	79	59
Dec. 15	Kentucky State	H	118	63
Dec. 18	Duke	N2	*92	95
Dec. 22	Indiana	N3	66	52
Dec. 29	Louisville	H	82	62
Jan. 2	Tulane	N4	101	67
Jan. 5	Mississippi State	A	*69	74
Jan. 9	Georgia	H	84	88
Jan. 12	South Carolina	A	51	50
Jan. 15	Ole Miss	H	87	64

Jan. 19	Notre Dame	A	72	65
Jan. 22	Auburn	A	69	62
Jan. 26	Alabama	H	61	64
Jan. 29	Florida	A	70	68
Feb. 2	South Carolina	H	91	74
Feb. 6	Tennessee	A	*74	76
Feb. 9	LSU	A	68	56
Feb. 13	Vanderbilt	H	67	59
Feb. 16	Georgia	A	69	78
Feb. 19	Tennessee	H	64	61
Feb. 23	Arkansas	H	71	58
Feb. 27	Vanderbilt	A	73	86
Mar. 2	Florida	H	70	67

SEC Tournament
(Atlanta, Ga.)

Mar. 8	South Carolina	57	70

NCAA East Regional First/Second Rounds
(St. Louis, Mo.)

Mar. 14	Valparaiso	83	68
Mar. 16	Tulsa	87	82

NCAA East Regional
(Syracuse, N.Y.)

Mar. 22	Maryland	68	78
		2460	2183

(N1) Cincinnati   (N3) Indianapolis
(N2) East Rutherford N.J.(N4) Louisville

— Leading Scorers —

Tayshaun Prince (6-9 Sr. F) 17.5
Keith Bogans (6-5 Jr. G) 11.6
Marquis Estill (6-9 Jr. F) 8.9
Gerald Fitch (6-3 So. G) 8.9
Cliff Hawkins (6-1 So. G) 7.1

2002-2003 — Won 32, Lost 4

SEC Eastern Division Champ (16-0)
SEC Champions
SEC Tournament Champion
Ranked 1st AP, 4th ESPN/USA Today
Coach: Tubby Smith

Maui Invitational

Nov. 25	Arizona State	N	82	65
Nov. 26	Virginia	N	61	75
Nov. 27	Gonzaga	N	80	72
Dec. 3	High Point	H	84	64
Dec. 7	North Carolina	A	98	81
Dec. 10	Tulane	N	76	60
Dec. 14	Michigan State	H	67	71
Dec. 21	Indiana	N	70	64
Dec. 28	Louisville	A	63	81
Dec. 30	Tennessee State	H	115	87
Jan. 2	Alcorn State	H	94	63
Jan. 4	Ohio	N	83	75
Jan. 8	Tennessee	A	74	71
Jan. 11	South Carolina	H	62	55
Jan. 14	Vanderbilt	A	74	52
Jan. 18	Notre Dame	H	88	73
Jan. 22	Auburn	H	67	51
Jan. 25	Alabama	H	63	46
Feb. 1	South Carolina	A	87	69
Feb. 4	Florida	H	70	55
Feb. 8	Ole Miss	A	80	62
Feb. 11	Georgia	H	87	67
Feb. 15	LSU	H	68	57
Feb. 19	Arkansas	A	66	50
Feb. 23	Miss. State	H	70	62
Feb. 26	Tennessee	H	80	68
Mar. 2	Georgia	A	74	66
Mar. 5	Vanderbilt	H	106	44
Mar. 8	Florida	A	69	67

SEC Tournament
(New Orleans)

Mar. 14	Vanderbilt	N	81	63
Mar. 15	Auburn	N	78	58
Mar. 16	Miss. State	N	64	57

NCAA Tournament First/Second Rounds
(Nashville)

Mar. 21	IUPUI	N	95	64
Mar. 23	Utah	N	74	54

NCAA Regional
(Minneapolis)

Mar. 27	Wisconsin	N	63	57
Mar. 29	Marquette	N	69	83
			2782	2329

—Leading Scorers—

Keith Bogans (6-5, Sr. G) 15.7
Gerald Fitch (6-3, Jr. G) 12.3
Marquis Estill (6-9, Sr. F) 11.6
Erik Daniels (6-8, Jr. F) 9.5

2003-04 — Won 27, Lost 5

SEC East Champion (13-3)
SEC Tournament Champion
Ranked 2nd AP, 8th ESPN/USA Today
Coach: Tubby Smith

Nov. 21	Winthrop	H	65	44
Nov. 28	Tennessee Tech	H	108	81
Dec. 1	Marshall	N	89	76
Dec. 6	UCLA	N	52	50
Dec. 13	Michigan State	N	79	74
Dec. 20	Indiana	N	80	41
Dec. 23	EKU	H	101	72
Dec. 27	Louisville	H	56	65
Dec. 31	Austin Peay	N	61	53
Jan. 3	North Carolina	H	61	56
Jan. 10	Vanderbilt	H	75	63
Jan. 13	Miss. State	A	67	66
Jan. 17	Georgia	H	57	65
Jan. 20	Tennessee	A	69	*68
Jan. 25	Notre Dame	A	71	63
Jan. 28	Ole Miss	H	71	61
Jan. 31	Vanderbilt	A	60	66
Feb. 3	Florida	A	68	65
Feb. 7	South Carolina	H	65	64
Feb. 10	Alabama	H	68	55
Feb. 14	Georgia	A	68	74
Feb. 18	Arkansas	H	73	56
Feb. 21	Auburn	A	68	59
Feb. 25	Tennessee	H	92	65
Feb. 29	LSU	A	70	64
Mar. 3	South Carolina	A	84	65
Mar. 7	Florida	H	82	62

SEC Tournament
(Atlanta)

Mar. 12	Georgia	N	69	60
Mar. 13	South Carolina	N	78	63
Mar. 14	Florida	N	89	73

NCAA Tournament First/Second Rounds
(Columbus, Ohio)

Mar. 19	Florida A&M	N	96	76
Mar. 21	UAB	N	75	76
			2367	2036

—Leading Scorers—

Gerald Fitch (6-3, Sr. G) 16.2
Erik Daniels (6-8, Sr. F) 14.5
Kelenna Azubuike (6-5, So. G) 11.1
Chuck Hayes (6-6, Jr. F) 10.7
Cliff Hawkins (6-1, Sr. G) 10.3

2004-05 – Won 28, Lost 6

SEC Champion (14-2)
SEC East Champ
Ranked 7th, 5th ESPN/USA Today
Coach: Tubby Smith

Nov. 20	Coppin State	H	77	46
Nov. 23	Ball State	N	73	53
Nov. 26	Georgia State	H	77	59
Nov. 30	Tennessee Tech	H	92	63
Dec. 4	North Carolina	A	78	91
Dec. 8	Morehead St.	H	71	40
Dec. 11	Indiana	N	73	58
Dec. 18	Louisville	A	60	58
Dec. 22	William & Mary	H	92	47
Dec. 29	Campbell	H	82	50
Jan. 5	South Carolina	H	79	75
Jan. 9	Kansas	H	59	65
Jan. 12	Vanderbilt	H	69	54
Jan. 15	Georgia	A	76	55
Jan. 19	Ole Miss	A	53	50
Jan. 22	LSU	H	89	58
Jan. 25	Tennessee	A	84	62
Jan. 29	Arkansas	A	68	67
Feb. 5	Vanderbilt	A	84	70
Feb. 8	Florida	H	69	66
Feb. 12	Georgia	H	60	51
Feb. 15	South Carolina	A	61	73
Feb. 19	Miss. State	H	94	78
Feb. 23	Auburn	H	81	73
Feb. 26	Alabama	A	78	71
Mar. 2	Tennessee	H	73	61
Mar. 6	Florida	A	52	53

SEC Tournament (Atlanta)

Mar. 11	Tennessee	N	86	62
Mar. 12	LSU	N	79	*78
Mar. 13	Florida	N	53	70

NCAA Tournament First/Second Rounds
(Indianapolis)

Mar. 17	EKU	N	72	64
Mar. 19	Cincinnati	N	69	60

NCAA Regional
(Austin, Texas)

Mar. 25	Utah	N	62	52
Mar. 27	Michigan St.	N	88	**94
			2513	2127

—Leading Scorers—

Kelenna Azubuike (6-5, Jr. F) 14.7
Patrick Sparks (6-0, Jr. G) 11.0
Chuck Hayes (6-6, Sr. F) 10.9
Randolph Morris (6-10, F, C) 8.8
Rajon Rondo (6-1, Fr. G) 8.1

2005-06 – Won 22, Lost 13

Coach: Tubby Smith

Nov. 13	S. Dakota St.	H	71	54
Nov. 14	Lipscomb	H	67	49
Nov. 21	Iowa	N	63	67
Nov. 22	West Virginia	N	80	66
Nov. 25	Liberty	H	81	51
Nov. 29	High Point	H	75	55
Dec. 3	North Carolina	H	79	83
Dec. 6	Georgia State	N	73	46
Dec. 10	Indiana	N	53	79
Dec. 17	Louisville	H	73	61
Dec. 23	Iona	N	73	67
Dec. 30	Ohio	N	71	63
Jan. 3	UCF	H	59	57
Jan. 7	Kansas	A	46	73
Jan. 10	Vanderbilt	H	51	57
Jan. 14	Alabama	H	64	68
Jan. 17	Georgia	A	69	55
Jan. 21	South Carolina	H	80	78
Jan. 24	Auburn	A	71	62
Jan. 29	Arkansas	H	78	76
Feb. 1	Miss. State	A	81	66
Feb. 4	Florida	A	80	95
Feb. 7	Tennessee	H	67	75
Feb. 11	Vanderbilt	A	81	84
Feb. 15	Georgia	H	68	61
Feb. 18	South Carolina	A	79	66
Feb. 22	Ole Miss	H	80	40
Feb. 25	LSU	A	67	71
Mar. 1	Tennessee	A	80	78
Mar. 5	Florida	H	64	79
	SEC Tournament (Nashville)			
Mar. 9	Ole Miss	N	71	57
Mar. 10	Alabama	N	68	61
Mar. 11	South Carolina	N	61	65
	NCAA Tournament First/Second Rounds (Philadelphia)			
Mar. 17	UAB	N	69	64
Mar. 19	UConn	N	83	87
			2476	2190

—Leading Scorers—
Randolph Morris (6-10, So. C)13.3
Rajon Rondo (6-1, So. G)....11.2
Joe Crawford (6-4, So. G)....10.2
Patrick Sparks (6-0, Sr. G)....9.7
Ramel Bradley (6-1, So. G)....7.9

2006-07 – Won 22, Lost 12

Coach: Tubby Smith

Nov.15	Miami	H	57	46
Nov. 17	Miss, Valley St.	H	79	56
	Maui Invitational			
Nov. 20	DePaul	N	87	81
Nov. 21	UCLA	N	68	73
Nov. 22	Memphis	N	63	80
Nov. 28	College of Charleston	H	77	61
Dec. 2	North Carolina	A	63	75
Dec. 5	Chattanooga	N	79	63
Dec. 9	Indiana	H	59	54
Dec. 16	Louisville	A	61	49
Dec. 19	Santa Clara	H	74	60
Dec. 22	UMass	H	82	68
Dec. 29	EKU	H	78	65
Jan. 3	Houston	H	77	70
Jan. 6	Ole Miss	A	68	58
Jan. 10	Auburn	H	84	57
Jan. 13	Miss. State	H	64	60
Jan. 16	South Carolina	A	87	49
Jan. 20	Vanderbilt	H	67	72
Jan. 24	Georgia	A	69	78
Jan. 28	Tennessee	H	76	57
Feb. 3	Arkansas	A	82	74
Feb. 7	South Carolina	H	95	89
Feb. 10	Florida	H	61	64
Feb. 13	Tennessee	A	85	89
Feb. 17	Alabama	A	61	72
Feb. 20	LSU	H	70	63
Feb. 25	Vanderbilt	A	65	67
Feb. 28	Georgia	H	82	70
Mar. 4	Florida	A	72	85
	SEC Tournament (Atlanta)			
Mar. 8	Alabama	N	79	67
Mar. 9	Miss. State	N	82	84
	NCAA Tournament First/Second Rounds (Chicago)			
Mar. 16	Villanova	N	67	58
Mar. 18	Kansas	N	76	88
			2496	2314

—Leading Scorers—
Randolph Morris (6-11, Jr. C)....16.1
Joe Crawford (6-5, Jr. G)....14.0
Ramel Bradley (6-2, Jr. G)....13.4
Jodie Meeks (6-5, Fr. G)....8.7
Bobby Perry (6-8, Sr. F)....8.4

BILLY GILLISPIE ERA

2007-08 – Won 18, Lost 13

Coach: Billy Gillispie

Nov. 6	Cent. Arkansas	H	67	40
Nov. 7	Gardner-Webb	H	68	84
Nov. 21	Liberty	H	80	54
Nov. 24	Texas Southern	H	83	35
Nov. 27	Stony Brook	H	62	52
Dec. 1	North Carolina	H	77	86
Dec. 8	Indiana	A	51	70
Dec. 15	UAB	N	76	79
Dec. 18	Houston	A	69	83
Dec. 22	Tenn. Tech	H	69	47
Dec. 29	San Diego	H	72	81
Dec. 31	Fla. International	H	92	49
Jan. 5	Louisville	H	75	89
Jan. 12	Vanderbilt	H	79	73
Jan. 15	Miss. State	A	64	69
Jan. 19	Florida	A	70	81
Jan. 22	Tennessee	H	72	66
Jan. 26	South Carolina	H	78	70
Feb. 2	Georgia	A	63	58
Feb. 6	Auburn	A	66	63
Feb. 9	Alabama	H	62	52
Feb. 12	Vanderbilt	A	52	93
Feb. 16	LSU	A	67	63
Feb. 19	Georgia	H	61	55
Feb. 23	Arkansas	H	63	58
Feb. 27	Ole Miss	H	58	54
Mar. 2	Tennessee	A	60	63
Mar. 5	South Carolina	A	71	63
Mar. 9	Florida	H	75	70
	SEC Tournament (Atlanta)			
Mar. 15	Georgia	N	56	60
	NCAA Tournament First/Second Rounds (Anaheim, Calif.)			
Mar. 20	Marquette	N	66	74
			2118	2038

—Leading Scorers—
Joe Crawford (6-5, Sr. G)....17.9
Patrick Patterson (6-8, F, C)....16.4
Ramel Bradley (6-2, Sr. G)....15.9
Jodie Meeks (6-5, So. G)....8.8

2008-09 – Won 22, Lost 14

Coach: Billy Gillispie

Nov. 14	VMI	H	103	111
Nov. 18	North Carolina	A	58	77
Nov. 22	Delaware St.	H	71	42
Nov. 24	Longwood	H	91	57
	Las Vegas Invitational			
Nov. 28	Kansas St.	N	74	72
Nov. 29	West Virginia	N	54	43
Dec. 3	Lamar	H	103	61
Dec. 6	Miami (Fla.)	H	67	73
Dec. 7	Miss. Valley St.	H	88	65
Dec. 13	Indiana	H	72	54
Dec. 20	Appalachian St.	N	93	69
Dec. 22	Tennessee St.	H	102	58
Dec. 27	Fla. Atlantic	H	76	69
Dec. 29	Central Michigan	H	84	52
Jan. 4	Louisville	A	71	74
Jan. 10	Vanderbilt	H	70	60
Jan. 13	Tennessee	A	90	72
Jan. 18	Georgia	A	68	45
Jan. 21	Auburn	H	73	64
Jan. 24	Alabama	A	61	51
Jan. 27	Ole Miss	A	80	85
Jan. 31	South Carolina	H	77	78
Feb. 3	Miss. State	H	57	66
Feb. 10	Florida	H	68	65
Feb. 14	Arkansas	A	79	63
Feb. 17	Vanderbilt	A	64	77
Feb. 21	Tennessee	H	77	58
Feb. 25	South Carolina	A	59	77
Feb. 28	LSU	H	70	73
Mar. 4	Georgia	H	85	90
Mar. 7	Florida	A	53	60
	SEC Tournament (Tampa, Fla.)			
Mar. 12	Ole Miss	N	71	58
Mar. 13	LSU	N	58	67
	National Invitational Tournament			
Mar. 17	UNLV	H	70	60
Mar. 23	Creighton	A	65	63
Mar. 25	Notre Dame	A	67	77
			2669	2390

—Leading Scorers—
Jodie Meeks (6-5, Jr. G)....23.7
Patrick Patterson (6-8, So. C)....17.9
Perry Stevenson (6-9, Jr., F)....7.8
Ramon Harris (6-7, Jr. F)....5.5

JOHN CALIPARI ERA

2009-10 – Won 35, Lost 3

SEC Champion
SEC Eastern Division Champ (14-2)
SEC Tournament Champion
Ranked 2nd AP, 2nd ESPN/USA Today

Coach: John Calipari

Nov. 13	Morehead St.	H	75	59
Nov. 16	Miami (Ohio)	H	72	70
	Cancun Challenge			
Nov. 19	Sam Houston St.	H	102	92
Nov. 21	Rider	H	92	63
Nov. 24	Cleveland St.	N	73	49
Nov. 25	Stanford	N	73	*65
Nov. 30	UNC Asheville	N	94	57
Dec. 5	North Carolina	H	68	66
Dec. 9	UConn	N	64	61
Dec. 12	Indiana	A	90	73
Dec. 19	Austin Peay	H	90	69
Dec. 21	Drexel	H	88	44
Dec. 23	Long Beach St.	H	86	73
Dec. 29	Hartford	H	104	61
Jan. 2	Louisville	H	71	62
Jan. 9	Georgia	H	76	68
Jan. 12	Florida	A	89	77
Jan. 16	Auburn	A	72	67
Jan. 23	Arkansas	H	101	70
Jan. 26	South Carolina	A	62	68
Jan. 30	Vanderbilt	H	85	72
Feb. 2	Ole Miss	H	85	75
Feb. 6	LSU	A	81	55
Feb. 9	Alabama	H	66	55
Feb. 13	Tennessee	H	73	62
Feb. 16	Miss. State	A	81	*75
Feb. 20	Vanderbilt	A	58	56
Feb. 25	South Carolina	H	82	61
Feb. 27	Tennessee	A	65	74
Mar. 3	Georgia	A	80	68
Mar. 7	Florida	H	74	66
	SEC Tournament (Nashville)			
Mar. 12	Alabama	N	73	67
Mar. 13	Tennessee	N	74	45
Mar. 14	Miss. State	N	75	*74
	NCAA Tournament First/Second Rounds (New Orleans)			
Mar. 18	E. Tenn. St.	N	100	71
Mar. 20	Wake Forest	N	90	60
	NCAA Regional (Syracuse, N.Y.)			
Mar. 25	Cornell	N	62	45
Mar. 27	West Virginia	N	66	73
			3012	2468

—Leading Scorers—
John Wall (6-4, Fr. G)....16.6
DeMarcus Cousins (6-11, Fr. C)....15.1
Patrick Patterson (6-8, Jr. F)....14.3
Eric Bledsoe (6-1, Fr. G)....11.3
Darius Miller (6-7, So. G)....6.5

2010-11 – Won 29, Lost 9

SEC Tournament Champion

Coach: John Calipari

Nov. 12	ETSU	H	88	65
Nov. 19	Portland	A	79	48
Nov. 22	Oklahoma	N	76	64
Nov. 23	Washington	N	74	67
Nov. 24	Connecticut	N	67	84
Nov. 30	Boston U	H	91	57
Dec. 4	North Carolina	A	73	75
Dec. 8	Notre Dame	N	72	58
Dec. 11	Indiana	H	81	62
Dec. 18	Miss. Valley St.	H	85	60
Dec. 22	Winthrop	H	89	52
Dec. 28	Coppin State	H	91	61
Dec. 31	Louisville	A	78	63
Jan. 3	Penn	H	86	62
Jan. 8	Georgia	A	70	77
Jan. 11	Auburn	H	78	54
Jan. 15	LSU	H	82	44
Jan. 18	Alabama	A	66	68
Jan. 22	South Carolina	A	67	58
Jan. 29	Georgia	H	66	60
Feb. 1	Ole Miss	A	69	71
Feb. 5	Florida	A	68	70
Feb. 8	Tennessee	H	73	61
Feb. 12	Vanderbilt	A	77	81
Feb. 15	Miss. State	H	85	79
Feb. 19	South Carolina	H	90	59
Feb. 23	Arkansas	A	76	*77
Feb. 26	Florida	H	76	68
Mar. 1	Vanderbilt	H	68	66
Mar. 6	Tennessee	A	64	58
	SEC Tournament (Atlanta, Ga.)			
Mar. 11	Ole Miss	N	75	66
Mar. 12	Alabama	N	72	58
Mar. 13	Florida	N	70	54
	NCAA East Regional First/Second Rounds (Tampa, Fla.)			
Mar. 17	Princeton	N	59	57
Mar. 19	West Virginia	N	71	63
	NCAA East Regional (Newark, N.J.)			
Mar. 25	Ohio State	N	62	60
Mar. 27	North Carolina	N	76	69
	NCAA Final Four (Houston, Texas)			
Apr. 2	Connecticut	N	55	56
			2845	2353

—Leading Scorers—
Brandon Knight (6-3, Fr. G)....17.3
Terrence Jones (6-8, Fr. F)....15.7
Doron Lamb (6-4, Fr. G)....12.3
Darius Miller (6-7, Jr. G)....10.9
DeAndre Liggins (6-6, Jr. F)....8.6

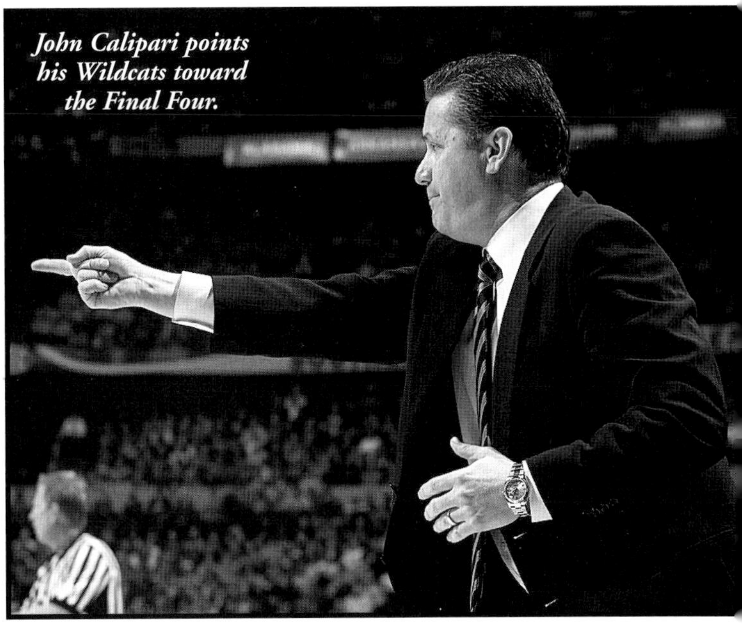

John Calipari points his Wildcats toward the Final Four.

All-Time Results – 1903-2016

UK's eight national championship trophies.

2011-12 – Won 38, Lost 2

National Champions
SEC East Champions
Coach: John Calipari

Nov. 11	Marist	H	108	58
Nov. 15	Kansas	N	75	65
Nov. 19	Penn State	N	85	47
Nov. 20	Old Dominion	N	62	52
Nov. 23	Radford	H	88	40
Nov. 26	Portland	H	87	63
Dec. 1	St. John's	H	81	59
Dec. 3	North Carolina	H	73	72
Dec. 10	Indiana	A	72	73
Dec. 17	Chattanooga	H	87	62
Dec. 20	Samford	H	82	50
Dec. 22	Loyola	H	87	63
Dec. 28	Lamar	H	86	64
Dec. 31	Louisville	H	69	62
Jan. 3	Ark.-Little Rock	N	73	51
Jan. 11	Auburn	A	68	53
Jan. 14	Tennessee	A	65	62
Jan. 17	Arkansas	H	86	63
Jan. 21	Alabama	H	77	71
Jan. 24	Georgia	A	57	44
Jan. 28	LSU	A	74	50
Jan. 31	Tennessee	H	69	44
Feb. 4	South Carolina	A	86	52
Feb. 7	Florida	H	78	58
Feb. 11	Vanderbilt	A	69	63
Feb. 18	Ole Miss	H	77	62
Feb. 21	Miss. State	A	73	64
Feb. 25	Vanderbilt	H	83	74
Mar. 1	Georgia	H	79	49
Mar. 4	Florida	A	74	59

(SEC Tournament)
(New Orleans)

Mar. 9	LSU	N	60	51
Mar. 10	Florida	N	74	71
Mar. 11	Vanderbilt	N	64	71

(NCAA East Regional)
(First/Second Rounds)
(Louisville)

Mar. 15	WKU	N	81	66
Mar. 17	Iowa State	N	87	71

(NCAA East Regional)
(Atlanta)

Mar. 23	Indiana	N	102	90
Mar. 25	Baylor	N	82	70

(NCAA Final Four)
(New Orleans)

Mar. 31	Louisville	N	69	61
Apr. 2	Kansas	N	67	59

—Leading Scorers—
Anthony Davis (6-10 Fr. F) 14.2
Doron Lamb (6-4 So. G) 13.7
Terrence Jones (6-9 So. F) 12.3
Michael Kidd-Gilchrist (6-7 Fr. F).............11.0
Marquis Teague (6-2 Fr. G).......................10.0

2012-13 – Won 21, Lost 12

Coach: John Calipari

Nov. 9	Maryland	N	72	69
Nov. 13	Duke	N	68	75
Nov. 16	Lafayette	A	101	49
Nov. 21	Morehead	H	81	70
Nov. 23	LIU-Brooklyn	H	104	75
Nov. 29	Notre Dame	A	50	64
Dec. 1	Baylor	H	55	64
Dec. 4	Samford	H	88	56
Dec. 8	Portland	H	74	46
Dec. 15	Lipscomb	H	88	50
Dec. 22	Marshall	H	82	54
Dec. 29	Louisville	A	77	80
Jan. 2	E. Michigan	A	90	38
Jan. 10	Vanderbilt	A	60	58
Jan. 12	Texas A&M	H	71	83
Jan. 15	Tennessee	H	75	65
Jan. 19	Auburn	A	73	53
Jan. 22	Alabama	A	55	59
Jan. 26	LSU	H	75	70
Jan. 29	Ole Miss	A	87	74
Feb. 2	Texas A&M	A	68	*72
Feb. 5	South Carolina	H	77	55
Feb. 9	Auburn	H	72	62
Feb. 12	Florida	A	52	69
Feb. 16	Tennessee	A	58	88
Feb. 20	Vanderbilt	H	74	70
Feb. 23	Missouri	H	90	*83
Feb. 27	Miss. State	H	85	55
Mar. 2	Arkansas	A	60	73
Mar. 7	Georgia	A	62	72
Mar. 9	Florida	H	61	57

(SEC Tournament)
(Nashville)

Mar. 15	Vanderbilt	N	48	64

(NIT First Round)
Moon Township, Pa.)

Mar. 19	Robert Morris	N	57	59

—Leading Scorers—
Archie Goodwin (6-4 Fr. G) 14.1
Alex Poythress (6-8 Fr. F) 11.2
Nerlens Noel (6-10 Fr. F) 10.5
Kyle Wiltjer (6-10 So. F) 10.2
Ryan Harrow (6-2 So. G) 9.9

2013-14 – Won 29, Lost 11

National Runner-Up
Coach: John Calipari

Nov. 8	UNC Asheville	H	89	57
Nov. 10	N. Kentucky	H	93	63
Nov. 12	Michigan State	N	74	78
Nov. 17	Robert Morris	H	87	49
Nov. 19	UT-Arlington	H	105	76
Nov. 25	Cleveland State	H	68	61
Nov. 27	E. Michigan	H	81	63
Dec. 1	Providence	N	79	65
Dec. 6	Baylor	N	62	67
Dec. 10	Boise State	H	70	55
Dec. 14	North Carolina	A	77	82
Dec. 21	Belmont	H	93	80
Dec. 28	Louisville	H	73	66
Jan. 8	Miss. State	H	85	63
Jan. 11	Vanderbilt	H	71	62
Jan. 14	Arkansas	A	85	*87
Jan. 18	Tennessee	H	74	66
Jan. 21	Texas A&M	H	68	51
Jan. 25	Georgia	H	79	54
Jan. 28	LSU	A	82	87
Feb. 1	Missouri	A	84	79
Feb. 4	Ole Miss	H	80	64
Feb. 8	Miss. State	A	69	59

Feb. 12	Auburn	A	64	56
Feb. 15	Florida	H	59	69
Feb. 18	Ole Miss	A	84	70
Feb. 22	LSU	H	77	*76
Feb. 27	Arkansas	H	71	*67
Mar. 1	South Carolina	A	67	72
Mar. 4	Alabama	H	55	48
Mar. 8	Florida	A	65	84

(SEC Tournament)
(Atlanta)

Mar. 14	LSU	N	85	67
Mar. 15	Georgia	N	70	58
Mar. 16	Florida	N	60	61

(NCAA East Regional)
(Second/Third Rounds)
(St. Louis)

Mar. 21	Kansas State	N	56	49
Mar. 23	Wichita State	N	78	76

(NCAA Regional Round)
(Indianapolis)

Mar. 28	Louisville	N	74	69
Mar. 30	Michigan	N	75	72

(NCAA Final Four)
(Arlington, Texas)

Apr. 5	Wisconsin	N	74	73
Apr. 7	UConn	N	54	60

—Leading Scorers—
Julius Randle (6-9 Fr. F) 15.0
James Young (6-4 Fr. G/F) 14.3
Aaron Harrison (6-6 Fr. G) 13.7
Andrew Harrison (6-6 Fr. G) 10.9
Willie Cauley Stein (7-0 So. F) 6.8

2014-15 – Won 38, Lost 1

NCAA Final Four
SEC Champion
SEC Tournament Champion
Coach: John Calipari

Nov. 14	Grand Canyon	H	85	45
Nov. 16	Buffalo	H	71	52
Nov. 18	Kansas	N	72	40
Nov. 21	Boston	H	89	65
Nov. 23	Montana State	H	86	28
Nov. 25	UT-Arlington	H	92	44
Nov. 30	Providence	H	58	38
Dec. 5	Texas	H	63	51
Dec. 7	E. Kentucky	H	82	49
Dec. 10	Columbia	H	56	46
Dec. 13	North Carolina	H	84	70
Dec. 20	UCLA	A	83	44
Dec. 27	Louisville	A	58	50
Jan. 6	Ole Miss	H	89	*86
Jan. 10	Texas A&M	A	70	**64
Jan. 13	Missouri	H	86	37
Jan. 17	Alabama	A	70	48
Jan. 20	Vanderbilt	H	65	57
Jan. 24	South Carolina	A	58	43
Jan. 29	Missouri	A	69	53
Jan. 31	Alabama	H	70	55
Feb. 3	Georgia	H	69	58
Feb. 7	Florida	A	68	61
Feb. 10	LSU	A	71	69
Feb. 14	South Carolina	H	77	43
Feb. 17	Tennessee	A	66	48
Feb. 21	Auburn	H	110	75
Feb. 25	Miss. State	A	74	56
Feb. 28	Arkansas	H	84	67
Mar. 3	Georgia	A	72	64
Mar. 7	Florida	H	67	50

(SEC Tournament)
(Nashville)

Mar. 13	Florida	N	64	49
Mar. 14	Auburn	N	91	67
Mar. 15	Arkansas	N	78	63

(NCAA Regional)
(Second/Third Rounds)
(Louisville)

Mar. 19	Hampton	N	79	56
Mar. 21	Cincinnati	N	64	51

(NCAA Regional Round)
(Cleveland)

Mar. 26	West Virginia	N	78	39

Mar. 28	Notre Dame	N	68	66

(NCAA Final Four)
(Indianapolis)

Apr. 4	Wisconsin	N	64	71

—Leading Scorers—
Aaron Harrison (6-6 So. G) 11.0
Karl-Anthony Towns (6-11 Fr. F) 10.3
Devin Booker (6-6 Fr. G) 10.0
Andrew Harrison (6-6 So. G) 9.3
Willie Cauley Stein (7-0 Jr. F) 8.98

2015-16 – Won 27, Lost 9

SEC East Co-Champions
SEC Tournament Champions
Coach: John Calipari

Nov. 13	Albany	H	78	65
Nov. 14	NJIT	H	87	57
Nov. 17	Duke	N	74	63
Nov. 20	Wright State	H	78	63
Nov. 24	Boston U	H	82	62
Nov. 27	South Florida	A	84	63
Nov. 30	Illinois State	H	75	63
Dec. 3	UCLA	A	77	87
Dec. 9	EKU	H	88	67
Dec. 12	Arizona State	H	72	58
Dec. 19	Ohio State	N	67	74
Dec. 26	Louisville	H	75	73
Jan. 2	Ole Miss	H	83	61
Jan. 5	LSU	A	67	85
Jan. 9	Alabama	A	77	61
Jan. 12	Miss. State	H	80	74
Jan. 16	Auburn	A	70	75
Jan. 21	Arkansas	A	80	66
Jan. 23	Vanderbilt	H	76	57
Jan. 27	Missouri	H	88	54
Jan. 30	Kansas	A	84	90
Feb. 2	Tennessee	A	77	84
Feb. 6	Florida	H	80	61
Feb. 9	Georgia	H	82	48
Feb. 13	South Carolina	A	89	62
Feb. 18	Tennessee	H	80	70
Feb. 20	Texas A&M	A	77	*79
Feb. 23	Alabama	H	78	53
Feb. 27	Vanderbilt	A	62	74
Mar. 1	Florida	A	88	79
Mar. 5	LSU	H	94	77

(SEC Tournament)
(Nashville)

Mar. 11	Alabama	N	85	59
Mar. 12	Georgia	N	93	80
Mar. 13	Texas A&M	N	82	*77

(NCAA East Regional)
(First/Second Rounds)
(Des Moines, Iowa)

Mar. 17	Stony Brook	N	85	57
Mar. 19	Indiana	N	67	73

—Leading Scorers—
Jamal Murray (6-4 Fr. G.) 20.0
Tyler Ulis (5-9 So. G) 17.3
Alex Poythress (6-8 Sr. F) 10.2
Isaiah Briscoe (6-3 Fr. G) 9.6
Derek Willis (6-9 Jr. F) 7.7

Tyler Ulis offers instructions to Jamal Murray, Isaiah Briscoe, Marcus Lee and Derek Willis.

Deron Feldhaus, Richie Farmer and their families couldn't hold back the tears during an emotional Senior Night ceremony.

Author's Bio

Tom Wallace is a former award-winning sportswriter who covered UK basketball while working for legendary broadcaster Cawood Ledford and as a columnist for *The Cats' Pause*. He is the author of several sports-related books, including the highly successful *Kentucky Basketball Encyclopedia*, now out in its fourth edition. He has also written books with former Wildcats Travis Ford and Jeff Sheppard.

As a freelance writer, Tom has written seven mystery/thriller novels, the most recent being *The Poker Game*. His other novels include *The Fire of Heaven*, *The List*, *Gnosis*, *Heirs of Cain*, *The Devil's Racket* and *What Matters Blood*.

A graduate of Western Kentucky University, Tom spent many years as a successful sportswriter. From 1983-86, he served as sports editor for the Gleaner in Henderson, Kentucky, where he was twice honored by the Kentucky Press Association for writing the best sports story in the state.

Tom, a Vietnam vet, lives in Lexington. He is a member of Mystery Writers of America. His website is www.tomwallacenovels.com.